BASEBALL

CONNECT WITH US!

f **/USABaseball**

Join the more than 200,000 fans who like us on Facebook.

🐦 **@USABaseball**

Over 50,000 people receive breaking news and special offers by following us on Twitter.

📷 **@USABaseball**

Follow us on Instagram for a behind-the-scenes look at USA Baseball's events.

OUR PASTIME'S FUTURE.

usabaseball.com

Baseball america®
DIRECTORY

Editor
JOSH NORRIS

Assistant Editors
HUDSON BELINSKY, J.J. COOPER, MICHAEL LANANNA,
VINCE LARA-CINISOMO, JIM SHONERD

Database and Application Development
BRENT LEWIS

Photo Editor
JIM SHONERD

Design & Production
SARA HIATT MCDANIEL, LINWOOD WEBB

Programming & Technical Development
BRENT LEWIS

Cover Photo
ANDREW WOOLLEY

DISTRIBUTED BY SIMON & SCHUSTER ISBN-13: 978-1-932391-62-6

Baseball america

ESTABLISHED 1981
P.O. Box 12877, Durham, NC 27709 • Phone (919) 682-9635

THE TEAM
GENERAL MANAGER Will Lingo *@willingo*

EDITORIAL
EDITOR IN CHIEF John Manuel *@johnmanuelba*
MANAGING EDITOR J.J. Cooper *@jjcoop36*
ASSOCIATE EDITOR Matt Eddy *@matteddyba*
NEWS EDITOR Josh Norris *@jnorris427*
WEB EDITOR Vincent Lara-Cinisomo *@vincelara*
NATIONAL WRITERS Ben Badler *@benbadler*
Teddy Cahill *@tedcahill*
ASSISTANT EDITORS Michael Lananna *@mlananna*
Jim Shonerd *@jimshonerdba*
EDITORIAL ASSISTANT Hudson Belinsky *@hudsonbelinsky*

PRODUCTION
DESIGN & PRODUCTION DIRECTOR Sara Hiatt McDaniel
MULTIMEDIA MANAGER Linwood Webb

ADVERTISING
ADVERTISING DIRECTOR George Shelton
DIRECT MARKETING MANAGER Ximena Caceres
DIGITAL SALES MANAGER Larry Sarzyniak
MARKETPLACE MANAGER Kristopher M. Lull
ADVERTISING ACCOUNT EXECUTIVE Abbey Langdon

BUSINESS
CUSTOMER SERVICE Ronnie McCabe, C.J. McPhatter
ACCOUNTING/OFFICE MANAGER Hailey Carpenter
TECHNOLOGY MANAGER Brent Lewis

STATISTICAL SERVICE
MAJOR LEAGUE BASEBALL ADVANCED MEDIA

ACTION/OUTDOOR GROUP
MANAGEMENT
PRODUCTION DIRECTOR Kasey Kelley
FINANCE DIRECTOR Adam Miner
DIRECTOR OF VIDEO Chris Mauro

DESIGN
CREATIVE DIRECTOR Marc Hostetter
CREATIVE DIRECTOR Peter Tracy

SALES & MARKETING
VP, SALES Kristen Ude
SR. MARKETING DIRECTOR Adam Cozens

EVENTS
DIRECTOR, EVENTS Scott Desiderio
VP, EVENT SALES Sean Nielsen

DIGITAL GROUP
DIGITAL DIRECTOR, ENGINEERING Jeff Kimmel
SENIOR PRODUCT MANAGER Rishi Kumar
SENIOR PRODUCT MANAGER Marc Bartell

FACILITIES
MANAGER Randy Ward
OFFICE COORDINATOR Ruth Hosea
IT SUPPORT SPECIALIST Mike Bradley

MANUFACTURING & PRODUCTION OPERATIONS
VP, MANUFACTURING
& AD OPERATIONS Greg Parnell
SENIOR DIRECTOR, AD OPERATIONS Pauline Atwood
ARCHIVIST Thomas Voehringer

 THE ENTHUSIAST NETWORK™

TEN: THE ENTHUSIAST NETWORK, LLC
CHAIRMAN Peter Englehart
CHIEF EXECUTIVE OFFICER Scott P. Dickey
EVP, CHIEF FINANCIAL OFFICER Bill Sutman
PRESIDENT, AUTOMOTIVE Scott Bailey
EVP, CHIEF CREATIVE OFFICER Alan Alpanian
EVP, SPORTS & ENTERTAINMENT Norb Garrett
EVP, CHIEF CONTENT OFFICER Angus MacKenzie
EVP, OPERATIONS Kevin Mullan
EVP, SALES & MARKETING Eric Schwab
SVP, DIGITAL OPERATIONS Dan Bednar
SVP & GM, AUTOMOTIVE
AFTERMARKET Matt Boice
SVP, FINANCIAL PLANNING Mike Cummings
SVP, AUTOMOTIVE DIGITAL Geoff DeFrance
VP, EDITORIAL OPERATIONS Amy Diamond
SVP, CONTENT STRATEGY,
AUTOMOTIVE David Freiburger
SVP, DIGITAL, SPORTS &
ENTERTAINMENT Greg Morrow
VP, DIGITAL MONETIZATION Elisabeth Murray
SVP, MARKETING Ryan Payne
EVP, MIND OVER EYE Bill Wadsworth

CONSUMER MARKETING, ENTHUSIAST MEDIA SUBSCRIPTION COMPANY, INC.
SVP, CIRCULATION Tom Slater
VP, RETENTION &
OPERATIONS FULFILLMENT Donald T. Robinson III

Experience baseball history year-round
VISIT US IN COOPERSTOWN
and at
BASEBALLHALL.ORG

PRESERVING HISTORY. HONORING EXCELLENCE. CONNECTING GENERATIONS.

NATIONAL
BASEBALL
HALL OF FAME®

TABLE OF CONTENTS

TD Ameritrade Park, Omaha

ANDREW WOOLLEY

Marlins Park

WHAT'S NEW IN 2016

DOUBLE-A
Ballpark: Hartford (Eastern) — Dunkin Donuts Field
Franchise Move: Hartford Yard Goats (Eastern) replace New Britain Rock Cats.

LOW CLASS A
Franchise Move: Columbia Fireflies (South Atlantic) replace Savannah Sand Gnats

ROOKIE
Affiliation Additions: Tigers add second Gulf Coast League team

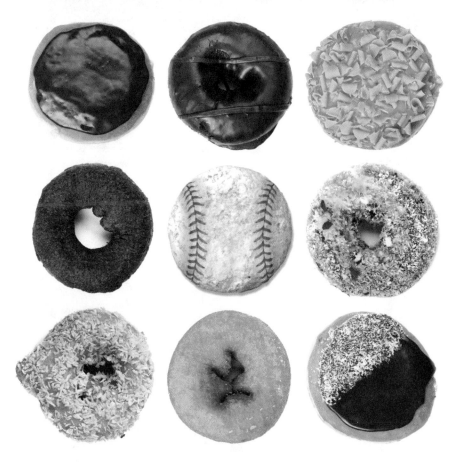

LIVE BASEBALL EVERY NIGHT? SWEET.

LIVE LOOK–INS AND ANALYSIS ON MLB TONIGHT™ PLUS 5 LIVE GAMES EACH WEEK

MLB NETWORK

OUR NATIONAL PASTIME ALL THE TIME®

   GO TO FINDMLBNETWORK.COM FOR CHANNEL NUMBER

Map illustrations by Paul Trap

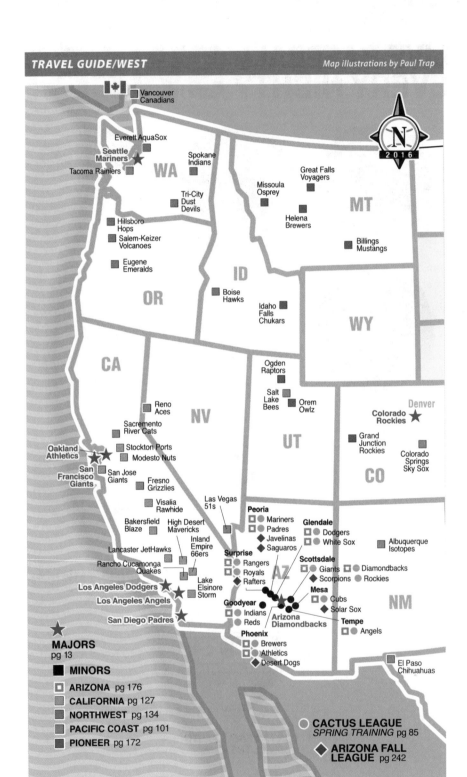

Vancouver
Canadians

Everett AquaSox

Seattle
Mariners

Tacoma Rainiers

Spokane
Indians

WA

Tri-City
Dust
Devils

Missoula
Osprey

Great Falls
Voyagers

MT

Hillsboro
Hops

Salem-Keizer
Volcanoes

Helena
Brewers

Eugene
Emeralds

Billings
Mustangs

ID

OR

Boise
Hawks

Idaho
Falls
Chukars

WY

Ogden
Raptors

CA

Salt
Lake
Bees

Orem
Owlz

Reno
Aces

Denver

Colorado
Rockies

Sacramento
River Cats

NV

Grand
Junction
Rockies

Stockton Ports

Modesto Nuts

UT

Colorado
Springs
Sky Sox

Oakland
Athletics

San Jose
Giants

Fresno
Grizzlies

CO

San
Francisco
Giants

Visalia
Rawhide

Las Vegas
51s

Bakersfield
Blaze

High Desert
Mavericks

Peoria

Mariners

Padres

Glendale

Dodgers

White Sox

Albuquerque
Isotopes

Lancaster JetHawks

Inland
Empire
66ers

Javelinas

Saguaros

Rancho Cucamonga
Quakes

Surprise

Rangers

Royals

Scottsdale

Giants

Diamondbacks

Scorpions

Rockies

AZ

Lake
Elsinore
Storm

Rafters

Los Angeles Dodgers

Mesa

Cubs

Los Angeles Angels

Goodyear

Solar Sox

NM

San Diego Padres

Indians

Reds

Arizona
Diamondbacks

Tempe

Angels

Phoenix

Brewers

Athletics

El Paso
Chihuahuas

Desert Dogs

MAJORS
pg 13

■ MINORS

□ **ARIZONA** pg 176

■ **CALIFORNIA** pg 127

■ **NORTHWEST** pg 134

■ **PACIFIC COAST** pg 101

■ **PIONEER** pg 172

○ **CACTUS LEAGUE**
SPRING TRAINING pg 85

◆ **ARIZONA FALL
LEAGUE** pg 242

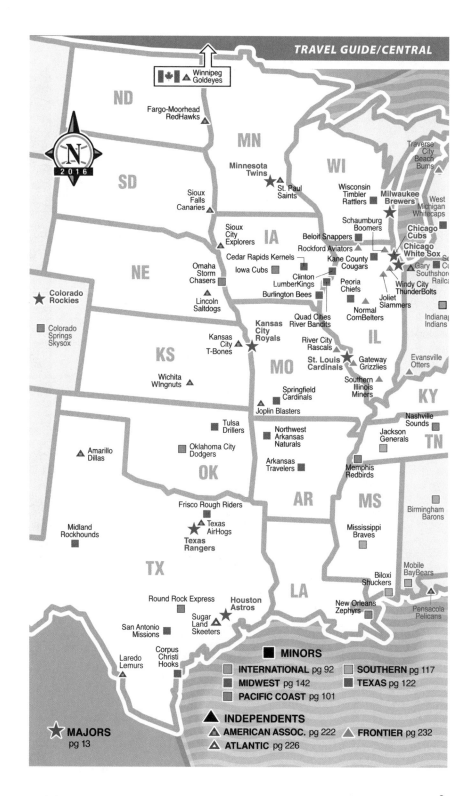

Winnipeg Goldeyes

N 2016

ND

Fargo-Moorhead RedHawks

MN

Minnesota Twins

St. Paul Saints

WI

Traverse City Beach Bums

SD

Sioux Falls Canaries

Wisconsin Timbler Rattlers

Milwaukee Brewers

West Michigan Whitecaps

Schaumburg Boomers

Sioux City Explorers

IA

Beloit Snappers

Chicago Cubs

Rockford Aviators

Chicago White Sox

NE

Cedar Rapids Kernels

Kane County Cougars

Gary Southshore Railca

Omaha Storm Chasers

Iowa Cubs

Clinton LumberKings

Peoria Chiefs

Windy City ThunderBolts

Colorado Rockies

Lincoln Saltdogs

Burlington Bees

Joliet Slammers

Indiana Indians

Colorado Springs Skysox

Quad Cities River Bandits

Normal CornBelters

Kansas City Royals

Kansas City T-Bones

River City Rascals

IL

KS

St. Louis Cardinals

Gateway Grizzlies

Evansville Otters

KY

Wichita Wingnuts

MO

Southern Illinois Miners

Springfield Cardinals

Joplin Blasters

Nashville Sounds

Amarillo Dillas

Tulsa Drillers

Northwest Arkansas Naturals

Jackson Generals

TN

Oklahoma City Dodgers

Arkansas Travelers

Memphis Redbirds

OK

AR

MS

Frisco Rough Riders

Birmingham Barons

Midland Rockhounds

Texas AirHogs

Texas Rangers

Mississippi Braves

TX

Mobile BayBears

Round Rock Express

Houston Astros

LA

Biloxi Shuckers

San Antonio Missions

Sugar Land Skeeters

New Orleans Zephyrs

Pensacola Pelicans

Laredo Lemurs

Corpus Christi Hooks

■ MINORS

☐ INTERNATIONAL pg 92   ☐ SOUTHERN pg 117

■ MIDWEST pg 142   ■ TEXAS pg 122

■ PACIFIC COAST pg 101

★ MAJORS
pg 13

▲ INDEPENDENTS

▲ AMERICAN ASSOC. pg 222   △ FRONTIER pg 232

△ ATLANTIC pg 226

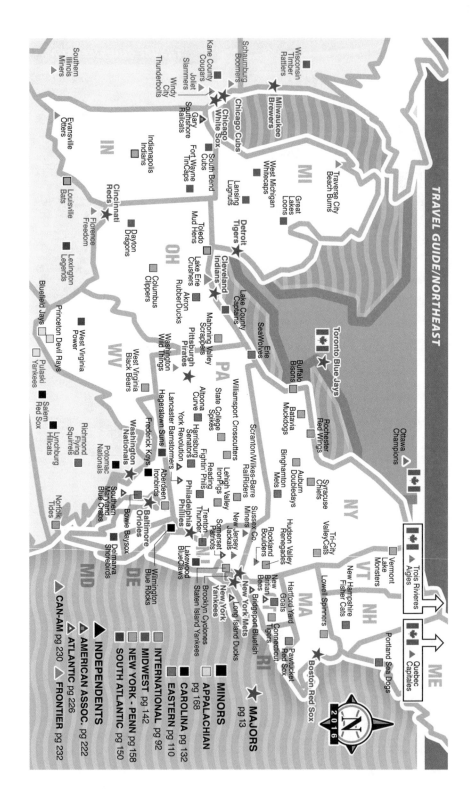

Southern Illinois Miners
Wisconsin Timber Rattlers
Schaumburg Boomers
Kane County Cougars
Joliet Slammers
Windy City Thunderbolts
Gary SouthShore Railcats
Chicago White Sox
Chicago Cubs
Milwaukee Brewers
Traverse City Beach Bums
Evansville Otters
Indianapolis Indians
South Bend Cubs
Fort Wayne TinCaps
Lansing Lugnuts
Great Lakes Loons
West Michigan Whitecaps
Detroit Tigers
IN
Louisville Bats
Cincinnati Reds
Florence Freedom
Lexington Legends
Dayton Dragons
Toledo Mud Hens
Lake Erie Crushers
Akron RubberDucks
Columbus Clippers
Cleveland Indians
Lake County Captains
Erie SeaWolves
OH
MI
Bluefield Jays
Princeton Devil Rays
Pulaski Yankees
Salem Red Sox
Lynchburg Hillcats
Norfolk Tides
West Virginia Power
West Virginia Black Bears
Washington Wild Things
Pittsburgh Pirates
Mahoning Valley Scrappers
Altoona Curve
State College Spikes
Williamsport Crosscutters
WV
Richmond Flying Squirrels
Potomac Nationals
Washington Nationals
Southern Maryland Blue Crabs
Frederick Keys
Hagerstown Suns
Lancaster Barnstormers
York Revolution
Harrisburg Senators
Reading Fightin' Phils
Lehigh Valley IronPigs
Scranton/Wilkes-Barre RailRiders
PA
Buffalo Bisons
Batavia Muckdogs
Rochester Red Wings
Auburn Doubledays
Binghamton Mets
Syracuse Chiefs
Toronto Blue Jays
Ottawa Champions
MD
DE
Delmarva Shorebirds
Bowie Baysox
Baltimore Orioles
Aberdeen Ironbirds
Wilmington Blue Rocks
Philadelphia Phillies
Trenton Thunder
Lakewood BlueClaws
Somerset Patriots
New Jersey Jackals
Sussex Co. Miners
Rockland Boulders
Hudson Valley Renegades
Tri-City ValleyCats
NY
NJ
Bridgeport Bluefish
New Britain Bees
Hartford Yard Goats
Connecticut Tigers
New York Yankees
New York Mets
Long Island Ducks
Brooklyn Cyclones
Staten Island Yankees
Vermont Lake Monsters
New Hampshire Fisher Cats
Lowell Spinners
Pawtucket Red Sox
Boston Red Sox
Portland Sea Dogs
Trois Rivieres Aigles
Quebec Capitales
VT
NH
MA
RI
ME

Trois Rivieres Aigles
Quebec Capitales

★ MAJORS pg 13

MINORS
INTERNATIONAL pg 92
EASTERN pg 110
CAROLINA pg 132
APPALACHIAN
MIDWEST pg 142
NEW YORK - PENN pg 158
SOUTH ATLANTIC pg 150

INDEPENDENTS
AMERICAN ASSOC. pg 222
ATLANTIC pg 226
CAN-AM pg 230
FRONTIER pg 232

2016 N

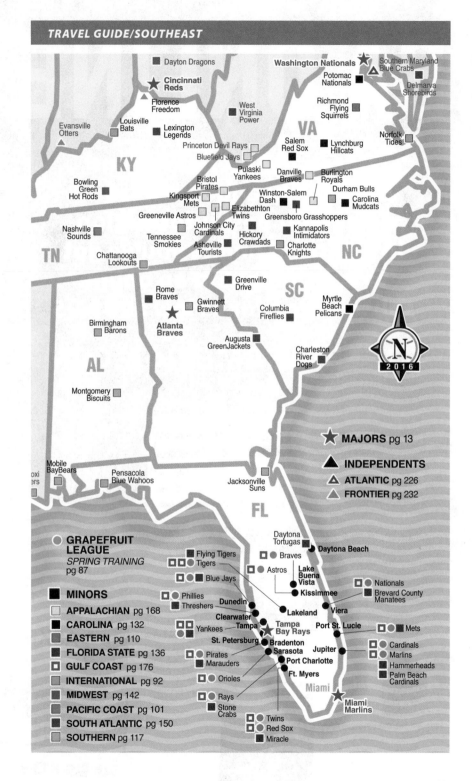

Dayton Dragons

Washington Nationals

Southern Maryland Blue Crabs

Cincinnati Reds

Florence Freedom

Potomac Nationals

Delmarva Shorebirds

Richmond Flying Squirrels

Evansville Otters

Louisville Bats

Lexington Legends

West Virginia Power

VA

Norfolk Tides

Salem Red Sox

Lynchburg Hillcats

Princeton Devil Rays

Bluefield Jays

KY

Pulaski Yankees

Danville Braves

Burlington Royals

Bowling Green Hot Rods

Bristol Pirates

Kingsport Mets

Winston-Salem Dash

Durham Bulls

Carolina Mudcats

Greeneville Astros

Elizabethton Twins

Greensboro Grasshoppers

Nashville Sounds

Johnson City Cardinals

Kannapolis Intimidators

TN

Tennessee Smokies

Hickory Crawdads

Asheville Tourists

Chattanooga Lookouts

Charlotte Knights

NC

Greenville Drive

Rome Braves

SC

Myrtle Beach Pelicans

Gwinnett Braves

Columbia Fireflies

Birmingham Barons

Atlanta Braves

Augusta GreenJackets

Charleston River Dogs

AL

N 2016

Montgomery Biscuits

★ MAJORS pg 13

▲ INDEPENDENTS

Mobile BayBears

oxi ers

Pensacola Blue Wahoos

Jacksonville Suns

△ ATLANTIC pg 226

△ FRONTIER pg 232

FL

Daytona Tortugas

GRAPEFRUIT LEAGUE
SPRING TRAINING
pg 87

Flying Tigers

Daytona Beach

Tigers

Braves

Blue Jays

Astros

Lake Buena Vista

Nationals

Brevard County Manatees

MINORS

Phillies

APPALACHIAN pg 168

Threshers

Dunedin

Kissimmee

Viera

CAROLINA pg 132

Clearwater

Lakeland

Port St. Lucie

EASTERN pg 110

Yankees

Tampa

Mets

FLORIDA STATE pg 136

St. Petersburg

Tampa Bay Rays

GULF COAST pg 176

Pirates

Bradenton

Sarasota

Jupiter

Cardinals

INTERNATIONAL pg 92

Marauders

Port Charlotte

Marlins

MIDWEST pg 142

Orioles

Ft. Myers

Hammerheads

PACIFIC COAST pg 101

Miami

Palm Beach Cardinals

SOUTH ATLANTIC pg 150

Rays

SOUTHERN pg 117

Stone Crabs

Twins

Miami Marlins

Red Sox

Miracle

BA ONLINE

Baseball America is your baseball headquarters, and to get our best information in print and online you've got to subscribe! Get an online subscription for as low as $9.95

BASEBALLAMERICA.COM

MAJOR LEAGUES

MAJOR LEAGUE BASEBALL

Rob Manfred

Mailing Address: 245 Park Ave. New York, NY 10167.
Telephone: (212) 931-7800. **Website:** www.mlb.com.
Commissioner of Baseball: Rob Manfred.
Commissioner Emeritus: Allan H. (Bud) Selig.
President, Business/Media: Bob Bowman.
Chief Communications Officer: Pat Courtney. **Chief Legal Officer:** Dan Halem. **Chief Investment Officer:** Jonathan Mariner. **Chief Operating Officer:** Tony Petitti. **Chief Financial Officer:** Bob Starkey.

BASEBALL OPERATIONS

Chief Baseball Officer: Joe Torre.
Senior VP, Baseball Operations: Kim Ng, Peter Woodfork. **Senior VP, Standards/ Operations:** Joe Garagiola Jr.
Senior Director, Major League Operations: Roy Krasik. **Director, International Baseball Operations:** Chris Haydock. **Senior Director, Baseball Operations:** Jeff Pfeifer. **Director, Minor League Operations:** Fred Seymour. **Manager, Amateur Relations:** Chuck Fox. **Senior Manager, Latin American Game Development:** Joel Araujo. **Manager, International Baseball Operations:** Giovanni Hernandez. **Manager, International Baseball Investigation & Compliance:** Melissa Bristol. **Specialist, Umpire Administration:** Cathy Davis. **Specialist, International Baseball Operations:** Rebecca Seesel. **Senior Coordinator, International Baseball Operations:** Shane Barclay. **Coordinator, Major League Operations:** Gina Liento. **Pace of Game Analyst:** Chris Knettel. **Coordinator, On Field Operations:** Stephen Mara, Michael Sansarran.
Coordinator, Baseball Operations: Garrett Horan. **Coordinator, International Baseball Operations:** Max Thomas. **Registration Analyst:** William Clements. **Executive Assistant, Baseball Operations:** Chris Romanello. **Senior Administrative Assistant:** Llubia Reyes-Bussey.
Director, Major League Umpiring: Randy Marsh. **Director, Umpiring Development:** Rich Rieker. **Director, Umpire Medical Services:** Mark Letendre. **Director, Umpire Administration:** Matt McKendry. **Director, Instant Replay:** Justin Klemm.
Umpiring Supervisors: Cris Jones, Tom Leppard, Chuck Meriwether, Ed Montague, Steve Palermo, Charlie Reliford, Larry Young. **Umpire Evaluator:** Ed Rapuano. **Special Assistant, Umpiring:** Bruce Froemming. **Instant Replay Coordinator:** Ross Larson. **Coordinator, Umpire Administration:** Raquel Wagner. **Video Coordinator:** Freddie Hernandez. **Baseball Systems:** Nancy Crofts.
Director, Dominican Operations: Rafael Perez. **Director, Arizona Fall League:** Steve Cobb. **Senior Director, Major League Scouting Bureau:** Bill Bavasi. **Assistant Director, Scouting Bureau:** Rick Oliver..

COMMUNICATIONS

Telephone: (212) 931-7878. **Fax:** (212) 949-5654.
VP, Communications: John Blundell, Mike Teevan. **VP, Business Communications:** Matt Bourne. **Director, Communications:** Donald Muller. **Director, Business Communications:** Steve Arocho, Dan Queen. **Manager, Business Communications:** Jen Zudonyi Specialist, **Communications:** Lydia Devlin. **Specialist, Business Communications:** David Hochman. **Coordinator, Business Communications:** Sarah Leer. **Executive Assistant, Communications:** Ginger Dillon. **Official Historian:** John Thorn.

CLUB RELATIONS

Senior VP, Scheduling/Club Relations: Katy Feeney. **Senior VP, Club Relations:** Phyllis Merhige.

AMERICAN LEAGUE

Year League Founded: 1901.
2016 Opening Date: April 3. **Closing Date:** Oct. 2.
Regular Season: 162 games.
Division Structure: East—Baltimore, Boston, New York, Tampa Bay, Toronto.
Central—Chicago, Cleveland, Detroit, Kansas City, Minnesota. **West**—Houston, Los Angeles, Oakland, Seattle, Texas.
Playoff Format: Two non-division winners with best records meet in one-game wildcard playoff. Wildcard winner and three division champions meet in two best-of-five Division Series. Winners meet in best-of-seven Championship Series.
All-Star Game: July 12, Petco Park, San Diego (National League vs. American League).
Roster Limit: 25, through Aug 31, when rosters expand to 40.
Brand of Baseball: Rawlings.
Statistician: MLB Advanced Media, 75 Ninth Ave., 5th Floor, New York, NY 10011.

STADIUM INFORMATION

Team	Stadium	LF	CF	RF	Capacity	2015 Att.
Baltimore	Oriole Park at Camden Yards	333	410	318	45,971	2,320,588
Boston	Fenway Park	310	390	302	37,673	2,880,694
Chicago	U.S. Cellular Field	330	400	335	40,615	1,755,810
Cleveland	Progressive Field	325	405	325	37,675	1,388,905
Detroit	Comerica Park	345	420	330	41,782	2,726,048
Houston	Minute Maid Park	315	435	326	40,976	2,153,585
Kansas City	Kauffman Stadium	330	410	330	37,903	2,708,549
Los Angeles	Angel Stadium	333	404	333	45,050	3,012,765
Minnesota	Target Field	339	404	328	39,504	2,220,054
New York	Yankee Stadium	318	408	314	50,291	3,193,795
Oakland	O.co Coliseum	330	400	367	35,067	1,768,175
Seattle	Safeco Field	331	401	326	47,447	2,193,581
Tampa Bay	Tropicana Field	315	404	322	41,315	1,247,668
Texas	Globe Life Park in Arlington	332	400	325	48,114	2,491,875
Toronto	Rogers Centre	328	400	328	50,598	2,794,891

NATIONAL LEAGUE

Year League Founded: 1876.
2016 Opening Date: April 3. **Closing Date:** Oct. 2.
Regular Season: 162 games.
Division Structure: East—Atlanta, Miami, New York, Philadelphia, Washington.
Central—Chicago, Cincinnati, Milwaukee, Pittsburgh, St. Louis. **West**—Arizona, Colorado, Los Angeles, San Diego, San Francisco.
Playoff Format: Two non-division winners with best records meet in one-game wildcard playoff. Wildcard winner and three division champions meet in two best-of-five Division Series. Winners meet in best-of-seven Championship Series.
All-Star Game: July 12, Petco Park, San Diego (National League vs. American League).
Roster Limit: 25, through Aug. 31 when rosters expand to 40.
Brand of Baseball: Rawlings.
Statistician: MLB Advanced Media, 75 Ninth Ave., 5th Floor, New York, NY 10011.

STADIUM INFORMATION

Team	Stadium	LF	CF	RF	Capacity	2015 Att.
Arizona	Chase Field	330	407	334	49,033	2,080,145
Atlanta	Turner Field	335	400	330	49,743	2,001,392
Chicago	Wrigley Field	355	400	353	41,160	2,959,812
Cincinnati	Great American Ball Park	328	404	325	42,319	2,419,506
Colorado	Coors Field	347	415	350	50,499	2,506,789
Los Angeles	Dodger Stadium	330	395	330	56,000	3,764,815
Miami	Marlins Park	344	407	335	36,742	1,752,235
Milwaukee	Miller Park	344	400	345	41,900	2,542,558
New York	Citi Field	335	408	330	42,200	2,569,753
Philadelphia	Citizens Bank Park	329	401	330	43,647	1,831,080
Pittsburgh	PNC Park	325	399	320	38,496	2,498,596
St. Louis	Busch Stadium	336	400	335	46,681	3,520,889
San Diego	Petco Park	336	396	322	42,685	2,459,742
San Francisco	AT&T Park	339	399	309	41,503	3,375,882
Washington	Nationals Park	336	402	335	41,888	2,619,843

Arizona Diamondbacks

Office Address: Chase Field, 401 E. Jefferson St, Phoenix, AZ 85004.
Mailing Address: P.O. Box 2095, Phoenix, AZ 85001.
Telephone: (602) 462-6500. **Fax:** (602) 462-6599. **Website:** www.dbacks.com

OWNERSHIP
Managing General Partner: Ken Kendrick. **General Partners:** Mike Chipman, Jeff Royer.

BUSINESS OPERATIONS
President/CEO: Derrick Hall. **Executive Vice President, Business Operations:** Cullen Maxey. **Special Assistants to President/CEO:** Roland Hemond, Luis Gonzalez, Randy Johnson, J.J. Putz. **Military Affairs Specialist:** Captain Jack Ensch. **Executive Assistant to President/CEO:** Brooke Mitchell.

Ken Kendrick

BROADCASTING
VP, Broadcasting: Scott Geyer. **Senior Director, Game Operations/Multi-Media Productions:** Rob Weinheimer.

CORPORATE PARTNERSHIPS/MARKETING
VP, Corporate Partnerships: Judd Norris. **Director, Corporate Partnership Services:** Kerri White. **Director, Advertising:** Rayme Lofgren. **Manager, Hispanic & Emerging Markets:** Jerry Romo.

FINANCE/LEGAL
Executive VP/CFO: Tom Harris. **VP, Finance:** Craig Bradley. **Director, Financial Management/Purchasing:** Jeff Jacobs. **Director, Accounting:** Chris James. **Executive Assistant to Managing General Partner/CFO:** Sandy Cox. **Senior VP/General Counsel:** Nona Lee. **Senior Director, Legal Affairs/Associate General Counsel:** Caleb Jay.

COMMUNITY AFFAIRS
VP, Corporate/Community Impact: Debbie Castaldo.

COMMUNICATION/MEDIA RELATIONS
SVP, Communications: Josh Rawitch. **Senior Director, Player/Media Relations:** Casey Wilcox. **Senior Manager, Player/Media Relations:** Patrick O'Connell. **Senior Manager, Corporate Communications:** Katie Krause.

SPECIAL PROJECTS/FAN EXPERIENCE
VP, Special Projects: Graham Rossini. **Director, Special Projects/Brand Development:** Matt Helmeid. **Director, Baseball Outreach/Development:** Jeff Rodin. **General Manager, Salt River Fields:** David Dunne.

STADIUM OPERATIONS
VP, Facility Operations/Event Services: Russ Amaral. **Senior Director, Security:** Sean Maguire. **Director, Facility Services:** Jose Montoya. **Director, Facilities Engineering:** Jim White. **Director, Event Services:** Bryan White.

2016 SCHEDULE
Standard Game Times: 6:40 p.m.; Sun. 1:10.

APRIL		JULY	
4-6 . . . . .Colorado	20-22 . . . . . . .at St. Louis	1-3. . . . . . San Francisco	22-25 . . . . Atlanta
7-10 . . . . . Chicago (NL)	24-26 . . . . . at Pittsburgh	4-6. . . . . San Diego	26-28 . . . . Cincinnati
12-14 . at Los Angeles (NL)	27-29 . . . . San Diego	8-10 . . . at San Francisco	30-31 . . at San Francisco
15-17 . . . . . at San Diego	30-31 . . . . Houston	15-17 . . .Los Angeles (NL)	**SEPTEMBER**
18-21 . . . at San Francisco		19-20 . . . . .Toronto	2-4. . . . . at Colorado
22-24 . . . . . . .Pittsburgh	**JUNE**	22-24 . . . . . .at Cincinnati	5-7. . . at Los Angeles (NL)
25-28 . . . . St. Louis	1-2. . . . . . . .at Houston	25-28 . . . . at Milwaukee	9-11. . . . . .San Francisco
29-30 . . . . .Colorado	3-5. . . . . .at Chicago (NL)	29-31 . at Los Angeles (NL)	12-14 . . . . .Colorado
	6-8. . . . . .Tampa Bay		15-18 . . .Los Angeles (NL)
MAY	10-12 . . . . .Miami	**AUGUST**	19-21 . . . . . at San Diego
1 . . . . .Colorado	13-15 . . .Los Angeles (NL)	1-3. . . . . . . .Washington	23-25 . . . . . at Baltimore
3-5. . . . . at Miami	17-20 . . . . at Philadelphia	5-7. . . . . .Milwaukee	26-29 . . . . at Washington
6-8. . . . . at Atlanta	21-22 . . . . . . at Toronto	9-11. . . . at New York (NL)	30 . . . . San Diego
9-11 . . . . . . .at Colorado	23-26 . . . . . at Colorado	12-14 . . . . . . .at Boston	
12-15 . . . . .San Francisco	27-29 . . . . .Philadelphia	15-17 . . . .New York (NL)	**OCTOBER**
16-18 . . . .New York (AL)		18-21 . . . . . at San Diego	1-2. . . . . San Diego

GENERAL INFORMATION
Stadium (year opened): Chase Field (1998). **Player Representative:** Brad Ziegler.
Team Colors: Sedona Red, Sonoran Sand and Black. **Home Dugout:** Third Base.
Playing Surface: Grass.

Telephone: (602) 514-8400. **Fax:** (602) 462-4141.
Senior VP, Ticket Sales/Marketing: John Fisher. **VP, Business Strategy/Operations:** Kenny Farrell.

BASEBALL OPERATIONS

Chief Baseball Officer: Tony La Russa.
Senior VP/General Manager: Dave Stewart. **Senior VP, Baseball Operations:** De Jon Watson. **Assistant GM:** Bryan Minniti. **VP/Special Assistant to GM:** Bob Gebhard. **Special Assistant to GM/Major League Scout:** Bill Bryk, Todd Greene, Mike Piatnik. **Special Assistants to GM:** Joe Carter, David Duncan, Craig Shipley, Mark Snipp, Tim Wilken. **Special Assistant to VP, Latin America Operations:** Junior Noboa. **Director, Baseball Analytics/ Research:** Dr. Ed Lewis. **Manager, Baseball Operations:** Sam Eaton. **Data Analyst:** John Krazit. **Major League Video Coordinator:** Allen Campbell. **Executive Assistant, Baseball Operations:** Kristyn Pierce. **Assistant, Baseball Operations:** Ian Rebhan. **Mathematical Modeler, Baseball Analytics:** Cody Callahan. **Quantitative Researcher, Baseball Analytics:** Max Glick.

Tony La Russa

MAJOR LEAGUE STAFF
Manager: Chip Hale.
Coaches: Bench—Glenn Sherlock; **Pitching**—Mike Butcher; **Hitting**—Dave Magadan; **First Base**—Dave McKay; **Third Base**—Matt Williams; **Bullpen**— Garvin Alston; **Assistant Hitting**—Mark Grace; **Coach/Translator**—Ariel Prieto.

MEDICAL/TRAINING
Club Physician: Dr. Gary Waslewski. **Head Trainer:** Ken Crenshaw. **Assistant Trainer:** Ryan DiPanfilo. **Strength/ Conditioning Coordinator:** Nate Shaw. **Physical Therapist:** Ben Hagar.

PLAYER DEVELOPMENT
Telephone: (602) 462-6500. **Fax:** (602) 462-6425.
Director, Player Development: Mike Bell. **Assistant Director, Player Development:** TJ Lasita. **Senior Manager, Player Development:** Shawn Marette. **Coordinators:** Tony Perezchica (field/infield), Luis Urueta (short-season field), Dan Carlson (pitching), Wellington Cepeda (short-season pitching), Chris Cron (hitting), Joel Youngblood (outfield/ baserunning), Bill Plummer (catching), Mark Grudzielanek (assistant), Audo Vicente (coach – short-season/AZL/DSL) Hatuey Mendoza (Latin American Operations), Wilfredo Tejada (Dominican field), Brad Arnsberg (rehab pitching), Kyle Torgerson (medical), Paul Porter (assistant medical), Vaughn Robinson (strength), Jim Currigan (video), Alex Cultice (video assistant), Bob Bensinger (complex).

FARM SYSTEM

Class	Club (League)	Manager	Hitting Coach	Pitching Coach
Triple-A	Reno (PCL)	Phil Nevin	Greg Gross	Gil Heredia
Double-A	Mobile (SL)	Robby Hammock	Jason Camilli	Doug Drabek
High A	Visalia (CAL)	J.R. House	Vince Harrison	Jeff Bajenaru
Low A	Kane County (MWL)	Mike Benjamin	Jonathan Mathews	Rich Sauveur
Short-season	Hillsboro (NWL)	Shelley Duncan	Jose Amado	Mike Parrott
Rookie	Missoula (PIO)	Joe Mather	Franklin Stubbs	Darwin Peguero
Rookie	Diamondbacks (AZL)	Darrin Garner	Jacob Cruz	Manny Garcia

SCOUTING
Telephone: (602) 462-6500. **Fax:** (602) 462-6425.
Director, Scouting: Deric Ladnier. **Assistant Director, Scouting:** Brendan Domaracki. **Special Assistant to Senior VP, Baseball Operations/Coordinator, Pro Scouting:** Mike Russell. **Coordinator, Scout Ahead Development Program:** Peter Wardell. **Assistant, Scout Ahead Development Program:** Cory Hahn.
Major League Scouts: Bill Bryk (Schererville, IN), Todd Greene (Alpharetta, GA), Mike Piatnik (Winter Haven, FL). **Pro Scouts:** Josh Barfield (Scottsdale, AZ), Mike Brown (Naples, FL), Ray Crone (Waxahachie, TX), Bob Cummings (Oak Lawn, IL), Clay Daniel (Jacksonville, FL), Jeff Gardner (Costa Mesa, CA), Bill Gayton (San Diego, CA), Ben Johnson (Litchfield Park, AZ), Brad Kelley (Scottsdale, AZ), Howard McCullough (Greenville, NC), Tom Romenesko (Santee, CA), Scipio Spinks (Sugarland, TX), Wade Taylor (Oviedo, FL), John Vander Wal (Grand Rapids, MI), Peter Vuckovich (Johnstown, PA). **Independent Leagues, Coordinator:** Chris Carminucci (Southbury, CT).
National Crosscheckers: Greg Lonigro (Connellsville, PA), James Merriweather III. (Glendale, AZ).
Regional Supervisors: Steve Connelly (Emerald Isle, NC), Clark Crist (Tucson, AZ), Steve McAllister (Chillicothe, IL), Jeff Mousser (Huntington Beach, CA), Joe Robinson (St Louis, MO), Frankie Thon Jr (Miami, FL).
Area Scouts: John Bartsch (Rocklin, CA), Nathan Birtwell (Nashville, TN), Frank Damas (Miami Lakes, FL), Orsino Hill (Elk Grove, CA), Kerry Jenkins (Birmingham, AL), Hal Kurtzman (Lake Balboa, CA), TR Lewis (Marietta, GA), Joe Mason (Millbrook, AL), Rick Matsko (Davidsville, PA), Rusty Pendergrass (Missouri City, MO), Donnie Reynolds (Portland, OR), Tony Piazza (Springfield, MO), JR Salinas (Dallas, TX), Dennis Sheehan (Glasco, NY), Rick Short (Peoria, IL), Doyle Wilson (Phoenix, AZ), George Swain (Wilmington, NC), Luke Wrenn (Lakeland, FL).
Part-Time Scouts: Doug Mathieson (Aldergrove, BC), Homer Newlin (Tallahassee, FL), Joe Rodriguez (Nashville, TN).
Director, Pacific Rim Operations: Mack Hayashi. **Special Assistant, Pacific Rim Operations:** Jim Marshall.
Coordinator, Latin America: Francisco Cartaya. **International Scouting Supervisor:** Luis Baez (Santo Domingo, DR).
International Scouts: Dominican Republic—Gabriel Berroa, José Ortiz, Rafael Mateo; **Panama**—José Díaz Perez; **Mexico** – Rodrigo Aguierre, Ray Padilla; **Nicaragua**—Julio Sanchez; **Colombia**—Luis Gonzalez; **Venezuela**—Didimo Bracho Jr., Andres Garcia, Alfonso Mora.

Atlanta Braves

Office Address: 755 Hank Aaron Dr., Atlanta, GA 30315.
Mailing Address: PO Box 4064, Atlanta, GA 30302.
Telephone: (404) 522-7630. **Website:** www.braves.com.

OWNERSHIP

Operated/Owned By: Liberty Media.
Chairman/CEO: Terry McGuirk. **Chairman Emeritus:** Bill Bartholomay. **President:** John Schuerholz. **Senior Vice President:** Henry Aaron.

BUSINESS OPERATIONS

Executive VP, Business Operations: Mike Plant. **Senior VP/General Counsel:** Greg Heller.

FINANCE

Senior VP/Chief Financial Officer: Chip Moore.

MARKETING/SALES

Executive VP, Sales/Marketing: Derek Schiller. **VP, Marketing:** Adam Zimmerman. **VP, Ticket Sales:** Paul Adams. **VP, Corporate Sales:** Jim Allen.

MEDIA RELATIONS/PUBLIC RELATIONS

Telephone: (404) 614-1556. **Fax:** (404) 614-1391.
Senior Director, Public Relations: Beth Marshall. **Public Relations Manager:** Kelly Barnes.
Director, Media Relations: Brad Hainje. **Publications Manager:** Andy Littlefield. **Media Relations Manager:** Adrienne Midgley. **Media Relations Coordinator:** Jonathan Kerber.
Media Relations Assistant: Jared Burleyson.

Terry McGuirk

STADIUM OPERATIONS

VP, Stadium Operations/Security: Larry Bowman. **Field Director:** Ed Mangan. **Senior Director, Game Entertainment:** Scott Cunningham. **PA Announcer:** Casey Motter. **Official Scorers:** Richard Musterer, Mike Stamus.

TICKETING

Telephone: (404) 577-9100. **Fax:** (404) 614-2480. **Email:** ticketsales@braves.com.
Senior Director, Ticket Operations: Anthony Esposito.

TRAVEL/CLUBHOUSE

Traveling Secretary: Chris Van Zant. **Visiting Clubhouse Manager:** John Holland.

2016 SCHEDULE

Standard Game Times: 7:10 p.m.; Fri. 7:35; Sun. 1:35.

APRIL
4-6	Washington
8-10	St. Louis
11-14	at Washington
15-17	at Miami
19-21	Los Angeles
22-24	New York
25-26	Boston
27-28	at Boston
29-30	at Chicago

MAY
1	at Chicago
2-4	at New York
6-8	Arizona
10-12	Philadelphia
13-15	at Kansas City
16-19	at Pittsburgh
20-22	at Philadelphia
24-26	Milwaukee
27-29	Miami
30-31	San Francisco

JUNE
1-2	San Francisco
3-5	at Los Angeles
6-8	at San Diego
10-12	Chicago
13-16	Cincinnati
17-19	at New York
21-22	at Miami
23-26	New York
27-29	Cleveland
30	Miami

JULY
1-3	Miami
4-6	at Philadelphia
8-10	at Chicago
15-17	Colorado
18-20	at Cincinnati
21-24	at Colorado
26-27	at Minnesota
28-31	Philadelphia

AUGUST
2-4	Pittsburgh
5-7	at St. Louis
8-11	at Milwaukee
12-14	at Washington
16-17	Minnesota
18-21	Washington
22-25	at Arizona
26-28	at San Francisco
30-31	San Diego

SEPTEMBER
1	San Diego
2-4	at Philadelphia
5-7	at Washington
9-11	New York
12-14	Miami
16-18	Washington
19-21	at New York
22-25	at Miami
27-29	Philadelphia
30	Detroit

OCTOBER
1-2	Detroit

GENERAL INFORMATION

Stadium (year opened): Turner Field (1997).
Team Colors: Red, white and blue.
Player Representative: Unavailable.
Home Dugout: First Base.
Playing Surface: Grass.

BASEBALL OPERATIONS

Telephone: (404) 522-7630. **Fax:** (404) 614-3308.
President, Baseball Operations: John Hart.
General Manager/Director, Pro Scouting: John Coppolella. **Director, Baseball Operations:** Billy Ryan. **Assistant Director, Pro Scouting/Analytics:** Matt Grabowski. **Assistant Director, Baseball Operations:** Kiley McDaniel. **Manager, Baseball Video Operations:** Rob Smith. **Executive Assistants:** Chris Rice, Eli Jimenez. **Assistant, Baseball Operations:** Danielle Monday. **Analyst, Baseball Operations:** Garrett Wilson. **Analyst, Major League Operations:** Noah Woodward.

John Hart

MAJOR LEAGUE STAFF

Manager: Fredi Gonzalez.
Coaches: Bench—Carlos Tosca; **Pitching**—Roger McDowell; **Hitting**—Kevin Seitzer; **Assistant Hitting Coach**—Jose Castro; **First Base**—Terry Pendleton; **Third Base**—Bo Porter; **Bullpen Coach**—Eddie Perez; **Bullpen Catcher**—Alan Butts; **Assistant Coach**—Horacio Ramirez.

MEDICAL/TRAINING

Director, Player Health & Performance: Andrew Hauser. **Head Team Physician:** Dr. Xavier Duralde. **Trainer:** Jeff Porter. **Assistant Trainer:** Jim Lovell. **Major League Strength/Conditioning Coach:** Phil Falco.

PLAYER DEVELOPMENT

Telephone: (404) 522-7630. **Fax:** (404) 614-1350.
Director, Player Development: Dave Trembley. **Assistant Director, Player Development:** Jonathan Schuerholz. **Manager, Minor League Administration:** Ron Knight. **Manager, Minor League Operations:** A.J. Scola. **Senior Advisors, Player Development:** Lee Elia, Lebi Ochoa.
Pitching Coordinator: Chuck Hernandez. **Hitting Coordinator:** John Pierson. **Roving Coordinators:** Joe Breeden (catching), Luis Lopez (infield), Joe Metz (medical); Rick Slate (strength/conditioning); Chris Dayton (assistant, strength/conditioning); Kyle Clements (video). **Minor League Equipment Manager:** Jeff Pink. **Rehab Pitching Coordinator:** Mike Maroth; **Assistant Rehab Instructor:** Kenny Dominguez. **Physical Therapist:** Marc Oceguera. **Pitching Consultant:** Steve Webber.

FARM SYSTEM

Class	Club (League)	Manager	Hitting Coach	Pitching Coach
Triple-A	Gwinnett (IL)	Brian Snitker	John Moses	Marty Reed
Double-A	Mississippi (SL)	Luis Salazar	Garey Ingram	Dennis Lewallyn
High A	Carolina (CL)	Rocket Wheeler	Carlos Mendez	Derrick Lewis
Low A	Rome (SAL)	Randy Ingle	Bobby Moore	Gabe Luckett
Rookie	Danville (APP)	Robinson Cancel	Ivan Cruz	Dan Meyer
Rookie	Braves (GCL)	Nestor Perez, Jr.	Rick Albert	Mike Alvarez
Rookie	Braves (DSL)	Francisco Santiesteban	Jefferson Romero	Chris Roque

SCOUTING

Telephone: (404) 522-7630. **Fax:** (404) 614-1350.
Special Assistants to GM: Gordon Blakeley (Newnan, GA), Roy Clark (Marietta, GA), Chad MacDonald (Arlington, TX), Rick Williams (Tampa, FL), Tom Giordano (Orlando, FL); Chipper Jones (Roswell, GA); Fred McGriff (Tampa, FL); Greg Walker (Pearson, GA). **Major League Scouts:** Matt Carroll (Erdenheim, PA), Dennis Haren (San Diego, CA), Dave Holliday (Bixby, OK), Matt Kinzer (Hammond, LA), Leon Wurth (Lenoir City, TN), Ted Simmons (Wildwood, MO) Terry R Tripp (Harrisburg, IL). **Professional Scouts:** Rod Gilbreath (Lilburn, GA), Pat Shortt (South Hempstead, NY), Rick Arnold (Spring Mills, PA), Devlin McConnell (Merion Station, PA), Patrick Lowery (Silver Spring, MD), Zeke Fine (San Francisco, CA).
Director, Scouting: Brian Bridges. **Manager, Scouting Operations:** Dixie Keller. **Assistant, Scouting:** Chris Lionetti **National Crosscheckers:** Tom Battista (Westlake Village, CA), Sean Rooney (Apex, NC), Deron Rombach (Arlington, TX). **Regional Crosscheckers: West**—Tom Davis (Ripon, CA), **East**—Reed Dunn (Nashville, TN), **Midwest**—Terry C Tripp (Norris, IL). **Southern Supervisor:** Dustin Evans (Acworth, GA).
Area Scouts: Kevin Barry (Kinmundy, IL), Billy Best (Holly Spings, NC), Hugh Buchanan (Snellville, GA), Justin Clark (Lakeland, FL), Dan Cox (Huntington Beach, CA), Nate Dion (Edmond, OK), Brett Evert (Salem, OR), Ralph Garr (Richmond, TX), Gene Kerns (Hagerstown, MD), Kevin Martin (Los Angeles, CA), Greg Morhardt (South Windsor, CT), Lou Sanchez (Miami, FL), Rick Sellers (Remus, MI), Don Thomas (Geismar, LA), Darin Vaughan (Kingwood, TX), Ricky Wilson (Buckeye, AZ).

Baltimore Orioles

Office Address: 333 W Camden St., Baltimore, MD 21201.
Telephone: (888) 848-BIRD. **Fax:** (410) 547-6272.
E-mail Address: birdmail@orioles.com. **Website:** www.orioles.com.

OWNERSHIP
Operated By: The Baltimore Orioles Limited Partnership Inc.
Chairman/CEO: Peter Angelos.

BUSINESS OPERATIONS
Executive Vice President: John Angelos. **VP/Special Liaison to Chairman:** Lou Kousouris.
General Legal Counsel: Russell Smouse. **Director, Human Resources:** Lisa Tolson. **Director, Information Systems:** James Kline.

FINANCE
Executive VP/CFO: Robert Ames. **VP, Finance:** Michael D. Hoppes, CPA.

PUBLIC RELATIONS/COMMUNICATIONS
Telephone: (410) 547-6150. **Fax:** (410) 547-6272.
VP, Communications/Marketing: Greg Bader. **Director, Public Relations:** Kristen Hudak.
Manager, Media Relations: Jim Misudek. **Coordinator, Public Relations:** Chris Martrich.
Coordinator, Digital Communications: Amanda Sarver. **Public Relations Assistant:** Jim Hogan. **Public Relations Assistant:** Elizabeth Ayers. **Director, Community Relations/ Promotions:** Kristen Schultz.

Peter Angelos

BALLPARK OPERATIONS
Director, Ballpark Operations: Kevin Cummings. **Head Groundskeeper:** Nicole McFadyen. **PA Announcer:** Ryan Wagner. **Official Scorers:** Jim Henneman, Marc Jacobson, Ryan Eigenbrode.

TICKETING
Telephone: (888) 848-BIRD. **Fax:** (410) 547-6270.
VP, Ticketing/Fan Services: Neil Aloise. **Assistant Director, Sales:** Mark Hromalik.

TRAVEL/CLUBHOUSE
Director, Team Travel: Kevin Buck.
Equipment Manager (Home): Chris Guth. **Equipment Manager (Road):** Fred Tyler.

2016 SCHEDULE
Standard Game Times: 7:05 p.m; Sun. 1:35

APRIL		JULY	
4-7 . . . . .Minnesota	20-22 . at Los Angeles (AL)	1-3 . . . . .at Seattle	22-23 . . . . . .Washington
8-10 . . . . . . .Tampa Bay	24-26 . . . . . .at Houston	4-6. . . at Los Angeles (NL)	24-25 . . . . at Washington
11-13 . . . . .at Boston	27-29 . . . .at Cleveland	8-10 . . . . Los Angeles (AL)	26-28 . . . at New York (AL)
14-17 . . . . .at Texas	30-31 . . . . Boston	15-17 . . . . . at Tampa Bay	29-31 . . . . .Toronto
19-21 . . . . .Toronto	**JUNE**	18-21 . . . at New York (AL)	**SEPTEMBER**
22-24 . . . .at Kansas City	1-2. . . . . Boston	22-24 . . . . . . Cleveland	2-4. . . . . . . .New York (AL)
25-27 . . . . . at Tampa Bay	3-5. . . . . .New York (AL)	25-27 . . . . .Colorado	5-7. . . . . . at Tampa Bay
28-30 . . . . . Chicago (AL)	6-8. . . . . Kansas City	29-31 . . . . . . at Toronto	9-11 . . . . .at Detroit
MAY	9-12 . . . . at Toronto		12-14 . . . . . . .at Boston
1 . . . . Chicago (AL)	14-16 . . . . .at Boston	**AUGUST**	15-18 . . . . . . .Tampa Bay
3-5. . . . . .New York (AL)	17-19 . . . . .Toronto	2-4. . . . . Texas	19-22 . . . . Boston
6-8. . . . . Oakland	21-22 . . . . . . San Diego	5-7. . . . .at Chicago (AL)	23-25 . . . . .Arizona
9-11 . . . . at Minnesota	24-26 . . . . . .Tampa Bay	8-11 . . . . . . .at Oakland	27-29 . . . . . at Toronto
12-15 . . . . Detroit	28-29 . . . . at San Diego	12-14 . . at San Francisco	30 . . . . . at New York (AL)
17-19 . . . . Seattle	30 . . . . .at Seattle	16-17 . . . . Boston	**OCTOBER**
		18-21 . . . . Houston	1-2. . . . . at New York (AL)

GENERAL INFORMATION
Stadium (year opened): Oriole Park at Camden Yards (1992).
Team Colors: Orange, black and white.

Player Representative: Darren O'Day.
Home Dugout: First Base.
Playing Surface: Grass.

BASEBALL OPERATIONS

Telephone: (410) 547-6107. **Fax:** (410) 547-6271.
Executive VP, Baseball Operations: Dan Duquette.
VP, Baseball Operations: Brady Anderson. **Special Assistant to Executive VP, Baseball Operations:** Lee Thomas. **Assistant Director, Major League Administration/Pro Scouting:** Bill Wilkes. **Director, Player Personnel:** John Stockstill. **Director, Baseball Operations:** Tripp Norton. **Director, Pacific Rim Operations/Baseball Development:** Mike Snyder. **Director, Baseball Analytics:** Sarah Gelles. **Coordinator, Baseball Operations:** Pat DiGregory. **Coordinator, Video:** Michael Silverman. **Coordinator, Advance Scouting:** Ben Werthan. **Coordinator, Pro Scouting:** Matt Koizim.

Dan Duquette

MAJOR LEAGUE STAFF

Manager: Buck Showalter.
Coaches: Bench—John Russell; **Pitching**—Dave Wallace; **Hitting**—Scott Coolbaugh; **Assistant Hitting**—Mark Quinn; **First Base**—Wayne Kirby; **Third Base**—Bobby Dickerson; **Bullpen**—Dom Chiti; **Coach**—Einar Diaz.

MEDICAL/TRAINING

Club Physician/Medical Director: Dr. William Goldiner. **Club Physician, Orthopedics:** Dr. Michael Jacobs. **Head Athletic Trainer:** Richie Bancells. **Assistant Athletic Trainers:** Brian Ebel, Chris Correnti. **Strength/Conditioning Coaches:** Joe Hogarty, Ryo Naito.

PLAYER DEVELOPMENT

Telephone: (410) 547-6120. **Fax:** (410) 547-6298.
Director, Player Development: Brian Graham. **Director, Minor League Operations:** Kent Qualls. **Coordinator, Minor League Administration:** J. Maria Arellano. **Coordinator, Player Development:** Cale Cox. **Director, Pitching Development:** Rick Peterson. **Coordinator, Minor League Hitting:** Jeff Manto. **Organizational Hitting Instructor/Evaluator:** Terry Crowley. **Coordinator, Minor League Catching:** Don Werner. **Coordinator, Minor League Infield:** Kevin Bradshaw. **Roving Instructor, Outfield/Baserunning/Strength:** Scott Beerer.
Medical Coordinator: Dave Walker. **Latin American Medical Coordinator:** Manny Lopez. **Coordinator, Strength/Conditioning—Sarasota:** Ryan Driscoll. **Coordinator, Minor League Rehab Pitching:** Scott McGregor. **Minor League Equipment Manager:** Jake Parker. **Pitching Administrator, Florida/DSL:** Dave Schmidt. **Administrator, Sarasota Operations:** Len Johnston.

FARM SYSTEM

Class	Club (League)	Manager	Hitting Coach	Pitching Coach
Triple-A	Norfolk (IL)	Ron Johnson	Sean Berry	Mike Griffin
Double-A	Bowie (EL)	Gary Kendall	Howie Clark	Alan Mills
High A	Frederick (CL)	Keith Bodie	Erik Pappas	Kennie Steenstra
Low A	Delmarva (SAL)	Ryan Minor	Kyle Moore	Blaine Beatty
Short-season	Aberdeen (NYP)	Luis Pujols	Scott Beerer	Justin Lord
Rookie	Orioles (GCL)	Orlando Gomez	M. May/K. Bradshaw	Wilson Alvarez
Rookie	Orioles (DSL)	Unavailable	Unavailable	Unavailable
Rookie	Orioles (DSL2)	Unavailable	Unavailable	Unavailable

SCOUTING

Telephone: (410) 547-6212. **Fax:** 410-547-6928.
Director, Amateur Scouting: Gary Rajsich.
Scouting Administrator: Brad Ciolek. **Special Assistant to the GM/Scouting:** Danny Haas (Fort Myers, FL). **National Crosschecker Supervisor:** Matt Haas (Cincinnati, OH). **West Coast Supervisor:** David Blume (Elk Grove, CA). **Midwest Supervisor:** Jim Richardson (Marlow, OK). **Upper Midwest Supervisor:** Ernie Jacobs (Wichita, KS).
Area Scouts: Dean Albany (Baltimore, MD), Mike Boulanger (Broken Arrow, OK), Kelvin Colon (Miami, FL), Adrian Dorsey (Nashville, TN), Thom Dreier (The Woodlands, TX), Dan Durst (Rockford, IL), Kirk Fredriksson (Torrington, CT), John Gillette (Gilbert, AZ), Ken Guthrie (Sanger, TX), David Jennings (Spanish Fort, AL), Arthur McConnehead (Atlanta, GA), Rich Morales (Blacksburg, VA), Mark Ralston (Carlsbad, CA), Jeff Stevens (Walnut Creek, CA), Jim Thrift (Sarasota, FL), Brandon Verley (White Salmon, WA), Scott Walter (Manhattan Beach, CA).
Special Assignment Scouts: Wayne Britton (Waynesboro, VA), Dave Machemer (Stevensville, MI). **Major League Scouts:** Dave Engle (San Diego, CA), Jim Howard (Clifton Park, NY), Bruce Kison (Bradenton, FL). **Professional Scouts:** Todd Frohwirth (Waukesha, WI).
Executive Director, International Recruiting: Fred Ferreira. **Director, Baseball Operations for the Dominican Republic:** Nelson Norman. **Academy Director, Dominican Republic:** Felipe Rojas Alou. **International Scouts:** Joel Bradley, Enrique Constante, Calvin Maduro, Brett Ward.

Boston Red Sox

Office Address: Fenway Park, 4 Yawkey Way, Boston, MA 02215.
Telephone: (617) 226-6000. **Fax:** (617) 226-6416. **Website:** www.redsox.com

OWNERSHIP
Principal Owner: John Henry. **Chairman:** Thomas C. Werner. **Club President:** Sam Kennedy. **President/CEO Emeritus:** Larry Lucchino.

BUSINESS OPERATIONS
EVP/ FSG Corporate Strategy & General Counsel: Ed Weiss. **EVP/Business Affairs:** Jonathan Gilula. **EVP/Partnerships:** Troup Parkinson. **SVP/Strategic Planning & Senior Counsel:** Dave Beeston.

Sam Kennedy

BALLPARK OPERATIONS
VP/Ballpark Operations: Peter Nesbit. **VP/Fan Services & Entertainment:** Sarah McKenna. **VP/Florida Business Operations:** Katie Haas. **VP/Fenway Park Tours:** Marcita Thompson.

FINANCE, STRATEGY, & ANALYTICS
SVP/Finance, Strategy & Analytics: Tim Zue. **SVP/CFO:** Steve Fitch. **Financial Advisor to the President:** Jeff White.

HUMAN RESOURCES/INFORMATION TECHNOLOGY
SVP/Human Resources: Amy Waryas. **VP/Information Technology:** Brian Shield.

LEGAL
SVP/Government Affairs & Special Counsel: David Friedman. **VP/Club Counsel:** Elaine Weddington Steward.

MARKETING/COMMUNICATIONS
SVP/Chief Marketing Officer: Adam Grossman. **Senior Director/Media Relations:** Kevin Gregg. **Senior Advisor to the President:** Charles Steinberg.

PARTNERSHIPS/CLIENT SERVICES
VP/Client Services: Marcell Bhangoo. **VP/Community, Alumni & Player Relations:** Pam Kenn.

TICKETING/SALES/EVENTS
SVP/Ticketing, Concerts, & Events: Ron Bumgarner. **SVP/Fenway Concerts & Entertainment:** Larry Cancro. **VP/Ticketing:** Richard Beaton. VP/Ticketing Services & Operations. Naomi Calder. **VP/Ticket Sales:** William Droste. **VP/Fenway Enterprises:** Carrie Campbell.

RED SOX FOUNDATION
Honorary Chairman: Tim Wakefield. **Executive Director:** Gena Borson.

2016 SCHEDULE
Standard Game Times: 7:10 p.m.; Sun. 1:35

APRIL
4-7 . . . . .at Cleveland
8-10 . . . . at Toronto
11-13 . . . . Baltimore
15-18 . . . . .Toronto
19-21 . . . . . . .Tampa Bay
22-24 . . . . . . .at Houston
25-26 . . . . at Atlanta
27-28 . . . . Atlanta
29-30 . . . . .New York

MAY
1 . . . . .New York
3-5 . . . . .at Chicago
6-8 . . . . at New York
9-11 . . . . Oakland
12-15 . . . . Houston

16-18 . . . . .at Kansas City
20-22 . . . . . . Cleveland
24-26 . . . . .Colorado
27-29 . . . . . . at Toronto
30-31 . . . . . .at Baltimore

JUNE
1-2 . . . . .at Baltimore
3-5 . . . . .Toronto
7-8 . . . . . at San Francisco
10-12 . . . . . at Minnesota
14-16 . . . . Baltimore
17-19 . . . . Seattle
20-23 . . . . Chicago
24-26 . . . . .at Texas
27-29 . . . . .at Tampa Bay

JULY
1-3 . . . . Los Angeles
4-6 . . . . Texas
8-10 . . . . .Tampa Bay
15-17 . . . . . at New York
19-20 . . . . .San Francisco
21-24 . . . . . . .Minnesota
25-27 . . . . Detroit
28-31 . . . . at Los Angeles

AUGUST
1-4 . . . . .at Seattle
5-7 . . . . . at Los Angeles
9-11 . . . . .New York
12-14 . . . . .Arizona
16-17 . . . . . .at Baltimore
18-21 . . . . .at Detroit

22-25 . . . . . at Tampa Bay
26-28 . . . . . . Kansas City
29-31 . . . . . . .Tampa Bay

SEPTEMBER
2-4 . . . . .at Oakland
5-7 . . . . at San Diego
9-11 . . . . at Toronto
12-14 . . . . Baltimore
15-18 . . . . .New York
19-22 . . . . . .at Baltimore
23-25 . . . . at Tampa Bay
27-29 . . . . . at New York
30 . . . . .Toronto

OCTOBER
1-2 . . . . .Toronto

GENERAL INFORMATION
Stadium (year opened):
Fenway Park (1912).
Team Colors: Navy blue, red and white.

Player Representative: Unavailable.
Home Dugout: First Base.
Playing Surface: Grass.

BASEBALL OPERATIONS

President, Baseball Operations: Dave Dombrowski
SVP/GM: Mike Hazen. **SVP/Assistant GM:** Brian O'Halloran. **SVP/Player Personnel:**
Allard Baird. **SVP/Baseball Operations:** Frank Wren. **VP/Amateur & International Scouting:**
Amiel Sawdaye. **VP/Baseball Administration:** Raquel Ferreira. **Traveling Secretary:** Jack
McCormick. **Director, Major League Operations:** Zack Scott. **Director, Pitching Analysis &
Development:** Brian Bannister. **Senior Baseball Analyst:** Tom Tippett. **Baseball Operations
Analysts:** Greg Rybarczyk and Joe McDonald. **Coordinator, Baseball Operations:** Mike
Regan. **Coordinator Baseball Systems Development:** Shawn O'Rourke. **Executive Assistant:**
Erin Cox. **Senior Advisor:** Bill James. **Special Assistants to GM:** Pedro Martinez, Jason Varitek.

Dave Dombrowski

MAJOR LEAGUE STAFF

Manager: John Farrell.
Coaches: Bench—Torey Lovullo; **Pitching**—Carl Willis; **Hitting**—Chili Davis; **First Base**—
Ruben Amaro Jr.; **Third Base**—Brian Butterfield; **Bullpen**—Dana LeVangie. **Assistant Hitting Coach:** Victor Rodriguez.
Bullpen Catchers: Mani Martinez & Michael Brenly. **BP Thrower:** Matt Noone.

SPORTS MEDICINE SERVICE

Director, Sports Medicine Service: Dan Dyrek. **Medical Director:** Dr. Larry Ronan. **Head Team Orthopedist:**
Dr. Peter Asnis. **Head Athletic Trainer:** Brad Pearson. **Assistant Trainers:** Paul Buchheit, Masai Takahashi. **Strength/
Conditioning Coach:** Kiyoshi Momose. **Assistant Strength/Conditioning Coach:** Mike Roose. **Massage Therapists:**
Russell Nua, Shinichiro Uchikubo. **Physical Therapist:** Adam Thomas. **Head Minor League Physician:** Dr. Brian
Busconi. Director, **Behavioral Health Program:** Dr. Richard Ginsburg. **Mental Skills Coordinators:** Bob Tewksbury, Laz
Gutierrez, Justin Su'a. **Sports Medicine Administrative Manager:** Elana Webb.

PLAYER DEVELOPMENT

Director, Player Development: Ben Crockett. **Assistant Director, Player Development:** Brian Abraham. **Assistant
Director, Florida Baseball Operations:** Ethan Faggett. **Minor League Equipment Manager:** Mike Stelmach. **Field
Coordinator:** David Howard. **Latin American Pitching Coordinator/GCL Pitching Coach:** Goose Gregson. **Minor
League Medical Coordinator:** Brandon Henry. **Minor League Strength/Conditioning Coordinator:** Edgar Barreto. **Latin
Medical Coordinator:** David Herrera. **Physical Therapist/Clinical Educator:** Jason Bartley. **Roving Instructors:** Andy Fox
(infield), Chad Epperson (catching), Greg Norton(hitting), Ralph Treuel (pitching), Billy McMillon(outfield/baserunning).

FARM SYSTEM

Class	Club (League)	Manager	Hitting Coach	Pitching Coach
Triple-A	Pawtucket (IL)	Kevin Boles	Rich Gedman	Bob Kipper
Double-A	Portland (EL)	Carlos Febles	Jon Nunnally	Kevin Walker
High A	Salem (CL)	Joe Oliver	Nelson Paulino	Paul Abbott
Low A	Greenville (SAL)	Darren Fenster	Lee May Jr.	Walter Miranda
Short-season	Lowell (NYP)	Iggy Suarez	Wilton Veras	Lance Carter
Rookie	Red Sox (GCL)	Tom Kotchman	Junior Zamora	Dick Such
Rookie	Red Sox 1 (DSL)	Jose Zapata	Carlos Adolfo	Aquilino Lopez
Rookie	Red Sox 2 (DSL)	Aly Gonzalez	Ozzie Chavez	Oscar Lira

SCOUTING

VP/International Scouting: Eddie Romero. Director, **Professional Scouting:** Gus Quattlebaum. **Director, Amateur
Scouting:** Michael Rikard. **Director, Player Personnel:** Jared Banner. **Assistant Director, Amateur Scouting:**
Steve Sanders. **Coordinator, Advance Scouting:** Harrison Slutsky. **Scouting Coordinator:** Brian Cruz. **Assistant,
Professional Scouting:** Alex Gimenez. **Special Assignment Scouts:** Eddie Bane, Steve Peck, Brad Sloan.
Special Assistant, Player Personnel: Mark Wasinger. **Global Crosschecker:** Paul Fryer.
Major League Advance Scout: Steve Langone. **Major League Scouts:** Jaymie Bane, Nate Field, Gary Hughes, Bob
Hamelin, John Lombardo, Joe McDonald, Matt Mahoney, Anthony Turco.
Crosscheckers: John Booher (National), Fred Petersen (Southeast), Jim Robinson (South), Quincy Boyd (Northeast),
Dan Madsen (West), Chris Mears (Pitching), Tom Kotchman (Florida). **Area Scouts:** Chris Calciano (Rehoboth, DE), Tim
Collinsworth (Katy, TX), Lane Decker (Piedmont, OK), Raymond Fagnant (East Granby, CT), Todd Gold (Charlotte, NC),
Stephen Hargett (Jacksonville, FL), Blair Henry (Eagan, MN), Justin Horowitz (Seattle, WA), Josh Labandeira, (Fresno, CA),
Brian Moehler (Marietta, GA), Edgar Perez (Vega Baja, PR), John Pyle (Lexington, KY), Willie Romay (Miami Springs, FL),
Demond Smith (Elk Grove, CA), Paul Toboni (Dallas, TX), Danny Watkins (Daphne, AL), Vaughn Williams (Gilbert, AZ), Jim
Woodward (Claremont, CA). **Part Time Scouts:** Rob English, Tim Martin, Jay Oliver, Keith Prager, David Scrivines, Dick
Sorkin, Adam Stern, Terry Sullivan.
International Crosschecker & Coordinator, Latin American Scouting: Todd Claus. **International Crosschecker:**
Rolando Pino. Coordinator, **Pacific Rim Scouting:** Jon Deeble. **Coordinator, International Scouting:** Adrian Lorenzo.
Director, Dominican Academy: Jesus Alou. **Assistant Director, Dominican Academy:** Javier Hernandez. **Dominican
Republic Scouting Supervisor:** Manny Nanita. Coordinator, **Venezuela Scouting/Venezuela Scout:** Manny Padron.
International Scouts: Jonathan Cruz (Dominican Republic), Michel DeJesus (Dominican Republic), Angel Escobar
(Venezuela), Steve Fish (Australia), Cris Garibaldo (Panama), Ernesto Gomez (Venezuela), James Kang (Mexico), Toshi
Kato (Japan), John Kennedy (Brazil), John Kim (Korea), Louie Lin (Taiwan), Wilder Lobo (Venezuela), Esau Medina
(Dominican Republic), Rafael Mendoza (Nicaragua), Ramon Mora (Venezuela), Dennis Neuman (Aruba/Curacao),
Francisco Polanco (Dominican Republic), Santiago Prada (Colombia), Alex Requena (Venezuela), Lenin Rodriguez
(Venezuela), Rene Saggiadi (Europe), Darryn Smith (South Africa), Sotero Torres (Mexico). **International Pro Scouts:**
David Cortes (Mexico), Shun Kakazu (Japan).

Chicago Cubs

Office Address: Wrigley Field, 1060 W. Addison St., Chicago, IL 60613.
Telephone: (773) 404-2827. **Website:** www.cubs.com.

OWNERSHIP
Executive Chairman: Tom Ricketts. **Board of Directors:** Laura Ricketts, Pete Ricketts, Todd Ricketts and Tribune Company.

BUSINESS OPERATIONS

Tom Ricketts

President, Business Operations: Crane Kenney. **Executive VP, Government and Community Affairs/General Counsel:** Michael Lufrano. **Senior VP, Strategy/Ballpark Operations:** Alex Sugarman. **Senior VP/CFO:** Jon Greifenkamp. **VP, Sales/Partnerships:** Colin Faulkner. **VP, Wrigley Field Restoration and Expansion:** Carl Rice. **VP, Human Resources:** Bryan Robinson. **VP, Communications/Community:** Julian Green. **VP, General Counsel:** Lydia Wahlke. Senior Advisor, **Business Operations:** Mark McGuire. **Executive Assistant to the Chairman:** Lorraine Swiatly. **Manager, Board and Stakeholder Relations:** Sarah Poontong. **Executive Coordinator, Business Operations:** Michele Dietz.

BALLPARK OPERATIONS
Senior Director, Facilities/Procurement: Patrick Meenan. **Senior Director, Wrigley Field Event Operations:** Matt Kenny. **Director, Security/Safety Operations:** James Reynolds. **Assistant Director, Guest Services:** Hannah Basinger. **Assistant Director, Event Operations/ Security:** Derek Crawford. **Assistant Director, Facilities:** Roger Baird. **Manager, Facility Maintenance:** Russell Johnson. **Public Address Announcer:** Andrew Belleson. **Organist:** Gary Pressy.

MARKETING/COMMUNICATIONS
Senior Director, Marketing: Alison Miller. **Assistant Director, Organizational Communications:** Lindsay Bago. **Manager, Communications:** Kevin Saghy. **Coordinator, Public Relations:** Alyson Cohen.

CORPORATE PARTNERSHIPS
Senior Director, Corporate Partnerships: Allen Hermeling. **Assistant Director, Corporate Partnerships Sales Operations:** Brian O'Connor. **Controller:** Melissa Shields.

INFORMATION TECHNOLOGY/HUMAN RESOURCES
Vice President, Technology: Andrew McIntyre. **Assistant Director, Human Resources:** Rachel O'Connell. **HR Manager, Ballpark Operations:** Danielle Alexa. **HR Staffing Lead:** Marisol Widmayer.

LEGAL/COMMUNITY AFFAIRS
Counsel: Mike Feldman. **Director, Community Affairs:** Connie Falcone.

TICKET SALES/SERVICE/OPERATIONS
Director, Ticket Sales: Andy Blackburn. **Director, Ticket Service:** Brian Garza. **Senior Director, Ticketing:** Cale Vennum.

2016 SCHEDULE
Standard Game Times: 7:05 p.m.; Sun. 1:20

APRIL		JULY		
4-5 . . . . . . at Los Angeles	20-22 . . . at San Francisco	1-3 . . . . at New York	19-21 . . . . . . at Colorado	
7-10 . . . . at Arizona	23-25 . . . . . . .at St. Louis	4-6 . . . . Cincinnati	22-24 . . . . . at San Diego	
11-14 . . . . Cincinnati	27-29 . . . . .Philadelphia	8-10 . . . . . at Pittsburgh	26-28 . . . . at Los Angeles	
15-17 . . . . .Colorado	30-31 . . . . . . Los Angeles	15-17 . . . . Texas	29-31 . . . . Pittsburgh	
18-20 . . . . . .at St. Louis		18-20 . . . . .New York	SEPTEMBER	
21-24 . . . . .at Cincinnati	JUNE	22-24 . . . . . at Milwaukee	1-4 . . . . . . San Francisco	
26-28 . . . . . .Milwaukee	1-2 . . . . Los Angeles	25-26 . . . . . . .at Chicago	5-7 . . . . . . at Milwaukee	
29-30 . . . . Atlanta	3-5 . . . . .Arizona	27-28 . . . . Chicago	9-11 . . . . . . .at Houston	
	6-8 . . . . . at Philadelphia	29-31 . . . . Seattle	12-14 . . . . . .at St. Louis	
MAY	10-12 . . . . . at Atlanta		15-18 . . . . . .Milwaukee	
1 . . . . Atlanta	13-15 . . . . at Washington	AUGUST	19-21 . . . . Cincinnati	
2-4 . . . . . . at Pittsburgh	17-19 . . . . . . Pittsburgh	1-3 . . . . .Miami	23-25 . . . . St. Louis	
5-8 . . . . Washington	20-22 . . . . St. Louis	5-7 . . . . . . .at Oakland	26-29 . . . . at Pittsburgh	
9-11 . . . . San Diego	23-26 . . . . . at Miami	9-10 . . . . . . Los Angeles	30 . . . . . . .at Cincinnati	
13-15 . . . . . .Pittsburgh	27-29 . . . . .at Cincinnati	11-14 . . . . St. Louis	OCTOBER	
17-19 . . . . at Milwaukee	30 . . . . at New York	16-18 . . . . . .Milwaukee	1-2 . . . . . . .at Cincinnati	

GENERAL INFORMATION
Stadium (year opened): Wrigley Field (1914). **Home Dugout:** Third Base.
Team Colors: Royal blue, red and white. **Playing Surface:** Grass.
Player Representative: Unavailable.

BASEBALL OPERATIONS

Telephone: (773) 404-2827. **Fax:** (773) 404-4147.
President, Baseball Operations: Theo Epstein.
Executive VP/General Manager: Jed Hoyer. **Assistant GMs:** Randy Bush, Shiraz Rehman.
Special Assistant to GM/Director, International Scouting: Louis Eljaua. **Special Assistant
to GM/Director, Major League Scouting:** Kyle Evans. **Director, Baseball Operations:** Scott
Harris. **Director, Research/Development:** Chris Moore.
Assistant to the GM: Jeff Greenberg. Coordinator, **Major League Video/Pacific Rim Liaison:**
Naoto Masamoto. **Coordinator, Advance Scouting:** Nate Halm. **Coordinator, Advance Scouting:**
Tommy Hottovy. **Coordinator, Player Development/Scouting Video:** Mitch Duggins. **Baseball
Systems Architect:** Ryan Kruse. Analyst, **Research/Development:** Chris Jones. **Analyst, Research/
Development:** Sean Ahmed. **Assistants, Baseball Operations:** Greg Davey, Alex Smith, John
Baker. **Special Assistants:** Ryan Dempster, Ted Lilly, Kerry Wood, Kevin Youkilis.

Theo Epstein

MAJOR LEAGUE STAFF

Manager: Joe Maddon.
Coaches: Bench—Dave Martinez; **Pitching**—Chris Bosio; **Hitting**—John Mallee; **Assistant Hitting**—Eric Hinske;
Third Base—Gary Jones; **First Base**—Brandon Hyde; **Bullpen**—Lester Strode; **Quality Assurance Coach**—Henry
Blanco; **Catching Coach**—Mike Borzello; Staff Assistant–Franklin Font; **Bullpen Catcher**—Chad Noble.

MEDICAL/TRAINING

Team Physician: Dr. Stephen Adams. **Team Orthopedist:** Dr. Stephen Gryzlo. Director, **Medical Administration:**
Mark O'Neal. **Head Athletic Trainer:** P.J. Mainville. **Assistant Athletic Trainers:** Ed Halbur, Matt Johnson.

MEDIA RELATIONS

Director, Media Relations: Peter Chase. Assistant Director, **Media Relations:** Jason Carr. Coordinator, **Media
Relations:** Safdar Khan. Assistant, **Media Relations:** Alex Wilcox.

PLAYER DEVELOPMENT

Telephone: (773) 404-4035. **Fax:** (773) 404-4147.
Senior VP, Amateur Scouting/Player Development: Jason McLeod. **Director, Player Development:** Jaron Madison.
Assistant Director, Player Development/International Scouting: Alex Suarez. **Assistant Director, Minor League
Operations:** Bobby Basham. **Coordinator, Minor League Administration:** Derrick Fong. **Assistant, Player Development/
International Scouting:** Kenny Socorro. **Director, Mental Skills Program:** Josh Lifrak. **Coordinator, Mental Skills Program:**
Darnell McDonald. **Latin Coordinator, Mental Skills Program:** Rey Fuentes. **Field Coordinator:** Tim Cossins. **Coordinators:**
Jim Brower (pitching), Andy Haines (hitting), Doug Dascenzo (outfield/baserunning), Jose Flores (infield), Dave Keller (Latin
American field), Tom Beyers (assistant hitting), Mike Mason (assistant pitching).

FARM SYSTEM

Class	Club (League)	Manager	Hitting Coach	Pitching Coach
Triple-A	Iowa (PCL)	Marty Pevey	Brian Harper	Rod Nichols
Double-A	Tennessee (SL)	Mark Johnson	Desi Wilson	Terry Clark
High A	Myrtle Beach (CL)	Buddy Bailey	Mariano Duncan	Anderson Tavarez
Low A	South Bend (MWL)	Jimmy Gonzalez	Guillermo Martinez	David Rosario
Short-season	Eugene (NWL)	Jesus Feliciano	Ty Wright	Brian Lawrence
Rookie	Cubs (AZL)	Carmelo Martinez	J. Farrell/C.Valaika	Ron Villone
Rookie	Cubs 1 (DSL)	Claudio Almonte	Carlos Ramirez	E. Villacis/J. Cueto
Rookie	Cubs 2 (DSL)	Pedro Gonzalez	Franklin Blanco	Armando Gabino

SCOUTING

Director, Amateur Scouting: Matt Dorey (Seattle, WA). Assistant Director, **Amateur Scouting:** Lukas McKnight
(Libertyville, IL). **Amateur Scouting Assistant:** Shane Farrell (Chicago, IL). **Director, Professional Scouting:** Jared
Porter (Chicago, IL). **Coordinator, Pro Scouting:** Andrew Bassett (Chicago, IL). **Major League Scouts:** Terry Kennedy
(Chandler, AZ), Jason Karegeannes (De Pere, WI), Adam Wogan (Brooklyn, NY). **Pro Scouts:** Billy Blitzer (Brooklyn, NY),
Steve Boros (Kingwood, TX), Jake Ciarrachi (Chicago, IL), Matt Hahn (Tampa, FL), Dennis Henderson (Orange, CA), Mark
Kiefer (Hunt, TX), Robert Lofrano (Woodland Hills, CA), Kyle Phillips (Alpine, CA), Mark Servais (La Crosse, WI), Keith Stohr
(Satellite Beach, FL). **Pro/Amateur Scout:** Jason Parks (Scottsdale, AZ). **Special Assignment Scouts:** Jason Cooper
(Kirkland, WA), Dave Klipstein (Keller, TX).
National Supervisors: Sam Hughes (Atlanta, GA), Ron Tostenson (El Dorado Hills, CA). **Crosscheckers:** Southeast-
Bobby Filotei (Mobile, AL); Central-Trey Forkerway (Houston, TX); West-Mark Adair (Irvine, CA); Midwest/Northeast-
Tim Adkins (Huntington, WV). **Area Scouts:** Daniel Carte (Hurricane, WV), Tom Clark (Lake City, FL), Chris Clemons
(Robinson, TX), Kevin Ellis (Houston, TX), Al Geddes (Canby, OR), Edwards Guzman (Toa Baja, PR) Greg Hopkins (Camas,
WA), John Koronka (Clermont, FL), Alex Levitt (Nashville, TN), Keith Lockhart (Dacula, GA), Alex Lontayo (Chula Vista,
CA), Steve McFarland (Scottsdale, AZ), Tom Myers (Santa Barbara, CA), Ty Nichols (Broken Arrow, OK), Eric Servais
(Minneapolis, MN), Matt Sherman (Kingston, MA), Billy Swoope (Norfolk, VA), Gabe Zappin (Walnut Creek, CA), Stan
Zielinski (Winfield, IL).
Director, Dominican Republic Operations: Jose Serra. **Scouting Coordinator, Dominican Republic:** Gian Guzman.
Venezuelan Scouting Supervisor: Hector Ortega. **Coordinator, Pacific Rim Scouting:** Min Kyu Sung. **International
Scouts:** Cirillo Cumberbatch (Panama), Mario Encarnacion (Dominican Republic), Jose Estevez (Dominican Republic),
Carlos Figueroa (Venezuela), Julio Figueroa (Venezuela), Valerio Heredia (Dominican Republic), Sergio Hernandez
(Mexico), Rafael Jimenez (Venezuela), Miguel Mijares (Venezuela), Juan DeDios Moncion (Dominican Republic), Manuel
Pestana (Venezuela), Brent Phelan (Australia), Carlos Reyes (Dominican Republic).

Chicago White Sox

Office Address: U.S. Cellular, Field, 333 W. 35th St., Chicago, IL 60616.
Telephone: (312) 674-1000. **Fax:** (312) 674-5116. **Website:** whitesox.com, orgullosox.com.

OWNERSHIP

Chairman: Jerry Reinsdorf. **Vice Chairman:** Eddie Einhorn.
Board of Directors: Robert Judelson, Judd Malkin, Allan Muchin, Jay Pinsky, Lee Stern, Burton Ury, Charles Walsh.
Special Assistant to Chairman: Dennis Gilbert. **Assistant to Chairman:** Barb Reincke. **Coordinator, Administration/Investor Relations:** Katie Hermle.

BUSINESS OPERATIONS

Senior Executive Vice President: Howard Pizer.
Senior Director, Information Services: Don Brown. **Vice President, Human Resources:** Moira Foy. **Senior Coordinator, Human Resources:** Leslie Gaggiano.

Jerry Reinsdorf

FINANCE

Senior VP, Administration/Finance: Tim Buzard. **Vice President, Finance:** Bill Waters.
Accounting Manager: Chris Taylor.

MARKETING/SALES

Senior VP, Sales/Marketing: Brooks Boyer. **Senior Director, Business Development/Broadcasting:** Bob Grim. Director, **Game Presentation:** Cris Quintana. **Senior Manager, Scoreboard Operations/Production:** Jeff Szynal. Manager, **Game Operations:** Dan Mielke.
Senior Coordinator, Manager, Multimedia/Design: Lauren Markiewicz.
Director, Corporate Partnerships Sales Development: George McDoniel. **Director, Corporate Partnerships Activation:** Gail Tucker. Manager, **Corporate Partnerships Development:** Jeff Floerke.
Coordinators, Corporate Partnership Activation: Arden Reed, Kat Claeys. **Senior Director, Ticket Sales:** Tom Sheridan. **Manager, Premium Seating Sales:** Rob Boaz.

MEDIA RELATIONS/PUBLIC RELATIONS

Telephone: (312) 674-5300. **Fax:** (312) 674-5116.
Senior VP, Communications: Scott Reifert.
Senior Director, Media Relations: Bob Beghtol. **Director, Public Relations:** Sheena Quinn. **Assistant Director, Media Relations:** Ray Garcia. **Coordinator, Public Relations:** Julianne Bartosz. **Coordinators, Media Relations/Services:** Joe Roti, Megan Golden.
Vice President, Community Relations/Executive Director, CWS Charities: Christine O'Reilly. **Managers, Community Relations:** Sarah Marten, Lauren Pesqueda. **Director, Youth Baseball Initiatives:** Kevin Coe. **Director, Digital Communications:** Brad Boron. **Director, Advertising/Design Services:** Gareth Breunlin. **Manager, Online Communications:** Dakin Dugaw.

STADIUM OPERATIONS

Senior VP, Stadium Operations: Terry Savarise. **Senior Director, Park Operations:** Greg Hopwood. **Senior**

2016 SCHEDULE

Standard Game Times: 7:10 p.m.; Sun. 1:10.

APRIL		
4-7 . . . . .at Oakland	20-22 . . . . . Kansas City	4-6. . . . . .New York	25-28 . . . . Seattle
8-10 . . . . Cleveland	23-25 . . . . . . Cleveland	8-10 . . . . Atlanta	29-31 . . . . . . .at Detroit
11-14 . . . at Minnesota	26-29 . . . .at Kansas City	15-17 . . . . at Los Angeles	
15-17 . . . . at Tampa Bay	30-31 . . . . at New York	18-20 . . . . . . .at Seattle	**SEPTEMBER**
18-21 . . . . . Los Angeles	**JUNE**	21-24 . . . . Detroit	1-4. . . . . . . at Minnesota
22-24 . . . . Texas	1 . . . . at New York	25-26 . . . . Chicago	5-7. . . . . Detroit
25-27 . . . . . . at Toronto	3-5. . . . . .at Detroit	27-28 . . . . . .at Chicago	9-11 . . . . . . Kansas City
28-30 . . . . . .at Baltimore	7-9. . . . . . .Washington	29-31 . . . . at Minnesota	12-15 . . . . Cleveland
	10-12 . . . . . . Kansas City		16-18 . . . .at Kansas City
MAY	13-15 . . . . Detroit	**AUGUST**	20-21 . . . . at Philadelphia
1 . . . . .at Baltimore	17-19 . . . . .at Cleveland	2-4. . . . . .at Detroit	23-25 . . . . . .at Cleveland
3-5. . . . . Boston	20-23 . . . . . . .at Boston	5-7. . . . . Baltimore	26-29 . . . . .Tampa Bay
6-8. . . . . . . .Minnesota	24-26 . . . . .Toronto	9-11 . . . . .at Kansas City	30 . . . . .Minnesota
9-11 . . . . .at Texas	28-30 . . . . . .Minnesota	12-14 . . . . at Miami	
13-15 . . . at New York	**JULY**	16-18 . . . . .at Cleveland	**OCTOBER**
17-19 . . . . Houston	1-3. . . . . . . .at Houston	19-21 . . . . . . Oakland	1-2. . . . . .Minnesota
		23-24 . . . . . .Philadelphia	

GENERAL INFORMATION

Stadium (year opened): U.S. Cellular Field (1991).
Team Colors: Black, white and silver.

Player Representative: Unavailable.
Home Dugout: Third Base.
Playing Surface: Grass.

Director, Guest Services/Diamond Suite Operations: Julie Taylor. **Head Groundskeeper:** Roger Bossard. **PA Announcer:** Gene Honda. **Official Scorers:** Bob Rosenberg, Don Friske.

TICKETING
Director, Ticket Operations: Mike Mazza. Manager, **Ticket Accounting Administration:** Ken Wisz.

TRAVEL/CLUBHOUSE
Director, Team Travel: Ed Cassin.
Manager, White Sox Clubhouse: Rob Warren. **Manager, Visiting Clubhouse:** Gabe Morell. **Manager, Umpires Clubhouse:** Joe McNamara Jr.

BASEBALL OPERATIONS
Executive Vice President: Ken Williams.
Senior VP/General Manager: Rick Hahn.
VP/Assistant GM: Buddy Bell. **Assistant GM:** Jeremy Haber. **Special Assistants:** Bill Scherrer, Dave Yoakum, Marco Paddy. **Major League Advance Scout:** Bryan Little. **Executive Assistant to GM:** Nancy Nesnidal. **Senior Director, Baseball Operations:** Dan Fabian. **Assistant Director, Baseball Operations:** Daniel Zien. **Coordinator Baseball Information:** Dan Strittmatter.

Rick Hahn

MAJOR LEAGUE STAFF
Manager: Robin Ventura
Coaches: Bench—Rick Renteria; **Pitching**—Don Cooper; **Batting**—Todd Steverson; **First Base**—Daryl Boston; **Third Base**—Joe McEwing; **Bullpen**—Bobby Thigpen. **Assistant Hitting Coach:** Greg Sparks. **Manager of Cultural Development:** Luis Sierra.

MEDICAL/TRAINING
Senior Team Physician: Dr. Charles Bush-Joseph. **Head Athletic Trainer:** Herm Schneider. **Assistant Athletic Trainer:** Brian Ball. **Director, Strength/Conditioning:** Allen Thomas. **Physical Therapist:** Brett Walker.

PLAYER DEVELOPMENT
Director, Player Development: Nick Capra. **Assistant Director, Player Development/Scouting:** Del Matthews. **Senior Director, Minor League Operations:** Grace Guerrero Zwit. **Senior Coordinator, Minor League Administration:** Kathy Potoski. **Coordinator Latin American Operations:** Arturo Perez. **Manager, Clubhouse/Equipment:** Dan Flood.
Minor League Field Coordinator: Kirk Champion. **Pitching Coordinator:** Curt Hasler. **Hitting Coordinator:** Vance Law. **Instructors:** Aaron Rowand (outfield/baserunning), Vince Coleman (Base Stealing Advisor), Everado Magallanes (infield), John Orton (catching), Dale Torborg (conditioning coordinator). **Minor League Medical/Rehabilitation Coordinator:** Scott Takao. **Physical Therapist:** Sean Bardenett. **Coaching Assistants:** Jerry Hairston, Anthony Santiago. **Dominican Republic Academy and Field Coordinator:** Rafael Santana.

FARM SYSTEM

Class	Club (League)	Manager	Hitting Coach	Pitching Coach
Triple-A	Charlotte (IL)	Julio Vinas	Andy Tomberlin	Richard Dotson
Double-A	Birmingham (SL)	Ryan Newman	Jaime Dismuke	J.R. Perdew
High A	Winston-Salem (CL)	Joel Skinner	Charlie Poe	Jose Bautista
Low A	Kannapolis (SAL)	Cole Armstrong	Justin Jirschele	Brian Drahman
Rookie	Great Falls (PL)	Tommy Thompson	Willie Harris	Matt Zaleski
Rookie	White Sox (AZL)	Mike Gellinger	Gary Ward	Felipe Lira

SCOUTING
Telephone: (312) 674-1000. **Fax:** (312) 674-5105.
Director, Amateur Scouting: Nick Hostetler (Hebron, KY). **Senior Advisor, Scouting Operations:** Doug Laumann.
National Crosscheckers: Nathan Durst (Sycamore, IL), Ed Pebley (Brigham City, UT). **Regional Crosscheckers: East**—Joe Siers (Wesley Chapel, FL), **Midwest**—Mike Shirley (Anderson, IN), **West**—Derek Valenzuela (Temecula, CA).
Advisor to Baseball Department: Larry Monroe (Schaumburg, IL).
Area Scouts: Mike Baker (Santa Ana, CA), Kevin Burrell (Sharpsburg, GA), Robbie Cummings (Portland, OR), Ryan Dorsey (Dallas, TX), Abe Fernandez (Fort Mill, SC), Joel Grampietro (Revere, MA), Garret Guest (Frankfort, IL), Phil Gulley (Morehead, KY), Warren Hughes (Mobile, AL), J.J. Lally (Denison, IA), George Kachigian (Coronado, CA), John Kazanas (Phoenix, AZ), Steve Nichols (Mount Dora, FL), Glenn Murdock (Livonia, MI), Jose Ortega (Fort Lauderdale, FL), Clay Overcash (Oologan, OK), Noah St. Urbain (Stockton, CA), Adam Virchis (Modesto, CA), Chris Walker (Houston, TX), Justin Wechsler (Niles, MI), Kenny Williams, Jr. (Los Angeles, CA).
Pro Scouts: Bruce Benedict (Atlanta, GA), Kevin Bootay (Sacramento, CA), Joe Butler (Long Beach, CA), Chris Lein (Jacksonville, FL), Alan Regier (Gilbert, AZ), Daraka Shaheed (Vallejo, CA), Keith Staab (College Station, TX), John Tumminia (Newburgh, NY), Bill Young (Scottsdale, AZ).
International Scouts: Amador Arias (Venezuela), Marino DeLeon (Dominican Republic), Robinson Garces (Venezuela), Tomas Herrera (Mexico), Reydel Hernandez (Venezuela), Miguel Peguero (Dominican Republic), Guillermo Peralta (Dominican Republic), Omar Sanchez (Venezuela), Fermin Ubri (Dominican Republic).

Cincinnati Reds

Office Address: 100 Joe Nuxhall Way, Cincinnati, OH 45202.
Telephone: (513) 765-7000. **Fax:** (513) 765-7342.
Website: www.reds.com.

OWNERSHIP

Operated by: The Cincinnati Reds LLC.
President/CEO: Robert H. Castellini. **Chairman:** W. Joseph Williams Jr. **Vice Chairman/Treasurer:** Thomas L. Williams. **COO:** Phillip J. Castellini. **Executive Operations Manager to the COO:** Tasha Hughes. **Secretary:** Christopher L. Fister.

BUSINESS OPERATIONS

Senior Vice President, Business Operations: Karen Forgus. **Business Operations Assistant/Speakers Bureau:** Emily Mahle. **Business Operations Assistant:** Alex Heekin. **Senior Advisor, Business Operations:** Joe Morgan.

FINANCE/ADMINISTRATION

VP, Finance/CFO: Doug Healy. **Chief Legal Counsel:** James Marx. **Controller:** Bentley Viator. **Assistant to General Counsel/CFO:** Teena Schweier. **Accounting Manager:** Jill Niemeyer. **Director, Human Resources:** Allison Stortz. **Employee Relations Manager:** Garry McGuire. **VP, Technology:** Brian Keys.

SALES/TICKETING

VP, Corporate Sales: Bill Reinberger. Director, **Sponsorship Development:** Dave Collins. **VP, Ticketing/Business Development:** Aaron Eisel. **Senior Director, Ticket Sales/Service:** Mark Schueler. **Director, Premium Sales/Service:** Chris Bausano. **Director, Customer Service:** Craig Warman. **Ticket Marketing Manager:** Kristen Meyers. **Senior Director, Ticket Operations:** John O'Brien. **Season Ticket Manager:** Bev Bonavita. **Director, Group Sales/Service:** Jacob Widerschein. **Director, Season Sales/Retention:** Patrick Montague.

Bob Castellini

MEDIA RELATIONS

Director, Media Relations: Rob Butcher. Assistant Director, **Media Relations:** Larry Herms. Assistant Director, **Media Relations/Digital Content:** Jamie Ramsey.

COMMUNICATIONS/MARKETING

VP, Communications/Marketing: Ralph Mitchell. **Director, Digital Media:** Lisa Braun. **Director, Marketing:** Audra Sordyl. **Senior Manager, Communications/Web Content:** Jarrod Rollins. **Public Relations Manager:** Michael Anderson. **Promotional Purchasing/Broadcasting Administration:** Lori Watt. **Communications Coordinator:** Brendan Hader. **Senior Director, Productions/Creative:** Adam Lane. **Director, Creative Operations:** Jansen Dell. **Director, Productions:** Jami Itiavkase. **Senior Director, Promo Events/Player Relations:** Zach Bonkowski. **Director, Promo Events/Player Relations:** Corey Hawthorne.

2016 SCHEDULE

Standard Game Times: 7:10 p.m.; Sun. 1:10

APRIL		JULY	
4-7 . . . . .Philadelphia	18-19 . . . . Cleveland	1-3. . . . . . at Washington	23-24 . . . . Texas
8-10 . . . . Pittsburgh	20-22 . . . . Seattle	4-6. . . . . .at Chicago	26-28 . . . . at Arizona
11-14 . . . . . . at Chicago	23-25 . . . . at Los Angeles	8-10 . . . . at Miami	29-31 . . . at Los Angeles
15-17 . . . . . . .at St. Louis	27-29 . . . . . at Milwaukee	15-17 . . . . . .Milwaukee	SEPTEMBER
18-20 . . . . .Colorado	30-31 . . . . . . at Colorado	18-20 . . . . Atlanta	2-4. . . . . St. Louis
21-24 . . . . Chicago	JUNE	22-24 . . . . Arizona	5-7. . . . . .New York
25-27 . . . . . . at New York	1-2. . . . . . . at Colorado	25-27 . . . at San Francisco	8-11 . . . . . . at Pittsburgh
29-30 . . . . . at Pittsburgh	3-5. . . . . . . Washington	29-31 . . . . . at San Diego	12-14 . . . . . . .Milwaukee
	7-9. . . . . St. Louis		16-18 . . . . . . Pittsburgh
MAY	10-12 . . . . Oakland	AUGUST	19-21 . . . . . .at Chicago
1 . . . . . . at Pittsburgh	13-16 . . . . . . at Atlanta	2-4. . . . . St. Louis	23-25 . . . . . at Milwaukee
2-4. . . . . . San Francisco	17-19 . . . . . .at Houston	5-7. . . . . . at Pittsburgh	26-29 . . . . . .at St. Louis
5-8. . . . . .Milwaukee	21-22 . . . . .at Texas	8-10 . . . . .at St. Louis	30 . . . . Chicago
9-11 . . . . Pittsburgh	23-26 . . . . . San Diego	12-14 . . . . . at Milwaukee	OCTOBER
13-15 . . . . at Philadelphia	27-29 . . . . Chicago	15-18 . . . . .Miami	1-2. . . . . Chicago
16-17 . . . . . .at Cleveland	30 . . . . . . at Washington	19-22 . . . . . . Los Angeles	

GENERAL INFORMATION

Stadium (year opened): Great American Ball Park (2003). **Playing Surface:** Grass.
Home Dugout: First Base. **Team Colors:** Red, white
Player Representative: Unavailable. and black.

COMMUNITY RELATIONS

Executive Director, Community Fund: Charley Frank. **Director, Community Relations:** Lindsey Dingeldein. **Diversity Relations Coordinator:** Phylicia McCorkle. **Executive Director, Reds Hall of Fame:** Rick Walls. **Operations Manager/Chief Curator, Reds Hall of Fame:** Chris Eckes.

BALLPARK OPERATIONS

VP, Ballpark Operations: Tim O'Connell. **Senior Director, Ballpark Operations:** Sean Brown. **Director, Ballpark Administration:** Colleen Rodenberg. **Ballpark Operations Superintendent:** Bob Harrison. **Senior Manager, Guest/Event Ops:** Jan Koshover. **Facility Services Coordinator:** Jen Clemens. **Senior Manager, Security:** Keith Cook. **Chief Engineer:** Roger Smith. **Assistant Chief Engineer:** Gary Goddard. **Head Groundskeeper:** Stephen Lord. **Assistant Head Groundskeeper:** Derrik Grubbs. **Grounds Supervisor:** Robbie Dworkin.

BASEBALL OPERATIONS

President, Baseball Operations: Walt Jocketty.

Senior VP, Baseball Operations/General Manager: Dick Williams. **Assistant GMs:** Sam Grossman, Nick Krall. **Executive Assistant to GM:** Melissa Hill. **VP/Special Assistant to the GM:** Jerry Walker. **Special Assistants to the GM:** Miguel Cairo, Eric Davis, Barry Larkin, Mario Soto. **Manager, Baseball Systems Development:** Brett Elkins. **Apps Development Specialist, Baseball Systems:** Ryan Barger. **Manager, Video Scouting:** Rob Coughlin. **Manager, Baseball Operations:** Eric Lee. **Baseball Operations Analysts:** Joshua Schaffer, Bo Thompson.

MEDICAL/TRAINING

Medical Director: Dr. Timothy Kremchek. **Assistant Medical Director:** Dr. Angel Velazquez. **Head Athletic Trainer:** Steve Baumann. **Assistant Athletic Trainers:** Jimmy Mattocks, Tomas Vera. **Stength/Conditioning Coordinator:** Sean Marohn.

Walt Jocketty

MAJOR LEAGUE STAFF

Manager: Bryan Price.
Coaches: Bench—Jim Riggleman; **Hitting**—Don Long; **Pitching**—Mark Riggins; **First Base**—Freddie Benavides; **Third Base**—Billy Hatcher; **Bullpen**—Mack Jenkins; **Catching**—Mike Stefanski.

PLAYER DEVELOPMENT

Director, Player Development: Jeff Graupe. Director, **Minor League Administration:** Lois Hudson. **Arizona Operations Manager:** Mike Saverino. **Assistant to Arizona Operations Manager:** Charlie Rodriguez. **Minor League Equipment Manager:** Jonathan Snyder. **Minor League Clubhouse Assistant:** John Bryk. **Field Coordinator:** Bill Doran. **Latin America Field Coordinator:** Joel Noboa. **Coordinators:** Ryan Jackson (hitting), Tony Fossas (pitching), Darren Bragg (outfield/baserunning), Corky Miller (catching), Richard Stark (medical), Patrick Serbus (athletic training). **Director, Dominican Republic Academy:** Juan Peralta. **Physical Therapist/Rehab Coordinator:** Brad Epstein.

FARM SYSTEM

Class	Club (League)	Manager	Hitting Coach	Pitching Coach
Triple-A	Louisville (IL)	Delino DeShields	Jody Davis	Ted Power
Double-A	Pensacola (SL)	Pat Kelly	Alex Pelaez	Danny Darwin
High A	Daytona (FSL)	Eli Marrero	Gookie Dawkins	Tom Brown
Low A	Dayton (MWL)	Dick Schofield	Luis Bolivar	Derrin Ebert
Rookie	Billings (PIO)	Ray Martinez	Joe Thurston	Seth Etherton
Rookie	Reds (AZL)	Jose Nieves	Daryle Ward	Elmer Dessens
Rookie	Reds 1 (DSL)	Jose Castro	Unavailable	Luis Montano
Rookie	Reds 2 (DSL)	Luis Saturria	Cristobal Rodriguez	Luis Andujar

SCOUTING

Senior Director, Pro Scouting: Terry Reynolds. **Senior Director, Amateur Scouting:** Chris Buckley. **Assistant Director, Amateur Scouting:** Paul Pierson. **Special Assistants:** Cam Bonifay, J. Harrison, Marty Maier, John Morris, Jeff Schugel, Kevin Towers. **Major League Scout:** Shawn Pender. **Professional Scouts:** Will Harford, Joe Jocketty, Bruce Manno, Jeff Morris, Jonathan Reynolds, Steve Roadcap.

Crosscheckers: Bill Byckowski (Ontario, Canada), Rex De La Nuez (Burbank, CA), Jerry Flowers (Cypress, TX), Joe Katuska (Cincinnati, OH), Mark McKnight (Tega Cay, SC). **Scouting Supervisors:** Tony Arias (Miami Lakes, FL), Rich Bordi (Rohnert Park, CA), Jeff Brookens (Chambersburg, PA), John Ceprini, Dan Cholowsky, Byron Ewing (Haslet, TX), Rick Ingalls (Long Beach, CA), Rick Jacques, Ben Jones (Alexandria, LA), Mike Keenan (Manhattan, KS), Brad Meador (Cincinnati, OH), Mike Misuraca (Murrieta, CA), Hector Otero, John Poloni (Tarpon Springs, FL), J.R. Reynolds, Lee Seras (Flanders, NJ), Perry Smith (Charlotte, NC), Andy Stack (Hartford, WI), Greg Zunino (Cape Coral, FL). **Scouts:** Larry Barton (Crestwood, KY), Dan Bleiwas (Thornhill, Ontario), Jamie Bodaly (Langley, BC), Ed Daub (Binghamton, NY), Dave Dawson (Santa Clarita, CA), Jim Grief (Paducah, KY), Bill Killian (Stanwood, MI), Denny Nagel (Cincinnati, OH), Lou Snipp (Humble, TX), Marlon Styles (Cincinnati, OH), Mike Wallace (Escondido, CA), Roger Weberg (Bemidji, MN).

Director, International Scouting: Tony Arias. **Assistant Director, International Scouting:** Miguel Machado. **Director, Global Scouting:** Jim Stoeckel. **Scouting Coordinator, Dominican Republic:** Enmanuel Cartagena. **Scouting Coordinator, Venezuela:** Jose Fuentes.

International Scouts: Edward Bens (Dominican Republic), Geronimo Blanco (Colombia), Jean Paul Conde (Venezuela), Auguido Gonzalez (Venezuela), Edgar Melo (Dominican Republic), Victor Nova (Dominican Republic), Victor Oramas (Venezuela), Gary Peralta (Dominican Republic), Ricard Quintero (Venezuela) Anibal Reluz (Panama), Felix Romero (Dominican Republic), Jose Valdelamar (Colombia).

Cleveland Indians

Office Address: Progressive Field, 2401 Ontario St., Cleveland, OH 44115.
Telephone: (216) 420-4200. **Fax:** (216) 420-4396.
Website: www.indians.com.

OWNERSHIP
Owner: Larry Dolan. **Chairman/Chief Executive Officer:** Paul Dolan.

BUSINESS OPERATIONS
Senior Vice President, Strategy/Business Analytics: Andrew Miller. **Executive Administrative Assistant:** Marlene Lehky. **Executive VP, Business:** Dennis Lehman. **Executive VP, Sales/Marketing:** Brian Barren. **Executive Administrative Assistant, Business:** Dru Kosik.

CORPORATE PARTNERSHIPS/FINANCE
Senior Director, Corporate Partnership: Ted Baugh. **Manager, Corporate Partnership Services:** Sam Zelasko. **Partnership Manager:** Bryan Hoffart. **Account Executives, Corporate Partnerships:** Dominic Polito, Penny Forster, Julie Weaver, Raphael Collins. **Administrative Assistant:** Kim Scott.
VP, Finance/CFO: Ken Stefanov. **VP/General Counsel:** Joe Znidarsic. **Controller:** Sarah Taylor. **Senior Director, Planning, Analysis/Reporting:** Rich Dorffer. **Manager, Accounting:** Karen Menzing. **Manager, Payroll Accounting/Services:** Mary Forkapa. **Concessions Accounting Manager:** Diane Turner.

HUMAN RESOURCES
VP, Human Resources/Chief Diversity Officer: Sara Lehrke. **Assistant Director, Talent Acquisition:** Mailynh Vu. **Assistant Director, Talent Development/Engagement:** Jennifer Gibson. **Manager, Talent Acquisition - Seasonal:** Valencia Kimbrough. **Coordinator, Benefits:** Crystal Basile. **Coordinator, Talent Development:** Nate Daymut.

MARKETING
VP, Marketing/Brand Management: Alex King. **Assistant Director, Brand Management:** Nicole Schmidt. **Manager, Advertising & Promotions:** Anne Madzelan. **Brand Analyst:** Evan Prose.

COMMUNICATIONS/BASEBALL INFORMATION
Telephone: (216) 420-4380. **Fax:** (216) 420-4430.
Senior VP, Public Affairs: Bob DiBiasio. **Senior Director, Communications:** Curtis Danburg. **Director, Baseball Information:** Bart Swain. **Assistant Director, Baseball Information:** Court Berry-Tripp. **Assistant Director, Communications:** Joel Hammond. **Team Photographer:** Dan Mendlik.

BALLPARK OPERATIONS
VP, Ballpark Operations: Jim Folk. **Senior Director, Ballpark Operations:** Jerry Crabb. **Senior Director,**

Larry Dolan

2016 SCHEDULE
Standard Game Times: 7:05 p.m.; Sun. 1:05.

APRIL		JULY	
4-7 . . . . Boston	18-19 . . . . . .at Cincinnati	1-3 . . . . at Toronto	22-24 . . . . . . .at Oakland
8-10 . . . . .at Chicago	20-22 . . . . . . .at Boston	4-6 . . . . Detroit	25-28 . . . . .at Texas
12-14 . . . . . at Tampa Bay	23-25 . . . . . .at Chicago	7-10 . . . . .New York	29-31 . . . . Minnesota
15-17 . . . . .New York	27-29 . . . . . . Baltimore	15-17 . . . . at Minnesota	
19-21 . . . . Seattle	30-31 . . . . Texas	18-20 . . . .at Kansas City	**SEPTEMBER**
22-24 . . . . . . .at Detroit		22-24 . . . . .at Baltimore	2-4 . . . . Miami
25-27 . . . . at Minnesota	**JUNE**	26-27 . . . . . Washington	5-8 . . . . Houston
29-30 . . . at Philadelphia	1 . . . . Texas	29-31 . . . . Oakland	9-11 . . . . . at Minnesota
	2-5 . . . . Kansas City		12-15 . . . . . . .at Chicago
MAY	6-9 . . . . .at Seattle	**AUGUST**	16-18 . . . . Detroit
1 . . . . . . at Philadelphia	10-12 . . . . at Los Angeles	1-4 . . . . Minnesota	20-22 . . . . . Kansas City
3-5 . . . . Detroit	13-15 . . . .at Kansas City	5-7 . . . . at New York	23-25 . . . . Chicago
6-8 . . . . Kansas City	17-19 . . . . Chicago	9-10 . . . . at Washington	26-29 . . . . . . .at Detroit
9-11 . . . . .at Houston	20-22 . . . . . . .Tampa Bay	11-14 . . . . . Los Angeles	30 . . . . . . .at Kansas City
13-15 . . . . . .Minnesota	24-26 . . . . . . .at Detroit	16-18 . . . . Chicago	
16-17 . . . . Cincinnati	27-29 . . . . . . at Atlanta	19-21 . . . . .Toronto	**OCTOBER**
	30 . . . . at Toronto		1-2 . . . . . .at Kansas City

GENERAL INFORMATION

Stadium (year opened): Progressive Field (1994). **Home Dugout:** Third Base.
Team Colors: Navy blue, red and silver. **Playing Surface:** Grass.
Player Representative: Corey Kluber.

Facility Operations: Seth Cooper. **Head Groundskeeper:** Brandon Koehnke. **Manager, Game Day Staff:** Renee VanLaningham. **Manager, Ballpark Operations:** Steve Walters. **Manager, Security:** Omar Jufko. **Manager, Arizona Operations:** Ryan Lantz.

INFORMATION SYSTEMS
Senior VP, Technology/Chief Information Officer: Neil Weiss. **Director, Software Development:** Matt Tagliaferri. **Director, Infrastructure/Operations:** Whitney Kuszmaul. **Manager, End User Support:** Kevin Dean. **Network Support Analyst:** Al Fisher. **Data Architect, Business Systems:** Plamen Kouzov.

TICKETING
Telephone: (216) 420-4487. **Fax:** (216) 420-4481.
Director, Ticket Services: Andrea Jirousek. **Ticket Services Manager:** Shedrick Taylor. **Ticket Office Manager:** Jennifer McGee. **Ticket Operations Manager:** Seth Fuller. **Ticket Services Coordinator:** Tamara Bell.

TEAM OPERATIONS/CLUBHOUSE
Director, Team Travel: Mike Seghi. **Home Clubhouse Manager:** Tony Amato. **Assistant Home Clubhouse Manager:** Marty Bokovitz. **Manager, Video Operations:** Bob Chester.

BASEBALL OPERATIONS

President, Baseball Operations: Chris Antonetti.
General Manager: Mike Chernoff. **Assistant General Manager:** Derek Falvey. **Director, Baseball Operations:** Matt Forman. **Assistant, Baseball Operations:** Alex Merberg. **Senior Director, Baseball Research and Development:** Sky Andrecheck. **Principal Data Scientist:** Keith Woolner. **Baseball Analyst:** Max Marchi. **Director, Baseball Administration:** Wendy Hoppel. **Executive Administrative Assistant:** Marlene Lehky.

MAJOR LEAGUE STAFF
Manager: Terry Francona. **Coaches: Bench**—Brad Mills; **Pitching**—Mickey Callaway; **Hitting**—Ty Van Burkleo; **First Base**—Sandy Alomar Jr.; **Third Base**—Mike Sarbaugh; **Bullpen**—Jason Bere; **Assistant Hitting Coach**—Matt Quatraro. **Assistants, Major League Staff:** Mike Barnett, Armando Camacaro, Ricky Pacione.

Chris Antonetti

MEDICAL/TRAINING
Head Team Physician: Dr. Mark Schickendantz. **Senior Director, Medical Services:** Lonnie Soloff. **Head Athletic Trainer:** James Quinlan. **Assistant Athletic Trainers:** Jeff Desjardins, Michael Salazar.

PLAYER DEVELOPMENT
Telephone: (216) 420-4308. **Fax:** (216) 420-4321.
Director, Player Development: Carter Hawkins. **Assistant Directors, Player Development:** Eric Binder, Alex Eckelman. **Administrative Assistant:** Nilda Taffanelli. **Advisors:** Minnie Mendoza, Johnny Goryl, Tim Tolman, Travis Fryman. **Special Assistants:** Travis Hafner, Tim Belcher. **Field Coordinator:** Tom Wiedenbauer. **Assistant Field Coordinator:** Julio Rangel. **Coordinators:** Ruben Niebla (pitching), Jim Rickon (hitting), John McDonald (infield), Scooter Tucker (catching), Todd Kubacki (strength/conditioning), Matt Blake (lower level pitching), Ken Knutson (pitching programs/rehab), Bruce Chen (cultural development). **Latin America Strength/Conditioning Coordinator:** Nelson Perez. **Performance Coaches:** Ceci Clark, Brian Miles, Oscar Gutierrez.

FARM SYSTEM

Class	Club	Manager	Hitting Coach	Pitching Coach
Triple-A	Columbus (IL)	Chris Tremie	Rouglas Odor	Steve Karsay
Double-A	Akron (EL)	Dave Wallace	Tim Laker	Tony Arnold
High A	Lynchburg (CL)	Mark Budzinski	Larry Day	Rigo Beltran
Low A	Lake County (MWL)	Tony Mansolino	Junior Betances	Steve McCatty
Short-season	Mahoning Valley (NYP)	Edwin Rodriguez	Kevin Howard	Tighe Dickinson
Rookie	Indians (AZL)	Anthony Medrano	B. Magallanes/D. Malave	Mark Allen
Rookie	Indians (DSL)	Jose Mejia	Freddy Tiburcio	Jesus Sanchez

SCOUTING
Senior Director, Scouting Operations: John Mirabelli.
Special Assistants to the GM: Steve Lubratich, Dave Malpass, Don Poplin.
Director, Amateur Scouting: Brad Grant. **Assistant Director, Amateur Scouting:** Scott Barnsby. **Senior Adviser, Amateur Scouting:** Bo Hughes (Sherman Oaks, CA). **Coordinator, Amateur Scouting:** Clint Longenecker. **Assistant, Amateur Scouting:** Rob Cerfolio. **National Crosschecker:** Scott Meaney (Apex, NC). **Regional Crosscheckers:** Jon Heuerman (Chandler, AZ), Kevin Cullen (Frisco, TX), Jason Smith (Long Beach, CA), Mike Soper (Tampa, FL), Brad Tyler (Bishop, GA). **Area Scouts:** Steve Abney (Lawrence, KS), Chuck Bartlett (Starkville, MS), CT Bradford (Stamford, CT), Mike Bradford (Irvine, CA), Conor Glassey (Woodinville, WA), Mike Kanen (Hoboken, NJ), Blaze Lambert (Azle, TX), Don Lyle (Sacramento, CA), Bob Mayer (Somerset, PA), Junie Melendez (North Ridgeville, OH), Carlos Muniz (San Pedro, CA), Les Pajari (Angora, MN), Ryan Perry (Keller, TX), Steffan Segui (Tampa, FL), Kyle Van Hook (Brenham, TX). **Part-Time Scouts:** Bob Malkmus, Bill Schudlich, Adam Stahl, Jose Trujillo, Ryan MacPhail, Clint Brown, Joe DeMarco.
Director, Pro Scouting: Paul Gillispie. **Assistant Director, Pro Scouting:** Victor Wang. **Pro Scouts:** Mike Calitri (Tampa, FL), Doug Carpenter (North Palm Beach, FL), Chris Gale (Austin, TX), Trey Hendricks (Cleveland, OH), Dave Miller (Wilmington, NC), Brent Urcheck (Philadelphia, PA).
Assistant Director, International Scouting: Jason Lynn. **International Crosschecker:** Koby Perez. **Latin America Crosschecker/South Florida Area Scout:** Juan Alvarez.

Colorado Rockies

Office Address: 2001 Blake St., Denver, CO 80205.
Telephone: (303) 292-0200. **Fax:** (303) 312-2116.
Website: www.coloradorockies.com.

OWNERSHIP
Operated by: Colorado Rockies Baseball Club Ltd.
Owner/General Partner: Charles K. Monfort. **Owner/Chairman/Chief Executive Officer:** Richard L. Monfort.
Executive Assistant to the Owner/General Partner: Patricia Penfold. **Executive Assistant to the Owner/Chairman/Chief Executive Officer:** Terry Douglass.

BUSINESS OPERATIONS

Richard Monfort

Executive Vice President/Chief Operating Officer: Greg Feasel. **Assistant to Executive VP/Chief Operating Officer:** Kim Olson. **VP, Human Resources:** Elizabeth Stecklein.

FINANCE
Executive VP/CFO/General Counsel: Hal Roth. **VP, Finance:** Michael Kent. **Senior Director, Purchasing:** Gary Lawrence. **Coordinator, Purchasing:** Gloria Giraldi. **Senior Director, Accounting:** Phil Emerson. **Accountants:** Joel Binfet, Laine Campbell. **Payroll Administrator:** Juli Daedelow.

SALES
VP, Corporate Sales: Walker Monfort. **Assistant to VP, Corporate Sales:** Nicole Ortiz. **Assistant Director, Corporate Sales:** Kari Anderson. **Account Executive:** Nate VanderWal. **VP Community/Retail Operations:** James P. Kellogg. Director, **Retail Operations:** Aaron Heinrich. **Director, Promotions/Special Events:** Jason Fleming.
Director, In-Game Entertainment/Broadcasting: Kent Krosbakken.

MARKETING/COMMUNICATIONS
Telephone: (303) 312-2325. **Fax:** (303) 312-2319.
VP, Marketing/Communications: Jill Campbell. **Supervisor, Advertising/Marketing:** Sarah Topf.
Assistant Director, Digital Media/Publications: Julian Valentin. **Assistant, Social Media/Publications:** Lauren Jacaruso. **Coordinator, Communications/ Marketing:** Erin Shneider. **Director, Communications:** Warren Miller. **Coordinators, Communications:** Cory Little, Nick Parson.

BALLPARK OPERATIONS
VP, Ballpark Operations: Kevin Kahn. **Senior Director, Food Service Operations/Development:** Albert Valdes. **Senior Director, Guest Services:** Steven Burke. **Head Groundskeeper:** Mark Razum. **Assistant Head Groundskeeper:** Jon Larson. **Senior Director, Engineering/Facilities:** Allyson Gutierrez. **Director, Engineering:** Randy Carlill. **Director, Facilities:** Oly Olsen.
Senior Director, Information Systems: Bill Stephani.

2016 SCHEDULE
Standard Game Times: 6:40 p.m.; Sat. 6:10; Sun. 1:10.

APRIL			
4-6 . . . . at Arizona	20-22 . . . . . at Pittsburgh	4-6. . . . . at San Francisco	26-28 . . . . at Washington
8-10 . . . . . . San Diego	24-26 . . . . .at Boston	7-10 . . . . . . .Philadelphia	29-31 . . . . . Los Angeles
12-14 . . . . .San Francisco	27-29 . . . . .San Francisco	15-17 . . . . at Atlanta	
15-17 . . . . . .at Chicago	30-31 . . . . Cincinnati	18-20 . . . . . .Tampa Bay	**SEPTEMBER**
18-20 . . . . .at Cincinnati		21-24 . . . . Atlanta	2-4. . . . . .Arizona
22-24 . . . . . Los Angeles	**JUNE**	25-27 . . . .at Baltimore	5-7. . . . . . San Francisco
25-28 . . . . Pittsburgh	1-2. . . . . Cincinnati	28-31 . . . . . at New York	8-11 . . . . . . at San Diego
29-30 . . . . at Arizona	3-5. . . . . . at San Diego		12-14 . . . . at Arizona
	6-8. . . . . at Los Angeles	**AUGUST**	16-18 . . . . San Diego
MAY	10-12 . . . . . San Diego	2-4. . . . . Los Angeles	19-21 . . . . St. Louis
1 . . . . at Arizona	14-15 . . . . . . .New York	5-7. . . . . .Miami	22-25 . . . at Los Angeles
2-4. . . . . . at San Diego	17-20 . . . . at Miami	8-9. . . . . Texas	27-29 . . . at San Francisco
5-8. . . . . at San Francisco	21-22 . . . . . at New York	10-11 . . . . .at Texas	30 . . . . .Milwaukee
9-11 . . . . Arizona	23-26 . . . . .Arizona	12-14 . . . . at Philadelphia	
13-15 . . . . . .New York	27-29 . . . . .Toronto	15-17 . . . . . .Washington	**OCTOBER**
17-19 . . . . . .at St. Louis	**JULY**	19-21 . . . . . . Chicago	1-2. . . . . .Milwaukee
	1-3. . . . . at Los Angeles	22-24 . . . . . at Milwaukee	

GENERAL INFORMATION
Stadium (year opened): Coors Field (1995). **Home Dugout:** First Base.
Team Colors: Purple, black and silver. **Playing Surface:** Grass.
Player Representative: Unavailable.

Official Scorers: Dave Einspahr, Dave Plati. **Public Address Announcer:** Reed Saunders.

TICKETING

Telephone: (303) 762-5437, (800) 388-7625. **Fax:** (303) 312-2115.

VP, Ticket Operations/Sales/Services: Sue Ann McClaren. **Senior Director, Ticket Services/Finance/Technology:** Kent Hakes. **Assistant Director, Ticket Operations:** Kevin Flood. **Senior Director, Season Tickets/Renewals/Business Strategy:** Jeff Benner. **Assistant Director, Season Tickets:** Farrah Magee. **Senior Director, Groups/Outbound Sales/ Suites:** Matt Haddad. **Manager, Suites/Party Facilities:** Traci Abeyta. **Senior Account Executive:** Todd Thomas.

TRAVEL/CLUBHOUSE

Director, Major League Operations: Paul Egins. **Director, Clubhouse Operations:** Alan Bossart.

BASEBALL OPERATIONS

Senior VP/General Manager: Jeff Bridich.

Assistant to Senior VP/GM: Adele Armagost. **Assistant GM, Baseball Operations/ Assistant General Counsel:** Zack Rosenthal. **Assistant GM/Player Personnel:** Jon Weil. **Manager, Baseball Administration:** Domenic DiRicco. **Coordinator, Baseball Operations/ Staff Counsel:** Matt Obernauer. **Coordinator, Baseball Analytics:** Trevor Patch. **Baseball Data Architect:** Jamie Holowell. **Special Assistant to the GM:** Danny Montgomery.

MAJOR LEAGUE STAFF

Manager: Walt Weiss.

Coaches: Bench—Tom Runnells; **Pitching**—Steve Foster; **Hitting**—Blake Doyle; **Third Base**—Stu Cole; **First Base** —Eric Young, Sr.; **Bullpen**—Darren Holmes; **Catching/Defensive Coordinator**—Rene Lachemann; **Bullpen Catcher**—Pat Burgess; **Director, Physical Performance**—Gabe Bauer; **Physical Performance Coach**—Mike Jasperson; **Video**—Brian Jones.

Jeff Bridich

MEDICAL/TRAINING

Senior Director, Medical Operations/Special Projects: Tom Probst. **Medical Director:** Dr. Thomas Noonan. **Club Physicians:** Dr. Allen Schreiber, Dr. Douglas Wyland. **Head Trainer:** Keith Dugger. **Assistant Athletic Trainer:** Scott Gehret.

PLAYER DEVELOPMENT

Assistant Director, Player Development: Zach Wilson. **Manager, Player Development:** Chris Forbes. **Coordinator, Minor League Operations:** Jesse Stender. **Director, Pitching Operations:** Mark Wiley. **Head Pitching Coordinator:** Doug Linton. **Assistant Pitching Coordinator:** Bob Apodaca. **Hitting Coordinator:** Duane Espy. **Catching Coordinator:** Mark Strittmatter.

Latin America Field Coordinator: Edison Lora. **Head Rehabilitation Coordinator:** Scott Murayama. **Assistant Rehabilitation Coordinator:** Andy Stover. **Physical Performance Coordinator:** Brian Buck. **Cultural Development Coordinator:** Josh Rosenthal. **Cultural Development Teacher:** Angel Amparo. **Peak Performance Coordinator:** Doug Chadwick. **Equipment Manager:** Jerry Bass.

FARM SYSTEM

Class	Club (League)	Manager	Hitting Coach	Pitching Coach
Triple-A	Albuquerque (PCL)	Glenallen Hill	Unavailable	Darryl Scott
Double-A	Hartford (EL)	Darin Everson	Jeff Salazar	Dave Burba
High A	Modesto (CAL)	Fred Ocasio	Lee Stevens	Brandon Emanuel
Low A	Asheville (SAL)	Warren Schaeffer	Mike Devereaux	Mark Brewer
Short-season	Boise (NWL)	Andy Gonzalez	Unavailable	Doug Jones
Rookie	Grand Junction (PIO)	Frank Gonzales	Aaron Munoz	Ryan Kibler
Rookie	Rockies (DSL)	Mauricio Gonzalez	Eugenio Jose	Edison Lora

SCOUTING

VP, Scouting: Bill Schmidt.

Senior Director, Scouting Operations: Marc Gustafson. **Special Assistant, GM:** Danny Montgomery. **Assistant Scouting Director:** Damon Iannelli. **Special Assistant, Scouting:** Rick Mathews. **Assistant, Scouting/Field Operations:** Sterling Monfort. **Assistant, Scouting/Baseball Operations:** Irma Castaneda.

Advance Scouts: Chris Warren, Joe Little. **Special Assistant, Player Personnel:** Ty Coslow (Louisville, KY). **Major League Scouts:** Steve Fleming (Louisa, VA), Will George (Woolwich Township, NJ), Jack Gillis (Sarasota, FL), Mark Germann (Atkins, IA), Joe Housey (Hollywood, FL), Mike Paul (Tucson, AZ). **Professional Scout:** John Corbin (Hollywood, FL). **Part-Time Professional Scout:** Jim Pransky (Davenport, IA).

National Crosscheckers: Mike Ericson (Phoenix, AZ), Jay Matthews (Concord, NC). **Area Scouts:** Scott Alves (Phoenix, AZ), Brett Baldwin (Kansas City, MO), Julio Campos (Guaynabo, PR) John Cedarburg (Fort Myers, FL), Scott Corman (Lexington, KY), Jordan Czarniecki (Nashville, TN), Jeff Edwards (Fresno, TX), Sean Gamble (Atlanta, GA), Mike Garlatti (Edison, NJ), Matt Hattabaugh (Westminster, CA), Darin Holcomb (Woodland, CA), Jon Lukens (Dana Point, CA), Matt Pignataro (Seattle, WA), Jesse Retzlaff (Dallas, TX), Rafael Reyes (Miami, FL), Ed Santa (Powell, OH), Zack Zulli (Hammond, LA) **Part-Time Scouts:** Norm DeBriyn (Fayetteville, AR), Dave McQueen (Bossier City, LA), Greg Pullia (Plymouth, MA).

VP, International Scouting/Player Development: Rolando Fernandez. **Manager, Dominican Operations:** Jhonathan Leyba. **Supervisor, Venezuelan Scouting:** Orlando Medina. **International Scouts:** Phil Allen (Australia), Martin Cabrera (Dominican Republic), Carlos Gomez (Venezuela), Raul Gomez (International), Alving Mejias (International), Frank Roa (Dominican Republic), Jossher Suarez (Venezuela). **Part-Time International Scouts:** Rogers Figueroa (Colombia), Marius Loupadiere (Panama).

Detroit Tigers

Office Address: 2100 Woodward Ave, Detroit, MI 48201.
Telephone: (313) 471-2000. **Fax:** (313) 471-2138. **Website:** www.tigers.com

OWNERSHIP
Operated By: Detroit Tigers Inc. **Owner:** Michael Ilitch.
Executive Vice President, Baseball Operations and General Manager: Al Avila.
Special Assistants to the General Manager: Willie Horton, Al Kaline, Jim Leyland, Dick Egan, Alan Trammell.
Executive Assistant to Executive Vice President, Baseball Operations and General Manager: Marty Lyon.

BUSINESS OPERATIONS
Executive Vice President, Business Operations: Duane McLean.
Executive Assistant to Executive VP, Business Operations: Peggy Thompson.

FINANCE/ADMINISTRATION
VP/CFO: Stephen Quinn.
Senior Director, Finance: Kelli Kollman. **Director, Purchasing/Supplier Diversity:**
DeAndre Berry. **Accounting Manager:** Sheila Robine. **Financial Analyst:** Kristin Jorgensen.
Accounts Payable Coordinator: Debbi Sword. **Accounts Receivable Coordinator:** Monica
Basil. **Administrative Assistant:** Tina Sidney.
Senior Director, Human Resources: Karen Gruca. **Director, Payroll Administration:**
Maureen Kraatz. **Associate Counsel:** Amy Peterson. **Internal Audit Manager:** Candice Lentz.

PUBLIC/COMMUNITY AFFAIRS
VP, Community/Public Affairs: Elaine Lewis.
Director, Tigers Foundation: Jordan Field. **Manager, Player Relations:** Sam Abrams. **Manager, Community
Affairs:** Alexandrea Thrubis. **Community Affairs Coordinator:** Courtney Kaplan. **Foundation Coordinator:** Chandler
Gilbert. **Administrative Assistants:** Audrey Zielinski/Donna Bernardo.

Michael Ilitch

SALES/MARKETING
VP, Corporate Partnerships: Steve Harms.
Director, Corporate Sales: Steve Cleary. **Senior Director, Corporate Sales:** Kurt Buhler. **Corporate Sales
Managers:** Soula Burns, John Wolski. **Sponsorship Services Manager:** Angelita Hernandez. **Sponsorship Services
Coordinators:** Jessica Langolf, Ellyn Yurgalite.
VP, Marketing: Ellen Hill Zeringue. **Director, Marketing:** Ron Wade. **Social Media Specialist:** Mac Slavin.
Marketing/Promotions Coordinator: Angela Perez. **Director, Promotions/Special Events:** Eli Bayles. **Promotions
Coordinator:** Haley Kolff. **Director, Broadcasting/In-Game Entertainment:** Stan Fracker. **VP, Ticket/Suite Sales:** Scot
Pett.

2016 SCHEDULE
Standard Game Times: 7:08 p.m.; Sun. 1:08.

APRIL		
5-6 . . . . at Miami	16-18 . . . . Minnesota	23-25 . . . . . at Minnesota
8-10 . . . . New York	20-22 . . . . . . .Tampa Bay	26-28 . . . . . . Los Angeles
11-12 . . . . Pittsburgh	23-25 . . . . . .Philadelphia	29-31 . . . . Chicago
13-14 . . . . . at Pittsburgh	27-29 . . . . . . .at Oakland	
15-17 . . . . . . .at Houston	30-31 . . . . at Los Angeles	**SEPTEMBER**
19-21 . . . .at Kansas City	**JUNE**	2-4 . . . . . . .at Kansas City
22-24 . . . . Cleveland	1 . . . . . at Los Angeles	5-7 . . . . .at Chicago
25-28 . . . . Oakland	3-5 . . . . Chicago	9-11 . . . . Baltimore
29-30 . . . . . at Minnesota	6-8 . . . . .Toronto	12-15 . . . . . . .Minnesota
	10-12 . . . . . . at New York	16-18 . . . . . .at Cleveland
MAY	13-15 . . . . . .at Chicago	20-22 . . . . . at Minnesota
1 . . . . at Minnesota	16-19 . . . . .at Kansas City	23-25 . . . . . Kansas City
3-5 . . . . . . .at Cleveland	20-23 . . . . Seattle	26-29 . . . . . . Cleveland
6-8 . . . . Texas	24-26 . . . . . . Cleveland	30 . . . . at Atlanta
9-11 . . . . at Washington	28-29 . . . . . . .Miami	
12-15 . . . . . .at Baltimore	30 . . . . . . at Tampa Bay	**OCTOBER**
		1-2 . . . . at Atlanta

JULY	
1-3 . . . . at Tampa Bay	
4-6 . . . . . . .at Cleveland	
7-10 . . . . at Toronto	
15-17 . . . . . Kansas City	
18-20 . . . . . . Minnesota	
21-24 . . . . . . .at Chicago	
25-27 . . . . . . .at Boston	
29-31 . . . . Houston	

AUGUST	
2-4 . . . . Chicago	
5-7 . . . . .New York	
8-10 . . . . .at Seattle	
12-14 . . . . .at Texas	
15-17 . . . . . Kansas City	
18-21 . . . . Boston	

GENERAL INFORMATION

Stadium (year opened): Comerica Park (2000).
Team Colors: Navy blue, orange
and white.

Player Representative: Unavailable.
Home Dugout: Third Base.
Playing Surface: Grass.

MEDIA RELATIONS/COMMUNICATIONS

MEDIA RELATIONS/COMMUNICATIONS
Telephone: (313) 471-2114. **Fax:** (313) 471-2138.
VP, Communications: Ron Colangelo. **Director, Baseball Media Relations:** Aileen Villarreal. **Manager, Baseball Media Relations:** Chad Crunk. **Coordinator, Media Relations:** Michele Wysocki.

BASEBALL OPERATIONS

Telephone: (313) 471-2000. **Fax:** (313) 471-2099.
Executive Vice President, Baseball Operations and General Manager: Al Avila.
VP/Assistant GM/General Counsel: John Westhoff. **VP/Assistant GM:** David Chadd. **VP, Player Personnel:** Scott Bream. **VP, Player Development:** Dave Littlefield. **Senior Director, Baseball Operations:** Jay Sartori. **Director, Baseball Operations:** Sam Menzin. **Baseball Operations Analyst:** Andrew Koo. **Assistant Counsel, Baseball Operations:** Alan Avila. **Executive Assistant to the Executive Vice President, Baseball Operations & General Manager:** Marty Lyon. **Executive Assistant to the Assistant GM's:** Eileen Surma.

MAJOR LEAGUE STAFF
Manager: Brad Ausmus.
Coaches: Pitching—Rich Dubee; **Batting**—Wally Joyner; **First Base**—Omar Vizquel; **Third Base**—Dave Clark; **Bullpen**—Mick Billmeyer; **Bench**—Gene Lamont; **Assistant Hitting**—David Newhan.

Al Avila

MEDICAL/TRAINING
Director, Medical Services/Head Athletic Trainer: Kevin Rand. **Assistant Athletic Trainers:** Matt Rankin, Doug Teter. **Strength/Conditioning Coordinator:** Chris Walter. **Assistant Strength/Conditioning:** Yousef Zamat. **Team Physicians:** Dr. Michael Workings, Dr. Stephen Lemos, Dr. Louis Saco (Florida). **Coordinator, Medical Services:** Gwen Keating.

PLAYER DEVELOPMENT
Director, Minor League Operations: Dan Lunetta. **Director, Player Development:** Dave Owen. **Director, Minor League/Scouting Administration:** Cheryl Evans. **Director, Latin American Player Development:** Manny Crespo. **Director, Latin American Operations:** Miguel Garcia. **Director Dominican Republic Operations:** Ramon Perez. **Coordinator, Minor League Operations:** Avi Becher. **Coordinator, International Player Programs:** Sharon Lockwood. **ESL/Cultural Assimilation Instructor:** Israel Javalera Diaz. **Administrative Assistant, Minor League Operations:** Marilyn Acevedo. **Minor League Field Coordinator:** Bill Dancy. **Minor League Medical Coordinator:** Corey Tremble. **Minor League Strength/Conditioning Coordinator:** Steve Chase. **International Medical Coordinator:** Steve Melendez. **Minor League Video Operations Assistant:** David Allende.
Roving Instructors: Bruce Fields (hitting), Scott Fletcher (infield), AJ Sager (pitching), Joe DePastino (catching), Gene Roof (outfield/baserunning), Brian Peterson (performance enhancement), Robert "Ghost" Frutchey (minor league clubhouse manager), Bo Bianco (assistant minor league clubhouse manager).

FARM SYSTEM

Class	Club	Manager	Hitting Coach	Pitching Coach
Triple-A	Toledo (IL)	Lloyd McClendon	Leon Durham	Jeff Pico
Double-A	Erie (EL)	Lance Parrish	Phil Clark	Willie Blair
High A	Lakeland (FSL)	Dave Huppert	Nelson Santovenia	Jorge Cordova
Low A	West Michigan (MWL)	Andrew Graham	Edgar Alfonzo	Mark Johnson
Short-season	Connecticut (NYP)	Mike Rabelo	Mike Hessman	Ace Adams
Rookie	Tigers West (GCL)	Rafael Martinez	G. Geigel/J.Robles	Nick Avila
Rookie	Tigers East (GCL)	Rafael Gil	Carmelo Jaime	Carlos Bohorquez

SCOUTING
Telephone: (863) 413-4103. **Fax:** (863) 413-1954.
VP, Assistant General Manager: David Chadd
Director, Amateur Scouting: Scott Pleis. **Director, Minor League & Scouting Administration:** Cheryl Evans. **Assistant, Amateur Scouting:** Clayton Zoellner.
VP, Player Personnel: Scott Bream. **Major League Scouts:** Ray Crone (Cedar Hill,TX),Joe Ferrone (Grosse Pointe, MI),Randy Johnson (Valley Center, CA),Jim Olander (Vail, AZ), Jim Rough (Ocala, FL), Bruce Tanner (New Castle, PA), Jeff Wetherby (Wesley Chapel, FL). **Senior Advisors:** Scott Reid (Phoenix,AZ), Murray Cook (Orlando, FL). **National Crosscheckers:** Tim Hallgren (Cape Girardeau, MO). Steve Hinton (Mather, CA): **Regional Crosscheckers: East**—James Orr (Orlando, FL); **Central**—Tim Grieve (New Braunfels, TX); **Midwest**—Mike Hankins (Lee's Summit, MO); **West**—Marti Wolever (Scottsdale, AZ).
Area Scouts: Nick Avila (Pembroke Pines, FL), Bryson Barber (Pensacola, FL), Jim Bretz (South Windsor, CT), Grant Brittain (Hickory, NC), RJ Burgess (St. Petersburg, FL), Scott Cerny (Rocklin, CA), Dave Dangler (Camas, WA), Oneri Fleita (Niles, IL), Justin Henry (Vicksburg, MS), Ryan Johnson (Wichita, KS), Jeff Kunkel (Ann Arbor, MI), Matt Lea (Austin, TX), Tim McWilliam (San Diego, CA), Steve Pack (San Marcos, CA), Brian Reid (Gilbert, AZ), Harold Zonder (Louisville, KY).
Director, International Operations: Tom Moore. **Director, Latin American Player Development:** Manny Crespo. **Director, Latin American Scouting:** Miguel Garcia. **Coordinator, Pacific Rim:** Kevin Hooker. **Director, Dominican Republic Operations:** Ramon Perez. **Director, Dominican Academy:** Oliver Arias. **Venezuelan Scouting Supervisor:** Alejandro Rodriguez. **Venezuelan Academy Administrator:** Oscar Garcia. **International Crosschecker:** Oneri Fleita. **Scouting Assistant, International Operations:** Eric Nieto.

Houston Astros

Office Address: Minute Maid Park, Union Station, 501 Crawford, Suite 400, Houston, TX 77002.
Mailing Address: PO Box 288, Houston, TX 77001. **Telephone:** (713) 259-8000. **Fax:** (713) 259-8981. **Email Address:** fanfeedback@astros.mlb.com. **Website:** www.astros.com.

OWNERSHIP
Owner/Chairman: Jim Crane.

BUSINESS OPERATIONS

Jim Crane

President, Business Operations: Reid Ryan. **Executive Advisor:** Nolan Ryan. **Executive Assistant:** Eileen Colgin.
Senior VP, Business Operations: Marcel Braithwaite. **Senior VP, Corporate Partnerships:** Matt Brand. **Executive Director, Astros Foundation/Community Relations:** Twila Carter. **Senior VP, Broadcasting/Alumni Relations:** Jamie Hildreth. **Senior VP, Ticket Sales/Strategy:** Jason Howard. **General Counsel:** Giles Kibbe. **Senior VP, Marketing/ Communications:** Anita Sehgal. **Chief Financial Officer:** Michael Slaughter. **VP, Media Relations:** Gene Dias. **VP, Strategy/Analytics:** Michael Dillon. **VP, Stadium Operations:** Bobby Forrest. **VP, Foundation Development:** Marian Harper. **VP, Human Resources:** Vivian Mora. **VP, Finance:** Doug Seckel. **VP, Event Sales/Operations:** Stephanie Stegall. **VP, Marketing:** Jason Wooden. **Director, Business Development:** Samir Mayur.

MEDIA RELATIONS/COMMUNITY RELATIONS
Telephone: (713) 259-8900. **Fax:** (713) 259-8025.
Managers, Media Relations: Steve Grande, Dena Propis. **Coordinators, Media Relations:** Jake Holtrop, Chris Peixoto. **Manager, Broadcasting:** Ginny Gotcher. **Coordinator, Community Relations:** Rachel Bubier. **Astros Foundation, Community Affairs:** Christina Frewin. **Director, Urban Youth Academy:** Daryl Wade.

MARKETING/ANALYTICS
Director, Promotions/Grassroots Marketing: Christie Feliz. **Director, Business Strategy/Analytics:** Jay Verrill. **Director, Ballpark Entertainment:** Chris E. Garcia. **Director, Creative Services:** Chris David Garcia. **Senior Manager, Media Strategy/Marketing:** Ryan Smith. **Senior Manager, Marketing Entertainment:** Kyle Hamsher. **Manager, Promotions/Events:** Brianna Carbonell. **Manager, Social Media:** Amanda Rykoff.

CORPORATE PARTNERSHIPS
Senior Director, Corporate Partnerships: Creighton Kahoalii. **National Partnership Development, Corporate Partnerships:** Enrique Cruz. **Account Executives, Corporate Sponsorships:** Keshia Dupas, Matt Richardson, Jeff Stewart. **Account Managers, Corporate Partnerships:** Melissa Hahn, Chris Leahy, Andrew Shipp, Megan Wisniewski.

STADIUM OPERATIONS
Senior Director, Major League Field Operations: Dan Bergstrom. **Director, Stadium Operations:** Dave McKenzie. **Director, Security:** Ben Williams. **Director, Parking:** Gary Rowberry. **Director, Engineering:** Philip Pizzo.

2016 SCHEDULE
Standard Game Times: 7:10 p.m.; Sat. 6:10; Sun. 1:10.

APRIL
4-7 . . . . . at New York (AL)
8-10 . . . . . at Milwaukee
11-14 . . . . . Kansas City
15-17 . . . . Detroit
19-21 . . . . .at Texas
22-24 . . . . Boston
25-27 . . . . . . .at Seattle
29-30 . . . . . .at Oakland

MAY
1 . . . . .at Oakland
2-4 . . . . Minnesota
5-8 . . . . Seattle
9-11 . . . . Cleveland
12-15 . . . . . . .at Boston
17-19 . . . .at Chicago (AL)

20-22 . . . . Texas
24-26 . . . . . . Baltimore
27-29 . at Los Angeles (AL)
30-31 . . . . at Arizona

JUNE
1-2 . . . . .Arizona
3-5 . . . . Oakland
6-9 . . . . .at Texas
10-12 . . . . . at Tampa Bay
14-15 . . . . . .at St. Louis
17-19 . . . . Cincinnati
20-22 . . . Los Angeles (AL)
24-26 . . . .at Kansas City
27-29 . at Los Angeles (AL)

JULY
1-3 . . . . Chicago
4-6 . . . . Seattle
7-10 . . . . Oakland
15-17 . . . . .at Seattle
18-20 . . . . . .at Oakland
22-24 . . . Los Angeles (AL)
25-27 . . . .New York (AL)
29-31 . . . . . . .at Detroit

AUGUST
1-4 . . . . .Toronto
5-7 . . . . Texas
8-11 . . . . . . at Minnesota
12-14 . . . . . . at Toronto
16-17 . . . . St. Louis
18-21 . . . . . .at Baltimore

22-24 . . . . . at Pittsburgh
26-28 . . . . . . .Tampa Bay
29-31 . . . . Oakland

SEPTEMBER
2-4 . . . . .at Texas
5-8 . . . . . . .at Cleveland
9-11 . . . . . Chicago (NL)
12-14 . . . . Texas
16-18 . . . . .at Seattle
19-21 . . . . . . .at Oakland
22-25 . . . Los Angeles (AL)
26-28 . . . . Seattle
30 . . . . . . at Los Angeles

OCTOBER
1-2 . . . at Los Angeles (AL)

GENERAL INFORMATION

Stadium (year opened):
Minute Maid Park (2000).
Team Colors: Navy and orange.

Player Representative: Unavailable.
Home Dugout: First Base.
Playing Surface: Grass.

TICKETING

Senior Director, Group Sales/Inside Sales: P.J. Keene. **Senior Director, Season Ticket Services/Operations:** Alan Latkovic. **Director, Box Office Operations:** Bill Cannon. **Director, Ticket Operations:** Mark Cole. **Director, Premium Sales/Service:** Clay Kowalski. **Director, Season Ticket Sales:** Andre Luck.

BASEBALL OPERATIONS

General Manager: Jeff Luhnow. **Special Assistant to the General Manager, Process Improvement:** Sig Mejdal. **Special Assistants:** Craig Biggio, Roger Clemens, Enos Cabell. **Director, Player Personnel:** Quinton McCracken. **Director, Baseball Operations:** Brandon Taubman. **Director, Research and Development:** Mike Fast. **Senior Technical Architect:** Ryan Hallahan. **Analytics Developer:** Darren DeFreeuw. **Coordinator, International Operations:** Eve Rosenbaum. **Coordinator, Baseball Operations:** Armando Velasco. **Mathematical Modeler:** Colin Wyers.

Jeff Luhnow

MAJOR LEAGUE STAFF

Manager: A.J. Hinch.

Coaches: Bench—Trey Hillman; **Pitching**—Brent Strom; **Hitting**—Dave Hudgens; **First Base**—Rich Dauer; **Third Base**—Gary Pettis; **Bullpen**—Craig Bjornson; **Assistant Hitting Coach**—Alonzo Powell; **Bullpen Catcher**—Javier Bracamonte, Carlos Muñoz.

TEAM OPERATIONS/CLUBHOUSE

Director, Team Operations: Dan O'Neill. **Manager, Major League Advance Information:** Tom Koch-Weser. **Coordinator, Major League Advance Information:** Matt Hogan. **Clubhouse Manager:** Carl Schneider. **Visiting Clubhouse Manager:** Steve Perry. **Major League Video Coordinator/Analyst:** Evan Stackpole.

MEDICAL/TRAINING

Director, Sports Medicine & Performance: Bill Firkus. **Head Team Physician:** Dr. David Lintner. **Team Physicians:** Dr. Thomas Mehlhoff, Dr. James Muntz, Dr. Pat McCulloch. **Head Athletic Trainer:** Jeremiah Randall. **Assistant Athletic Trainers:** James Ready, Daniel Roberts. **Minor League Medical Coordinator:** Scott Barringer. Head Strength & **Conditioning Coach:** Jacob Beiting. Minor League Strength & **Conditioning Coordinator:** Brendan Verner.

PLAYER DEVELOPMENT

Director, Minor League Operations: Allen Rowin. **Assistant Director, Minor League Operations:** Pete Putila. **Director, Florida Operations:** Jay Edmiston. **Supervisor, Education and Acculturation:** Doris Gonzalez. **Field Coordinator:** Paul Runge. **Minor League Coordinators:** Jeff Albert (hitting), Doug White (pitching), Mark Bailey (catching), Adam Everett (infield). **Roving Outfield Instructor:** Leon Roberts. **Development Coaches:** Morgan Ensberg, Aaron DelGiudice, Tommy Kawamura. **GCL Coach:** Wladimir Sutil. **Complex Pitching Coordinator:** Josh Miller. **DSL Program Coordinator:** Charlie Romero. **DSL Outfield Specialist:** Melvi Ortega. **DSL Hitting Specialist:** Omar Rosario. **DSL Infield Specialist:** Alejandro Martinez. **DSL Assistant:** Hassan Wessin.

FARM SYSTEM

Class	Club	Manager	Hitting Coach	Pitching Coach
Triple-A	Fresno (PCL)	Tony DeFrancesco	Ralph Dickenson	Dyar Miller
Double-A	Corpus Christi (TL)	Rodney Linares	Dan Radison	Dave Borkowski
High A	Lancaster (CAL)	Ramon Vazquez	Darryl Robinson	Michael Burns
Low A	Quad Cities (SAL)	Omar Lopez	Joel Chimelis	Chris Holt
Short-season	Tri-City (NYP)	Lamarr Rogers	Dillon Lawson	Drew French
Rookie	Greeneville (APP)	Josh Bonifay	Cesar Cedeno	Bill Murphy
Rookie	Astros (GCL)	Marty Malloy	Luis Mateo	Erick Abreu
Rookie	Astros 1 (DSL)	Russ Steinhorn	Sixto Ortega	Rick Aponte
Rookie	Astros 2 (DSL)	Carlos Lugo	Rene Rojas	Gerardo Olivares

SCOUTING

Director, Amateur Scouting: Mike Elias. Director, **Pro Scouting:** Kevin Goldstein. **Coordinator, Amateur Scouting:** Paul Cusick. **Pro Scouts:** Hank Allen (Upper Marlboro, MD), Tucker Blair (Elkridge, MD), Paul Gale (Rockford, IL), Alex Jacobs (Lakeland, FL), Spike Lundberg (Murrieta, CA), Tim Moore (Greenville, NC), Will Sharp (Athens, GA), Aaron Tassano (Glendale, AZ), Everett Teaford (Nashville, TN), Mike Wickham (Hoboken, NJ), Chris Young (Georgetown TX). **Senior Scouting Advisor:** Charlie Gonzalez (Davie, FL). **Eastern Supervisor:** JD Alleva (Charlotte, NC). **Western Supervisor:** Kris Gross (Mission Viejo, CA). **Midwest Crosschecker:** Ralph Bratton (Dripping Springs, TX). **FL/PR/NE Crosschecker:** Evan Brannon. **West Crosschecker:** Brad Budzinski (Laguna Niguel, CA). **East Crosschecker:** Gavin Dickey (Atlanta, GA). **Area Scouts:** Tim Bittner (Mechanicsville, VA), Bryan Byrne (Walnut Creek, CA), Zach Clark (Lawrenceville, NJ), Tim Costic (Stevenson Ranch, CA), Justin Cryer (Oxford, MS), Noel Gonzales (Houston, TX), Ryan Leake (San Diego, CA), John Martin (Tampa, FL), Mark Ross (Tucson, AZ), Bobby St. Pierre (Atlanta, GA), Jim Stevenson (Tulsa, OK), Nick Venuto (Newton Falls, OH). **Senior Advising Scout:** Bob King (La Mesa, CA). **Part-Time Scouts:** Robert Gutierrez (Miami Gardens, FL), John Lee (Oglesby, IL), Donnie Marbut (Issaquah, WA), Marcus Rodgers (Chicago, IL), Ross Smith (Valdosta, GA), Joey Sola (Caguas, PR). **Director, International:** Oz Ocampo. **Manager, International Development and Special Assignment Scout:** Carlos Alfonso (Gilbert, AZ). **Senior Advisor, Latin American Development:** Julio Linares. **Supervisor, Latin American Development and Operations:** Caridad Cabrera. **DR Admin:** Sam Visser. **International Scouts: Crosscheckers**—Tom Shafer (Lockport, IL), Roman Ocumarez (DR); **Dominican Republic**—Francis Mojica, Johan Maya, Rene Rojas, Jose Lima, Leocadio Guevara, David Brito; **Venezuela**—Daniel Acuna, Jose Palacios, Enrique Brito, Carlos Barrios; **Mexico**–Raul Lopez, Ruben Amaro Sr., Edgar Lizarraga, Miguel Pintor; **Colombia**—Neder Horta; **Curacao**—Quincy Martina; **Panama**—Carlos Gonzalez; Pacific Rim–Isao O'Jimi.

Kansas City Royals

Office Address: One Royal Way, Kansas City, MO 64129.
Mailing Address: PO Box 419969, Kansas City, MO 64141.
Telephone: (816) 921-8000. **Fax:** (816) 924-0347. **Website:** www.royals.com.

OWNERSHIP

Operated By: Kansas City Royals Baseball Club, Inc.
Chairman/CEO: David Glass. **President:** Dan Glass. **Board of Directors:** Ruth Glass, Don Glass, Dayna Martz, Julia Irene Kauffman.
Executive Assistant to the President: Lora Grosshans

BUSINESS OPERATIONS

Senior Vice President, Business Operations: Kevin Uhlich. **Executive Administrative Assistant:** Cindy Hamilton. **Director, Royals Hall of Fame:** Curt Nelson. **Director, Authentic Merchandise Sales:** Justin Villarreal.

David Glass

FINANCE/ADMINISTRATION

VP, Finance/Administration: David Laverentz. **Director, Finance:** Adam Tyhurst. **Director, Human Resources:** Johnna Meyer. **Director, Risk Management:** Patrick Fleischmann. **Director Payroll:** Jodi Parsons. **Senior Director, Information Systems:** Brian Himstedt. **Senior Director, Ticket Operations:** Anthony Blue. **Director, Ticket Operations:** Chris Darr.

COMMUNICATIONS/BROADCASTING

VP, Communications/Broadcasting: Mike Swanson. **Assistant Director, Communications:** Mike Cummings. **Coordinator, Media Relations/Alumni:** Dina Blevins. **Coordinator, Communications/Broadcasting:** Colby Curry.

PUBLICITY/COMMUNITY RELATIONS

VP, Publicity: Toby Cook. **VP, Community Relations:** Ben Aken. **Director, Royals Charities:** Marie Dispenza. **Director, Community Outreach:** Betty Kaegel.

BALLPARK OPERATIONS

VP, Ballpark Operations/Development: Bob Rice. **Senior Director, Groundskeeping/Landscaping:** Trevor Vance. **Senior Director, Stadium Engineering:** Todd Burrow. **Director, Ballpark Services:** Johnny Williams. **Director, Event Operations:** Isaac Riffel. **Director, Guest Services/Experience:** Anthony Mozzicato.

MARKETING/BUSINESS DEVELOPMENT

VP, Marketing/Business Development: Michael Bucek. **Senior Director, Event Presentation/Production:** Don Costante. **Director, Event Presentation/Production:** Steven Funke. **Director, Marketing/Advertising:** Brad Zollars. **Director, Digital/Social Media:** Erin Sleddens. **Senior Director, Corporate Partnerships/Broadcast Sales:** Jason Booker. **Senior Director, Client Services:** Michele Kammerer. **Senior Director, Sales/Service:** Steve Shiffman. **Director, Sales/Service:** Scott Wadsworth.

2016 SCHEDULE

Standard Game Times: 7:10 p.m.; Sat. 6:10; Sun. 1:10.

APRIL		JULY	
3-5 . . . . . .New York (NL)	20-22 . . . . . . .at Chicago	1-3 . . . . . at Philadelphia	23-25 . . . . at Miami
8-10 . . . . Minnesota	23-25 . . . . . at Minnesota	4-6 . . . . at Toronto	26-28 . . . . .at Boston
11-14 . . . . . .at Houston	26-29 . . . . Chicago	7-10 . . . . Seattle	29-31 . . . . .New York
15-17 . . . . . .at Oakland	30-31 . . . . . . .Tampa Bay	15-17 . . . . . . .at Detroit	
19-21 . . . . Detroit		18-20 . . . . . . Cleveland	SEPTEMBER
22-24 . . . . . . Baltimore	JUNE	22-24 . . . . Texas	2-4 . . . . Detroit
25-27 . . . at Los Angeles	1 . . . . .Tampa Bay	25-27 . . . . . Los Angeles	5-7 . . . . . . at Minnesota
29-30 . . . . .at Seattle	2-5 . . . . . . .at Cleveland	28-31 . . . . .at Texas	9-11 . . . . .at Chicago
	6-8 . . . . at Baltimore		12-15 . . . . Oakland
MAY	10-12 . . . . . .at Chicago	AUGUST	16-18 . . . . Chicago
1 . . . . .at Seattle	13-15 . . . . . . Cleveland	1-4 . . . . . . at Tampa Bay	20-22 . . . . .at Cleveland
2-4 . . . . Washington	16-19 . . . . Detroit	5-7 . . . . .Toronto	23-25 . . . . .at Detroit
6-8 . . . . . .at Cleveland	21-22 . . . at New York (NL)	9-11 . . . . Chicago	27-29 . . . . . . .Minnesota
9-12 . . . . . . at New York	24-26 . . . . Houston	12-14 . . . . . at Minnesota	30 . . . . Cleveland
13-15 . . . . Atlanta	27-28 . . . . St. Louis	15-17 . . . . . .at Detroit	
16-18 . . . . Boston	29-30 . . . . . .at St. Louis	18-21 . . . . . . .Minnesota	OCTOBER
			1-2 . . . . Cleveland

GENERAL INFORMATION

Stadium (year opened): Ewing M. Kauffman Stadium (1973). **Team Colors:** Royal blue and white.

Player Representative: Unavailable. **Home Dugout:** First Base. **Playing Surface:** Grass.

BASEBALL OPERATIONS
Telephone: (816) 921-8000. **Fax:** (816) 924-0347.
Senior VP, Baseball Operations/General Manager: Dayton Moore.
VP/Assistant GM, Player Personnel: J.J. Picollo. **VP/Assistant GM, International Operations:** Rene Francisco. **VP, Baseball Operations:** George Brett. **Assistant GM, Baseball Administration:** Jin Wong. **Assistant GM, Baseball Operations:** Scott Sharp. **Senior Advisor to GM, Scouting/Player Development:** Mike Arbuckle. **Director, Baseball Operations/Analytics:** Mike Groopman.
    Director, Baseball Administration: Kyle Vena. **Director, Baseball Analytics/Player Personnel:** John Williams. **Director, Baseball Analytics/Research Science:** Daniel Mack. **Senior Advisors:** Art Stewart, Donnie Williams. **Advisor:** Rafael Belliard. **Special Assistants to GM:** Louie Medina, Pat Jones, Mike Toomey, Mike Pazik, Jim Fregosi, Jr., Tim Conroy. **Special Assistant to Baseball Operations:** Mike Sweeney. **Executive Assistant to the GM:** Emily Penning. **Assistant to Analytics:** Guy Stevens. **Systems Architect:** Harper Weaver.

Dayton Moore

TRAVEL/CLUBHOUSE
    Senior Director, Clubhouse Operations/Team Travel: Jeff Davenport. **Assistant Equipment Manager:** Patrick Gorman. **Visiting Clubhouse Manager:** Chuck Hawke. **Video Coordinator:** Mark Topping.

MAJOR LEAGUE STAFF
    Manager: Ned Yost.
    Coaches: Bench—Don Wakamatsu; **Pitching**—Dave Eiland; **Hitting**—Dale Sveum; **First Base**—Rusty Kuntz; **Third Base**—Mike Jirschele; **Bullpen**—Doug Henry; **Coach**—Pedro Grifol; **Replay/Advance Scouting Coordinator**—Bill Duplissea; **Bullpen Catcher**—Cody Clark.

MEDICAL/TRAINING
    Team Physician: Dr. Vincent Key. **Head Athletic Trainer:** Nick Kenney. **Assistant Athletic Trainer:** Kyle Turner. **Strength/Conditioning:** Ryan Stoneberg. **Physical Therapist:** Jeff Blum.

PLAYER DEVELOPMENT
    Telephone: (816) 921-8000. **Fax:** (816) 924-0347.
    Director, Minor League Operations: Ronnie Richardson.
    Baseball Operations Assistant/Player Development: Chris Getz. **Minor League/Amateur Video Coordinator:** Nick Relic. **Senior Coordinator:** Chino Cadahia. **Senior Pitching Advisor:** Bill Fischer. **Special Assistant, Player Development:** John Wathan, Harry Spilman. **Coordinators:** Larry Carter (pitching), Terry Bradshaw (hitting), Rafael Belliard (infield), Milt Thompson (bunting/baserunning), Chris DeLucia (medical), Tony Medina (Latin America Medical), Garrett Sherrill (strength/conditioning), Luis Perez (Latin America strength/conditioning), Justin Hahn (rehab), Jeff Diskin (cultural development), Freddy Sandoval (mental skills).

FARM SYSTEM

Class	Club (League)	Manager	Hitting Coach	Pitching Coach
Triple-A	Omaha (PCL)	Brian Poldberg	Tommy Gregg	Andy Hawkins
Double-A	Northwest Arkansas (TL)	Vance Wilson	Brian Buchanan	Steve Luebber
High A	Wilmington (CL)	Jamie Quirk	Abraham Nunez	Charlie Corbell
Low A	Lexington (SAL)	Omar Ramirez	Damon Hollins	Mitch Stetter
Rookie	Idaho Falls (PIO)	Justin Gemoll	Andre David	Jeff Suppan
Rookie	Burlington (APP)	Scott Thorman	Jesus Azuaje	Carlos Martinez
Rookie	Royals (AZL)	Darryl Kennedy	Nelson Liriano	Mark Davis
Rookie	Royals (DSL)	Miguel Bernard	Onil Joseph	Gustavo Martinez

SCOUTING
    Telephone: (816) 921-8000. **Fax:** (816) 924-0347.
    Director, Scouting: Lonnie Goldberg. **Director, Pro Scouting:** Gene Watson.
    Manager, Scouting Operations: Linda Smith. **Assistant to Amateur Scouting:** Jack Monahan.
    Professional Scouts: Dennis Cardoza (Munds Park, AZ), Mike Pazik (Bethesda, MD), Tony Tijerina (Newark Valley, NY); Jon Williams (Imperial, MO), Ron Toenjes (Georgetown, TX), Mitch Webster (Kansas City, MO), Alec Zumwalt (Hiddenite, NC). **National Supervisors:** Paul Gibson (Center Moriches, NY), Dan Ontiveros (Laguna Niguel, CA), Junior Vizcaino (Raleigh, NC). **Regional Supervisors: Midwest**—Gregg Miller (Meeker, OK), **Southeast**—Gregg Kilby (Tampa, FL), **West**—Gary Wilson (Sacramento, CA), **Northeast**—Keith Connolly (Fair Haven, NJ). **Area Supervisors:** Rich Amaral (Huntington Beach, CA), Jim Buckley (Tampa, FL), Travis Ezi (New Orleans, LA), Casey Fahy (Clayton, NJ), Jim Farr (Williamsburg, VA), Mike Farrell (Indianapolis, IN), Sean Gibbs (Santa Rosa Beach, FL), Colin Gonzales (Dana Point, CA), Josh Hallgren (Keller, TX), Chad Lee (Norman, OK), Justin Lehr (The Woodlands, TX), Joel Matthews (Concord, NC), Scott Melvin (Quincy, IL), Alex Mesa (Miami, FL), Ken Munoz (Scottsdale, AZ), Matt Price (Mission, KS), Joe Ross (Kirkland, WA).
    Part-Time Scouts: Kirk Barclay (Wyoming, ON), Eric Briggs (Bolivar, MO), Rick Clendenin (Clendenin, WV), Louis Collier (Chicago, IL), Corey Eckstein (Abbotsford, BC), Nick Hamilton (Avon Lake, OH), Jerry Lafferty (Kansas City, MO), Brittan Motley (Grandview, MO), Chad Raley (Baton Rouge, LA), Johnny Ramos (Carolina, PR).
    Latin America Supervisor: Orlando Estevez. **International Scouts:** Neil Burke (Australia), Richard Castro (Venezuela), Alberto Garcia (Venezuela), Jose Gualdron (Venezuela); Joelvis Gonzalez (Venezuela), Edson Kelly (Aruba), Juan Lopez (Nicaragua), Nathan Miller (Taiwan), Rafael Miranda (Colombia), Fausto Morel (Dominican Republic), Ricardo Ortiz (Panama), Edis Perez (Dominican Republic), Rafael Vasquez (Dominican Republic), Franco Wawoe (Curacao).

Los Angeles Angels

Office Address: 2000 Gene Autry Way, Anaheim, CA 92806.
Mailing Address: 2000 Gene Autry Way, Anaheim, CA 92803.
Telephone: (714) 940-2000. **Fax:** (714) 940-2205.
Website: www.angels.com.

OWNERSHIP
Owner: Arte Moreno. **Chairman:** Dennis Kuhl. **President:** John Carpino.

BUSINESS OPERATIONS
Chief Financial Officer: Bill Beverage. **Senior Vice President, Finance/Administration:** Molly Jolly. **Director, Legal Affairs/Risk Management:** Alex Winsberg. **Controller:** Cris Lacoste. **Benefits Manager:** Cecilia Schneider. **Accountants:** Lorelei Schlitz, Kylie McManus, Jennifer Whynott. **Financial Analyst:** Jennifer Jeanblanc. **Accounts Payable Specialist:** Sarah Talamonte. **Payroll Assistant:** Alison Kelso.
    Director, Human Resources: Deborah Johnston. **Human Resources Generalist:** Brittany Johnson. **Human Resources Representative:** Mayra Castro. **Staffing Manager:** Kristin Machuca. **Assistant Scheduler:** Kendra Rodriguez.
    Director, Information Services: Al Castro. **Senior Network Engineer:** Neil Fariss. **Senior Desktop Support Analyst:** David Yun. **Technology Integration Specialist:** Paramjit 'Tiny' Singh. **Helpdesk Support Assistant:** Mike Gallant.

Arte Moreno

CORPORATE SALES
Vice President of Sales: Neil Viserto. **Senior Director, Business Development:** Mike Fach. **Senior Corporate Account Executives:** Nicole Provansal, Rick Turner. **Corporate Account Executive:** Drew Zinser. Senior Manager, **Partner Services:** Bobby Kowan. **Supervisor, Sponsorship Services:** Vanessa Vega. **Sponsorship Services Coordinators:** Andie Mitsuda, Erin Morey, Adam Overgaard.

MARKETING/ENTERTAINMENT
Director, Marketing: Jenn Bauer. **Senior Manager, Ticket Marketing:** Ryan Vance. **Marketing Manager:** Kevin Shaw. **Marketing Representative:** Alex Tinyo. **Graphic Designer:** Jeff Lee. **Social Media Coordinator:** Tara Nicodemo. **Graphic Design Coordinator:** Erin Goforth. **Team Photographer:** Matt Brown.
    Director, Entertainment/Production: Peter Bull. **Producer, Video Operations:** David Tsuruda. **Associate Producer:** Danny Pitts. **Entertainment Coordinator:** Samantha Andersen.

PUBLIC/MEDIA RELATIONS/COMMUNICATIONS
Telephone: (714) 940-2014. **Fax:** (714) 940-2205.
Vice President, Communications: Tim Mead. **Director, Communications:** Eric Kay. **Media Relations Representative:** Adam Chodzko. **Communications Assistant:** Matt Birch.
    Senior Director, Community Relations: Jenny Price. **Community Relations Coordinator:** Chrissy Vaughn.

2016 SCHEDULE
Standard Game Times: 7:05 p.m.; Sun. 12:35.

APRIL		JULY	
4-5 . . . . Chicago	18-19 . . . . . . Los Angeles	1-3 . . . . .at Boston	23-25 . . . . at Toronto
7-10 . . . . Texas	20-22 . . . . Baltimore	4-7 . . . . at Tampa Bay	26-28 . . . . .at Detroit
11-13 . . . . . .at Oakland	23-25 . . . . .at Texas	8-10 . . . . . .at Baltimore	29-31 . . . . Cincinnati
15-17 . . . . . at Minnesota	27-29 . . . . Houston	15-17 . . . . Chicago	SEPTEMBER
18-21 . . . . . .at Chicago	30-31 . . . . Detroit	18-20 . . . . Texas	2-4 . . . . .at Seattle
22-24 . . . . Seattle	JUNE	22-24 . . . . .at Houston	5-7 . . . . .at Oakland
25-27 . . . . . Kansas City	1 . . . . Detroit	25-27 . . . .at Kansas City	9-11 . . . . Texas
29-30 . . . . .at Texas	3-5 . . . . . . at Pittsburgh	28-31 . . . . Boston	12-14 . . . . Seattle
MAY	6-9 . . . . at New York	AUGUST	15-18 . . . . .Toronto
1 . . . . .at Texas	10-12 . . . . Cleveland	2-4 . . . . Oakland	19-21 . . . . .at Texas
2-4 . . . . . . at Milwaukee	13-15 . . . . . . .Minnesota	5-7 . . . . .at Seattle	22-25 . . . . . .at Houston
6-8 . . . . .Tampa Bay	17-19 . . . . . .at Oakland	9-10 . . . . . . .at Chicago	26-28 . . . . Oakland
10-12 . . . . St. Louis	20-22 . . . . . .at Houston	11-14 . . . . .at Cleveland	30 . . . . Houston
13-15 . . . . . . .at Seattle	23-26 . . . . Oakland	15-18 . . . . Seattle	OCTOBER
16-17 . . . . at Los Angeles	27-29 . . . . Houston	19-21 . . . . . . .New York	1-2 . . . . Houston

GENERAL INFORMATION
Stadium (year opened): Angel Stadium of Anaheim (1966). **Home Dugout:** Third Base.
Team Colors: Red, dark red, blue and silver. **Playing Surface:** Grass.
Player Representative: C.J. Wilson.

BALLPARK OPERATIONS/FACILITIES

Senior Director, Ballpark Operations: Brian Sanders. **Director, Ballpark Operations:** Sam Maida. **Senior Manager, Stadium Events and Operations:** Calvin Ching. **Guest Experience Manager:** Travis Roberts. **Security Manager:** Mark Macias. **Event Sales/Service Manager:** Courtney Wallace. **Manager, Field/Ground Maintenance:** Barney Lopas. **Turf Grass Manager:** Greg Laesch. **Receptionists:** Margie Walsh, Marty Valles.

Director, Stadium Facilities: Mike McKay. **Purchasing Manager:** Suzanne Peters. **Asset Coordinator:** Daniel Angulo. **Manager, Facility Maintenance:** Steve Preston. **Custodial Supervisors:** Nathan Bautista, Ray Nells. **Custodial Shift Supervisor:** Pedro Del Castillo. **Office Assistant:** Jose Padilla.

TICKETING

Director, Ticketing Operations: Sheila Brazelton. **Manager, Ticket Office:** Susan Weiss. **Ticketing Supervisor:** Armando Reyna. **Director, Ticket Sales/Services:** Tom DeTemple. **Manager, Premium Sales & Service:** Kyle Haygood. **Premium Seating Coordinator:** Cierra Lane. **Ticket Marketing Coordinator:** Julie Henrick. **Manager, Ticket Sales:** Josh Hunhoff. **Manager, Client Services:** Justin Hallenbeck.

TRAVEL/CLUBHOUSE

Clubhouse Manager: Keith Tarter. **Assistant Clubhouse Manager:** Shane Demmitt. **Visiting Clubhouse Manager:** Brian 'Bubba' Harkins. **Senior Video Coordinator:** Diego Lopez. **Video Coordinator:** Ruben Montano.

BASEBALL OPERATIONS

General Manager: Billy Eppler.

Assistant GMs: Jonathan Strangio, Steve Martone. **Special Advisor:** Bill Stoneman. **Special Assistants to GM:** Eric Chavez, Tim Huff, Marcel Lachemann, Bobby Scales. **Director, Player Personnel:** Justin Hollander. **Director, Analytics:** Jonathan Luman. **Assistant Director, Scouting:** Nate Horowitz. **Coordinator, Baseball Administration:** Adam Cali.

MAJOR LEAGUE STAFF

Manager: Mike Scioscia.

Coaches: Bench—Dino Ebel; **Pitching**—Charles Nagy; **Batting**—Dave Hansen; **First Base**—Gary Disarcina; **Third Base**—Ron Roenicke; **Infield**—Alfredo Griffin; **Bullpen**—Scott Radinsky; **Bullpen Catcher**—Tom Gregorio; **Assistant Hitting**—Paul Sorrento; **Catching And Player Information**—Steve Soliz.

Billy Eppler

MEDICAL/TRAINING

Team Physician: Dr. Craig Milhouse. **Team Orthopedists:** Dr. Robert Grumet, Dr. Michael Shepard. **Head Athletic Trainer:** Adam Nevala. **Assistant Athletic Trainer:** Rick Smith. **Strength/Conditioning Coach:** T.J. Harrington.

PLAYER DEVELOPMENT

Director, Player Development: Bobby Scales.

Assistant Director, Player Development: Mike LaCassa. **Minor League Equipment Manager, Arizona:** Brett Crane. **Field Coordinator:** Mike Micucci. **Roving Instructors:** Paul Sorrento (Hitting), Jim Eppard (Assistant Hitting), Bill Lachemann (Catching/Special Assignment), Tyrone Boykin (Outfield/Baserunning/Bunting), Jim Gott (Pitching), Kernan Ronan (Rehab Pitching), Keith Johnson (Infield), Pete Harnisch (Special Assignment Pitching), Bobby Knoop (Special Assignment Infield), Geoff Hostetter (Training Coordinator), Al Sandoval (Strength/Conditioning), Eric Munson (Rehab).

FARM SYSTEM

Class	Club	Manager	Hitting Coach	Pitching Coach
Triple-A	Salt Lake (PCL)	Keith Johnson	Tom Torrincasa	Erik Bennett
Double-A	Arkansas (TL)	Mark Parent	Brenton Del Chiaro	Scott Budner
High A	Inland Empire (CAL)	Chad Tracy	Ryan Barba	Michael Wuertz
Low A	Burlington (MWL)	Adam Melhuse	Buck Coats	Jairo Cuevas
Rookie	Orem (PIO)	Dave Stapleton	T. Adair/A. Gomez	J.Slusarz/H. Astacio
Rookie	Angels (AZL)	Elio Sarmiento	B. Betancourth/P. Mcanulty	M. Wise/J. Van Eaton
Rookie	Angels (DSL)	Hector De La Cruz	Anel De Los Santo	Nerio De Los Santos Rodriguez

SCOUTING

Director, Pro Scouting: Hal Morris.

Major League/Special Assignment Scout: Timothy Schmidt (San Bernardino, CA). **Professional Scouts:** Jeff Cirillo (Medina, WA), Chris Fetter (Carmel, IN), Travis Ice (Lawrence, KS), Kevin Jarvis (Franklin, TN), Mike Koplove (Haddonfield, NJ), Tim McIntosh (Stockton, CA), Ken Stauffer (Katy, TX), Gary Varsho (Chili, WI), Bobby Williams (Sarasota, FL).

Director, Amateur Scouting: Ric Wilson.

National Crosscheckers: Jeff Malinoff (Lopez, WA), Mike Koplove (Haddonfield, Nj), Steffan Wilson (Wayne, Pa). **Regional Supervisors: Northeast**—Jason Baker (Lynchburg, VA); **Southeast**—Chris McAlpin (Moultrie, GA); **Northern Midwest**—Joel Murrie (Evergreen, CO); **Southern Midwest**—Kevin Ham (Cypress, TX); **Northwest**—Scott Richardson (Sacramento, CA); **Southwest**—Jayson Durocher (Phoenix, AZ).

Area Scouts: Don Archer (Canada), Jared Barnes (South Bend, IN), John Burden (Fairfield, OH), Drew Chadd (Wichita, KS), Tim Corcoran (LaVerne, CA), Ben Diggins (Newport Beach, CA), Jason Ellison (Issaquah, WA), Nick Gorneault (Springfield, MA), John Gracio (Mesa, AZ), Chad Hermansen (Henderson, NV), Todd Hogan (Dublin, GA), Ryan Leahy (Beverly, MA), Brandon McArthur (Kennesaw, GA), Ralph Reyes (Miami, FL), Omar Rodriguez (Puerto Rico), Brian Tripp (Walnut Creek, CA), Rudy Vasquez (San Antonio, TX), Rob Wilfong (San Dimas, CA), J.T. Zink (Hoover, AL).

Director, International Scouting: Carlos Gomez. **International Scouting Supervisors:** Marlon Urdaneta (Venezuela), Alfredo Ulloa (Dominican Republic). **International Scouts:** Jochy Cabrera (Dominican Republic), Domingo Garcia (Dominican Republic), Carlos Ramirez (Venezuela), Franciso Tejeda (Dominican Republic).

Los Angeles Dodgers

Office Address: 1000 Elysian Park Ave., Los Angeles, CA 90012.
Telephone: (323) 224-1500. **Fax:** (323) 224-1269. **Website:** www.dodgers.com.

OWNERSHIP/EXECUTIVE OFFICE

Chairman: Mark Walter.
Partners: Earvin 'Magic' Johnson, Peter Guber, Todd Boehly, Robert 'Bobby' Patton, Jr.
President/CEO: Stan Kasten. **Special Advisors to Chairman:** Tommy Lasorda, Sandy Koufax, Don Newcombe.
Senior Advisor to President/CEO: Ned Colletti. **Special Assistant to President/CEO:** Vance Lovelace.

BUSINESS OPERATIONS

Executive Vice President: Bob Wolfe. **Executive VP/Chief Marketing Officer:** Lon Rosen.
CFO: Tucker Kain. **Senior VP/General Counsel:** Sam Fernandez. **Senior VP, Planning/
Development:** Janet Marie Smith. **Senior VP, Corporate Partnerships:** Michael Young.
Senior VP, Stadium Operations: Steve Ethier. **Vice President, Finance:** Eric Hernandez.
Director, Financial Planning/Analysis: Gregory Buonaccorsi.

SALES/PARTNERSHIP

VP, Ticket Sales: David Siegel. **Senior Director, Partnership Administration:** Jenny Oh.
Vice President, Corporate Partnerships: Lorenzo Sciarrino. **Director, Season Sales:** David
Kirkpatrick. **Director, Partnership Sales Administration/Service:** Paige Kirkpatrick. **Vice
President, Premium Sales/Services:** Antonio Morici.

Mark Walter

MARKETING/BROADCASTING

VP, Marketing/Broadcasting: Erik Braverman. **Director, Advertising/Promotions:** Shelley
Wagner. **Director, Production:** Greg Taylor. **Director, Graphic Design:** Ross Yoshida. **Director, Broadcast Engineering:**
Tom Darin.

HUMAN RESOURCES/LEGAL

Senior Director, Human Resources: Leonor Romero. **Senior Counsel:** Chad Gunderson.

COMMUNICATIONS/COMMUNITY AFFAIRS

Director, Public Relations: Joe Jareck. **Assistant Director, Public Relations:** Yvonne Carrasco. **Director, Digital/
Print Content:** Jon Weisman. **Senior Director, External Affairs/Community Relations:** Naomi Rodriguez.

INFORMATION TECHNOLOGY/STADIUM OPERATIONS/SECURITY

VP, Information Technology: Ralph Esquibel. VP, **Security/Guest Services:** Shahram Ariane. Director, **Facilities:**
David Edford. **Assistant Director, Turf/Grounds:** Eric Hansen.

TICKETING

Telephone: (323) 224-1471. **Fax:** (323) 224-2609.
VP, Ticket Operations: Bill Hunter. VP, **Ticket Development:** Seth Bluman.

2016 SCHEDULE

Standard Game Times: 7:10 p.m.; Sun. 1:10

APRIL
4-6 . . . . at San Diego
7-10 . . . . at San Francisco
12-14 . . . . Arizona
15-17 . . . . . San Francisco
19-21 . . . . at Atlanta
22-24 . . . . . at Colorado
25-28 . . . . Miami
29-30 . . . . San Diego

MAY
1 . . . . San Diego
3-4 . . . . . . at Tampa Bay
6-8 . . . . at Toronto
9-12 . . . . .New York (NL)
13-15 . . . . St. Louis
16-17 . . . Los Angeles (AL)

18-19 . at Los Angeles (AL)
20-22 . . . . . at San Diego
23-25 . . . . Cincinnati
27-29 . . . at New York (NL)
30-31 . . . .at Chicago (NL)

JUNE
1-2 . . . . . .at Chicago (NL)
3-5 . . . . Atlanta
6-8 . . . . .Colorado
10-12 . . . at San Francisco
13-15 . . . . at Arizona
16-19 . . . . . . .Milwaukee
20-22 . . . . Washington
24-27 . . . . . at Pittsburgh
28-30 . . . . . at Milwaukee

JULY
1-3 . . . . .Colorado
4-6 . . . . Baltimore
7-10 . . . . San Diego
15-17 . . . . at Arizona
19-21 . . . . at Washington
22-24 . . . . . .at St. Louis
26-27 . . . . . .Tampa Bay
29-31 . . . . .Arizona

AUGUST
2-4 . . . . . . at Colorado
5-7 . . . . Boston
8-10 . . . . . .Philadelphia
12-14 . . . . . . Pittsburgh
16-18 . . . at Philadelphia
19-22 . . . .at Cincinnati

23-25 . . . . . San Francisco
26-28 . . . . . Chicago (NL)
29-31 . . . . . . at Colorado

SEPTEMBER
2-4 . . . . San Diego
5-7 . . . . Arizona
9-11 . . . . at Miami
12-14 . . . at New York (AL)
15-18 . . . . at Arizona
19-21 . . . . . San Francisco
22-25 . . . . .Colorado
27-29 . . . . . at San Diego
30 . . . . . at San Francisco

OCTOBER
1-2 . . . . . at San Francisco

GENERAL INFORMATION

Stadium (year opened):
Dodger Stadium (1962).
Team Colors: Dodger blue and white.

Player Representative: Unavailable.
Home Dugout: Third Base.
Playing Surface: Grass

BASEBALL OPERATIONS
Telephone: (323) 224-1500. **Fax:** (323) 224-1463.
President, Baseball Operations: Andrew Friedman.
General Manager: Farhan Zaidi. **Senior VP, Baseball Operations:** Josh Byrnes. **VP, Baseball Operations:** Alex Anthopoulos. **Director, Baseball Operations:** Alex Tamin. **Director, Baseball Administration:** Ellen Harrigan. **Director, Team Travel:** Scott Akasaki. **Senior Advisor, Baseball Operations:** Gerry Hunsicker. **Special Assistant:** Pat Corrales. **Major League Video Coordinator:** John Pratt. **Assistant, Baseball Operations/Analysis:** Emilee Fragapane. **Analysts, Baseball Operations:** Ethan Levitt, Doug Wachter.

Farhan Zaidi

MAJOR LEAGUE STAFF
Manager: Dave Roberts.
Coaches: Bench—Bob Geren; **Pitching**—Rick Honeycutt; **Hitting**—Turner Ward; **First Base**—George Lombard; **Third Base**—Chris Woodward; **Bullpen**—Josh Bard. **Assistant Hitting Coach**—Tim Hyers. **Quality Assurance**—Juan Castro. **Catching Instructor**—Steve Yeager. **Bullpen Catchers**—Rob Flippo, Steve Cilladi.

MEDICAL/TRAINING
Head Athletic Trainer: Neil Rampe. **Assistant Athletic Trainer:** Nate Lucero. **Assistant Athletic Trainer:** Thomas Albert. **Strength/Conditioning Coach:** Brandon McDaniel. **Physical Therapist:** Steve Smith. **Massage Therapist:** Yosuke Nakajima. **Head Team Physician:** Dr. Neal ElAttrache. **Coordinator, Medical & Billing:** Andrew Otovic.

PLAYER DEVELOPMENT
Telephone: (323) 224-1500. **Fax:** (323) 224-1359.
Director, Player Development: Gabe Kapler.
Assistant Director, Player Development: Nick Francona. **Senior Advisor to Player Development:** Charlie Hough. **Senior Manager, Player Development:** Jeremy Zoll. **Manager, Minor League Administration:** Adriana Urzua. **Coordinator, Player Development:** Matt McGrath. **Coordinator, Strong Mind Program:** AJ LaLonde. **Field Coordinator:** Clayton McCullough. **Coordinators:** Damon Mashore (hitting), Paco Figueroa (assistant hitting), Rick Knapp (pitching), Travis Barbary (catching), Kremlin Martinez (assistant pitching), Ryan Sienko (assistant catching). **Instructors:** Austin Chubb, Robert Fick, Maury Wills. **Minor League Medical Coordinator:** Mauricio Elizondo. **Performance Coordinator:** Brian Stoneberg. **Strength & Conditioning Coordinator:** Travis Smith. **Assistant Minor League Medical Coordinator:** Kevin Orloski. **Latin American Strength and Conditioning Coordinator:** Lauren Green. **Skills Development Coordinator:** Shaun Larkin. **Assistant, Player Development:** Drew MacPhail.

FARM SYSTEM

Class	Club (League)	Manager	Hitting Coach	Pitching Coach
Triple-A	Oklahoma City (PCL)	Bill Haselman	Shawn Wooten	Matt Herges
Double-A	Tulsa (TL)	Ryan Garko	Termel Sledge	Bill Simas
High A	Rancho Cucamonga (CAL)	Drew Saylor	Jay Gibbons	Kip Wells
Low A	Great Lakes (MWL)	Gil Velazquez	John Valentin	Bobby Cuellar
Rookie	Ogden (PIO)	Shaun Larkin	Unavailable	Don Alexander
Rookie	Dodgers (AZL)	John Shoemaker	A. Bates/R. Fick	G. Sabat/S. Andrade
Rookie	Dodgers (DSL)	Pedro Mega	Unavailable	Unavailable

SCOUTING
VP, Amateur/International Scouting: David Finley.
Director, Amateur Scouting: Billy Gasparino. **National Crosschecker:** John Green. **National Crosschecker:** Brian Stephenson. **Advisor to Scouting Director:** Gib Bodet. **Advisor to Scouting Director:** Gary Nickels. **Pitching Crosschecker:** Jack Cressend. **North East Regional Crosschecker:** Jon Adkins. **South East Regional Crosschecker:** Alan Matthews. **Midwest Regional Crosschecker:** Rob St. Julien. **Western Regional Crosschecker/Special Assistant to Scouting:** Paul Cogan. **Manager, Scouting/Travel Administration:** Jane Capobianco. **Scouting Coordinator:** Zachary Fitzpatrick. **Coordinator, Video Scouting:** Jabari Barnett.
Area Scouts: Garrett Ball (GA), Clint Bowers (Southern TX), Adrian Casanova (Southern FL, Puerto Rico), Brian Compton (AZ, UT, CO, NM), Bobby Darwin (Inner City Los Angeles Specialist), Rich Delucia (Eastern PA, ME, NH, MA, RI, VT, NY, NJ), Stephen Head (NE, KS, IA, MO), Scott Hennessey (Northern FL, Southern GA), Josh Herzenberg (OK, AR, Northern TX), Henry Jones (ID, OR, AK, HI, WA), Lon Joyce (NC, SC), Tom Kunis (Northern CA, Northern NV), Marty Lamb (IN, KY, OH, TN), Trey Magnuson (MT, ND, WY, SD, MN , WI, IL, MI,), Brent Mayne (Southern CA, Orange and San Diego Co.), Dennis Moeller (Central and Southern CA), Jonah Rosenthal (Western PA, MD, DE, WV, VA, DC), Philip Stringer (LA, MS, AL, Western FLA).
Director, Player Personnel: Galen Carr. **Professional Scouts:** Peter Bergeron, Greg Booker, Lou Colletti, Scott Groot, Toney Howell, Bill Latham, Vance Lovelace, Tydus Meadows, Steve Pope, Will Rhymes, John Sanders, Doug Skiles, Chris Smith, Matt Smith, Les Walrond. **Special Assistant, Player Personnel:** Aaron Sele, Jose Vizcaino. **Special Assistant, Pro Scouting/Player Development:** Jeff Pickler. **Senior Assistant Director, Scouting:** Alex Slater. **Pro Scouting Coordinator:** Derek O'Hara. **Video Advance Scout:** Daniel Lehmann.
VP, International Scouting: Ismael Cruz. **Senior Scouting Advisor, Dominican Republic:** Ralph Avila.

Miami Marlins

Office Address: Marlins Park, 501 Marlins Way, Miami, FL 33125
Telephone: (305) 480-1300. **Fax:** (305) 480-3012.
Website: www.marlins.com.

OWNERSHIP

Owner/CEO: Jeffrey H. Loria. **Vice Chairman:** Joel A. Mael. **President:** David P. Samson. **Special Assistants to the Owner:** Bill Beck, Jack McKeon. **Special Assistants to the President:** Jeff Conine, Andre Dawson, Tony Perez.

BUSINESS OPERATIONS

Executive Vice President/Chief Financial Officer: Michel Bussiere. **Executive VP, Operations/Events:** Claude Delorme.
Executive Assistant to Owner/Vice Chairman/President: Beth McConville. **Executive Assistant to the Executive VP/CFO:** Lisa Milk. **Executive Assistant to the Executive VP, Operations/Events:** Teresita Garcia.

ADMINISTRATION

VP, Human Resources: Ana Hernández. **Manager, Human Resources:** Michelle Casanova. **Administrative Coordinator, Human Resources:** Giselle Lopez. **Director, Risk Management:** Fred Espinoza.

Jeffrey Loria

FINANCE

Senior VP, Finance: Susan Jaison. **Payroll Administrator:** Carolina Calderon. **Assistant, Payroll:** Edgar Perez. **Manager, Accounting:** Michael Mullane. Coordinators, **Accounts Payable:** Nick Kautz, Anthony Paneque. **Coordinator, Accounting:** John Cantalupo. **Assistant, Accounting:** Mary Horton, Jose Paez.

MARKETING

Director, Multicultural Marketing: Juan Martinez. **Director, Marketing/Promotions:** Matthew Britten. **Manager, Multicultural Marketing:** Darling Jarquin. **Manager, Marketing:** Boris Menier. **Supervisor, Promotions:** Rafael Capdevila.

LEGAL

Senior Counsel: Ashwin Krishnan. **Executive Assistant, Legal:** Sade Diaz.

SALES/TICKETING

Senior VP, Corporate Partnerships: Brendan Cunningham. **VP, Business Development:** Dale Hendricks. **Senior Director, Corporate Partnerships:** David Murphy. **VP, Sales/Service:** Ryan McCoy. **Director, Ticket Operations:** Mardi Dilger.

GAME PRESENTATION/EVENTS/BALLPARK OPERATIONS

Senior Director, Game Presentation/Events: Larry Blocker. **Assistant Engineering Director, Game Presentation & Events:** Chad Messina. **VP, Facilities:** Jeffrey King. **Senior Director, Ballpark Operations:** Michael Hurt. **Director,**

2016 SCHEDULE

Standard Game Times: 7:10 p.m.; Sun. 1:10

APRIL
5-6	Detroit
7-10	at Washington
11-13	at New York
15-17	Atlanta
18-21	Washington
22-24	at San Francisco
25-28	at Los Angeles
29-30	at Milwaukee

MAY
1	at Milwaukee
3-5	Arizona
6-8	Philadelphia
9-11	Milwaukee
13-15	at Washington
16-18	at Philadelphia

20-22	Washington
23-24	Tampa Bay
25-26	at Tampa Bay
27-29	at Atlanta
30-31	Pittsburgh

JUNE
1-2	Pittsburgh
3-5	New York
7-9	at Minnesota
10-12	at Arizona
13-15	at San Diego
17-20	Colorado
21-22	Atlanta
23-26	Chicago
28-29	at Detroit
30	at Atlanta

JULY
1-3	at Atlanta
4-6	at New York
8-10	Cincinnati
15-17	at St. Louis
18-21	at Philadelphia
22-24	New York
25-27	Philadelphia
28-31	St. Louis

AUGUST
1-3	at Chicago
5-7	at Colorado
8-10	San Francisco
12-14	Chicago
15-18	at Cincinnati
19-21	at Pittsburgh

23-25	Kansas City
26-28	San Diego
29-31	at New York

SEPTEMBER
1	at New York
2-4	at Cleveland
5-7	Philadelphia
9-11	Los Angeles
12-14	at Atlanta
16-18	at Philadelphia
19-21	Washington
22-25	Atlanta
26-28	New York
30	at Washington

OCTOBER
1-2	at Washington

GENERAL INFORMATION

Stadium (year opened): Marlins Park (2012).
Team Colors: Red-Orange, Yellow, Blue, Black, White.
Player Representative: Steve Cishek.

Home Dugout: Third Base.
Playing Surface: Grass.

Parking: Michael McKeon. Director, **Game Services:** Antonio Torres-Roman.

COMMUNICATIONS/MEDIA RELATIONS

Senior VP, Communications/Broadcasting: P.J. Loyello. **Senior Director, Communications:** Matt Roebuck. **Director, Publications & Baseball Information:** Marty Sewell. **Manager, Baseball Information:** Joe Vieira. **Manager, Communications:** Jon Erik Alvarez. **Coordinator, Communications:** Maria Armella. **Director, Broadcasting:** Emmanuel Muñoz. **Coordinator, Broadcasting:** Kyle Sielaff. **Senior Director, Community Outreach:** Angela Smith. **Director, Creative Services:** Eddie Fernandez. **VP/Executive Director, Marlins Foundation:** Alfredo Mesa. **Director, Marlins Foundation:** Alan Alvarez.

TRAVEL/CLUBHOUSE

Director, Team Travel: Manny Colon. **Equipment Manager:** John Silverman. **Visiting Clubhouse Manager:** Rock Hughes. **Assistant Clubhouse Manager:** Michael Diaz. **Assistant,** Clubhouse

BASEBALL OPERATIONS

Michael Hill

President, Baseball Operations: Michael Hill.
VP/Assistant General Manager: Mike Berger.
Executive Assistant to the President, Baseball Operations: Nancy Berry. **Assistant GM:** Brian Chattin. **VP, Player Personnel:** Jeff McAvoy. **Senior Advisor, Player Personnel:** Orrin Freeman. **VP, Special Assistant:** Marty Scott. **VP, Special Assistant:** Craig Weissmann. **Senior Director, Analytics:** Jason Paré. **Director of Analytics:** Dan Noffsinger. **Director, Team Travel:** Manny Colon. **Video Coaching Coordinator:** Dan Budreika.

MAJOR LEAGUE STAFF

Manager: Don Mattingly
Coaches: Bench—Tim Wallach; **Pitching**—Juan Nieves; **Hitting**—Barry Bonds; **First Base/Infield**—Perry Hill; **Third Base**—Lenny Harris; **Outfield**—Lorenzo Bundy; **Catching**— Brian Schneider; **Assistant Hitting**—Frank Menechino; **Bullpen**—Reid Cornelius; **Bullpen Coordinator**—Jeff Urgelles.

MEDICAL/TRAINING

Head Trainer: Sean Cunningham. **Assistant Trainers:** Mike Kozak, Dustin Luepker. **Strength/Conditioning Coach:** Ty Hill. **Team Psychologist:** Robert Seifer, Ph.D.

PLAYER DEVELOPMENT

VP, Player Development: Marc DelPiano. **VP, Pitching Development:** Jim Benedict. **Senior Advisor, Pitching development:** Joe Coleman. **Assistant Director, Player Development/International Operations:** Marc Lippman. **Senior Advisor, Player Development:** Tommy Thompson. **Assistant Director, Player Development:** Brett West. **Minor League Video Coordinator:** Joe Lisewski. **Field Coordinator:** Gary Cathcart. **Pitching Coordinator:** Mike Cather. **Assistant Pitching Coordinator:** Jeff Schwarz. **Hitting Coordinator:** Joe Dillon. **Infield Coordinator:** Jorge Hernandez. **Catching Coordinator:** Bobby Ramos. **Training/Rehab Coordinator:** Gene Basham. **Strength/Conditioning Coordinator:** Mark Brennan. **Rehab Pitching Coordinator:** John Duffy. **Minor League Equipment/Clubhouse Manager:** Mark Brown.

FARM SYSTEM

Class	Club (League)	Manager	Hitting Coach	Pitching Coach
Triple-A	New Orleans (PCL)	Arnie Beyeler	Paul Phillips	Derek Botelho
Double-A	Jacksonville (SL)	Dave Berg	Rich Arena	Storm Davis
High A	Jupiter (FSL)	Randy Ready	Frank Moore	Jeremy Powell
Low A	Greensboro (SAL)	Kevin Randel	Rigoberto Silverio	Brendan Sagara
Short-season	Batavia (NYP)	Angel Espada	Luis Quinones	Unavailable
Rookie	Marlins (GCL)	Julio Bruno	Daniel Santin	Manny Olivera

SCOUTING

VP, Scouting: Stan Meek.
Assistant Director, Scouting Administration: Gregg Leonard. **Assistant Director, Amateur Scouting:** Michael Youngberg.
Director, Pro Scouting: David Keller. **Assistant, Pro Scouting:** Andrew Leon. **Advance Scout:** Willie Fraser (Hopewell Junction, NY). **Special Assignment Scout:** Dominic Viola (Holly Springs, NC). **Special Assignment Scout:** Jim Cuthbert (Breinigsville, PA). **Advisor, Player Personnel:** Paul Ricciarini (Pittsfield, MA). **Professional Scouts:** Pierre Arsenault (Pierrefonds, QC), Matt Gaski (Tempe, AZ), Benny Latino (Hammond, LA), Gary Pellant (Chandeler, AZ), Dave Roberts (Fort Worth, TX), Phil Rossi (Jessup, PA), **Independent League Scout:** David Espinosa (Miami, FL).
National Crosschecker: David Crowson (College Station, TX). **Regional Supervisors:** Southeast, Mike Cadahia (Miami, FL); Northeast, Carmen Carcone (Woodstock, GA); Central, Steve Taylor (Shawnee, OK); West, Scott Goldby (Yuba City, CA); Canada, Steve Payne (Barrington, RI). **Area Scouts:** Eric Brock (Indianapolis, IN), Christian Castorri (Dacula, GA), Robby Corsaro (Victorville, CA), Donovan O'Dowd (Delray Beach, FL), Alex Smith (Abingdon, MD), John Hughes (Walnut Creek, CA), Brian Kraft (Bixby, OK), Adrian Puig (Miami, FL), Blake Newsome (Florence, SC), Tim McDonnell (Westminster, CA), Bob Oldis (Iowa City, Iowa), Gabe Sandy (Damascus, OR), Scott Stanley (Peoria, AZ), Ryan Wardinsky (The Woodlands, TX), Mark Willoughby (Hammond, LA), Nick Zumsande (Fairfax, IA).
Director, International Operations: Albert Gonzalez. **International Supervisors:** Sandy Nin (Santo Domingo, Dominican Republic), Wilmer Castillo (Maracay, VZ). **International Scouts:** Hugo Aquero (Dominican Republic), Carlos Avila (Venezuela), Luis Cordoba (Panama), Edgarluis J Fuentes (Venezuela), Alvaro Julio (Colombia), Alix Martinez (Dominican Republic), Domingo Ortega (Dominican Republic), Robin Ordonez (Venezuela).

Milwaukee Brewers

Office Address: Miller Park, One Brewers Way, Milwaukee, WI 53214.
Telephone: (414) 902-4400. **Fax:** (414) 902-4053.
Website: www.brewers.com.

OWNERSHIP
Operated By: Milwaukee Brewers Baseball Club.
Chairman/Principal Owner: Mark Attanasio.

BUSINESS OPERATIONS

Mark Attanasio

Chief Operating Officer: Rick Schlesinger. **Executive Vice President, Finance/ Administration:** Bob Quinn. **VP, General Counsel:** Marti Wronski. **VP, Marketing/Business Development:** Teddy Werner. **Executive Assistant:** Adela Reeve. **Executive Assistant, Ownership Group:** Samantha Ernest. **Executive Assistant/Paralegal:** Kate Rock.

FINANCE/ACCOUNTING
VP, Finance/Accounting: Jamie Norton. **Accounting Director:** Vicki Wise. **Senior Manager, Payroll:** Vickie Nikoley. **VP, Human Resources/Office Management:** Sally Andrist.
VP, Technology/Information Systems: Nick Watson. **Director, Network Services:** Corey Kmichik. **Manager, Infrastructure/Information Security:** Adam Bauer. **Manager, Baseball Systems Development:** Josh Krowiorz.

MARKETING/CORPORATE SPONSORSHIPS
VP, Corporate Marketing: Tom Hecht. **Senior Director, Corporate Marketing:** Andrew Pauls. **Director, Corporate Marketing:** Joe Robinson. **VP, Consumer Marketing:** Jim Bathey. **Senior Director, Merchandise Branding:** Jill Aronoff. **Senior Director, Marketing:** Kathy Schwab. **Director, Suite Services:** Kristin Miller. **Coordinator, Marketing/Promotions:** Brittany Luznicky.
VP, Broadcasting/Entertainment: Aleta Mercer. **Director, Audio/Video Productions:** Deron Anderson. **Manager, Entertainment/Broadcasting:** Tim Shea. **Manager, Electronic Displays:** Cory Wilson. **Coordinator, Audio/Video Production:** Matt Morell.

MEDIA RELATIONS/COMMUNICATIONS
VP, Communications: Tyler Barnes. **Senior Director, Media Relations:** Mike Vassallo. **Director, New Media:** Caitlin Moyer. **Senior Manager, Media Relations:** Ken Spindler. **Manager, Media Relations:** Zach Weber. **Publications Assistant:** Robbin Barnes. **Senior Director, Community Relations:** Katina Shaw. **Director, Alumni Relations:** Dave Nelson. **Manager, Community Relations:** Erica Bowring. **Executive Director, Brewers Community Foundation:** Cecelia Gore.

2016 SCHEDULE
Standard Game Times: 7:10 p.m.; Sun. 1:10.

APRIL		JULY	
4-6 . . . . . . San Francisco	17-19 . . . . Chicago	1-3 . . . . .at St. Louis	22-24 . . . . .Colorado
8-10 . . . . Houston	20-22 . . . . . at New York	4-6 . . . . . . at Washington	25-28 . . . . Pittsburgh
11-14 . . . . . .at St. Louis	24-26 . . . . at Atlanta	8-10 . . . . St. Louis	29-31 . . . . St. Louis
15-17 . . . . at Pittsburgh	27-29 . . . . Cincinnati	15-17 . . . . . .at Cincinnati	**SEPTEMBER**
18-19 . . . . at Minnesota	30-31 . . . . St. Louis	19-21 . . . . at Pittsburgh	2-4 . . . . at Pittsburgh
20-21 . . . . . . Minnesota	**JUNE**	22-24 . . . . Chicago	5-7 . . . . Chicago
22-24 . . . . .Philadelphia	1 . . . . St. Louis	25-28 . . . . Arizona	8-11 . . . . . . .at St. Louis
26-28 . . . . . . .at Chicago	2-5 . . . . . at Philadelphia	29-31 . . . . . . Pittsburgh	12-14 . . . . .at Cincinnati
29-30 . . . . .Miami	7-8 . . . . Oakland		15-18 . . . . . .at Chicago
MAY	9-12 . . . . .New York	**AUGUST**	20-22 . . . . . . Pittsburgh
1 . . . . .Miami	13-15 . . . at San Francisco	1-3 . . . . . . at San Diego	23-25 . . . . Cincinnati
2-4 . . . . Los Angeles	16-19 . . . . at Los Angeles	5-7 . . . . at Arizona	26-28 . . . . .at Texas
5-8 . . . . . . .at Cincinnati	21-22 . . . . . . .at Oakland	8-11 . . . . Atlanta	30 . . . . at Colorado
9-11 . . . . at Miami	24-26 . . . . . Washington	12-14 . . . . Cincinnati	**OCTOBER**
12-15 . . . . . . San Diego	28-30 . . . . . Los Angeles	16-18 . . . . . .at Chicago	1-2 . . . . at Colorado
		19-21 . . . . .at Seattle	

GENERAL INFORMATION
Stadium (year opened): Miller Park (2001).
Team Colors: Navy blue, gold and white.

Player Representative: Unavailable.
Home Dugout: First Base.
Playing Surface: Grass.

STADIUM OPERATIONS
VP, Stadium Operations: Bob Hallas. **Director, Grounds:** Michael Boettcher. **Manager, Warehouse:** John Weyer. **Director, Brewers Special Events:** Tai Pauls. **Senior Manager, Event Services:** Matt Lehmann. **Senior Manager, Guest Relations:** Jennacy Frey. **Receptionists:** Jody McBee, Susan Ramsdell.

TICKETING
Telephone: (414) 902-4000. **Fax:** (414) 902-4056.
Vice President, Ticket Services: Regis Bane. **Senior Director, Ticket Sales:** Billy Friess. **Director, Group Ticket Sales:** Chris Kimball. **Administrative Assistant:** Irene Bolton.

BASEBALL OPERATIONS
Telephone: (414) 902-4400. **Fax:** (414) 902-4515.
General Manager: David Stearns
VP/Assistant GM: Matt Arnold. **Senior Advisor:** Doug Melvin. **VP Baseball Projects:** Gord Ash.
Special Assistant to GM/Pro Scouting/Player Personnel: Dick Groch. **Director, Baseball Operations:** Karl Mueller. **Assistant Director, Video Scouting:** Scott Campbell. **Video Coordinator:** Joe Crawford. **Manager-Baseball Operations:** Matt Kleine. **Manager-Advance Scouting:** Brian Powalish. **Manager-Baseball Research & Quantitative Analysis:** Nick Davis. **Senior Administrator, Baseball Operations:** Barb Stark. **Senior Director, Team Travel & Clubhouse Operations:** Dan Larrea.

David Stearns

MAJOR LEAGUE STAFF
Manager: Craig Counsell. **Coaches: Bench**—Pat Murphy; **Pitching**—Derek Johnson; **Hitting**—Darnell Coles; **First Base**—Carlos Subero; **Third Base**—Ed Sedar; **Bullpen**—Lee Tunnell; **Coach**—Jason Lane.

MEDICAL/TRAINING
Head Team Physician: Dr. William Raasch. **Head Athletic Trainer:** Dan Wright. **Assistant Athletic Trainer:** Dave Yeager. **Strength/Conditioning Specialist:** Josh Seligman. **Director, Medical Operations:** Roger Caplinger.

PLAYER DEVELOPMENT
Farm Director: Tom Flanagan. **Assistant Farm Director:** Eduardo Brizuela. **Manager, Administration/Player Development:** Mark Mueller. **Assistant to Director, Staff/Player Development/OF Instructor:** Tony Diggs. **Coordinator, Arizona Complex/Video Operations:** Matt Kerls. **Field Coordinator & Catching Instructor:** Charlie Greene. **Coordinators:** Frank Neville (athletic training), Rick Tomlin (pitching), Jeremy Reed (hitting), Bob Miscik (infield), Mark Dewey (assistant pitching).

FARM SYSTEM

Class	Club (League)	Manager	Coach	Pitching Coach
Triple-A	Colorado Springs (PCL)	Rick Sweet	Bob Skube	Fred Dabney
Double-A	Biloxi (SL)	Mike Guerrero	Sandy Guerrero	Chris Hook
High A	Brevard County (FSL)	Joe Ayrault	Ned Yost IV	David Chavarria
Low A	Wisconsin (MWL)	Matt Erickson	Al LeBoeuf	Gary Lucas
Rookie	Helena (PIO)	Nestor Corredor	Liu Rodriguez	Mark Dewey
Rookie	Brewers (AZL)	Tony Diggs	Hanley Statia	Steve Cline
Rookie	Brewers (DSL)	Victor Estevez	Luis De Los Santos	Geraldo Obispo

SCOUTING
Telephone: (414) 902-4400. **Fax:** (414) 902-4059.
VP, Amateur Scouting/Special Assistant to the GM: Ray Montgomery.
Director, Professional Scouting: Zack Minasian. **Assistant Director, Amateur Scouting:** Tod Johnson. **Manager, Administration/Amateur Scouting:** Amanda Kropp. **Coordinator, Pro Scouting:** Ben McDonough.
National Supervisors: Doug Reynolds (Tallahassee, FL), Steve Riha (Houston, TX). **National Pitching Supervisor:** Jim Rooney (Berwyn, IL). **Regional Supervisors:** Josh Belovsky (Orange, CA), Tim McIlvaine (Franklin, TN), Corey Rodriguez (Palo Verdes Estates, CA), Brian Sankey (The Hills, TX), Mike Serbalik (Clifton Park, NY).
Pro Scouts: Lary Aaron (Fayetteville, GA), Brad Del Barba (Fort Mitchell, KY), Bryan Gale (Philadelphia, PA), Taylor Green (Gilbert, AZ), Joe Kowal (Yardley, PA), Cory Melvin (Tampa, FL), Tom Mooney (Pittsfield, MA), Ross Pruitt (Jupiter, FL), Marv Thompson (West Jordan, UT), Ryan Thompson (Scottsdale, AZ), Derek Watson (Milwaukee, WI).
Area Scouts: Drew Anderson (Kansas City, MO), Joe Graham (Roseville, CA), KJ Hendricks (Arlington, TX), Dan Huston (Westlake Village, CA), Harvey Kuenn, Jr (New Berlin, WI), Jay Lapp (London, Ontario, Canada), Mark Muzzi (Grand Prairie, TX), Dan Nellum (Crofton, MD), Scott Nichols (Richland, MS), Mike Rouse (Trabuco Canyon, CA), Brian Sankey (The Hills, TX), Jeff Scholzen (Santa Clara, UT), Mike Serbalik (Clifton Park, NY), John T. Shelby III (Tampa, FL), Jeff Simpson (Nashville, TN), Steve Smith (Kennesaw, GA), Charles Sullivan (Weston, FL), Shawn Whalen (Vancouver, WA). **Junior Scouts:** Bryan Corey (Mesa, AZ), Taylor Frederick (Raleigh, NC), Wynn Pelzer (Atlanta, GA).
Part-Time Scouts: Ted Brzenk (Waukesha, WI), Richard Colpaert (Shelby Township, MI), Don Fontana (Pittsburgh, PA), Joe Hodges (Rockwood, TN), Ernie Rogers (Chesapeake, VA), JP Roy (Saint Nicolas, Quebec, Canada), Lee Seid (Las Vegas, NV), Brad Stoll (Lawrence, KS), Nathan Trosky (Carmel, CA).
Director, Latin America Scouting: Manny Batista (Vega Alta, PR). **Latin America Scout Supervisors:** Eduardo Sanchez (Dominican Republic), Fernando Veracierto (Venezuela). **Latin America Scouts:** Julio De La Cruz (Dominican Republic), Reinaldo Hidalgo (Venezuela), Alcides Melendez (Venezuela), Jose Morales (Dominican Republic), Clifford Nuitter (Central America), Edgar Suarez (Venezuela).

Minnesota Twins

Office Address: Target Field, 1 Twins Way, Minneapolis, MN 55403.
Telephone: (612) 659-3400. **Fax:** 612-659-4025. **Website:** www.twinsbaseball.com.

OWNERSHIP
Operated By: The Minnesota Twins.
Chief Executive Officer: Jim Pohlad.
Executive Board: Jim Pohlad, Bob Pohlad, Bill Pohlad, Dave St. Peter.

BUSINESS OPERATIONS
President, Minnesota Twins: Dave St. Peter. **Executive Vice President, Business Development:** Laura Day. **Executive VP, Business Administration/CFO:** Kip Elliott.
    Special Assistant to the President/GM: Bill Smith. **Director, Ballpark Development/ Planning:** Dan Starkey. **Executive Assistants:** Danielle Berg, Joan Boeser, Lynette Gittins.

Jim Pohlad

HUMAN RESOURCES/FINANCE/TECHNOLOGY
    VP, Human Resources/Diversity: Raenell Dorn. **Director, Payroll:** Lori Beasley. **Director, Benefits:** Leticia Silva. **Human Resources Generalist:** Holly Corbin. **Senior Director, Finance:** Andy Weinstein. **Senior Manager, Ticket Accounting:** Jerry McLaughlin. **Senior Manager, Accounting:** Lori Windschitl. **Senior Manager, Financial Planning/Analysis:** Mike Kramer. **Senior Director, Procurement:** Bud Hanley. **Manager, Procurement:** Mike Sather.
    VP, Technology: John Avenson. **Senior Director, Technology:** Wade Navratil.

MARKETING
    VP, Brand Marketing: Nancy O'Brien. **Senior Manager, Marketing/Promotions Manager:** Julie Okland. **Director, Diversity Marketing:** Miguel Ramos. **Senior Manager, Twins Productions:** Sam Henschen. **Manager, Creative Services:** Matt Semke.

CORPORATE PARTNERSHIPS
    Senior Director, Corporate Partnership: Jeff Jurgella. **Senior Account Executives:** Doug Beck, Karen Cleary, Jordan Woodcroft, Chad Jackson. **Manager, Client Services:** Amelia Johnson. **Coordinators, Corporate Client Services:** Ann Drapcho, Brittany Kennedy, Joe Morin.

COMMUNICATIONS
    Telephone: (612) 659-3471. **Fax:** (612) 659-4029.
    Senior Director, Communications: Dustin Morse. **Senior Manager, Communications:** Mitch Hestad. **Manager, Communications/Publications:** Mike Kennedy. **Communications Assistant:** Cori Frankenberg.

COMMUNITY RELATIONS
    Senior Director, Community Affairs: Bryan Donaldson. **Manager, Community Relations:** Stephanie Johnson. **Manager, Community Programs:** Josh Ortiz. **Coordinator, Community Relations:** Gloria Westerdahl.

2016 SCHEDULE
Standard Game Times: 7:10 p.m.; Sun 1:10.

APRIL
4-7 . . . . at Baltimore
8-10 . . . . . at Kansas City
11-14 . . . . Chicago
15-17 . . . . . . Los Angeles
18-19 . . . . . . Milwaukee
20-21 . . . . . at Milwaukee
22-24 . . . . at Washington
25-27 . . . . Cleveland
29-30 . . . . Detroit

MAY
1 . . . . Detroit
2-4 . . . . at Houston
6-8 . . . . at Chicago
9-11 . . . . Baltimore
13-15 . . . . . at Cleveland

16-18 . . . . . . .at Detroit
19-22 . . . . Toronto
23-25 . . . . . Kansas City
27-29 . . . . . . .at Seattle
30-31 . . . . . . .at Oakland

JUNE
1 . . . . at Oakland
2-5 . . . . Tampa Bay
7-9 . . . . Miami
10-12 . . . . Boston
13-15 . . . . at Los Angeles
16-19 . . . . New York
21-23 . . . . . Philadelphia
24-26 . . . . . at New York
28-30 . . . . . . at Chicago

JULY
1-3 . . . . Texas
4-6 . . . . Oakland
7-10 . . . . .at Texas
15-17 . . . . . . Cleveland
18-20 . . . . . . at Detroit
21-24 . . . . . . .at Boston
26-27 . . . . Atlanta
29-31 . . . . Chicago

AUGUST
1-4 . . . . . . .at Cleveland
5-7 . . . . . . at Tampa Bay
8-11 . . . . Houston
12-14 . . . . . Kansas City
16-17 . . . . . . at Atlanta
18-21 . . . . .at Kansas City

23-25 . . . . Detroit
26-28 . . . . . . at Toronto
29-31 . . . . .at Cleveland

SEPTEMBER
1-4 . . . . Chicago
5-7 . . . . Kansas City
9-11 . . . . Cleveland
12-15 . . . . . . .at Detroit
16-18 . . . . . at New York
20-22 . . . . Detroit
23-25 . . . . Seattle
27-29 . . . .at Kansas City
30 . . . . .at Chicago

OCTOBER
1-2 . . . . .at Chicago

GENERAL INFORMATION
Stadium (year opened): Target Field (2010).
Team Colors: Red, navy blue and white.
Player Representative: Glen Perkins.

Home Dugout: First Base.
Playing Surface: Four-way blend of Kentucky Bluegrass.

TICKETING/EVENTS

Telephone: 1-800-33-TWINS. **Fax:** (612) 659-4030.

VP, Ticket Sales/Service: Mike Clough. **Director, Suite/Premium Seat Sales/Service:** Scott O'Connell. **Director, Season Sales/Service:** Eric Hudson. **VP, Ticket Operations:** Paul Froehle. **Director, Box Office:** Mike Stiles. **Director, Target Field Events/Tours:** David Christie.

BALLPARK OPERATIONS

Executive VP/General Manager: Terry Ryan.

VP, Player Personnel: Mike Radcliff. **VP/Assistant GM:** Rob Antony. **Special Assistant:** Tom Kelly. **Manager, Major League Administration/Baseball Research:** Jack Goin. **Administrative Assistant to the GM:** Lizz Downey. **Director, Team Travel:** Mike Herman. **Developer, Baseball Systems:** Jeremy Raadt. **Applications Programmer, Baseball Systems:** Jerad Parish, **Coordinator, Baseball Research:** Andrew Ettel, **Baseball Operations Assistant:** Nick Beauchamp.

BASEBALL OPERATIONS

Executive VP/General Manager: Terry Ryan.

VP, Player Personnel: Mike Radcliff. **VP/Assistant GM:** Rob Antony. **Special Assistant:** Tom Kelly. **Manager, Major League Administration/Baseball Research:** Jack Goin. **Administrative Assistant to the GM:** Lizz Downey. **Director, Team Travel:** Mike Herman. **Developer, Baseball Systems:** Jeremy Raadt. **Baseball Operations Assistant:** Nick Beauchamp. **Coordinator, Baseball Research:** Andrew Ettel.

MAJOR LEAGUE STAFF

Manager: Paul Molitor. **Coaches: Bench**—Joe Vavra; **Pitching**—Neil Allen; **Hitting**—Tom Brunansky; **First Base**—Butch Davis; **Third Base**—Gene Glynn; **Bullpen**—Eddie Guardado; **Assistant Hitting**—Rudy Hernandez. **Equipment Manager:** Rod McCormick. **Visitors Clubhouse:** Jason Lizakowski. **Director, Major League Video:** Sean Harlin.

Terry Ryan

MEDICAL/TRAINING

Club Physicians: Dr. John Steubs, Dr. Vijay Eyunni, Dr. Tom Jetzer, Dr. Jon Hallberg, Dr. Diane Dahm, Dr. Amy Beacom, Dr. Pearce McCarty, Dr. Rick Aberman. **Head Trainer:** Dave Pruemer. **Assistant Trainers:** Tony Leo, Lanning Tucker. **Strength/Conditioning Coach:** Perry Castellano.

PLAYER DEVELOPMENT

Telephone: (612) 659-3480. **Fax:** (612) 659-4026.

Director, Minor League Operations: Brad Steil.

Senior Manager, Minor League Administration: Kate Townley. **Senior Manager, Florida Operations:** Brian Maloney. **Assistant, Florida/International Operations:** Rafael Yanez. **Minor League Coordinators:** Joel Lepel (field), Eric Rasmussen (pitching), Sam Perlozzo (infield/baserunning), Erik Beiser (strength/conditioning), Jose Marzan (Latin American Operations), David Jeffrey (Video).

FARM SYSTEM

Class	Club (League)	Manager	Coach	Pitching Coach
Triple-A	Rochester (IL)	Mike Quade	Chad Allen	Stu Cliburn
Double-A	Chattanooga (SL)	Doug Mientkiewicz	Tommy Watkins	Ivan Arteaga
High A	Fort Myers (FSL)	Jeff Smith	Jim Dwyer	Henry Bonilla
Low A	Cedar Rapids (MWL)	Jake Mauer	Brian Dinkelman	J.P. Martinez
Rookie	Elizabethton (APP)	Ray Smith	Jeff Reed	Luis Ramirez
Rookie	Twins (GCL)	Ramon Borrego	S. Singleton/J. Valentin	C. Bello/V. Vasquez
Rookie	Twins (DSL)	Jimmy Alvarez	Ramon Nivar	Manuel Santana

SCOUTING

Director, Scouting: Deron Johnson.

Coordinator, Professional Scouting: Vern Followell. **Senior Manager, Scouting/International Administration:** Amanda Daley. **Administrative Assistant to Scouting:** Brittany Minder.

Major League Scouts: Ken Compton, Wayne Krivsky. **Pro Scouts:** Larry Corrigan, Bill Harford, Bob Hegman, Mike Larson, Bill Mele, Marty Miller, Bill Milos, Earl Winn. **Special Assignment Scout:** Earl Frishman.

National Crosschecker: Tim O'Neil. **Scouting Supervisors: East**—Mark Quimuyog; **West**—Sean Johnson; **Southeast**—Billy Corrigan; **Midwest**—Mike Ruth. **Area Scouts:** Trevor Brown (WA), Walt Burrows (Canada), Taylor Cameron (CA), JR DiMercurio (KS), Brett Dowdy (FL), Marty Esposito (TX), John Leavitt (CA), Jeff Pohl (IN), Jack Powell (GA), Greg Runser (TX), Alan Sandberg (TN), Elliott Strankman (CA), Ricky Taylor (NC), Freddie Thon (FL), Jay Weitzel (PA), Ted Williams (AZ), John Wilson (NJ), Mark Wilson (MN).

Coordinator, International Scouting: Howard Norsetter. **Coordinator, Latin American Scouting:** Fred Guerrero. **International Scouts—Full-Time:** Dave Bergman (Holland), Cary Broder (Taiwan), Glenn Godwin (Europe, Africa), David Kim (Pacific Rim), Luis Lajara (Dominican Republic), Jose Leon (**Supervisor**—Venezuela, Panama), Manuel Luciano (Dominican Republic), Eury Luis (Dominican Republic), Marlon Nava (Venezuela), Eduardo Soriano (Dominican Republic). **International Scouts—Part-Time:** Hector Barrios (Panama), Gavin Bennett (South Africa), John Cortese (Italy), Andy Johnson (Europe), Juan Padilla (Venezuela), Franklin Parra (Venezuela), Yan-Yu "Kenny" Su (Taiwan), Koji Takahashi (Japan), Pablo Torres (Venezuela), Lester Victoria (Curacao).

New York Mets

Office Address: Citi Field, 126th Street, Flushing, NY 11368.
Telephone: (718) 507-6387. **Fax:** (718) 507-6395.
Website: www.mets.com. **Twitter:** @mets.

OWNERSHIP

Operated By: Sterling Mets LP.
Chairman/Chief Executive Officer: Fred Wilpon. **President:** Saul Katz. **Chief Operating Officer:** Jeff Wilpon.

BUSINESS OPERATIONS

Executive VP/Chief Revenue Officer: Lou DePaoli. **Executive Director, Business Intelligence/Analytics:** John Morris.

LEGAL/HUMAN RESOURCES

Executive VP/Chief Legal Officer: David Cohen. **VP/Deputy General Counsel:** Neal Kaplan. **Senior Counsel:** James Denniston. **VP, Human Resources:** Holly Lindvall.

FINANCE

CFO: Mark Peskin. **VP/Controller:** Len Labita. **Assistant Controller/Director:** John Ventimiglia. **VP/Financial Planning:** Peter Woll

MARKETING/COMMUNICATIONS/SALES

Senior VP, Marketing/Communications: David Newman. **VP, Corporate Partnerships Sales/Services:** Wes Engram. **Executive Director, Entertainment Marketing & Productions:** Tim Gunkel. **Senior Director, Marketing:** Mark Fine. **Senior Director, Broadcasting/Special Events:** Lorraine Hamilton.

Fred Wilpon

MEDIA RELATIONS

Telephone: (718) 565-4330. **Fax:** (718) 639-3619.
VP, Media Relations: Jay Horwitz. **Executive Director, Communications:** Harold Kaufman. **Senior Director, Media Relations:** Shannon Forde.

TICKETING

Telephone: (718) 507-8499. **Fax:** (718) 507-6369.
VP, Ticket Sales/Services: Chris Zaber. **Senior Director, Group Sales:** Wade Graf. **Senior Director, Season Ticket Account Services:** Jamie Ozure. **Executive Director, Ticket Sales:** Katie Mahon.

VENUE SERVICES/OPERATIONS/TECHNOLOGY

Senior VP, Venue Services/Operations: Mike Landeen. **VP, Metropolitan Hospitality:** Heather Collamore. **VP, Ballpark Operations:** Sue Lucchi. **VP, Technology:** Tom Festa. **Executive Director, Venue Services:** Paul Schwartz. **Executive Director, Guest Experience:** Chris Brown. **Senior Director, Building Operations:** Peter Cassano.

2016 SCHEDULE

Standard Game Times: 7:10 p.m.; Sun. 1:10.

APRIL		
3-5 . . . . . .at Kansas City	23-25 . . . . at Washington	4-6 . . . . .Miami
8-10 . . . . . .Philadelphia	27-29 . . . . . Los Angeles	7-10 . . . . . . Washington
11-13 . . . . .Miami	30-31 . . . . Chicago	15-17 . . . at Philadelphia
15-17 . . . . .at Cleveland		18-20 . . . . . .at Chicago
18-20 . . . . at Philadelphia	**JUNE**	22-24 . . . . at Miami
22-24 . . . . at Atlanta	1 . . . . Chicago	25-27 . . . . St. Louis
25-27 . . . . . . Cincinnati	3-5 . . . . at Miami	28-31 . . . . .Colorado
29-30 . . . . .San Francisco	6-8 . . . . . . at Pittsburgh	
	9-12 . . . . . at Milwaukee	**AUGUST**
MAY	14-16 . . . . . . Pittsburgh	1-2 . . . . .New York
1 . . . . San Francisco	17-19 . . . . Atlanta	3-4 . . . . at New York
2-4 . . . . Atlanta	21-22 . . . . . Kansas City	5-7 . . . . .at Detroit
5-8 . . . . . . at San Diego	23-26 . . . . at Atlanta	9-11 . . . . .Arizona
9-12 . . . . at Los Angeles	27-29 . . . . at Washington	12-14 . . . . . . San Diego
13-15 . . . . . at Colorado	30 . . . . Chicago	15-17 . . . . at Arizona
17-19 . . . . . Washington		18-21 . . . at San Francisco
20-22 . . . . . . .Milwaukee	**JULY**	23-25 . . . . .at St. Louis
	1-3 . . . . Chicago	26-28 . . . . . .Philadelphia

SEPTEMBER		
29-31 . . . . .Miami		
SEPTEMBER		
1 . . . . .Miami		
2-4 . . . . Washington		
5-7 . . . . . . .at Cincinnati		
9-11 . . . . at Atlanta		
12-14 . . . . at Washington		
16-18 . . . . . . Minnesota		
19-21 . . . . Atlanta		
22-25 . . . . .Philadelphia		
26-28 . . . . at Miami		
30 . . . . . at Philadelphia		
OCTOBER		
1-2 . . . . . . at Philadelphia		

GENERAL INFORMATION

Stadium (year opened): Citi Field (2009).
Team Colors: Blue and orange.
Player Representative: Unavailable.
Home Dugout: First Base.
Playing Surface: Grass.

TRAVEL/CLUBHOUSE
Clubhouse Manager: Kevin Kierst. **Assistant Equipment Manager:** Dave Berni. **Visiting Clubhouse Manager:** Tony Carullo. **Director, Team Travel:** Brian Small.

BASEBALL OPERATIONS

Telephone: (718) 803-4013, (718) 565-4339. **Fax:** (718) 507-6391.
General Manager: Sandy Alderson.
VP/Assistant GM: John Ricco. **Special Assistant to GM:** J.P. Ricciardi. **Executive Assistant to GM:** June Napoli. **Director, Baseball Operations:** Adam Fisher. **Manager, Baseball Research/Development:** TJ Barra. **Coordinator, Baseball Systems Development:** Joe Lefkowitz. **Coordinator, Baseball Operations:** Jeffrey Lebow. **Assistant, Advance Scouting/ Replay Coordinator:** Jim Kelly. **Director, Player Relations/Programs & Community Outreach:** Donovan Mitchell.

Sandy Alderson

MAJOR LEAGUE STAFF
Manager: Terry Collins.
Coaches: Bench—Dick Scott; **Pitching**—Dan Warthen; **Batting**—Kevin Long; **Assistant Batting**—Pat Roessler; **First Base**—Tom Goodwin; **Third Base**—Tim Teufel; **Bullpen**—Ricky Bones.

MEDICAL/TRAINING
Medical Director: Dr. David Altchek. **Physician:** Dr. Struan Coleman. **Trainer:** Ray Ramirez. **Assistant Trainer:** Brian Chicklo. **Strength/Conditioning Coordinator:** Dustin Clarke. **Physical Therapist:** John Zajac. **Massage Therapist:** Yoshihiro Nishio.

PLAYER DEVELOPMENT
Telephone: (718) 565-4302. **Fax:** (718) 205-7920.
Director, Minor League Operations: Ian Levin. **Manager, St. Lucie Operations:** Ronny Reyes. **Equipment/ Operations Manager:** John Mullin. **Coordinator, Minor League/International Operations:** Jennifer Wolf. **Director, Latin American Operations:** Juan Henderson. **International Field Coordinator:** Rafael Landestoy. **Special Catching Instructor:** Ozzie Virgil.
Minor League Field Coordinator: Kevin Morgan. **Hitting Coordinator:** Lamar Johnson. **Short-Season Hitting Coordinator:** Ryan Ellis. **Full Season Pitching Coordinator:** Ron Romanick. **Short-Season Pitching Coordinator:** Miguel Valdes. **Catching Coordinator:** Bob Natal. **Outfield Coordinator:** Benny Distefano. **Rehab Pitching Coordinator:** Jon Debus. **Medical Coordinator:** Mike Herbst. **Rehab/Physical Therapist Coordinator:** Dave Pearson. **Strength/Conditioning Coordinator:** Jason Craig. **Senior Advisor:** Guy Conti. **Special Instructors:** Bobby Floyd, Al Jackson, Edgardo Alfonso.

FARM SYSTEM

Class	Club	Manager	Hitting Coach	Pitching Coach
Triple-A	Las Vegas (PCL)	Wally Backman	Jack Voigt	Frank Viola
Double-A	Binghamton (EL)	Pedro Lopez	Luis Natera	Glenn Abbott
High A	St. Lucie (FSL)	Luis Rojas	Val Pascucci	Marc Valdes
Low A	Savannah (SAL)	Jose Leger	Joel Fuentes	Jonathan Hurst
Short-season	Brooklyn (NYP)	Tom Gamboa	Sean Ratliff	Unavailable
Rookie	Kingsport (APP)	Luis Rivera	Ender Chavez	Unavailable
Rookie	Mets (GCL)	Jose Carreno	Yunir Garcia	Royce Ring
Rookie	Mets 1 (DSL)	Manny Martinez	Leo Hernandez	B. Marte/R. Roque
Rookie	Mets 2 (DSL)	David Davalillo	Rafael Fernandez	Francisco Martinez

SCOUTING
Telephone: (718) 565-4311. **Fax:** (718) 205-7920.
Senior Director, Amateur Scouting: Tommy Tanous. **Assistant Scouting Director:** Marc Tramuta (Fredonia, NY). **Coordinator, Amateur Scouting:** Bryan Hayes. **Regional Supervisors: Southeast**—Steve Barningham (Land O'Lakes, FL), **West**—Doug Thurman (San Jose, CA), **Northeast**—Marlin McPhail (Irmo, SC), **Midwest**—Mac Seibert (Cantonment, FL). **Area Supervisors:** Cesar Aranguren (Clermont, FL), Jet Butler (Jackson, MS), Daniel Coles (Carthage, NC), Ray Corbett (College Station, TX), Jarrett England (Murfreesboro, TN), , Chris HXXX (Ann Arbor, MI), Tyler Holmes (Roseville, CA), Tommy Jackson (Birmingham, AL), Fred Mazuca (Tustin, CA), Claude Pelletier (St. Lazare, Quebec), Michael Pesce (New Hyde Park, NY), Jim Reeves (Camas, WA), Kevin Roberson (Scottsdale, AZ), Justin Schwartz (Oklahoma City, OK), Max Semler (Allen, TX), Jim Thompson (Philadelphia, PA), Andrew Toussaint (Los Angeles, CA), Jon Updike (Sorrento, FL).
Senior Director, Pro Scouting: Jim D'Aloia. **Professional Scouts:** Bryn Alderson (New York, NY), Mack Babitt (Richmond, CA), Conor Brooks (Plymouth, MA), Thomas Clark (Shrewsbury, MA), Tim Fortugno (Elk Grove, CA), Ashley Lawson (Athens, TN), Shaun McNamara (Worcester, MA), Art Pontarelli (Lincoln, RI), Roy Smith (Chicago, IL), Rudy Terrasas (Santa Fe, TX).
Senior Director, International Scouting: Chris Becerra (Ventura, CA). **International Supervisors:** Gerardo Cabrera (Dominican Republic), Hector Rincones (Venezuela). Hilario Soriano (Senior Advisor, Dominican Republic), Harold Herrera (Coordinator, Latin American Scouting). **International Scouts:** Modesto Abreu (Dominican Republic), Marciano Alvarez (Dominican Republic), Alexis De La Cruz (Dominican Republic), Robert Espejo (Venezuela), Bon Kim (Asia), Gabriel Low (Mexico), Nestor Moreno (Venezuela), Daurys Nin (Dominican Republic), Ismael Perez (Venezuela), Carlos Perez (Venezuela), Ismael Perez (Venezuela), Sendly Reina (Curacao), Andrew Sallee (Europe).

New York Yankees

Office Address: Yankee Stadium, One East 161st St., Bronx, NY 10451.
Telephone: (718) 293-4300.
Website: www.yankees.com, www.yankeesbeisbol.com. **Twitter:** @Yankees, @YankeesPR, @LosYankees, @LosYankeesPR.

OWNERSHIP
Managing General Partner/Co-Chairperson: Harold Z. (Hal) Steinbrenner. **General Partner/Co-Chairperson:** Henry G. (Hank) Steinbrenner. **General Partner/Vice Chairperson:** Jennifer Steinbrenner Swindal. **General Partner/Vice Chairperson:** Jessica Steinbrenner. **Vice Chairperson:** Joan Steinbrenner.

BUSINESS OPERATIONS

Harold Steinbrenner

President: Randy Levine, Esq.
Chief Operating Officer/General Counsel: Lonn A. Trost, Esq.
Senior VP, Strategic Ventures: Marty Greenspun. **Senior VP, Chief Security Officer:** Sonny Hight. **Senior VP, Yankee Global Enterprises/Chief Financial Officer:** Anthony Bruno. **Senior VP, Corporate/Community Relations:** Brian E. Smith. **Senior VP, Corporate Sales/Sponsorship:** Michael J. Tusiani. **Senior VP, Marketing:** Deborah Tymon. **VP, Stadium Operations:** Doug Behar. **VP/Chief Financial Officer, Accounting:** Robert B. Brown. **Deputy General Counsel/VP, Legal Affairs:** Alan Chang. **Chief Financial Officer/VP, Financial Operations:** Scott M. Krug. **VP, Chief Information Officer:** Mike Lane.

COMMUNICATIONS/MEDIA RELATIONS
Telephone: (718) 579-4460. **Fax:** (718) 293-8414.
Executive Director, Communications/Media Relations: Jason Zillo. **Assistant Director, Baseball Information/Public Communications:** Michael Margolis. **Manager, Baseball Information:** Lauren Moran. **Manager, Communications/Media Relations, Yankee Stadium Events:** Kenny Leandry. **Senior Coordinator, Media Services:** Alexandra Trochanowski. **Coordinator, Communications/Media Relations:** Rob Morse. **Assistant, Communications/Media Relations:** Kaitlyn Brennan. **Administrative Assistant, Communications/Media Relations:** Dolores Hernandez. **Japanese Media Advisor:** Yoshiki Sato.

TICKET OPERATIONS
Telephone: (718) 293-6000.
VP, Ticket Sales/Service/Operations: Kevin Dart. **Senior Director, Ticket Operations:** Irfan Kirimca.

BASEBALL OPERATIONS
Senior VP/General Manager: Brian Cashman.
Senior VP/Assistant GM: Jean Afterman, Esq. **Senior VP, Special Advisor:** Gene Michael. **Assistant GM:** Michael Fishman. **VP, Baseball Operations:** Tim Naehring. **Special Advisors:** Reggie Jackson, Hideki Matsui.
Director, Team Travel & Player Services: Ben Tuliebitz. **Director, Quantitative Analysis:** David Grabiner. **Manager,**

2016 SCHEDULE
Standard Game Times: 7:05 p.m.; Sat.-Sun. 1:05.

APRIL		
4-7 . . . . Houston	19-22 . . . . . .at Oakland	4-6. . . . . .at Chicago
8-10 . . . . .at Detroit	24-26 . . . . .Toronto	7-10 . . . . . .at Cleveland
12-14 . . . . . . at Toronto	27-29 . . . . at Tampa Bay	15-17 . . . . Boston
15-17 . . . . Seattle	30-31 . . . . at Toronto	18-21 . . . . Baltimore
19-21 . . . . Oakland		22-24 . . . . San Francisco
22-24 . . . . . . .Tampa Bay	**JUNE**	25-27 . . . . . .at Houston
25-27 . . . . .at Texas	1 . . . . at Toronto	29-31 . . . . . at Tampa Bay
29-30 . . . . .at Boston	3-5. . . . . . . .at Baltimore	
	6-9. . . . . . . Los Angeles	**AUGUST**
MAY	10-12 . . . . Detroit	1-2. . . . . at New York
1 . . . . .at Boston	14-15 . . . . . at Colorado	3-4. . . . . .New York
3-5. . . . . . .at Baltimore	16-19 . . . . . at Minnesota	5-7. . . . . Cleveland
6-8. . . . . Boston	21-22 . . . . .Colorado	9-11 . . . . .at Boston
9-12 . . . . . . Kansas City	24-26 . . . . Minnesota	12-14 . . . . . . .Tampa Bay
13-15 . . . . Chicago	27-30 . . . . Texas	15-17 . . . . .Toronto
16-18 . . . . . . at Arizona		19-21 . . . . at Los Angeles
	JULY	22-24 . . . . .at Seattle
	1-3. . . . . . . at San Diego	

26-28 . . . . . . Baltimore	
29-31 . . . . .at Kansas City	
SEPTEMBER	
2-4. . . . . .at Baltimore	
5-7. . . . . .Toronto	
8-11 . . . . . . .Tampa Bay	
12-14 . . . . . . Los Angeles	
15-18 . . . . .at Boston	
20-22 . . . . at Tampa Bay	
23-26 . . . . at Toronto	
27-29 . . . . Boston	
30 . . . . Baltimore	
OCTOBER	
1-2. . . . . Baltimore	

GENERAL INFORMATION
Stadium (year opened):
Yankee Stadium (2009).
Team Colors: Navy blue and white.

Player Representative: Unavailable.
Home Dugout: First Base.
Playing Surface: Grass.

Baseball Operations: Matt Ferry. **Coordinator, Baseball Operations:** Stephen Swindal, Jr. **Assistant, Baseball Operations:** Timothy Choi. **Major League Systems Architect:** Brian Nicosia. **Senior Web Developer:** Nick Eby. **Senior iOS Developer:** Michael Traverso. **Special Assignment Scout:** Jim Hendry. **Senior Analyst, Quantitative Analysis:** Jim Logue. **Analysts, Quantitative Analysis:** John Benedetto, Justin Sims, Sam Waters. **Database Engineer, Baseball Operations:** Jesse Bradford. **Nutritional Consultant:** Cynthia Sass. **Director, Mental Conditioning:** Chad Bohling.

MAJOR LEAGUE STAFF
Manager: Joe Girardi.
Coaches: Bench— Rob Thomson; **Pitching**—Larry Rothschild; **Hitting**—Jeff Pentland; **Assistant Hitting**—Alan Cockrell; **First Base**—Tony Pena; **Third Base**—Joe Espada; **Bullpen**—Gary Tuck; **Bullpen Catcher**—Roman Rodriguez.

MEDICAL/TRAINING
Team Physician, New York: Dr. Christopher Ahmad.
Head Team Internist: Paul Lee, M.D., M.P.H. **Team Internist:** William Turner, M.D. **Senior Advisor, Orthopedics:** Stuart Hershon, M.D. **Head Athletic Trainer:** Steve Donohue. **Physical Therapist/Assistant Athletic Trainer:** Michael Schuk. **Assistant Athletic Trainer:** Tim Lentych. **Massage Therapist:** Doug Cecil. **Director, Strength/Conditioning:** Matthew Krause. **Assistant Director, Strength/Conditioning:** Orlando Crance.

PLAYER DEVELOPMENT
Vice President, Player Development: Gary Denbo.
Director, Performance Science: John Kremer. **Director, Minor League Operations:** Eric Schmitt. **Assistant Director, Minor League Operations Development:** Hadi Raad. **Enterprise Solutions Engineer:** Rob Owens. **Pitching Instructor:** Nardi Contreras. **Field Coordinator:** Jody Reed. **Assistant Field Coordinator/Infield Coordinator:** Carlos Mendoza. **Hitting Coordinator:** James Rowson. **Pitching Coordinator (upper level):** Scott Aldred. **Pitching Coordinator (lower level):** Danny Borrell. **Outfield/Baserunning Coordinator:** Reggie Willits. **Catching Coordinator:** Josh Paul. **Rehab Pitching Instructor:** Greg Pavlick. **Rehab Position Player Instructor:** Tom Nieto. **Player Development Consultant:** Marc Bombard. **Video Coordinator, Player Development:** Adam Hunt. **Player Development Analyst:** Dan Greenlee. **Assistant, Minor League Operations:** Vic Roldan. **Medical Coordinator, Preventative Programs:** Mike Wickland. **Medical Coordinator:** Mark Littlefield. **Strength/Conditioning Coordinator:** Rigo Febles. **Assistant Strength/Conditioning Coordinator:** Mike Kicia. **Assistant Head Athletic Trainer:** Greg Spratt. **Physical Therapist, Player Development:** David Colvin.

FARM SYSTEM
Class	Club (League)	Manager	Hitting Coach	Pitching Coach
Triple-A	Scranton/WB (IL)	Al Pedrique	Tommy Wilson	Tommy Phelps
Double-A	Trenton (EL)	Bobby Mitchell	PJ Pilittere	Jose Rosado
High A	Tampa (FSL)	Patrick Osborn	Tom Slater	Tim Norton
Low A	Charleston (SAL)	Luis Dorante	Greg Colbrunn	Justin Pope
Short-season	Staten Island (NYP)	Dave Bialas	Eric Duncan	Unavailable
Rookie	Pulaski (APP)	Tony Franklin	Edwar Gonzalez	Butch Henry
Rookie	Yankees I (GCL)	Julio Mosquera	Unavailable	Armando Galarraga
Rookie	Yankees II (GCL)	Raul Dominguez	Kevin Mahoney	Elvys Quezada
Rookie	Yankees I (DSL)	Carlos Mota	Christian Reyes	Gabriel Tatis
Rookie	Yankees II (DSL)	Sonder Encarnacion	Edwin Beard	Gerardo Casadiego

SCOUTING
Telephone: (813) 875-7569. **Fax:** (813) 873-2302.
VP, Amateur Scouting: Damon Oppenheimer.
Assistant Director, Amateur Scouting: Ben McIntyre. **Director, Professional Scouting:** Kevin Reese. **Assistant Director, Professional Scouting:** Dan Giese. **National Crosscheckers:** Brian Barber, Tim Kelly, Jeff Patterson, DJ Svihlik. **Pitching Analyst, Amateur Scouting:** Scott Lovekamp. **Hitting Analyst, Amateur Scouting:** Jeff Deardorff. **Analyst, Amateur Scouting:** Scott Benecke. **Draft Medical Coordinator:** Justin Sharpe. **Video Coordinator, Amateur Scouting:** Mitch Colahan.
Professional Scouts: Joe Caro, Kendall Carter, Matt Daley, Jay Darnell, Jeff Datz, Brandon Duckworth, Bill Emslie, Abe Flores, Kevin Hart, Drew Henson, Aaron Holbert, Pat Murtaugh, Greg Orr, JT Stotts, Alex Sunderland, Dennis Twombley.
Area Scouts: Troy Afenir, Denis Boucher, Bobby DeJardin, Phil Geisler, Mike Gibbons, Billy Godwin, Matt Hyde, David Keith, Steve Kmetko, Steve Lemke, Mike Leuzinger, Carlos Marti, Ronnie Merrill, Darryl Monroe, Nick Ortiz, Bill Pintard, Cesar Presbott, Matt Ranson, Brian Rhees, Stewart Smothers, Mike Thurman, Mike Wagner.
Director, International Player Development: Pat McMahon. **Director, International Scouting:** Donny Rowland. **Assistant Director, International Player Development:** Mario Garza. **Director, Latin Baseball Academy:** Joel Lithgow. **International Hitting Instructor:** Ty Hawkins. **International Pitching Instructor:** Miguel Bonilla. **Rehab Manager:** Jose Duran. **Rehab Pitching Coach:** Luis Brito. **Rehab Hitting Coach:** Roy Gomez. **Coordinator, Cultural Development:** Hector Gonzalez. **Video Coordinator, International Operations:** Taylor Emanuels. **International Crosschecker/Coordinator, Int' Scouting/Pacific Rim:** Steve Wilson. **Crosschecker, International Scouting:** Dennis Woody. **Scouting Coordinator, Dominican Republic:** Raymon Sanchez. **Crosscheckers, Latin America:** Miguel Benitez, Victor Mata. **International Crosschecker:** Ricardo Finol. **Assistant, International Scouting:** Yunior Tabares. **Supervisor, Venezuela:** Jose Gavidia. **Dominican Republic Scouts:** Esteban Castillo, Leobaldo Figueroa, Raul Gonzalez, Arturo Pena, Juan Piron, Juan Rosario, Jose Sabino. **Venezuela Scouts:** Alan Atacho, Darwin Bracho, Roney Calderon, Borman Landaeta, Cesar Suarez, Luis Tinoco. **Mexico Scouts:** Lee Sigman, Humberto Soto, David Tapia. **International Scouts:** Rudy Gomez, Chi Lee (South Korea), Hensley Josephina (Curacao), Carlos Levy (Panama), Edgard Rodriguez (Nicaragua), Luis Sierra (Colombia), Ken Su (Taiwan), John Wadsworth (Australia), Troy Williams (Europe).

Oakland Athletics

Office Address: 7000 Coliseum Way, Oakland, CA 94621.
Telephone: (510) 638-4900. **Fax:** (510) 562-1633. **Website:** www.oaklandathletics.com.

OWNERSHIP
Owner/Managing Partner: Lew Wolff.

BUSINESS OPERATIONS
President: Michael Crowley. **Vice President, Venue Development:** Keith Wolff. **Executive Assistant:** Carolyn Jones. **General Counsel:** Neil Kraetsch. **Assistant General Counsel:** Ryan Horning.

FINANCE/ADMINISTRATION
Vice President, Finance: Paul Wong. **Senior Director, Finance:** Kasey Jarcik. **Director, Finance:** John Anki. **Payroll Manager:** Rose Dancil. **Senior Accountant, Accounts Payable:** Isabelle Mahaffey. **Senior Staff Accountant:** Nick Cukar. **Senior Account:** Danna Mouat. **Director, Human Resources:** Kim Kubo. **Human Resources Manager:** Elizabeth Espinoza. **Human Resources Assistant:** Katie Strehlow. **Director, Information Technology:** Nathan Hayes. **IT Manager:** David Frieberg.

Lew Wolff

SALES/MARKETING
VP, Sales/Marketing: Jim Leahey. **Assistant, Sales/Marketing:** Elizabeth Staub. **Senior Director, Marketing:** Troy Smith. **Senior Manager, Marketing:** Travis LoDolce. **Marketing Coordinator:** Laiken Whitters. **Marketing Assistant:** Kate Hunts. **Creative Services Manager:** Mike Ono. **Team Photographer:** Michael Zagaris. **Senior Manager, Promotion/Events:** Heather Rajeski. **Special Events Assistant:** Jake Anderson.

PUBLIC RELATIONS/COMMUNICATIONS
VP, Communications/Broadcasting: Ken Pries. **Director, Corporate Communications:** Catherine Aker. **Baseball Information Manager:** Mike Selleck. **Player and Media Relations Manager:** Adam Loberstein. **Media Services Manager:** Debbie Gallas. **Media Relations/Broadcasting Coordinator:** Zak Basch. **Director, Community Relations:** Detra Paige. **Community Relations Coordinator:** Melissa Guzman. **Community Relations Assistant:** Amanda Young. **Senior Director, Multimedia Services:** David Don. **Public Address Announcer:** Dick Callahan.

STADIUM OPERATIONS
VP, Stadium Operations: David Rinetti. **Senior Director, Stadium Operations:** Paul La Veau. **Senior Manager, Stadium Operations Events:** Kristy Ledbetter. **Stadium Services Manager:** Randy Duran. **Guest Services Manager:** Elisabeth Aydelotte. **Stadium Operations Manager:** Matt Van Norton. **Stadium Operations Assistants:** Perry Constas, Jason Silva. **Head Groundskeeper:** Clay Wood.

TICKET SALES/OPERATIONS/SERVICES
Executive Director, Ticket Sales/Operations: Steve Fanelli. **Senior Director, Service/Retention:** Josh Ziegenbusch.

2016 SCHEDULE
Standard Game Times: 7:05 p.m.; Sat./Sun. 1:05.

APRIL		JULY	
4-7 . . . . Chicago	19-22 . . . . New York	1-3 . . . . Pittsburgh	22-24 . . . . Cleveland
8-10 . . . . .at Seattle	23-25 . . . . . .at Seattle	4-6 . . . . . . at Minnesota	26-28 . . . . . .at St. Louis
11-13 . . . . . . Los Angeles	27-29 . . . . Detroit	7-10 . . . . . . .at Houston	29-31 . . . . . .at Houston
15-17 . . . . . Kansas City	30-31 . . . . . .Minnesota	15-17 . . . . .Toronto	**SEPTEMBER**
19-21 . . . . . at New York	**JUNE**	18-20 . . . . Houston	2-4 . . . . Boston
22-24 . . . . . . at Toronto	1 . . . . .Minnesota	21-24 . . . . . .Tampa Bay	5-7 . . . . Los Angeles
25-28 . . . . . . .at Detroit	3-5 . . . . .at Houston	25-27 . . . . .at Texas	9-11 . . . . Seattle
29-30 . . . . . . Houston	7-8 . . . . . . at Milwaukee	29-31 . . . .at Cleveland	12-15 . . . . .at Kansas City
MAY	10-12 . . . . . .at Cincinnati	**AUGUST**	16-18 . . . . .at Texas
1 . . . . Houston	13-16 . . . . Texas	2-4 . . . . . at Los Angeles	19-21 . . . . Houston
2-4 . . . . Seattle	17-19 . . . . . Los Angeles	5-7 . . . . Chicago	23-25 . . . . Texas
6-8 . . . . . .at Baltimore	21-22 . . . . . . .Milwaukee	8-11 . . . . Baltimore	26-28 . . . . at Los Angeles
9-11 . . . . . . .at Boston	23-26 . . . . at Los Angeles	12-14 . . . . Seattle	29-30 . . . . . . .at Seattle
13-15 . . . . at Tampa Bay	27-28 . . . at San Francisco	15-17 . . . . .at Texas	**OCTOBER**
16-18 . . . . Texas	29-30 . . . . San Francisco	19-21 . . . . . .at Chicago	1-2 . . . . .at Seattle

GENERAL INFORMATION
Stadium (year opened):
O.co Coliseum (1968).
Team Colors: Kelly green and gold.

Player Representative: Unavailable.
Home Dugout: Third Base.
Playing Surface: Grass.

Director, Ticket Operations: David Adame. **Ticket Services Manager:** Catherine Glazier. **Premium Services Manager:** Matt Langseth. **Premium Services Coordinator:** Brianne Gidcumb. **Ticket Operations Manager:** Anuj Patel. **Client Services Manager:** Cathy Garcia. **Box Office Coordinator:** Patricia Heagy. **Director, Ticket Sales:** Brian DiTucci. **Group Sales Manager:** David Nosti.

TRAVEL/CLUBHOUSE
Director, Team Travel: Mickey Morabito. **Equipment Manager:** Steve Vucinich. **Visiting Clubhouse Manager:** Mike Thalblum. **Assistant Equipment Manager:** Brian Davis. **Umpire/Clubhouse Assistant:** Matt Weiss. **Arizona Clubhouse Manager:** James Gibson. **Arizona Assistant Clubhouse Managers:** Thomas Miller, Chad Yaconetti.

BASEBALL OPERATIONS
Executive Vice President, Baseball Operations: Billy Beane.
General Manager: David Forst. **Assistant GM:** Dan Kantrovitz. **Assistant GM, Pro Scouting & Player Personnel :** Dan Feinstein. **Assistant GM/Director, Player Personnel:** Billy Owens. **Director, Baseball Systems:** Rob Naberhaus. **Special Assistants to GM:** Grady Fuson, Chris Pittaro. **Executive Assistant:** Betty Shinoda. **Director, Baseball Administration:** Pamela Pitts. **Video Coordinator:** Adam Rhoden. **Special Assistant to Baseball Operations:** Scott Hatteberg. **Baseball Operations Analyst:** Michael Schatz.

Billy Beane

MAJOR LEAGUE STAFF
Manager: Bob Melvin.
Coaches: Bench—Mark Kotsay; **Pitching**—Curt Young; **Batting**—Darren Bush; **First Base**— Mike Aldrete; **Third Base**—Ron Washington; **Bullpen**—Scott Emerson; **Assistant Hitting/Catching Coach**—Marcus Jensen; **Bullpen Catcher**—Phil Pohl.

MEDICAL/TRAINING
Head Athletic Trainer: Nick Paparesta. **Assistant Athletic Trainers:** Walt Horn, Brian Schulman. **Strength/Conditioning Coach:** Michael Henriques. **Major League Massage Therapist:** Ozzie Lyles. **Team Physicians:** Dr. Allan Pont, Dr. Elliott Schwartz. **Team Orthopedist:** Dr. Jon Dickinson. **Associate Team Orthopedist:** Dr. Will Workman. **Arizona Team Physicians:** Dr. Fred Dicke, Dr. Doug Freedberg.

PLAYER DEVELOPMENT
Telephone: (510) 638-4900. **Fax:** (510) 563-2376.
Director, Player Development: Keith Lieppman. **Director, Minor League Operations:** Ted Polakowski. **Administrative Assistant, Player Development:** Nancy Moriuchi. **Minor League Roving Instructors:** Juan Navarrete (infield), Gil Patterson (pitching), Jim Eppard (hitting). **Minor League Video Coordinator:** Mark Smith. **Minor League Medical Coordinator:** Jeff Collins. **Coordinator, Medical Services:** Larry Davis. **Minor League Strength/Conditioning Coordinator:** Josh Cuffe. **Special Instructor, Pitching/Rehabilitation:** Craig Lefferts. **Minor League Rehabilitation Coordinator:** Nate Brooks.

FARM SYSTEM
Class	Club (League)	Manager	Coach	Pitching Coach
Triple-A	Nashville (PCL)	Steve Scarsone	Eric Martins	Rick Rodriguez
Double-A	Midland (TL)	Ryan Christenson	Brian McArn	John Wasdin
High A	Stockton (CAL)	Rick Magnante	Tommy Everidge	Steve Connelly
Low A	Beloit (MWL)	Fran Riordan	Juan Dilone	Don Schulze
Short-season	Vermont (NYP)	Aaron Nieckula	Lloyd Turner	Carlos Chavez
Rookie	Athletics (AZL)	Webster Garrison	Ruben Escalera	Unavailable
Rookie	Athletics (DSL)	Carlos Casimiro	Rahdames Perez	David Brito

SCOUTING
Director, Scouting: Eric Kubota (Rocklin, CA).
Assistant Director, Scouting: Michael Holmes (Winston Salem, NC). **Director, Pro Scouting/Baseball Development:** Dan Feinstein (Lafayette, CA). **Scouting Assistant:** Ben Lowry (Berkeley, CA). **West Coast Supervisor:** Scott Kidd (Folsom, CA). **Midwest Supervisor:** Ron Marigny (Cypress, TX).
East Coast Supervisor: Marc Sauer (Tampa, FL). **Northeast Supervisor:** Pat Portugal (Wake Forest, NC). **Pro Scouts:** Jeff Bittiger (Saylorsburg, PA), Dan Freed (Lexington, IL), Trevor Ryan (Walnut Creek, CA), Will Schock (Oakland, CA), Steve Sharpe (Kansas City, MO), Tom Thomas (Phoenix, AZ), Mike Ziegler (Orlando, FL). **Area Scouts:** Anthony Aloisi (Laguna Niguel, CA), Neil Avent (Charlotte, NC), Armann Brown (Austin, TX), Jermaine Clark (Discovery Bay, CA), Jim Coffman (Portland, OR), Ruben Escalera (Carolina, PR), Matt Higginson (Burlington, ON), Scott Cousins (Scottsdale, AZ), Craig Conklin (Malibu, CA), Kevin Mello (Chicago, IL), Kelcey Mucker (Baton Rouge, LA), Trevor Schaffer (Belleair, FL), Rich Sparks (Sterling Heights, MI), Al Skorupa (Overland Park, KS), Jemel Spearman (Lithonia, GA), Ron Vaughn (Windsor, CT).
Director, Latin American Operations: Raymond Abreu (Santo Domingo, DR). **Coordinator, Latin American Scouting:** Julio Franco (Carrizal, VZ). **International Scouts:** Ruben Barradas (Venezuela), Juan Carlos De La Cruz (Dominican Republic), Angel Eusebio (Dominican Republic), Andri Garcia (Venezuela), Adam Hislop (Taiwan), Lewis Kim (South Korea), Pablo Marmol (Dominican Republic), Juan Mosquera (Panama), Tito Quintero (Colombia), Amaurys Reyes (Dominican Republic), Oswaldo Troconis (Venezuela), Juan Villanueva (Venezuela).

Philadelphia Phillies

Office Address: Citizens Bank Park, One Citizens Bank Way, Philadelphia, PA 19148.
Telephone: (215) 463-6000. **Website:** www.phillies.com.

OWNERSHIP
Operated By: The Phillies.
President: Andy MacPhail. **Chairman:** David Montgomery. **Chairman Emeritus:** Bill Giles.

BUSINESS OPERATIONS
VP/General Counsel: Rick Strouse. **VP, Human Resources/Customer Services:** Kathy Killian. **Director, Ballpark Enterprises/Business Development:** Joe Giles. **Director, Information Systems:** Brian Lamoreaux. **Director, Human Resources/Benefits:** JoAnn Marano.

BALLPARK OPERATIONS
Executive VP/ COO: Michael Stiles. **Director, Operations/Facility:** Mike DiMuzio. **Director, Operations/Events:** Eric Tobin. **Director, Operations/Security:** Sal DeAngelis. **Director, Field Operations:** Mike Boekholder **Manager, Concessions Development:** Bruce Leith. **PA Announcer:** Dan Baker. **Official Scorers:** Jay Dunn, Mike Maconi, Dick Shute

COMMUNICATIONS
Telephone: (215) 463-6000. **Fax:** (215) 389-3050.
VP, Communications: Bonnie Clark. **Director, Baseball Communications:** Greg Casterioto.
Coordinator, Baseball Communications: Craig Hughner. **Baseball Communications Assistant:** Chris Ware.

David Montgomery

FINANCE
VP/CFO: John Nickolas. Director, **Payroll Services:** Karen Wright.

MARKETING/PROMOTIONS
Senior VP, Marketing/ AdSales: David Buck. **Manager, Client Services/Alumni Relations:** Debbie Nocito. **Director, Corporate Partnerships:** Rob MacPherson. **Director, Advertising Sales:** Brian Mahoney. **Director, Corporate Sales:** Scott Nickle. **Manager, Advertising Sales:** Tom Sullivan.
VP, Marketing Programs/Events: Kurt Funk. **Director, Entertainment:** Chris Long. **Manager, Broadcasting:** Rob Brooks. **Manager, Advertising/Internet Services:** Jo-Anne Levy-Lamoreaux.

SALES/TICKETS
Telephone: (215) 463-1000. **Fax:** (215) 463-9878.
VP, Sales/Ticket Operations: John Weber. **Director, Ticket Technology/Development:** Chris Pohl. **Director, Sales:** Derek Schuster. **Manager, Suite Sales/Services:** Tom Mashek. **Director, Ticket Services/Intern Program:** Phil Feather. **Manager, Season Ticket Services:** Mike Holdren.

2016 SCHEDULE
Standard Game Times: 7:05 p.m.; Sun. 1:35

APRIL		
4-7 . . . . . . .at Cincinnati	20-22 . . . . Atlanta	JULY
8-10 . . . . . . at New York	23-25 . . . . . . .at Detroit	1-3 . . . . . . Kansas City
11-14 . . . . . . San Diego	27-29 . . . . . . .at Chicago	4-6. . . . . Atlanta
15-17 . . . . . .Washington	30-31 . . . . . Washington	7-10 . . . . . at Colorado
18-20 . . . . . . .New York	JUNE	15-17 . . . . . . .New York
22-24 . . . . at Milwaukee	1 . . . . Washington	18-21 . . . . .Miami
26-28 . . . at Washington	2-5. . . . . . . .Milwaukee	22-24 . . . . . at Pittsburgh
29-30 . . . . Cleveland	6-8. . . . . Chicago	25-27 . . . . at Miami
MAY	10-12 . . . . at Washington	28-31 . . . . . at Atlanta
1 . . . . Cleveland	13-14 . . . . . . at Toronto	AUGUST
2-5. . . . . .at St. Louis	15-16 . . . . .Toronto	2-4. . . . . . . San Francisco
6-8. . . . . at Miami	17-20 . . . . .Arizona	5-7. . . . . . at San Diego
10-12 . . . . . at Atlanta	21-23 . . . at Minnesota	8-10 . . . . at Los Angeles
13-15 . . . . . . Cincinnati	24-26 . . . at San Francisco	12-14 . . . . . . .Colorado
16-18 . . . . .Miami	27-29 . . . . . . at Arizona	16-18 . . . . . Los Angeles
		19-21 . . . . St. Louis

23-24 . . . . . .at Chicago	
26-28 . . . . . at New York	
29-31 . . . . . Washington	
SEPTEMBER	
2-4. . . . . Atlanta	
5-7. . . . . at Miami	
8-11 . . . . . at Washington	
12-15 . . . . . .Pittsburgh	
16-18 . . . . .Miami	
20-21 . . . . Chicago	
22-25 . . . . at New York	
27-29 . . . . . . at Atlanta	
30 . . . . .New York	
OCTOBER	
1-2. . . . . .New York	

GENERAL INFORMATION

Stadium (year opened): Citizens Bank Park (2004).
Team Colors: Red, white and blue.
Player Representative: Unavailable.
Home Dugout: First Base.
Playing Surface: Natural Grass.

TRAVEL/CLUBHOUSE
Director, Team Travel/Clubhouse Services: Frank Coppenbarger.
Manager, Visiting Clubhouse: Kevin Steinhour. **Manager, Home Clubhouse:** Phil Sheridan. **Manager, Equipment/ Umpire Services:** Dan O'Rourke.

BASEBALL OPERATIONS
VP/General Manager: Matt Klentak
Assistant GM: Scott Proefrock. **Assistant GM:** Ned Rice. **Senior Advisor to the President/ GM:** Pat Gillick. **Senior Advisors to the GM:** Dallas Green, Charlie Manuel. **Senior Advisor, International Operations:** Benny Looper. **Special Assistants to GM:** Bart Braun, Charley Kerfeld. **Special Assistant, Baseball Operations:** Ed Wade. **Director, Team Travel/Clubhouse Services:** Frank Coppenbarger. **Director, Baseball Operations:** Scott Freedman. **Director, Baseball Research and Development:** Andy Galdi. **Director, Professional Scouting:** Mike Ondo. **Baseball Information Analyst:** Jay McLaughlin. **Advance Scouting Analyst:** Chris Cashman. **Analyst, Baseball Research and Development:** Lewis Pollis. **Administrative Assistant, Baseball Operations:** Adele MacDonald.

Matt Klentak

MAJOR LEAGUE STAFF
Manager: Pete Mackanin
Coaches: Bench—Larry Bowa; **Pitching**—Bob McClure; **Hitting**—Steve Henderson; **First Base**—Mickey Morandini; **Third Base**—Juan Samuel; **Bullpen** —Rick Kranitz; **Catching**—John McLaren; **Bullpen Catchers**—Jesus Tiamo & Bob Stumpo

MEDICAL/TRAINING
Director, Medical Services: Dr. Michael Ciccotti. **Head Athletic Trainer:** Scott Sheridan. **Assistant Athletic Trainers:** Shawn Fcasni, Chris Mudd. **Major LeagueConditioning Coordinator:** Paul Fournier. **Employee Assistance Professional:** Dickie Noles.

PLAYER DEVELOPMENT
Director, Player Development: Joe Jordan.
Director, Minor League Operations: Lee McDaniel. **Assistant Director, Player Development:** Steve Noworyta. **Special Assistant, Player Personnel:** Jorge Velandia. **Director, Florida Operations/GM. Clearwater Threshers:** John Timberlake. **Assistant Director, Minor League Operations/Florida Operations:** Joe Cynar. **Coordinator, International Operations:** Ray Robles.
Field Coordinator: Doug Mansolino. **Assistant Field Coordinator/Hitting:** Andy Tracy. **Pitching Coordinator:** Rafael Chaves. **Roving Pitching Coach:** Carlos Arroyo. **Infield Coordinator:** Chris Truby. **Outfield/Baserunning:** Andy Abad. **Catching:** Ernie Whitt. **Athletic Training coordinator:** Joe Rauch. **Strength/Conditioning Coordinator:** Jason Meredith.

FARM SYSTEM

Class	Club (League)	Manager	Hitting Coach	Pitching Coach
Triple-A	Lehigh Valley (IL)	Dave Brundage	Sal Rende	Dave Lundquist
Double-A	Reading (EL)	Dusty Wathan	Frank Cacciatore	Steve Schrenk
High A	Clearwater (FSL)	Greg Legg	Rob Ducey	Aaron Fultz
Low A	Lakewood (SAL)	Shawn Williams	Nelson Prada	Brian Sweeney
Short-season	Williamsport (NYP)	Pat Borders	John Mizerock	Hector Berrios
Rookie	Phillies (GCL)	Roly deArmas	R. DeLima/ E. Dennis	Hector Mercado
Rookie	Phillies (DSL)	Manny Amador	C. Henriquez/W. Santana	Alex Concepcion

SCOUTING
Director, Amateur Scouting: Johnny Almaraz (San Antonio, TX)
Director, Amateur Scouting Administration: Rob Holiday (Philadelphia, PA). **Coordinators, Scouting:** Mike Ledna (Arlington Heights, IL), Bill Moore (Alta Loma, CA).
Regional Supervisors: Darrell Conner (West/Riverside, CA), Gene Schall (Mid-Atlantic/Harleysville, PA), David Seifert (Paw Paw, IL), Eric Valent (Southeast/Wyomissing, PA)
Area Scouts: Alex Agostino (Quebec), Shane Bowers (La Verne, CA), Steve Cohen (Spring, TX), Joey Davis (Rocklin, CA), Mike Garcia (Moreno Valley, CA), Brad Holland (Gilbert, AZ), Aaron Jersild (Alpharetta, GA), Brian Kohlscheen (Norman, OK), Alan Marr (Sarasota, FL), Timi Moni (Nashville, TN), Paul Murphy (Wilmington, DE), Demerius Pittman (Corona, CA), Luis Raffan (Miami, FL), Hilton Richardson (Kirkland, WA), Paul Scott (Rockwall, TX), Mike Stauffer (Brandon, MS), Scott Trcka (Hobart, IN).
Director International Scouting: Sal Agostinelli (Kings Park, NY). **International Scouts:** Rafael Alvarez (Venezuela), Norman Anciani (Panama), Franklin Felida (Dominican Republic), Luis Garcia (Dominican Republic), Gene Grimaldi (Antiles), Tomas Herrera (Mexico), Andres Hiraldo (Dominican Republic), Gregory Manuel (Aruba), Jesus Mendez (Venezuela), Jairo Morelos (Colombia), Romulo Oliveros (Venezuela), Bernardo Perez (Dominican Republic), Philip Riccobono (Korea), Carlos Salas (Dominican Republic), Claudio Scerrato (Italy), Ebert Valazquez (Venezuela).
Director, Major League Scouting: Gordon Lakey (Barker, TX). **Special Assignment Scouts:** Howie Frieling (Apex, NC), Dave Hollins (Orchard Park, NY), Craig Colbert (Portland, OR), Dan Wright (Cave Springs, AR). **Professional Scouts:** Jeff Harris (Chico, CA), Steve Jongewaard (West Chester, OH), Jesse Levis (Fort Washington, PA), Jon Mercurio (Coraopolis, PA), Roy Tanner (Palatka , FL), Del Unser (Scottsdale, AZ).

Pittsburgh Pirates

Office Address: PNC Park at North Shore, 115 Federal St., Pittsburgh, PA, 15212.
Mailing Address: PO Box 7000, Pittsburgh, PA 15212.
Telephone: (412) 323-5000. **Fax:** (412) 325-4412. **Website:** www.pirates.com. **Twitter:** @Pirates.

OWNERSHIP
Chairman of the Board: Robert Nutting.
Board of Directors: Donald Beaver, Eric Mauck, G. Ogden Nutting, Robert Nutting, William Nutting, Duane Wittman.

BUSINESS OPERATIONS
President: Frank Coonelly. **Senior VP, Business Affairs/General Counsel:** Bryan Stroh.

COMMUNICATIONS
VP, Communications/Broadcasting: Brian Warecki. **Director, Baseball Communications:** Jim Trdinich. **Director, Broadcasting:** Marc Garda. **Director, Media Relations:** Dan Hart. **Manager, Business Communications/Social Media:** Terry Rodgers.

COMMUNITY RELATIONS
Senior VP, Community/Public Affairs: Patty Paytas. **Director, Community Relations:** Michelle Mejia. **Manager, Diversity Initiatives:** Unavailable. **Manager, Pirates Charities:** Jackie Hunter.

MARKETING
Senior Director, Marketing/Special Events: Brian Chiera. **Director, Alumni Affairs/Promotions/Licensing:** Joe Billetdeaux. **Director, Advertising/Creative Services:** Kiley Cauvel. **Director, Special Events/Game Presentation:** Christine Serkoch. **Director, PNC Park Events:** Ann Elder.

Frank Coonelly

CORPORATE SPONSORSHIPS
Senior Director, Corporate Sponsorship Sales/Service: Aaron Cohn.

STADIUM OPERATIONS
Executive VP/General Manager, PNC Park: Dennis DaPra. **Senior Director, Ballpark Operations:** Chris Hunter. **Senior Director, Security/Contract Services:** Jeff Podobnik. **Senior Director, Florida Operations:** Trevor Gooby. **Director, Field Maintenance:** Matt Brown.

FINANCE/ADMINISTRATION/INFORMATION TECHNOLOGY
Executive VP/CFO: Jim Plake. **Senior Director, IT:** Terry Zeigler. **Senior Director, Business Analytics:** Jim Alexander.

TICKETING
Telephone: (800) 289-2827.
Director, Suite Sales/Service: Terri Smith. **Director, New Business Development:** Nick McNeill. **Director, Season Ticket Service/Retention:** Jim Popovich. **Director, Ticket Operations:** Doug Vanderheyden.

2016 SCHEDULE
Standard Game Times: 7:05 p.m.; Sun. 1:35.

APRIL			
3-6 . . . . St. Louis	16-19 . . . . Atlanta	JULY	22-24 . . . . Houston
8-10 . . . . . .at Cincinnati	20-22 . . . . . . .Colorado	1-3. . . . . .at Oakland	25-28 . . . . . at Milwaukee
11-12 . . . . . . .at Detroit	24-26 . . . . Arizona	4-7. . . . . .at St. Louis	29-31 . . . . . . .at Chicago
13-14 . . . . Detroit	27-29 . . . . .at Texas	8-10 . . . . Chicago	
15-17 . . . . . .Milwaukee	30-31 . . . . . . at Miami	15-17 . . . at Washington	SEPTEMBER
19-21 . . . . at San Diego		19-21 . . . . . .Milwaukee	2-4. . . . . .Milwaukee
22-24 . . . . . . at Arizona	JUNE	22-24 . . . . . .Philadelphia	5-7. . . . . St. Louis
25-28 . . . . . at Colorado	1-2. . . . . at Miami	26-27 . . . . Seattle	8-11 . . . . Cincinnati
29-30 . . . . . . Cincinnati	3-5 . . . . Los Angeles	29-31 . . . . at Milwaukee	12-15 . . . at Philadelphia
	6-8. . . . . .New York		16-18 . . . . . .at Cincinnati
MAY	10-12 . . . . St. Louis	AUGUST	20-22 . . . . . at Milwaukee
1 . . . . Cincinnati	14-16 . . . . . at New York	2-4. . . . . at Atlanta	23-25 . . . . . Washington
2-4. . . . . Chicago	17-19 . . . . . . .at Chicago	5-7. . . . . Cincinnati	26-29 . . . . Chicago
6-8. . . . . . . .at St. Louis	20-23 . . . . San Francisco	9-11 . . . . San Diego	30 . . . . .at St. Louis
9-11 . . . . . .at Cincinnati	24-27 . . . . . Los Angeles	12-14 . . . at Los Angeles	
13-15 . . . . . . .at Chicago	28-29 . . . . . . .at Seattle	15-17 . . . at San Francisco	OCTOBER
		19-21 . . . . .Miami	1-2. . . . . .at St. Louis

GENERAL INFORMATION
Stadium (year opened): PNC Park (2001). **Team Colors:** Black and gold.
Player Representative: Neil Walker. **Home Dugout:** Third Base. **Playing Surface:** Grass.

BASEBALL OPERATIONS

Senior VP/General Manager: Neal Huntington.
Assistant GMs: Kevan Graves, Greg Smith, Kyle Stark. **Director, Baseball Informatics:** Dan Fox. **Special Assistants to GM:** Ron Hopkins, Matt Ruebel, Jax Robertson, Doug Strange. **Major League Scouts:** Mike Basso, Ricky Bennett, Jim Dedrick, Bob Minor, Steve Williams. **Pro Scouts:** Mike Baker, Carlos Berroa, Mal Fichman, Rodney Henderson, John Kosciak, Sean McNally, Alvin Rittman, Everett Russell, Lewis Shaw. **Special Assistants to Baseball Operations:** Jamey Carroll, Scott Elarton, James Harris, Grady Little, Kevin Young. **Assistant Director, Baseball Operations:** Will Lawton. **Baseball Operations Assistant:** Sean Kelly. **Quantitative Analyst:** Andrew Gibson, Mike Fitzgerald, Stuart Wallace. **Data Architect:** Josh Smith. **Software Developer:** Brian Hulick. **Video Coordinator:** Kevin Roach. **Video Advance Scout:** Joe Hultzen.

Neal Huntington

MAJOR LEAGUE STAFF

Manager: Clint Hurdle.
Coaches: Pitching—Ray Searage; **Hitting**—Jeff Branson; **First Base**—Nick Leyva; **Third Base**—Rick Sofield; **Bullpen**—Euclides Rojas; **Bench Coach**—David Jauss; **Coach**—Jeff Livesey; **Coach**—Brad Fischer.

MEDICAL/TRAINING

Medical Director: Dr. Patrick DeMeo. **Team Physician:** Dr. Edward Snell. **Director of Performance:** Dr. Chris Johnson. **Sports Science Coordinator:** Brendon Huttmann. **Head Major League Athletic Trainer:** Todd Tomczyk. **Assistant Major League Athletic Trainer:** Ben Potenziano. **Major League Strength/Conditioning Coach:** Ricky White. **Physical Therapist:** Kevin "Otis" Fitzgerald.

PLAYER DEVELOPMENT

Director, Minor League Operations: Larry Broadway.
Coordinator, Baseball Administration: Diane DePasquale. **Coordinator, Minor League Operations:** Brian Selman. **Field Coordinator:** Tom Prince. **Coordinator, Instruction:** Dave Turgeon. **Outfield/Baserunning Coordinator:** Kimera Bartee. **Pitching Coordinator:** Scott Mitchell. **Assistant Pitching Coordinator:** Tom Filer. **Latin American Pitching Coordinator:** Amaury Telemaco. **Catching Coordinator:** Milver Reyes. **Infield Coordinator:** Gary Green. **Hitting Coordinator:** Larry Sutton. **Assistant Hitting Coordinator:** Andy Barkett. **Minor League Video Coordinator:** Ryan Gaynor.
Senior Advisor, Latin American Operations: Luis Silverio. **Senior Advisor, Player Development:** Woody Huyke. **Senior Advisor, Player Development:** Mike Lum. **Dominican Academy Coordinator:** Gera Alvarez. **Medical Services Coordinator:** Carl Randolph. **Athletic Training Coordinator:** Bryan Housand. **Minor League Rehab Coordinator:** AJ Patrick. **Strength and Conditioning Coordinator:** Carlo Alvarez. **Strength/Conditioning Specialist:** Joe Hughes. **Director, Mental Conditioning:** Bernie Holliday. **Mental Conditioning Coordinators:** Tyson Holt, Hector Morales. **Coordinator, Personal/Professional Development:** Jon Hammermeister. **Minor League Equipment Manager:** Pat Hagerty. **Education Coordinator:** Mayu Fielding.

FARM SYSTEM

Class	Club (League)	Manager	Hitting Coach	Pitching Coach
Triple-A	Indianapolis (IL)	Dean Treanor	Butch Wynegar	Stan Kyles
Double-A	Altoona (EL)	Joey Cora	Kevin Riggs	Justin Meccage
High A	Bradenton (FSL)	Michael Ryan	Keoni De Renne	Jeff Johnson
Low A	West Virginia (SAL)	Brian Esposito	Ryan Long	Matt Ford
Short-season	West Virginia (NYP)	Wyatt Toregas	Jonathan Prieto	Mark DiFelice
Rookie	Bristol (APP)	Edgar Varela	Austin McClune	Tom Filer
Rookie	Pirates (GCL)	Milver Reyes	Kory DeHaan	Elvin Nina
Rookie	Pirates (DSL)	Mendy Lopez	C. Beltre/G. Picart	Dan Urbina

SCOUTING

Fax: (412) 325-4414.
Director, Amateur Scouting: Joe Delli Carri. **Assistant Director, Amateur Scouting:** Mike Mangan.
Coordinator, Amateur Scouting: Matt Skirving. **National Supervisors:** Jack Bowen (Bethel Park, PA), Jimmy Lester (Columbus, GA). **Regional Supervisors:** Jesse Flores (Sacramento, CA), Trevor Haley (Temperance, MI), Sean Heffernan (Florence, SC), Greg Schilz (Washington D.C.).
Area Supervisors: Rick Allen (Thousand Oaks, CA), Matt Bimeal (Olathe, KS), Adam Bourassa (Cincinnati, OH), Phil Huttmann, (McKinney, TX), Jerry Jordan (Kingsport, TN), Max Kwan (Kent, WA), Wayne Mathis (Cuero, TX), Darren Mazeroski (Panama City Beach, FL), Tim Osborne (Woodstock, GA), Nick Presto (Palm Beach Gardens, FL), Dan Radcliff (Palmyra, VA), Mike Sansoe (Fairfield, CA), Steve Skrinar (Framingham, MA), Brian Tracy (Yorba Linda, CA), Derrick Van Dusen (Phoenix, AZ), Anthony Wycklendt (Brookfield, WI). **Part-Time Scout:** Enrique Hernandez (Puerto Rico).
Director, Latin American Scouting: Rene Gayo. **Admin, Dominican Republic:** Emmanuel Gomez. **International Scouts: Full-time**—Fu-chun Chiang (Far East), Orlando Covo (Colombia), Julio Dominguez (Cuba), Tom Gillespie (Europe), Tony Harris (Australia), Nelson Llenas (Dominican Republic), Juan Mercado (Dominican Republic), Rodolfo Petit (Venezuela), Geron Sands (Bahamas), Victor Santana (Dominican Republic), Cristino Valdez (Dominican Republic), Jesus Valdez (Mexico); **Part-time**—John Akel (Ecuador), Esteban Alvarez (Dominican Republic), Amaro Costa (Argentina), Pablo Csorgi (Venezuela), Denny Diaz (Dominican Republic), Kwamane Ennis (Jamaica), Ruppert Fearon (Jamaica), Eugene Helder (Aruba), Jhoan Hidalgo (Venezuela), Jose Lavagnino (Mexico), Javier Magdaleno (Venezuela), Yeferson Mercado (Dominican Republic), Juan Morales (Venezuela), Jose Mosquera (Colombia), Robinson Ortega (Colombia), Jose Ortiz (Dominican Republic), Juan Perea (Mexico), Jose Pineda (Panama), Cesar Saba (Dominican Republic), Cristobal Santoya (Colombia), Leon Taylor (Jamaica), Jesus Valdez Jr. (Mexico), Mark Van Zanten (Curacao).

St. Louis Cardinals

Office Address: 700 Clark Street, St. Louis MO 63102.
Telephone: (314) 345-9600. **Fax:** (314) 345-9523. **Website:** www.cardinals.com.

OWNERSHIP
Operated By: St. Louis Cardinals, LLC.
Chairman/Chief Executive Officer: William DeWitt, Jr.
President: Bill DeWitt III. **Senior Administrative Assistant to Chairman:** Grace Kell. **Senior Administrative Assistant to President:** Julie Laningham.

BUSINESS OPERATIONS

Bill DeWitt III

FINANCE
Fax: (314) 345-9520.
Senior VP/Chief Financial Officer: Brad Wood. **Director, Finance:** Rex Carter. **Director, Human Resources:** Ann Seeney. **VP, Event Services/Merchandising:** Vicki Bryant. **Director, Special Events:** Julia Row.

MARKETING/SALES/COMMUNITY RELATIONS
Fax: (314) 345-9529.
Senior VP, Sales/Marketing: Dan Farrell. **Administrative Assistant, VP Sales/Marketing:** Gail Ruhling. **VP, Corporate Marketing/Stadium Entertainment:** Thane van Breusegen. **Director, Scoreboard Operations/Fan Entertainment/Senior Account Executive:** Tony Simokaitis. **Director, Publications:** Steve Zesch.
VP, Community Relations/Executive Director, Cardinals Care: Michael Hall. **Administrative Assistant:** Bonnie Parres.

COMMUNICATIONS
Fax: (314) 345-9530.
VP, Communications: Ron Watermon. **Director, Communications:** Brian Bartow. **Manager, Communications:** Melody Yount. **Manager, Photography:** Taka Yanagimoto. **Communications Coordinator:** Chris Tunno. **Administrative Assistant, Communications:** Marybeth Rae. **PA Announcer:** John Ulett. **Official Scorers:** Gary Muller, Jeff Durbin, Mike Smith.

STADIUM OPERATIONS
Fax: (314) 345-9535.
VP, Stadium Operations: Joe Abernathy. **Administrative Assistant:** Hope Baker. **Director, Security/Special Services:** Joe Walsh. **Director, Stadium Operations/Guest Services:** Mike Ball. **Director Facility, Security/Stadium Operations:** Hosei Maruyama. **Head Groundskeeper:** Bill Findley.

2016 SCHEDULE
Standard Game Times: 7:15 p.m.; Sun. 1:15.

APRIL		
3-6	at Pittsburgh
8-10	at Atlanta
11-14	Milwaukee
15-17	Cincinnati
18-20	Chicago
22-24	at San Diego
25-28	at Arizona
29-30	Washington

MAY
1 . . . . Washington
2-5 . . . . Philadelphia
6-8 . . . . Pittsburgh
10-12 . at Los Angeles (AL)
13-15 . at Los Angeles (NL)
17-19 . . . . Colorado

20-22 . . . . Arizona
23-25 . . . . Chicago
26-29 . . . at Washington
30-31 . . . . . at Milwaukee

JUNE
1 . . . . at Milwaukee
3-5 . . . . . . San Francisco
7-9 . . . . . . at Cincinnati
10-12 . . . . . at Pittsburgh
14-15 . . . . Houston
17-19 . . . . Texas
20-22 . . . . . at Chicago
24-26 . . . . . at Seattle
27-28 . . . . at Kansas City
29-30 . . . . . Kansas City

JULY
1-3 . . . . Milwaukee
4-7 . . . . Pittsburgh
8-10 . . . . . at Milwaukee
15-17 . . . . Miami
18-21 . . . . . San Diego
22-24 . . . . . Los Angeles
25-27 . . . . at New York
28-31 . . . . . at Miami

AUGUST
2-4 . . . . at Cincinnati
5-7 . . . . Atlanta
8-10 . . . . Cincinnati
11-14 . . . . . at Chicago
16-17 . . . . . at Houston
19-21 . . . at Philadelphia

23-25 . . . . New York
26-28 . . . . Oakland
29-31 . . . . at Milwaukee

SEPTEMBER
2-4 . . . . at Cincinnati
5-7 . . . . . . at Pittsburgh
8-11 . . . . Milwaukee
12-14 . . . . Chicago
15-18 . . . at San Francisco
19-21 . . . . . at Colorado
23-25 . . . . at Chicago
26-29 . . . . . Cincinnati
30 . . . . Pittsburgh

OCTOBER
1-2 . . . . Pittsburgh

GENERAL INFORMATION
Stadium (year opened): Busch Stadium (2006).
Team Colors: Red and white.
Player Representative: Unavailable.
Home Dugout: First Base.
Playing Surface: Grass.

TICKETING
Fax: (314) 345-9522.
VP, Ticket Sales/Service: Joe Strohm.

TRAVEL/CLUBHOUSE
Fax: (314) 345-9523.
Traveling Secretary: C.J. Cherre. **Equipment Manager:** Rip Rowan. **Assistant Equipment Manager:** Ernie Moore.
Visiting Clubhouse Manger: Jerry Risch. **Video Coordinator:** Chad Blair.

BASEBALL OPERATIONS
Senior VP/General Manager: John Mozeliak.
Assistant GM: Mike Girsch. **Senior Executive Assistant:** Linda Brauer. **Senior Special Assistant to GM:** Mike Jorgensen. **Special Assistant to GM:** Ryan Franklin, Willie McGee. **Director, Player Personnel:** Matt Slater. **Director, Major League Administration:** Judy Carpenter-Barada. **Director, Baseball Administration:** John Vuch. **Manager, Baseball Information:** Jeremy Cohen. **Quantitative Analysts:** Matt Bayer, Patrick Casanta, Kevin Seats, Brian Seyfert, Dane Sorensen

MAJOR LEAGUE STAFF
Telephone: (314) 345-9600.
Manager: Mike Matheny.
Coaches: Bench—David Bell; **Pitching**—Derek Lilliquist; **Hitting**—John Mabry; **Assistant Hitting Instructor**—Bill Mueller; **First Base**—Chris Maloney; **Third Base**—Jose Oquendo; **Bullpen**—Blaise Ilsley; **Bullpen Catchers**—Jamie Pogue, Kleininger Teran.

John Mozeliak

MEDICAL/TRAINING
Head Team Physician: Dr. Michael Milne. **Head Trainer:** Adam Olsen. **Assistant Trainers:** Jeremy Clipperton, Chris Conroy. **Assistant Trainer/Rehabilitation Coordinator:** Adam Olsen. **Strength/Conditioning Coach:** Pete Prinzi. **Director of Performance:** Robert Butler. **Performance Physical Therapist:** Jason Shutt

PLAYER DEVELOPMENT
Director, Player Development: Gary LaRocque.
Administrator Minor League Operations: Tony Ferreira.
Special Assistant, Player Development: Gaylen Pitts. **Minor League Field Coordinator:** Mark DeJohn.
Coordinators: Tim Leveque (pitching), Derrick May (hitting), Ron Warner (roving infield), Luis Aguayo (Latin America coordinator), Paul Davis (asst. pitching coach), George Greer (offensive strategist), Barry Weinberg (senior medical advisor), David Meyer (minor league medical/rehab), Frank Daversa (asst. minor league rehab). **Minor League Equipment Manager:** Dave Vondarhaar.

FARM SYSTEM

Class	Club (League)	Manager	Hitting Coach	Pitching Coach
Triple-A	Memphis (PCL)	Mike Shildt	Mark Budaska	Bryan Eversgerd
Double-A	Springfield (TL)	Dann Bilardello	Ramon Ortiz	Jason Simontacchi
High A	Palm Beach (FSL)	Oliver Marmol	Donnie Ecker	Randy Niemann
Low A	Peoria (MWL)	Joe Kruzel	Jobel Jimenez	Dernier Orozco
Short-season	State College (NYP)	Johnny Rodriguez	Roger LaFrancois	Darwin Marrero
Rookie	Johnson City (APP)	Chris Swauger	Roberto Espinoza	Cale Johnson
Rookie	Cardinals (GCL)	Steve Turco	Cody Gabella (coach)	Giovanni Carrara
Rookie	Cardinals (DSL)	Fray Peniche	Erik Almonte/John Matos	Billy Villanueva

SCOUTING
Fax: (314) 345-9519.
Director, Scouting: Randy Flores
Coordinator, Baseball Operations/Scouting: Jared Odom. **Special Assistant to Amateur Scouting:** Mike Roberts.
Professional Scouts: Patrick Elkins (Baltimore, MD), Jeff Ishii (Chino, CA), Mike Jorgensen (Fenton, MO), Marty Keough (Scottsdale, AZ), Deric McKamey (Bluffton, OH), Ricky Meinhold (Tampa, FL), Joe Rigoli (Parsippany, NJ), Kerry Robinson (Ballwin, MO).
Crosscheckers: Joe Almaraz (San Antonio, TX), Brian Hopkins (Holly Springs, NC), Jeremy Schied (Temecula, CA), Roger Smith (Eastman, GA), Jamal Strong (Surprise, AZ), Matt Swanson (Round Rock, TX).
Area Scouts: Dominic "Ty" Boyles (Atlanta, GA) Jason Bryans (Windsor, Ontario), Mike Dibiase (Tampa, FL), Rob Fidler (Seattle, WA), Mike Garciaparra (Orange, CA), Ralph Garr Jr. (Houston, TX), Dirk Kinney (Kansas City, MO), Aaron Krawiec (Gilbert, AZ), Aaron Looper (Shawnee, OK), Tom Lipari (Omaha, NE), Marcus McBeth (Chandler, AZ), Sean Moran (Levittown, PA), Zach Mortimer (Sacramento, CA), Jared Odom (St. Louis, MO), Charles Peterson (Memphis, TN), Juan Ramos (Carolina, PR).
Part-Time Scouts: Karl Sakuda (Honolulu, HI), Steve Walsh (St. Louis, MO).
Director, International Operations: Moises Rodriguez. **Assistant Director, International Scouting:** Luis Morales.
International Crosschecker: Cesar Geronimo, Jr. **Scouting Supervisor, Dominican Republic:** Angel Ovalles.
Administrator, Dominican Republic Operations: Aaron Rodriguez. **International Scouts:** Jean Carlos Alvarez (Dominican Republic), Braly Guzman (Dominican Republic), Omar Rogers (Dominican Republic), Ezequiel Sepulveda (Dominican Republic), Jose Gonzalez (Venezuela), Adel Granadillo (Venezuela), Estuar Ruiz (Venezuela), Carlos Balcazar (Colombia), Crysthiam Blanco (Nicaragua), Damaso Espino (Latin America), Ramon Garcia (Mexico).

San Diego Padres

Office Address: Petco Park, 100 Park Blvd, San Diego, CA 92101.
Mailing Address: PO Box 122000, San Diego, CA 92112.
Telephone: (619) 795-5000. **E-mail address:** comments@padres.com. **Website:** www.padres.com.
Twitter: @padres. **Facebook:** www.facebook.com/padres. **Instagram:** www.instagram.com/padres

OWNERSHIP

Operated By: Padres LP. **Managing Partner, Ownership:** Peter Seidler. **Executive Chairman:** Ron Fowler.
Ownership: Tom Seidler. **President/CEO:** Mike Dee.

BUSINESS OPERATIONS

Executive Vice President, Business Administration/General Counsel: Erik Greupner. **Vice President, Strategy/Innovation:** Ryan Gustafson. **Deputy General Counsel:** Caroline Perry.

FINANCE/ADMINISTRATION/INFORMATION TECHNOLOGY/HUMAN RESOURCES

Senior VP/CFO: Ronda Sedillo. **Director, Accounting:** Todd Bollman. **Director, Information Technology:** Ray Chan. **Director, Human Resources:** Sara Greenspan.

COMMUNITY RELATIONS/MILITARY AFFAIRS

Telephone: (619) 795-5265. **Fax:** (619) 795-5266.
VP, Community Relations: Sue Botos. **Military Affairs Advisor:** J.J. Quinn. **Managers, Community Relations:** Allison Eddy, Veronica Nogueira, Christina Papasedero.

Ron Fowler

ENTERTAINMENT/MARKETING/COMMUNICATIONS/CREATIVE SERVICES

Senior VP/Chief Marketing Officer: Wayne Partello. **Senior Director, Game Day Presentation:** Matt Coy. **Director, Marketing/Brand Activation:** Katie Jackson. **Director, Content:** Nicky Patriarca. **Manager, Media Relations:** Josh Ishoo. **Manager, Advertising:** Nicole Miller. **Manager, Community Marketing:** Darryl Mendoza. **Manager, Fan Programs Technology:** Alex Williams. **Manager, In-Park Entertainment:** Mike Grace. **Manager, Entertainment/Production Engineer:** Hendrik Jaehn. **Manager, Scoreboard Operations:** Jeff Praught. **Multimedia Producer:** Seth Foster. **Coordinator, Communications:** Danny Sanchez.

BALLPARK OPERATIONS/HOSPITALITY

VP, Ballpark Operations/GM, Petco Park: Mark Guglielmo. **VP, Chief Hospitality Officer:** Scott Marshall. **Senior Director, Ballpark Operations:** Nick Capo. **Director, Security:** John Leas. **Director, Event Operations:** Ken Kawachi. **Director, Field Operations:** Matt Balough. **Director, Guest Services:** Kameron Durham.

TICKETING

Telephone: (619) 795-5500. **Fax:** (619) 795-5034.
VP, Corporate & Event Revenue: Jeremy Horowitz. **VP, Corporate Partnerships:** Sergio Del Prado. **VP, Ticket Sales:** Eric McKenzie. **Director, Ticket Operations:** Jim Kiersnowski. **Director, Partnership Services:** Danielle Sergeant. **Director, Membership Services:** Sindi Edelstein. **Director, Group Tickets & Hospitality:** Curt Waugh.

2016 SCHEDULE

Standard Game Times: 7:10 p.m.; Sat. 5:40; Sun. 1:10

APRIL
4-6 . . . . Los Angeles
8-10 . . . . at Colorado
11-14 . . . . at Philadelphia
15-17 . . . . Arizona
19-21 . . . . Pittsburgh
22-24 . . . . St. Louis
25-27 . . . at San Francisco
29-30 . . . . at Los Angeles

MAY
1 . . . . at Los Angeles
2-4 . . . . Colorado
5-8 . . . . New York
9-11 . . . . at Chicago
12-15 . . . . . at Milwaukee
17-19 . . . . San Francisco

20-22 . . . . . Los Angeles
23-25 . . . at San Francisco
27-29 . . . . at Arizona
30-31 . . . . .at Seattle

JUNE
1-2 . . . . Seattle
3-5 . . . . Colorado
6-8 . . . . Atlanta
10-12 . . . . . at Colorado
13-15 . . . . Miami
16-19 . . . . . Washington
21-22 . . . . . at Baltimore
23-26 . . . . .at Cincinnati
28-29 . . . . . . Baltimore

JULY
1-3 . . . . New York

4-6 . . . . at Arizona
7-10 . . . . at Los Angeles
15-17 . . . . San Francisco
18-21 . . . . . . at St. Louis
22-24 . . . at Washington
25-27 . . . . . . at Toronto
29-31 . . . . . . Cincinnati

AUGUST
1-3 . . . . Milwaukee
5-7 . . . . Philadelphia
9-11 . . . . . at Pittsburgh
12-14 . . . . . at New York
15-17 . . . . at Tampa Bay
18-21 . . . . Arizona
22-24 . . . . Chicago
26-28 . . . . at Miami

30-31 . . . . at Atlanta

SEPTEMBER
1 . . . . at Atlanta
2-4 . . . . at Los Angeles
5-7 . . . . Boston
8-11 . . . . Colorado
12-14 . . . at San Francisco
16-18 . . . . . . at Colorado
19-21 . . . . Arizona
22-25 . . . . . San Francisco
27-29 . . . . . Los Angeles
30 . . . . at Arizona

OCTOBER
1-2 . . . . at Arizona

GENERAL INFORMATION

Stadium (year opened): Petco Park (2004).
Team Colors: Blue, white, tan and gray

Player Representative: Tyson Ross.
Home Dugout: First Base.
Playing Surface: Grass.

TRAVEL/CLUBHOUSE

Director, Team Travel: Brian Prilaman. **Manager, Equipment & Clubhouse:** Spencer Dallin. **Assistant Equipment Manager/Umpire Room Attendant:** Tony Petricca. **Visiting Clubhouse Manager:** David Bacharach.

BASEBALL OPERATIONS

Telephone: (619) 795-5077. **Fax:** (619) 795-5361.
Executive VP/General Manager: A.J. Preller.
VP/Assistant GM: Fred Uhlman Jr. **VP, Scouting Operations:** Don Welke. **Assistant GM:** Josh Stein. **Senior Advisor to GM/Director, Player Personnel:** Logan White. **Director, Baseball Operations:** Nick Ennis. **Director, Baseball Research & Development:** Brian McBurney. **Director, Baseball Information:** Matt Klotsche. **Senior Advisor, Baseball Operations:** Trevor Hoffman. **Special Assistant, Baseball Operations:** Mark Loretta. **Special Assistant, Scouting:** David Post. **Special Assistant, Player Development:** Moises Alou. **Special Assistant/Special Assignment Scout:** Randy Smith.

A.J. Preller

MAJOR LEAGUE STAFF

Manager: Andy Green.
Coaches: Bench—Mark McGwire; **Pitching**—Darren Balsey; **Hitting**—Alan Zinter; **First Base**—Tarrik Brock; **Third Base**—Glenn Hoffman; **Bullpen**—Doug Bochtler; **Coach**—Eddie Rodriguez.

MEDICAL/TRAINING

Club Physician: Scripps Clinic Medical Staff. **Assistant Athletic Trainers:** Paul Navarro & Will Sinon. **Massage Therapist:** Philip Kerr. **Strength/Conditioning Coach:** Brett McCabe.

PLAYER DEVELOPMENT

Telephone: (619) 795-5343. **Fax:** (619) 795-5036.
Director, Player Development: Sam Geaney. **Assistant Director, Player Development:** Ben Sestanovich. **Manager, Minor Leagues:** Todd Stephenson. **Manager, International Operations:** Cesar Rizik. **Equipment Manager, Player Development:** Zach Nelson. **Administrator, Dominican Republic Operations:** Jesus Negrette. **Roving Instructors:** Luis Ortiz (Field/Hitting Coordinator), Ryley Westman (Coordinator, Instruction), Mark Prior (Pitching Coordinator), Kevin Hooper (Infield Coordinator), Tony Tarasco (Outfield/Baserunning Coordinator), Gorman Heimueller (Roving Pitching Instructor), Eric Junge (Minor League Pitching Instructor), John Nester (Minor League Catching Instructor), Evaristo Lantigua (Coordinator, Latin American Instruction), Dave Bingham (Instructor, Player Development), Shaun Cole (Coordinator, Player Development), Dan Cepin (Coordinator, Int'l Player Development), Joseph Tarantino (Medical Coordinator), Jordan Wolf (Strength/Conditioning Coordinator), Ryan Bitzel (Rehab Coordinator). **Director, Professional Development:** Jason Amoroso.

FARM SYSTEM

Class	Farm Club (League)	Manager	Hitting Coach	Pitching Coach
Triple-A	El Paso (PCL)	Rod Barajas	Morgan Burkhart	Bronswell Patrick
Double-A	San Antonio (TL)	Phil Wellman	Johnny Washington	Jimmy Jones
High A	Lake Elsinore (CAL)	Francisco Morales	Xavier Nady	Glendon Rusch
Low A	Fort Wayne (MWL)	Anthony Contreras	Lance Burkhart	Burt Hooton
Short-season	Tri-City (NWL)	Brandon Wood	Oscar Bernard	Pete Zamora
Rookie	Padres (AZL)	Michael Collins	Doug Banks	Ben Fritz
Rookie	Padres (DSL)	Jeremy Rodriguez	J. Ramirez/J. Pozo	N. Cruz/J. Quezada

SCOUTING

Director, Amateur Scouting: Mark Conner (Hendersonville, TN). **Director, Professional Scouting:** Pete DeYoung (San Diego, CA). **Director, International Scouting:** Chris Kemp (Charlotte, NC). **Assistant to Director, Scouting:** Eddie Ciafardini (San Diego, CA). **National Crosschecker:** Kurt Kemp (Peachtree City, GA).
Director, Scouting: Mark Conner (Gallatin, TN). **Director, International Scouting:** Chris Kemp. **Assistant to Director, Scouting:** Eddie Ciafardini (San Diego, CA). **National Crosschecker:** Kurt Kemp (Peachtree City, GA).
Supervisors: Yancy Ayres (Topeka, KS), Josh Emmerick (Orange, CA), Chip Lawrence (Palmetto, FL), Andrew Salvo (Pace, FL). **Amateur Scouts:** Stephen Baker (Houston, TX), Doug Banks (Scottsdale, AZ), Justin Baughman (Portland, OR), Willie Bosque (Winter Garden, FL), Nick Brannon (Huntersville, NC), Troy Hoerner (Greenville, WI), Dustin Johnson (Alexandria, VA), Chris Kelly (Sarasota, FL), Nick Long (Rancho Santa Margarita, CA), Matt Maloney (Granville, OH), Steve Moritz (Kennesaw, GA), Sam Ray (San Francisco, CA), Matt Schaffner (Dallas, TX), Michael Silva (Broken Arrow, OK), Jeff Stevens (Manhattan Beach, CA), John Stewart (Granville, NY), Tyler Stubblefield (Canton, GA). **Part-Time Scouts:** Willie Ronda (Las Lomas Rio Piedras, PR), Murray Zuk (Souris, Manitoba).
Special Assignment Scouts: Senior Advisor/Special Assignment Scout: Randy Smith (Scottsdale, AZ), Steve Lyons (Winter Park, FL). **Professional Scouts:** Keith Boeck (Phoenix, AZ), Chris Bourjos (Scottsdale, AZ), Jim Elliott (Winston-Salem, NC), Spencer Graham (Gresham, OR), Al Hargesheimer (Arlington Heights, IL), Tim Holt (Allen, TX), Mark Merila (Minneapolis, MN), Dominic Scavone (Palm Harbor, FL), Duane Shaffer (Goodyear, AZ), Tyler Tufts (Macedonia, OH), Mike Venafro (Fort Myers, FL), Cory Wade (Zionsville, IN).
Director, Pacific Rim Operations: Acey Kohrogi. **Coordinator, Latin American Scouting:** Felix Feliz. **Supervisor, Venezuela:** Yfrain Linares. **International Supervisor:** Trevor Schumm. **International Scouts & Part Time Scouts:** Antonio Alejos (Venezuela), Andres Cabadias (Colombia), Milton Croes (Aruba), Emenejildo Diaz (Dominican Republic), Alvin Duran (Dominican Republic), Jonatthan Feliz (Dominican Republic), Martin Jose (Dominican Republic), Victor Magdaleno (Venezuela), Bill McLaughlin (Mexico), Ricardo Montenegro (Panama), Takashi Muto (Japan), Hoon NamGung (South Korea), Luis Prieto (Venezuela), Ysrael Rojas (Dominican Republic), Jose Salado (Dominican Republic), Damian Shanahan (Australia).

San Francisco Giants

Office Address: AT&T Park, 24 Willie Mays Plaza, San Francisco, CA 94107.
Telephone: (415) 972-2000. **Fax:** (415) 947-2800. **Website:** sfgiants.com, sfgigantes.com.

OWNERSHIP
Operated by: San Francisco Baseball Associates L.P.

BUSINESS OPERATIONS
President/Chief Executive Officer: Laurence M. Baer. **Special Assistants:** Will Clark, Willie Mays. **Senior Advisor:** Willie McCovey.

FINANCE
Senior Vice President, Finance/Treasurer: Lisa Pantages. **Senior VP/Chief Information Officer:** Bill Schlough. **Vice President, Information Technology:** Ken Logan.

HUMAN RESOURCES/LEGAL
Senior VP, Chief People Officer: Leilani Gayles. **Senior Advisor, Benefits/Compliance:** Joyce Thomas. **Benefits Senior Manager:** Nicole Bivetto. **Executive VP/General Counsel:** Jack F. Bair.

Laurence M. Baer

COMMUNICATIONS
Telephone: (415) 972-2445. **Fax:** (415) 947-2800.
Senior VP, Communications/Senior Advisor to the CEO: Staci Slaughter. **Senior Director, Broadcast Services:** Maria Jacinto. **Senior Director, Media Relations:** Matt Chisholm. **Manager, Hispanic Marketing/Media Relations:** Erwin Higueros. **Media Relations Manager:** Liam Connolly.

BUSINESS OPERATIONS
Executive VP, Business Operations: Mario Alioto. **Senior VP, Business Development:** Jason Pearl. **Director, Strategic Accounts/Business Development:** Bill Lawrence. **VP, Marketing/Advertising:** Danny Dann. **Senior Director: Promotions/Special Events:** Faham Zakariaei. **Director, Promotions/Event Production:** Valerie McGuire. **Director, Sponsorship Activation/Business Development:** Kristin Shaff. **VP, Retail Operations:** Dave Martinez.

TICKETING
Telephone: (415) 972-2000. **Fax:** (415) 972-2500.
Managing VP, Ticket Sales/Services: Russ Stanley. **VP, Ticket Sales:** Jeff Tucker.
VP, Strategic Revenue Services: Jerry Drobny. **Senior Director, Ticket Services:** Devin Lutes.

MARKETING
Executive Producer, Marketing/Advertising: Matt McKee. **Project Manager, Marketing/Advertising:** Kara Gilmore. **Executive Producer, SFG Productions:** Keith Macri. **PA Announcer:** Renel Brooks-Moon.

2016 SCHEDULE
Standard Game Times: 7:15 p.m.; Sun. 1:05

APRIL
4-6 . . . . . . at Milwaukee
7-10 . . . . Los Angeles (NL)
12-14 . . . . . . at Colorado
15-17 . at Los Angeles (NL)
18-21 . . . . Arizona
22-24 . . . . Miami
25-27 . . . . . San Diego
29-30 . . . at New York (NL)

MAY
1 . . . . . at New York (NL)
2-4 . . . . at Cincinnati
5-8 . . . . Colorado
9-11 . . . . Toronto
12-15 . . . . . . at Arizona
17-19 . . . . . at San Diego

20-22 . . . . . Chicago (NL)
23-25 . . . . . . San Diego
27-29 . . . . . at Colorado
30-31 . . . . . . at Atlanta

JUNE
1-2 . . . . at Atlanta
3-5 . . . . at St. Louis
7-8 . . . . Boston
10-12 . . . Los Angeles (NL)
13-15 . . . . . . Milwaukee
17-19 . . . . at Tampa Bay
20-23 . . . at Pittsburgh
24-26 . . . . . Philadelphia
27-28 . . . . Oakland
29-30 . . . . . . at Oakland

JULY
1-3 . . . . at Arizona
4-6 . . . . Colorado
8-10 . . . . Arizona
15-17 . . . . at San Diego
19-20 . . . . . . at Boston
22-24 . . at New York (AL)
25-27 . . . . . . Cincinnati
28-31 . . . . . Washington

AUGUST
2-4 . . . . . at Philadelphia
5-7 . . . . . at Washington
8-10 . . . . at Miami
12-14 . . . . . . Baltimore
15-17 . . . . . . Pittsburgh
18-21 . . . New York (NL)

23-25 . at Los Angeles (NL)
26-28 . . . . Atlanta
30-31 . . . . Arizona

SEPTEMBER
1-4 . . . . . at Chicago (NL)
5-7 . . . . at Colorado
9-11 . . . . . . at Arizona
12-14 . . . . . . San Diego
15-18 . . . . St. Louis
19-21 . at Los Angeles (NL)
22-25 . . . . at San Diego
27-29 . . . . Colorado
30 . . . . . Los Angeles (NL)

OCTOBER
1-2 . . . . . Los Angeles (NL)

GENERAL INFORMATION
Stadium (year opened): AT&T Park (2000).
Team Colors: Black, orange and cream.
Player Representative: Matt Cain.
Home Dugout: Third Base.
Playing Surface: Grass.

BASEBALL OPERATIONS

Telephone: (415) 972-1922. **Fax:** (415) 947-2929.
Executive Vice President, Baseball Operations: Brian R. Sabean.
Senior VP/ General Manager: Bobby Evans. **Senior VP/Assistant GM, Player Personnel:**
Dick Tidrow. **Special Assistant to GM:** Felipe Alou. **VP, Assistant GM:** Jeremy Shelley.
Vice President of Baseball Operations: Yeshayah Goldfarb. **Exec Assistant to Baseball
Operations & Administration:** Karen Sweeney.

Brian Sabean

MAJOR LEAGUE STAFF

Manager: Bruce Bochy.
Coaches: Bench—Ron Wotus; **Pitching**—Dave Righetti; **Hitting**—Hensley Meulens/Steve
Decker; **First Base**—Bill Hayes; **Third Base**—Roberto Kelly; **Bullpen**—Mark Gardner.
Bullpen Catchers: Eli Whiteside, Taira Uematsu. **Assistant Coach/Video Replay Analyst:**
Shawon Dunston. **Batting Practice Pitcher/Video Replay Analyst:** Chad Chop. **Manager of
Professional Video Systems:** Yo Miyamoto. **Assistant, Pro Video Systems:** Patrick Yount.

MEDICAL/TRAINING

Team Physicians: Dr. Anthony Saglimbeni, Dr. Robert Murray, Dr. Ken Akizuki, Dr. Tim McAdams. **Head Trainer:** Dave
Groeschner. **Assistant Trainers:** Anthony Reyes, Eric Ortega. **Strength/Conditioning Coaches:** Carl Kochan. **Sports
Science Specialist:** Geoff Head. **ML Physical Therapist:** Antonio Reale. **Massage Therapist:** Haro Ogawa. **Coordinator,
Medical Administration:** Chrissy Yuen. **Coordinator of Minor League Trainers:** Mark Gruesbeck. **Director of
Employee Assistance Program:** Michael Mombrea.
Coordinator of Minor League Strength & Conditioning: Brad Lawson. **Minor League Physical Therapist:** Frank
Perez. **Latin American Coordinator of Strength & Conditioning:** Saul Martinez.

PLAYER DEVELOPMENT

Director, Player Development: Shane Turner. **Coordinator, Minor League Pitching:** Bert Bradley. **Coordinator,
Minor League Hitting:** Andy Skeels. **Special Assistants, Player Development:** Joe Amalfitano, Will Clark, Jim
Davenport, Fred Stanley, Gene Clines. **Minor League Coach:** Tom Trebelhorn. **Minor League Roving Instructors:** Jeff
Tackett (catching), Randy Winn (OF & Baserunning), Alvaro Espinoza (Infield), Gary Davenport (Coach), Lee Smith (pitch-
ing), Kirt Manwaring (catching).

FARM SYSTEM

Class	Farm Club (League)	Manager	Hitting Coach	Pitching Coach
Triple-A	Sacramento (PCL)	Jose Alguacil	Damon Minor	Dwight Bernard
Double-A	Richmond (EL)	Miguel Ojeda	Ken Joyce	Steve Kline
High A	San Jose (CAL)	Lipso Nava	Todd Linden	Michael Couchee
Low A	Augusta (SAL)	Nestor Rojas	Doug Clark	Jerry Cram
Short-season	Salem-Keizer (NWL)	Kyle Haines	Ricky Ward	Matt Yourkin
Rookie	Giants (AZL)	Henry Cotto	Billy Horton	Mario Rodriguez
Rookie	Giants (DSL)	Carlos Valderrama	Juan Parra	Marcos Aguasvivas

SCOUTING

Telephone: (415) 972-2360. **Fax:** (415) 947-2929.
VP/Assistant GM, Scouting/International Operations: John Barr (Haddonfield, NJ).
Manager, Pro and Amateur Scouting: Adam Nieting.
Pro Scouting—Senior Advisors, Scouting: Lee Elder (Ocean Springs, MS), Joe Lefebvre (Concord, NH), Matt
Nerland (Modesto, CA), Paul Turco Sr. (Sarasota, FL). **Advance Scouts:** Steve Balboni (Berkeley Heights, NJ), Keith
Champion (Ballwin, MO). **Special Assignment Scouts:** Joe Bochy (Plant City, FL), John Cox (Yucaipa, CA), Darren
Wittcke (Sherwood, OR). **Major League Scouts:** Brian Johnson (Detroit, MI), Michael Kendall (Rancho Palos Verde, CA),
Jalal Leach (Sacramento, CA), Bob Mariano (Fountain Hills, AZ), Glenn Tufts (Bridgewater, MA), Paul Turco Jr (Chicago, IL),
Tom Zimmer (Seminole, FL).
Amateur Scouting—Senior Advisors, Scouting: Ed Creech (Moultrie, GA), John Flannery (Austin, TX), Doug
Mapson (Chandler, AZ). **East Coast Crosschecker:** John Castleberry (High Point, NC), **West Coast Crosschecker:** Joe
Strain (Englewood, CO). **Supervisors: Northeast**—Arnold Brathwaite (Linthicum Heights, MD); **Midwest**—Andrew
Jefferson (St. Louis, MO); **Southeast**—Mike Metcalf (Sarasota, FL); **West**— Matt Woodward (Camas, WA).
Area Scouts: Northeast—Ray Callari (Cote Saint Luc, Quebec), Kevin Christman (Noblesville, IN), John DiCarlo
(Glenwood, NJ), Mark O'Sullivan (Haverhill, MA), Donnie Suttles (Marion, NC); **Southeast**—Jose Alou (Boynton Beach,
FL), Jim Gabella (Deltona, FL), Luke Murton (McDonough, GA), Jeff Wood (Birmingham, AL); **Midwest**—Todd Coryell
(Aurora, IL), James Mouton (Missouri City, TX), Daniel Murray (Prairie Village, KS), Todd Thomas (Dallas, TX); **West**—
Brad Cameron (Los Alamitos, CA), Larry Casian (Salem, OR), Chuck Fick (Newbury Park, CA), Chuck Hensley Jr. (Mesa,
AZ), Keith Snider (Stockton, CA). **Part-Time Scouts:** Jorge Posada Sr. (Rio Piedras, PR), Tim Rock (Orlando, FL). **Senior
Consultants, Scouting:** Dick Cole (Costa Mesa, CA).
Director, International Operations: Joe Salermo (Hallandale Beach, FL). **Director, Dominican Operations:** Pablo
Peguero. **Assistant Director, Dominican Operations:** Felix Peguero. **Latin America Crosschecker:** Junior Roman
(San Sebastian, PR). **Venezuela Supervisor:** Ciro Villalobos Sr. **International Scouts:** Jonathan Arraiz (Venezuela),
Jonathan Bautista (Dominican Republic), Rogelio Castillo (Panama), Phillip Elhage (Curacao/Bonaire/Aruba), Gabriel
Elias (Dominican Republic), Edgar Fernandez (Venezuela), Jeff Kusumoto (Japan), Juan Marquez (Venezuela), Daniel
Mavarez (Colombia), Oscar Montero (Venezuela), Sandy Moreno (Nicaragua), Ruddy Moretta (Dominican Republic), Jim
Patterson (Australia), Luis Pena (Mexico), Jesus Stephens (Dominican Republic), Ciro Villalobos Jr. (Venezuela), Edgar
Ferreira (Dominican Republic, Video)

Seattle Mariners

Office Address: 1250 First Ave. South, Seattle, WA 98134.
Mailing Address: PO Box 4100, Seattle, WA 98194.
Telephone: (206) 346-4000. **Fax:** (206) 346-4400. **Website:** www.mariners.com.

OWNERSHIP

Board of Directors: Minoru Arakawa, John Ellis, Buck Ferguson, Chris Larson, Howard Lincoln, Wayne Perry, Frank Shrontz.
Chair/CEO: Howard Lincoln.
President/Chief Operating Officer: Kevin Mather.

BUSINESS OPERATIONS

FINANCE
Senior VP, Finance: Tim Kornegay. **Controller:** Greg Massey. **Senior VP, Human Resources:** Marianne Short.

CORPORATE BUSINESS/MARKETING
Executive VP, Business/Operations: Bob Aylward. **VP, Corporate Business/Community Relations:** Joe Chard. **Senior Director, Corporate Business:** Ingrid Russell-Narcisse. **Senior Director, Community Relations:** Gina Hasson. **Manager, Community Programs:** Sean Grindley. **VP, Marketing:** Kevin Martinez. **Senior Director, Marketing:** Gregg Greene.

SALES
VP, Sales: Frances Traisman. **Director, Ticket Sales:** Cory Carbary. **Director, Group Business Development:** Bob Hellinger.

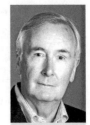
Howard Lincoln

BASEBALL INFORMATION/COMMUNICATIONS
Telephone: (206) 346-4000. **Fax:** (206) 346-4400.
Senior VP, Communications: Randy Adamack.
Senior Director, Baseball Information: Tim Hevly. **Senior Manager, Baseball Information:** Kelly Munro. **Manager, Baseball Information:** Fernando Alcala.
Director, Public Information: Rebecca Hale. **Director, Graphic Design:** Carl Morton.

TICKETING
Telephone: (206) 346-4001. **Fax:** (206) 346-4100.
Senior Director, Ticketing/Parking Operations: Malcolm Rogel. **Director, Ticket Services:** Jennifer Sweigert.

STADIUM OPERATIONS
VP, Ballpark Operations: Joe Myhra. **Senior Director, Safeco Field Operations:** Tony Pereira. **Director, Engineering/Maintenance:** Ryan van Maarth. **Director, Ballpark Sales and Marketing:** Alisia Anderson. **VP, Information Services:** Dave Curry. **Director, Information Systems:** Oliver Roy. **Director, Database/Applications:**

2016 SCHEDULE
Standard Game Times: 7:10 p.m.; Sun. 1:10.

APRIL
4-6 . . . . .at Texas
8-10 . . . . Oakland
11-13 . . . . Texas
15-17 . . . . . at New York
19-21 . . . . .at Cleveland
22-24 . . . . at Los Angeles
25-27 . . . . Houston
29-30 . . . . . Kansas City

MAY
1 . . . . Kansas City
2-4 . . . . .at Oakland
5-8 . . . . .at Houston
9-11 . . . . . .Tampa Bay
13-15 . . . . . Los Angeles
17-19 . . . . .at Baltimore

20-22 . . . . . .at Cincinnati
23-25 . . . . Oakland
27-29 . . . . . .Minnesota
30-31 . . . . . . San Diego

JUNE
1-2 . . . . . . at San Diego
3-5 . . . . .at Texas
6-9 . . . . Cleveland
10-12 . . . . Texas
14-16 . . . . . at Tampa Bay
17-19 . . . . . . .at Boston
20-23 . . . . . . .at Detroit
24-26 . . . . . . St. Louis
28-29 . . . . . . Pittsburgh
30 . . . . Baltimore

JULY
1-3 . . . . Baltimore
4-6 . . . . .at Houston
7-10 . . . . .at Kansas City
15-17 . . . . Houston
18-20 . . . . Chicago
22-24 . . . . . . at Toronto
26-27 . . at Pittsburgh
29-31 . . . . .at Chicago

AUGUST
1-4 . . . . Boston
5-7 . . . . Los Angeles
8-10 . . . . Detroit
12-14 . . . . .at Oakland
15-18 . . . . at Los Angeles
19-21 . . . . . .Milwaukee

22-24 . . . . . . .New York
25-28 . . . . . .at Chicago
29-31 . . . . .at Texas

SEPTEMBER
2-4 . . . . Los Angeles
5-8 . . . . Texas
9-11 . . . . . . .at Oakland
12-14 . . . . at Los Angeles
16-18 . . . . Houston
19-21 . . . . .Toronto
23-25 . . . . . at Minnesota
26-28 . . . . .at Houston
29-30 . . . . Oakland

OCTOBER
1-2 . . . . Oakland

GENERAL INFORMATION
Stadium (year opened): Safeco Field (1999).
Team Colors: Northwest green, silver and navy blue.
Player Representative: Charlie Furbush.
Home Dugout: First Base.
Playing Surface: Grass.

Justin Stolmeier. **Director, Procurement:** Norma Cantu. **Head Groundskeeper:** Bob Christofferson. **Assistant Head Groundskeepers:** Tim Wilson, Leo Liebert. **PA Announcer:** Tom Hutyler. **Official Scorer:** Eric Radovich.

MERCHANDISING
Senior Director, Merchandise: Jim LaShell. **Director, Retail Merchandising:** Julie McGillivray. **Director, Retail Stores:** Craig Geffrey.

TRAVEL/CLUBHOUSE
Director, Team Travel: Ron Spellecy.
Clubhouse Manager: Ryan Stiles. **Visiting Clubhouse Manager:** Unavailable. **Video Coordinator:** Jimmy Hartley. **Assistant Video Coordinator:** Craig Manning.

BASEBALL OPERATIONS
Executive VP/General Manager: Jerry Dipoto.
VP, Assistant GM: Jeff Kingston. **Special Assistants to the GM:** Joe Bohringer, Roger Hansen, Ken Madeja. **Manager, Baseball Operations:** Caleb Peiffer. **Administrator, Baseball Operations:** Debbie Larsen.

Jerry Dipoto

MAJOR LEAGUE STAFF
Manager: Scott Servais. **Bench**—Tim Bogar. **Pitching**—Mel Stottlemyre, Jr.; **Hitting**—Edgar Martinez; **First Base**—Casey Candaele; **Third Base**—Manny Acta; **Bullpen**—Mike Hampton.

MEDICAL/TRAINING
Medical Director: Ed Khalfayan. **Club Physician:** Mitch Storey. **Head Trainer:** Rick Griffin. **Assistant Trainers:** Rob Nodine, Matt Toth, Yoshi Nakazawa. **Strength & Conditioning:** James Clifford, Chad Uihlein.

PLAYER DEVELOPMENT
Telephone: (206) 346-4316. **Fax:** (206) 346-4300.
Director, Player Development: Andy McKay.
Administrator, Player Development: Jan Plein. **Assistant, Player Development:** Jack Mosimann. **Special Asst., Player Development:** Peter Harnisch. **Special Assistant, Player Development/Scouting:** John Hester. **Coordinator, Minor League Instruction:** Mike Micuci. **Coordinator, International Player Programs:** David Macias. **Coordinator, Athletic Trainers:** James Southard. **Latin Athletic Trainer Coordinator:** Javier Alvidrez. **Assistant Athletic Trainer Coordinator:** Ben Fraser. **Rehab Pitching Coordinator:** Gary Wheelock.
Roving Instructors: Pitching—Rick Waits; **Catching**—Dan Wilson; **Hitting**—Brant Brown; **Infield**—Jim Pankovits; **Special Assignment**—Alvin Davis; **Latin America Field Coordinator**—Jose Moreno; **Latin America Pitching Coordinator**—Carlos Chantres.

FARM SYSTEM

Class	Club (League)	Manager	Hitting Coach	Pitching Coach
Triple-A	Tacoma (PCL)	Pat Listach	Scott Brosius	Lance Painter
Double-A	Jackson (SL)	Daren Brown	Roy Howell	Andrew Lorraine
High A	Bakersfield (CAL)	Eddie Menchaca	Max Venable	Ethan Katz
Low A	Clinton (MWL)	Mitch Canham	Cesar Nicolas	Rich Dorman
Short-season	Everett (NWL)	Rob Mummau	Brian Hunter	Moises Hernandez
Rookie	Peoria (AZL)	Zac Livingston	Andy Bottin	Yoel Monzon
Rookie	Mariners (DSL)	Jose Umbria	Jose Guillen	Danielin Acevedo

SCOUTING
Telephone: (206) 346-4314. **Fax:** (206) 346-4300.
Director, Professional Scouting: Lee MacPhail. **Assistant Director, Player Personnel:** Todd Donovan. **Pro Scouting Assistant:** Jordan Bley. **Director, Amateur Scouting:** Tom McNamara. **Assistant Scouting Director/Senior National Crosschecker:** Mark Lummus. **National Crosschecker:** Devitt Moore. **Scouting Administrator:** Hallie Larson. **Amateur Scouting Assistant:** Ken Wade.
Major League Scouts: Micah Franklin (Gilbert, AZ), Greg Hunter (Seattle, WA), Jason Lefkowitz (Dallas, TX), Nick Manno (Columbia Station, OH), Bill Masse (Manchester, CT), John McMichen (Cincinnati, OH), Joe Nelson (West Palm Beach, FL), Woody Woodward (Palm Coast, FL).
Amateur Scouts/Territorial Supervisors: West—Chris Pelekoudas (Mesa, AZ); **Midwest**—Ben Collman (Austin, TX); **Canada**—Brian Nichols (Taunton, MA); **Northeast**—Mike Moriarty (Marlton, NJ); **Southeast**—Jesse Kapellusch (Emporia, KS).
Area Supervisors: Tyrus Bowman (Oklahoma City, OK), Jay Catalano (Nashville, TN), Dennis Gonsalves (Torrance, CA), Ryan Holmes (Moorpark, CA), Amanda Hopkins (Phoenix, AZ), John Hughes (Thiells, NY), Jackson Laumann (Union, KY), Steve Markovich (Highlands, NJ), Rob Mummau (Palm Harbor, FL), Dana Papasedero (Chelan, WA), Gary Patchett (Murrieta, CA), Stacey Pettis (Brentwood, CA), Myron Pines (Garden Grove, CA), Tony Russo (Montgomery, IL), Jeff Sakamoto (Tualatin, OR), Rafael Santo Domingo (San Juan, PR), Noel Sevilla (Miami, FL), Bob Steinkamp (Beatrice, NE), Taylor Terrasas (Sant Fe, TX), Stephen Tromblee (San Antonio, TX), Ross Vecchio (Canonsburg, PA), John Wiedenbauer (Johns Creek, GA).
Director, International: Tim Kissner (Kirkland, WA). **Supervisor, Dominican Republic:** Eddy Toledo (Sato Domingo, DR). **Coordinator, Pacific Rim/Mexico:** Ted Heid (Peoria, AZ). **Administrative Director, Dominican Operations:** Martin Valerio (Santo Domingo, Dominican Republic). **Coordinator, Venezuelan Operations:** Emilio Carrasquel (Barquisimeto, Venezuela). **International Crosschecker:** Scott Hunter (Mt. Lauerel, NJ). **Canada/Europe Advisor:** Wayne Norton.
International Scouts: Tristan Loetzsch (Australia), Manabu Noto (Saitama, Japan).

Tampa Bay Rays

Office Address: Tropicana Field, One Tropicana Drive, St. Petersburg, FL 33705.
Telephone: (727) 825-3137. **Fax:** (727) 825-3111. **Website:** www.raysbaseball.com.

OWNERSHIP
Principal Owner: Stuart Sternberg. **President:** Brian Auld.

BUSINESS OPERATIONS
Senior Vice President, Administration/General Counsel: John Higgins. **Chief Business Officer:** Jeff Cogen. **Senior VP, Strategy/Development:** Melanie Lenz. **VP, Strategy/Development:** William Walsh. **VP, Human Resources/Administration:** Bill Wiener, Jr. **VP, IT:** Juan Ramirez. **Senior Director, Human Resources:** Jennifer Tran. **Senior Director, Guest Relations:** Cass Halpin.

FINANCE
Chief Financial Officer: Rob Gagliardi. **Controller:** Patrick Smith. **Director, Financial Planning/Analysis:** Jason Gray.

MARKETING/COMMUNITY RELATIONS
Senior Director, Community Relations: Suzanne Luecke.

COMMUNICATIONS/BROADCASTING
Phone: (727) 825-3242.
VP, Communications: Rick Vaughn. **Senior Director, Communications:** Dave Haller. **Senior Director, Broadcasting:** Larry McCabe.

CORPORATE PARTNERSHIPS
VP, Corporate Partnerships: Josh Bullock. **Director, Corporate Partnership Services:** Sean Liston.

TICKET SALES
Phone: (888) FAN-RAYS. **VP, Ticket Sales/Marketing:** Brian Richeson. **Director, Marketing:** Amy Miller. **Director, Promotions:** Stephon Thomas. **Senior Director, Ticket Development and Services:** Jeff Tanzer. **Director, Ticket Operations:** Robert Bennett. **Assistant Director, Ticket Operations:** Ken Mallory.

STADIUM OPERATIONS
VP, Operations/Facilities: Rick Nafe. **Senior Director, Stadium Operations:** Scott Kelyman, Tom Karac. **Director, Stadium Operations:** Chris Raineri. **Head Groundskeeper:** Dan Moeller. **Senior Director, Fan Experience:** Eric Weisberg.

TRAVEL/CLUBHOUSE
Director, Team Travel/Clubhouse Operations: Chris Westmoreland. **Manager, Home Clubhouse:** Jose Fernandez. **Manager, Visitor Clubhouse:** Guy Gallagher. **Video Coordinator:** Chris Fernandez.

Stuart Sternberg

2016 SCHEDULE
Standard Game Times: 7:10 p.m.; Sun. 1:40.

APRIL		
3-6 . . . . .Toronto	20-22 . . . . .at Detroit	**JULY**
8-10 . . . . . .at Baltimore	23-24 . . . . at Miami	1-3 . . . . Detroit
12-14 . . . . Cleveland	25-26 . . . . .Miami	4-7 . . . . Los Angeles (AL)
15-17 . . . . . Chicago (AL)	27-29 . . . .New York (AL)	8-10 . . . . .at Boston
19-21 . . . . .at Boston	30-31 . . . . .at Kansas City	15-17 . . . . Baltimore
22-24 . . . at New York (AL)		18-20 . . . . at Colorado
25-27 . . . . Baltimore	**JUNE**	21-24 . . . . . .at Oakland
29-30 . . . . .Toronto	1 . . . . . . .at Kansas City	26-27 . at Los Angeles (NL)
	2-5 . . . . . . at Minnesota	29-31 . . . . .New York (AL)
MAY	6-8 . . . . at Arizona	
1 . . . . .Toronto	10-12 . . . . Houston	**AUGUST**
3-4 . . . . .Los Angeles (NL)	14-16 . . . . Seattle	1-4 . . . . Kansas City
6-8 . . at Los Angeles (AL)	17-19 . . . . .San Francisco	5-7 . . . . .Minnesota
9-11 . . . . .at Seattle	20-22 . . . . . .at Cleveland	8-10 . . . . at Toronto
13-15 . . . . Oakland	24-26 . . . . . .at Baltimore	12-14 . . . at New York (AL)
16-18 . . . . at Toronto	27-29 . . . . Boston	15-17 . . . . San Diego
	30 . . . . Detroit	19-21 . . . . Texas
		22-25 . . . . Boston
		26-28 . . . . .at Houston
		29-31 . . . . .at Boston
		SEPTEMBER
		2-4 . . . . .Toronto
		5-7 . . . . Baltimore
		8-11 . . . at New York (AL)
		12-14 . . . . . at Toronto
		15-18 . . . . .at Baltimore
		20-22 . . . . .New York (AL)
		23-25 . . . . Boston
		26-29 . . . . . .at Chicago
		30 . . . . .at Texas
		OCTOBER
		1-2 . . . . .at Texas

GENERAL INFORMATION
Stadium (year opened): Tropicana Field (1998). **Home Dugout:** First Base.
Team Colors: Dark blue, light blue, yellow. **Playing Surface:** AstroTurf
Player Representative: Matt Moore. Game Day Grass 3D-60 H.

BASEBALL OPERATIONS

President, Baseball Operations: Matt Silverman.

VPs, Baseball Operations: Chaim Bloom, Erik Neander. **Director, Baseball Operations:** James Click. **Administrator, Baseball Operations:** Sandy Dengler. **Special Assistant, Baseball Operations:** Bobby Heck. **Director, Baseball Systems:** Brian Plexico. **Director, Baseball Development:** Peter Bendix. **Developers, Baseball Systems:** Bradley Ankrom, Ryan Kelley. **Analytics Developer, Baseball Systems:** Michael Vanger. **Director, Scouting Analytics:** Shawn Hoffman. **Director, Pitching Research & Development:** Joshua Kalk. **Analysts, Baseball Research/Development:** Jonathan Erlichman, Will Cousins. **Junior Developer, Baseball Systems:** Nick Siefken. **Coordinator, Baseball Operations:** Graham Tyler. **Video Coordinator, Baseball Operations:** Ryan Bristow. **Assistant, Baseball Research/ Development:** Adam Esquer, Kevin Ferris. **Assistant, Baseball Operations:** Andrew Ball, Tyler Chamberlain-Simon, Hamilton Marx, Jeremey Sowers.

Matthew Silverman

MAJOR LEAGUE STAFF

Manager: Kevin Cash.

Coaches: Bench—Tom Foley; **Pitching**—Jim Hickey; **Hitting**—Derek Shelton; **First Base**—Rocco Baldelli; **Third Base**—Charlie Montoyo; **Bullpen**—Stan Boroski; **Hitting/Catching**—Jamie Nelson.

MEDICAL/TRAINING

Medical Director: Dr. James Andrews. **Medical Team Physician:** Dr. Michael Reilly. **Orthopedic Team Physician:** Dr. Koco Eaton. **Head Athletic Trainer:** Ron Porterfield. **Assistant Athletic Trainers:** Paul Harker, Mark Vinson. **Strength/ Conditioning Coach:** Kevin Barr.

PLAYER DEVELOPMENT

Telephone: (727) 825-3267. **Fax:** (727) 825-3493.

Director, Minor League Operations: Mitch Lukevics.

Assistant Director, Minor League Operations: Jeff McLerran. **Administrator, International/Minor League Operations:** Giovanna Rodriguez. **Field Coordinators:** Jim Hoff, Bill Evers. **Minor League Coordinators:** Skeeter Barnes (outfield/baserunning), Dick Bosman (pitching), Dewey Robinson (pitching), Jorge Moncada (pitching), Charlie Haeger (pitching), Steve Livesey (hitting), Chad Mottola (hitting), Paul Hoover (catching), Joe Benge (medical), Joel Smith (rehabilitation), Chris Tomashoff (Latin American medical), Trung Cao (strength/conditioning), James Schwabach (mental skills).

FARM SYSTEM

Class	Club (League)	Manager	Hitting Coach	Pitching Coach
Triple-A	Durham (IL)	Jared Sandberg	Ozzie Timmons	Kyle Snyder
Double-A	Montgomery (SL)	Brady Williams	Dan Dement	R.C. Lichtenstein
High A	Charlotte (FSL)	Michael Johns	Joe Szekely	Steve Watson
Low A	Bowling Green (MWL)	Reinaldo Ruiz	Manny Castillo	Bill Moloney
Short-season	Hudson Valley (NYP)	Tim Parenton	Craig Albernaz	Brian Reith
Rookie	Princeton (APP)	Danny Sheaffer	Wuarnner Rincones	Jose Gonzalez
Rookie	Rays (GCL)	Jim Morrison	Tomas Francisco	Marty DeMerritt
Rookie	Rays 1 (DSL)	Julio Zorrilla	Rafael Guerrero	Roberto Yil
Rookie	Rays 2 (DSL)	German Melendez	Ivan Ochoa	Alberto Bastardo

SCOUTING

Director, Pro Scouting: Kevin Ibach (Geneva, IL).

Director, Amateur Scouting: Rob Metzler. **Senior Advisor, Scouting/Baseball Operations:** R.J. Harrison (Phoenix, AZ). **Assistant, Amateur Scouting:** Tim Steggall. **Administrator, Scouting:** Samantha Bireley.

Special Assignment Scouts: Mike Juhl (Indian Train, NC), Fred Repke (Carson City, NV).

Major League Scouts: Bob Cluck (San Diego, CA). **Pro Scouts:** Michael Brown (Chandler, AZ), Ken Califano (Aberdeen, MD), Jason Cole (Austin, TX), Brent Gates (Grand Rapids, MI), Jason Grey (Mesa, AZ), Brian Keegan (Matthews, NC), Ken Kravec (Sarasota, FL), Dave Myers (Seattle, WA), Jeff Stewart (Normal, IL), Tyler Stohr (Jacksonville, FL).

National Crosschecker: Chuck Ricci (Williamsburg, VA). **Midwest Regional Supervisor:** Jeff Cornell (Lee's Summitt, MO). **Northeastern Regional Supervisor:** Brian Hickman (Fort Mill, SC). **Southeastern Regional Supervisor:** Kevin Elfering (Wesley Chapel, FL). **Western Regional Supervisor:** Jake Wilson (Ramona, CA). **Scout Supervisors:** Tim Alexander (Jamesville, NY), Matt Alison (Lenexa, KS), James Bonnici (Auburn Hills, MI), Tom Couston (St. Petersburg, FL), Rickey Drexler (New Iberia, LA), J.D. Elliby (Mansfield, TX), Brett Foley (Trinity, FL), Joe Hastings (Charlotte, NC), Ryan Henderson (Gilbert, AZ), Milt Hill (Cumming, GA), Alan Hull (Foster City, CA), Jamie Jones (Poway, CA), Paul Kirsch (Wilsonville, OR), Pat Murphy (Marble Falls, TX), Victor Rodriguez (Miramar, FL), Greg Whitworth (Los Angeles, CA), Lou Wieben (Little Ferry, NJ). **Part-Time Area Scouts:** Jose Hernandez (Miami, FL), Gil Martinez (San Juan, PR), Graig Merritt (Pitts Meadow, Canada), Casey Onaga (Honolulu, HI), Ethan Purser (Rockmart, GA), Jack Sharp (Dallas, TX), Donald Turley (Spring, TX).

Director, International Scouting: Carlos Rodriguez (Tampa, FL). **Coordinator, International Operations:** Patrick Walters (Tampa, FL). **International Crosschecker:** Steve Miller (Tampa, FL). **Coordinator, South American Operations:** Ronnie Blanco. **Consultant, International Operations:** John Gilmore. **Coordinator, Colombia:** Angel Contreras. **Scouting Supervisor, Mexico:** Eddie Diaz. **Scouting Supervisor, Dominican Republic:** Danny Santana. **Scouting Supervisor, Venezuela:** Marlon Roche. **International Scouts:** Aaron Acosta (Mexico), William Bergolla (Venezuela), Orlando Cabrera (Brazil), Juan Francisco Castillo (Venezuela), Alfredo Celestin (Dominican Republic), Adriano De Souza (Brazil), Jose Gomez (Dominican Republic), Carlos Herazo (Dominican Republic), Keith Hsu (Taiwan), Chairon Isenia (Curacao), Eric Ramirez (Dominican Republic), Miguel Richardson (Dominican Republic), Victor Torres (Dominican Republic), Tateki Uchibori (Japan), Jiri Vitt (Czech Republic), Ulli Wermuth (Germany), Gustavo Zapata (Panama).

Texas Rangers

Office Address: 1000 Ballpark Way, Arlington, TX 76011. **Mailing Address:** P.O. Box 90111, Arlington, TX 76011.
Telephone: (817) 273-5222. **Fax:** (817) 273-5110. **Website:** www.texasrangers.com.

OWNERSHIP
Co-Chairman: Ray C. Davis, Bob R. Simpson. **Chairman, Ownership Committee:** Neil Leibman.

BUSINESS OPERATIONS

Ray Davis

Executive Vice President, Business Partnerships/Development: Joe Januszewski.
Executive VP, Business Operations: Rob Matwick. **Executive VP/CFO:** Kellie Fischer.
Executive VP, Communications: John Blake. **Executive VP, Entertainment/Productions:**
Chuck Morgan. **Executive Assistant to Co-Chairman:** Keli West. **Executive Assistant
to Business Operations/Finance:** Gabrielle Stokes. **Executive Assistant to Business
Partnerships/Development:** Courtney Rowell. **Manager, Ownership Concierge Services:**
Amy Beam.

FINANCE/ACCOUNTING
VP/Controller: Starr Gulledge. **Assistant Controller:** Brian Thompson.

HUMAN RESOURCES/LEGAL/INFORMATION TECHNOLOGY
Senior VP, Human Resources/Risk Management: Terry Turner. **Associate Counsel:** Kate
Cassidy. **Director, Human Resources:** Mercedes Riley. **VP, Information Technology:** Mike
Bullock.

BALLPARK/EVENT OPERATIONS
VP, Security/Parking: Blake Miller. **Assistant VP, Customer Service:** Donnie Pordash. **Assistant VP, Business
Operations:** Richard Price. **Director, Parking/Security:** Mike Smith.

COMMUNICATIONS/COMMUNITY RELATIONS
Assistant VP, Broadcasting/Communications: Angie Swint. **Assistant VP, Player and Alumni Relations:** Taunee
Paur Taylor. **Senior Director, Media Relations:** Rich Rice. **Director, Social Media:** Kaylan Eastepp. **Assistant Director,
Player Relations:** Melia Wood. **Manager, Photography:** Kelly Gavin. **Manager, Media Relations:** Brian SanFilippo.
Manager, Broadcast Operations: Madison Pelletier. **Coordinator, Communications:** Kate Munson. **Coordinator,
Player Relations:** Stephanie Gentile. **VP, Community Outreach/Executive Director, Foundation:** Karin Morris.
Director, Youth Baseball Programs: Homer Bush.

FACILITIES
VP, Ballpark Operations: Sean Decker. **Senior Director, Maintenance:** Mike Call. **Senior Director, Facility
Operations:** Duane Arber. **Director, Grounds:** Dennis Klein. **Director, Complex Grounds:** Steve Ballard.

MARKETING/GAME PRESENTATION
VP, Marketing: Becky Kimbro. **Director, Senior Director, Game Entertainment/Productions:** Chris DeRuyscher.

2016 SCHEDULE
Standard Game Times: 7:05 p.m.; Sun. 2:05.

APRIL		
4-6. . . . . Seattle	20-22 . . . . . .at Houston	4-6. . . . . .at Boston	25-28 . . . . . . Cleveland
7-10 . . . . at Los Angeles	23-25 . . . . Los Angeles	7-10 . . . . . . .Minnesota	29-31 . . . . Seattle
11-13 . . . . . . .at Seattle	27-29 . . . . . . Pittsburgh	15-17 . . . . . .at Chicago	
14-17 . . . . . . Baltimore	30-31 . . . . .at Cleveland	18-20 . . . . at Los Angeles	**SEPTEMBER**
19-21 . . . . Houston		22-24 . . . . .at Kansas City	2-4. . . . . Houston
22-24 . . . . . .at Chicago	**JUNE**	25-27 . . . . . . Oakland	5-8. . . . . .at Seattle
25-27 . . . . . . .New York	1. . . . . .at Cleveland	28-31 . . . . . Kansas City	9-11 . . . . at Los Angeles
29-30 . . . . . Los Angeles	3-5. . . . . Seattle		12-14 . . . . . .at Houston
	6-9. . . . . Houston	**AUGUST**	16-18 . . . . Oakland
MAY	10-12 . . . . . .at Seattle	2-4. . . . . . . .at Baltimore	19-21 . . . . . Los Angeles
1. . . . . Los Angeles	13-16 . . . . . .at Oakland	5-7. . . . . . . .at Houston	23-25 . . . . . . .at Oakland
2-5. . . . . at Toronto	17-19 . . . . . .at St. Louis	8-9. . . . . . at Colorado	26-28 . . . . . .Milwaukee
6-8. . . . . .at Detroit	21-22 . . . . . . Cincinnati	10-11 . . . . .Colorado	30 . . . . .Tampa Bay
9-11 . . . . Chicago	24-26 . . . . Boston	12-14 . . . . Detroit	
13-15 . . . . .Toronto	27-30 . . . . . at New York	15-17 . . . . Oakland	**OCTOBER**
16-18 . . . . . .at Oakland	**JULY**	19-21 . . . . .at Tampa Bay	1-2. . . . . .Tampa Bay
	1-3. . . . . . at Minnesota	23-24 . . . . .at Cincinnati	

GENERAL INFORMATION
Stadium (year opened): Globe
Life Park in Arlington (1994).
Team Colors: Royal blue and red.
Player Representative: Derek Holland.
Home Dugout: First Base.
Playing Surface: Grass.

Senior VP, Partnerships/Client Service: Jim Cochrane. **Senior Director, Media Sales:** Wade Howell. **Senior VP, Ticket Sales/Service:** Paige Farragut. **Senior Director, Ticket Services:** Mike Lentz.

BASEBALL OPERATIONS

Telephone: (817) 273-5222. **Fax:** (817) 273-5285.
President, Baseball Operations/General Manager: Jon Daniels.
Assistant GM: Thad Levine. **Special Assistants to the GM:** Darren Oliver, Ivan Rodriguez, Michael Young. **Director, Baseball Operations:** Matt Vinnola. **Director, Baseball Information Services:** Todd Slavinsky. **Executive Assistant to President, Baseball Operations/GM:** Joda Parent. **Special Assistant, Scouting:** Scott Littlefield.

MAJOR LEAGUE STAFF
Manager: Jeff Banister.
Coaches: Bench—Steve Buechele; **Pitching**—Doug Brocail; **Hitting**—Anthony Iapoce; **First Base**—Hector Ortiz; **Third Base**—Tony Beasley; **Field Coordinator**—Jayce Tingler; **Bullpen**—Brad Holman; **Assistant Hitting Coach**—Justin Mashore; **Replay Coach**--Bobby Jones.

Jon Daniels

MEDICAL/TRAINING
Team Physician: Dr. Keith Meister. **Team Internist:** Dr. David Hunter.
Spine Consultant: Dr. Andrew Dossett. **Senior Director, Medical Operations:** Jamie Reed. **Head Trainer:** Kevin Harmon. **Assistant Trainer:** Matt Lucero. **Director, Strength/Conditioning:** Jose Vazquez.

PLAYER DEVELOPMENT
Telephone: (817) 436-5999. **Fax:** (817) 273-5285.
Senior Director, Player Development: Mike Daly.
Manager, Minor League Operations: Paul Kruger. **Field Coordinator:** Corey Ragsdale. **Pitching Coordinator:** Danny Clark. **Coordinators:** Josue Perez (hitting), Dwayne Murphy (assistant hitting/Outfield), Chris Briones (catching), Jeff Andrews (assistant pitching), Keith Comstock (rehab pitching), Kenny Holmberg (infield), Brian Dayett (special assignment coach), Napoleon Pichardo (strength/conditioning), Jason Roberts (medical), Sean Fields (rehab). **Assistant, Arizona Operations:** Stosh Hoover. **Minor League Equipment Manager:** Chris Ackerman.

FARM SYSTEM

Class	Club (League)	Manager	Coach	Pitching Coach
Triple-A	Round Rock (PCL)	Jason Wood	Jim Presley	Greg Hibbard
Double-A	Frisco (TL)	Joe Mikulik	Jason Hart	Steve Mintz
High A	High Desert (CAL)	Howard Johnson	Oscar Marin	Bobby Rose
Low A	Hickory (SAL)	Spike Owen	Francisco Matos	Jose Jaimes
Short-season	Spokane (NWL)	Tim Hulett	Kenny Hook	Brian Shouse
Rookie	Rangers (AZL)	Matt Siegel	Chae Lambin	Joey Seaver
Rookie	Ranger s (DSL)	Carlos Cardoza	Guillermo Mercedes	Jesus Delgado

SCOUTING
Senior Director, Amateur Scouting: Kip Fagg. **Senior Director, Player Personnel:** Josh Boyd.
Assistant, Pro Scouting: Mike Parnell. **Major League Scouts:** Russ Ardolina (Rockville, MD), Mike Anderson (Austin, TX). **Pro Scouts:** Scot Engler (Montgomery, IL), Jay Eddings (Tulsa, OK), Ross Fenstermaker (Granite Bay, CA), Mike Grouse (Lubbock,TX), Todd Walther (Hurst, TX), Brian Sikorski (Fraser, MI), Jonathan George (Pittsburgh, PA).
Manager, Amateur Scouting: Ben Baroody. **National Crosschecker:** Clarence Johns (Atlanta, GA). **Special Assistant to the General Manager:** James Keller (Sacramento, CA). **West Coast Crosschecker:** Casey Harvie (Lake Stevens, WA). **Midwest Crosschecker:** Randy Taylor (Katy, TX). **Eastern Crosschecker:** Ryan Coe (Acworth, GA). **Southeast Crosschecker:** Brian Williams (Cincinnati, OH). **Special Assignment Crosschecker:** Jake Krug (Flower Mound, TX). **Area Scouts:** Josh Simpson (Hobbs, NM), Brett Campbell (Orlando, FL), Roger Coryell (Ypsilanti, MI), Bobby Crook (Fort Worth, TX), Steve Flores (Temecula, CA), Brian Matthews (Mount Joy, PA), Todd Guggiana (Long Beach, CA), Jay Heafner (Charlotte, NC), Bob Laurie (Plano, TX), Gary McGraw (Gaston, OR), Michael Medici (Danville, IN), Butch Metzger (Sacramento, CA), Brian Morrison (Birmingham, AL), Takeshi Sakurayama (Manchester, CT), Dustin Smith (Olathe, KS), Cliff Terracuso (Jupiter, FL), Derrick Tucker (Kennesaw, GA). **Part-Time Scouts:** Chris Collias (Oak Park, MI), Buzzie Keller (Seguin, TX), Rick Schroeder (Phoenix, AZ).
Senior Advisor, Pacific Rim Operations: Jim Colborn. **Coordinator, Pacific Rim Operations:** Joe Furukawa (Japan). **Director, Latin America Scouting:** Rafic Saab. **Latin America Supervisor:** Roberto Aquino. **Dominican Program Coordinator/Scout:** Danilo Troncosco. **Manager, Pacific Rim Operations:** Curtis Jung. **Latin America Crosschecker:** Chu Halabi (Aruba).
DR Complex Administrator: Jose Vargas. **International Scouts:** Rafael Belen (Dominican Republic), Willy Espinal (Dominican Republic), Jose Felomina (Curacao), Jose Fernandez (Florida), Jhonny Gomez (Venezuela), Juan Salazar (Venezuela) Carlos Gonzalez (Venezuela), Rodolfo Rosario (Dominican Republic), Hamilton Sarabia (Colombia), Eduardo Thomas (Panama), Manuel Velez (Mexico), Hajime Watabe (Japan).

Toronto Blue Jays

Office/Mailing Address: 1 Blue Jays Way, Suite 3200, Toronto, Ontario M5V 1J1.
Telephone: (416) 341-1000. **Fax:** (416) 341-1245. **Website:** www.bluejays.com.

OWNERSHIP

Operated by: Toronto Blue Jays Baseball Club. **Principal Owner:** Rogers Communications Inc. **Chairman, Toronto Blue Jays:** Edward Rogers. **Vice Chairman, Rogers Communications Inc.:** Phil Lind. **President, Media Business Unit:** Rick Brace.

BUSINESS OPERATIONS

President/CEO: Mark Shapiro. **Senior Vice President, Business Operations:** Stephen Brooks. **Consultant:** Howard Starkman. **Executive Assistant to the President/CEO:** Gail Ricci.

FINANCE/ADMINISTRATION

Senior Vice President, Business Operations: Stephen Brooks. **Executive Assistant:** Donna Kuzoff. **Senior Director, Finance:** Lynda Kolody. **Director, Payroll and Benefits:** Brenda Dimmer. **Director, Risk Management:** Suzanne Joncas. **Senior Manager:** David J. Hill. **Accounting Manager:** Tanya Proctor. **Financial Business Manager (RC):** Leslie Galant-Gardiner. **Manager, Stadium Payroll:** Sharon Dykstra. **Manager, Ticket Receipts and Vault Services:** Joseph Roach. **Accountant:** Emerita Flores. **Financial Analyst:** Pier-Luc Nappert. **Financial Analyst:** Melissa Paterson. **Payroll and Finance Analyst:** Tony Phung. **Payroll Analyst:** Joyce Chan.

Mark Shapiro

MARKETING/COMMUNITY RELATIONS

Vice President, Marketing and Merchandising: Anthony Partipilo. **Executive Assistant, Marketing:** Maria Cresswell. **Director, Game Entertainment and Promotions:** Marnie Starkman. **Manager, Community Marketing and Player Relations:** Holly Gentemann. **Manager, Direct Marketing:** Sherry Oosterhuis. **Manager, Promotions and Fan Activation:** Michelle Seniuk. **Manager, Special Events:** Kristy-Leigh Boone. **Manager, Stadium Entertainment:** Daniel Joseph. **Sr. Graphic Designer:** Corey McDonald. **Sr. Motion Graphics Designer:** Ryan Stone. **Motion Graphics Designer:** Andrew Gyorgyfi. **Graphic Designer:** Greg O'Brien. **Coordinator, Amateur Baseball:** T.J. Burton. **Coordinator, Marketing:** Maureen Kinghorn. **Coordinator, Promotions and Stadium Entertainment:** Stefanie Wright.

COMMUNICATIONS

Vice President, Communications: Jay Stenhouse. **Manager, Baseball Information:** Mal Romanin. **Coordinator, Baseball Information:** Erik Grosman. **Coordinator, Communications:** Sue Mallabon

STADIUM OPERATIONS

Vice President, Stadium Operations and Security: Mario Coutinho. **Manager, Event Services:** Julie Minott. **Manager, Game Operations:** Karyn Gottschalk. **Supervisor, Guest Experience:** Matt Black. **Coordinator, Guest Experience:** Lisa Simons. **Administrative Assistant:** Marion Farrell.

2016 SCHEDULE

Standard Game Times: 7:07 p.m.; Sat/Sun: 1:07

APRIL
3-6 . . . . . . at Tampa Bay
8-10 . . . . Boston
12-14 . . . . . . .New York
15-18 . . . . . .at Boston
19-21 . . . . . .at Baltimore
22-24 . . . . Oakland
25-27 . . . . Chicago
29-30 . . . . . at Tampa Bay

MAY
1 . . . . at Tampa Bay
2-5 . . . . Texas
6-8 . . . . Los Angeles
9-11 . . . at San Francisco
13-15 . . . . . .at Texas
16-18 . . . . . . .Tampa Bay

19-22 . . . . . at Minnesota
24-26 . . . . . . at New York
27-29 . . . . Boston
30-31 . . . . . . .New York

JUNE
1 . . . . .New York
3-5 . . . . .at Boston
6-8 . . . . .at Detroit
9-12 . . . . Baltimore
13-14 . . . . . .Philadelphia
15-16 . . at Philadelphia
17-19 . . . . .at Baltimore
21-22 . . . . . .Arizona
24-26 . . . . . .at Chicago
27-29 . . . . at Colorado
30 . . . . Cleveland

JULY
1-3 . . . . Cleveland
4-6 . . . . Kansas City
7-10 . . . . Detroit
15-17 . . . . . .at Oakland
19-20 . . . . . at Arizona
22-24 . . . . Seattle
25-27 . . . . . San Diego
29-31 . . . . . . Baltimore

AUGUST
1-4 . . . . .at Houston
5-7 . . . . . .at Kansas City
8-10 . . . . . . .Tampa Bay
12-14 . . . . Houston
15-17 . . . . . at New York
19-21 . . . . .at Cleveland

23-25 . . . . . Los Angeles
26-28 . . . . Minnesota
29-31 . . . . .at Baltimore

SEPTEMBER
2-4 . . . . . . at Tampa Bay
5-7 . . . . at New York
9-11 . . . . Boston
12-14 . . . . .Tampa Bay
15-18 . . . . at Los Angeles
19-21 . . . . .at Seattle
23-26 . . . . . . .New York
27-29 . . . . . Baltimore
30 . . . . .at Boston

OCTOBER
1-2 . . . . .at Boston

GENERAL INFORMATION

Stadium (year opened):
Rogers Centre (1989).
Team Colors: Blue and white.

Player Representative: Unavailable.
Home Dugout: Third Base.
Playing Surface: AstroTurf 3DXtreme 60 Product.

TICKET OPERATIONS

Director, Ticket Operations: Justin Hay. **Director, Ticket Services and Fulfillment:** Sheila Stella. **Manager, Box Office:** Christina Dodge.

TICKET SALES/SERVICE

Vice President, Ticket Sales and Service: Jason Diplock. **Executive Assistant:** Stacey Jackson. **Director, Luxury Suite Sales and Service:** Michael Hook. **Manager, Group Sales:** Ryan Gustavel. **Manager, Season Ticket Services:** Erik Bobson. **Manager, Ticket Sales:** John Santana.

TRAVEL/CLUBHOUSE

Director, Team Travel/Clubhouse Operations: Mike Shaw. **Equipment Manager:** Jeff Ross. **Clubhouse Manager:** Kevin Malloy. **Visiting Clubhouse Manager:** Len Frejlich. **Video Operations:** Robert Baumander. **Major League Advance Scouting Coordinator:** Ryan Mittleman. **Team Employee Assistance Program:** Brian Shaw. **Coordinator, Advance Scouting/Video:** Harry Einbinder.

BASEBALL OPERATIONS

Executive Vice President, Baseball Operations/General Manager: Ross Atkins.
Senior Vice President, Baseball Operations/Assistant General Manager: Tony LaCava.
Assistant General Manager: Andrew Tinnish. **Special Assistant to the General Manager:** Dana Brown. **Director, Analytics:** Joe Sheehan. **Director, Baseball Operations:** Mike Murov. **Director, Team Safety:** Ron Sandelli. **Director, Team Travel and Clubhouse Operations:** Mike Shaw. **Manager, Major League Administration:** Heather Connolly.

MAJOR LEAGUE STAFF

Manager: John Gibbons.
Coaches: Bench—DeMarlo Hale; **Pitching**—Pete Walker; **Hitting**—Brook Jacoby; **First Base**—Tim Leiper; **Third Base**—Luis Rivera; **Bullpen**—Dane Johnson; **Assistant Hitting**—Eric Owens. **Bullpen Catchers:** Alex Andreopoulos, Jason Phillips.

Ross Atkins

MEDICAL/TRAINING

Medical Advisor: Dr. Bernie Gosevitz. **Consulting Physician:** Dr. Ron Taylor. **Consulting Team Physicians:** Dr. Irv Feferman, Dr. Noah Forman. **Head Trainer:** George Poulis. **Assistant Trainers:** Mike Frostad, Jeff Stevenson. **Strength/Conditioning Coordinator:** Chris Joyner.

PLAYER DEVELOPMENT

Telephone: (727) 734-8007. **Fax:** (727) 734-8162.
Director, Player Development: Gil Kim. **Director, Minor League Operations:** Charlie Wilson. **Minor League Field Coordinator:** Doug Davis. **Senior Advisor:** Rich Miller. **Advisor:** Eric Wedge. **Senior Pitching Advisor:** Rick Langford. **Rehab Pitching Coach:** Darold Knowles. **Coordinators:** John Tamargo Jr., (hitting), Kenny Graham (hitting), Mike Mordecai (instruction), Tim Raines (outfield/baserunning), Sal Fasano (pitching), Scott Weberg (strength/conditioning). **Infield Coach:** Danny Solano. **Hitting Instructor:** Steve Springer. **Athletic Training Coordinator:** Jose Ministral. **Equipment Manager:** Billy Wardlow. **Player Development Assistants:** Megan Evans, Mike Nielsen. **Assistant, Latin American Administration:** Blake Bentley. **Administrative Assistant:** Kim Marsh.

FARM SYSTEM

Class	Club (League)	Manager	Hitting Coach	Pitching Coach
Triple-A	Buffalo (IL)	Gary Allenson	Richie Hebner	Bob Stanley
Double-A	New Hampshire (EL)	Bobby Meacham	Stubby Clapp	Vince Horsman
High A	Dunedin (FSL)	Ken Huckaby	Corey Hart	Jim Czajkowski
Low A	Lansing (MWL)	John Schneider	Donnie Murphy	Jeff Ware
Short-season	Vancouver (NWL)	John Tamargo Jr.	Dave Pano	Willie Collazo
Rookie	Bluefield (APP)	Dennis Holmberg	Aaron Mathews	Antonio Caceres
Rookie	Blue Jays (GCL)	Cesar Martin	Paul Elliott	Juan Rincon
Rookie	Blue Jays (DSL)	Jose Mateo	Carlos Villalobos	Rafael Lazo

SCOUTING

Director, Professional Scouting: Perry Minasian. **Director, Amateur Scouting:** Brian Parker. **Special Assistant, Amateur Scouting:** Chuck LaMar. **Coordinator, Professional Scouting:** David Haynes. **Special Assignment Scout:** Russ Bove. **Major League Scouts:** Jim Beattie, Sal Butera, Dan Evans, Ed Lynch, Jim Skaalen. **Senior Advisor/Professional Scout:** Mel Didier. **Professional Crosscheckers:** Kevin Briand, Dean Decillis, Jon Lalonde. **Professional Scouts:** Matt Anderson, Jon Bunnell, Kimball Crossley, Kevin Fox, Bryan Lambe, Ted Lekas, Brad Matthews, David May Jr. **Crosscheckers:** Blake Crosby, Blake Davis, C.J. Ebarb, Tim Rooney, Paul Tinnell. **Area Scouts:** Mike Alberts (Leominster, MA), Joey Aversa (Fountain Valley, CA), Coulson Barbiche (Milford, OH), Matt Bishoff (Tampa, FL), Dallas Black (Springdale, AR), Darold Brown (Elk Grove, CA), Ryan Fox (Yakima, WA), Pete Holmes (Phoenix, AZ), Jeff Johnson (Carmel, IN), Brian Johnston (Baton Rouge, LA), Chris Kline (Beaufort, NC), Randy Kramer (Aptos, CA), Jamie Lehman (Liverpool, NY), Jim Lentine (San Clemente, CA), Nate Murrie (Bowling Green, KY), Don Norris (Hoover, AL), Matt O'Brien (Clermont, FL), Wes Penick (Clive, IA), Bud Smith (Lakewood, CA), Mike Tidick (Statesboro, GA), Gerald Turner (Euless, TX), Doug Witt (Brooklyn, MD). **Canada Scout:** Don Cowan (Delta, BC).
Director, Latin American Operations: Sandy Rosario. **International Crosschecker:** Luis Marquez. **Supervisor, Dominican Republic:** Lorenzo Perez. **Supervisor, Venezuela:** Henry Sandoval. **International Scouts:** Jairo Castillo (San Cristobal, DR), Jose Contreras (Miranda, VZ), Alexis de la Cruz (Santo Domingo, DR), Luciano del Rosario (Santo Domingo, DR), Enrique Falcon (Cartagena, COL), Francisco Plasencia (Aragua, VZ), Daniel Sotelo (Managua, Nicaragua), Marino Tejada (Santo Domingo, DR), Alex Zapata (Colon, Panama).

Washington Nationals

Office Address: 1500 South Capitol Street SE, Washington, DC 20003.
Telephone: (202) 640-7000. **Fax:** (202) 547-0025.
Website: www.nationals.com.

OWNERSHIP
Managing Principal Owner: Theodore Lerner.
Principal Owners: Annette Lerner, Mark Lerner, Judy Lenkin Lerner, Edward Cohen, Debra Lerner Cohen, Robert Tanenbaum, Marla Lerner Tanenbaum.

BUSINESS OPERATIONS

Ted Lerner

Chief Operating Officer, Lerner Sports: Alan Gottlieb. **Chief Revenue & Marketing Officer:** Valerie Camillo. **Chief Financial Officer:** Lori Creasy. **Senior Vice President:** Elise Holman.

BALLPARK ENTERPRISES
Senior Director, Ballpark Enterprises: Maggie Gessner.

LEGAL
Senior Vice President & General Counsel: Damon T. Jones. **Vice President & Deputy General Counsel:** Amy Inlander Minniti.

HUMAN RESOURCES
Vice President, Human Resources: Alexa Herndon. **Director, Benefits:** Stephanie Giroux. **Director, Human Resources:** Steve Reed. **Manager, Human Resources:** Alan Gromest.

COMMUNICATIONS
Vice President, Communications: Jennifer Giglio. **Executive Director, Communications:** Elizabeth Alexander. **Senior Director, Baseball Communications:** Amanda Comak. **Manager, Communications:** Kyle Brostowitz. **Manager, Communications:** Carly Rolfe. **Coordinator, Communications:** Christopher Browne.

COMMUNITY RELATIONS
Vice President, Community Engagement: Gregory McCarthy. **Senior Director, Community Relations:** Shawn Bertani. **Senior Manager, Community Relations:** Nicole Murray.

MARKETING/BROADCASTING
Vice President, Brand Marketing: Kristine Friend. **Vice President, Broadcasting & Game Presentation:** Jacqueline Coleman. **Director, Production & Operations:** Dave Lundin. **Manager, Promotions & Events:** Lindsey Norris.

TICKETING/SALES
Vice President, Ticket Sales, Membership Services & Operations: David McElwee. **Director, Ticket Sales:** Joseph Dellwo. **Manager, Group Sales:** Brian Beck. **Director, Premium Sales & Service:** Kai Murray. **Director, Ticket Services & Sales Development:** Ben Cobleigh. **Senior Director, Ticket Operations:** Andrew Bragman.

2016 SCHEDULE
Standard Game Times: 7:05 p.m.; Sun. 1:35

APRIL
4-6 . . . . at Atlanta
7-10 . . . . .Miami
11-14 . . . . Atlanta
15-17 . . . . at Philadelphia
18-21 . . . . at Miami
22-24 . . . . . . .Minnesota
26-28 . . . . .Philadelphia
29-30 . . . . . . .at St. Louis

MAY
1 . . . . .at St. Louis
2-4 . . . . . .at Kansas City
5-8 . . . . .at Chicago
9-11 . . . . Detroit
13-15 . . . . .Miami
17-19 . . . . . . at New York

20-22 . . . . at Miami
23-25 . . . . .New York
26-29 . . . . St. Louis
30-31 . . . . at Philadelphia

JUNE
1 . . . . at Philadelphia
3-5 . . . . . . .at Cincinnati
7-9 . . . . .at Chicago
10-12 . . . .Philadelphia
13-15 . . . . Chicago
16-19 . . . . at San Diego
20-22 . . . . at Los Angeles
24-26 . . . . at Milwaukee
27-29 . . . . . . .New York
30 . . . . Cincinnati

JULY
1-3 . . . . Cincinnati
4-6 . . . . .Milwaukee
7-10 . . . . . . at New York
15-17 . . . . . . Pittsburgh
19-21 . . . . . Los Angeles
22-24 . . . . . . San Diego
26-27 . . . . .at Cleveland
28-31 . . . at San Francisco

AUGUST
1-3 . . . . at Arizona
5-7 . . . . . . San Francisco
9-10 . . . . Cleveland
12-14 . . . . Atlanta
15-17 . . . . . at Colorado
18-21 . . . . . . at Atlanta

22-23 . . . . . at Baltimore
24-25 . . . . . . Baltimore
26-28 . . . . .Colorado
29-31 . . . . at Philadelphia

SEPTEMBER
2-4 . . . . at New York
5-7 . . . . Atlanta
8-11 . . . . . .Philadelphia
12-14 . . . . .New York
16-18 . . . . . . at Atlanta
19-21 . . . . at Miami
23-25 . . . . . at Pittsburgh
26-29 . . . . .Arizona
30 . . . . .Miami

OCTOBER
1-2 . . . . .Miami

GENERAL INFORMATION

Stadium (year opened): Nationals Park (2008).
Team Colors: Red, white and blue.

Player Representative: Unavailable.
Home Dugout: First Base.
Playing Surface: Grass.

BUSINESS STRATEGY & ANALYTICS
Executive Director, Strategy & Analytics: Mike Shane. **Senior Director, Strategy:** Mike Carney.

BALLPARK OPERATIONS
Vice President, Ballpark Operations: Frank Gambino. **Executive Director, Ballpark Operations & Guest Experience:** Jonathan Stahl. **Director, Security:** Sylvester Servance. **Director, Field Operations:** John Turnour.

BASEBALL OPERATIONS

General Manager/President, Baseball Operations: Mike Rizzo.
Assistant GM/VP, Baseball Operations: Bob Miller. **Assistant GM/VP, Baseball Operations:** Adam Cromie. **Assistant GM/VP, Finance:** Ted Towne. **Senior Advisor to GM:** Phillip Rizzo. **Special Assistant to the GM/Major League Administration:** Harolyn Cardozo. **VP, Clubhouse Operations/Team Travel:** Rob McDonald. **Director, Baseball Operations:** Michael DeBartolo. **Director, Baseball Research/Development:** Sam Mondry-Cohen.
Analysts, Baseball Research/Development: Lee Mendelowitz, Josh Weinstock. **Developers, Baseball Research/Development:** Isaac Gerhart-Hines, Jay Liu. **Assistant, Baseball Operations:** John Wulf. **Director, Advance Scouting:** Erick Dalton. **Manager, Advance Scouting:** Christopher Rosenbaum. **Coordinator, Advance Scouting:** Jonathan Tosches. **Clubhouse Manager:** Mike Wallace. **Visiting Clubhouse Manager:** Matt Rosenthal. **Equipment Manager:** Dan Wallin. **Assistant, Clubhouse/Team Travel:** Ryan Wiebe.

Mike Rizzo

MAJOR LEAGUE STAFF
Manager: Dusty Baker.
Coaches: Bench—Chris Speier; **Pitching**—Mike Maddux; **Hitting**—Rick Schu; **First Base**—Davey Lopez; **Third Base**—Bob Henley; **Bullpen**—Dan Firova; **Assistant Hitting Coach:** Jacque Jones.

MEDICAL/TRAINING
Executive Director, Medical Services: Harvey Sharman. **Lead Team Physician:** Dr. Robin West. **Chairman, Medical Services Advisory Board:** Dr. Keith Pyne.
Director, Athletic Trainer: Paul Lessard. **Athletic Trainers:** Gary Barajas, Dale Gilbert. **Assistant, Athletic Training:** John Hsu. **Head Strength/Conditioning Coach:** Matt Eiden. **Corrective Exercise Specialists:** Joe Cancellieri, Patrick Panico. **Team Physician/Internist:** Dr. Dennis Cullen. **Team Physician, Florida:** Dr. Bruce Thomas.

PLAYER DEVELOPMENT
Assistant GM/VP, Player Personnel: Doug Harris.
Director, Player Development: Mark Scialabba. **Director, Minor League Operations:** Ryan Thomas. **Assistant, Player Development:** JJ Estevez. **Senior Advisor to the GM:** Bob Boone. **Senior Advisor to the GM, Player Development:** Randy Knorr. **Senior Advisor, Player Development:** Spin Williams. **Director, Florida Operations:** Thomas Bell.
Field Coordinators: Jeff Garber, Tommy Shields. **Hitting Coordinator:** Troy Gingrich. **Pitching Coordinator:** Paul Menhart. **Catching Coordinator:** Michael Barrett. **Outfield/Baserunning Coordinator:** Gary Thurman. **DR Field Coordinator:** Sandy Martinez. **Rehabilitation Pitching Coordinator:** Mark Grater. **Medical/Rehabilitation Coordinator:** Jon Kotredes. **Strength/Conditioning Coordinator:** Landon Brandes.

FARM SYSTEM

Class	Club	Manager	Hitting Coach	Pitching Coach
Triple-A	Syracuse (IL)	Billy Gardner Jr.	Brian Daubach	Bob Milacki
Double-A	Harrisburg (EL)	Matthew Lecroy	Brian Rupp	Chris Michalak
High A	Potomac (CL)	Tripp Keister	Luis Ordaz	Franklin Bravo
Low A	Hagerstown (SAL)	Patrick Anderson	Amaury Garcia	Sam Narron
Short-season	Auburn (NYP)	Jerad Head	Mark Harris	Tim Redding
Rookie	Nationals (GCL)	Josh Johnson	Jorge Mejia	Michael Tejera
Rookie	Nationals (DSL)	Sandy Martinez	Jose Herrera	Pablo Frias

SCOUTING
Assistant GM/VP, Scouting Operations: Kris Kline.
Director, Scouting Operations: Eddie Longosz. **Director, Player Procurement:** Kasey McKeon. **Special Assistants to GM:** Steve Arnieri, Chuck Cottier, Mike Cubbage, Mike Daughtry, Dan Jennings, Ron Rizzi, Jay Robertson, Bob Schaefer, Terry Wetzel.
Professional Scout: Aron Weston. **Special Assistant to GM/National Crosschecker, East:** Jeff Zona. **National Supervisor:** Mark Baca. **National Crosschecker, Midwest:** Jimmy Gonzales. **National Crosschecker, West:** Fred Costello.
Area Supervisors: Ray Blanco (Miami, FL), Justin Bloxom (Indianapolis, IN), Brian Cleary (Cincinnati, OH), Paul Faulk (Myrtle Beach, SC), Ben Gallo (Encinitas, CA) Ed Gustafson (Denton, TX), Buddy Hernandez (Windermere, FL), Brandon Larson (San Antonio, TX), Steve Leavitt (Huntington Beach, CA), John Malzone (Needham, MA), Alex Morales (Wellington, FL), Bobby Myrick (Colonial Heights, VA), Scott Ramsay (Valley, WA), Eric Robinson (Acworth, GA), Alex Rodriguez (Miami, FL), Mitch Sokol (Phoenix, AZ), Everett Stull (Elk Grove, CA), Tyler Wilt (Willis, TX).
VP, International Operations: Johnny DiPuglia. **Dominican Crosschecker:** Fausto Severino. **Latin American Crosschecker:** Moises De La Mota. **Academy Administrator and Scout, Puerto Rico:** Alex Rodriguez. **Coordinator, Venezuela:** German Robles. **Coordinator, Pacific Rim:** Marty Brown. **Assistant, International Scouting:** Taisuke Sato.
International Scouts: Carlos Ulloa (Dominican Republic), Modesto Ulloa (Dominican Republic), Pablo Arias (Dominican Republic), Virgilio De Leon (Dominican Republic). Eduardo Rosario (Venezuela), Juan Indriago (Venezuela), Juan Munoz (Venezuela), Ronald Morillo (Venezuela), Salvador Donadelli (Venezuela). **Part-Time International Scouts:** Caryl Van Zanten (Curacao), Miguel Ruiz (Panama), Eduardo Cabrera (Colombia).

MEDIA INFORMATION

LOCAL MEDIA INFORMATION

AMERICAN LEAGUE

BALTIMORE ORIOLES
Radio Announcers: Joe Angel, Fred Manfra. **Flagship Station:** WJZ-FM 105.7 The Fan.
TV Announcers: Mike Bordick, Rick Dempsey, Jim Hunter, Jim Palmer, Gary Thorne. **Flagship Station:** Mid-Atlantic Sports Network (MASN).

BOSTON RED SOX
Radio Announcers: Joe Castiglione, Tim Neverett. **Flagship Station:** WEEI (93.7 FM/850 AM).
TV Announcers: Dave O'Brien, Jerry Remy. **Flagship Station:** New England Sports Network (regional cable).

CHICAGO WHITE SOX
Radio Announcers: Ed Farmer, Darrin Jackson, Chris Rongey (pre/post). **Flagship Station:** WSCR The Score 670-AM.
TV Announcers: Ken Harrelson, Steve Stone, Jason Benetti. **Flagship Stations:** WGN TV-9, WCIU-TV, Comcast SportsNet Chicago (regional cable).

CLEVELAND INDIANS
Radio Announcers: Tom Hamilton, Jim Rosenhaus. **Flagship Station:** WTAM 1100-AM.
TV Announcers: Rick Manning, Matt Underwood, Al Pawlowski (Pre/post). **Flagship Station:** SportsTime Ohio.

DETROIT TIGERS
Radio Announcers: Dan Dickerson, Jim Price. **Flagship Station:** WXYT 97.1 FM and AM 1270.
TV Announcers: Mario Impemba, Rod Allen, Kirk Gibson, Jack Morris, Craig Monroe. **Flagship Station:** FOX Sports Detroit (regional cable).

HOUSTON ASTROS
Radio Announcers: Steve Sparks, Robert Ford. **Spanish:** Alex Trevino, Francisco Romero. **Flagship Stations:** KBME 790-AM, KLAT 1010-AM (Spanish).
TV Announcers: Bill Brown, Alan Ashby, Geoff Blum. **Flagship Station:** ROOT Sports Houston.

KANSAS CITY ROYALS
Radio Announcers: Denny Matthews, Steve Physioc, Steve Stewart. **Kansas City affiliate:** KCSP 610-AM.
TV Announcers: Ryan Lefebvre, Rex Hudler, Joel Goldberg, Jeff Montgomery (pre-game). **Flagship Station:** FOX Sports Kansas City.

LOS ANGELES ANGELS
Radio Announcers: Terry Smith, Mark Langston. **Flagship Station:** AM 830, 1330 KWKW (Spanish).
TV Announcers: Victor Rojas, Mark Gubicza. **Spanish TV Announcers:** Jose Mota, Amaury Pi-Gonzalez. **Flagship TV Station:** Fox Sports West (regional cable).

MINNESOTA TWINS
Radio Announcers: Cory Provus, Dan Gladden. **Radio Network Studio Host:** Kris Atteberry. **Radio Engineer:** Kyle Hammer. Spanish Radio **Play-by-Play:** Alfonso Fernandez. **Spanish Radio Analyst:** Tony Oliva. **Flagship Station:** 1500 ESPN.
TV Announcers: Bert Blyleven, Dick Bremer. **Flagship Station:** Fox Sports North.

NEW YORK YANKEES
Radio Announcers: John Sterling, Suzyn Waldman. **Flagship Station:** WFAN 660-AM, WADO 1280-AM. **Spanish Radio Announcers:** Francisco Rivera, Rickie Ricardo.
TV Announcers: David Cone, Jack Curry, John Flaherty, Michael Kay, Al Leiter, Bob Lorenz, Meredith Marakovits, Paul O'Neill, Ken Singleton. **Flagship Station:** YES Network (Yankees Entertainment & Sports).

OAKLAND ATHLETICS
Radio Announcers: Vince Cotroneo, Ken Korach. **Flagship Station:** KGMZ 95.7 The Game, FM.
TV Announcers: Ray Fosse, Glen Kuiper. **Flagship Stations:** Comcast Sports Net California.

SEATTLE MARINERS
Radio Announcers: Rick Rizzs, Aaron Goldsmith. **Flagship Station:** 710 ESPN Seattle (KIRO-AM 710).
TV Announcers: Mike Blowers, Dave Sims. **Flagship Station:** ROOT Sports Northwest.

TAMPA BAY RAYS
Radio Announcers: Andy Freed, Dave Wills. **Flagship Station:** Sports Animal WDAE 620 AM.
TV Announcers: Brian Anderson, Dewayne Staats, Todd Kalas. **Flagship Station:** FOX Sports Sun.

TEXAS RANGERS
Radio Announcers: Eric Nadel, Matt Hicks; Spanish-Eleno Ornelas, Jose Guzman. **Flagship Station:** 105.3 The Fan FM, KZMP 1540 AM (Spanish).
TV Announcers: Steve Busby, Tom Grieve, Dave Raymond, Emily Jones; **Flagship Stations:** FOX Sports Southwest (regional cable), Time Warner (Spanish).

TORONTO BLUE JAYS
Radio Announcers: Jerry Howarth, Joe Siddal, Mike Wilner. **Flagship Station:** SportsNet Radio Fan 590-AM.
TV Announcers: Buck Martinez, Pat Tabler, Dan Shulman. **Flagship Station:** Rogers Sportsnet.

NATIONAL LEAGUE

ARIZONA DIAMONDBACKS
Radio Announcers: Greg Schulte, Tom Candiotti, Mike Ferrin, Rodrigo Lopez (Spanish), Oscar Soria (Spanish), Richard Saenz (Spanish), Arturo Ochoa (Spanish). **Flagship Stations:** Arizona Sports 98.7 FM & KSUN Radio Fiesta 1400 AM (Spanish).
TV Announcers: Steve Berthiaume, Bob Brenly. **Flagship Stations:** FOX Sports Arizona (regional cable).

ATLANTA BRAVES
Radio Announcers: Jim Powell, Don Sutton. **Flagship Stations:** WCNN-AM 680, The Fan (93.7 FM), WYAY-FM (106.7).
TV Announcers: Chip Caray, Joe Simpson. **Flagship Stations:** FOX Sports South/SportSouth (regional cable).

CHICAGO CUBS
Radio Announcers: Pat Hughes, Ron Coomer. **Flagship Station:** WGN 720-AM.
TV Announcers: Len Kasper, Jim Deshaies. **Flagship Stations:** WGN Channel 9 (national cable), Comcast SportsNet Chicago (regional cable), WCIU-TV Channel 26.

CINCINNATI REDS
Radio Announcers: Marty Brennaman, Thom Brennaman, Jeff Brantley, Jim Kelch, Chris Welsh, Doug Flynn. **Flagship Station:** WLW 700-AM.
TV Announcers: Chris Welsh, Thom Brennaman, Jeff Brantley, George Grande. **Flagship Station:** Fox Sports Ohio (regional cable).

COLORADO ROCKIES
Radio Announcers: Jack Corrigan, Jerry Schemmel. **Flagship Station:** KOA 850-AM.
TV Announcers: Drew Goodman, George Frazier, Jeff Huson.

LOS ANGELES DODGERS
Radio Announcers: Vin Scully, Rick Monday, Charley Steiner, Nomar Garciaparra. **Spanish:** Jaime Jarrín, Fernando Valenzuela, Pepe Yñiguez. **Flagship Stations:** AM570 Fox Sports LA, KTNQ 1020-AM (Spanish).
TV Announcers: Vin Scully, Charley Steiner, Orel Hershiser, Nomar Garciaparra, Alanna Rizzo, John Hartung, Jerry Hairston, Jr. **Spanish:** Jorge Jarrin, Manny Mota. **Flagship Stations:** SportsNet LA (regional cable).

MIAMI MARLINS
Radio Announcers: Dave Van Horne, Glenn Geffner. **Flagship Stations:** WINZ 940-AM, WAQI 710-AM (Spanish). **Spanish Radio Announcers:** Felo Ramirez, Yiky Quintana.
TV Announcers: Carl Pavano, Rich Waltz, Jeff Conine, Craig Minervini, Preston Wilson. **Spanish TV Announcers:** Raul Striker Jr. **Flagship Stations:** FSN Florida (regional cable).

MILWAUKEE BREWERS
Radio Announcers: Bob Uecker, Jeff Levering. **Flagship Station:** WTMJ 620-AM.
TV Announcers: Bill Schroeder, Brian Anderson. **Flagship Station:** Fox Sports Net North.

NEW YORK METS
Radio Announcers: Howie Rose, Josh Lewin. **Flagship Station:** WOR 710-AM.
TV Announcers: Gary Cohen, Keith Hernandez, Ron Darling, Steve Gelbs. **Flagship Stations:** Sports Net New York (regional cable), PIX11-TV.

PHILADELPHIA PHILLIES
Radio Announcers: Scott Franzke, Larry Andersen, Jim Jackson. **Flagship Station:** SportsRadio 94WIP (94.1 FM)
TV Announcers: Tom McCarthy, Ben Davis, Matt Stairs, Gregg Murphy, Mike Schmidt. **Flagship Stations:** Comcast SportsNet, NBC 10

PITTSBURGH PIRATES
Radio Announcers: Joe Block, Steve Blass, Greg Brown, Bob Walk, John Wehner. **Flagship Station:** Sports Radio 93.7 FM The Fan.
TV Announcers: Joe Block, Steve Blass, Greg Brown, Bob Walk, John Wehner. **Flagship Station:** ROOT SPORTS (regional cable).

ST. LOUIS CARDINALS
Radio Announcers: Mike Shannon, John Rooney. **Flagship Station:** KMOX 1120 AM.
TV Announcers: Rick Horton, Al Hrabosky, Dan McLaughlin. **Flagship Stations:** Fox Sports Midwest.

SAN DIEGO PADRES
Radio Announcers: Ted Leitner, Jesse Agler, Don Orsillo. **Flagship Stations:** The Mighty 1090-AM/ESPN 1700-AM.
TV Announcers: Dick Enberg, Mark Grant and Don Orsillo. **Flagship Station:** Fox Sports San Diego. **Spanish Announcers:** Eduardo Ortega, Carlos Hernandez XEMO-860-AM

SAN FRANCISCO GIANTS
Radio Announcers: Mike Krukow, Duane Kuiper, Jon Miller, Dave Flemming. **Spanish:** Tito Fuentes, Erwin Higueros. **Flagship Station:** KNBR 680-AM (English); ESPN Deportes-860AM (Spanish).
TV Announcers: CSN Bay Area-Mike Krukow, Duane Kuiper; **KNTV-NBC 11**—Jon Miller, Mike Krukow. **Flagship Stations:** KNTV-NBC 11, CSN Bay Area (regional cable).

WASHINGTON NATIONALS
Radio Announcers: Charlie Slowes, Dave Jageler. **Flagship Station:** WJFK 106.7 FM.
TV Announcers: Bob Carpenter, FP Santangelo, Dan Kolko. **Flagship Station:** Mid-Atlantic Sports Network (MASN).

NATIONAL MEDIA INFORMATION

BASEBALL STATISTICS

ELIAS SPORTS BUREAU INC. NATIONAL MEDIA BASEBALL STATISTICS

Official Major League Statistician Mailing Address: 500 Fifth Ave., Suite 2140, New York, NY 10110. **Telephone:** (212) 869-1530. **Fax:** (212) 354-0980. **Website:** www.esb.com.

President: Seymour Siwoff.

Executive Vice President: Steve Hirdt. **Vice President:** Peter Hirdt. **Data Processing Manager:** Chris Thorn.

MLB ADVANCED MEDIA

Official Minor League Statistician Mailing Address: 75 Ninth Ave., New York, NY 10011. **Telephone:** (212) 485-3444. **Fax:** (212) 485-3456. **Website:** MiLB.com.

Director, Stats: Chris Lentine. **Senior Manager, Stats:** Shawn Geraghty.

Senior Stats Supervisors: Jason Rigatti, Ian Schwartz. **Stats Supervisors:** Lawrence Fischer, Jake Fox, Dominic French, Kelvin Lee.

MILB.COM OFFICIAL WEBSITE OF MINOR LEAGUE BASEBALL

Mailing Address: 75 Ninth Ave, New York, NY 10011. **Telephone:** (212) 485-3444. **Fax:** (212) 485-3456. **Website:** MiLB.com.

Director, Minor League Club Initiatives: Nathan Blackmon. **Managing Producer, MiLB.com:** Brendon Desrochers. **Club Producers:** Dan Marinis, Danny Wild. **Columnist:** Ben Hill. **Prospects Reporter:** Sam Dykstra.

STATS LLC

Mailing Address: 2775 Shermer Road, Northbrook, IL 60062. **Telephone:** (847) 583-2100. **Fax:** (847) 470-9140. **Website:** www.stats.com. **Email:** sales@stats.com. **Twitter:** @STATSBiznews; @STATS_MLB. **CEO:** Ken Fuchs. **Chief Operating Officer:** Robert Schur. **EVP, Global Sales & Marketing:** Greg Kirkorsky. **SVP, Products:** Jim Corelis. **VP, Marketing:** Kirsten Porter. **Associate Vice President, Data Operations:** Allan Spear. **Manager, Baseball Operations:** Jeff Chernow

TELEVISION NETWORKS

ESPN INC.

Mailing Address: ESPN Plaza, Bristol, CT 06010. **Telephone:** (860) 766-2000.

ESPN, INC., & ABC NEW YORK EXECUTIVE OFFICES

Mailing Address: 77 W 66th Street New York, NY 10023. **Telephone:** (212) 456-7777. **Co-Chairman Disney Media Networks & President ESPN:** John Skipper. **Executive VP, Administration:** Ed Durso. **Executive VP, Production & Programming:** John Wildhack. **Executive VP, Production:** Norby Williamson. **Executive VP, Programming & Scheduling:** Burke Magnus. **Senior VP, Production Innovation:** Jed Drake. **Senior VP Production & Remote Events:** Mark Gross. **VP, Studio Production:** Mike McQuade. **Senior Coordinating Producer, MLB:** Phil Orlins. **Coordinating Producer, Baseball Tonight:** Fernando Lopez. **Senior Publicist, Communications:** Gianina Thompson. **Vice President, Production:** Jay Rothman. **Publicist, Communications:** Michael Skarka.

FOX SPORTS/FOX SPORTS 1

Mailing Address, Los Angeles: Fox Network Center, Building 101, Fifth floor, 10201 West Pico Blvd., Los Angeles, CA 90035. **Telephone:** (310) 369-6000. **Fax:** (310) 969-6700.

Mailing Address, New York: 1211 Avenue of the Americas, 20th Floor, New York, NY 10036. **Telephone:** (212) 556-2500. **Fax:** (212) 354-6902.

Website: www.foxsports.com. **President and COO:** Eric Shanks. **Executive Vice President and Executive Producer:** John Entz. **General Manager and COO, FOX Sports 1:** David Nathanson. **Executive VP, News:** Scott Ackerson. **Executive VP, Field Operations and Engineering:** Ed Delaney. **Executive VP/Creative Director:** Gary Hartley. **Executive VP, Programming and Research:** Bill Wanger. **Senior VP, Production:** Jack Simmons. **VP, Production:** Judy Boyd. **VP, Field Operations and Engineering:** Mike Davies. **Coordinating Producer, MLB on FOX:** Pete Macheska. **Game Director, MLB on FOX:** Bill Webb. **Senior VP, Communications and Media Relations:** Lou D'Ermilio. **VP, Communications:** Dan Bell. **Director, Communications:** Ileana Pena. **Manager:** Eddie Motl. **Publicist:** Valerie Krebs.

MLB NETWORK

Mailing Address: One MLB Network Plaza, Secaucus, NJ 07094. **Telephone:** (201) 520-6400. **President:** Rob McGlarry. **Executive VP, Advertising/Sales:** Bill Morningstar. **Senior VP, Production:** Dave Patterson. **Senior VP, Marketing/Promotion:** Mary Beck. **Senior VP, Finance/Administration:** Tony Santomauro. **Senior VP, Operations/Engineering:** Susan Stone. **VP, Production:** Mike Santini. **VP, Programming:** Andy Butters. **VP, Engineering/I.T.:** Mark Haden. **VP, Distribution/Affiliate Sales/Marketing:** Brent Fisher. **VP, Studio and Broadcast Operations:** Bob Mincieli. **VP, Creative Services:** Chris Mallory. **VP, Business Public Relations, Major League Baseball:** Matt Bourne. **Director, Media Relations, MLB Network:** Lorraine Fisher. **Specialist, Media Relations, MLB Network:** Lou Barricelli.

OTHER TELEVISION NETWORKS

CBS SPORTS
Mailing Address: 51 W 52nd St., New York, NY 10019. **Telephone:** (212) 975-5230. **Fax:** (212) 975-4063. **Chairman:** Sean McManus. **President:** David Berson. **Executive VP, Programming:** Rob Correa. **Executive Producer/VP, Production:** Harold Bryant. **Senior VP, Communications:** Jennifer Sabatelle.

CNN SPORTS
Mailing Address: One CNN Center, Atlanta, GA 30303. **Telephone:** (404) 878-1600. **Fax:** (404) 878-0011. **Vice President, Production:** Jeffrey Green.

HBO SPORTS
Mailing Address: 1100 Avenue of the Americas, New York, NY 10036. **Telephone:** (212) 512-1000. **Fax:** (212) 512-1751. **President, HBO Sports:** Ken Hershman.

NBC SPORTS GROUP
Mailing Address: 1 Blachley Road, Stamford, CT 06902. **Telephone:** (203) 356-7000. **Chairman:** Mark Lazarus. **Group President:** David Preschlack. **President, Programing:** Jon Miller. **CMO, Olympics:** John D. Miller. **CMO:** Jenny Storms. **EVP, Sales:** Seth Winter. **SVP and GM, Digital Media:** Rick Cordella. **Executive Producer:** Sam Flood. **Senior VP, Communications:** Greg Hughes.

ROGERS SPORTSNET (CANADA)
Mailing Address: 9 Channel Nine Court, Toronto, ON M1S 4B5. **Telephone:** (416) 332-5600. **Fax:** (416) 332-5629. **Website:** www.sportsnet.ca. **President, Rogers Media:** Keith Pelley. **President, Rogers Sportsnet:** Scott Moore. **Director, Communications/Promotions:** Dave Rashford.

THE SPORTS NETWORK (CANADA)
Mailing Address: 9 Channel Nine Court, Toronto, ON M1S 4B5. **Telephone:** (416) 384-5000. **Fax:** (416) 332-4337. **Website:** www.tsn.ca.

RADIO NETWORKS

ESPN RADIO
Mailing Address: ESPN Plaza Bristol, CT 06010. **Telephone:** (860) 766-2000, (800) 999-9985. **Fax:** (860) 766-4505. **Website:** espn.go.com/espnradio. **Senior VP, Production Business Divisions/Audio & Deportes:** Traug Keller. **Vice President, Network Content:** David Roberts. **Vice President, Deportes Programming & Business Units:** Freddy Rolon. **Executive Producer II Radio:** John Martin. **Senior Director, Daytime Programming:** Amanda Gifford. **Senior Director, Radio Programming Operations:** Peter Gianesini. **Director Affiliate Relations:** Jeff Martindale. **Director Audio Event Production:** Steven Haddad

SIRIUS XM SATELLITE RADIO
Mailing Address: 1500 Eckington Place NE, Washington, DC 20002. **Telephone:** (202) 380-4000. **Fax:** 202-380-4500. **Hotline:** (866) 652-6696. **E-Mail Address:** mlb@siriusxm.com. **Website:** www.siriusxm.com. **President/Chief Content Officer:** Scott Greenstein. **Senior VP, Sports:** Steve Cohen. **VP, Sports:** Brian Hamilton. **Director, MLB programming:** Chris Eno. **Senior Director, Communications/Sports Programming:** Andrew Fitzpatrick.

SPORTS BYLINE USA
Mailing Address: 300 Broadway, Suite 8, San Francisco, CA 94133. **Telephone:** (415) 434-8300. **Guest Line:** (800) 358-4457. **Studio Line:** (800) 878-7529. **Fax:** (415) 391-2569. **E-Mail Address:** editor@sportsbyline.com. **Website:** www.sportsbyline.com. **President:** Darren Peck. **Executive Producer:** Ira Hankin.

YAHOO SPORTS RADIO
Mailing Address: 5353 West Alabama St., Suite 415, Houston, TX 77056. **Telephone:** (800) 224-2004. **Fax:** (713) 479-5333. **Website:** www.yahoosportsradio.com.

GENERAL INFORMATION

SCOUTING

MAJOR LEAGUE BASEBALL SCOUTING BUREAU
Mailing Address: 3500 Porsche Way, Suite 100, Ontario, CA 91764. **Telephone:** (909) 980-1881. **Fax:** (909) 980-7794. **Year Founded:** 1974.
Senior Director: Bill Bavasi. **Scouting Director:** Bob Fontaine. **Assistant Director:** Rick Oliver. **Office and Scout School Coordinator:** Debbie Keedy. **Coordinator-Scouting Operations:** Will Clements.
Scouts: Tom Burns (Harrisburg, PA) Andy Campbell (Gilbert, AZ), Travis Coleman (Birmingham, AL), Dan Dixon (Temecula, CA), Brad Fidler (Douglassville, PA), Rusty Gerhardt (New London, TX), Chris Heidt (Rockford, IL), Gil Kubski (Los Angeles, CA), Paul Mirocke (Tampa, FL), Carl Moesche (Gresham, OR), Gary Randall (Rock Hill, SC), Kevin Saucier (Pensacola, FL), Harry Shelton (Ocoee, FL), Craig Smajstrla (Pearland, TX), George Vranau (Sacramento, CA), Robin Wallace (Newburyport, MA),.
Canadian Scouts: Jason Chee-Aloy (Toronto), Jasmin Roy (Longueuil, Quebec), Bob Smyth (Ladysmith, BC), Tony Wylie (Anchorage, AK).

PROFESSIONAL BASEBALL SCOUTS FOUNDATION
Mailing Address: 5010 N. Parkway Calabasas, Suite 201, Calabasas, CA 91302. **Telephone:** (818) 224-3906 / **Fax** (818) 267-5516. **Email:** cindy.pbsf@yahoo.com. **Website:** www.pbsfonline.com
Chairman: Dennis J. Gilbert. **Executive Director:** Cindy Picerni. **Board of Directors:** Bill "Chief" Gayton, Pat Gillick, Derrick Hall, Roland Hemond, Gary Hughes, Jeff Idelson, Dan Jennings, JJ Lally, Tommy Lasorda, Frank Marcos, Roberta Mazur, Harry Minor, Bob Nightengale, Damon Oppenheimer, Jared Porter, Tracy Ringolsby, John Scotti, Dale Sutherland, Kevin Towers, Dave Yoakum, John Young.

SCOUT OF THE YEAR FOUNDATION
Mailing Address: P.O. Box 211585, West Palm Beach, FL 33421. **Telephone:** (561) 798-5897, (561) 818-4329. **E-mail Address:** bertmazur@aol.com.
President: Roberta Mazur. **Vice President:** Tracy Ringolsby. **Treasurer:** Ron Mazur II. **Board of Advisers:** Pat Gillick, Roland Hemond, Gary Hughes, Tommy Lasorda. **Scout of the Year Program Advisory Board:** Tony DeMacio, Joe Klein, Roland Hemond, Gary Hughes, Dan Jennings, Linda Pereira.

UMPIRES

JIM EVANS ACADEMY
Mailing Address: 200 South Wilcox St., #508, Castle Rock, CO 80104. **Telephone:** (303) 290-7411. **E-mail Address:** jim@umpireacademy.com. **Website:** www.umpireacademy.com.
Operator: Jim Evans.

MINOR LEAGUE BASEBALL UMPIRE TRAINING ACADEMY
Mailing Address: P.O. Box A, St. Petersburg, FL, 33731-1950. **Telephone:** (877) 799-UMPS. **Fax:** (727) 456-1745. **Email:** info@MiLBUmpireAcademy.com. **Website:** www.MiLBUmpireAcademy.com
Director: Dusty Dellinger. **Chief of Instruction:** Mike Felt. **Curriculum Coordinator:** Larry Reveal. **Lead Classroom Instructor:** Jorge Bauza. **Lead Field Instructor:** Darren Spagnardi. **Lead Cage Instructor:** Tyler Funneman. **Classroom Instructor:** Brian Sinclair. **Field Leader:** Mark Lollo. **Medical Coordinator:** Mark Stubblefield. **Administrator:** Andy Shultz.

MINOR LEAGUE BASEBALL UMPIRE DEVELOPMENT
Street Address: 9550 16th Street North, St Petersburg, FL 33716. **Mailing Address:** P.O. Box A, St. Petersburg, FL 33731-1950. **Telephone:** (727) 822-6937. **Fax:** (727) 821-5819.
President/CEO: Pat O'Conner. **Secretary/VP, Legal Affairs/General Counsel:** D. Scott Poley. **Director, Umpire Development:** Dusty Dellinger. **Chief, Instruction/Umpire Development Evaluator:** Mike Felt. **Field Evaluators/Instructors:** Jorge Bauza, Tyler Funneman, Larry Reveal, Darren Spagnardi, Brian Sinclair and Mark Lollo. **Medical Coordinator:** Mark Stubblefield. **Special Assistant, Umpire Development:** Lillian Patterson.

WENDELSTEDT UMPIRE SCHOOL
Mailing Address: P.O. Box 1079 Albion, MI, 49224. **Telephone:** 800-818-1690. **Fax:** 888-881-9801. **Email Address:** admin@umpireschool.com. **Website:** www.umpireschool.com.

WORLD UMPIRES ASSOCIATION
Year Founded: 2000.
President: Joe West. **Vice President:** Fieldin Culbreth. **Secretary/Treasurer:** Jim Reynolds. **Governing Board:** Dan Bellino, Dan Iassogna, Jeff Kellogg, Bill Miller, Tim Timmons, Bill Welke. **Labor Counsel:** TBA. **Administrator:** Phil Janssen.

TRAINERS

PROFESSIONAL BASEBALL ATHLETIC TRAINERS SOCIETY
Mailing Address: 1201 Peachtree St., 400 Colony Square, Suite 1750, Atlanta, GA 30361. **Telephone:** (404) 875-4000, ext. 1. **Fax:** (404) 892-8560. **E-mail Address:** rmallernee@mallernee-branch.com or sam@theromanogroup.com. **Website:** www.pbats.com
Year Founded: 1983

MAJOR LEAGUES

President: Mark O'Neal (Chicago Cubs). **Secretary:** Ron Porterfield (Tampa Bay Rays). **Treasurer:** Tom Probst (Colorado Rockies). American League Head. **Athletic Trainer Representative:** Nick Kenney (Kansas City Royals). **American League Assistant Athletic Trainer Representative:** Brian Ball. (Chicago White Sox). **National League Head Athletic Trainer Representative:** Keith Dugger (Colorado Rockies). National League Assistant Athletic. **Trainer Representative:** Ben Potenziano (Pittsburgh Pirates). **Immediate Past President:** Richie Bancells (Baltimore Orioles). **General Counsel:** Rollin Mallernee II. **Communications and Public Relations:** Neil Romano.

MUSEUMS

BABE RUTH BIRTHPLACE
Office Address: 216 Emory St., Baltimore, MD 21230. **Telephone:** (410) 727-1539. **Fax:** (410) 727-1652. **E-mail Address:** info@baberuthmuseum.org. **Website:** www.baberuthmuseum.com.
Year Founded: 1973.
Executive Director: Mike Gibbons. **Curator:** Amanda Peacock. **Communications:** John Hein
Fall/Winter Hours: Museum open Tuesday-Sunday, 10 a.m. to 5 p.m. **Closed:** New Year's Day, Thanksgiving and Christmas. **Spring/Summer Hours:** Museum open Monday-Sunday, 10 a.m. to 5 p.m. **Open until 7 on Oriole Night Game Days

CANADIAN BASEBALL HALL OF FAME AND MUSEUM
Museum Address: 386 Church St. South, St. Marys, Ontario N4X 1C2. **Mailing Address:** P.O. Box 1838, St. Marys, Ontario N4X 1C2. **Telephone:** (519) 284-1838. **Fax:** (519) 284-1234. **E-mail Address:** baseball@baseballhalloffame.ca. **Website:** www.baseballhalloffame.ca.
Year Founded: 1983.
Director Operations: Scott Crawford.
Hours: May-weekends **only-Saturday 10:**30-4pm; Sunday noon-4pm. June 1-August 31-Monday-Saturday, **10:**30-4pm; Sunday, noon-4pm. Sept 1 - Oct 8 - **Thursday-**Saturday **10:**30-4pm; Sunday noon-4pm

FIELD OF DREAMS MOVIE SITE
Address: 28995 Lansing Rd., **Mailing Address:** PO BOX 300 Dyersville, IA 52040. **Telephone:** (563) 875-8404; (888) 875-8404. **Fax:** (888.519.2254). **E-mail Address:** info@fodmoviesite.com. **Website:** www.fodmoviesite.com.
Year Founded: 1989.
Gift Shop Office/Business Manager: Betty Boeckenstedt. **Hours:** April-November, 9 a.m.-6 p.m.

WORLD OF LITTLE LEAGUE: PETER J. MCGOVERN MUSEUM AND OFFICIAL STORE
Office Address: 525 US 15, South Williamsport, PA 17702. **Mailing Address:** P.O. Box 3485, Williamsport, PA 17701. **Telephone:** (570) 326-3607. **Fax:** (570) 326-2267. **E-mail Address:** museum@littleleague.org. **Website:** www. LittleLeagueMuseum.org. **Facebook:** LittleLeagueMuseum
Year Founded: 1982.
Vice President/Executive Director: Lance Van Auken. **Director, Public Programming/Outreach:** Janice Ogurcak. **Curator:** Adam Thompson.
Museum Hours: Open 9 a.m. to 5 p.m., Monday-Sunday. **Closed:** Easter, Thanksgiving, Dec. 24, 25, 31 and New Year's Day

LOUISVILLE SLUGGER MUSEUM AND FACTORY
Office Address: 800 W. Main St., Louisville, KY 40202. **Telephone:** (502) 588-7228, (877) 775-8443. **Fax:** (502) 585-1179. **Website:** www.sluggermuseum.com.
Year Founded: 1996.
Executive Director: Anne Jewell.
Museum Hours: Jan. 1-June 30/Aug. 10-Dec. 31-Mon-Sat 9 a.m.-5 p.m., Sun. 11 a.m.-5 p.m.; July 1-Aug. 9-Sun-Thurs 9 a.m.-6 p.m., Fri-Sat 9 a.m.-8 p.m. **Closed:** Thanksgiving/Christmas Day.

NATIONAL BASEBALL HALL OF FAME AND MUSEUM
Address: 25 Main St., Cooperstown, NY 13326. **Telephone:** (888) 425-5633, (607) 547-7200. **Fax:** (607) 547-2044. **E-mail Address:** info@baseballhalloffame.org. **Website:** www.baseballhall.org.
Year Founded: 1939.
Chairman: Jane Forbes Clark. **Vice Chairman:** Joe Morgan. **President:** Jeff Idelson.
Museum Hours: Open daily, year-round, closed only Thanksgiving, Christmas and New Year's Day. 9 a.m.-5 p.m. Summer hours, 9 a.m.-9 p.m. (Memorial Day weekend through the day before Labor Day.)
2015 Hall of Fame Induction Weekend: July 24-27, Cooperstown, NY.

NEGRO LEAGUES BASEBALL MUSEUM
Mailing Address: 1616 E. 18th St., Kansas City, MO 64108. **Telephone:** (816) 221-1920. **Fax:** (816) 221-8424. **E-mail Address:** bkendrick@nlbm.com. **Website:** www.nlbm.com.
Year Founded: 1990.
President: Bob Kendrick. **Executive Director Emeritus:** Don Motley.
Museum Hours: Tues.-Sat. 9 a.m.-6 p.m.; Sun. noon-6 p.m.

NOLAN RYAN FOUNDATION AND EXHIBIT CENTER
Mailing Address: 2925 South Bypass 35, Alvin, TX 77511. **Telephone:** (281) 388-1134. **FAX:** (281) 388-1135. **Website:** www.nolanryanfoundation.org.
Hours: Mon.-Fri. 9 a.m.-4 p.m. The exhibit is closed Saturdays and Sundays.

RESEARCH

SOCIETY FOR AMERICAN BASEBALL RESEARCH

Mailing Address: Cronkite School at ASU, 555 N Central Ave., #416 , Phoenix, AZ 85004. **Website:** www.sabr.org.
Year Founded: 1971.
President: Vince Gennaro. **Vice President:** Bill Nowlin. **Secretary:** Todd Lebowitz. **Treasurer:** F.X. Flinn. **Directors:** Ty Waterman, Chris Dial, Emily Hawks, Leslie Heaphy. **CEO:** Marc Appleman. **Director of Editorial Content:** Jacob Pomrenke.

ALUMNI ASSOCIATIONS

MAJOR LEAGUE BASEBALL PLAYERS ALUMNI ASSOCIATION

Mailing Address: 1631 Mesa Ave., Copper Building, Suite D, Colorado Springs, CO 80906. **Telephone:** (719) 477-1870. **Fax:** (719) 477-1875. **E-mail Address:** postoffice@mlbpaa.com. **Website:** www.baseballalumni.com. **Facebook:** facebook.com/majorleaguebaseballplayersalumniassociation. **Twitter:** @MLBPAA.
Chief Executive Officer: Dan Foster (dan@mlbpaa.com). **Chief Operating Officer:** Geoffrey Hixson (geoff@mlbpaa.com). **Vice President, Operations:** Mike Groll (mikeg@mlbpaa.com). **Director, Communications:** Nikki Warner (nikki@mlbpaa.com). **Director, Membership:** Kate Hutchinson (Kate@mlbpaa.com). **Director, Memorabilia:** Greg Thomas (greg@mlbpaa.com). **Public Relations Assistant:** Rachel Levitsky (Rachel@mlbpaa.com). **Database Administrator:** Chris Burkeen (cburkeen@mlbpaa.com)

MAJOR LEAGUE ALUMNI MARKETING

Chief Executive Officer: Dan Foster (dan@mlbpaa.com). **Chief Operating Officer:** Geoffrey Hixson (geoff@mlbpaa.com). **Vice President, Legends Entertainment Group:** Chris Torgusen (chris@mlbpaa.com). **Vice President of Operations:** Mike Groll (mikeg@mlbpaa.com). **Marketing Coordinator, Legends Entertainment Group:** Ryan Thomas (rthomas@mlbpaa.com). **Director of New Business Development:** Pete Kelly (pete@mlbpaa.com). **Memorabilia Coordinator:** Chris Spomer (cspomer@mlbpaa.com). **Sales Manager:** Amy Wagner (Amy@mlbpaa.com).

MINOR LEAGUE BASEBALL ALUMNI ASSOCIATION

Mailing Address: P.O. Box A, St. Petersburg, FL 33731-1950. **Telephone:** (727) 822-6937. **Fax:** (727) 821-5819. **E-Mail Address:** alumni@MiLB.com. **Website:** www.milb.com.

BASEBALL ASSISTANCE TEAM (B.A.T.)

Mailing Address: 245 Park Ave., 31st Floor, New York, NY 10167. **Telephone:** (212) 931-7822, **Fax:** (212) 949-5433. **Website:** www.baseballassistanceteam.com.
Year Founded: 1986.
To Make a Donation: (866) 605-4594.
President: Randy Winn. **Vice President:** Bob Watson. **Board of Directors:** Sal Bando, Dick Freeman, Steve Garvey, Luis Gonzalez, Raul Ibanez, Adam Jones, Mark Letendre, Diane Margolin, Buck Martinez, Alan Nahmias, Christine O'Reilly, Staci Slaughter, Gary Thorne, Bob Watson, Greg Wilcox, Randy Winn. **Director:** Erik Nilsen. **Secretary:** Thomas Ostertag. **Treasurer:** Scott Stamp. **Advisor:** Laurel Prieb. **Consultant:** Sam McDowell. **Consultant:** Tim McDowell. **Consultant:** Dr. Genoveva Javier. **Consultant:** Benny Ayala. **Operations:** Vladimir Cruz, Michelle Fucich.

ASSOCIATION OF PROFESSIONAL BALL PLAYERS OF AMERICA

Address: 101 S. Kraemer Blvd., Suite 112 Placentia, CA 92870. **Phone:** 714-528-2012. **Fax:** 714-528-2037. **Website:** www.apbpa.org. **E-mail:** ballplayersassn@aol.com
President: Jim Rantz. **1st Vice President:** Del Crandall. **2nd Vice President:** Marti Wolever. **Secretary-Treasurer:** Dick Beverage. **Directors:** Dusty Baker, Tony LaRussa, Bobby Grich, Brooks Robinson, Ryne Sandberg, Tom Lasorda Wes Parker, Cal Ripken Jr., Nolan Ryan, Mike Scioscia. **Advisory Council:** Jay Johnstone, Tal Smith, Chuck Stevens. **Membership Services Manager:** Patty Joost (patty@apbpa.org)

MINISTRY

BASEBALL CHAPEL

Mailing Address: P.O. Box 10102, Largo FL 33773. **Telephone:** (610) 999-3600. **E-mail Address:** office@baseballchapel.org. **Website:** www.baseballchapel.org.
Year Founded: 1973.
President: Vince Nauss. **Hispanic Ministry:** Cali Magallanes, Gio Llerena. **Ministry Operations:** Rob Crose, Steve Sisco. **Board of Directors:** Don Christensen, Greg Groh, Dave Howard, Vince Nauss, Walt Wiley.

CATHOLIC ATHLETES FOR CHRIST

Mailing Address: 3703 Cameron Mills Road, Alexandria, VA 22305. **Telephone:** (703) 239-3070. **E-mail Address:** info@catholicathletesforchrist.org. **Website:** www.catholicathletesforchrist.org.
Year Founded: 2006.
President: Ray McKenna. **MLB Ministry Coordinator:** Kevin O'Malley. **MLB Athlete Advisory Board Members:** Mike Sweeney (Chairman), Jeff Suppan (Vice Chairman), Sal Bando, Tom Carroll, David Eckstein, Terry Kennedy, Jack McKeon, Darrell Miller, Mike Piazza, Vinny Rottino, Craig Stammen.Bando, David Eckstein, Terry Kennedy, Jack McKeon, Darrell Miller, Mike Piazza, Vinny Rottino, Craig Stammen.

TRADE/EMPLOYMENT

BASEBALL WINTER MEETINGS

Mailing Address: P.O. Box A, St. Petersburg, FL 33731. **Telephone:** (727) 822-6937. **Fax:** (727) 821-5819. **E-Mail Address:** BaseballWinterMeetings@milb.com. **Website:** www.baseballwintermeetings.com.
2016 Convention: Dec. 4-8, Gaylord National Resort and Convention Center, Washington, D.C.

BASEBALL TRADE SHOW

Mailing Address: P.O. Box A, St. Petersburg, FL 33731-1950. **Telephone:** (866) 926-6452. **Fax:** (727) 683-9865. **E-Mail Address:** TradeShow@MiLB.com. **Website:** www.BaseballTradeShow.com. **Contact:** Noreen Brantner, Sr. Asst. Director, Exhibition Services & Sponsorships.
2016 Show: Dec. 4-8, Gaylord National Resort and Convention Center, Washington, D.C.

PROFESSIONAL BASEBALL EMPLOYMENT OPPORTUNITIES

Mailing Address: P.O. Box A, St. Petersburg, FL 33731-1950. **Telephone:** 866-WE-R-PBEO. **Fax:** 727-821-5819.
Website: www.PBEO.com. **Email:** info@PBEO.com. **Contact:** Mark Labban, Manager, Business Development.

BASEBALL CARD MANUFACTURERS

PANINI AMERICA INC.

Mailing Address: Panini America, 5325 FAA Blvd., Suite 100, Irving TX 75061. **Telephone:** (817) 662-5300, (800) 852-8833. **Website:** www.paniniamerica.net. **Email:** RM_Marketing@paniniamerica.net. **Marketing Manager:** Scott Prusha.

GRANDSTAND CARDS

Mailing Address: 22647 Ventura Blvd., #192, Woodland Hills, CA 91364. **Telephone:** (818) 992-5642. **Fax:** (818) 348-9122. **E-mail Address:** gscards1@pacbell.net.

BRANDT SPORTS MARKETING (FORMERLY MULTIAD SPORTS)

Mailing Address: 8914 N. Prairie Pointe Ct., Peoria, IL 61615. **Telephone:** (800) 720-9740. **Fax:** (563) 386-4817. **Website:** http://www.brandtco.com/sports.
Contact: Jim Dougas, jim.douglas@brandtco.com. **Phone:** 309-215-9243. **Fax:** 563-386-4817. **Contact:** Dave Mateer, dave.mateer@brandtco.com. **Phone:** 309-215-9248. **Fax:** 563-386-4817.

TOPPS

Mailing Address: One Whitehall St., New York, NY 10004. **Telephone:** (212) 376-0300. **Fax:** (212) 376-0573. **Website:** www.topps.com.

UPPER DECK

Mailing Address: 2251 Rutherford Rd., Carlsbad, CA 92008. **Telephone:** (800) 873-7332. **Fax:** (760) 929-6548.
E-mail Address: customer_service@upperdeck.com. **Website:** www.upperdeck.com.

SPRING TRAINING

CACTUS LEAGUE

For spring training schedules, see page 240

ARIZONA DIAMONDBACKS

MAJOR LEAGUE
Complex Address: Salt River Fields at Talking Stick, 7555 North Pima Road, Scottsdale, AZ 85256. **Telephone:** (480) 270-5000. **Seating Capacity:** 11,000 (7,000 fixed seats, 4,000 lawn seats). **Location:** From Loop-101, use exit 44 (Indian Bend Road) and proceed west for approximately one-half mile; turn right at Pima Road to travel north and proceed one-quarter mile; three entrances to Salt River Fields will be available on the right-hand side.

MINOR LEAGUE
Complex Address: Same as major league club.

CHICAGO CUBS

MAJOR LEAGUE
Complex Address: Cubs Park, 2330 West Rio Salado Parkway, Mesa, AZ 85201. **Telephone:** (480) 668-0500. **Seating Capacity:** 15,000.
Location: on the land of the former Riverview Golf Course, bordered by the 101 and 202 interchange in Mesa.

MINOR LEAGUE
Complex Address: Same as major league club.

CHICAGO WHITE SOX

MAJOR LEAGUE
Complex Address: Camelback Ranch-Glendale, 10710 West Camelback Road, Phoenix, AZ 85037. **Telephone:** (623) 302-5000. **Seating Capacity:** 13,000.
Hotel Address: Comfort Suites Glendale, 9824 W Camelback Rd, Glendale, AZ 85305. **Telephone:** (623) 271-9005. **Hotel Address:** Renaissance Glendale Hotel & Spa, 9495 W Coyotes Blvd, Glendale, AZ 85305. **Telephone:** 629-937-3700.

MINOR LEAGUE
Complex/Hotel Address: Same as major league club.

CINCINNATI REDS

MAJOR LEAGUE
Complex Address: Cincinnati Reds Player Development Complex, 3125 S Wood Blvd, Goodyear, AZ 85338. **Telephone:** (623) 932-6590. **Ballpark Address:** Goodyear Ballpark, 1933 S Ballpark Way, Goodyear, AZ 85338. **Telephone:** (623) 882-3120.
Hotel Address: Marriott Residence Inn, 7350 N Zanjero Blvd, Glendale, AZ 85305. **Telephone:** (623) 772-8900. **Fax:** (623) 772-8905.

MINOR LEAGUE
Complex/Hotel Address: Same as major league club.

CLEVELAND INDIANS
Complex Address: Cleveland Indians Player Development Complex 2601 S Wood Blvd, Goodyear, AZ 85338; Goodyear Ballpark 1933 S Ballpark Way, Goodyear, AZ 85338. **Telephone:** (623) 882-3120.
Location: From Downtown Phoenix/East Valley: West on I-10 to Exit 127, Bullard Avenue and proceed

south (left off exit), Bullard Avenue turns into West Lower Buckeye Road. Turn left on to Wood Blvd.
Hotel Address: (Media) Hampton Inn and Suites, 2000 N Litchfield Rd, Goodyear, AZ 85395. **Telephone:** (623) 536-1313. **Hotel Address:** Holiday Inn Express, 1313 N Litchfield Rd, Goodyear, AZ 85395. **Telephone:** (623) 535-1313. **Hotel Address:** TownePlace Suites, 13971 West Celebrate Life Way, Goodyear, AZ 85338. **Telephone:** (623) 535-5009. **Hotel Address:** Residence Inn by Marriott, 2020 N Litchfield Rd, Goodyear, AZ 85395. **Telephone:** (623) 866-1313.

MINOR LEAGUE
Complex Address: Same as major league club.

COLORADO ROCKIES

MAJOR LEAGUE
Complex Address: Salt River Fields at Talking Stick, 7555 North Pima Rd, Scottsdale, AZ 85258. **Telephone:** (480) 270-5800. **Seating Capacity:** 11,000 (7,000 fixed seats, 4,000 lawn seats). **Location:** From Loop-101, use exit 44 (Indian Bend Road) and proceed west for approximately one-half mile; turn right at Pima Road to travel north and proceed one-quarter mile; three entrances to Salt River Fields will be available on the right-hand side. **Visiting Team Hotel:** The Scottsdale Plaza Resort, 7200 North Scottsdale Road, Scottsdale, AZ 85253. **Telephone:** (480) 948-5000. **Fax:** (480) 951-5100.

MINOR LEAGUE
Complex/Hotel Address: Same as major league club.

KANSAS CITY ROYALS

MAJOR LEAGUE
Complex Address: Surprise Stadium, 15850 North Bullard Ave, Surprise, AZ 85374. **Telephone:** (623) 222-2000. **Seating Capacity:** 10,700. **Location:** I-10 West to Route 101 North, 101 North to Bell Road, left on Bell for five miles, stadium on left.
Hotel Address: Wigwam Resort, 300 East Wigwam Blvd, Litchfield Park, Arizona 85340. **Telephone:** (623) 935-3811.

MINOR LEAGUE
Complex Address: Same as major league club. **Hotel Address:** Comfort Hotel and Suites, 13337 W Grand Ave, Surprise, AZ 85374. **Telephone:** (623) 583-3500.

LOS ANGELES ANGELS

MAJOR LEAGUE
Complex Address: Tempe Diablo Stadium, 2200 West Alameda Drive, Tempe, AZ 85282. **Telephone:** (480) 858-7500. **Fax:** (480) 438-7583. **Seating Capacity:** 9,558. **Location:** I-10 to exit 153B (48th Street), south one mile on 48th Street to Alameda Drive, left on Alameda.

MINOR LEAGUE
Complex Address: Tempe Diablo Minor League Complex, 2225 W Westcourt Way, Tempe, AZ 85282. **Telephone:** (480) 858-7558.
Hotel Address: Sheraton Phoenix Airport, 1600 South 52nd Street, Tempe, AZ 85281. **Telephone:** (480) 967-6600.

LOS ANGELES DODGERS

MAJOR LEAGUE

Complex Address: Camelback Ranch, 10710 West Camelback Rd, Phoenix, AZ 85037. **Seating Capacity:** 13,000, plus standing room.

Location: I-10 or I-17 to Loop 101 West or North, Take Exit 5, Camelback Road West to ballpark. **Telephone:** (623) 302-5000. **Hotel:** Unavailable.

MINOR LEAGUE

Complex/Hotel Address: Same as major league club.

MILWAUKEE BREWERS

MAJOR LEAGUE

Complex Address: Maryvale Baseball Park, 3600 N 51st Ave, Phoenix, AZ 85031. **Telephone:** (623) 245-5555. **Seating Capacity:** 9,000. **Location:** I-10 to 51st Ave, north on 51st Ave
Hotel Address: Unavailable.

MINOR LEAGUE

Complex Address: Maryvale Baseball Complex, 3805 N 53rd Ave, Phoenix, AZ 85031. **Telephone:** (623) 245-5600. **Hotel Address:** Unavailable.

OAKLAND ATHLETICS

MAJOR LEAGUE

Complex Address: Hohokam Stadium, 1235 North Center Street, Mesa, AZ 85201. **Telephone:** 480-907-5489. **Seating Capacity:** 10,000.

MINOR LEAGUE

Complex Address: Fitch Park, 160 East 6th Place, Mesa, AZ 85201. **Telephone:** 480-387-5800.
Hotel Address: Unavailable.

SAN DIEGO PADRES

MAJOR LEAGUE

Complex Address: Peoria Sports Complex, 8131 West Paradise Lane, Peoria, AZ 85382. **Telephone:** (623) 773-8700. **Fax:** (623) 486-7154. **Seating Capacity:** 12,000.

Location: I-17 to Bell Road exit, west on Bell to 83rd Ave. **Hotel Address:** La Quinta Inn & Suites (623) 487-1900, 16321 N 83rd Avenue, Peoria, AZ 85382.

MINOR LEAGUE

Complex/Hotel: Country Inn and Suites (623) 879-9000, 20221 N 29th Avenue, Phoenix, AZ 85027.

SAN FRANCISCO GIANTS

MAJOR LEAGUE

Complex Address: Scottsdale Stadium, 7408 East Osborn Rd, Scottsdale, AZ 85251. **Telephone:** (480) 990-7972. **Fax:** (480) 990-2643. **Seating Capacity:** 11,500. **Location:** Scottsdale Road to Osborne Road, east on Osborne for A 1/2 mile. **Hotel Address:** Hilton Garden Inn Scottsdale Old Town, 7324 East Indian School Rd, Scottsdale, AZ 85251. **Telephone:** (480) 481-0400.

MINOR LEAGUE

Complex Address: Giants Minor League Complex 8045 E Camelback Road, Scottsdale, AZ 85251. **Telephone:** (480) 990-0052. **Fax:** (480) 990-2349.

SEATTLE MARINERS

MAJOR LEAGUE

Complex Address: Seattle Mariners, 15707 North 83rd Street, Peoria, AZ 85382. **Telephone:** (623) 776-4800. **Fax:** (623) 776-4829. **Seating Capacity:** 12,339. **Location:** Hwy 101 to Bell Road exit, east on Bell to 83rd Ave, south on 83rd Ave. **Hotel Address:** La Quinta Inn & Suites, 16321 N 83rd Ave, Peoria, AZ 85382. **Telephone:** (623) 487-1900.

MINOR LEAGUE

Complex Address: Peoria Sports Complex (1993), 15707 N 83rd Ave, Peoria, AZ 85382. **Telephone:** (623) 776-4800. **Fax:** (623) 776-4828. **Hotel Address:** Hampton Inn, 8408 W Paradise Lane, Peoria, AZ 85382. **Telephone:** (623) 486-9918.

TEXAS RANGERS

MAJOR LEAGUE

Complex Address: Surprise Stadium, 15754 North Bullard Ave, Surprise, AZ 85374. **Telephone:** (623) 266-8100. **Seating Capacity:** 10,714. **Location:** I-10 West to Route 101 North, 101 North to Bell Road, left at Bell for seven miles, stadium on left. **Hotel Address:** Residence Inn Surprise, 16418 N Bullard Ave, Surprise, AZ 85374. **Telephone:** (623) 249-6333.

MINOR LEAGUE

Complex Address: Same as major league club. **Hotel Address:** Holiday Inn Express and Suites Surprise, 16549 North Bullard Ave, Surprise AZ 85374. **Telephone:** (800) 939-4249.

GRAPEFRUIT LEAGUE

For spring training schedules, see page 240

ATLANTA BRAVES

MAJOR LEAGUE
Stadium Address: Champion Stadium at ESPN Wide World of Sports Complex, 700 S Victory Way, Kissimmee, FL 34747. **Telephone:** (407) 939-1500.
Seating Capacity: 9,500. **Location:** I-4 to exit 25B (Highway 192 West), follow signs to Magic Kingdom/ Wide World of Sports Complex, right on Victory Way.
Hotel Address: World Center Marriott, World Center Drive, Orlando, FL 32821. **Telephone:** (407) 239-4200.

MINOR LEAGUE
Complex Address: Same as major league club. **Telephone:** (407) 939-2232. **Fax:** (407) 939-2225.
Hotel Address: Marriot Village at Lake Buena Vista, 8623 Vineland Ave, Orlando, FL 32821. **Telephone:** (407) 938-9001.

BALTIMORE ORIOLES

MAJOR LEAGUE
Complex Address: Ed Smith Stadium, 2700 12th Street, Sarasota, FL 34237. **Telephone:** (941) 893-6300. **Fax:** (941) 893-6377. **Seating Capacity:** 7,500. **Location:** I-75 to exit 210, West on Fruitville Road, right on Tuttle Avenue.

MINOR LEAGUE
Complex Address: Buck O'Neil Baseball Complex at Twin Lakes Park, 6700 Clark Rd, Sarasota, FL 34241. **Telephone:** (941) 923-1996.

BOSTON RED SOX

MAJOR LEAGUE
Complex Address: JetBlue Park at Fenway South, 11500 Fenway South Drive, Fort Myers, FL 33913.
Telephone: (239) 334-4700. **Directions: From the North:** Take I-75 South to Exit 131 (Daniels Parkway); Make a left off the exit and go east for approximately two miles; JetBlue Park will be on your left. **From the South:** Take I-75 North to Exit 131 (Daniels Parkway); Make a right off exit and go east for approximately two miles; JetBlue Park will be on your left.

MINOR LEAGUE
Complex/Hotel Address: Fenway South, 11500 Fenway South Drive, Fort Myers, FL 33913.

DETROIT TIGERS

MAJOR LEAGUE
Complex Address: Joker Marchant Stadium, 2301 Lakeland Hills Blvd, Lakeland, FL 33805. **Telephone:** (863) 686-8075. **Seating Capacity:** 9,000. **Location:** I-4 to exit 33 (Lakeland Hills Boulevard).

MINOR LEAGUE
Complex Address: Tigertown, 2125 N Lake Ave, Lakeland, FL 33805. **Telephone:** (863) 686-8075.

HOUSTON ASTROS

MAJOR LEAGUE
Complex Address: Osceola County Stadium, 631 Heritage Park Way, Kissimmee, FL 34744. **Telephone:** (321) 697-3200. **Fax:** (321) 697-3197. **Seating Capacity:** 5,300. **Location:** From Florida Turnpike South, take exit 244, west on US 192, right on Bill Bec... 'd. **Hotel Address:** Embassy Suites Orlando-Lak ...sta South, 4955 Kyngs Heath Rd, Kissim' **Telephone:** (407) 597-4000.

MINOR LEAGUE
Complex Information: Same as club. **Hotel Address:** Holiday Inn Ma ... 5711 W Irlo Bronson Memorial Hwy, Kissimn ... .746. **Telephone:** (407) 396-4222.

MIAMI MARLINS

MAJOR LEAGUE
Complex Address: Roger Dean Stadium, 4751 Main Street, Jupiter, FL 33458. **Telephone:** (561) 775-1818. **Telephone:** (561) 799-1346. **Seating Capacity:** 7,000. **Location:** I-95 to exit 83, east on Donald Ross Road for one mile to Central Blvd, left at light, follow Central Boulevard to circle and take Main Street to Roger Dean Stadium. **Hotel Address:** Palm Beach Gardens Marriott, 4000 RCA Boulevard, Palm Beach Gardens, FL 33410. **Telephone:** (561) 622-8888. **Fax:** (561) 622-0052.

MINOR LEAGUE
Complex/Hotel Address: Same as major league club.

MINNESOTA TWINS

MAJOR LEAGUE
Complex Address: Centurylink Sports Complex/ Hammond Stadium, 14100 Six Mile Cypress Parkway, Fort Myers, FL 33912. **Telephone:** (239) 533-7610. **Seating Capacity:** 8,100. **Location:** Exit 21 off I-75, west on Daniels Parkway, left on Six Mile Cypress Parkway. **Hotel Address:** Four Points by Sheraton, 13600 Treeline Avenue South, Ft. Myers, FL 33913. **Telephone:** (800) 338-9467.

MINOR LEAGUE
Complex/Hotel Address: Same as major league club.

NEW YORK METS

MAJOR LEAGUE
Complex Address: Tradition Field, 525 NW Peacock Blvd, Port St. Lucie, FL 34986. **Telephone:** (772) 871-2100. **Seating Capacity:** 7,000. **Location:** Exit 121C (St Lucie West Blvd) off I-95, east 1/4 mile, left onto NW Peacock. **Hotel Address:** Hilton Hotel, 8542 Commerce Centre Drive, Port St. Lucie, FL 34986. **Telephone:** (772) 871-6850.

MINOR LEAGUE
Complex Address: Same as major league club. **Hotel Address:** Main Stay Suites, 8501 Champions Way, Port St. Lucie, FL 34986. **Telephone:** (772) 460-8882.

NEW YORK YANKEES

MAJOR LEAGUE
Complex Address: George M. Steinbrenner Field, One Steinbrenner Drive, Tampa, FL 33614. **Telephone:** (813) 875-7753. **Seating Capacity:** 11,076. **Hotel:** Unavailable.

MINOR LEAGUE
Complex Address: Yankees Player Development/ Scouting Complex, 3102 N Himes Ave, Tampa, FL 33607. **Telephone:** (813) 875-7569. **Hotel:** Unavailable.

PHILADELPHIA PHILLIES

MAJOR LEAGUE
Complex Address: Bright House Networks Field, 601 North Old Coachman Road, Clearwater, FL 33765. **Telephone:** (727) 467-4457. **Fax:** (727) 712-4498. **Seating Capacity:** 8,500. **Location:** Route 60 West, right on Old Coachman Road, ballpark on right after Drew Street. **Hotel Address:** Holiday Inn Express, 2580 Gulf to Bay Blvd, Clearwater, FL 33765. **Telephone:** (727) 797-6300. **Hotel Address:** La Quinta Inn, 21338 US 19 North, Clearwater, FL 33765. **Telephone:** (727) 799-1565.

MINOR LEAGUE
Complex Address: Carpenter Complex, 651 N Old Coachman Rd, Clearwater, FL 33765. **Telephone:** (727) 799-0503. **Fax:** (727) 726-1793. **Hotel Addresses:** Hampton Inn, 21030 US Highway 19 North, Clearwater, FL 34625. **Telephone:** (727) 797-8173. **Hotel Address:** Econolodge, 21252 US Hwy 19, Clearwater, FL 34625. **Telephone:** (727) 799-1569.

PITTSBURGH PIRATES

MAJOR LEAGUE
Stadium Address: McKechnie Field, 17th Ave West and Ninth Street West, Bradenton, FL 34205. **Seating Capacity:** 8,500. **Location:** US 41 to 17th Ave, west to 9th Street. **Telephone:** (941) 747-3031. **Fax:** (941) 747-9549.

MINOR LEAGUE
Complex: Pirate City, 1701 27th St E, Bradenton, FL 34208.

ST. LOUIS CARDINALS

MAJOR LEAGUE
Complex Address: Roger Dean Stadium, 4751 Main Street, Jupiter, FL 33458. **Telephone:** (561) 775-1818. **Fax:** (561) 799-1380. **Seating Capacity:** 7,000. **Location:** I-95 to exit 58, east on Donald Ross Road for 1/4 mile. **Hotel Address:** Embassy Suites, 4350 PGA Blvd, Palm Beach Gardens, FL 33410. **Telephone:** (561) 622-1000.

MINOR LEAGUE
Complex: Same as major league club. **Hotel:** Double Tree Palm Beach Gardens. **Telephone:** (561) 622-2260.

TAMPA BAY RAYS

MAJOR LEAGUE
Stadium Address: Charlotte Sports Park, 2300 El Jobean Road, Port Charlotte, FL 33948. **Telephone:** (941) 206-4487. **Seating Capacity:** 6,823 (5,028 fixed seats). **Location:** I-75 to US-17 to US-41, turn left onto El Jobean Rd. **Hotel Address:** None.

MINOR LEAGUE
Complex/Hotel Address: None.

TORONTO BLUE JAYS

MAJOR LEAGUE
Stadium Address: Florida Auto Exchange Stadium, 373 Douglas Ave, Dunedin, FL 34698. **Telephone:** (727) 733-9302. **Seating Capacity:** 5,509. **Location:** US 19 North to Sunset Point; west on Sunset Point to Douglas Avenue; north on Douglas to Stadium; ballpark is on the southeast corner of Douglas and Beltrees.

MINOR LEAGUE
Complex Address: Bobby Mattick Training Center at Englebert Complex, 1700 Solon Ave, Dunedin, FL 34698. **Telephone:** (727) 734-8007. **Hotel Address:** Clarion Inn & Suites, 20967 US Highway 19 North Clearwater, FL 33765. **Telephone:** (727) 799-1181.

WASHINGTON NATIONALS

MAJOR LEAGUE
Complex Address: Space Coast Stadium, 5800 Stadium Parkway, Melbourne, FL 32940. **Telephone:** (321) 633-9200. **Seating Capacity:** 8,100. **Location:** I-95 southbound to Fiske Blvd (exit 74), south on Fiske/ Stadium Parkway to stadium; I-95 northbound to State Road #509/Wickham Road (exit 73), left off exit, right on Lake Andrew Drive; turn right on Stadium Parkway, stadium is 1/2 mile on left. **Hotel Address:** Hampton Inn, 130 Sheriff Drive, Viera, FL. **Telephone:** (321) 255-6868.

MINOR LEAGUE
Complex Address: Carl Barger Complex, 5600 Stadium Pkwy, Melbourne, FL 32940. **Telephone:** (321) 633-8119. **Hotel:** Same as major league club.

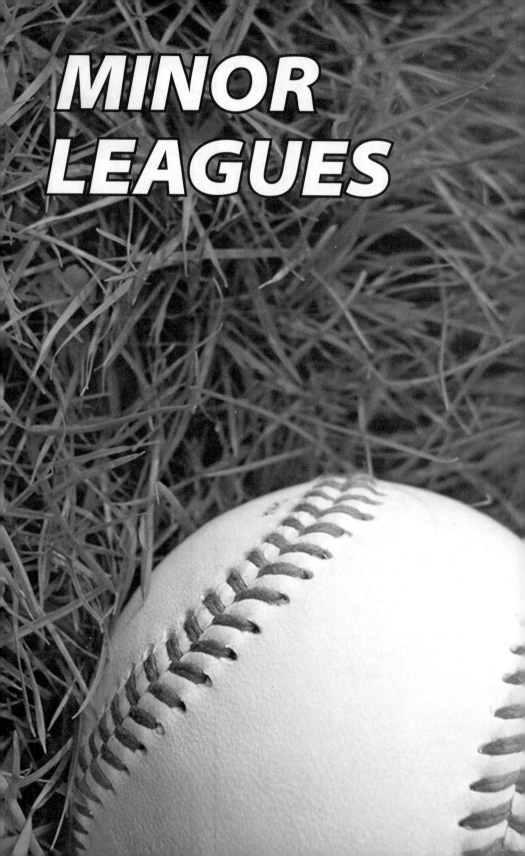

MINOR
LEAGUES

MINOR LEAGUE BASEBALL

THE NATIONAL ASSOCIATION OF PROFESSIONAL BASEBALL LEAGUES

Street Address: 9550 16th St. North, St. Petersburg, FL 33716. **Mailing Address:** PO Box A, St. Petersburg, FL 33731-1950. **Telephone:** (727) 822-6937. **Fax:** (727) 821-5819. **Fax/Marketing:** (727) 894-4227. **Fax/Licensing:** (727) 825-3785. **President/CEO:** Pat O'Conner.

MINOR LEAGUE BASEBALL ™

Vice President: Stan Brand. **Chief Operating Officer:** Brian Earle. **Chief Financial Officer:** Sean Brown. **Chief Marketing & Commercial Officer:** David Wright.

Pat O'Conner

Senior VP, Legal Affairs/General Counsel: Scott Poley. **Special Counsel:** George Yund. **VP, Baseball/Business Operations:** Tim Brunswick.

VP, Marketing Strategy: Kurt Hunzeker. **VP, National/Regional Sales:** Rod Meadows. **Senior Director, Communications:** Jeff Lantz. **Director, Digital Properties:** Stefanie Loncarich. **Director, Information Technology:** Rob Colamarino. **Director, Security/Facility Operations:** Earnell Lucas. **Director, Licensing:** Sandie Hebert. **Director, Business Development:** Scott Kravchuk. **Assistant Director, Legal Affairs:** Louis Brown. **Manager, Baseball Operations/Executive Assistant to the President:** Mary Wooters. **Controller:** James Dispanet. **Senior Assistant Director, Event Services:** Kelly Butler. **Assistant Director, Licensing:** Carrie Adams. **Assistant Director, Legal Affairs:** Louis Brown. **Assistant Director, Business Development:** Courtney Jantz. **Assistant Director, Corporate Communications:** Mary Marandi. **Assistant Director, Account Services:** Heather Raburn. **Associate Counsel:** Robert Fountain. **Manager, Human Resources:** Amber Kukulya. **Manager, Baseball/Business Operations:** Andy Shultz. **Manager, Business Development:** Mark Labban. **Contract Manager/Legal Assistant:** Jeannette Machicote. **Manager, Sales/Account Services:** Gabe Rendon. **Manager, Trade Show Services:** Eileen Sahin-Murphy. **Manager, Strategy/Analytics:** Cory Bernstine. **Graphic Designer:** Ashley Allphin. **Senior Accountant:** Michelle Heystek. **Coordinator, Licensing/Contracts:** Jessica Merrick. **Coordinator, E-Commerce/Business Services:** Jill Philippi. **Coordinator, Trademarks/Intellectual Properties:** Jess Schneider. **Receptionist:** Kim Bradbury.

AFFILIATED MEMBERS/COUNCIL OF LEAGUE PRESIDENTS

Triple-A

League	President	Telephone	Fax Number
International	Randy Mobley	(614) 791-9300	(614) 791-9009
Mexican	Plinio Escalante	011-52-555-557-1007	011-52-555-395-2454
Pacific Coast	Branch Rickey	(512) 310-2900	(512) 310-8300

Double-A

League	President	Telephone	Fax Number
Eastern	Joe McEacharn	(207) 761-2700	(207) 761-7064
Southern	Lori Webb	(770) 321-0400	(770) 321-0037
Texas	Tom Kayser	(210) 545-5297	(210) 545-5298

High Class A

League	President	Telephone	Fax Number
California	Charlie Blaney	(805) 985-8585	(805) 985-8580
Carolina	John Hopkins	(336) 691-9030	(336) 464-2737
Florida State	Ken Carson	(727) 224-8244	(386) 252-7495

Low Class A

League	President	Telephone	Fax Number
Midwest	Dick Nussbaum	(574) 231-3000	(574) 231-3000
South Atlantic	Eric Krupa	(727) 538-4270	(727) 499-6853

Short-Season

League	President	Telephone	Fax Number
New York-Penn	Ben Hayes	(727) 289-7112	(727) 683-9691
Northwest	Mike Ellis	(406) 541-9301	(406) 543-9463

Rookie Advanced

League	President	Telephone	Fax Number
Appalachian	Lee Landers	(704) 252-2656	Unavailable
Pioneer	Jim McCurdy	(509) 456-7615	(509) 456-0136

Rookie

League	President	Telephone	Fax Number
Arizona	Bob Richmond	(208) 429-1511	(208) 429-1525
Dominican Summer	Orlando Diaz	(809) 532-3619	(809) 532-3619
Gulf Coast	Operated by MiLB	(727) 456-1734	(727) 821-5819

NATIONAL ASSOCIATION BOARD OF TRUSTEES

TRIPLE-A
At-large: Ken Young (Norfolk). **International League:** Ken Schnacke, Vice Chairman (Columbus). **Pacific Coast League:** Sam Bernabe, Chairman (Iowa). **Mexican League:** Chito Rodriguez (Quintana Roo).

DOUBLE-A
Eastern League: Joe Finley (Trenton). **Southern League:** Stan Logan, Secretary (Birmingham). **Texas League:** Reid Ryan (Corpus Christi).

CLASS A
California League: Tom Volpe (Stockton). **Carolina League:** Chuck Greenberg (Myrtle Beach). **Florida State League:** Ron Myers (Lakeland).
Midwest League: Tom Dickson (Lansing). **South Atlantic League:** Chip Moore (Rome).

SHORT-SEASON
New York-Penn League: Marv Goldklang (Hudson Valley). **Northwest League:** Bobby Brett (Spokane).

ROOKIE
Appalachian League: Mitch Lukevics (Princeton). **Pioneer League:** Dave Elmore, (Idaho Falls). **Gulf Coast League:** Bill Smith (Twins).

PROFESSIONAL BASEBALL UMPIRE CORP.
President/CEO: Pat O'Conner.
Secretary/Vice President, Legal Affairs/General Counsel: Scott Poley.
Director, MiLBUD: Dusty Dellinger. **Chief, Instruction/MiLBUD Evaluator:** Mike Felt. **Field Evaluators/Instructors:** Jorge Bauza, Tyler Funneman, Mark Lollo, Larry Reveal, Brian Sinclair, Darren Spagnardi. **Medical Coordinator:** Mark Stubblefield. **Special Assistant, MiLBUD:** Lillian Patterson.

GENERAL INFORMATION

			Regular Season		All-Star Games	
	Teams	Games	Opening Day	Closing Day	Date	Host
International	14	144	April 7	Sept. 5	*July 13	Charlotte
Pacific Coast	16	144	April 7	Sept. 5	*July 13	Charlotte
Eastern	12	142	April 7	Sept. 5	July 13	Akron
Southern	10	140	April 7	Sept. 5	June 21	Mississippi
Texas	8	140	April 7	Sept. 5	June 28	Springfield
California	10	140	April 7	Sept. 5	#June 21	Lake Elsinore
Carolina	8	140	April 7	Sept. 5	#June 21	Lake Elsinore
Florida State	12	140	April 7	Sept. 4	June 18	Fort Myers
Midwest	16	140	April 7	Sept. 5	June 21	Cedar Rapids
South Atlantic	14	140	April 7	Sept. 5	June 21	Lexington
New York-Penn	14	76	June 17	Sept. 5	Aug. 16	Hudson Valley
Northwest	8	76	June 17	Sept. 5	^Aug. 2	Ogden
Appalachian	10	68	June 23	Sept. 1	None	
Pioneer	8	76	June 17	Sept. 8	^Aug. 4	Ogden
Arizona	TBD	56	June 20	Aug. 29	None	
Gulf Coast	17	60	June 24	Sept. 1	None	

*Triple-A All-Star Game. #California League vs. Carolina League. ^Northwest League vs. Pioneer League.

INTERNATIONAL LEAGUE

Address: 55 South High St., Suite 202, Dublin, Ohio 43017.
Telephone: (614) 791-9300. **Fax:** (614) 791-9009.
E-Mail Address: office@ilbaseball.com. **Website:** www.ilbaseball.com.
Years League Active: 1884-

President/Treasurer: Randy Mobley.
Vice President: Dave Rosenfield. **League Administrator:** Chris Sprague. **Corporate Secretary:** Max Schumacher.
Directors: Don Beaver (Charlotte), Bill Dutch (Syracuse), Joe Finley (Lehigh Valley), George Habel (Durham), Erik Ibsen (Toledo), North Johnson (Gwinnett), Stuart Katzoff (Louisville), Bob Rich Jr. (Buffalo), Dave Rosenfield (Norfolk), Jeremy Ruby (Scranton/Wilkes-Barre), Ken Schnacke (Columbus), Max Schumacher (Indianapolis), Naomi Silver (Rochester), Mike Tamburro (Pawtucket). **Office Manager:** Gretchen Addison.
Division Structure: North-Buffalo, Lehigh Valley, Pawtucket, Rochester, Scranton/Wilkes-Barre, Syracuse. West-Columbus, Indianapolis, Louisville, Toledo. South-Charlotte, Durham, Gwinnett, Norfolk.
Regular Season: 144 games. **2015 Opening Date:** April 7. **Closing Date:** Sept 5.
All-Star Game: July 13 at Charlotte (IL vs Pacific Coast League).

Randy Mobley

Playoff Format: South winner meets West winner in best of five series; wild card (non-division winner with best winning percentage) meets North winner in best of five series. Winners meet in best-of-five series for Governors' Cup championship.
Triple-A Championship Game: Sept. 20 at Memphis (IL vs Pacific Coast League).
Roster Limit: 25. **Player Eligibility:** No restrictions.
Official Baseball: Rawlings ROM-INT.
Umpires: Joey Amaral (Baltimore, MD), John Bacon (Sherrodsville, OH), Jonathan Bailey (Lithia Springs, GA), Sean Barber (Lakeland, FL), Toby Basner (Snellville, GA), Joe Born (Lafayette, IN), Ryan Clark (McDonough, GA), Clint Fagan (Tomball, TX), Eric Gillam (Roscoe, IL), Max Guyll (Fort Wayne,IN), Adam Hamari (Marquette, MI), Nic Lentz (Holland, MI), Shane Livensparger (Jacksonville Beach, FL), Ben May (Racine, WI), Matt McCoy (Ellis Grove, IL), Daniel Merzel (Hopkinton, MA), Derek Mollica (Lake Worth, FL), Robert Moreno (Cumana, Venezuela), Roberto Ortiz (Orlando, FL), Jeremie Rehak (Monroesville, PA), Jeremy Riggs (Suffolk, VA), Chris Segal (Burke, VA), Carlos Torres (Acarigua, Venezuela), John Tumpane (Chicago, IL), Jansen Visconti (Latrobe, PA), Chad Whitson (Dublin, OH).

STADIUM INFORMATION

Club	Stadium	Opened	Dimensions LF	CF	RF	Capacity	2015 Att.
Buffalo	Coca-Cola Field	1988	325	404	325	18,025	551.303
Charlotte	BB&T Ballpark	2015	325	400	315	10,002	669,398
Columbus	Huntington Park	2009	325	400	318	10,100	622,096
Durham	Durham Bulls Athletic Park	1995	305	400	327	10,000	554,788
Gwinnett	Coolray Field	2009	335	400	335	10,427	270,336
Indianapolis	Victory Field	1996	320	402	320	14,500	662,536
Lehigh Valley	Coca-Cola Park	2008	336	400	325	10,000	613,815
Louisville	Louisville Slugger Field	2000	325	400	340	13,131	527,588
Norfolk	Harbor Park	1993	333	400	318	12,067	386,402
Pawtucket	McCoy Stadium	1946	325	400	325	10,031	466,600
Rochester	Frontier Field	1997	335	402	325	10,840	440,360
Scranton/WB	PNC Field	2013	330	408	330	10,000	402,731
Syracuse	NBT Bank Stadium	1997	330	400	330	11,671	262,408
Toledo	Fifth Third Field	2002	320	408	315	10,300	531,249

BUFFALO BISONS

Address: Coca-Cola Field, One James D. Griffin Plaza, Buffalo, NY 14203.
Telephone: (716) 846-2000. **Fax:** (716) 852-6530.
E-Mail Address: info@bisons.com. **Website:** www.bisons.com.
Affiliation (first year): Toronto Blue Jays (2013). **Years in League:** 1886-90, 1912-70, 1998-

OWNERSHIP/MANAGEMENT

Operated By: Rich Products Corp. **Principal Owner/President:** Robert Rich Jr. **President, Rich Entertainment Group:** Melinda Rich. **Vice President/Chief Operating Officer, Rich Entertainment Group:** Joseph Segarra. **President, Rich Baseball Operations:** Jon Dandes.
VP/General Manager: Mike Buczkowski. **VP/Secretary:** William Gisel. **Corporate Counsel:** Jill Bond, William Grieshober. **Director, Sales:** Anthony Sprague. **Director, Stadium Operations:** Tom Sciarrino. **Controller:** Kevin Parkinson. **Senior Accountants:** Chas Fiscella. **Accountants:** Amy Delaney, Tori Dwyer. **Director, Ticket Operations:**

Mike Poreda. **Director, Public Relations:** Brad Bisbing. **Director, Entertainment/Marketing Services:** Matt La Sota. **Creative Services/Website Marketing Coordinator:** Ashley Whitehead. **Director, Corporate Sales:** Jim Harrington. **Group Sales Manager:** Geoff Lundquist. **Sponsorship/Promotions Coordinator:** Mike Simoncelli. **Sales Coordinators:** Rachel Osucha. **Account Executives:** Mark Gordon, Nick Iacona, Robert Kates, Burt Mirti, Beth Potozniak. **Manager, Merchandise:** Victoria Rebmann. **Manager, Office Services:** Margaret Russo. **Executive Assistant:** Tina Lesher. **Community Relations:** Gail Hodges. **Director, Food Services:** Robert Free. **General Manager, Food Service Operations:** Sean Regan. **Food Service Operations Supervisor:** Curt Anderson. **Head Groundskeeper:** Chad Laurie. **Chief Engineer:** Pat Chella. **Home Clubhouse/Baseball Operations Coordinator:** Scott Lesher. **Visiting Clubhouse Manager:** Steve Morris.

FIELD STAFF

Manager: Gary Allenson. **Hitting Coach:** Richie Hebner. **Pitching Coach:** Bob Stanley. **Athletic Trainer:** Voon Chong. **Strength/Conditioning Coach:** Jason Dowse.

GAME INFORMATION

Radio Announcers: Ben Wagner, Duke McGuire. **No of Games Broadcast:** 144. **Flagship Station:** ESPN 1520. **PA Announcer:** Jerry Reo, Tom Burns. **Official Scorers:** Kevin Lester, Jon Dare.
Stadium Name: Coca-Cola Field. **Location:** From north, take I-190 to Elm Street exit, left onto Swan Street; From east, take I-190 West to exit 51 (Route 33) to end, exit at Oak Street, right onto Swan Street; From west, take I-190 East, exit 53 to I-90 North, exit at Elm Street, left onto Swan Street. **Standard Game Times:** 7:05 pm, Sun 1:05. **Ticket Price Range:** $9-15.
Visiting Club Hotel: Adams Mark, 120 Church St, Buffalo, NY 14202. **Telephone:** (716) 845-5100.

CHARLOTTE KNIGHTS

Address: BB&T Ballpark, 324 S. Mint St., Charlotte, NC 28202.
Telephone: (704) 274-8300. **Fax:** 704-274-8330.
E-Mail Address: knights@charlotteknights.com. **Website:** www.charlotteknights.com.
Affiliation (first year): Chicago White Sox (1999). **Years in League:** 1993-

OWNERSHIP/MANAGEMENT

Operated by: Knights Baseball, LLC. **Principal Owners:** Don Beaver, Bill Allen.
Executive Vice President/Chief Operating Officer: Dan Rajkowski. **General Manager, Baseball Operations:** Scotty Brown. **VP, Marketing:** Mark Smith. **VP, Sales:** Chris Semmens. **Director, Special Programs/Events:** Julie Clark. **Director, PR/Media Relations:** Tommy Viola. **Director, Broadcasting/Team Travel:** Matt Swierad. **Business Manager:** Michael Sanger. **Director, Stadium Operations:** Mark McKinnon. **Facility Manager:** Tom Gorter. **Merchandise Manager:** Ryan Petrere. **Director, Ticket Sales/Operations:** Matt Millward. **Director, Community/Team Relations:** Lindsey Roycraft. **Video Director:** David Ruckman. **Assistant Director, Video Production:** Drew DeMarcantonio. **Creative Director:** Bill Walker. **Promotions Manager:** Philip Norvell. **Entertainment Specialist:** Brittany Egan. **Corporate Sales Executives:** Jeremy Auker, Damon Roschke. **Director, Group Sales:** Kathryn Bobel. **Director, Season Ticket Sales:** Brett Butler. **Season Ticket Sales Representatives:** Brandon Batts, David Burns, Ian Holmes. **Group Sales Representatives:** J.J. Briceno, Kevin Hughes. **Ticket Operations Assistant:** Jonathan English. **Special Events Manager:** Katherine Anderson. **Premium Services Manager:** Bess LaMay. **Partnership Services Coordinator:** Ashley Warshauer. **Head Groundskeeper:** Eddie Busque. **Stadium Operations Associate:** Nick Braun. **Front Desk Receptionist:** Megan Smithers.

FIELD STAFF

Manager: Julio Vinas. **Pitching Coach:** Richard Dotson. **Hitting Coach:** Andy Tomberlin. **Coach:** Tim Esmay. **Trainer:** Scott Johnson. **Conditioning:** Shawn Powell.

GAME INFORMATION

Radio Announcers: Matt Swierad, Mike Pacheco. **No. of Games Broadcast:** 144. **Flagship Station:** ESPN 730 AM. **PA Announcer: Official Scorers:** Jerry Bowers, Dave Friedman, Karl Lyles, David McDowell.
Stadium Name: BB&T. **Ballpark Location:** Exit 10 off Interstate 77. **Ticket Price Range:** $8-$19.
Visiting Club Hotel: Doubletree by Hilton Charlotte, 895 W. Trade St., Charlotte, NC 28202.

COLUMBUS CLIPPERS

Address: 330 Huntington Park Lane, Columbus, OH 43215.
Telephone: (614) 462-5250. **Fax:** (614) 462-3271. **Tickets:** (614) 462-2757.
E-Mail Address: info@clippersbaseball.com. **Website:** www.clippersbaseball.com.
Affiliation (first year): Cleveland Indians (2009). **Years in League:** 1955-70, 1977-

OWNERSHIP/MANAGEMENT

Operated By: Columbus Baseball Team Inc. **Principal Owner:** CBT Inc. **Board of Directors:** Steven Francis, Tom Fries, Wayne Harer, Thomas Katzenmeyer, David Leland, Cathy Lyttle, Gary Schaeffer, Jeffrey Sopp, McCullough Williams.
President/General Manager: Ken Schnacke. **Assistant GM:** Mark Warren. **Director, Ballpark Operations:** Steve Dalin. **Assistant Director, Ballpark Operations:** Tom Rinto. **Director, Ticket Operations:** Scott Ziegler. **Assistant**

BaseballAmerica.com   Baseball America 2016 Directory • **93**

Director, Ticket Operations: Eddie Langhenry. **Assistant Directors, Ticket Sales:** Kevin Daniels, George Robinson. **Director, Marketing/Sales:** Mark Galuska. **Assistant Director, Marketing:** Emily Poynter. **Assistant Director, Sales:** Chelsea Gilman.

    Director, Promotions/In-Game Entertainment: Seth Rhodes. **Assistant Director, Promotions/Mascots:** Steve Kuilder. **Director, Communications/Media/Historian:** Joe Santry. **Assistant Director, Media Relations/Statistics:** Anthony Slosser. **Director, Social Media/Website Communication:** Matt Leininger. **Directors, Broadcasting:** Ryan Mitchell, Scott Leo. **Director, Merchandising:** Krista Oberlander. **Assistant Director, Merchandising:** Eric Dameron. **Director, Group Sales:** Ben Keller. **Assistant Directors, Group Sales:** Kevin Smith, Robert Freese. **Director, Multimedia:** Larry Mitchell. **Assistant Directors, Multimedia:** Yoshi Ando, Pat Welch. **Director, Finance/ Administration:** Bonnie Badgley. **Assistant Director, Finance:** Ashley Ramirez. **Executive Assistant to President/GM:** Ashley Held.

    Office Manager: Melissa Schrader. **Director, Sponsor Relationships:** Joyce Martin. **Director, Event Planning:** Micki Shier. **Assistant Director, Event Planning/Catering/Suites:** Shannon O'Boyle. **Clubhouse Manager:** Matt Pruzinsky. **Ballpark Superintendent:** Gary Delozier. **Head Groundskeeper:** Wes Ganobcik.

FIELD STAFF

    Field Manager: Chris Tremie. **Pitching Coach:** Steve Karsay. **Hitting Coach:** Rouglas Odor. **Trainer:** Chad Wolfe. **Strength/Conditioning Coach:** Ed Subel.

GAME INFORMATION

    Radio Announcers: Ryan Mitchell, Scott Leo. **No of Games Broadcast:** 144. **Flagship Station:** WMNI 920 AM. **PA Announcer:** Matt Leininger. **Official Scorer:** Jim Habermehl, Ray Thomas, Ty Debevoise and Paul Pennell.

    Stadium Name: Huntington Park. **Location:** From north: South on I-71 to I-670 west, exit at Neil Avenue, turn left at intersection onto Neil Avenue; From south: North on I-71, exit at Front Street (#100A), turn left at intersection onto Front Street, turn left onto Nationwide Blvd; From east: West on I-70, exit at Fourth Street, continue on Fulton Street to Front Street, turn right onto Front Street, turn left onto Nationwide Blvd; From west: East on I-70, exit at Fourth Street, continue on Fulton Street to Front Street, turn right onto Front Street, turn left onto Nationwide Blvd. **Ticket Price Range:** $4-20.

    Visiting Club Hotel: Crowne Plaza, 33 East Nationwide Blvd, Columbus, OH 43215. **Telephone:** (877) 348-2424. **Visiting Club Hotel:** Drury Hotels Columbus Convention Center, 88 East Nationwide Blvd, Columbus, OH 43215. **Telephone:** (614) 221-7008. **Visiting Club Hotel:** Hyatt Regency Downtown, 350 North High Street, Columbus, OH 43215. **Telephone:** (614) 463-1234.

DURHAM BULLS

    Office Address: 409 Blackwell St., Durham, NC 27701. **Mailing Address:** PO Box 507, Durham, NC 27702

    Telephone: (919) 687-6500. **Fax:** (919) 687-6560.

    Website: durhambulls.com. **Twitter:** @DurhamBulls

    Affiliation (first year): Tampa Bay Rays (1998). **Years in League:** 1998-

OWNERSHIP/MANAGEMENT

    Operated By: Capitol Broadcasting Company, Inc.

    President/CEO: Jim Goodmon. **Vice President:** George Habel.

    General Manager: Mike Birling. **Director, Corporate Partnerships:** Chip Allen. **Director, Ticket Sales:** Peter Wallace. **Director, Promotions:** Krista Boyd. **Director, Food and Beverage:** Dave Levey. **Director, Stadium Operations:** Scott Strickland. **Director, Merchandise/Team Travel:** Bryan Wilson. **Director, Communications:** Matt Sutor. **Business Manager:** Rhonda Carlile. **Accounting Supervisor:** Theresa Stocking. **Staff Accountant:** Alicia McMillen. **Receptionist:** Natasha Jessup. **Manager, Corporate Partnerships:** Morgan Weber. **Senior Sponsorship Account Executive:** Nick Bavin. **Sponsorship Account Executives:** Andrew Ferrier, Patrick Kinas, Jenn Paonessa. **Head Groundskeeper, DBAP:** Cameron Brendle. **Multimedia Manager:** Walmer Medina. **Mascot/Community Relations Coordinator:** Nicholas Tennant. **Production Designer:** Bryan Smith. **Group Sales Manager:** Brian Simorka. **Premium Ticket Sales Manager:** Eli Starkey. **Corporate Sales Executives:** Brandon Cates, Michele Fox, Chris Jones, Sol Prensky. **Assistant Managers, Group Sales:** Aaron Edgell, Cassie Fowler. **Inside Sales Consultants:** Melissa Balbach, Bryant Strader. **Box Office Manager:** Daniel Nobles. **Concessions Manager:** Todd Feneley. **Catering Manager:** Erin Swanson. **Operations Managers:** Cortlund Beneke, Roger Rose. **Manager, Home Clubhouse:** Colin Saunders. **Manager, Visiting Clubhouse:** Aaron Kuehner. **Team Ambassador:** Bill Law.

FIELD STAFF

    Manager: Jared Sandberg. **Hitting Coach:** Ozzie Timmons. **Pitching Coach:** Kyle Snyder. **Athletic Trainer:** Mike Sandoval. **Strength and Conditioning Coach:** Bryan King.

GAME INFORMATION

    Broadcasters: Patrick Kinas, Scott Pose. **No. of Games Broadcast:** 144. **Flagship Station:** 96.5 FM and 99.3 FM **PA Announcer:** Tony Riggsbee. **Official Scorer:** Brent Belvin.

    Stadium Name: Durham Bulls Athletic Park. **Location:** From Raleigh, I-40 West to Highway 147 North, exit 12B to Willard, two blocks on Willard to stadium; From I-85, Gregson Street exit to downtown, left on Chapel Hill Street, right on Mangum Street. **Standard Game Times:** 7:05 pm, Sunday 5:05. **Ticket Price Range:** $7-14.

    Visiting Club Hotel: Hilton Durham Near Duke University; 3800 Hillsborough Road, Durham, NC 27705. **Telephone:** (919) 383-8033.

GWINNETT BRAVES

Office Address: 2500 Buford Drive, Lawrenceville, GA 30043. Mailing Address: P.O. Box 490310, Lawrenceville, GA 30049.
Telephone: (678) 277-0300. Fax: (678) 277-0338.
E-Mail Address: gwinnettinfo@braves.com. Website: www.gwinnettbraves.com.
Affiliation (first year): Atlanta Braves (1966). Years in League: 1884, 1915-17, 1954-64, 1966-

OWNERSHIP/MANAGEMENT

General Manager: North Johnson. Assistant GM: Shari Massengill. Office Manager: Tyra Williams. Manager, Corporate Partnerships: Ande Sadtler. Corporate Partnerships Account Representative: Aaron Morrison. Partnership Services Coordinator: Halle Machitar. Director, Ticket Sales: Todd Pund. Assistant Ticket Sales Manager: Jerry Pennington. Sr. Ticket Operations Coordinator: Julian Perez-Dowdy. Account Executives: Andrew Behr, Malcolm Chapman, Erik Holst, Josh Wilson, Jason Wright. Media Relations Manager: Dave Lezotte. Community Affairs and Promotions Coordinator: Jillian Ward. Game Entertainment Manager: Chris Jones. Creative Services Coordinator: Casey Comeaux. Director, Stadium Operations: Ryan Stoltenberg. Stadium Operations Coordinator: Rick Fultz. Facilities Engineer: Gary Hoopaugh. Director, Sports Turf Management: Chris Ball. Team Store Manager: Mary Lupoli. Clubhouse Manager: Nick Dixon.

FIELD STAFF

Manager: Brian Snitker. Pitching Coach: Marty Reed. Hitting Coach: John Moses. Trainer: Ricky Alcantara.

GAME INFORMATION

Radio Announcer: Tony Schiavone. No. of Games Broadcast: 144. Flagship Station: 97.7 FM.
PA Announcer: Kevin Kraus. Official Scorers: Guy Curtright, Jack Woodard, Tim Gaines.
Stadium Name: Coolray Field. Location: I-85 (at Exit 115, State Road 20 West) and I-985 (at Exit 4), follow signs to park. Ticket Price Range: $6-40.
Visiting Club Hotel: Courtyard by Marriott Buford/Mall of Georgia, 1405 Mall of Georgia Boulevard, Buford, GA 30519. Telephone: (678) 215-8007.

INDIANAPOLIS INDIANS

Address: 501 W Maryland Street, Indianapolis, IN 46225.
Telephone: (317) 269-3542. Fax: (317) 269-3541.
E-Mail Address: Indians@IndyIndians.com. Website: www.indyindians.com.
Affiliation (first year): Pittsburgh Pirates (2005). Years in League: 1963, 1998-

OWNERSHIP/MANAGEMENT

Operated By: Indians Inc. President/Chairman of the Board: Max Schumacher.
Vice President, Baseball/Administrative Affairs: Cal Burleson. General Manager: Randy Lewandowski. VP, Corporate Affairs: Bruce Schumacher. Director, Business Operations: Brad Morris. Voice of the Indians: Howard Kellman. Director, Corporate Sales/Marketing: Joel Zawacki. Director, Merchandising: Mark Schumacher. Director, Facilities: Tim Hughes. Director, Tickets/Operations: Matt Guay. Senior Manager, Communications/Retail: Jon Glesing. Senior Manager, Ticket/Premium Services: Kerry Vick.
Office Manager: Julie Rumschlag. Manager, Community Relations/Promotions: Brian McLaughlin. Manager, Telecast/Productions: Scott Templin. Manager, Marketing: Kim Stoebick. Manager, Creative Services: Adam Pintar. Manager, IT: Sean Couse. Manager, Stadium Maintenance: Allan Danehy. Manager, Operations: Andrew Jackson. Manager, Facilities: Matt Rapp. Manager, Ticket Sales: Chad Bohm. Manager, Ticket Services/Internship Coordinator: Bryan Spisak. Coordinator, Community Relations/Promotions: Chelsea Lowman. Coordinator, Media/Communications: Ryan Sheets. Coordinators, Partnership Activation: Kylie Iadicicco, Hayden Hammersley. Sponsorship Sales Account Executives: Chris Inderstrodt, Christina Toler. Marketing/Design Specialist: Whitney Alderson. Graphic Designer: Jessica Davis. Senior Ticket Sales Executives: Ryan Barrett, Jonathan Howard. Sponsorship Sales Account Executive: Nathan Butler. Ticket Sales Executives: Noelle Cook, Ty Eaton, Alex Moormeier. Garrett Rosh. Premium Service/Events Coordinator: Sarah McKinney. Merchandise Coordinator: Katarina Burns. Operations Support: Ricky Floyd, Sandra Johnson. Head Groundskeeper: Joey Stevenson. Assistant Groundskeeper: Adam Basinger. ARAMARK General Manager: Chris Scherrer. Home Clubhouse Manager: Bob Martin. Visiting Clubhouse Manager: Jeremy Martin. Guest Relations Coordinator: Eddie Acheson.

FIELD STAFF

Manager: Dean Treanor. Hitting Coach: Butch Wynegar. Pitching Coach: Stan Kyles. Trainer: Lee Slagle. Strength/Conditioning Coach: Furey Leva.

GAME INFORMATION

Radio Announcers: Howard Kellman, Andrew Kappes. Flagship Station: Fox Sports 97.5 FM/1260 AM.
PA Announcer: David Pygman. Official Scorers: Bill McAfee, Bill Potter, Kim Rogers, Ed Holdaway.
Stadium Name: Victory Field. Location: I-70 to West Street exit, north on West Street to ballpark; I-65 to Martin Luther King and West Street exit, south on West Street to ballpark. Standard Game Times: 7:05 pm; 1:35 (Wed/Sun), 7:15 (Fri). Ticket Price Range: $10-16.
Visiting Club Hotel: Comfort Suites, 515 S. West Street, Indianapolis, IN 46225. Telephone: (317) 631-9000.

LEHIGH VALLEY IRONPIGS

Address: 1050 IronPigs Way, Allentown, PA 18109.
Telephone: (610) 841-7447. **Fax:** (610) 841-1509.
E-Mail Address: info@ironpigsbaseball.com. **Website:** www.ironpigsbaseball.com.
Affiliation (first year): Philadelphia Phillies (2008). **Years in League:** 2008-

OWNERSHIP/MANAGEMENT

Ownership: LV Baseball LP. **President/General Manager:** Kurt Landes.
Assistant GM: Howard Scharf. **Vice President, Media/Communications:** Jon Schaeffer. **Vice President, Marketing/ Entertainment:** Lindsey Knupp. **Director, Media Relations:** Matt Provence. **Media Relations Assistant:** Joe Fitzhenry. **Director, Community Relations:** Dana DeFilippo. **Manager, Community Relations:** Hannah Ishida. **Director, Merchandise:** Unavailable. **Merchandise Associate:** Kesha Patterson. **Director, Ticket Sales:** Scott Evans. **Director, Group Sales:** Don Wilson. **Director, Marketing:** Ron Rushe. **Marketing Services Managers:** Elizabeth Latinsky, Mallory Miles. **Director, Creative Services:** Terrance Breen. **Manager, Creative Services:** Justin Vrona. **Director, Special Events:** Allison Valentine. **Director, Concessions/Catering:** Alex Rivera. **Manager, Concessions:** Brock Hartranft. **Manager, Catering:** Steve Agosti. **Executive Chef:** Jerry Rogers. **Controller:** Deb Landes. **Manager, Finance:** Michelle Perl. **Manager, Promotions/Entertainment:** Tanner Buchas. **Director, Stadium Operations:** Jason Kiesel. **Stadium Operations Managers:** Matt Cheesman, Kyle Walbert. **Managers, Sponsorship:** Chris Kobela, Andy Wood. **Manager, Ticket Operations:** Brittany Balonis. **Ticket Representatives:** Steve Carhart, Andrew Klein, Rory Muth, Patrick Walker. **Manager, Group Sales:** Brad Ludwig. **Group Reps:** Liz DiBerardino, Ryan Hines, Nick Wootsick. **Director, Field Operations:** Ryan Hills. **Receptionist:** Pat Golden.

FIELD STAFF

Manager: Dave Brundage. **Hitting Coach:** Sal Rende. **Pitching Coach:** David Lundquist. **Trainers:** Jon May. **Strength/Conditioning:** Dong Lien.

GAME INFORMATION

Radio Announcers: Matt Provence, Jon Schaeffer. **No. of Games Broadcast:** 144. **Flagship Radio Station:** ESPN 1160/1240/1320 AM. **Television Station:** TV2. **Television Announcers:** Mike Zambelli, Steve Degler, Matt Provence, Doug Heater. **No. of Games Televised:** 72 (all home games).
PA Announcer: Jim Walck. **Official Scorers:** Mike Falk, Jack Logic, David Sheriff, Dick Shute.
Stadium Name: Coca-Cola Park. **Location:** Take US 22 to exit for Airport Road South, head south, make right on American Parkway, left into stadium. **Standard Game Times:** 7:05 pm, Sat. 6:35, Sun 1:35.

LOUISVILLE BATS

Address: 401 E Main St, Louisville, KY 40202.
Telephone: (502) 212-2287. **Fax:** (502) 515-2255.
E-Mail Address: info@batsbaseball.com. **Website:** www.batsbaseball.com.
Affiliation (first year): Cincinnati Reds (2000). **Years in League:** 1998-

OWNERSHIP/MANAGEMENT

Chairman: Stuart and Jerry Katzoff (MC Sports).
Board of Directors: Dan Ulmer Jr., Edward Glasscock, Gary Ulmer, Kenny Huber, Steve Trager, Michael Brown. **President/CEO:** Gary Ulmer. **Senior Vice President:** Greg Galiette. **Vice President, Stadium Operations/Technology:** Scott Shoemaker. **Vice President, Business Operations:** James Breeding. **Controller:** Michelle Anderson. **Accounting Assistant:** Becky Reeves. **Director, Media/Public Relations:** Chadwick Fischer. **Media Relations Assistant:** Ryan Ritchey. **Director, Broadcasting:** Matt Andrews. **Assistant Director, Broadcasting:** Nick Curran. **Director, Baseball Operations:** Josh Hargreaves. **Director, Online Media/Design:** Tony Brown. **Director, Sponsorships:** Sarah Nordman. **Director, Business Development:** Bryan McBride. **Director, Business Operations:** Kyle Reh. **Director, Corporate Suites:** Malcolm Jollie. **Director, Group Sales:** Evan Patrick. **Assistant Director, Ticket Operations:** Andrew Siers. **Senior Account Executive:** Hal Norwood. **Corporate Marketing Manager:** Brian Knight. **Corporate Marketing Manager:** Michael Harmon. **Corporate Marketing Manager:** Karly King. **Manager, Team Store/Merchandise:** Katherine Steponovich. **Manager/Coordinator, Stadium Operations:** Nathan Renfrow. **Head Clubhouse Manager:** Derrick Jewell. **Visiting Clubhouse Manager:** Ryan Dammeyer. **Head Groundskeeper:** Tom Nielsen. **Assistant Groundskeeper:** Charlie Krips. **Club Physicians:** Walter Badenhausen, M.D.; John A. Lach, Jr., M.D. **Club Dentist:** Pat Carroll, D.M.D. **Chaplains:** Bob Bailey, Jose Castillo.

FIELD STAFF

Manager: Delino DeShields. **Pitching Coach:** Ted Power. **Hitting Coach:** Jody Davis. **Trainer:** Steve Gober. **Strength/Conditioning Coach:** Unavailable.

GAME INFORMATION

Radio Announcers: Matt Andrews, Nick Curran. **No. of Games Broadcast:** 144. **Flagship Station:** WKRD 790-AM.
PA Announcer: Charles Gazaway. **Official Scorer:** Neil Rohrer. **Organist:** Bob Ramsey.
Stadium Name: Louisville Slugger Field. **Location:** I-64 and I-71 to I-65 South/North to Brook Street exit, right on Market Street, left on Jackson Street; stadium on Main Street between Jackson and Preston. **Ticket Price Range:** $8-18.
Visiting Club Hotel: Galt House Hotel, 140 North Fourth Street, Louisville, KY 40202. **Telephone:** (502) 589-5200.

NORFOLK TIDES

Address: 150 Park Ave, Norfolk, VA 23510.
Telephone: (757) 622-2222. **Fax:** (757) 624-9090.
E-Mail Address: receptionist@norfolktides.com. **Website:** www.norfolktides.com.
Affiliation (first year): Baltimore Orioles (2007). **Years in League:** 1969-

OWNERSHIP/MANAGEMENT

Operated By: Tides Baseball Club Inc. **President:** Ken Young. **General Manager:** Joe Gregory. **Executive Vice President/Senior Advisor to President:** Dave Rosenfield.

Assistant GM: Ben Giancola. **Director, Media Relations:** Ian Locke. **Director, Community Relations:** Heather McKeating. **Director, Ticket Operations:** Gretchen Todd. **Director, Group Sales:** John Muszkewycz. **Director, Premium Services:** Stephanie Hierstein. **Director, Stadium Operations:** Mike Zeman. **Business Manager:** Andrew Garrelts. **Director, Business Development/Gameday Experience:** Mike Watkins. **Corporate Sponsorships/Promotions:** Jonathan Mensink, John Rogerson. **Manager, Merchandising:** AnnMarie Piddisi Ambler. **Assistant Director, Stadium Operations:** Mike Cardwell. **Assistant to Director, Tickets:** Sze Fong. **Administrative Assistant:** Lisa Blocker. **Event Staff Manager:** Joanna Wauhop.

Head Groundskeeper: Kenny Magner. **Assistant Groundskeeper:** Derek Trueblood. **Home Clubhouse Manager:** Kevin Casey. **Visiting Clubhouse Manager:** Jack Brenner. **Media Relations Assistant:** Joshua Kay. **Community Relations Assistant:** Michelle Black. **Group Sales Representatives:** Morgan Kaplan, Denzel Davis.

FIELD STAFF

Manager: Ron Johnson. **Hitting Coach:** Sean Berry. **Pitching Coach:** Mike Griffin. **Field Coach:** Jose Hernandez. **Athletic Trainer:** Mark Shires. **Strength/Conditioning Coach:** Trevor Howell.

GAME INFORMATION

Radio Announcers: Pete Michaud, Dave Rosenfield. **No. of Games Broadcast:** 144. **Flagship Station:** ESPN 94.1 FM. **PA Announcer:** Jack Ankerson. **Official Scorers:** Mike Holtzclaw, Dave Lewis.

Stadium Name: Harbor Park. **Location:** Exit 9, 11A or 11B off I-264, adjacent to the Elizabeth River in downtown Norfolk. **Standard Game Times:** 6:35 pm during weekdays in April & May, 7:05 pm, Sun 1:05 pm (first half of season), 6:05 pm (second half of season). **Ticket Price Range:** $10-15.

Visiting Club Hotel: Sheraton Waterside, 777 Waterside Dr, Norfolk, VA 23510. **Telephone:** (757) 622-6664.

PAWTUCKET RED SOX

Office Address: One Ben Mondor Way, Pawtucket, RI 02860. **Mailing Address:** PO Box 2365, Pawtucket, RI 02861.
Telephone: (401) 724-7300. **Fax:** (401) 724-2140.
E-Mail Address: info@pawsox.com. **Website:** www.pawsox.com.
Affiliation (first year): Boston Red Sox (1973). **Years in League:** 1973-

OWNERSHIP/MANAGEMENT

Operated by: Pawtucket Red Sox Baseball Club, Inc.

Chairman: Larry Lucchino. **Vice Chairman:** Mike Tamburro. **Senior Vice President/General Manager:** Dan Rea. **Treasurer:** Jeff White. **VP, Sales/Sponsorship:** Michael Gwynn. **VP, Communications and Community Relations:** Bill Wanless. **VP, Sales:** Rob Crain. **Director, Merchandising:** Brooke Coderre. **Director, Media Creation:** Kevin Galligan. **Director, Ticket Sales:** John Wilson. **Director, Warehouse Operations:** Dave Johnson. **Special Assistant to President:** Jackie Dempsey. **Special Assistant to President/GM:** Joseph Bradlee. **Director, Fan Services:** Rick Medeiros. **Director, Corporate Sponsorship:** Geoff Sinott Jr. **Manager, McCoy Enterprises:** Grace Eng. **Manager, Accounting/Data Analytics:** Matt Levin. **Account Executives:** Tom Linehan, Sam Sousa, Mike Lyons, Brian Airoldi, Nick Narodowy, Chris Tedesco, Nicole Rosenberg. **Field Superintendant:** Matt McKinnon. **Director, Clubhouse Operations:** Carl Goodreau. **Executive Chef:** Ken Bowdish.

FIELD STAFF

Manager: Kevin Boles. **Hitting Coach:** Rich Gedman. **Pitching Coach:** Dick Such. **Coach:** Bruce Crabbe. **Trainer:** Jon Jochim. **Strength/Conditioning Coach:** Kirby Retzer

GAME INFORMATION

Radio Announcers: Josh Maurer, Will Flemming. **No. of Games Broadcast:** 144. **Flagship Station:** WHJJ 920-AM. **PA Announcers:** Jim Martin, Scott Fraser. **Official Scorer:** Bruce Guindon.

Stadium Name: McCoy Stadium. **Location:** From north, 95 South to exit 2A in Massachusetts (Newport Ave), follow Newport Ave for 2 miles, right on Columbus Ave, follow one mile, stadium on right; From south, 95 North to exit 28 (School Street), right at bottom of exit ramp, through two sets of lights, left onto Pond Street, right on Columbus Ave, stadium entrance on left; From west (Worcester), 295 North to 95 South and follow directions from north; From east (Fall River), 195 West to 95 North and follow directions from south. **Standard Game Times:** 7 pm, Sat. 6, Sun 1. **Ticket Price Range:** $5-11.

Visiting Club Hotel: Wyndham Garden Providence, 220 India Street, Providence, RI 02903. **Telephone:** (401) 272-5577.

ROCHESTER RED WINGS

Address: One Morrie Silver Way, Rochester, NY 14608.
Telephone: (585) 454-1001. **Fax:** (585) 454-1056.
E-Mail: info@redwingsbaseball.com. **Website:** RedWingsBaseball.com.
Affiliation (first year): Minnesota Twins (2003). **Years in League:** 1885-89,
1891-92, 1895-

OWNERSHIP/MANAGEMENT

Operated by: Rochester Community Baseball, Inc. **President/CEO/COO:** Naomi Silver.
Chairman: Gary Larder. **General Manager:** Dan Mason. **Assistant GM:** Will Rumbold. **Controller:** Christina Duquin.
Director, Human Resources: Paula LoVerde. **Manager, Ticket Office:** Dave Welker. **Manager, Executive Services:**
Marcia DeHond. **Director, Communications:** Nate Rowan. **Director, Corporate Development:** Nick Sciarratta.
Manager, Social Media/Promotions: Tim Doohan. **Director, Group Sales:** Bob Craig. **Account Executives:** Kevin Lute
& Mike Ewing. **Senior Director, Sales:** Matt Cipro. **Director, Ticket Operations:** Rob Dermody. **Assistant Director,
Ticket Operations:** Eric Friedman. **Director, Video Production:** John Blotzer. **Manager, Merchandising:** Kathy Bills.
Manager, Team Store: Casey Sanders.
Head Groundskeeper: Gene P Buonomo. **Assistant Groundskeeper:** Geno Buonomo. **Administrative
Assistant:** Gini Darden. **GM, Food/Beverage:** Jeff Dodge. **Business Manager, Food/Beverage:** Dave Bills. **Manager,
Concessions:** Jeff DeSantis. **Director, Catering:** Courtney Trawitz. **Sales Manager, Catering:** Steve Gonzalez.
Executive Chef: Dan Shea. **Manager, Warehouse:** Rob Burgett.

FIELD STAFF

Manager: Mike Quade. **Hitting Coach:** Chad Allen. **Pitching Coach:** Stu Cliburn. **Trainer:** Larry Bennese. **Strength
Coach:** Dax Fiore.

GAME INFORMATION

Radio Announcer: Josh Whetzel. **No. of Games Broadcast:** 144. **Flagship Stations:** WHTK 1280-AM, WYSL 1040-
AM.
PA Announcers: Kevin Spears, Rocky Perrotta. **Official Scorers:** Warren Kozireski, Brendan Harrington, Craig
Bodensteiner.
Stadium Name: Frontier Field. **Location:** I-490 East to exit 12 (Brown/Broad Street) and follow signs; I-490 West to
exit 14 (Plymouth Ave) and follow signs. **Standard Game Times:** 7:05 pm, Sun 1:35. **Ticket Price Range:** $8-12.
Visiting Club Hotel: Rochester Plaza, 70 State St, Rochester, NY 14608. **Telephone:** (585) 546-3450.

SCRANTON/WILKES-BARRE RAILRIDERS

Address: 235 Montage Mountain Rd., Moosic, PA 18507.
Telephone: (570) 969-2255. **Fax:** (570) 963-6564.
E-Mail Address: info@swbrailriders.com. **Website:** www.swbrailriders.com
Affiliation (first year): New York Yankees (2007). **Years in League:** 1989-

OWNERSHIP/MANAGEMENT

Owned by: SWB Yankees, LLC. **Operated by:** SWB Yankees, LLC.
General Manager: Jeremy Ruby. **Chief Operating Officer:** Josh Olerud. **VP, Marketing/Corporate Services:** Katie
Beekman. **VP, Baseball Operations:** Curt Camoni.
Director, Media Relations/Broadcasting: John Sadak. **Assistant Director, Media Relations/Broadcasting:** TBA.
Director, Gameday Operations: William Steiner. **Corporate Partnerships Executive:** Josh Dilts. **Director, Special
Events/Graphic Design:** Kristina Knight. **Director, Community Relations:** Rachel Mark. **Corporate Services Manager:**
Lindsey Graham. **Corporate Services/Analytics Manager:** Karen Luciano. **CRM & Business Analytics:** Chase Mattioli.
Fan Services Manager: Noelle Richard. **Video/Website Manager:** Victor Sweet. **Director, Marketing/Promotions:**
Barry Snyder. **Director, Ticket Operations:** Felicia Adamus. **Assistant Ticket Operations Manager:** Bryant Guilmette.
Senior Director, Ticket Sales: Robert McLane. **Regional Corporate Sales Managers:** Giovanni Fricchione, Alyssa
Novick. **Regional Group Sales Manager:** Mike Harvey, **Senior Inside Sales Representative:** Kelly Cusick. **Inside
Sales Representatives:** Nick Ciaglia. **Sales Representatives:** Joe Rocco, Sean Magee. **Sales Coordinator:** Robby
Judge. **Group Sales Coordinator:** Tim Duggan. **Director, Field Operations:** Steve Horne. **Operations Manager/Ass't
Groundskeeper:** Paul Tumavitch. **Director, Ballpark Operations:** Joe Villano. **Receptionist/Office Manager:** Maggie
Rowlands.

FIELD STAFF

Manager: Al Pedrique. **Hitting Coach:** Tommy Wilson. **Pitching Coach:** Tommy Phelps. **Bullpen Coach:** Jason
Brown. **Trainer:** Darren London. **Strength Coach:** Brad Hyde. **Video Manager:** Tyler DeClerck. **Clubhouse Manager:**
Mike Macciocco.

GAME INFORMATION

Radio Announcer: John Sadak. **No. of Games Broadcast:** 144. **Flagship Stations:** 100.7 FM, 1340 WYCK-AM, 1400 WICK-AM, 1440 WCDL-AM, 106.7 FM. **Television Announcer:** John Sadak. **No. of Games Broadcast:** 20. **Flagship Station:** WQMY-TV.

PA Announcer: Unavailable. **Official Scorers:** Dave Lauriha, John Errico, Armand Rosamilia.

Stadium Name: PNC Field. **Location:** Exit 182 off Interstate 18; stadium is on Montage Mountain Road. **Standard Game Times:** 6:35 pm (April/May) 7:05 pm (June-August), Sun 1:05 pm. **Ticket Price Range:** $7-$12.

Visiting Club Hotel: Radisson Lackawanna Station. **Telephone:** (570) 342-8300.

SYRACUSE CHIEFS

Address: One Tex Simone Drive, Syracuse, NY 13208.

Telephone: (315) 474-7833. **Fax:** (315) 474-2658.

E-Mail Address: baseball@syracusechiefs.com. **Website:** www.syracusechiefs.com.

Affiliation (first year): Washington Nationals (2009). **Years in League:** 1885-89, 1891-92, 1894-1901, 1918 1920-27, 1934-55, 1961-

OWNERSHIP/MANAGEMENT

Operated by: Community Owned Baseball Club of Central New York, Inc.

Chairman: Robert Julian, Esq. **President:** William Dutch. **First Executive Vice President:** Paul Solomon.

General Manager: Jason Smorol. **Director, Sales/Marketing:** Kathleen McCormick. **Director, Finance:** Frank Santoro. **Director, Group Sales:** Arnold Malloy. **Director, Broadcasting/Public Relations:** Kevin Brown. **Director, Ticket Sales:** Will Commisso. **Director, Multimedia Production:** Anthony Cianchetta. **Manager, Corporate Sales:** Julie Cardinali. **Manager, Luxury Suites/Guest Relations:** Bill Ryan. **Director, Community Relations/Social Media:** Jeffrey Irizarry. **Head Groundskeeper:** John Stewart.

FIELD STAFF

Manager: Billy Gardner, Jr. **Hitting Coach:** Brian Daubach. **Pitching Coach:** Bob Milacki. **Trainer:** Jeff Allred. **Strength Coordinator:** Brett Henry.

GAME INFORMATION

Radio Announcers: Kevin Brown/Eric Gallanty. **No. of Games Broadcast:** 144. **Flagship Station:** The Score 1260 AM.

PA Announcers: Nick Aversa. **Official Scorer:** Dom Leo.

Stadium Name: NBT Bank Stadium. **Location:** New York State Thruway to exit 36 (I-81 South), to 7th North Street exit, left on 7th North, right on Hiawatha Boulevard. **Standard Game Times:** 7:05 pm, Sun 1:05 pm. **Ticket Price Range:** $7-13.

Visiting Club Hotel: Crowne Plaza Syracuse, 701 E Genesee St, Syracuse, NY 13210. **Telephone:** (315) 479-7000.

TOLEDO MUD HENS

Address: 406 Washington St., Toledo, OH 43604.

Telephone: (419) 725-4367. **Fax:** (419) 725-4368.

E-Mail Address: mudhens@mudhens.com. **Website:** www.mudhens.com.

Affiliation (first year): Detroit Tigers (1987). **Years in League:** 1889, 1965-

OWNERSHIP/MANAGEMENT

Operated By: Toledo Mud Hens Baseball Club, Inc.

Chairman of the Board: Michael Miller. **Vice President:** David Huey. **Secretary/Treasurer:** Charles Bracken. **President/CEO:** Joseph Napoli. **Chief Marketing Officer:** Kim McBroom.

GM/Executive Vice President: Erik Ibsen, **President, A Cut Above Catering:** Craig Nelson. **CFO:** Brian Leverenz. **Director, Events/Entertainment:** Michael Keedy. **Communications/Media Director:** Andi Roman.

Director, Ticket Sales/Services: Thomas Townley. **Accounting:** Sheri Kelly, Tom Mitchell.

Gameday Operations Manager: Greg Setola. **Corporate Sales Associate:** Ed Sintic. **Director, Ticket Sales/Services:** Thom Townley. **Game Plan Consultants:** Phil Bargardi, Becky Fitts, Adam Haman, John Manzoian, McKay Phillips. **Group Sales Manager: Kyle Moll, Group Consultant:** Scott McGorty, Hannah Tyson, Brian Wilson; **Manager, Digital Communications:** Nathan Steinmetz. **Game Plan Advisor:** Colleen Rerucha. **Special Events Coordinator:** Emily Croll. **Director, Game Day Coordinator:** Tony Bibler. **Broadcast Services:** Greg Tye. **Creative Director:** Dan Royer. **Graphic Design Assistants:** Will Melon, Alex Dartt, Director, **Merchandise & Licensing:** Craig Katz. **Manager, Swamp Shop:** Stephanie Miller. **Manager, Office Manager:** Carol Hamilton. **Executive Assistants:** Tracy Evans, Brenda Murphy, Pam Miranda. **Turf Manager:** Jake Tyler. **Assistant Turf Manager:** Cory Myers. **Clubhouse Manager:** Joe Sarkisian. **Team Historian:** John Husman.

FIELD STAFF

Manager: Lloyd McClendon. **Hitting:** Leon Durham. **Pitching Coach:** Jeff Pico. **Trainer:** Chris McDonald.

GAME INFORMATION

Radio Announcer: Jim Weber. **No. of Games Broadcast:** 144. **Flagship Station:** WCWA 1230-AM. **TV Announcers:** Jim Weber, Matt Melzak. **No. of Games Broadcast:** 72 (all home games). **TV Flagship:** Buckeye Cable Sports Network (BCSN).

PA Announcer: Unavailable. **Official Scorers:** Jeff Businger, Ron Kleinfelter, Guy Lammers, John Malkoski Jr.

Stadium Name: Fifth Third Field. **Location:** From Ohio Turnpike 80/90, exit 54 (4A) to I-75 North, follow I-75 North to exit 201-B, left onto Erie Street, right onto Washington Street; From Detroit, I-75 South to exit 202-A, right onto Washington Street; From Dayton, I-75 North to exit 201-B, left onto Erie Street, right on Washington Street; From Ann Arbor, Route 23 South to I-475 East, I-475 east to I-75 South, I-75 South to exit 202-A, right onto Washington Street. **Ticket Price Range:** $10.

Visiting Club Hotel: Park Inn, 101 North Summit, Toledo, OH 43604. **Telephone:** (419) 241-3000.

PACIFIC COAST LEAGUE

PACIFIC COAST LEAGUE

Address: One Chisholm Trail, Suite 4200, Round Rock, Texas 78681.
Telephone: (512) 310-2900. **Fax:** (512) 310-8300.
E-Mail Address: office@pclbaseball.com. **Website:** www.pclbaseball.com.
President: Branch B. Rickey.

Vice President: Don Logan (Las Vegas).

Directors: Don Beaver (New Orleans), Sam Bernabe (Iowa), John Pontius John Mozeliak (Memphis), Chris Cummings (Fresno), Dave Elmore (Colorado Springs), Aaron Artman (Tacoma), Don Logan (Las Vegas), Chris Almendarez (Round Rock), Marc Amicone (Salt Lake), Gary Green (Omaha), Art Matin Larry Freedman (Oklahoma), Josh Hunt (El Paso), Jeff Savage (Sacramento), John Traub (Albuquerque), Frank Ward (Nashville), Stuart Katzoff Herb Simon (Reno).

Director, Business: Melanie Fiore. **Director, Baseball Operations:** Dwight Hall. **Media/Operations Assistant:** Andrew Cockrum.

Division Structure: American Conference—Northern: Colorado Springs, Iowa, Omaha, Oklahoma City. **Southern:** Memphis, Nashville, New Orleans, Round Rock. **Pacific Conference—Northern:** Fresno, Reno, Sacramento, Tacoma. **Southern:** Albuquerque, El Paso, Las Vegas, Salt Lake.

Regular Season: 144 games. **2015 Opening Date:** April 9. **Closing Date:** Sept 7.
All-Star Game: July 15 at Omaha (PCL vs International League).

Playoff Format: Pacific Conference/Northern winner meets Southern winner, and American Conference/Northern winner meets Southern winner in best-of-five semifinal series. Winners meet in best-of-five series for league championship.

Triple-A Championship Game: Sept. 20 at Memphis (IL vs Pacific Coast League).

Roster Limit: 24. **Player Eligibility Rule:** No restrictions. **Brand of Baseball:** Rawlings ROM.

Umpires: Nick Bailey (Big Spring, TX), Jordan Baker (Shawnee, OK), Lance Barrett (Fort Worth, TX), Ryan Blakney (Wenatchee, WA), Cory Blaser (Westminster, CO), Blake Davis (Englewood, CO), Jordan Ferrell (Clarksville, TN), Spencer Flynn, (Plymouth, MN Forney, TX), Hal Gibson (Marysville, WA), Brian Hertzog (Lake Stevens, WA), Patrick Hoberg (Urbandale, IA), Joel Hospodka (Omaha, NE), Kolin Kline (Arvada, CO), Shaun Lampe (Phoenix, AZ Dubuque, IA), Patrick Mahoney (Pittsburg, CA), Brandon Misun (Edmond, OK), Gabriel Morales (Livermore, CA), Jeffrey Morrow (Fenton, MO) Michael Muchlinski (Ephrata, WA), Alex Ortiz (Los Angeles, CA), Marcus Pattillo (Jonesboro, AR), Daniel Reyburn (Franklin, TN), Mark Ripperger (Carlsbad, CA), Stuart Scheurwater (Regina, Saskatchewan, Canada), Adam Schwarz (Riverside Nuevo, CA), Chris Segal (Burke, VA), Gregory Stanzak (Phoenix, AZ Tulsa, OK), Quinn Wolcott (Puyallup, WA), Thomas Woodring (Boulder, Las Vegas, NV); Ramon De Jesus (Santo Domingo, DR), Travis Eggert (Pine, AZ), Chris Gonzalez (San Jose, CA); Ryan Goodman (Encino, CA), Brandon Henson (Gowrie, IA), Anthony Johnson (McComb, MS), Nicholas Mahrley (Phoenix, AZ) Thomas Newsom (King, NC), Robert Ortiz (Hopkinsville, KY), Alberto Ruiz (Las Vegas, NV).

Branch Rickey

STADIUM INFORMATION

Club	Stadium	Opened	Dimensions LF	CF	RF	Capacity	2015 Att.
Albuquerque	Isotopes Park	2003	340	400	340	13,279	560, 519
Colorado Springs	Security Service Field	1988	350	410	350	8,400	300,209
El Paso	Southwest University Park	2014	322	406	322	9,650	578,952
Fresno	Chukchansi Park	2002	324	402	335	12,500	458,431
Iowa	Principal Park	1992	335	400	335	11,000	504,577
Las Vegas	Cashman Field	1983	328	433	328	9,334	333,520
Memphis	AutoZone Park	2000	319	400	322	14,500	278,579
*Nashville	First Tennessee Park	2015	327	400	327	10,000	565,548
New Orleans	Zephyr Field	1997	325	400	325	10,000	324,973
Oklahoma City	Chickasaw Bricktown Ballpark	1998	325	400	325	9,000	471,996
Omaha	Werner Park	2011	310	402	315	9,023	386,141
Reno	Aces Ballpark	2009	339	410	340	9,100	376,422
Round Rock	Dell Diamond	2000	330	405	325	8,722	595,012
Sacramento	Raley Field	2000	330	405	325	14,014	672,354
Salt Lake	Salt Lake Smith's Ballpark	1994	345	420	315	15,411	470,760
Tacoma	Cheney Stadium	1960	325	425	325	7,200	352,521

ALBUQUERQUE ISOTOPES

Address: 1601 Avenida Cesar Chavez SE, Albuquerque, NM 87106.
Telephone: (505) 924-2255. **Fax:** (505) 242-8899.
E-Mail Address: info@abqisotopes.com. **Website:** www.abqisotopes.com.
Affiliation (first year): Colorado Rockies (2015). **Years in League:** 1972-2000, 2003-

OWNERSHIP/MANAGEMENT

President: Ken Young. **Vice President/Secretary/Treasurer:** Emmett Hammond. **VP/GM:** John Traub. **VP, Corporate Development:** Nick LoBue. **Assistant GM, Business Operation:** Chrissy Baines. **Assistant GM, Sales/ Marketing:** Adam Beggs. **Director, Stadium Operations:** Bobby Atencio. **Director, Public Relations:** Kevin Collins. **Director, Accounting/Human Resources:** Cynthia DiFrancesco. **Director, Retail Operations:** Kara Hayes. **Box Office/ Administration Manager:** Mark Otero. **Community Relations Manager:** Michelle Montoya. **Season Tickets/Group Sales Manager:** Jason Buchta. **Marketing/Promotions Manager:** Kasen Dudley. **Game Production Manager:** Kris Shepard. **Suite Relations Manager:** Paul Hartenberger. **Event Operations Manager:** Nick Orn. **Facility Operations Manager:** Andrew Garrison. **Broadcaster:** Josh Suchon. **Corporate Sales Executive:** Dylan Storm. **Ticket Sales Executive:** Terry Clark. **Ticket Sales Executive:** Bryan Pruitt. **Ticket Sales Executive:** Aaron Robinson. **Ticket Sales Executive:** Malcolm Smith. **Public Relations Assistant:** Andrew Cockrum. **Front Office Assistant:** Margaret Harris. **Retail Operations Assistant:** Michael Malgieri. **Travel Coordinator/Home Clubhouse Manager:** Ryan Maxwell. **Director, Field Operations:** Casey Griffin. **Assistant Groundskeeper:** Clint Belau. **GM, Spectra Food & Hospitality:** Patrick Queeney. **Office Manager:** Angela Goniea. **Catering Manager, Spectra Food/ Hospitality:** Amanda Baca. **Concession Manager, Spectra Food & Hospitality:** Kevin Reiniche. **Head Chef:** Mario D'Elia.

FIELD STAFF

Manager: Glenallen Hill. **Hitting Coach:** Unavailable. **Pitching Coach:** Darryl Scott.

GAME INFORMATION

Radio Announcer: Josh Suchon. **No. of Games Broadcast:** 144. **Flagship Station:** KNML 610-AM. **PA Announcer:** TBA. **Official Scorers:** Gary Herron. **Stadium Name:** Isotopes Park. **Location:** From 1-25, exit east on Avenida Cesar Chavez SE to University. Boulevard; From I-40, exit south on University Boulevard SE to Avenida Cesar Chavez. **Standard Game Times:** 7:05 pm. Sun 1:35/6:05 pm. **Ticket Price Range:** $8-$27. **Visiting Club Hotel:** Sheraton Albuquerque Airport Hotel, 2910 Yale Blvd SE, Albuquerque, NM 87106. **Telephone:** (505) 843-7000.

COLORADO SPRINGS SKY SOX

Address: 4385 Tutt Blvd., Colorado Springs, CO 80922.
Telephone: (719) 597-1449. **Fax:** (719) 597-2491.
E-Mail address: info@skysox.com. **Website:** www.skysox.com.
Affiliation (first year): Milwaukee Brewers (2015). **Years in League:** 1988-

OWNERSHIP/MANAGEMENT

Operated By: Colorado Springs Sky Sox Inc.
Principal Owner: David Elmore. **President/General Manager:** Tony Ensor. **Director, Public Relations:** Nick Dobreff. **Assistant GM/Senior Director, Corporate Sales:** Chris Phillips. **Senior Director, Ticketing/Merchandise:** Whitney Shellem. **Senior Director, Group Sales:** Keith Hodges. **Director, Broadcasting:** Dan Karcher. **Director, Accounting:** Kelly Hanlon. **Director, Promotions:** Ben Taylor. **Director, Marketing:** Kyle Fritzke. **Vice President, Field Operations:** Steve DeLeon. **Manager, Graphics/Community Relations:** Tricia Metzger. **Manager, Stadium Operations:** Eric Martin. **Manager, Corporate Sales:** Spencer Molnar. **Assistant Director, Group Sales:** Kevin Soto. **Manager, Group Sales:** Dustin True. **Manager, Military Group Sales:** Justin Krause. **Manager, Box Office:** Jake Cooke. **Event Manager:** Brien Smith. **GM, Diamond Creations:** Don Giuliano. **Executive Chef:** Chris Evans.
Home Clubhouse Manager: Cole Filosa. **Visiting Clubhouse Manager:** Steve Martin.

FIELD STAFF

Manager: Rick Sweet. **Coach:** Bob Skube. **Pitching Coach:** Fred Dabney.

GAME INFORMATION

Radio Announcer: Dan Karcher. **No. of Games Broadcast:** 144. **Flagship Station:** AM 1300 The Animal. **PA Announcer:** Josh Howe. **Official Scorer:** Marty Grantz, Rich Wastler. **Stadium Name:** Security Service Field. **Location:** I-25 South to Woodmen Road exit, east on Woodmen to Powers Blvd., right on Powers to Barnes Road. **Standard Game Times:** 7:05 pm, Sat. 6:05, Sun 1:35. **Ticket Price Range:** $5-13. **Visiting Club Hotel:** Hilton Garden Inn, 1810 Briargate Parkway, Colorado Springs, CO 80920. **Telephone:** (719) 598-6866.

EL PASO CHIHUAHUAS

Address: 1 Ballpark Plaza, El Paso, TX 79901.
Telephone: (915) 533-2273. **Fax:** (915) 242-2031.
E-Mail Address: info@epchihuahuas.com. **Website:** www.epchihuahuas.com.
Affiliation (first year): San Diego Padres (2014). **Years in League:** 2014-

OWNERSHIP/MANAGEMENT

Owner/Chairman of the Board: Paul Foster. **Owner/CEO/Vice Chairman:** Josh Hunt. **Owners:** Alejandra de la Vega Foster, Woody Hunt.
President: Alan Ledford. **General Manager:** Brad Taylor.
Head Groundskeeper: Andy Beggs. **Director, Finance/Administration:** Pamela De La O. **Director, Ballpark**

Operations: Douglas Galeano. **Manager, Broadcasting/Media Relations:** Tim Hagerty. **Account Executive, Ticket Sales:** Ryan Knox, Alex Lakinske, Primo Martinez, Nick Seckerson, Ryan Veinotte. **Manager, Ticket Operations:** Rebecca Jacobsen. **Assistant Ticket Operations Supervisor:** Maya Horsman. **Director, Corporate Partnerships:** Becky Lee. **Senior Account Executive, Ticket Sales:** Colby Miller. **Director, Marketing Communications:** Angela Olivas. **Director, Ticket Sales:** Aaron Johnson. **Account Executive, Corporate Partnerships:** Judge Scott. **Manager, Retail/Database/Special Projects:** Jon Staub. **Manager, Promotions/Community Relations:** Andy Imfeld. **Account Executive, Group Sales:** AJ Barbalace, Brittany Morgan. **Special Events/Military Groups Coordinator:** Monica Castillo. **Director, Guest Services/Baseball Operations:** Lizette Espinosa. **Manager, Facilities Operations:** Will Forney. **Administrative Services Coordinator:** Bethany Schopper.

Mascot/Entertainment Coordinator: Grant Gorham. **Manager, Video/Digital Production:** Juan Gutierrez. **Accounting Assistant:** Heather Hagerty. **Account Services Executive, Corporate Partnerships:** Ashley Hermosillo. **Promotions/Community Relations Specialist:** Rebecca Gutierrez. **Assistant Head Groundskeeping Supervisor:** Nate Jones. **Senior Account Executive, Group Sales:** Yari Marte Natal. **Operations/Event Sales/Service Representative:** David Meza. **Baseball Operations Assistant:** Mike Raymundo. **Account Services Executive, Ticket Sales:** Nick Seckerson.

FIELD STAFF
Manager: Rod Barajas. **Hitting Coach:** Morgan Burkhart. **Pitching Coach:** Bronswell Patrick. **Trainers:** Nathan Stewart, Isak Yoon.

GAME INFORMATION
Radio Announcer: Tim Hagerty. **No. of Games Broadcast:** 144. **Flagship Station:** ESPN 600 AM El Paso. **PA Announcer:** Ray Adauto. **Official Scorer:** Bernie Ricono. **Stadium Name:** Southwest University Park. **Standard Game Times:** 7:05 pm, Sun 1:05. **Ticket Price Range:** $5-10.50.
Visiting Club Hotel: Hilton Garden Inn.

FRESNO GRIZZLIES

Address: 1800 Tulare St, Fresno, CA 93721.
Telephone: (559) 320-4487. **Fax:** (559) 264-0795.
E-Mail Address: info@fresnogrizzlies.com. **Website:** www.FresnoGrizzlies.com.
Affiliation (first year): Houston Astros (2015). **Years in League:** 1998-

OWNERSHIP/MANAGEMENT
Operated By: Fresno Baseball Club, LLC.
President: Chris Cummings. **General Manager/Executive Vice President:** Derek Franks. **Assistant General Manager:** Unavailable. **VP, Revenue:** Jerry James. **Director, Marketing:** Sam Hansen.
Director, Operations: Joe Castillo. **Director, Sales:** Andrew Milios. **Director, Stadium Maintenance:** Harvey Kawasaki. **Community Fund Director:** Whitney Campbell. **Director, Corporate Sales:** Andrew Melrose. **Director, Business Operations:** Chris Wilson. **Ticket Sales Manager:** Cody Holden. **Entertainment Manager:** Ray Ortiz. **Inside Sales Manager:** Andrew Hacnik. **Stadium Maintenance Manager:** Ira Calvin. **Merchandise Manager:** Lalonnie Calderon. **Premium Seating Sales Manager:** Jon Stockton. **Assistant Ticket Sales Manager:** Brian Boden.
Finance Manager: Monica DeLacerda. **Entertainment/Mascot Coordinator:** Troy Simeon. **Group Sales Account Executive:** Eric Moreno. **Corporate Partnership Executive:** Kyle Esty. **Group Sales Manager:** Kyle Kleiman. **Community Fund Assistant:** Chris Ortiz. **Ticket Sales Assistant:** Kendra Coy. **Administrative Assistant:** Yanet Richardson. **Head Groundskeeper:** David Jacinto.

FIELD STAFF
Manager: Tony DeFrancesco. **Hitting Coach:** Ralph Dickenson. **Pitching Coach:** Dyar Miller. **Athletic Trainer:** Unavailable. **Strength/Conditioning Coach:** Unavailable.

GAME INFORMATION
Radio Announcer: Doug Greenwald. **No. of Games Broadcast:** 144. **Flagship Radio Station:** 1430 AM KYNO. **Flagship TV Station:** ABC 30.1.
Stadium Name: Chukchansi Park. **Location:** 1800 Tulare St, Fresno, CA 93721. **Directions:** From 99 North, take Fresno Street exit, left on Fresno Street, left on Inyo or Tulare to stadium. From 99 South, take Fresno Street exit, left on Fresno Street, right on Broadway to H Street. From 41 North, take Van Ness exit toward Fresno, left on Van Ness, left on Inyo or Tulare, stadium is straight ahead. From 41 South, take Tulare exit, stadium is located at Tulare and H Streets, or take Van Ness exit, right on Van Ness, left on Inyo or Tulare, stadium is straight ahead. **Ticket Price Range:** $9-19.
Visiting Club Hotel: University Square Hotel of Fresno, 4961 North Cedar Avenue, Fresno, CA 93726). **Telephone:** (559) 224-4200.

IOWA CUBS

Address: One Line Drive, Des Moines IA 50309.
Telephone: (515) 243-6111. **Fax:** (515) 243-5152.
Website: www.iowacubs.com
Affiliation (first year): Chicago Cubs (1981). **Years in League:** 1969-

OWNERSHIP/MANAGEMENT
Operated By: Raccoon Baseball Inc.
Chairman/Principal Owner: Michael Gartner. **Executive Vice President:** Michael Giudicessi. **President/General Manager:** Sam Bernabe. **Shareholder:** Mike Gartner. **Executive VP/Assistant GM:** Nate Teut. **VP/CFO:** Sue Tollefson. **VP/Director, Broadcast Operations:** Deene Ehlis. **Director, Media Relations:** Randy Wehofer. **Manager, Media Relations:** Shelby Cravens. **Director, Communications:** Scott Sailor. **Director, Multimedia Arts:** Justin Walters. **Director, Ticket Operations:** Kenny Houser. **Director, Luxury Suites:** Brent Conkel. **Assistant Ticket Manager:** Aaron Roland Jason Gellis. **Director, Stadium Operations:** Jeff Tilley. **Manager, Stadium Operations:** Nic Peters, Andrew Quillin. **Corporate Relations:** Red Hollis, Eric Hammes, Brianne Westlake. **Head Groundskeeper:** Chris Schlosser. **Director, Merchandise:** Shelby Heimbuch. **Director, Special Events:** KC Routos. **Accountant:** Lori Auten. **Director, Information Technology:** Ryan Clutter. **Landscape Coordinator:** Shari Kramer.

FIELD STAFF
Manager: Marty Pevey. **Hitting Coach:** Brian Harper. **Pitching Coach:** Rod Nichols. **Athletic Trainer:** Scott Barringer Shane Nelson. **Strength/Conditioning:** Ryan Clausen.

GAME INFORMATION
Radio Announcers: Deene Ehlis, Randy Wehofer. **No. of Games Broadcast:** 144. **Flagship Station:** AM 940 KPSZ.
PA Announcers: Aaron Johnson, Mark Pierce, Corey Coon, Rick Stageman, Joe Hammen. **Official Scorers:** Jayme Adam, Doug Howard, Michael Pecina, James Hilchen, Steve Mohr.
Stadium Name: Principal Park. **Location:** I- 80 or I-35 to Third Street exit, south on Third Street, left on Line Drive. **Standard Game Times:** 7:08 pm, Sun 1:08. **Ticket Price Range:** $4-14. $5-16.
Visiting Club Hotel: Renaissance Savery Hotel, 401 Locust Street, Des Moines IA 50309. **Telephone:** (515) 244-2151.

LAS VEGAS 51S

Address: 850 Las Vegas Blvd North, Las Vegas, NV 89101.
Telephone: (702) 943-7200. **Fax:** (702) 943-7214.
E-Mail Address: info@lv51.com. **Website:** www.lv51.com.
Affiliation (first year): New York Mets (2013). **Years in League:** 1983-

OWNERSHIP/MANAGEMENT
Operated By: Summerlin Las Vegas Baseball Club LLC.
President/COO: Don Logan. **General Manager/Vice President, Sales/Marketing:** Chuck Johnson. **VP, Ticket Operations:** Mike Rodriguez. **VP, Operations/Security:** Nick Fitzenreider. **Director, Sponsorships:** James Jensen. **Senior Accountant/Analyst:** Scott Montes. **Staff Accountant:** Harrison Allen. **Director, Broadcasting:** Russ Langer. **Director, Ticket Sales:** Erik Eisenberg. **Director, Community Relations/Customer Service:** Melissa Harkavy. **Business Development:** Larry Brown. **Media Relations Director:** Jim Gemma. **Ticket Operations Assistant:** Michelle Taggart. **Administrative Assistants:** Jan Dillard, Pat Dressel. **Account Executives, Ticket Sales:** Bryan Frey, TJ Thedinga. **Retail Operations Manager:** Jason Weber. **Operations Manager:** Chip Vespe.

FIELD STAFF
Manager: Wally Backman. **Hitting Coach:** Jack Voigt. **Pitching Coach:** Frank Viola. **Athletic Trainer:** Joe Golia. **Strength/Conditioning Coach:** Jon Cioffi.

GAME INFORMATION
Radio Announcer: Russ Langer. **No. of Games Broadcast:** 144. **Flagship Station:** Sports 920 (AM) The Game.
PA Announcer: Dan Bickmore. **Official Scorers:** Peter Legner, Mark Wasik.
Stadium Name: Cashman Field. **Location:** I-15 to US 95 exit (downtown), east to Las Vegas Boulevard North exit, one-half mile north to stadium. **Standard Game Time:** 7:05 pm. **Ticket Price Range:** $11-16.
Visiting Club Hotel: Golden Nugget Hotel & Casino, 129 Fremont Street, Las Vegas, NV 89101. **Telephone:** (702) 385-7111.

MEMPHIS REDBIRDS

Office Address: 198 Union, Memphis, TN 38103. **Stadium Address:** 200 Union Ave, Memphis, TN 38103.
Telephone: (901) 721-6000. **Fax:** (901) 328-1102.
Website: www.memphisredbirds.com.
Affiliation (first year): St. Louis Cardinals (1998). **Years in League:** 1998-

OWNERSHIP/MANAGEMENT

Ownership: St. Louis Cardinals.
General Manager: Craig Unger. **Director, Operations:** Mark Anderson. **Coordinator, Operations:** Kevin Rooney. **Season Ticket Sales Manager:** S.J. Tucker. **Group Sales Ticket Manager:** Lisa Peterson. **Director, Media Relations:** Michael Whitty. **Corporate Sales Executive:** Phil Abernathy. **Corporate Sales Executive:** Tiffany Oatis. **Manager, Fan Engagement:** Taylor Noon. **Graphic Designer:** Martheus Wade. **After Effects/Video Editor:** Dillan Wavra. **Accounting Manager:** Cindy Neal. **Groundskeeper: Office Manager:** Jackie Likens. **Groundskeeper:** Ben Young. **Assistant Groundskeeper:** Brian Bowe. **Facilities Manager:** Spencer Shields. **Community Relations Coordinator:** Isaiah Bell.

FIELD STAFF

Manager: Mike Shildt. **Hitting Coach:** Mark Budaska. **Pitching Coach:** Bryan Eversgerd. **Trainer:** Unavailable.

GAME INFORMATION

Radio Announcer: Steve Selby. **No. of Games Broadcast:** 144. **Flagship Station:** WHBQ 560-AM.
PA Announcer: Unavailable. **Official Scorer:** J.J. Guinozzo, Eric Opperman.
Stadium Name: AutoZone Park. **Location:** North on I-240, exit at Union Avenue West, one and half mile to park.
Standard Game Times: 7:05 pm, Sat. 6:05, Sun 2:05. **Ticket Price Range:** $6-23.
Visiting Club Hotel: Sleep Inn at Court Square, 40 N Front, Memphis, TN 38103. **Telephone:** (901) 522-9700.

NASHVILLE SOUNDS

Address: 19 Junior Gilliam Way, Nashville, TN 37219.
Telephone: (615) 690-4487. **Fax:** (615) 256-5684.
E-Mail address: info@nashvillesounds.com. **Website:** www.nashvillesounds.com.
Affiliation (first year): Oakland Athletics (2015). **Years in League:** 1998-

OWNERSHIP/MANAGEMENT

Operated By: MFP Baseball. **Owners:** Frank Ward, Masahiro Honzawa. **Chief Operating Officer:** Garry Arthur.
Vice Presdient, Operations: Doug Scopel. **VP, Corporate Sales/Marketing:** Paul Hemingway. **VP, Ticket Operations:** Chris Sprunger. **VP, Human Resources:** Amy Schoch. **Director, Accounting:** Barb Walker. **Director, Multimedia Productions:** Brett Ausbrooks. **Director, Entertainment:** Mary Hegley. **Director, Community Relations:** Dani Ward. **Director, Stadium Operations:** Jeremy Wells. **Director, Merchandise:** Katie Ward. **Director, Special Events:** Nicole Santelman. **Senior Manager, Premium Sales:** Justin Webster. **Managers, Premium Sales:** Jillian Brake, Wilson Korte, Tim Nemes, Eric Sundvold. **Manager, Accounting:** Halie Montgomery. **Manager, Guest Services:** Katherine Dunn. **Manager, Ticket Operations:** Leon McCathen. **Manager, Premium Services:** Teresa Moscati. **Manager, Advertising:** Ryan Madar. **Managers, Corporate Partnerships Activations:** Andi Grindley, Danielle Gaw. **Manager, Creative Services:** Alex Wassel. **Manager, Media Relations:** Chad Seely. **Head Groundskeeper:** Thomas Trotter. **Assistant Groundskeepers:** Patrick Barnaby, Matt Goff. **Assistant Manager, Stadium Operations:** Austin Brunk. **Assistant, Multimedia Production:** Erik Sharpnack. **Account Executives, Premium Sales:** Evan Elkins, Mandy Valentine, Greg Pai. **Coordinator, Ticket Operations:** Cooper Fazio. **Mascot Coordinator:** Buddy Yelton. **Executive Assistant:** Jane Nicholson. **Team Photographer:** Mike Strasinger.

FIELD STAFF

Manager: Steve Scarsone. **Hitting Coach:** Eric Martins. **Pitching Coach:** Rick Rodriguez. **Trainer:** Brad LaRosa. **Strength/Conditioning Coach:** A.J. Seeliger. **Clubhouse/Equipment Manager:** Matt Gallant.

GAME INFORMATION

Radio Announcer: Jeff Hem. **No. of Games Broadcast:** 144. **Flagship Station:** 102.5 FM The Game.
PA Announcer: Eric Berner. **Official Scorers:** Eric Jones, Kyle Parkinson, Cody Bush.
Stadium Name: First Tennessee Park. **Location:** I-65 to exit 85 (Rosa L Parks Blvd) and head south; turn left on Jefferson St, then turn right onto 5th Ave North, then turn left on Jackson St. **Standard Game Times:** 7:05 pm, Sat. 6:35/7:05 pm, Sun 2:05 (April-June 19), 6:35 (June 26-August 14). **Ticket Price Range:** $9-35.
Visiting Club Hotel: Millennium Maxwell House, 2025 Rosa L Parks Blvd, Nashville, TN, 37228.

NEW ORLEANS ZEPHYRS

Address: 6000 Airline Dr, Metairie, LA 70003.
Telephone: (504) 734-5155. **Fax:** (504) 734-5118.
E-Mail Address: zephyrs@zephyrsbaseball.com. **Website:** www.zephyrsbaseball.com.
Affiliation (first year): Miami Marlins (2009). **Years in League:** 1998-

OWNERSHIP/MANAGEMENT

President/Owner: Lou Schewechheimer. **Co-Owner:** Don Beaver.
Senior Vice President/General Manager: Augusto "Cookie" Rojas. **VP, Baseball Operations:** Mike Schline. **VP/General Counsel:** Walter Leger. **Executive Director, Business Development:** David Warner. **Director, Broadcasting/Team Travel:** Tim Grubbs. **Director, Media Relations:** Dave Sachs. **Director, Community Relations/Promotions:** Rachel Whitley. **Director, Finance:** Donna Light. **Director, Stadium Operations:** Craig Schaffer. **Merchandise/Special Events:** Will Hall. **Box Office Director:** Hillary Dazzo. **Clubhouse Director:** Brett Herbert. **Group Sales:** Hunter Whitfield, Daniel Staney, Kyle Guille. **Corporate Sales:** Jesse Bastian. **Head Groundskeeper:** Thomas Marks. **Assistant**

Groundskeeper: Jared Schaffer. **Color Analyst/Speaking Bureau:** Ron Swoboda. **Administrative Assistant:** Susan Radkovich.

FIELD STAFF

Manager: Andy Haines. **Hitting Coach:** Damon Minor. **Pitching Coach:** Charlie Corbell. **Trainer:** Chris Olson.

GAME INFORMATION

Radio Announcers: Tim Grubbs, Ron Swoboda. **No. of Games Broadcast:** 144. **Flagship Station:** WMTI 106.1 FM. **PA Announcer:** Doug Moreau. **Official Scorer:** JL Vangilder.
Stadium Name: Zephyr Field. **Location:** I-10 West toward Baton Rouge, exit at Clearview Pkwy (exit 226) and continues south, right on Airline Drive (US 61 North) for 1 mile, stadium on left; From airport, take Airline Drive (US 61) east for 4 miles, stadium on right. **Standard Game Times:** 7 pm, Sat. 6, Sun 2 (April-May), 6 (June-Sept). **Ticket Price Range:** $6-10.
Visiting Club Hotel: Sheraton Four Points, 6401 Veterans Memorial Blvd, Metairie, LA 70003. **Telephone:** (504) 885-5700.

OKLAHOMA CITY DODGERS

Address: 2 S Mickey Mantle Dr., Oklahoma City, OK 73104.
Telephone: (405) 218-1000. **Fax:** (405) 218-1001.
E-Mail Address: info@okcdodgers.com. **Website:** www.okcdodgers.com.
Affiliation (first year): Los Angeles Dodgers (2015). **Years in League:** 1963-1968, 1998-

OWNERSHIP/MANAGEMENT

Operated By: MB OKC LLC. **Principal Owner:** Mandalay Baseball
President/General Manager: Michael Byrnes. **Senior Vice President:** Jenna Byrnes. **Senior Marketing Director:** Armando Reyes. **Director, Finance/Accounting:** Jon Shaw. **Senior Director, Corporate Partnerships:** Matt Taylor. **Director, Sales Strategies:** Ben Beecken. **Director, Business Development:** Kyle Daugherty. **Director, Group Initiatives:** Kyle Logan. **Director, Operations:** Mitch Stubenhofer. **Director, Facility Operations:** Harlan Budde. **Director, Media Relations/Broadcasting:** Alex Freedman. **Director, Entertainment:** Shannon Landers. **Director, Partner Services:** Zack Collins. **Senior Director, Food/Beverage:** Travis Johnson. **Managing Director, OKC Dodgers Baseball Foundation:** Jennifer Van Tuyl. **Baseball Operations Manager:** Josh Ingram. **Manager, Special Events:** Carolyn Gadboys. **Office Manager:** Travis Hunter. **Head Groundskeeper:** Monte McCoy.

FIELD STAFF

Manager: Bill Haselman. **Hitting Coach:** Unavailable. **Pitching Coach:** Unavailable. **Athletic Trainer:** Greg Harrel. **Strength/Conditioning Coach:** Unavailable.

GAME INFORMATION

Radio Announcer: Alex Freedman. **No. of Games Broadcast:** 144. **Station:** KGHM-AM 1340 (www.1340thegame.com).
PA Announcer: Unavailable. **Official Scorers:** Jim Byers, Ryan McGhee, Rich Tortorelli.
Stadium Name: Chicasaw Bricktown Ballpark. **Location:** Bricktown area in downtown Oklahoma City, near interchange of I-235 and I-40, off I-235 take Sheridan exit to Bricktown; off I-40 take Shields exit, north to Bricktown. **Standard Game Times:** 7:05 pm, Sun 2:05 (April-May), 6:05 (June-Aug). **Ticket Price Range:** $8-20.
Visiting Club Hotel: Courtyard Oklahoma City Downtown, 2 West Reno Ave., Oklahoma City, OK 73102. **Telephone:** (405) 232-2290.

OMAHA STORM CHASERS

Address: Werner Park, 12356 Ballpark Way, Papillion, NE 68046.
Administrative Office Phone: (402) 734-2550. **Ticket Office Phone:** (402) 738-5100. **Fax:** (402) 734-7166.
E-mail Address: info@omahastormchasers.com. **Website:** www.omahastorm-chasers.com.
Affiliation (first year): Kansas City Royals (1969). **Years in League:** 1998-

OWNERSHIP/MANAGEMENT

Operated By: Alliance Baseball Managing Partners. **Owners:** Gary Green, Larry Botel, Eric Foss, Brian Callaghan, Stephen Alepa, Alan Stein, Peter Huff.
CEO: Gary Green. **President/General Manager:** Martie Cordaro. **Assistant GM:** Laurie Schlender. **Assistant GM, Operations:** Andrea Stava. **Office Manager:** Keri Feyerherm. **Director, Broadcasting:** Mark Nasser. **Director, Business Development:** Dave Endress. **Director, Marketing/Communications:** Rob Sternberg. **Director, Sales:** Sean Olson. **Director, Ballpark Operations:** Brett Myers. **Broadcaster/Director, Baseball Operations:** Brett Pollock.. **Senior Corporate Account Manager:** Jason Kinney. **Client Services Manager:** Kaci Long. **Marketing/Promotions Manager:** Rob Sternberg. **Group Sales Manager:** Alex Beck. **Senior Group Sales Executives:** Ryan Worthen, Alex Jerden, Lauren Teer, Andy Baker. **Ticket Operations Manager:** Zach Daw. **Media Relations Manager:** Andrew Green.

Manager, Production/Design: Adam McLaughlin. Multimedia Producer: Cody Hall. Special Events Coordinator: Shawn Fitzpatrick. Community Relations Manager: Megan Burdek. Mascot Coordinator: Taylor Edmonds. Ballpark Operations Coordinator: Matt Owen. Head Groundskeeper: Noah Diercks. Front Office Assistant: Donna Kostal.

FIELD STAFF

Manager: Brian Poldberg. Hitting Coach: Tommy Gregg. Pitching Coach: Andy Hawkins. Athletic Trainer: Dave Iannicca. Strength Coach: Joe Greany.

GAME INFORMATION

Radio Announcers: Mark Nasser, Brett Pollock. No. of Games Broadcast: 144. Flagship Station: KZOT-AM 1180. PA Announcer: Craig Evans. Official Scorers: Frank Adkisson, Steve Pivovar, Ryan White.
Stadium Name: Werner Park. Location: Highway 370, just east of I-80 (exit 439). Standard Game Times: 6:35 pm (April-May), 7:05 (June-Sept), Fri/Sat 7:05, Sun 2:05.
Visiting Club Hotel: Courtyard Omaha La Vista, 12560 Westport Parkway, La Vista, NE 68128. Telephone: (402) 339-4900. Fax: (402) 339-4901.

RENO ACES

Address: 250 Evans Ave, Reno, NV 89501.
Telephone: (775) 334-4700. Fax: (775) 334-4701.
Website: www.renoaces.com.
Affiliation (first year): Arizona Diamondbacks (2009). Years in League: 2009-

OWNERSHIP/MANAGEMENT

Managing Partner: Herb Simon.
Partners: Jerry Katzoff, Stuart Katzoff, Steve Simon. Chief Financial Officer: Chris Gelfuso. General Counsel: Craig Etem. President: Eric Edelstein. Vice President, Executive: Andrew Daugherty. Vice President, Ticket Sales: Samantha Hicks. Manager, Ballpark Operations: Kyle Titus. Director, Broadcasting: Ryan Radtke. Manager, Communications: Cheyne Reiter. Director, Marketing: Audrey Hill. Coordinator, Communications: Ryan Schmitz. Coordinator, Graphic Design/Entertainment: Stephanie Godlewski. Coordinator, Promotions/Community Relations: Jennifer Kastenholz.
Vice President, Business Development: Brian Moss. Manager, Development: Chris Holland. Vice President, Corporate Partnerships: Emily Jaenson. Coordinator, Corporate Partnership Services: Erin Saunders. Account Executives, Corporate Partnerships: Brian Hill, Max Margulies. Manager, Ticket Operations: Sarah Bliss. Coordinator, Ticket Operations: Liz Bell. Manager, Group Sales: Kris Morrow. Account Executives, Outside Sales: Aaron Harmon, Jeff Turner. Account Executives, Group Sales: Nick Gassner, Miles Hendrick, Jillian Stoker. Account Executive: Megan Mazzoni, Ross Melen, Ian Ueltschi. Account Executive, USL Reno: John Wermeling. Coordinator, Sales: Will Hurlburt. Manager, Grounds: Joe Hill. Assistant Groundskeeper: Danny Losito. Coordinator, Ballpark Operations: Anthony Altamura. Manager, Facilities: Miguel Paredes. Director, Merchandise: Jordan Teixeira. Retail Buyer: Stacey Little. Manager, Human Resources/Senior Staff Accountant: Melinda Jessee. Senior Staff Accountant: Jamie Smith. Junior Staff Accountant: Jacquie Menicucci.

FIELD STAFF

Manager: Phil Nevin. Hitting Coach: Greg Gross. Pitching Coach: Gil Heredia. Coach: Tack Wilson. Athletic Trainer: Masa Abe. Strength/Conditioning Coach: Matt Tenney.

GAME INFORMATION

Radio Announcer: Ryan Radtke. No. of Games Broadcast: 144. Flagship Station: Fox Sports 630 AM.
PA Announcer: Unavailable. Official Scorer: Billy Lee, Nick Saccomanno, Katie Rihn, Gregg Zive.
Stadium Name: Aces Ballpark. Location: From north, south and east: I-80 West, Exit 14 (Wells Ave.), left on Wells, right at Kuenzli St., ballpark on right; From West, I-80 East to Exit 13 (Virginia St.), right on Virginia, left on Second, ballpark on left. Standard Game Times: 7:05 pm, 6:35, 1:05. Ticket Price Range: $7-30.
Visiting Club Hotel: Silver Legacy Resort Casino. Telephone: 775-325-7401.

ROUND ROCK EXPRESS

Address: 3400 East Palm Valley Blvd, Round Rock, TX 78665.
Telephone: (512) 255-2255. Fax: (512) 255-1558.
E-Mail Address: info@rrexpress.com. Website: www.roundrockexpress.com.
Affiliation (first year): Texas Rangers (2011). Year in League: 2005-

OWNERSHIP/MANAGEMENT

Operated By: Ryan Sanders Baseball, LP. Principal Owners: Nolan Ryan, Don Sanders. Owners: Reese Ryan, Reid Ryan, Brad Sanders, Bret Sanders, Eddie Maloney.
CEO, Ryan Sanders Baseball: Reese Ryan. Chief Operating Officer, Ryan Sanders Baseball: JJ Gottsch. Executive Assistant, Ryan Sanders Baseball: Debbie Bowman. Administrative Assistant, Ryan Sanders Baseball: Jacqueline Bowman. Special Events Coordinator, Ryan Sanders Baseball: Desa Swaim.
President: Chris Almendarez. General Manager: Tim Jackson. Advisor to President/GM: Dave Fendrick. Senior Vice President, Marketing: Laura Fragoso. VP, Corporate Sales: Henry Green. VP, Ticket Sales: Gary Franke. VP,

MINOR LEAGUES

Business Development: Gregg Miller. **VP, Administration/Accounting:** Debbie Coughlin. **VP, Communications/ PR:** Jill Cacic. **Senior Director, Stadium Operations:** David Powers. **Senior Director, United Heritage Center:** Scott Allen. **Senior Director, Ticket Operations:** Ross Scott. **Director, Broadcasting:** Mike Capps. **Director, Ballpark Entertainment:** Steve Richards. **Director, Stadium Maintenance:** Aurelio Martinez. **Retail Manager:** Joe Belger. **Community Relations Coordinator:** Cassidy MacQuarrie. **Creative Marketing Coordinator:** Randi Null. **Grassroots Marketing Coordinator:** Casey Schnautz. **Client Services:** Zach Pustka. **IT Manager:** Sam Isham.

Stadium Operations Manager: Corey Woods. **Manager, Ticket Sales:** Stuart Scally. **Dell Account Manager:** Julia Benavides. **Account Executives:** Ahnna Moore, Sam Presley, Alyssa Coggins. **Head Groundskeeper:** Garrett Reddehase. **Clubhouse Manager:** Kenny Bufton. **Maintenance Staff:** Ofelia Gonzalez. **Electrician/HVAC Maintenance Staff:** Leslie Hitt. **Office Manager:** Wendy Abrahamsen.

FIELD STAFF

Manager: Jason Woods. **Hitting Coach:** Jim Presley. **Pitching Coach:** Greg Hibbard. **Trainer:** Carlos Olivas. **Strength Coach:** Ric Mabie.

GAME INFORMATION

Radio Announcers: Mike Capps. **No. of Games Broadcast:** 144. **Flagship Station:** The Horn 104.9 FM. **PA Announcer:** Glen Norman. **Official Scorer:** Tommy Tate. **Stadium Name:** Dell Diamond. **Location:** US Highway 79, 3.5 miles east of Interstate 35 (exit 253) or 1.5 miles west of Texas Tollway 130. **Standard Game Times:** 7:05 pm, 6:05, 1:05. **Ticket Price Range:** $7-$30. **Visiting Club Hotel:** Hilton Garden Inn, 2310 North IH-35, Round Rock, TX 78681. **Telephone:** (512) 341-8200.

SACRAMENTO RIVER CATS

Address: 400 Ballpark Drive, West Sacramento, CA 95691
Telephone: (916) 376-4700. **Fax:** (916) 376-4710
E-Mail Address: reception@rivercats.com. **Website:** www.rivercats.com
Affiliation (first year): San Francisco Giants (2015). **Years in League:** 1903, 1909-11, 1918-60, 1974-76, 2000-

OWNERSHIP/MANAGEMENT

Majority Owner/CEO: Susan Savage. **President:** Jeff Savage.

General Manager: Chip Maxson. **Senior Director, Human Resources:** Grace Bailey. **Controller:** Maddie Strika. **Accounting Assistant:** Michelle Agurto. **Executive Assistant:** Bobbi Gallagher. **Receptionist:** Anne Dalisay. **Director, Corporate Partnerships:** Greg Coletti. **Manager, Corporate Partnerships:** Ross Richards. **Coordinator, Partnership Activation:** Barbara Turpen. **Coordinator, Partnership Activation:** Ellese Dias. **Director, Marketing:** Erin O'Donnell. **Manager, Marketing:** Emily Williams. **Coordinator, Multimedia/Graphic Design:** Mike Villarreal. **Baseball Operations Coordinator:** Daniel Emmons. **Media Relations Coordinator:** Robert Barsanti. **Community Relations Coordinator:** Mike Osborn. **Mascot Coordinator:** Lee Warner. **Manager, Merchandise:** Rose Holland.

Assistant Manager, On Deck Shop: Erin Kilby. **Coordinator, Website/Research:** Brent Savage. **Manager, Events/ Entertainment:** Courtney Tyler. **Coordinator, Events/Entertainment:** Erika Busch. **Head Groundskeeper:** Chris Shastid. **Coordinator, Grounds:** Marcello Clamar. **Landscaper:** Rafael Quiroz. **Facility Supervisor:** Anthony Hernandez. **Facility Operations:** Mike Correa, Manual Chavez. **Senior Director, Ticket Sales:** Adam English. **Manager, Corporate Sales:** John Watts. **Manager, Inside Sales:** Joey Van Cleave. **Manager, Group Sales:** Eddie Eixenberger. **Senior Account Executive, Premium Sales/Suites:** Andrew Dean. **Senior Coordinator, Service:** Amanda Holland. **Corporate Account Executives:** DuMaurier Jordan, Michael Stewart, Jennica Berry, Jack Barbour. **Group Events Account Executives:** Alejandro Lacayo, Alexis Stevens, Jeff Goldsmith, Garrett Backhaus. **Inside Sales Representatives:** Zach Moseley, Alannah Bonalos.

FIELD STAFF

Manager: Jose Alguacil. **Hitting Coach:** Damon Minor. **Pitching Coach:** Dwight Bernard. **Athletic Trainer:** James Petra. **Strength Coach:** Adam Vish. **Clubhouse Manager:** Pablo Lopez.

GAME INFORMATION

Radio Broadcaster: Johnny Doskow. **No. of Games Broadcast:** 144. **PA Announcer:** Greg Lawson. **Official Scorers:** Brian Berger, Mark Honbo, Andrew Tomsky. **Stadium Name:** Raley Field. **Location:** I-5 to Business-80 West, exit at Jefferson Boulevard. **Standard Game Time:** 7:05 pm. **Ticket Price Range:** $10-$70. **Visiting Club Hotel:** Holiday Inn Capitol Plaza.

SALT LAKE BEES

Address: 77 W 1300 South, Salt Lake City, UT 84115.
Telephone: (801) 325-2337. **Fax:** (801) 485-6818.
E-Mail Address: info@slbees.com. **Website:** www.slbees.com.

Affiliation (first year): Los Angeles Angels (2001). **Years in League:** 1915-25, 1958-65, 1970-84, 1994-.

OWNERSHIP/MANAGEMENT

Operated by: Larry H. Miller Baseball Inc. **Principal Owner:** Gail Miller. **President, Miller Sports & Entertainment:** Steve Starks. **President, Miller Management Corporation:** Clark Whitworth. **Chief Operating Officer:** Jim Olson. **Chief Revenue Officer:** Don Stirling. **Chief Marketing Officer:** Craig Sanders. **Chief Financial Officer:** John Larson.

Vice President/General Manager: Marc Amicone. **Senior VP, Corporate Partnerships:** Chris Baum. **Senior VP, Ticket Sales:** Clay Jensen. **Senior VP, Communications:** Frank Zang. **General Counsel:** Sam Harkness. **VP, Corporate Partnerships:** Greg Tanner. **Director, Broadcasting:** Steve Klauke. **Director, Ticket Sales/Services:** Brad Jacoway. **Director, Corporate Partnerships:** Ted Roberts. **Senior Director, Marketing:** Kevin Dalton. **Director, Ticket Operations:** Laura Russell. **Communications Manager:** Kraig Williams. **Manager, Game Operations:** Renata Hadden.

Marketing Manager: Brady Brown. **Manager, Baseball Operations:** Bryan Kinneberg. **Ticket/Group Sales Manager:** Collin Forbes. **VP, Public Safety:** Jim Bell. **VP, Food Services:** Mark Stedman. **Director, Food Services:** Dave Dalton. **Youth Programs Coordinator:** Nate Martinez. **Clubhouse Manager:** Eli Rice. **Head Groundskeeper:** Brian Soukup.

FIELD STAFF

Manager: Keith Johnson. **Hitting Coach:** Tom Tornincasa. **Pitching Coach:** Erik Bennett. **Trainer:** Brian Reinker.

GAME INFORMATION

Radio Announcer: Steve Klauke. **No. of Games Broadcast:** 144. **Flagship Station:** 1280 AM.

PA Announcer: Jeff Reeves. **Official Scorers:** Howard Nakagama, Jeff Cluff.

Stadium Name: Smith's Ballpark. **Location:** I-15 North/South to 1300 South exit, east to ballpark at West Temple. **Standard Game Times:** 6:35 (April-May), 7:05 (June-Sept), Sun 1:05 (April-May), 7:05 (June-Sept). **Ticket Price Range:** $10-24.

Visiting Club Hotel: Sheraton City Centre, 150 W 500 South, Salt Lake City, UT 84101. **Telephone:** (801) 401-2000.

TACOMA RAINIERS

Address: 2502 South Tyler St, Tacoma, WA 98405.
Telephone: (253) 752-7707. **Fax:** (253) 752-7135.
Website: www.tacomarainiers.com.
Affiliation: Seattle Mariners (1995). **Years in League:** 1960-

OWNERSHIP/MANAGEMENT

Owners: The Baseball Club of Tacoma.

President: Aaron Artman. **Director, Administration/Assistant to President:** Patti Stacy. **Vice President, Business Development:** Jim Flavin. **VP, Sales:** Shane Santman. **Controller:** Brian Coombe. **Director, Ballpark Operations:** Nick Cherniske. **Creative Director:** Tony Canepa. **Media Relations Coordinator:** Brett Gleason. **Director, Partner Development:** Julia Falvey. **Director, Baseball Operations/Merchandise:** Ashley Schutt. **Director, Ticket Operations:** Cameron Badgett. **Director, Marketing/Partner Services:** Betsy Hechtner.

Manager, Suite Services/Events: Taryn Duncan. **Corporate Sales Managers:** Andrew Barry, Isaiah Dowdell, Kevin Drugge, Jordan Leister, Tyler Olsson. **Senior Corporate Sales Managers:** Ben Nelson, Tim O'Hollaren. **Coordinator, Box Office:** Necia Borba. **Coordinator, Event Sales:** Byron Pullen. **Coordinator, Corporate Partner Services:** Yvette Yzaguirre. **Senior Group Event Coordinator:** Chris Aubertin. **Group Event Coordinators:** Caitlin Calnan, Charlotte Freed, Natalie Hostetter, Lohren Stitt. **Director, Game Entertainment:** Casey Catherwood. **Technical Coordinator:** Anthony Phinney. **Senior Accountant:** Elise Schorr. **Head Groundskeeper:** Michael Huie. **Receptionist:** Taylor Barham. **Home Clubhouse Manager:** Shane Hickenbottom.

FIELD STAFF

Manager: Pat Listach. **Hitting Coach:** Scott Brosius. **Pitching Coach:** Lance Painter. **Trainers:** Tom Newberg, BJ Downie. **Performance Specialist:** Derek Mendoza.

GAME INFORMATION

Radio Broadcaster: Mike Curto. **No. of Games Broadcast:** 144. **Flagship Station:** KHHO 850-AM.

PA Announcer: Randy McNair. **Official Scorers:** Kevin Kalal, Gary Brooks, Michael Jessee.

Stadium Name: Cheney Stadium. **Location:** From I-5, take exit 132 (Highway 16 West) for 1.2 miles to 19th Street East exit, merge right onto 19th Street, right onto Clay Huntington Way and follow into parking lot of ballpark. **Standard Game Times:** 7:05, Sun 1:35. **Ticket Price Range:** $7.50-$25.50.

Visiting Club Hotel: Hotel Murano, 1320 Broadway Plaza, Tacoma, WA 98402. **Telephone:** (253) 238-8000.

EASTERN LEAGUE

Address: 30 Danforth St, Suite 208, Portland, ME 04101.
Telephone: (207) 761-2700. **Fax:** (207) 761-7064.
E-Mail Address: elpb@easternleague.com. **Website:** www.easternleague.com.
Years League Active: 1923-

President/Treasurer: Joe McEacharn.
Vice President/Secretary: Charlie Eshbach. **VP:** Chuck Domino. **Assistant to President:**
Bill Rosario. **Directors:** Fernando Aguirre (Erie), Ken Babby (Akron), Rick Brenner (New
Hampshire), Mark Butler (Harrisburg), Lou DiBella (Richmond), Geoff Iacuessa (Portland), Joe
Finley (Trenton), John Hughes (Binghamton), Bob Lozinak (Altoona), Brian Shallcross (Bowie),
Josh Solomon (Hartford), Craig Stein (Reading).

Division Structure: Eastern—Binghamton, Hartford, New Hampshire, Portland, Reading,
Trenton. **Western**—Akron, Altoona, Bowie, Erie, Harrisburg, Richmond.

Regular Season: 142 games. **2016 Opening Date:** April 7. **Closing Date:** Sept 5.
All-Star Game: July 13 at Akron.

Playoff Format: Top two teams in each division meet in best-of-five series. Winners meet in
best-of-five series for league championship.

Roster Limit: 25. **Player Eligibility Rule:** No restrictions.
Brand of Baseball: Rawlings.

Joe McEacharn

Umpires: Erich Bacchus (Germantown, MD), Ryan Benson (Danbury, CT), Paul Clemons
(Oxford, KS), Scott Costello (Barrie, Ontario), Doug Del Bello (Hamburg, NY), Christopher
Graham (Newmarket, Ontario), Rich Grassa (Lindenhurst, NY), Ben Levin (Cincinnati, OH), John Libka (Port Huron, MI),
John Mang (Youngstown, OH), Brian Peterson (Seaside Heights, NJ), Michael Provine (Newtown, PA), Charlie Ramos
(Grand Rapids, MI), Sean Ryan (Waunakee, WI), Jorge Teran (Barquisimeto, Venezuela), Alex Tosi (Chicago, IL), Ryan Wills
(Williamsburg, VA), Michael Wiseman (White Lake, MI).

STADIUM INFORMATION

Club	Stadium	Opened	Dimensions LF	Dimensions CF	Dimensions RF	Capacity	2015 Att.
Akron	Canal Park	1997	331	400	337	7,630	340,916
Altoona	Peoples Natural Gas Field	1999	325	405	325	7,210	302,761
Binghamton	NYSEG Stadium	1992	330	400	330	6,012	188,104
Bowie	Prince George's Stadium	1994	309	405	309	10,000	256,865
Erie	Jerry Uht Park	1995	317	400	328	6,000	203,655
Harrisburg	Metro Bank Park	1987	325	400	325	6,300	301,588
Hartford*	Dunkin Donuts Park	2016	325	400	325	6,146	267,377
New Hampshire	Northeast Delta Dental Stadium	2005	326	400	306	6,500	368,291
Portland	Hadlock Field	1994	315	400	330	7,368	359,427
Reading	FirstEnergy Stadium	1951	330	400	330	9,000	417,010
Richmond	The Diamond	1985	330	402	330	9,560	417,828
Trenton	Arm & Hammer Park	1994	330	407	330	6,150	347,231

*Team operated as New Britain Rock Cats in 2015

AKRON RUBBERDUCKS

Address: 300 S Main St, Akron, OH 44308.
Telephone: (330) 253-5151. **Fax:** (330) 253-3300.
E-Mail Address: information@akronrubberducks.com. **Web site:** www.akronrub-
berducks.com.
Affiliation (first year): Cleveland Indians (1989). **Years in League:** 1989-

OWNERSHIP/MANAGEMENT

Operated By: Akron Baseball, LLC. **Principal Owner:** Ken Babby.
General Manager/COO: Jim Pfander. **Assistant GM:** Scott Riley. **Controller:** Leslie Wenzlawsh. **Financial Analyst:**
Sean Flowerday. **Coordinator, Promotions:** Christina Urycki. **Director, Public/Media Relations:** Adam Liberman.
Director, Broadcasting/Baseball Information: Dave Wilson. **Coordinator, Merchandise:** Jeff Campano . **Manager,
Creative Services:** Marissa Forcina. **Director, Stadium Operations:** Adam Horner. **Head Groundskeeper:** Chris Walsh.
Assistant Director, Ballpark Operations: Taylor Englebaugh. **Director, Food/Beverage:** Brian Manning. **Assistant
Director, Food/Beverage:** Colin Tulley. Director, **Suites & Special Events:** Sam Dankoff. **Office Manager:** Missy Dies.
Coordinator, Community Relations: Alex Hawks. **Box Office Manager:** Pete Nugent. **Director, Ticket Operations:**
Brian Flenner. **Director, Ticket Sales:** Jeremy Heit. **Senior Group Sales Manager:** Mitch Cromes. **Senior Account
Executive:** Dee Shilling. **Ticket Sales Executives:** Craig Wilson, Mark Carlozzi, Jenna Reed. **Director, Corporate
Partnerships:** Brent DeCoster. **Manager, Corporate Partnerships:** Juli Donlen. **Graphic Designer:** Taylor Myers.
Director, Player Facilities: Shad Gross.

FIELD STAFF

Manager: Dave Wallace. **Hitting Coach:** Tim Laker. **Pitching Coach:** Tony Arnold. **Trainer:** Jeremy Heller. **Strength/Conditioning Coach:** TBD.

GAME INFORMATION

Radio Announcers: Jim Clark, Dave Wilson. **No of Games Broadcast:** 142. **Flagship Station:** Fox Sports Radio 1350-AM.

PA Announcer: TBD. **Official Scorer:** Tom Giffen.

Stadium Name: Canal Park. **Location:** From I-76 East or I-77 South, exit onto Route 59 East, exit at Exchange/Cedar, right onto Cedar, left at Main Street; From I-76 West or I-77 North, exit at Main Street/Downtown, follow exit onto Broadway Street, left onto Exchange Street, right at Main Street. **Standard Game Time:** 6:35 (April-May); 7:05 pm (June-Sept), Sun 2:05. **Ticket Price Range:** $5-9. **Visiting Club Hotel:** TBD. **Telephone:** TBD.

ALTOONA CURVE

Address: Peoples Natural Gas Field, 1000 Park Avenue, Altoona, PA 16602
Telephone: (814) 943-5400. **Fax:** (814) 942-9132
E-Mail Address: frontoffice@**altoonacurve.com Website: http://**www.altoonacurve.com/
Affiliation (first year): Pittsburgh Pirates (1999). **Years in League:** 1999-

OWNERSHIP/MANAGEMENT

Operated By: Lozinak Professional Baseball. **Managing Members:** Bob and Joan Lozinak. **COO:** David Lozinak. **CFO:** Mike Lozinak. **Chief Administrative Officer:** Steve Lozinak. **General Manager:** Rob Egan. **Senior Advisor:** Sal Baglieri. **Director, Finance:** Mary Lamb. **Assistant Director, Finance:** Katie Cence. **Administrative Assistant:** Donna Harpster. **Director, Ticket Operations:** Corey Homan. **Box Office Manager:** Steffan Langguth. **Senior Ticket Associate:** Nathan Bowen. **Ticket Associate:** Jess Knott. **Sponsorship Sales Executive:** Adam Erikson. Director, **Marketing & Promotions:** Mike Kessling. **Manager, Communications/Broadcasting:** Trey Wilson. **Manager, Community Relations/Special Events:** Emily Rosencrants. **Ballpark Operations Manager:** Doug Mattern. **Head Groundskeeper:** McClain Murphy. **Manager of Concessions:** Glenn McComas. **Assistant Manager, Concessions:** Michelle Anna. **Mascot Development/Marketing Coordinator:** Isaiah Arpino. **Merchandise Manager:** Michelle Gravert.

FIELD STAFF

Manager: Joey Cora. **Hitting Coach:** Kevin Riggs. **Pitching Coach:** Justin Meccage. **Trainer:** Dru Scott. **Strength/Conditioning:** Alan Burr.

GAME INFORMATION

Radio Announcers: Trey Wilson, Nathan Bowen. **No. of Games Broadcast:** 142. **Flagship Station:** ESPN Radio 1430-AM, WVAM. **PA Announcer:** Rich DeLeo. **Official Scorers:** Ted Beam, Dick Wagner. **Stadium Name:** Peoples Natural Gas Field. **Location:** Located just off the Frankstown Road Exit off I-99. **Standard Game Times:** 7 p.m., 6 p.m. (April-May); Sat. 6 p.m., Sun 6 p.m. **Ticket Price Range:** $5-12. **Visiting Club Hotel:** Altoona Grand Hotel.

BINGHAMTON METS

Office Address: 211 Henry St., Binghamton, NY 13901. **Mailing Address:** PO Box 598, Binghamton, NY 13902.
Telephone: (607) 723-6387. **Fax:** (607) 723-7779.
E-Mail Address: bmets@bmets.com. **Website:** www.bmets.com.
Affiliation (first year): New York Mets (1992). **Years in League:** 1923-37, 1940-63, 1966-68, 1992-

OWNERSHIP/MANAGEMENT

President: John Hughes. **General Manager:** Jim Weed. Director, **Broadcasting & Media Relations:** Tim Heiman. **Director, Community Relations:** Connor Gates
Director, Marketing: Eddie Saunders. **Director, Sales:** Amber Coyne. **Director, Stadium Operations:** Richard Tylicki. **Director, Video Production:** Joe Campione. **Box Office Manager:** Jordan Jicha. **Sports Turf Manager:** Tyler Jennings. **Office Manager, Senior Accountant:** Karen Micalizzi. **Scholastic Programs Coordinator:** Lou Ferarro. **Special Events Coordinators:** Connor Gates. **Merchandise Manager:** Lisa Shattuck.

FIELD STAFF

Manager: Pedro Lopez. **Hitting Coach:** Luis Natera. **Pitching Coach:** Glenn Abbott.

GAME INFORMATION

Radio Announcer: Tim Heiman. **No. of Games Broadcast:** 142. **Flagship Station:** WNBF 1290-AM. **PA Announcer:** Chris Schmidt, Roger Neel. **Official Scorer:** Steve Kraly. **Stadium Name:** NYSEG Stadium. **Location:** I-81 to exit 4S (Binghamton), Route 11 exit to Henry Street. **Standard Game Times:** 6:35, 7:05 (Fri-Sat), 1:05 (Day Games). **Ticket Price Range:** $7 - $12.
Visiting Club Hotel: Best Western, 569 Harry L Drive, Johnson City, NY 13790. **Telephone:** (607) 729-9194.

BOWIE BAYSOX

Address: Prince George's Stadium, 4101 NE Crain Hwy, Bowie, MD 20716.
Telephone: (301) 805-6000. Fax: (301) 464-4911.
E-Mail Address: info@baysox.com. Website: www.baysox.com.
Affiliation (first year): Baltimore Orioles (1993). Years in League: 1993-

OWNERSHIP/MANAGEMENT

Owned By: Bowie Baysox Baseball Club LLC.
President: Ken Young. General Manager: Brian Shallcross. Assistant GM: Phil Wrye. Director, Marketing: Brandan Kaiser. Director, Field/Facility Operations: Matt Parrott. Director, Ticket Operations: Charlene Fewer. Director, Sponsorships: Matt McLaughlin. Assistant Director, Ticket Operations: Sam Colein. Promotions Manager: Chris Rogers. Communications Manager: Matt Wilson. Sponsorship Account Manager: Adam Pohl. Group Events Managers: Patrick Gotimer, Seph Moeder. Box Office Manager: Landon Ferrell. Director, Video Production: Mitchell Block. Stadium Operations Manager: Austin Ingersoll. Assistant Head Groundskeeper: Andrew Lawing. Director, Gameday Personnel: Darlene Mingioli. Clubhouse Manager: Andy Maalouf. Bookkeeper: Carol Terwilliger.

FIELD STAFF

Manager: Gary Kendall. Coach: Howie Clark. Pitching Coach: Alan Mills.

GAME INFORMATION

Radio Announcer: Adam Pohl. No. of Games Broadcast: 142. Flagship Station: www.1430wnav.com.
PA Announcer: Adrienne Roberson. Official Scorers: Peter O'Reilly, Carl Smith, Ted Black, Herb Martinson.
Stadium Name: Prince George's Stadium. Location: 1/4 mile south of US 50/Route 301 Interchange in Bowie.
Standard Game Times: Mon-Thu, Sat. 6:35 pm, Fri 7:05 pm, Sun 2:05 pm. Ticket Price Range: $7-17.
Visiting Club Hotel: Best Western Annapolis, 2520 Riva Rd, Annapolis, MD 21401. Telephone: (410) 224-2800

ERIE SEAWOLVES

Address: 110 E 10th St, Erie, PA 16501.
Telephone: (814) 456-1300. Fax: (814) 456-7520.
E-Mail Address: seawolves@seawolves.com. Website: www.seawolves.com.
Affiliation (first year): Detroit Tigers (2001). Years in League: 1999-

OWNERSHIP/MANAGEMENT

Principal Owners: At Bat Group, LLC. CEO: Fernando Aguirre. President: Greg Coleman. Assistant GM, Communications: Greg Gania. Assistant GM, Sales: Mark Pirrello. Director, Accounting/Finance: Amy McArdle. Director, Operation: Chris McDonald. Director, Entertainment: Scott Ciaccia. Director, Group Sales: Dan Torf. Account Executive: Megan Allen. Ticket Operations Manager: Justin Cartor. Director, Food/Beverage: Mike Riffle.

FIELD STAFF

Manager: Lance Parrish. Hitting Coach: Phil Clark. Pitching Coach: Willie Blair. Trainer: T.J. Saunders. Strength/Conditioning Coach: David Snedden.

GAME INFORMATION

Radio Announcer: Greg Gania. No. of Games Broadcast: 142. Flagship Station: Fox Sports Radio WFNN 1330-AM.
PA Announcer: Bob Shreve. Official Scorer: Les Caldwell. Stadium Name: Jerry Uht Park. Location: US 79 North to East 12th Street exit, left on State Street, right on 10th Street. Standard Game Times: 7:05 p.m., 6:35 p.m. (April-May), Sun 1:35 p.m. Ticket Price Range: $9-15.
Visiting Club Hotel: Clarion Lake Erie, 2800 West 8th St., Erie, PA 16505.
Telephone: (814) 833-1116.

HARRISBURG SENATORS

Office Address: FNB Field, City Island, Harrisburg, PA 17101.
Mailing Address: PO Box 15757, Harrisburg, PA 17105. Telephone: (717) 231-4444. Fax: (717) 231-4445.
E-Mail address: information@senatorsbaseball.com. Website: www.senators-baseball.com.
Affiliation (first year): Washington Nationals (2005). Years in League: 1924-35, 1987-

OWNERSHIP, MANAGEMENT

Operated By: Senators Partners, LLC. Principal Owner: Mark Butler. President: Kevin Kulp. General Manager: Randy Whitaker. Assistant GM, Game Operations: Aaron Margolis. Accounting Manager: Donna Demczak. Accounting, Assistant: Izzy Carter. Senior Corporate Sales Executive: Todd Matthews. Senior Sales Executive of Corporate Development: Nate DeFazio. Director of Ticket Sales: Jonathan Boles. Senior Account Executive: Jessica Moyer. Account Executive: Kevin Dougherty, Brian Becka, Josh Mohn. Sales Service Coordinator: Madeline

BaseballAmerica.com

Moreno. **Box Office Manager:** Matt McGrady. **Box Office Intern:** Josh Bleyer. **General Business Intern:** Miguel Acri-Rodriguez. **Ticket Sales and Service Interns:** John Fellon, Nathan Joyce, Daniel Jones, and L.K. Thompson. **Director, Merchandise:** Ann Marie Naumes. **Director, Stadium Operations:** Tim Foreman. **Head Groundskeeper:** Brandon Forsburg. **Director, Broadcasting/Media Relations:** Terry Byrom. **Broadcaster/Media Relations Assistant:** Perry Mattern. **Community Relations Coordinator:** Blair Jewell. **Community Relations Intern:** Alex Brandt. **Director, Digital/New Media:** Ashley Grotte. **Game Entertainment and Production Coordinator:** Sami Lesniak.

FIELD STAFF

Manager: Matt LeCroy. **Coach:** Brian Rupp. **Pitching Coach:** Chris Michalak. **Trainer:** Eric Montague. **Strength Coach:** Tony Rogowski.

GAME INFORMATION

Radio Announcers: Terry Byrom & Perry Mattern. **No. of Games Broadcast:** Home-71 Road-71. **Flagship Station:** 1460-AM. **PA Announcer:** Chris Andree. **Official Scorers:** Andy Linker and Mick Reinhard. **Stadium Name:** FNB Field. **Location:** I-83, exit 23 (Second Street) to Market Street, bridge to City Island. **Ticket Price Range:** $9-17. **Visiting Club Hotel:** Park Inn by Radisson, 5401 Carlisle Pike, Mechanicsburg, PA 17050. **Telephone:** (800) 772-7829. **Visiting Team Workout Facility:** Gold's Gym, 3401 Hartzdale Dr., Camp Hill, PA 17011. **Telephone:** (717) 303-2070.

HARTFORD YARD GOATS

Dunkin' Donuts Park: 1214 Main Street, Hartford CT 06103
Telephone: (860) 246-4628 **Fax:** (860) 247-4628
E-Mail Address: info@yardgoatsbaseball.com. **Website:** www.YardGoatsBaseball.com
Affiliation (second year): Colorado Rockies (2015). **Years in League:** (First Season)

OWNERSHIP/MANAGEMENT

Operated By: Connecticut Double Play LLC. **Directors:** Josh Solomon, Jim Solomon, Jennifer Goorno.
General Manager: Tim Restall. **Assistant General Manager:** Mike Ambramson. **Executive Director, Tickets:** Josh Montinieri. **Executive Director, Corporate Partnership:** Dean Zappalorti. Director, **Broadcasting & Media Relations:** Jeff Dooley. **Director, Business Development:** Steve Given. Director, **Hospitality & Events:** Andres Levy. **Director, Creative Services:** Ted Seavey. **Director,Stadium Operations:** Pat Kennedy. **Director, Community Partnerships:** Tiffany Young. **Controller:** Jim Bonfiglio. **Client & Sponsorship Relations Manager:** Amanda Goldsmith. **Ticket Operations Manager:** Dylan Conway. **Corporate Partnership Executive:** Steve Mekkelsen. **Marketing Coordinator:** Lori Soltis. **Ticket Sales Account Executive:** Matt DiBona. **Ticket Sales Account Executive:** Shawn Perry. **Marketing & Sponsor Relationship Manager:** Kathy Damato. **Stadium Operations Manager:** Dave Onusko. **Ticket Sales Account Executive:** Eric Eisenberg. **Merchandise Manager:** Eric Lorenzen. **Ticket Sales Account Executive:** Tom Baxter. **Ticket Sales Account Executive:** Matt Lafrennie. **Sports Turf Manager:** Kyle Calhoon. **Ticket Sales Account Executive:** Aisha Petteway. **Professional Sports Catering Director of Food & Beverage:** Austin Sagolla. **Senior Concessions Manager:** Zack Hermayer. **Executive Chef:** Chris Micci. **Catering & Business Manager:** Denise Picard.

FIELD STAFF

Manager: Darin Everson. **Coach:** Ron Gideon. **Pitching Coach:** Dave Burba. **Hitting Coach:** Jeff Salazar. **Trainer:** Billy Whitehead.

GAME INFORMATION

Radio Announcers: Jeff Dooley, Dan Lovallo. **No. of Games Broadcast:** 142. **Flagship Station:** News Radio 1410. **PA Announcer:** John Sheatsley. **Official Scorer:** Ed Smith.
Stadium Name: Dunkin' Donuts Park. **Directions: From the West:** Take 84 East to Exit 50 (Main Street). Take Exit 50 toward Main St. Use the left lane to merge onto Chapel S. Turn left onto Trumbull St. Use the middle lane to turn left onto Main St. **From the East:** Take 84 West to Exit 50 (US-44 W/Morgan Street). Follow I-91 S/Main St. Take a slight right onto Main St. **From the North:** Take 91 South to Exit 32A - 32B (Trumbull St). Turn left onto Market St. Turn right onto Morgan St. Take a slight right onto Main St. **From the South:** Take 91 North to Exit 32A - 32B (Market St). Use the left lane to take Exit 32A-32B for Trumbull St. Use the middle lane to turn left onto Market St. Turn right onto Morgan St. Take a slight right onto Main St. **Ticket Price Range:** $6-22. **Visiting Club Hotel:** Holiday Inn Express, 2553 Berlin Turnpike, Newington, CT 06111. (860) 372-4000.

NEW HAMPSHIRE
FISHER CATS

Address: 1 Line Dr, Manchester, NH 03101.
Telephone: (603) 641-2005. **Fax:** (603) 641-2055.
E-Mail Address: info@nhfishercats.com. **Website:** www.nhfishercats.com.
Affiliation (first year): Toronto Blue Jays (2004). **Years in League:** 2004-

OWNERSHIP/MANAGEMENT

Operated By: DSF Sports. **Owner:** Art Solomon. **President/General Manager:** Rick Brenner. **Senior VP, Sales:** Mike Ramshaw. **Senior VP/Assistant GM:** Jenna Raizes. **General Counsel/VP, Business Operations:** Steve Pratt. **VP, Stadium Operations:** Tim Hough. **VP, Ticket Sales:** Rob Vota. Executive Director, **Finance & Human Resources:** Debbie Morin. **Executive Director, Sales:** Erik Lesniak. **Executive Director, Broadcast/Media Relations:** Tom Gauthier. **Director, Merchandise:** John Egan. **Director, Hospitality/Special Events:** Stephanie Fournier. **Director, Creative Services:** Patrick Wallace. **Sports Turf Manager:** Dan Boyle. **Manager, Group Sales:** Matt Freeman. **Manager, Ticket Sales:** Michael Frissore. **Manager, Box Office:** Ryan Hyjek. **Manager, Business Development:** Jon Mersereau. Manager, **Community & Corporate Sales:** Tamara O'Donnell. **Manager, Facility Operations:** D.J. Peer. Coordinator, Media Relations/**Broadcasting & Account Executive:** Ben Gellman. Coordinator, **Group Sales & Account Executive:** Tom Devarenne. **Inside Sales Representatives:** John Evans, Zachary Weiner. Professional Sports Catering, Director, **Food & Beverage:** Kyle Lindquist.

FIELD STAFF

Manager: TBA. **Hitting Coach:** TBA. **Pitching Coach:** TBA. **Athletic Trainer:** TBA. **Strength/Conditioning:** TBA.

GAME INFORMATION

Radio Announcers: Tom Gauthier, Bob Lipman, Ben Gellman. **No. of Games Broadcast:** 142. **Flagship Station:** WGIR 610-AM.

PA Announcer: Ben Altsher, Eric Coplin, John Vitale. **Official Scorers:** Chick Smith, Lenny Parker, Pete Dupuis. **Stadium Name:** Northeast Delta Dental Stadium. **Location:** From I-93 North, take I-293 North to exit 5 (Granite Street), right on Granite Street, right on South Commercial Street, right on Line Drive. **Ticket Price Range:** $6-12. **Visiting Club Hotel:** Country Inn & Suites, 250 South River Rd., Bedford, N.H. 03110. **Telephone:** (603) 666-4600.

PORTLAND SEA DOGS

Office Address: 271 Park Ave, Portland, ME 04102. **Mailing Address:** PO Box 636, Portland, ME 04104.
Telephone: (207) 874-9300. **Fax:** (207) 780-0317.
E-Mail address: seadogs@seadogs.com. **Website:** www.seadogs.com.
Affiliation (first year): Boston Red Sox (2003). **Years in League:** 1994-

OWNERSHIP/MANAGEMENT

Operated By: Portland, Maine Baseball, Inc. **Chairman:** Bill Burke. **Treasurer:** Sally McNamara. **President:** Charles Eshbach. **Executive Vice President/General Manager:** Geoff Iacuessa. **Senior VP:** John Kameisha. **VP, Financial Affairs/Game Operations:** Jim Heffley. **Assistant GM, Media Relations:** Chris Cameron. **Executive Director, Sales:** Dennis Meehan. **Ticket Office Manager:** Dennis Carter. **Account Executive, Sales/Promotions:** Courtney Rague. **Account Executives, Sales:** Justin Phillips, John Muzzy. **Assistant Ticket Manager:** Bryan Pahigian. **Creative Services Manager:** Sammi Gorman. **Mascot Coordinator:** Tim Jorn. **Director, Broadcasting:** Mike Antonellis. **Director, Food Services:** Mike Scorza. **Assistant Director, Food Services:** Greg Moyes. **Office Manager:** Lyndsey Berry. **Clubhouse Managers:** Craig Candage Sr, Mike Coziahr. **Head Groundskeeper:** Rick Anderson.

FIELD STAFF

Manager: Carlos Febles. **Coach:** Jon Nunnally. **Pitching Coach:** Kevin Walker. **Trainer:** TBA.

GAME INFORMATION

Radio Announcer: Mike Antonellis. **No. of Games Broadcast:** 142. **Flagship Station:** WPEI 95.9 FM. **PA Announcer:** Paul Coughlin. **Official Scorer:** Thom Hinton. **Stadium Name:** Hadlock Field. **Location:** From South, I-295 to exit 5, merge onto Congress Street, left at St John Street, merge right onto Park Ave; From North, I-295 to exit 6A, right onto Park Ave. **Ticket Price Range:** $6-11.
Visiting Club Hotel: Fireside Inn & Suites, 81 Riverside St., Portland, ME 04103. **Telephone:** (207) 774-5601.

READING FIGHTIN PHILS

Office Address: Route 61 South/1900 Centre Ave, Reading, PA 19605. **Mailing Address:** PO Box 15050, Reading, PA 19612.
Telephone: (610) 370-2255. **Fax:** (610) 373-5868.
E-Mail Address: info@fightins.com. **Website:** www.fightins.com.
Affiliation (first year): Philadelphia Phillies (1967). **Years in League:** 1933-35, 1952-61, 1963-65, 1967-

OWNERSHIP/MANAGEMENT

Operated By: E&J Baseball Club, Inc. **Principal Owner:** Reading Baseball LP. **Managing Partner:** Craig Stein. **General Manager:** Scott Hunsicker. **Executive Director, Sales:** Joe Bialek. **Executive Director, Operations:** Matt Hoffmaster. **Executive Director, Baseball Operations & Merchandise:** Kevin Sklenarik. **Executive Director, Graphic Arts/Game Entertainment:** Matt Jackson. **Executive Director, Tickets:** Mike Becker. **Executive Director, Community Relations/Fan Development:** Mike Robinson. **Controller:** Kristyne Haver. **Head Groundskeeper:** Dan "Dirt" Douglas. **Director, Business Development:** Anthony Pignetti. **Video Director:** Andy Kauffman. **Office Manager:** Deneen Giesen. Director, **Food & Beverage:** Travis Hart. **Director, Educational Programs/Music/Game Presentation:**

Todd Hunsicker. **Director, Groups:** Jon Nally. **Director, Public Relations/Media Relations:** Eric Scarcella. **Director, Fundraising/Clubhouse Operations:** Andrew Nelson. **Manager, Groups/Extra Events/Game Presentation:** Stephen Thomas. **Managers, Groups:** Bill Richards, Derek Lupia. **Manager, Operations/Sales Representative:** Brian Hoeper. Merchandising Manager/Sales Rep.: Ryan Springborn. **Director, Marketing:** Tonya Petrunak.

FIELD STAFF
Manager: Dusty Wathan. **Coach:** Frank Cacciatore. **Pitching Coach:** Steve Schrenk.

GAME INFORMATION
Radio Announcer: Mike Ventola. **No. of Games Broadcast:** 142. **Flagship Station:** CBS Sports Radio 1240 AM.
PA Announcer: Justin Choate. **Official Scorers:** Paul Jones, Brian Kopetsky, Josh Leiboff, Dick Shute.
Stadium Name: FirstEnergy Stadium. **Location:** From east, take Pennsylvania Turnpike West to Morgantown exit, to 176 North, to 422 West, to Route 12 East, to Route 61 South exit; From west, take 422 East to Route 12 East, to Route 61 South exit; From north, take 222 South to Route 12 exit, to Route 61 South exit; From south, take 222 North to 422 West, to Route 12 East exit at Route 61 South. **Standard Game Times:** 7:05 pm, 6:35 (April-May), Sun. 2:05. **Ticket Price Range:** $5-11.
Visiting Club Hotel: Crowne Plaza Reading Hotel 1741 Papermill Road, Wyomissing, PA 19610. **Telephone:** (610) 376-3811.

RICHMOND FLYING SQUIRRELS

Address: 3001 N Boulevard, Richmond, VA 23230.
Telephone: (804) 359-3866. **Fax:** (804) 359-1373.
E-Mail Address: info@squirrelsbaseball.com. **Website:** www.squirrelsbaseball.com.
Affiliation: San Francisco Giants (2009). **Years in League:** 2009-

OWNERSHIP/MANAGEMENT
Operated By: Navigators Baseball LP. **President/Managing Partner:** Lou DiBella.
CEO: Chuck Domino. **Vice President/COO:** Todd "Parney" Parnell.
General Manager: Bill Papierniak. **Controller:** Faith Casey. **Director, Corporate Sales:** Mike Murphy. **Corporate Sales Executives:** Will Bell. **Assistant GM, Sales:** Brendon Porter. **Director, Tickets:** Patrick Flower. **Box Office Manager:** Andy Webb. **Director, Suite Sales/Client Relations:** Jerrine Lee. **Director, Business Development:** Marty Steele. Director of Broadcasting, **Communications & Marketing:** Jay Burnham. Director, Promotions/In-**Game Entertainment/Creative Services Manager:** Kellye Semonich. **Community Relations Manager:** Megan Angstadt. **Director of Group Sales:** Camp Peery, Assistant Director of Group Sales Chris Walker. Group Sales Executives Garrett Erwin, Deidre Geroni. **Corporate Sales Executive: Erin McDonald, Ticket Sales Executive Rebecca Lynch:** AG of Operations Ben Rothrock. **Director of Food/Beverage:** Mike Caddell. **Director, Tasty Goodness/Chef/Catering:** Josh Barban. **Director, Field Operations:** Steve Ruckman. **Assistant Director, Field Operations:** Kody Tingler. **Director, Stadium Operations:** Steve Pump.

FIELD STAFF
Manager: Miguel Ojeda. **Hitting Coach:** Ken Joyce. **Pitching Coach:** Steve Kline. **Athletic Trainer:** David Getsoff. **Strength/Conditioning Coach:** Mike Lidge.

GAME INFORMATION
Radio Announcers: Jay Burnham & Gregg Caserta. **No. of Games Broadcast:** 142. **Flagship Station:** Fox Sports Richmond WRNL-AM.
PA Announcer: Jimmy Barrett. **Official Scorer:** Scott Day.
Stadium Name: The Diamond. **Location:** Right off I-64 at the Boulevard exit. **Standard Game Times:** 7:05 pm, Sat. 6:35, Sun. 5:05. **Ticket Price Range:** $7-12.
Visiting Club Hotel: Comfort Suites at Virginia Center Commons, 10601 Telegraph Road, Glen Allen, VA. **Telephone:** (804) 262-2000.

TRENTON THUNDER

Address: One Thunder Road, Trenton, NJ 08611.
Telephone: (609) 394-3300. **Fax:** (609) 394-9666.
E-Mail address: fun@trentonthunder.com. **Website:** www.trentonthunder.com.
Affiliation (first year): New York Yankees (2003). **Years in League:** 1994-

OWNERSHIP/MANAGEMENT

Operated By: Garden State Baseball, LLP. **General Manager/COO:** Jeff Hurley.
Senior VP, Corporate Sales/Partnerships: Eric Lipsman. **Senior Director, Ticket Operations and Baseball Operations:** Matt Pentima. **Director, Merchandising:** Joe Pappalardo. **Director, Marketing/Sponsorship:** Lydia Rios. **Director, Food/Beverage:** Chris Champion. **Director, Stadium Operations:** Steve Brokowsky. **Director, Creative Services:** Chris Foster. **Director, Broadcast/Media Relations:** Adam Giardino. **Director, Grounds:** Mike Kerns. **Controller:** Trevor Hain. **Manager, Public Relations:** Jon Mozes. **Manager, Community Relations and Corporate Sales:** Vince Marcucci. **Manager, Stadium Operations:** Bryan Rock. **Manager, Group Sales:** Jon Bodnar. **Ticket Sales Account Executive:** Janelle Alfano, Sean O'Brien. **Group Sales Account Executive:** Jack Rymal, Nick Luongo, Chuck Keller, Michael Heyer. **Ticket Sales Account Representative:** Steven Carpenter. **Group Sales Account Representative:** Brian Davis. **Chef:** Corey Anderson. **Office Manager:** Mary Genthe.

FIELD STAFF

Manager: Bobby Mitchell . **Hitting Coach:** P.J. Pilittere. **Pitching Coach:** Jose Rosado. **Defensive Coach:** Justin Tordi. **Bullpen Coach:** JD Closser. **Trainer:** Lee Meyer. **Strength/Conditioning Coach:** TBA.

GAME INFORMATION

Radio Announcers: Adam Giardino, Jon Mozes. **No. of Games Broadcast:** 142. **Flagship Station:** WTSR 91.3 FM. **PA Announcer:** Kevin Scholla. **Official Scorers:** Jay Dunn, Greg Zak. **Greg Zak Sr. Stadium Name:** ARM & HAMMER Park. **Location:** From I-95, take Route 1 North to Route 29 South, stadium entrance just before tunnel; From NJ Turnpike, take Exit 7A and follow I-195 West, Road will become Rte 29, Follow through tunnel and ballpark is on left. **Standard Game Times:** Monday-Friday 1030/11/12/7, Sat. **5/7, Sun 1/5. Ticket Price Range:** $11-13.Visiting Club Hotel: Wyndham Garden Trenton. **Telephone:** (609) 421-4000.

SOUTHERN LEAGUE

Mailing Address: 2551 Roswell Rd, Suite 330, Marietta, GA 30062.
Telephone: (770) 321-0400. **Fax:** (770) 321-0037.
E-Mail Address: loriwebb@southernleague.com. **Website:** www.southernleague.com.
Years League Active: 1964-

President: Lori Webb.
Vice President: Steve DeSalvo. **Directors:** Ken Young (Biloxi), Jonathan Nelson (Birmingham), Jason Freier (Chattanooga), Reese Smith (Jackson), Ken Babby (Jacksonville), Steve DeSalvo (Mississippi), Mike Savit (Mobile), Sherrie Myers(Montgomery), Bruce Baldwin (Pensacola), Doug Kirchhofer (Tennessee).
Director, Operations: John Harris.
Division Structure: North—Birmingham, Chattanooga, Jackson, Montgomery, Tennessee. **South**—Biloxi, Jacksonville, Mississippi, Mobile, Pensacola.
Regular Season: 140 games (split schedule). **2016 Opening Date:** April 7. **Closing Date:** Sept. 5.
All-Star Game: June 21 in Pearl, MS.
Playoff Format: First-half division winners meet second-half division winners in best-of-five series. Winners meet in best of five series for league championship.
Roster Limit: 25. **Player Eligibility Rule:** No restrictions.
Brand of Baseball: Rawlings.
Umpires: Unavailable.

Lori Webb

STADIUM INFORMATION

Dimensions

Club	Stadium	Opened	LF	CF	RF	Capacity	2015 Att.
*Biloxi	MGM Stadium	2015	335	400	335	6,000	164,076
Birmingham	Regions Field	2013	320	400	325	8,500	444,639
Chattanooga	AT&T Field	2000	325	400	330	6,362	218,512
Jackson	Ballpark at Jackson	1998	310	395	320	6,000	136,918
Jacksonville	Baseball Grounds of Jacksonville	2003	321	420	317	11,000	272,422
Mississippi	Trustmark Park	2005	335	402	332	7,416	216,917
Mobile	Hank Aaron Stadium	1997	325	400	310	6,000	96,260
Montgomery	Riverwalk Stadium	2004	314	380	332	7,000	232,466
Pensacola	Bayfront Stadium	2012	325	400	335	6,000	305,063
Tennessee	Smokies Park	2000	330	400	330	6,000	277,606

* Team played all games on road until June 6, 2015.

BILOXI SHUCKERS

Address: 105 Cailavet Street, Biloxi, MS 39530
Telephone: (228) 233-3465.
E-Mail Address: info@biloxishuckers.com. **Website:**www.biloxishuckers.com.
Affiliation (second year): Milwaukee Brewers (1999). **Years in League:** 1985-

OWNERSHIP/MANAGEMENT
Operated By: Biloxi Baseball LLC. **President:** Ken Young. **General Manager:** Chuck Arnold.
Director, Media/Broadcaster: Chris Harris. **Director, Community Relations:** Cristina Coca. **Director, Sales:** Chris Birch. **Retail Manager:** Megan Ondrey. **Box Office Manager:** Allan Lusk. **Ticket Sales Executives:** Kevin Trembley, Theo Bacot, Deven Matthews, Kennedy Helms, Jenifer Truong. **Director, Stadium Operations:** Trevor Matifes. **Head Groundkeeper:** Jamie Hill. **Office Manager:** Lisa Turner. **Administrative Assistant:** Jourdan Natale.

FIELD STAFF
Manager: Mike Guerrero. **Coach:** Sandy Guerrero. **Pitching Coach:** Chris Hook. **Athletic Trainer:** Steve Patera. **Strength/Conditioning Coach:** Nate Dine.

GAME INFORMATION
PA Announcer: Kyle Curley. **Official Scorer:** Unavailable at this time.
Stadium Name: MGM Park. **Location:** I-10 to I-110 South toward beach, take Ocean Springs exit onto US 90 (Beach Blvd), travel east one block, turn left on Caillavet Street, stadium is on left. **Ticket Price Range:** $10-$27. **Visiting Club Hotel:** Double Tree by Hilton Biloxi on Beach Blvd.

BIRMINGHAM BARONS

Office Address: 1401 1st Ave South, Birmingham, AL, 35233. Mailing Address: PO Box 877, Birmingham, AL, 35233.
Telephone: (205) 988-3200. Fax: (205) 988-9698.
E-Mail Address: barons@barons.com. Website: www.barons.com.
Affiliation (first year): Chicago White Sox (1986). Years in League: 1964-65, 1967-75, 1981-

OWNERSHIP/MANAGEMENT

Principal Owners: Don Logan, Jeff Logan, Stan Logan.
General Manager: Jonathan Nelson. Chief Financial Officer: Randy Prince. Director, Broadcasting: Curt Bloom. Director, Customer Service: George Chavous. Media Relations Manager: Michael Guzman. Director, Production: Mike Ferko. Director, Retail Sales: Becky York. Director, Sales: John Cook. Director, Stadium Operations: Nick Lampasona. Director, Tickets: David Madison. Director, Group Sales: Charlie Santiago. Assistant Director of Group Sales: Jessica O'Rear. Premium Sales Manager: Brett Oats. Director of Events: Jennifer McGee. Corporate Event Planner: Emily Stuenkel. Group Sales Managers: Fabian Truss, Claire Griffith. Special Events Coordinators: Tyler Gore, Shawna Boswell. Premium Services Manager: Tay Bailey. Head Groundskeeper: Daniel Ruggiero. Assistant Groundskeeper: Eric Taylor. Office Manager: Rachelle Lawhorn. Corporate Sales Manager: Don Leo. Inventory Control Accountant: Ruth Allison. Accountant: Pam Autrey.
Director of Food and Beverage: David Montgomery. Executive Chef: Matt Jett. Catering Managers: Ginny Bryant, Matt Mullinax.

FIELD STAFF

Manager: Ryan Newman. Hitting Coach: Jaime Dismuke. Pitching Coach: J.R. Perdew.

GAME INFORMATION

Radio Announcer: Curt Bloom. No of Games Broadcast: 140. Flagship Station: News Radio 105.5 WERC-FM.
PA Announcers: Derek Scudder, Andy Parish. Official Scorers: AA Moore, David Tompkins.
Stadium Name: Regions Field. Location: I-65 (exit 259B) in Birmingham. Standard Game Times: 7:05 pm, Sat. 6:30, Sun 3:00. Ticket Price Range: $7-14.
Visiting Club Hotel: Sheraton Birmingham Hotel, 2101 Richard Arrington Junior Boulevard North, Birmingham, AL 35203. Telephone: (205) 324-5000.

CHATTANOOGA LOOKOUTS

Office Address: 201 Power Alley, Chattanooga, TN 37402. Mailing Address: PO Box 11002, Chattanooga, TN 37401.
Telephone: (423) 267-2208. Fax: (423) 267-4258.
E-Mail Address: lookouts@lookouts.com. Website: www.lookouts.com.
Affiliation (first year): Minnesota Twins (2015). Years in League: 1964-65, 1976-

OWNERSHIP/MANAGEMENT

Operated By: Chattanooga Lookouts, LLC
Principal Owner: Hardball Capital, Managing Partner Jason Freier
President: Rich Mozingo. Creative/Retail Manager: Emily Dillard. Public/Media Relations Manager: Dan Kopf. Head Groundskeeper: Brandon Moore. Marketing & Promotions Manager: Alex Tainsh. Director of Broadcasting: Larry Ward. Business & Ticket Operations Manager: Anastasia McCowan. Director, Food/Beverage: Steve Sullivan. Operations/Concessions Manager: Anthony Polito. Ticket Partnership Director: Andrew Zito. Ticket Partnership Manager: Jennifer Crum. Corporate Partnership Manager: Jennifer Crum.

FIELD STAFF

Manager: Doug Mientkiewicz. Hitting Coach: Tommy Watkins. Pitching Coach: Ivan Arteaga.

GAME INFORMATION

Radio Announcers: Larry Ward No. of Games Broadcast: 140. Flagship Station: 105.1 WALV-FM.
PA Announcer: Ron Hall. Official Scorers: Andy Paul, David Jenkins.
Stadium Name: AT&T Field. Location: From I-24, take US 27 North to exit 1C (4th Street), first left onto Chestnut Street, left onto Third Street. Ticket Price Range: $5-10.
Visiting Club Hotel: Holiday Inn, 2232 Center Street, Chattanooga, TN 37421. Telephone: (423) 485-1185.

JACKSON GENERALS

Address: 4 Fun Place, Jackson, TN 38305.
Telephone: (731) 988-5299. Fax: (731) 988-5246.
E-Mail Address: sarge@jacksongeneralsbaseball.com. Website: www.jacksongeneralsbaseball.com.

OWNERSHIP/MANAGEMENT

Operated by: Jackson Baseball Club LP.

Chairman: David Freeman. **President:** Reese Smith. **General Manager:** Jason Compton.

Vice President, Sales/Marketing: Mike Peasley. **Vice President, Finance:** Charles Ferrell. **Assistant General Manager, Game Operations:** Nick Hall. **Assistant General Manager, Sales:** Chris Freeman. **Turf Manager:** Marty Wallace. **Manager, Media Relations/Broadcasting:** Brandon Liebhaber. **Manager, Ticket Operations:** Mike Widay. **Manager, Stadium Operations and Stadium Security:** Lewis Crider. **Manager, Catering/Concessions:** Jeremy Wyatt. **Manager, Community Relations:** Tabitha Causey. **Manager, Clubhouse Operations:** CJ Fedewa.

FIELD STAFF

Manager: Daren Brown. **Coach:** Roy Howell. **Pitching Coach:** Lance Andrew Lorraine. **Trainer:** Geoff Swanson.

GAME INFORMATION

Radio Announcer: Brandon Liebhaber. **No. of Games Broadcast:** 140.

PA Announcer: Dan Reeves. **Official Scorer:** Mike Henson.

Stadium Name: The Ballpark at Jackson. **Location:** From I-40, take exit 85 South on FE Wright Drive, left onto Ridgecrest Road. **Standard Game Times:** 7:05 pm, Sat. 6:05, Sun. 2:05 or 6:05. **Ticket Price Range:** $6-12. **Visiting Club Hotel:** Doubletree by Hilton Jackson, 1770 Hwy 45 Bypass, Jackson, TN 38305. **Telephone:** (731) 664-6900.

JACKSONVILLE SUNS

Office Address: 301 A. Philip Randolph Blvd, Jacksonville, FL 32202.
Telephone: (904) 358-2846. **Fax:** (904) 358-2845.
E-Mail Address: info@jaxsuns.com. **Website:** www.jaxsuns.com.
Affiliation (first year): Miami Marlins (2009). **Years In League:** 1970-

OWNERSHIP/MANAGEMENT

Operated by: Jacksonville Baseball LLC

Owner & Chief Executive Officer: Ken Babby. **President, Fast Forward Sports Group:** Jim Pfander. **General Manager:** Harold Craw. **Assistant General Manager:** Noel Blaha. **Assistant General Manager, Food/Beverage:** Mary Nixon. **Vice President, Sales and Marketing:** Linda McNabb. **Director, Field Operations:** Christian Galen. **Director, Community Relations:** Andrea Williams. **Stadium Operations Manager:** Weill Casey. **Creative Services Manager:** Brian DeLettre. **Merchandise Manager:** Brennan Earley. **Food/ Beverage Manager:** Tina Gray-Young. **Business Manager:** Wanda James. **Groups Sales Manager:** Trevor Johnson. **Promotions Manager:** Devin Jones. **Media/ Public Relations Manager:** Marco LaNave. **Senior Corporate Account Manager:** Gary Nevolis. **Box Office Manager:** Theresa Viets. **Account Executive:** Clayton Edwards. **Account Executive:** Peter Ercey. **Sales and Marketing Coordinator:** Ashley McCallen. **Front Office Coordinator:** Lorie Tipton.

FIELD STAFF

Manager: David Berg. **Pitching Coach:** Storm Davis. **Hitting Coach:** Rich Arena. **Coach:** John Pachot. **Athletic Trainer:** Cesar Roman. **Strength & Conditioning Coach:** Robert Reichert. **Video Assistant:** Keanan Lamb.

GAME INFORMATION

Radio Announcer: Roger Hoover. **No. of Games Broadcast:** 140. **Flagship Station:** TBA.

PA Announcer: TBA. **Official Scorer:** Jason Eliopulos.

Stadium Name: Bragan Field at The Baseball Grounds of Jacksonville.

Location: I-95 South to Martin Luther King Parkway exit, follow Gator Bowl Blvd around Everbank Field; I-95 North to Exit 347 (Emerson Street), go right to Hart Bridge Expressway, take Sports Complex exit, left at light to stop sign, take left and follow around Everbank Field; From Mathews Bridge, take A Philip Randolph exit, right on A Philip Randolph, straight to stadium.

Standard Game Times: 7:05 pm, Sat. 6:05 pm, Sun. 3:05 pm. **Ticket Price Range:** $5-$18.

Visiting Club Hotel: Hyatt Regency Jacksonville Riverfront, 225 Coastline Drive, Jacksonville, FL 32202. **Telephone:** (904) 360-8665.

MISSISSIPPI BRAVES

Office Address: Trustmark Park, 1 Braves Way, Pearl, MS 39208.
Mailing Address: PO Box 97389, Pearl, MS 39288.
Telephone: (601) 932-8788. **Fax:** (601) 936-3567.
E-Mail Address: mississippibraves@braves.com. **Web site:** www.mississippibraves.com.
Affiliation: Atlanta Braves (2005). **Years in League:** 2005-

OWNERSHIP/MANAGEMENT

Operated By: Atlanta National League Baseball Club Inc.

General Manager: Steve DeSalvo. **Assistant GM:** Jim Bishop. **Ticket Manager:** Nick Anderson. **Merchandise Manager:** Sarah Banta. **Media Relations Manager:** Miranda Black. **Director, Sales:** Dave Burke. **Sales Associates:** Marrieo Stovall. **Stadium Operations Manager:** Chris Hornberger. **Promotions/Entertainment Manager:** Dan Oleskowicz. **Concessions Manager:** Felicia Thompson. **Office Manager:** Christy Shaw. **Director, Field/Facility Operations:** Matt Taylor. **Corporate Hospitality Manager:** Jan Williams. **Graphic Designer:** Patrick Westrick.

Receptionist: Megan Causey.

FIELD STAFF

Manager: Luis Salazar. Coach: Garey Ingram. Pitching Coach: Dennis Lewallyn. Trainer: Kyle Damschroder.

GAME INFORMATION

Radio Announcer: Kyle Tate. No. of Games Broadcast: 140. Flagship Station: WYAB 103.9 FM. PA Announcer: Derrel Palmer. Official Scorer: Mark Beason.
Stadium Name: Trustmark Park. Location: I-20 to exit 48/Pearl (Pearson Road). Ticket Price Range: $6-$25.
Visiting Club Hotel: Hilton Garden Inn Jackson Flowood, 118 Laurel Park Cove, Flowood, MS 39232. Telephone: (601) 487-0800.

MOBILE BAYBEARS

Address: Hank Aaron Stadium, 755 Bolling Brothers Blvd., Mobile, AL 36606.
Telephone: (251) 479-2327. Fax: (251) 476-1147.
E-Mail Address: Info@mobilebaybears.com. Web site: www.MobileBayBears.com.
Affiliation (first year): Arizona Diamondbacks (2007). Years in League: 1966, 1970, 1997- current

OWNERSHIP/MANAGEMENT

Operated by: HWS Baseball Group. Principal Owner: Mike Savit. Executive Vice President: Mike Gorrasi. General Manager: Chris Morgan. Assistant General Manager: Ari Rosenbaum. Director of Sales: Kyne Sheehy. Director of Stadium Operations: Nathan Breiner. Director of Ticket Operations: Matt Baranofsky. Account Executive: Jackson Hamilton. Account Executive: Mike Murtha. Groundskeeper: Gulf Coast Sports Fields.

FIELD STAFF

Manager: Robby Hammock. Hitting Coach: Jason Camilli. Pitching Coach: Doug Drabek. Coach: Mike Lansing. Coach: Eddie Oropesa. Athletic Trainer: Rafael Freitas. Strength Coach: Sean Light. Home Clubhouse Manager: Dustin Hann.

GAME INFORMATION

Radio Announcer: Unavailable. No. of Games Broadcast: 140. Website: www.BayBearsRadio.com. PA Announcer: Unavailable. Official Scorer: Unavailable.
Stadium Name: Hank Aaron Stadium. Location: I-65 to exit 1 (Government Blvd East), right at Satchel Paige Drive, right at Bolling Bros Blvd. Standard Game Times: 6:35pm (Weekday), 7:05 (Fri-Sat) 7:05 (Sun), 2:05 (April-May), Sunday: 5:05 pm (June-Sept). Ticket Price Range: $6-16.
Visiting Club Hotel: Riverview Plaza, 64 S Water St, Mobile, AL 36602. Telephone: (251) 438-4000.

MONTGOMERY BISCUITS

Address: 200 Coosa St., Montgomery, AL 36104.
Telephone: (334) 323-2255. Fax: (334) 323-2225.
E-Mail address: info@biscuitsbaseball.com. Web site: www.biscuitsbaseball.com.
Affiliation (first year): Tampa Bay Rays (2004). Years in League: 1965-1980, 2004-

OWNERSHIP/MANAGEMENT

Operated By: Montgomery Professional Baseball LLC. Principal Owners: Sherrie Myers, Tom Dickson. President: Greg Rauch. General Manager: Scott Trible. Assistant GM, Food and Special Events: Dave Parker. Director, Marketing: Staci Wilkenson. Sponsorship Service Representative: Jordan Thomas, Caitlin Gerger. Group Sales Representatives: Greg Liebbe, PJ Carr. Special Events Manager: Nancy Mathis. Multimedia Specialist: Jared McCarthy. Marketing/Promotions Assistant: Nathan Gunnels. Broadcaster, Media Relations: Chris Adams-Wall. Director, Retail Operations: Steve Keller. Director, Stadium Operations: Steve Blackwell. Box Office Manager: Anna Del Castillo. Head Groundskeeper: Alex English. Executive Chef: Dwayne Gulley. Business Manager: Tracy Mims. Administrative Assistant: Jeannie Burke. Season Ticket Concierge: Pamela Heberer.

FIELD STAFF

Manager: Brady Williams. Hitting Coach: Dan DeMent. Pitching Coach: RC Lichtenstein.

GAME INFORMATION

Radio Announcer: Chris Adams-Wall. No of Games Broadcast: 140. Flagship Station: WLWI 1440-AM. PA Announcer: Rick Hendrick. Official Scorer: Brian Wilson. Stadium Name: Montgomery Riverwalk Stadium. Location: I-65 to exit 172, east on Herron Street, left on Coosa Street. Ticket Price Range: $9-13. Visiting Club Hotel: Candlewood Suites, 9151 Boyd-Cooper Pkwy, Montgomery, AL 36117. Telephone: (334) 277-0677.

PENSACOLA BLUE WAHOOS

Address: 351 West Cedar St., Pensacola, FL 32502.
Telephone: (850) 934-8444. **Fax:** (850) 791-6256.
E-Mail Address: info@bluewahoos.com. **Website:** www.bluewahoos.com.
Affiliation (fifth year): Cincinnati Reds (2012). **Years in League:** 2012-

OWNERSHIP/MANAGEMENT

Operated by: Northwest Florida Professional Baseball LLC. **Principal Owners:** Quint Studer, Rishy Studer. **Minority Owner:** Bubba Watson.
CEO: Bruce Baldwin. **President:** Jonathan Griffith. **Receptionist:** Pam Handlin. **Operations Coordinator:** Mike Crenshaw. **Director, Sports Turf Management:** Ray Sayre. **Sales Executive:** Brian Larkin. **Director, Human Relations:** Dick Baker. **Media Relations Manager:** Maryjane Gardner. **Broadcaster:** Tommy Thrall. **Creative Services Manager:** Adam Waldron. **Creative Services Assistant:** Derek Diamond. **Director, Guest Relations/Community Relations:** Donna Kirby. **Director, Merchandise:** Denise Richardson. **Box Office Manager:** Joey DiChiara. **Sales Executives:** Jamie Briggs, Tanner Tucker. **Director, Food/Beverage:** Affonso Jefferson. **Executive Chef:** Travis Wilson. **CFO:** Amber McClure. **Assistant CFO:** Sally Jewell.

FIELD STAFF

Manager: Pat Kelly. **Hitting Coach:** Alex Pelaez. **Pitching Coach:** Danny Darwin. **Athletic Trainer:** Tyler Moos. **Strength & Conditioning Coach:** Nate Tamargo.

GAME INFORMATION

Radio Announcer: Tommy Thrall. **No. of Games Broadcast:** 140. **Flagship Station:** TBD.
PA Announcer: Josh Gay. **Official Scorer:** Craig Cooper.
Stadium Name: Blue Wahoos Stadium. **Standard Game Times:** 6:30 pm, Sat. 6:30, Sun. 4 pm. **Ticket Price Range:** $7-$19.
Visiting Club Hotels: Hilton Garden Inn, Hampton Inn, Homewood Suites.

TENNESSEE SMOKIES

Address: 3540 Line Drive, Kodak, TN 37764.
Telephone: (865) 286-2300. **Fax:** (865) 523-9913.
E-Mail Address: info@smokiesbaseball.com. **Website:** www.smokiesbaseball.com.
Affiliation (ninth year): Chicago Cubs (2007-). **Years in League:** 1964-67, 1972-

OWNERSHIP/MANAGEMENT

Owners: Randy & Jenny Boyd. **CEO:** Doug Kirchhofer. **President:** Chris Allen. **Vice President:** Jeremy Boler. **General Manager of Baseball Operations:** Brian Cox.
Assistant General Manager of Business Operations: Tim Volk. **Director, Corporate Sales:** Chris Franklin. **Group Sales Manager:** Jason Moody. **Director, Community Relations:** Lauren Chesney. **Director, Field Maintenance:** Anthony DeFeo. **General Manager of Smokies Hospitality:** Scott Tallon. Director, **In-Game Entertainment:** Kristi Servais. **Director, Media Relations:** Justin Rocke. **Director, Merchandise:** Matt Strutner. **Director, Stadium Operations:** Bryan Webster. **Stadium Operations Assistant:** Josh Howe. **Box Office Manager:** Michael McMullen. **Sponsorship Service Manager:** Baylor Love. **Sponsorship Service Coordinator:** Allie Crain. **Business Manager:** Suzanne French. **Account Executives:** Brad Dehler, Matt Graves, Eric Harrell, Andrew O'Gara . **Corporate Sales Executive:** Thomas Kappel. **Corporate Sales Representative: Tanner Bates Receptionist:** Tolena Trout.

FIELD STAFF

Manager: Mark Johnson. **Hitting Coach:** Desi Wilson. **Pitching Coach:** Terry Clark. **Trainer:** Jon Fierro.

GAME INFORMATION

Radio Announcer: Mick Gillispie. **No. of Games Broadcast:** 140. **Flagship Station:** WNML 99.1-FM/990-AM.
PA Announcer: Unavailable. **Official Scorers:** Jared Smith, Jack Tate
Stadium Name: Smokies Stadium. **Location:** I-40 to exit 407, Highway 66 North. **Standard Game Times:** 7:05 pm, Sat. 7:05 pm, Sun 2/5. **Ticket Price Range:** $6-11.
Visiting Club Hotel: Hampton Inn & Suites Sevierville, 105 Stadium Drive, Kodak, TN 37764. **Telephone:** (865) 465-0590.

TEXAS LEAGUE

Mailing Address: 2442 Facet Oak, San Antonio, TX 78232.
Telephone: (210) 545-5297. **Fax:** (210) 545-5298.
E-Mail Address: texasleague@sbcglobal.net. **Website:** www.texas-league.com.
Years League Active: 1888-1890, 1892, 1895-1899, 1902-1942, 1946-
President/Treasurer: Tom Kayser. **Vice Presidents:** Matt Gifford, Bill Valentine.
Corporate Secretary: Ken Schrom. **Assistant to the President:** Casey Greene.
Directors: Jon Dandes (Northwest Arkansas), Ken Schrom (Corpus Christi), William DeWitt III (Springfield), Dale Hubbard (Tulsa), Chuck Greenberg (Frisco), E. Miles Prentice (Midland), Russ Meeks (Arkansas), Burl Yarbrough (San Antonio).
Division Structure: North—Arkansas, Northwest Arkansas, Springfield, Tulsa. **South**—Corpus Christi, Frisco, Midland, San Antonio.
Regular Season: 140 games (split schedule). **2015 Opening Date:** April 9. **Closing Date:** Sept 7.
All-Star Game: June 30 at Corpus Christi.
Playoff Format: First-half division winners play second-half division winners in best of five series. Winners meet in best of five series for league championship.
Roster Limit: 25. **Player Eligibility Rule:** No restrictions.
Brand of Baseball: Rawlings.

Tom Kayser

Umpires: Mike Cascioppo (Escondido, CA), Nestor Ceja (Arleta, CA), Matt Czajak (Flower Mound, TX), Derek Eaton (Tracy, CA), Bryan Fields (Dallas, TX), Clayton Hamm (Spicewood, TX), Ramon Hernandez (Columbia, MD), Lee Meyers (Madera, CA), Clayton Park (Georgetown, TX), Ronnie Teague (Cypress, TX), Brett Terry (Beaverton OR), Jake Wilburn (Fort Worth, TX)

STADIUM INFORMATION

Club	Stadium	Opened	LF	CF	RF*	Capacity	2015 Att.
Arkansas	Dickey-Stephens Park	2007	332	413	330	5,842	337,566
Corpus Christi	Whataburger Field	2005	325	400	315	5,362	363,968
Frisco	Dr Pepper Ballpark	2003	335	409	335	10,216	477,354
Midland	Citibank Ballpark	2002	330	410	322	4,669	297,325
NW Arkansas	Arvest Ballpark	2008	325	400	325	6,500	290,471
San Antonio	Nelson Wolff Municipal Stadium	1994	310	402	340	6,200	308,564
Springfield	John Q. Hammons Field	2003	315	400	330	6,750	337,519
Tulsa	ONEOK Field	2010	330	400	307	7,833	380,759

ARKANSAS TRAVELERS

Office Address: Dickey-Stephens Park, 400 West Broadway, North Little Rock, AR 72114. **Mailing Address:** PO Box 3177, Little Rock, AR 72203.
Telephone: (501) 664-1555. **Fax:** (501) 664-1834.
E-Mail address: travs@travs.com. **Website:** www.travs.com.
Affiliation (first year): Los Angeles Angels (2001). **Years in League:** 1966-

OWNERSHIP/MANAGEMENT

Ownership: Arkansas Travelers Baseball Club, Inc. **President:** Russ Meeks.
General Manager: Paul Allen. **Director, Broadcasting/Media Relations:** Robbie Aaron. **Director, Finance:** Patti Clark. Director, **In-Game Entertainment:** Tommy Adam. **Assistant GM, Merchandise:** Rusty Meeks. **Park Superintendent:** Greg Johnston. **Assistant Park Superintendent:** Reggie Temple. **Director, Luxury Suites:** Evelyn White, Director of Guest Services: Jared Schein. **Assistant GM, Tickets:** Drew Williams. **Director, Marketing:** Lance Restum. **Corporate Event Planners:** Veronica Hernandez, Eric Schrader, Justin Phillips.

FIELD STAFF

Manager: Mark Parent. **Coach:** Brenton Del Chiaro. **Pitching Coach:** Scott Budner. **Trainer:** TBD. **Strength/Conditioning Coach:** Adam Auer.

GAME INFORMATION

Radio Announcers: Robbie Aaron. **No. of Games Broadcast:** 140. **Flagship Station:** KARN 920 AM.
PA Announcer: Russ McKinney. **Official Scorer:** Dan Floyd. **Stadium Name:** Dickey-Stephens Park. **Location:** I-30 to Broadway exit, proceed west to ballpark, located at Broadway Avenue and the Broadway Bridge. **Standard Game Time:** 7:10 pm. **Ticket Price Range:** $3-13. **Visiting Club Hotel:** Wyndham Riverfront, 2 Riverfront Place, N. Little Rock, AR 72114. **Telephone:** (501) 371-9000.

CORPUS CHRISTI HOOKS

Address: 734 East Port Ave, Corpus Christi, TX 78401.
Telephone: (361) 561-4665. **Fax:** (361) 561-4666.
E-Mail Address: info@cchooks.com. **Website:** www.cchooks.com.
Affiliation (first year): Houston Astros (2005). **Years in League:** 1958-59, 2005-

OWNERSHIP/MANAGEMENT
Owned/Operated By: Houston Astros.
President: Ken Schrom. **Vice President/General Manager:** Michael Wood.
Director, Sales/Marketing: Andy Steavens. **Senior Director, Sponsor Services:** Elisa Macias. **Senior Director, Communications:** Matt Rogers. **Director, Finance:** Kim Harris. **Director, Stadium Operations:** Jeremy Sturgeon. **Director, Ballpark Entertainment:** JD Davis. **Director, Season Ticket Services:** Jeff Mackor. **Director, Group Sales:** Amanda Pruett. **Media Relations Manager:** Michael Coffin. **Ticket Operations Manager:** Danielle O'Toole. **Customer Service Manager:** Brett Howsley. **Senior Service Desk Technician:** Jonathan Santana. **Media Relations Coordinator:** Chris Blake. **Community Relations Coordinator:** Courtney Merritt. **Social Media Coordinator:** Gil Perez. **Video Production Coordinator:** Amy Johnson. **Accounting Analyst:** Jessica Fearn. **Account Executive:** Zach Kaddatz. **Account Executive:** Tanner Twomey. **Retail Manager:** Rudy Soliz. **Maintenance Coordinator:** Fred Flores. **Stadium Operations:** Mike Shedd. **Clubhouse Manager:** Brad Starr. **Field Superintendent:** Nick Rozdilski. **Assistant Groundskeeper:** Andrew Batts

FIELD STAFF
Manager: Rodney Linares. **Hitting Coach:** Dan Radison. **Pitching Coach:** Dave Borkowski. **Development Coach:** Tommy Kawamura. **Athletic Trainer:** Grant Hufford. **Strength Coach:** Taylor Rhoades.

GAME INFORMATION
Radio Announcers: Michael Coffin, Chris Blake, Gene Kasprzyk. **No. of Games Broadcast:** 140. **Flagship Station:** KKTX-AM 1360.
Spanish Radio Announcer: Eduardo Becerra. **No. of Games Broadcast:** 70. **Station:** KUNO-AM 1440.
PA Announcer: Layne Berman. **Stadium Name:** Whataburger Field. **Location:** I-37 to end of interstate, left at Chaparral, left at Hirsh Ave. **Ticket Price Range:** $6-17.
Visiting Club Hotel: Holiday Inn Corpus Christi Downtown Marina, 707 North Shoreline Blvd, Corpus Christi, Texas, 78401. **Telephone:** (361) 882-1700.

FRISCO ROUGHRIDERS

Address: 7300 RoughRiders Trail, Frisco, TX 75034.
Telephone: (972) 731-9200. **Fax:** (972) 731-5355.
E-Mail Address: info@ridersbaseball.com. **Website:** www.ridersbaseball.com.
Affiliation (first year): Texas Rangers (2003). **Years in League:** 2003-

OWNERSHIP/MANAGEMENT
Operated by: Frisco RoughRiders LP. Chairman/**CEO/General Partner:** Chuck Greenberg. President & **Co-General Partner:** Scott Sonju. **Executive VP/General Manager:** Jason Dambach. **Chief Operating Officer:** Scott Burchett. **Chief Sales Officer:** Sam Torres. **VP, Accounting/Finance:** Dustin Alban.**VP, Community Development/Executive Director of RoughRiders Foundation:** Breon Dennis. Sr. **Director, Marketing/Promotions:** Matt Ratliff. **Director, Partner/Event Services:** Kristin Russell. **Director, Game Entertainment:** Regina Pierce. **Director, Ticket Operations:** TBD. **Director, Maintenance:** Alfonso Bailon. **Head Groundskeeper:** David Bicknell. **Senior Manager, Ticket Sales:** Ross Lanford. **Manager, Group Sales:** David Dwyer. **Operations Manager:** Scott Fults. **Manager, Partner Services:** David Kosydar. **Merchandise Manager:** Jennifer Adamczyk. **Executive Assistant and Office Manager:** Kelly Carr. **Manager, Broadcasting/Media Development:** Nathan Barnett.
Manager, Game Presentation: Garret Young. **Operations Coordinator:** Tyler Waddles. **Coordinator, Content/Video Production:** Bijan Zadeh. **Partner/Event Services Coordinator:** Kathryne Buckley. **Graphic Design Coordinator:** TBD. **Social Media and Database Coordinator:** Scott Beckendorf. **Ticket Operations Coordinator:** Adam Dolezal. **Account Executive, Corporate Development:** Lisa Gonzalez. **Corporate Marketing Managers:** Joshua Bray, Robert Brown, Kasey Carlock, Mike Cordisco, Tyler Ellis, Jonathan Fletcher, Matt Martin, Garret Randle, and Alyssa Sanchez. **Group Sales Executives:** Tom Baker, Sander Bryan, Austin Cain, Jeff Clark, Johnny Coenen, Kaitlyn Cox, Monica Man, Robert Sieb, Ryan Williams, Alex Wright, and Kanavis Wright. **Ticket Sales Coordinators:** Hilary Adams, LaJewelia Lewis, Jacob Sappington, and Tyler Marcotte. **Accounting Assistant:** Carole Bilse. **Customer Service Agents:** Jean Scherer,Vicki Sohn.

FIELD STAFF
Manager: Joe Mikulik. **Hitting Coach:** Jason Hart. **Pitching Coach:** Steve Mintz. **Trainer:** Jacob Newburn. **Strength/Conditioning:** Eric McMahon.

GAME INFORMATION
Broadcaster: Nathan Barnett. **No. of Games Broadcast:** 140. **Flagship Station:** www.RidersBaseball.com.
PA Announcer: John Clemens. **Official Scorer:** Larry Bump.
Stadium Name: Dr Pepper Ballpark. **Location:** Intersection of Dallas North Tollway & State Highway 121. **Standard**

Game Times: 7:05 pm, Sun. 4:05 (April-May) 6:05 (June-Sept).
    Visiting Club Hotel: Comfort Suites at Frisco Square, 9700 Dallas Parkway, Frisco, TX 75033. **Phone:** (972) 668-9700. **Fax:** (972) 668-9701.

MIDLAND ROCKHOUNDS

Address: Security Bank Ballpark, 5514 Champions Drive, Midland, TX 79706.
Telephone: (432) 520-2255. **Fax:** (432) 520-8326.
Website: www.midlandrockhounds.org.
Affiliation (first year): Oakland Athletics (1999). **Years in League:** 1972-

OWNERSHIP/MANAGEMENT

Operated By: Midland Sports, Inc. **Principal Owners:** Miles Prentice, Bob Richmond.
President: Miles Prentice. **Executive Vice President:** Bob Richmond. **General Manager:** Monty Hoppel.
Assistant GM: Jeff VonHolle. **Assistant GM, Marketing/Tickets:** Jamie Richardson. **Assistant GM, Operations:** Ray Fieldhouse. **Director, Broadcasting/Publications:** Bob Hards. **Director, Business Operations:** Eloisa Galvan. **Director, Group Sales:** Morgan Halpert. **Director, Ticket Operations:** Andrew Brown. **Office & Box Office Manager:** Christy Cole. **Director, Client Services:** Shelly Haenggi. **Director, Community Relations:** Courtnie Golden. **Director, Media Relations:** Frank Longobardo. **Director, Stadium Operations:** C.J. Bahr. **Assistant Director, Stadium Operations:** Joe Peters. **Stadium Operations/Sales Associate:** Matthew Bari. **Head Groundskeeper:** Monty Sowell. **Assistant Groundskeeper:** Andrew Petersen. **Game Entertainment/Video Board Coordinator:** Russ Pinkerton. **Sales Executive:** Blake Fosse. **Assistant Concessions Manager:** Preston Madill. Administrative Assistant, **Community & Media Relations:** Alex Kosman. **Group Sales Assistant:** Nick Sora. **Home Clubhouse Manager:** Derek Smith. **Visiting Clubhouse Manager:** Ari Vieira.

FIELD STAFF

Manager: Ryan Christenson. **Hitting Coach:** Brian McArn. **Pitching Coach:** John Wasdin. **Trainer:** Justin Whitehouse. **Strength/Conditioning:** Henry Torres.

GAME INFORMATION

Radio Announcer: Bob Hards. **No. of Games Broadcast:** 140. **Flagship Station:** KCRS 550 AM.
PA Announcer: Wes Coles. **Official Scorer:** Steve Marcum.
Stadium Name: Security Bank Ballpark. **Location:** From I-20, exit Loop 250 North to Highway 191 intersection.
Standard Game Times: 7 pm. **Ticket Price Range:** $7-16.
    Visiting Club Hotel: Springhill Suites by Marriott, 5716 Deauville Blvd, Midland, TX 79706. **Telephone:** (432) 695-6870.

NORTHWEST ARKANSAS
NATURALS

Address: 3000 S 56th Street, Springdale, AR 72762.
Telephone: (479) 927-4900. **Fax:** (479) 756-8088.
E-Mail Address: tickets@nwanaturals.com. **Website:** www.nwanaturals.com.
Affiliation (first year): Kansas City Royals (1995)
Years in League: 1987-Present

OWNERSHIP/MANAGEMENT

Principal Owner: Rich Products Corp. **Chairman:** Robert Rich Jr. **President, Rich Entertainment:** Melinda Rich. **President, Rich Baseball:** Jon Dandes. **General Manager:** Justin Cole. **Sales Manager:** Mark Zaiger. **Business Manager:** Morgan Helmer. **Marketing/PR Manager:** Dustin Dethlefs. **Ballpark Operations Director:** Jeff Windle. **Head Groundskeeper:** Brock White. **Ticket Office Coordinator:** Sam Ahern. **Broadcaster/Baseball Operations Coordinator:** Benjamin Kelly. **Promotions Coordinator:** Julie Fitzpatrick. **Production Coordinator:** Beth Salazar. **Ticket Sales Coordinator:** Jon Tucker. Sr. **Account Executive:** Brad Ziegler. **Account Executives:** Matt Fanning, Trey Garner. **Coordinator, Special Events:** TBA. **Coordinator, Operations:** Corey Lewis. **Merchandise Coordinator:** Paige Peugh. **Equipment Manager:** Danny Helmer.

FIELD STAFF

Manager: Vance Wilson. **Hitting Coach:** Brian Buchanan. **Pitching Coach:** Steve Luebber.

GAME INFORMATION

Radio Announcers: Benjamin Kelly. **No. of Games Broadcast:** 140. **Flagship:** KQSM 92.1-FM.
PA Announcer: Bill Rogers. **Official Scorer:** Kyle Stiles.
Stadium Name: Arvest Ballpark. **Location:** I-49 to US 412 West (Sunset Ave); Left on 56th St. **Ticket Price Range:** $8-13. **Standard Game Times:** 7:05 pm (Monday-Friday), 6:05 pm (Saturday), 2:05 pm (Sunday)
    Visiting Club Hotel: Holiday Inn Springdale, 1500 S 48th St, Springdale, AR 72762. **Telephone:** (479) 751-8300.

SAN ANTONIO MISSIONS

Address: 5757 Highway 90 West, San Antonio, TX 78227.
Telephone: (210) 675-7275. **Fax:** (210) 670-0001.
E-Mail Address: sainfo@samissions.com. **Website:** www.samissions.com.
Affiliation (first year): San Diego Padres (2007). **Years in League:** 1888, 1892, 1895-99, 1907-42, 1946-64, 1968-

OWNERSHIP/MANAGEMENT
Operated by: Elmore Sports Group. **Principal Owner:** David Elmore.
President: Burl Yarbrough. **General Manager:** Dave Gasaway. **Assistant GMs:** Mickey Holt, Jeff Long, Bill Gerlt. **GM, Diamond Concessions:** Mike Lindal. **Controller:** Eric Olivarez. **Director, Broadcasting:** Mike Saeger. **Office Manager:** Delia Rodriguez. **Box Office Manager:** Rob Gusick. **Director, Operations:** John Hernandez. **Director, Group Sales:** George Levandoski. **Director, Public Relations:** Rich Weimert. **Field Superintendent:** Craig Sampsell.

FIELD STAFF
Manager: Phillip Wellman. **Hitting Coach:** Johnny Washington. **Pitching Coach:** Jimmy Jones. **Trainer:** Daniel Turner.

GAME INFORMATION
Radio Announcer: Mike Saeger. **No. of Games Broadcast:** 140. **Flagship Station:** 860-AM.
PA Announcer: Roland Ruiz. **Official Scorer:** David Humphrey.
Stadium Name: Nelson Wolff Stadium. **Location:** From I-10, I-35 or I-37, take US Hwy 90 West to Callaghan Road exit. **Standard Game Times:** 7:05 pm, Sun 2:05/6:05.
Visiting Club Hotel: Holiday Inn Northwest/Sea World. **Telephone:** (210) 520-2508.

SPRINGFIELD CARDINALS

Address: 955 East Trafficway, Springfield, MO 65802.
Telephone: (417) 863-0395. **Fax:** (417) 832-3004.
E-Mail Address: springfield@cardinals.com. **Website:** springfieldcardinals.com.
Affiliation (first year): St. Louis Cardinals (2005). **Years in League:** 2005-

OWNERSHIP/MANAGEMENT
Operated By: St. Louis Cardinals.
Vice President/General Manager: Matt Gifford. **VP, Baseball/Business Operations:** Scott Smulczenski. **VP, Facility Operations:** Bill Fischer. **Director, Ticket Operations:** Angela Deke. **VP, Sales/Marketing:** Dan Reiter. **Manager, Promotions/Productions:** Kent Shelton. **Manager, Market Development:** Scott Bailes. **Director, Stadium Operations:** Aaron Lowrey. **Manager, Public Relations/Broadcaster:** Andrew Buchbinder. **Manager, Sales/Marketing:** Zack Pemberton. **Manager, Fan Interaction:** Faith Lorhan. **Box Office Supervisor/Office Assistant:** Liz Blase. **Head Groundskeeper:** Brock Phipps. **Assistant Head Groundskeeper:** Derek Edwards.

FIELD STAFF
Manager: Dann Bilardello. **Hitting Coach:** Ramon Ortiz. **Pitching Coach:** Jason Simontacchi. **Trainer:** Scott Ensell. **Assistant Coach/Scout:** T.C. Calhoun.

GAME INFORMATION
Radio Announcer: Andrew Buchbinder. **No. of Games Broadcast:** 140. **Flagship Station:** JOCK 98.7 FM.
PA Announcer: Unavailable. **Official Scorers:** Mark Stillwell, Tim Tourville.
Stadium Name: Hammons Field. **Location:** Highway 65 to Chestnut Expressway exit, west to National, south on National, west on Trafficway. **Standard Game Time:** 7:10 pm. **Ticket Price Range:** $6-28.
Visiting Club Hotel: University Plaza Hotel, 333 John Q Hammons Parkway, Springfield, MO 65806. **Telephone:** (417) 864-7333.

TULSA DRILLERS

Address: 201 N. Elgin, Tulsa, OK 74120.
Telephone: (918) 744-5998. **Fax:** (918) 747-3267.
E-Mail Address: mail@tulsadrillers.com. **Website:** www.tulsadrillers.com.
Affiliation (second year): Los Angeles Dodgers (2015). **Years in League:** 1933-42, 1946-65, 1977-

OWNERSHIP/MANAGEMENT
Operated By: Tulsa Baseball Inc. **Co-Chairmen:** Dale Hubbard, Jeff Hubbard.
President/GM: Mike Melega. **Executive VP/Assistant GM:** Jason George. **Bookkeeper:** Cheryll Couey. **Executive Assistant:** Kara Biden. **VP, Stadium Operations:** Mark Hilliard. **VP, Media/Public Relations:** Brian Carroll. **VP,**

MINOR LEAGUES

Marketing/Business Development: Rob Gardenhire. **Director, Merchandise:** Tom Jones. VP, **Ticket Sales & Analytics:** Zach Brockman Director, **Promotions/Game Entertainment:** Justin Gorski. **Director, Video Production:** Alan Ramseyer. Asst. **Director Media/Public Relations:** Wesley Leander. **Head Groundskeeper:** Gary Shepherd. **Assistant Bookkeeper:** Jenna Savill. **Manager, Ticket Sales:** Joanna Hubbard. **Account Executive:** David Kirk. **Account Executive:** Matt Johnson. **Mascot Coordinator:** Vincent Pace. **Manager, Facilities:** Stevelan Hamilton. **Manager, Stadium Operations:** Marshall Schellhardt. **Manager, Graphic Design/Social Media:** Kevin Rhatican. **Manager, Video Production:** Jase Chilcoat. **Manager, Digital Media/Special Events:** Courtney Gemmett

Receptionist: Lynda Davis. **Ticket Office Asst:** Matt Bishop. **Ticket Office Intern:** John Rhodes. **Ticket Office Intern:** Armando Ramirez. **Ticket Office Intern:** Terrance Wingo. **Ticket Office Intern:** Philip Sidoti. **Group Sales Intern:** Sean Piper. **Stadium Operations Intern:** Jeff Stocker. **Merchandise Intern:** Greg Stanzak. **Promotions Asst:** Justin Johnston. **Video Production Asst:** Hunter Weaver. **Director, Food Services:** Cody Malone. **Director, Concessions:** Wayne Campbell. **Concessions Manager:** Sara Bush. **Catering Manager:** Jasmine Wilson. **Clubhouse Manager:** Sam Salabura.

FIELD STAFF

Manager: Ryan Garko. **Hitting Coach:** Terrmel Sledge. **Pitching Coach:** Bill Simas. **Coach:** Leo Garcia. **Trainer:** Aaron Schumacher. **Strength Coach:** Tyler Norton.

GAME INFORMATION

Radio Announcer: Dennis Higgins. **No. of Games Broadcast:** 140. **Flagship Station:** KTBZ 1430-AM.

PA Announcer: Kirk McAnany. **Official Scorers:** Bruce Howard, Duane DaPron, Larry Lewis, Barry Lewis.

Stadium Name: ONEOK Field. **Location:** I-244 to Cincinnati/Detroit Exit (6A); north on Detroit Ave, right onto John Hope Franklin Blvd, right on Elgin Ave. **Standard Game Times:** 7:05 pm, Sun. 2:05 (April-June), 7:05 (July-Aug).

Visiting Club Hotel: Hyatt Regency, 100 E 2nd St, Tulsa, OK 74103. **Telephone:** (918) 582-9000.

CALIFORNIA LEAGUE

Address: 3600 South Harbor Blvd, Suite 122, Oxnard, CA 93035.
Telephone: (805) 985-8585. **Fax:** (805) 985-8580.
Website: www.californialeague.com. **E-Mail:** info@californialeague.com.
Years League Active: 1941-1942, 1946-
President: Charlie Blaney. **Vice President:** Tom Volpe.

Directors: Bobby Brett (Rancho Cucamonga), Jake Kerr (Lancaster), Dave Elmore (Inland Empire), D.G. Elmore (Bakersfield), Dave Heller (High Desert), Gary Jacobs (Lake Elsinore), Mike Savit (Modesto), Tom Seidler (Visalia), Tom Volpe (Stockton), Dan Orum (San Jose).

Director, Operations/Marketing: Matt Blaney. **Historian:** Chris Lampe. **Legal Counsel:** Jonathan Light. **CPA:** Jeff Hass.

Division Structure: North—Bakersfield, Modesto, San Jose, Stockton, Visalia. **South**— High Desert, Inland Empire, Lake Elsinore, Lancaster, Rancho Cucamonga.

Regular Season: 140 games (split schedule). **2016 Opening Date:** April 7. **Closing Date:** Sept 5.

Playoff Format: Six teams make the playoffs. First-half winners in each division earn first-round bye; second-half winners meet wild cards with next best overall records in best of three quarterfinals. Winners meet first-half champions in best of five semifinals. Winners meet in best of five series for league championship.

All-Star Game: Cal League-Carolina League, June 21 at Lake Elsinore.

Roster Limit: 25 active (35 under control). **Player Eligibility:** No more than two players and one player/coach on active list may have more than six years experience.

Brand of Baseball: Rawlings.

Umpires: Brandon Butler.Andrew Chesnut, Jon Felczak, Richard Genera, Adrian Gonzalez, Taka Matsuda, Jacob Metz, Pat Sharshel, Alex Trujillo, Kyle Wallace.

Charlie Blaney

Club	Stadium	Opened	Dimensions LF	CF	RF	Capacity	2015 Att.
Bakersfield	Sam Lynn Ballpark	1941	328	354	328	2,700	51,789
High Desert	Mavericks Stadium	1991	340	401	340	3,808	94,065
Inland Empire	San Manuel Stadium	1996	330	410	330	5,000	196,962
Lake Elsinore	The Diamond	1994	330	400	310	7,866	213,932
Lancaster	Clear Channel Stadium	1996	350	410	350	4,500	158,435
Modesto	John Thurman Field	1952	312	400	319	4,000	166,719
Rancho Cucamonga	LoanMart Field	1993	335	400	335	6,615	167,318
San Jose	Municipal Stadium	1942	320	390	320	5,208	189,205
Stockton	Banner Island Ballpark	2005	300	399	326	5,200	191,611
Visalia	Rawhide Ballpark	1946	320	405	320	2,468	121,004

BAKERSFIELD BLAZE

Office Address: 4009 Chester Ave, Bakersfield, CA 93301. **Mailing Address:** PO Box 10031, Bakersfield, CA 93389.
Telephone: (661) 716-4487. **Fax:** (661) 322-6199.
E-Mail Address: blaze@bakersfieldblaze.com. **Website:** www.bakersfieldblaze.com.
Affiliation: Seattle Mariners (2015). **Years In League:** 1941-42, 1946-75, 1978-79, 1982-

OWNERSHIP/MANAGEMENT

Principal Owner: Elmore Sports Group/D.G. Elmore.

General Manager: Elizabeth Martin. **Assistant GM, Media/Marketing:** Dan Besbris. **Assistant GM, Ticketing/Groups:** Mike Candela. **Director, Concessions Marketing:** Chris Henstra. **Director, Stadium Operations:** Jeff MacDonald. **Director, Group/Ticket Sales:** Billy Brosemer. **Coordinator, Community Relations:** Emily Hintz. **Head Groundskeeper:** Billy Brosemer.

FIELD STAFF

Manager: Eddie Menchaca. **Hitting Coach:** Max Venable. **Pitching Coach:** Andrew Lorraine.

GAME INFORMATION

Radio: Dan Besbris. **Flagship Station:** 1230-AM.

PA Announcer: Mike Cushine. **Official Scorer:** Tim Wheeler.

Stadium Name: Sam Lynn Ballpark. **Location:** Highway 99 to California Avenue, east two miles to Chester Avenue, north two miles to stadium. **Standard Game Time:** Variable due to setting sun. 7:30 pm. **Ticket Price Range:** $7-13.

Visiting Club Hotel: Marriott at the Convention Center, 801 Truxtun Ave, Bakersfield, CA 93301. **Telephone:** (661) 323-1900.

HIGH DESERT MAVERICKS

Address: 12000 Stadium Way, Adelanto, CA 92301.
Telephone: (760) 246-6287.
E-Mail Address: info@hdmavs.com. **Website:** www.hdmavs.com.
Affiliation: Texas Rangers (2015). **Years in League:** 1991-

OWNERSHIP/MANAGEMENT
Operated By: Main Street California. **Managing Partner:** Dave Heller. **General Manager:** Ben Hemmen. **Assistant GM:** Sarah Bosso. **Head Groundskeeper:** Ryan Cowan. **Public Relations Manager:** Shane Philipps. **Director of Ticket Sales:** David Barry.

FIELD STAFF
Manager: Howard Johnson. **Hitting Coach:** Bobby Rose. **Pitching Coach:** Oscar Marin. **Coach:** Aaron Levin. **Trainer:** Alex Rodriguez. **Strength/Conditioning Coach:** Anthony Miller

GAME INFORMATION
Radio Announcer: N/A. **PA Announcer:** Unavailable. **Official Scorer:** Unavailable. **Stadium Name:** Heritage Field. **Location:** I-15 North to Highway 395 to Adelanto Road. **Standard Game Times:** 6:35 pm (April-May), 7:05 pm (June-Aug), **Sun 1:**05 (April-May), 5:05 (June-Aug). **Ticket Price Range:** $4-$10. **Visiting Club Hotel:** Unavailable.

INLAND EMPIRE 66ERS

Address: 280 South E St., San Bernardino, CA 92401.
Telephone: (909) 888-9922. **Fax:** (909) 888-5251.
Website: www.66ers.com.
Affiliation (first year): Los Angeles Angels (2011). **Years in League:** 1941, 1987-

OWNERSHIP/MANAGEMENT
Operated by: Inland Empire 66ers Baseball Club of San Bernardino. **Principal Owners:** David Elmore, Donna Tuttle. **President:** David Elmore. **Chairman:** Donna Tuttle.
General Manager: Joe Hudson. **Assistant GM:** Ryan English. **Senior Director, Operations and Security:** Jordan Smith, **Director, Broadcasting:** Steve Wendt. **Director, Group Sales:** Steve Pelle. **Director, Marketing:** Matt Kowallis. **Director, Promotions:** Adam Franey. **Director, Ticket Operations and Sales:** Seam Peterson, **Manager, Creative Services:** Mark Altenbach. Group Account Executive Jarrett Stark. **Group Account Executive:** Stephanie O' Quinn. **Coordinator, Promotions:** Aris Theofanopolous. **Coordinator, Group Services:** Anna Franzerb, **Coordinator, New Media:** Bianca Hill, **Administrative Assistant:** Marlena Avant. **Head Groundskeeper:** Dominick Guerrero. **CFO:** John Fonseca.

FIELD STAFF
Manager: Chad Tracy. **Hitting Coach:** Ryan Barba. **Pitching Coach:** Michael Wuertz. **First Base Coach:** Steven Hernandez. **Trainer:** Matt Morell. **Strength/Conditioning Coach:** Sergio Rojas.

GAME INFORMATION
Radio Announcer: Steve Wendt. **Flagship Station:** 66ers Radio on TuneIn.
PA Announcer: J.J. Gould. **Official Scorer:** Bill Maury-Holmes.
Stadium Name: San Manuel Stadium. **Location:** From south, I-215 to 2nd Street exit, east on 2nd, right on G Street; from north, I-215 to 3rd Street exit, left on Rialto, right on G Street. **Standard Game Times:** 7:05 pm; **Sun 2:**05 (April-June), 5:05 (July-Aug). **Ticket Price Range:** $7-15.
Visiting Club Hotel: Unavailable. **Telephone:** Unavailable.

LAKE ELSINORE STORM

Address: 500 Diamond Drive, Lake Elsinore, CA 92530
Telephone: (951) 245-4487. **Fax:** (951) 245-0305.
E-Mail Address: info@stormbaseball.com. **Website:** www.stormbaseball.com.
Affiliation (first year): San Diego Padres (2001). **Years in League:** 1994-.

OWNERSHIP/MANAGEMENT
Owners: Gary Jacobs, Len Simon.
General Manager: Raj Narayanan. **Asst. GM (Operations/Concessions):** Tim Arseneau. **Asst. GM (Marketing/Digital Media)/Senior Designer:** Mark Beskid. **Director of Broadcasting:** Sean McCall. **Director of Community Relations/Group Sales Manager:** Courtney Kessler. **Director of Digital Content/Media Relations:** Tyler Zickel. **Director, Merchandising:** Donna Grunow. **Assistant Director, Merchandising:** Lucas Wedgewood. **Director, Ticketing:** Eric Colunga. **Asst. Director, Ticketing:** Tanner Grabianowski. **Asst. Director, Ticketing:** Kelly Wilga. **Director, Finance:** Rick Riegler. **Assistant Director, Finance:** Andres Pagan. **Director, First Impressions:** Peggy Mitchell. **Account Executive:** Eric Theiss. **Account Executive/Promotions:** Kasey Rawitzer. **Director, Partnerships/Fulfillment:** Jeff

Romero. Director of Player-**Community Relations/Clubhouse Manager:** Terrance Tucker. **General Manager, Storm Events:** Ian Singleton. **Stadium Operations/Events Coordinator:** Casey Scott. **Director, Grounds/Maintenance:** Joe Jimenez. **Assistant Director, Grounds:** Dave Herd. **Maintenance Supervisor:** Jassiel Reza. **Director of Concessions:** Chris Kidder **Diamond Club Events Coordinator:** Margie McCloskey. **Official Scorer:** Lloyd Nixon. **PA Announcer:** Joe Martinez. **Broadcasters:** Sean McCall, Tyler Zickel.

FIELD STAFF
Manager: Francisco Morales. **Hitting Coach:** Xavier Nady. **Pitching Coach:** Glendon Rusch.

GAME INFORMATION
Radio Announcer: Sean McCall. **No. of Games Broadcast:** 140. Flagship
Station: Radio 94.5. **PA Announcer:** Joe Martinez. **Official Scorer:** Lloyd Nixon. **Stadium Name:** The Diamond. **Location:** From I-15, exit at Diamond Drive, west one mile to stadium. **Standard Game Times: Mon-Thurs:** 6 p.m. **Fri-Sat:** 7 p.m. Sunday (first half): 1 p.m. (second half) 5 p.m. **Ticket Price Range:** $13-16. **Visiting Club Hotel:** Lake Elsinore Hotel and Casino, 20930 Malaga St, Lake Elsinore, CA 92530. **Telephone:** (951) 674-3101.

LANCASTER JETHAWKS

Address: 45116 Valley Central Way, Lancaster, CA 93536.
Telephone: (661) 726-5400. **Fax:** (661) 726-5406.
Email Address: info@jethawks.com. **Website:** www.jethawks.com.
Affiliation (first year): Houston Astros (2009). **Years in League:** 1996-

OWNERSHIP/MANAGEMENT
Operated By: JetHawks Baseball, LP. **Principal Owner/Managing General Partner:** Jake Kerr. **Partner:** Jeff Mooney. **President:** Andy Dunn. **Executive Vice President:** Tom Backemeyer. **General Manager:** William Thornhill. **Director, Facility/Baseball Operations:** John Laferney. Sr. **Director, Ticket Sales and Promotions:** Buck Rogers, **Director, Group Sales:** Dylan Baker. **Director, Marketing:** Katie Woods. **Account Executive:** Taylor Dunn.

FIELD STAFF
Manager: Ramon Vazquez. **Coach:** Darryl Robinson. **Pitching Coach:** Mike Burns. **Athletic Trainer:** Michael Rendon

GAME INFORMATION
Radio Announcer: Jason Schwartz. **No. of Games Broadcast:** 140. **Flagship Station:** www.jethawks.com. **PA Announcer:** TBD. **Official Scorer:** David Guenther. **Stadium Name:** The Hangar. **Location:** Highway 14 in Lancaster to Avenue I exit, west one block to stadium. **Standard Game Times:** 6:35 pm, Sun. 2:05pm (April-June), 5:05pm (July-Sept). **Ticket Price Range:** $8-15. **Visiting Club Hotel:** Comfort Inn, 1825 W Avenue J-12, Lancaster CA 93534. **Telephone:** (661) 723-2001.

MODESTO NUTS

Office Address: 601 Neece Dr, Modesto, CA 95351. **Mailing Address:** PO Box 883, Modesto, CA 95353.
Telephone: (209) 572-4487. **Fax:** (209) 572-4490
E-Mail Address: fun@modestonuts.com**Website:** www.modestonuts.com.
Affiliation (first year): Colorado Rockies (2005). **Years in League:** 1946-64, 1966-

OWNERSHIP/MANAGEMENT
Operated by: HWS Group IV. **Principal Owner:** Mike Savit.
Executive Vice President: Michael Gorrasi. **General Manager:** TBD. **Vice President, HWS Beverage:** Ed Mack. **Director, Brand Management:** Robert Moullette. **Director, Ticket Sales :** Austin Weltner. Director, **In-Game Entertainment:** Joe Tichy. **Manager, Promotions:** Britni Hicks.

FIELD STAFF
Manager: Fred Ocasio. **Coach:** TBD. **Pitching Coach:** Brandon Emanuel.

GAME INFORMATION
Radio Announcer: Unavailable.
PA Announcer: Unavailable. **Official Scorer:** Unavailable.
Stadium Name: John Thurman Field. **Location:** Highway 99 in southwest Modesto to Tuolomne Boulevard exit, west on Tuolomne for one block to Neece Drive, left for 1/4 mile to stadium. **Standard Game Times:** 7:05 pm, Sun. 1:05pm/6:05 pm. **Ticket Price Range:** $7 -13.
Visiting Club Hotel: Unavailable.

RANCHO CUCAMONGA
QUAKES

Office Address: 8408 Rochester Ave., Rancho Cucamonga, CA 91730. Mailing Address: P.O. Box 4139, Rancho Cucamonga, CA 91729.
Telephone: (909) 481-5000. Fax: (909) 481-5005.
E-Mail Address: info@rcquakes.com. Website: www.rcquakes.com.
Affiliation (first year): Los Angeles Dodgers (2011). Years in League: 1993-

OWNERSHIP/MANAGEMENT

Operated By: Brett Sports & Entertainment. Principal Owner: Bobby Brett.
President: Brent Miles. Vice President/General Manager: Grant Riddle. Vice President/Tickets: Monica Ortega. Assistant General Manager, Group Sales: Linda Rathfon. Assistant General Manager, Sponsorships: Chris Pope. Sponsorship Manager: Dori Eisenthal. Sponsorship Account Executive: Kevin Cabori. Promotions Manager: Bobbi Salcido. Director, Group Sales: Kyle Burleson. Director, Season Tickets/Operations: Eric Jensen. Group Sales Coordinator: Roberta Watson, Austin Derryberry, Rebecca Cave. Director, Accounting: Amara McClellan. Director, Public Relations/Voice of the Quakes: Mike Lindskog. Office Manager: Shelley Scebbi. Director, Food/Beverage: Jose Reyna.

FIELD STAFF

Manager: Drew Saylor. Hitting Coach: Jay Gibbons. Pitching Coach: Kip Wells.

GAME INFORMATION

Radio Announcer: Mike Lindskog.
PA Announcer: Chris Albaugh. Official Scorer: Ryan Wilson.
Stadium Name: LoanMart Field. Location: I-10 to I-15 North, exit at Foothill Boulevard, left on Foothill, left on Rochester to Stadium. Standard Game Times: 7:05 pm; Sun. 2:05 (April-June), 5:05 (July-Sept.). Ticket Price Range: $8-12.
Visiting Club Hotel: Best Western Heritage Inn, 8179 Spruce Ave, Rancho Cucamonga, CA 91730. Telephone: (909) 466-1111.

SAN JOSE GIANTS

Office Address: 588 E Alma Ave, San Jose, CA 95112. Mailing Address: PO Box 21727, San Jose, CA 95151.
Telephone: (408) 297-1435. Fax: (408) 297-1453.
E-Mail Address: info@sjgiants.com. Website: www.sjgiants.com.
Affiliation (first year): San Francisco Giants (1988). Years in League: 1942, 1947-58, 1962-76, 1979-

OWNERSHIP/MANAGEMENT

Operated by: Progress Sports Management. Principal Owners: San Francisco Giants, Heidi Stamas, Richard Beahrs. President/CEO: Daniel Orum. Chief Operating Officer/General Manager: Mark Wilson. Senior VP, Communications/Chief Marketing Officer Juliana Paoli. VP, Ballpark Operations: Lance Motch. VP, Finance/Human Resources: Tyler Adair. Director, Player Personnel: Linda Pereira. Director, Broadcasting: Joe Ritzo. Manager, Group Sales: Jeff Di Giorgio. Manager, Marketing/Media: Matt Alongi. Manager, Ticket Operations: Jacquie Stuart. Manager, Finance/Payroll: Vito Sambuceto. Account Executive: Liana Louie. Coordinator, Marketing/Retail: Sarah Acosta. Coordinator, Food and Beverage: Ramiro Mijares. Coordinator, Corporate Sponsorships: Gabe Diamond. Assistant, Marketing/Media: Jeff Black. Supervisor, Food and Beverage: Tara Tallman. Head Groundskeeper: Chase Martin.

FIELD STAFF

Manager: Lipso Nava. Hitting Coach: Todd Linden. Pitching Coach: Mike Couchee. Trainer: Garrett Havig. Strength/Conditioning Coach: Andy King.

GAME INFORMATION

Radio Announcers: Joe Ritzo, Justin Allegri. No. of Games Broadcast: 140.
Flagship: sjgiants.com. Television Announcers: Joe Ritzo, Joe Castellano. No. of Games Broadcast: 25 home games on Comcast Hometown Network (CHN), 70 home games on MiLB.TV. PA Announcer: Russ Call. Official Scorer: Mike Hohler. Stadium Name: Municipal Stadium. Location: South on I-280, Take 10th/11th Street Exit, Turn right on 10th Street, Turn left on Alma Ave; North on I-280: Take the 10th/11th Street Exit, Turn left on 10th Street, Turn Left on Alma Ave. Standard Game Times: 7 p.m., 6:30 p.m, Sat. 5 p.m., Sun 1 p.m. (5 p.m. after June 30).
Ticket Price Range: $8-24.

STOCKTON PORTS

Address: 404 W Fremont St, Stockton, CA 95203.
Telephone: (209) 644-1900. **Fax:** (209) 644-1931.
E-Mail Address: info@stocktonports.com. **Website:** www.stocktonports.com.
Affiliation (first year): Oakland Athletics (2005). **Years in League:** 1941, 1946-72, 1978-

OWNERSHIP/MANAGEMENT
Operated By: 7th Inning Stretch LLC.
President: Pat Filippone. **General Manager:** Bryan Meadows. **Assistant General Manager, Tickets:** Tim Pollack. **Director, Marketing:** Taylor McCarthy. **Director, Corporate Sales:** Aaron Morales. **Community and Public Relations Manager:** Kellie Ryan. **Operations and Events Manager:** Max Bochman. **Ticket Operations Manager:** Scott Gillies. **Manager, Graphics/Website:** Maria Boyle. **Group Sales Manager:** Luke Johnson. **Group Sales Account Executive:** Justice Hoyt. **Sponsorship/Ticket Sales Executive:** Greg Bell. **Bookkeeper:** Vang Hang. **Front Office Manager:** Jessica Due. **Ovations General Manager:** Mike Bristow.

FIELD STAFF
Manager: Rick Magnante. **Hitting Coach:** Tommy Everidge. **Pitching Coach:** Steve Connelly. **Trainer:** Travis Tims.

GAME INFORMATION
Radio Announcer: Zack Bayrouty. **No of Games Broadcast:** 140. **Flagship Station:** KWSX 1280 AM. **TV:** Comcast Hometown Network, Channel 104, Regional Telecast.
PA Announcer: Mike Conway. **Official Scorer:** Paul Muyskens.
Stadium Name: Banner Island Ballpark. **Location:** From I-5/99, take Crosstown Freeway (Highway 4) exit El Dorado Street, north on El Dorado to Fremont Street, left on Fremont. **Standard Game Times:** 7:05 pm. **Ticket Price Range:** $6-$20.
Visiting Club Hotel: Hampton Inn Stockton, 5045 South State Route 99 East, Stockton, CA 95215. **Telephone:** (209) 946-1234.

VISALIA RAWHIDE

Address: 300 N Giddings St, Visalia, CA 93291.
Telephone: (559) 732-4433. **Fax:** (559) 739-7732.
E-Mail Address: info@rawhidebaseball.com. **Website:** www.rawhidebaseball.com.
Affiliation (first year): Arizona Diamondbacks (2007). **Years in League:** 1946-62, 1968-75, 1977-

OWNERSHIP/MANAGEMENT
President: Tom Seidler. **General Manager:** Jennifer Pendergraft. **Sales & Promotion Director:** Jill Webb. **Ballpark Operations Assistant:** Julian Rifkind. **Assistant GM, Ticketing/Groups/Events:** Charlie Saponara. **Ticketing Manager:** Heather Dominguez. **Event Manager:** Lauren Lopes. **Director, Broadcasting/Media Relations:** Donny Baarns. **Community Relations/Groups:** Jon Bueno. **Assistant GM, Ballpark Operations:** Cody Gray. **Director of Ballpark Operations:** Matt Cooper. **Head Groundskeeper:** James Templeton. **Food/Beverage Manager:** Jerry Verastegui. **Ballpark Operations Assistant:** Les Kissick.

FIELD STAFF
Manager: JR House. **Hitting Coach:** Vince Harrison. **Pitching Coach:** Jeff Bajenaru. **Bench Coach:** Javier Colina. **Trainer:** Chad Moeller.

GAME INFORMATION
Radio Announcers: Donny Baarns. **No. of Games Broadcast:** 140. **Flagship Station:** TBD.
PA Announcer: Brian Anthony. **Official Scorer:** Harry Kargenian. **Stadium Name:** Rawhide Ballpark. **Location:** From Highway 99, take 198 East to Mooney Boulevard exit, left at second signal on Giddings; four blocks to ballpark. **Standard Game Times:** 7 pm, Sun. 1pm (first half), 6 pm (second half). **Ticket Price Range:** $5-30.
Visiting Club Hotel: Charter Inn & Suites, 1016 E Prosperity Ave, Tulare, CA 93274. **Telephone:** (559) 685-9500.

CAROLINA LEAGUE

Address: 1806 Pembroke Rd., Suite 2-B, Greensboro, NC 27408.
Telephone: (336) 691-9030. **Fax:** (336) 464-2737.
 E-Mail Address: office@carolinaleague.com. **Website:** www.carolinaleague.com.
Years League Active: 1945-.
President/Treasurer: John Hopkins.
 Vice President: Billy Prim (Winston-Salem). **Executive VP:** Steve Bryant (Carolina).
Corporate Secretary: Ken Young (Frederick). **Directors:** Tim Zue (Salem), Paul Sunwall
(Lynchburg), Chuck Greenberg (Myrtle Beach), Dave Ziedelis (Frederick), Steve Bryant
(Carolina), Clark Minker (Wilmington), Billy Prim (Winston-Salem), Art Silber (Potomac).
Administrative Assistant: Marnee Larkins.
 Division Structure: North—Frederick, Lynchburg, Potomac, Wilmington. **South**—Carolina,
Myrtle Beach, Salem, Winston-Salem.
 Regular Season: 140 games (split schedule). **2016 Opening Date:** April 7. **Closing Date:**
Sept 5.
 All-Star Game: Carolina League vs California League, June 21 at Lake Elsinore.
 Playoff Format: First-half division winners play second-half division winners in best of
three series; if a team wins both halves, it plays division opponent with next-best second-half
record. Division series winners meet in best of five series for Mills Cup.
 Roster Limit: 25 active. **Player Eligibility Rule:** No age limit. No more than two players
and one player/coach on active list may have six or more years of prior minor league service.
 Brand of Baseball: Rawlings.
 Umpires: Brock Ballou (Mt. Juliet, TN), Matthew Bates (Ooltewah, TN), Justin Houser (Mattawan, MI), Christopher
Marco (Waterdown, ON), Tyler Olson (Overland Park, KS), Randy Rosenberg (Arlington, VA), Christopher Scott
(Davidsonville, MD), Zachery Tieche (Sebring, OH).

John Hopkins

STADIUM INFORMATION

Club	Stadium	Opened	Dimensions			Capacity	2015 Att.
			LF	CF	RF		
Carolina	Five County Stadium	1991	330	400	309	6,500	202,072
Frederick	Harry Grove Stadium	1990	325	400	325	5,400	328,789
Lynchburg	City Stadium	1939	325	390	325	4,281	157,464
Myrtle Beach	TicketReturn.com Field	1999	308	405	328	5,200	240,357
Potomac	Pfitzner Stadium	1984	315	400	315	6,000	217,892
Salem	Salem Memorial Stadium	1995	325	401	325	5,502	228,120
Wilmington	Frawley Stadium	1993	325	400	325	6,532	282,437
Winston-Salem	BB&T Ballpark	2010	315	399	323	5,500	289,637

CAROLINA MUDCATS

 Office Address: 1501 NC Hwy 39, Zebulon, NC 27597. **Mailing Address:** PO Drawer 1218,
Zebulon, NC 27597.
 Telephone: (919) 269-2287. **Fax:** (919) 269-4910.
 E-Mail Address: muddy@carolinamudcats.com. **Website:** www.carolinamudcats.com.
 Affiliation: Atlanta Braves (2015-). **Years in League:** 2012-

OWNERSHIP/MANAGEMENT
 Operated by: Mudcats Baseball, LLC.
 Majority Owner/President: Steve Bryant. **Vice President/General Manager:** Joe Kremer. **General Manager,
Operations:** Eric Gardner. **Director, Food/Beverage:** Dwayne Lucas. **Director, Merchandise/Box Office Manager:**
Janell Bullock. **Director, Stadium Operations:** Alan Spence. Director, In-**Game Entertainment/Video Production:** Don
Sill. **Director, Promotions/Sales Executive:** Patrick Ennis. **Director, Community Relations:** Becca Holtgreive. **Graphic
Production:** Brock Ross. **Corporate Sales Executive:** Gerrod Speer. Corporate and Group Sales/**On-field Announcer:**
Duke Sanders. **Director of Group Sales/Sales Executive:** Mike Link. **Director of Ticket Operations/Sales Executive:**
Josh Perry. **Sales Executive:** Yogi Brewington. **Director, Field Operations:** John Packer. **Director, Broadcasting/Media
Relations:** Greg Young. **Mascot Coordinator:** Corey Essman.

FIELD STAFF
 Manager: Rocket Wheeler. **Hitting Coach:** Carlos Mendez. **Pitching Coach:** Derrick Lewis. **Trainer:** Nick Flynn.

GAME INFORMATION
 Radio Announcer: Greg Young. **No. of Games Broadcast:** 140. **Flagship Station:** The Big Dawg 98.5 FM, WDWG.
PA Announcer: Hayes Permar. **Official Scorer:** Bill Woodward. **Stadium Name:** Five County Stadium. **Location:** From
Raleigh, US 64 East to 264 East, exit at Highway 39 in Zebulon. **Standard Game Times:** 7 pm, Sat. 6:00, Sun. 2:00. **Ticket
Price Range:** $10-11.
 Visiting Club Hotel: Holiday Inn Raleigh

FREDERICK KEYS

Address: 21 Stadium Dr., Frederick, MD 21703.
Telephone: (301) 662-0013. **Fax:** (301) 662-0018.
E-Mail Address: info@frederickkeys.com. **Website:** www.frederickkeys.com.
Affiliation (first year): Baltimore Orioles (1989). **Years in League:** 1989-

OWNERSHIP/MANAGEMENT
Ownership: Maryland Baseball Holding LLC.
President: Ken Young. **General Manager:** Dave Ziedelis. **Director, Ticket Operations:** Ben Sealy. **Director, Marketing:** Bridget McCabe. **Promotions Manager:** Christine Roy. **Manager, Broadcasting/Public Relations:** Geoff Arnold. **Marketing Assistant:** Catie Graf. **Director, Group Sales:** Matt Miller. **Account Managers:** Amanda Kostolansky, Chris Colletti, Casey O'Brien. **Director, Sponsorship/Broadcaster:** Doug Raftery. **Account Managers:** Taylor Fisher, Elizabeth Wenger. **Box Office Assistants:** Chris Williams, Matthew Baker. **Director, Stadium Operations:** Kari Collins. **Head Groundskeeper:** Mike Soper. **Clubhouse Manager:** Adam Barron. **Office Manager:** Katy Bobbitt. **Finance Manager:** Tami Hetrick. General **Manager-Ovations:** Alan Cranfill.

FIELD STAFF
Manager: Orlando Gomez. **Hitting Coach:** Unavailable. **Pitching Coach:** Kennie Steenstra. **Athletic Trainer:** Pat Wesley.

GAME INFORMATION
Radio Announcers: Geoff Arnold, Doug Raftery.
PA Announcer: Andy Redmond. **Official Scorers:** Bob Roberson, Dennis Hetrick, Luke Stillson.
Stadium Name: Harry Grove Stadium. **Location:** From I-70, take exit 54 (Market Street), left at light; From I-270, take exit 32 (I-70Baltimore/Hagerstown) toward Baltimore (I-70), to exit 54 at Market Street. **Ticket Price Range:** $9-12.
Visiting Club Hotel: Comfort Inn Frederick, 7300 Executive Way, Frederick, MD 21704. **Telephone:** (301) 668-7272.

LYNCHBURG HILLCATS

Office Address: Lynchburg City Stadium, 3180 Fort Ave, Lynchburg, VA 24501. **Mailing Address:** PO Box 10213, Lynchburg, VA 24506.
Telephone: (434) 528-1144. **Fax:** (434) 846-0768.
E-Mail Address: info@lynchburg-hillcats.com. **Website:** www.Lynchburg-hillcats.com.
Affiliation (secondt year): Cleveland Indians (2015). **Years in League:** 1966-

OWNERSHIP/MANAGEMENT
Operated By: Elmore Sports Group.
President: Chris Jones. **General Manager:** Ronnie Roberts. **Assistant General Manager:** Colt Riley. **General Manager of Concessions:** Arjun Suresh. **Director of Sales:** Zach Willis. **Head Groundskeeper:** Darren Johnson. **Director, Broadcasting:** Kyle West., **Promotions:** Ashley Stephenson. **Director, Group Sales:** Josh Duffy. **Operations/Clubhouse Manager:** John Hutt. **Office Manager:** Diane Arrington.

FIELD STAFF
Manager: Mark Budzinski. **Hitting Coach:** Larry Day. **Pitching Coach:** Rigo Beltran. **Trainer:** Bobby Ruiz.

GAME INFORMATION
Radio Announcer: Kyle West. **No. of Games Broadcast:** 140. **Flagship Station:** WVGM-93.3 FM.
PA Announcer: Chuck Young. **Official Scorers:** Malcolm Haley, Chuck Young.
Stadium Name: Calvin Falwell Field at Lynchburg City Stadium. **Location:** US 29 Business South to Lynchburg City Stadium (exit 6); US 29 Business North to Lynchburg City Stadium (exit 4). **Ticket Price Range:** $7-10.
Visiting Club Hotel: Microtel Inn & Suites by Wyndham, 5704 Seminole Ave., Lynchburg, VA 24502. **Telephone:** (434) 239-2300.

MYRTLE BEACH PELICANS

Mailing Address: 1251 21st Avenue N. Myrtle Beach, SC 29577.
Telephone: (843) 918-6000. **Fax:** (843) 918-6001.
E-Mail Address: info@myrtlebeachpelicans.com. **Website:** www.myrtlebeachpelicans.com.
Affiliation (first year): Chicago Cubs (2015). **Years in League:** 1999-

OWNERSHIP/MANAGEMENT
Operated By: Myrtle Beach Pelicans LP. **President/Managing Partner:** Chuck Greenberg.
President/General Manager: Andy Milovich. **Merchandise Manager:** Dan Bailey. **Senior Director, Business Development:** Guy Schuman. **Vice President, Business Development:** Ryan Moore. **Director, Business Development:** Katelyn Guild. **Media Relations/Broadcaster:** Scott Kornberg. **Sports Turf Manager:** Corey Russell.

Senior Director, Finance: Anne Frost. **Senior Director, Community Development:** Jen Borowski. **Senior Director, Marketing:** Kristin Call. **Administrative Assistant:** Beth Freitas. **Facility Operations Manager:** Mike Snow. **Director, Food/Beverage:** Brad Leininger. **Director, Video Production:** Kyle Guertin. **Assistant GM/Sales:** Zach Brockman. **Box Office Manager:** Shannon Samanka. **Group Sales Manager:** Justin Bennett. **Account Executives:** Gandy Henry, Todd Chapman, David Woodward, Patrick Girard, Ryan Cannella. **Corporate Sales Manager:** Katelyn Guild. **Official Scorer:** BJ Scott.

FIELD STAFF
Manager: Buddy Bailey. **Pitching Coach:** Anderson Taravez. **Hitting Coach:** Mariano Duncan. **Assistant Coach:** Juan Cabreja. **Athletic Trainer:** Toby Williams.

GAME INFORMATION
PA Announcer: Unavailable. **Official Scorer:** Steve Walsh.
Stadium Name: Ticketreturn.com Field at Pelicans Ballpark. **Location:** US Highway 17 Bypass to 21st Ave. North, half mile to stadium. **Standard Game Times:** Unavailable. **Ticket Price Range:** $9-$15.
Visiting Club Hotel: Hampton Inn-Broadway at the Beach, 1140 Celebrity Circle, Myrtle Beach, SC 29577. **Telephone:** (843) 916-0600.

POTOMAC NATIONALS

Office Address: 7 County Complex Ct, Woodbridge, VA 22192. **Mailing Address:** PO Box 2148, Woodbridge, VA 22195.
Telephone: (703) 590-2311. **Fax:** (703) 590-5716.
E-Mail Address: info@potomacnationals.com. **Website:**www.potomacnationals.com.
Affiliation (first year): Washington Nationals (2005). **Years in League:** 1978-

OWNERSHIP/MANAGEMENT
Operated By: Potomac Baseball LLC.
Principal Owner: Art Silber. **President:** Lani Silber Weiss.
Vice President/General Manager: Zach Prehn. Assistant GM, Director, **Food & Beverage:** Aaron Johnson. **Ticket Director:** Brett Adams. Director, Corporate Sales/**Media Relations & Broadcasting:** Bryan Holland. Director, **Stadium Operations & Merchandising:** Arthur Bouvier. **Group Sales Executives:** Ashlee Towns, Jacob Martinez, & Ricky Goykin. **Manager, Community Relations:** Ashlee Towns. **Director, Graphic Design:** Alexis Deegan. **Manager, Business Operations:** Shawna Hooke. **Box Office Manager:** Chris Bentivegna.

FIELD STAFF
Manager: Tripp Keister. **Hitting Coach:** Luis Ordaz. **Pitching Coach:** Franklin Bravo. **Trainer:** TD Swinford.

GAME INFORMATION
Radio Announcer: Bryan Holland. **No. of Games Broadcast:** 140. **Flagship:** www.potomacnationals.com.
PA Announcer: Jeremy Whitham. **Official Scorer:** David Vincent, Ben Trittipoe.
Stadium Name: G. Richard Pfitzner Stadium. **Location:** From I-95, take exit, 158B and continue on Prince William Parkway for five miles, right into County Complex Court. **Standard Game Times:** 7:05 pm, Sat. 6:35, Sun. 1:05 (first half), Sun 6:05 (second half). **Ticket Price Range:** $10-16.
Visiting Club Hotel: Country Inn and Suites, Prince William Parkway, Woodbridge, VA 22192. **Telephone:** (703) 492-6868.

SALEM RED SOX

Office Address: 1004 Texas St., Salem, VA 24153. **Mailing Address:** PO Box 842, Salem, VA 24153.
Telephone: (540) 389-3333. **Fax:** (540) 389-9710.
E-Mail Address: info@salemsox.com. **Website:** www.salemsox.com.
Affiliation (first year): Boston Red Sox (2009). **Years in League:** 1968-

OWNERSHIP/MANAGEMENT
Operated By: Carolina Baseball LLC/Fenway Sports Group.
President: Sam Kennedy. **Managing Director:** Tim Zue. **President/General Manager:** Ryan Shelton. **VP/Assistant GM:** Allen Lawrence. **VP of Operations:** Tim Anderson. **VP of Ticket Sales/Service:** Nathan Blum. **Director, Corporate Sponsorships:** Steven Elovich. **Marketing/Promotions Manager:** Samantha Barney. **Community Relations Manager:** Chelsea Booth. **Facilities Manager:** Matt Bird. **Group Sales Director:** Andrew Yarnall. **Ticket Operations/Retention Manager:** Keegan Moody. **Food/Beverage Manager:** Patrick Pelletier. **Head Groundskeeper:** Bobby Estienne. **Account Executive:** Andy Leisen. **Account Executive:** Glen Medcalf. **Account Executive:** HJ Adams. **Clubhouse Manager:** TBA.

FIELD STAFF
Manager: Joe Oliver. **Hitting Coach:** Nelson Paulino. **Pitching Coach:** Paul Abbott. **Trainer:** TBA.

GAME INFORMATION

Radio Announcer: Kevin Burke. **No. of Games Broadcast:** 140. **Flagship Station:** ESPN 1240-AM.
PA Announcer: Unavailable. **Official Scorer:** Billy Wells. **Stadium Name:** LewisGale Field at Salem Memorial Ballpark. **Location:** I-81 to exit 141 (Route 419), follow signs to Salem Civic Center Complex. **Standard Game Times:** 7:05 pm, Sat. /Sun. 6:05/4:05. **Ticket Price Range:** $7-13. **Visiting Club Hotel:** Comfort Suites Ridgewood Farms, 2898 Keagy Rd., Salem, VA 24153. **Telephone:** (540) 375-4800.

WILMINGTON BLUE ROCKS

Address: 801 Shipyard Drive, Wilmington, DE 19801.
Telephone: (302) 888-2015. **Fax:** (302) 888-2032.
E-Mail Address: info@bluerocks.com. **Website:** www.bluerocks.com.
Affiliation (first year): Kansas City Royals (2007). **Years in League:** 1993-

OWNERSHIP/MANAGEMENT

Operated by: Wilmington Blue Rocks LP.
Honorary President: Matt Minker. **Owners:** Main Street Baseball, Clark Minker
General Manager: Chris Kemple. **Assistant GM:** Andrew Layman. **Director, Broadcasting/Media Relations:** Matt Janus. **Director, Advertising Sales:** Brian Radle. **Director, Merchandise:** Jim Beck. **Director, Marketing:** Joe Valenti. **Director, Community Affairs:** Kevin Linton. **Manager, Game Entertainment:** Mike Diodati. **Director, Tickets:** Stefani Rash. **Box Office Manager:** Mark Cunningham. **Group Sales Executives:** Joe McCarthy, Mike Cipolini and Mike Dailey. **Box Office Manager:** Brent Kepner. **Director, Field Operations:** Steve Gold. **Office Manager:** Erin Del Negro.

FIELD STAFF

Manager: Jamie Quirk. **Hitting Coach:** Abraham Nunez. **Pitching Coach:** Charlie Corbell. **Athletic Trainer:** James Stone.

GAME INFORMATION

Radio Announcers: Matt Janus and TBA. **No. of Games Broadcast:** 140. **Flagship Station:** 89.7 WGLS-FM. **PA Announcer:** Kevin Linton. **Official Scorer:** Dick Shute.
Stadium Name: Judy Johnson Field at Daniel Frawley Stadium.
Location: I-95 North to Maryland Ave (exit 6), right on Maryland Ave, and through traffic light onto Martin Luther King Blvd, right at traffic light on Justison St, follow to Shipyard Dr; I-95 South to Maryland Ave (exit 6), left at fourth light on Martin Luther King Blvd, right at fourth light on Justison St, follow to Shipyard Dr.
Standard Game Times: 6:35 pm, (Mon-Thur) 7:05 (Fri/Sat), Sun. 1:35 p.m. **Ticket Price Range:** $6-$14.
Visiting Club Hotel: Clarion Belle, 1612 N DuPont Hwy, New Castle, DE 19720. **Telephone:** (302) 299-1408.

WINSTON-SALEM DASH

Office Address: 926 Brookstown Ave, Winston-Salem, NC 27101.
Stadium Address: 951 Ballpark Way, Winston-Salem, NC 27101.
Telephone: (336) 714-2287. **Fax:** (336) 714-2288.
E-Mail Address: info@wsdash.com. **Website:** www.wsdash.com.
Affiliation (first year): Chicago White Sox (1997). **Years in League:** 1945-

OWNERSHIP/MANAGEMENT

Operated by: W-S Dash. **Principal Owner:** Billy Prim. **President:** Geoff Lassiter.
Vice President/Chief Financial Officer: Kurt Gehsmann. **VP, Baseball Operations:** Ryan Manuel. **VP, Ticket Sales:** C.J. Johnson. **VP, Corporate Partnerships:** Corey Bugno.
Director, Corporate Partnerships: Darren Hill. **Director, Group Sales:** Russell Parmele. **Director, Entertainment/ Community Relations:** Annie Stoltenberg. **Director, Facility Management:** Jeff Brown. **Broadcaster:** Brian Boesch. **Head Groundskeeper:** Paul Johnson. **Staff Accountant:** Amanda Elbert. **Creative Services Manager:** Kristin DiSanti. **Sponsor Services Account Managers:** Mimi Driscoll, Will Marrs. **Business Development Representatives:** Devin Athan, Taylor Boyle, Paul Stephens. **Group Sales Representative:** Sean Aquadro, Thomas Clark, Ira Dogruyol. **Box Office Manager:** Kenny Lathan.

FIELD STAFF

Manager: Joel Skinner. **Hitting Coach:** Charlie Poe. **Pitching Coach:** Jose Bautista. **Trainer:** Josh Fallin. **Strength Coach:** George Timke.

GAME INFORMATION

Radio Announcer: Brian Boesch. **No. of Games Broadcast:** 140. **Flagship Station:** 600 AM-WSJS (Thursdays) or wsdash.com (all games).
PA Announcer: Jeffrey Griffin. **Official Scorer:** Bill Grainger.
Stadium Name: BB&T Ballpark. **Location:** I-40 Business to Peters Creek Parkway exit (exit 5A). **Standard Game Times:** 7 pm, Sat. 6:30 pm, Sun 2 or 5 pm. **Visiting Club Hotel:** TBD.

FLORIDA STATE LEAGUE

Office Address: 104 E Orange Ave Daytona Beach, FL 32114. **Mailing Address:** PO Box 349, Daytona Beach, FL 32115.

Telephone: (386) 252-7479. **Fax:** (386) 252-7495.

E-Mail Address: fslbaseball@cfl.rr.com. **Website:** www.floridastateleague.com.

Years League Active: 1919-1927, 1936-1941, 1946- .

Ken Carson

President/Treasurer: Ken Carson.

VPs: North—Ken Carson. **South**—Paul Taglieri. **Corporate Secretary:** Horace Smith Jr. **Special Adviser:** Ben Hayes.

Directors: Mike Bauer (Jupiter/Palm Beach), Ken Carson (Dunedin), Jared Forma (Charlotte), Trevor Gooby (Bradenton), Jason Hochberg (Fort Myers), Josh Lawther (Daytona), Ron Myers (Lakeland), Kyle Smith (Brevard County), Vance Smith (Tampa), Paul Taglieri (St. Lucie), John Timberlake (Clearwater).

Office Manager: Laura LeCras.

Division Structure: North—Brevard County, Clearwater, Daytona, Dunedin, Lakeland, Tampa. **South**—Bradenton, Charlotte, Fort Myers, Jupiter, Palm Beach, St. Lucie.

Regular Season: 140 games (split schedule). **2015 Opening Date:** April 9. **Closing Date:** September 6.

All-Star Game: June 20 at St. Lucie.

Playoff Format: First-half division winners meet second-half winners in best of three series. Winners meet in best of five series for league championship.

Roster Limit: 25. **Player Eligibility Rule:** No age limit. No more than two players and one player-coach on active list may have six or more years of prior minor league service.

Brand of Baseball: Rawlings.

Umpires: Jordan Albarado (Scott, LA), Ryan Benson (Danbury, CT), Scott Costello (Barrie, Ontario), Ryan Doherty (Littleton, CO), Joe George (Springfield, IL), Ben Levin (Cincinnati, OH), Alexander MacKay (Evergreen, CO), Brennan Miller (Fairfax Station, VA), Kirk Struble (Kirkland, WA), Nate Tomlinson (Ogdenburg, WI), Matt Winter (Hubbard, IA), Michael Wiseman (White Lake, MI).

STADIUM INFORMATION

			Dimensions				
Club	Stadium	Opened	LF	CF	RF	Capacity	2015 Att.
Bradenton	McKechnie Field	1923	335	400	335	8,654	102,914
Brevard County	Space Coast Stadium	1994	340	404	340	7,500	78,373
Charlotte	Charlotte Sports Park	2009	343	413	343	5,028	105,965
Clearwater	Bright House Field	2004	330	400	330	8,500	174,283
Daytona	Jackie Robinson Ballpark	1930	317	400	325	4,200	137,224
Dunedin	Florida Auto Exchange Stadium	1977	335	400	327	5,509	52,659
Fort Myers	Hammond Stadium	1991	330	405	330	7,900	133,817
Jupiter	Roger Dean Stadium	1998	330	400	325	6,871	67,194
Lakeland*	Joker Marchant Stadium	1966	340	420	340	7,828	61,328
Palm Beach	Roger Dean Stadium	1998	330	400	325	6,871	67,108
St. Lucie	Mets Stadium	1988	338	410	338	7,000	99,044
Tampa	Steinbrenner Field	1996	318	408	314	11,026	92,786

Lakeland will play 2016 at Henley Field while Joker Marchant undergoes renovations

BRADENTON MARAUDERS

Address: 1701 27th Street East, Bradenton, FL 34208.

Telephone: (941) 747-3031. **Fax:** (941) 747-9442.

E-Mail Address: MaraudersInfo@pirates.com. **Website:** www.BradentonMarauders.com.

Affiliation (first year): Pittsburgh Pirates (2010). **Years in League:** 1919-20, 1923-24, 1926, 2010-.

OWNERSHIP/MANAGEMENT

Operated By: Pittsburgh Associates.

Senior Director, Florida Operations: Trevor Gooby. **Director, Operations:** A.J. Grant. **General Manager, Director of Sales:** Rachelle Madrigal. Coordinator, Florida Operations, **Ray Morris Coordinator, Concessions:** Erika Rolando. **Coordinator, Sales:** Craig Warzcecha. **Coordinator, Sales:** Josh Knupp. **Manager, Sales:** Justin Kristich. **Coordinator, Sponsorship/Tickets:** Shaun Higgins. **Coordinator, Marketing/Community Relations:** Carley Paganelli. **Coordinator, Florida Operations:** Nick Long. **Coordinator, Communication/Broadcasting:** Nate March. **Head Groundskeeper:** Victor Madrigal.

FIELD STAFF

Manager: Michael Ryan. **Coach:** Keoni DeRenne. **Pitching Coach:** Jeff Johnson. **Athletic Trainer:** Justin Ahrens.

GAME INFORMATION

PA Announcer: Ric Russo. **Official Scorer:** Dave Taylor.
Stadium Name: McKechnie Field. **Location:** I-75 to exit 220 (220B from I-75N) to SR 64 West/Manatee Ave, Left onto 9th St West, McKechnie Field on the left. **Standard Game Times:** 6:30 pm, Sun 1 pm (1st half), 5 pm (second half). **Ticket Price Range:** $6-12.
Visiting Club Hotel: Holiday Inn Express East Bradenton-Lakewood Ranch, 5464 Lena Road, Bradenton, FL 34211. **Telephone:** (941) 755-0055.

BREVARD COUNTY MANATEES

Address: 5800 Stadium Pkwy, Suite 101, Viera, FL 32940.
Telephone: (321) 633-9200. **Fax:** (321) 633-4418.
E-Mail Address: info@spacecoaststadium.com. **Website:** www.manateesbaseball.com.
Affiliation (first year): Milwaukee Brewers (2005). **Years in League:** 1994-

OWNERSHIP/MANAGEMENT

Operated By: Manatees Baseball Club LLC.
Chairman: Tom Winters. **Vice Chairman: President:** Charlie Baumann. **General Manager:** Kyle Smith. **Assistant GM:** Chad Lovitt. **Director, Business Operations/Finance:** Kelley Wheeler. **Sales Manager:** Joey Capistran. **Promotions Manager:** Kyle Thweatt. **Inside Sales/Box Office Manager:** Tom Snyder. **Accounting Manager:** Max Caron. **Clubhouse Manager:** Matthew Forbes. **Head Groundskeeper:** Doug Lopas.

FIELD STAFF

Manager: Joe Ayrault. **Coaches:** Ned Yost IV, Edwin Maysonet. **Pitching Coach:** Dave Chavarria. **Trainer:** Tommy Craig. **Strength/Conditioning Coordinator:** Jonah Mergen.

GAME INFORMATION

PA Announcer: J.C. Meyerholz. **Official Scorer:** Unavailable.
Stadium Name: Space Coast Stadium. **Location:** I-95 North to Wickham Rd (exit 191), left onto Wickham, right at traffic circle onto Lake Andrew Drive for 1 1/2 miles through the Brevard County Government Office Complex to the four-way stop, right on Stadium Parkway, Space Coast Stadium 1/2 mile on the left; I-95 South to Rockledge exit (exit 195), left onto Stadium Parkway, Space Coast Stadium is 3 miles on right. **Standard Game Times:** 6:35 pm, Sun. 5:05. **Tickets:** $6 - $10.
Visiting Club Hotel: Holiday Inn Melbourne-Viera Hotel and Conference Center. **Telephone:** (321) 255-0077.

CHARLOTTE STONE CRABS

Address: 2300 El Jobean Road, Building A, Port Charlotte, FL 33948.
Telephone: (941) 206-4487. **Fax:** (941) 206-3599.
E-Mail Address: info@stonecrabsbaseball.com. **Website:** www.stonecrabsbaseball.com.
Affiliation (first year): Tampa Bay Rays (2009). **Years in League:** 2009-

OWNERSHIP/MANAGEMENT

Operated By: Ripken Baseball.
General Manager: Jared Forma. **Assistant GM:** Jeffrey Cook. **Director, Finance:** Lori Engleman. **Director, Corporate Sponsorship:** Nate Gosline. **Marketing Manager:** Coeli Danella. **Director, Community Relations/Promotions:** Brandon Apter. **Group Sales Manager:** Hallie Rubins. **Account Representatives:** Otto Loor, Colin Wrba. **Operations Manager:** Tyler Darby. **Director, Food/Beverage:** Eric Peterson.

FIELD STAFF

Manager: Michael Johns. **Coach:** Joe Szekely. **Pitching Coach:** Steve Watson. **Trainer:** Scott Thurston.

GAME INFORMATION

PA Announcer: Josh Grant. **Official Scorer:** Rich Spedaliere.
Stadium Name: Charlotte Sports Park. **Location:** I-75 to Exit 179, turn left onto Toldeo Blade Blvd then right on El Jobean Rd. **Ticket Price Range:** $7-12.
Visiting Club Hotel: Sleep Inn, 806 Kings Hwy., Port Charlotte, FL 33980. **Phone:** 941-613-6300.

CLEARWATER THRESHERS

Address: 601 N Old Coachman Road, Clearwater, FL 33765.
Telephone: (727) 712-4300. **Fax:** (727) 712-4498.
Website: www.threshersbaseball.com. **Affiliation (first year):** Philadelphia Phillies (1985).
Years in League: 1985-

OWNERSHIP/MANAGEMENT
Operated by: Philadelphia Phillies.
Director, Florida Operations/General Manager: John Timberlake. **Business Manager:** Dianne Gonzalez. **Assistant GM/Director, Sales:** Dan McDonough. Assistant GM,
Ticketing: Jason Adams. **Office Administration:** DeDe Angelillis. **Manager, Group Sales:** Dan Madden. **Senior Sales Associate:** Bobby Mitchell. **Manager, Ballpark Operations:** Jerry Warren. **Operations Assistant:** Sean McCarthy. **Corporate Sales Associate:** Cory Sipe. **Manager, Special Events:** Doug Kemp. **Manager, Community Relations/Promotions:** Amanda Koch. **Clubhouse Manager:** Mark Meschede. **Manager, Food/Beverage:** Brad Dudash. **Suites Manager:** Wendy Armstrong. **Ticket Office Managers:** Pat Privelege, Kyle Webb. **Group Sales Assistant:** Aaron Frey. **Audio/Video:** Nic Repper. **Buyer/Manager, Merchandise:** Robin Warner. **PR Assistant:** Rob Stretch.

FIELD STAFF
Manager: Greg Legg. **Coach:** Rob Ducey. **Pitching Coach:** Aaron Fultz.

GAME INFORMATION
PA Announcer: Don Guckian. **Official Scorer:** Larry Wiederecht.
Stadium Name: Bright House Field. **Location:** US 19 North and Drew Street in Clearwater. **Standard Game Times:** 7 pm, Fri./Sat. 6:30. **Ticket Price Range:**
$6-10. **Visiting Club Hotel:** La Quinta Inn, 21338 US Highway 19 N, Clearwater, FL 33765. **Telephone:** (727) 799-1565.

DAYTONA TORTUGAS

Address: 110 E Orange Ave, Daytona Beach, FL 32114.
Telephone: (386) 257-3172. **Fax:** (386) 523-9490.
E-Mail Address: info@daytonatortugas.com. **Website:** www.daytonatortugas.com.
Affiliation (second year): Cincinnati Reds (2015). **Years in League:** 1920-24,1928, 1936-41, 1946-73, 1977-87, 1993-

OWNERSHIP/MANAGEMENT
Operated By: Tortugas Baseball Club LLC. **Principal Owner/President:** Reese Smith III
General Manager: Josh Lawther. **Assistant GM:** Jim Jaworski. **Director, Broadcasting/Media Relations:** Luke Mauro. **Assistant GM, Stadium Operations:** JR Laub. **Director, Ticket Operations:** Paul Krenzer. **Manager, Food/Beverage:** Kevin Dwyer. **Director, Merchandise:** Wade Becker. **Office Manager:** Tammy Devine. **Head Groundskeeper:** Blake Chapman.

FIELD STAFF
Manager: Eli Marrero. **Hitting Coach:** Gookie Dawkins. **Pitching Coach:** Tom Brown. **Trainer:** Kyle Utne.

GAME INFORMATION
Radio Announcer: Luke Mauro. **No. of Games Broadcast:** 140. **Flagship Station:** AM-1230 WSBB.
PA Announcer: Tim Lecras. **Official Scorer:** Don Roberts.
Stadium Name: Jackie Robinson Ballpark. **Location:** I-95 to International Speedway Blvd Exit (Route 92), east to Beach Street, south to Magnolia Ave east to ballpark; A1A North/South to Orange Ave west to ballpark. **Standard Game Time:** 7:05 p.m. **Ticket Price Range:** $6-12.
Visiting Club Hotel: Holiday Inn Resort Daytona Beach Oceanfront, 1615 S. Atlantic Ave Daytona Beach, FL 32118. **Telephone:** (386) 255-0921.

DUNEDIN BLUE JAYS

Address: 373 Douglas Ave Dunedin, FL 34698.
Telephone: (727) 733-9302. **Fax:** (727) 734-7661.
E-Mail Address: dunedin@bluejays.com. **Website:** dunedinbluejays.com.
Affiliation (first year): Toronto Blue Jays (1987). **Years in League:** 1978-79, 1987-

OWNERSHIP/MANAGEMENT
Director/General Manager, Florida Operations: Shelby Nelson. **Assistant GM:** Mike Liberatore.

Accounting Manager: Gayle Gentry. **Manager, Group Sales/Retail/Community Relations:** Kathi Beckman. Supervisor, Ticket Operations Hunter Haas. **Manager, Sales and Promotions Administrative Assistant/Receptionist:** Michelle Smith. **Supervisor, Stadium Operations:** Zac Phelps. **Head Superintendent:** Patrick Skunda. Clubhouse Supervisor, Jeff Jennings.

FIELD STAFF
Manager: Omar Malavé. **Hitting Coach:** John Tamargo Jr. **Pitching Coach:** Vince Horsman. **Trainer:** Shawn McDermott.

GAME INFORMATION
PA Announcer: Bill Christie. **Official Scorer:** Unavailable.
Stadium Name: Florida Auto Exchange Stadium. **Location:** From I-275, north on Highway 19, left on Sunset Point Rd for 4.5 miles, right on Douglas Ave; stadium is on right. **Standard Game Times:** 6:30 pm, Sun. 5 pm. **Ticket Price Range:** $7.
Visiting Club Hotel: La Quinta, 21338 US Highway 19 North, Clearwater, FL. **Telephone:** (727) 799-1565.

FORT MYERS MIRACLE

Address: 14400 Six Mile Cypress Pkwy, Fort Myers, FL 33912.
Telephone: (239) 768-4210. **Fax:** (239) 768-4211.
E-Mail Address: miracle@miraclebaseball.com. **Website:** www.miraclebaseball.com.
Affiliation (first year): Minnesota Twins (1993). **Years in League:** 1926, 1978-87, 1991-

OWNERSHIP/MANAGEMENT
Operated By: SJS Beacon Baseball. **Owner:** Jason Hochberg. **Chief Operating Officer:** Steve Gliner.
General Manager: Andrew Seymour. **Senior Director, Business Operations:** Suzanne Reaves. **Senior Director, Business Development:** John Kuhn. **Director, Broadcasting/Media Relations:** Brice Zimmerman. **Director, Food/Beverage:** Kevin Bush. **Director, Ticket Operations/Sales Advisor:** Bill Levy. **Sales Advisor:** Delroy Gay. **Assistant, Food/Beverage:** Danny Barbosa. **Head Groundskeeper:** Keith Blasingim. **Clubhouse Manager:** Brock Rasmussen.

FIELD STAFF
Manager: Jeff Smith. **Coach:** Jim Dwyer. **Pitching Coach:** Henry Bonilla. **Trainer:** Alan Rail.

GAME INFORMATION
Radio Announcer: Brice Zimmerman. **No. of Games Broadcast:** 140. **Internet Broadcast:** www.miraclebaseball.com.
PA Announcer: Bill Banfield. **Official Scorer:** Scott Pedersen.
Stadium Name: William H. Hammond Stadium at the CenturyLink Sports Complex. **Location:** Exit 131 off I-75, west on Daniels Parkway, left on Six Mile Cypress Parkway. **Standard Game Times:** 7:05 pm, Sat. 6:05; Sun. 4:05. **Ticket Price Range:** $6-12.
Visiting Club Hotel: Unavailable.

JUPITER HAMMERHEADS

Address: 4751 Main Street, Jupiter, FL 33458.
Telephone: (561) 775-1818. **Fax:** (561) 691-6886.
E-Mail Address: f.desk@rogerdeanstadium.com. **Website:** www.jupiterhammerheads.com.
Affiliation (first year): Miami Marlins (2002). **Years in League:** 1998-

OWNERSHIP/MANAGEMENT
Owned By: Miami Marlins, Jupiter Stadium, LTD.
General Manager, **Jupiter Stadium, LTD:** Mike Bauer. **Executive Assistant:** Kacey Wilcoxson. **Assistant GM, Jupiter Stadium LTD/GM Jupiter Hammerheads:** Jason Cantone. **Assistant GM, Jupiter Stadium:** Alex Inman. **Director, Accounting:** John McCahan. **Director, Corporate Partnerships/Marketing:** Katherine Deal. **Director, Ticketing:** Haile Urquhart. **Director, Community Relations/Promotions:** Marissa Korth. **Manager, Event Services:** Alex Inman. **Director, Grounds:** Jordan Treadway. **Assistant Directors, Grounds:** Micah Bennett, Drew Wolcott. **Stadium Building Manager:** Walter Herrera. **Merchandise Manager:** Chelsea Galbraith. **Ticket Manager:** Dustin Davis. **Press Box:** Jeff Bowe. **Office Manager:** Dianne Detling.

FIELD STAFF
Manager: Randy Ready. **Coach:** Frank Moore. **Pitching Coach:** Jeremy Powell.

GAME INFORMATION
PA Announcers: Dick Sanford, John Frost, Lou Palmer. **Official Scorer:** Brennan McDonald. **Stadium Name:** Roger Dean Stadium. **Location:** I-95 to exit 83, east on Donald Ross Road for 1/4 mile. **Standard Game Times:** 6:30 p.m., Sat. 5:30 p.m., Sun. 1:00 p.m. **Ticket Price Range:** $7-$10. **Visiting Club Hotel:** Fairfield Inn by Marriott, 6748 Indiantown Road, Jupiter, FL 33458. **Telephone:** (561) 748-5252.

LAKELAND FLYING TIGERS

Address: 2125 N Lake Ave, Lakeland, FL 33805.
Telephone: (863) 686-8075. **Fax:** (863) 688-9589.
Website: www.lakelandflyingtigers.com.
Affiliation (first year): Detroit Tigers (1967). **Years in League:** 1919-26, 1953-55, 1960, 1962-64, 1967-.

OWNERSHIP/MANAGEMENT

Owned By: Detroit Tigers, Inc. **Principal Owner:** Mike Ilitch. Please delete President **Director, Florida Operations:** Ron Myers. **General Manager:** Zach Burek. **Manager, Administration/Operations:** Shannon Follett. **Ticket Manager:** Ryan Eason. **Assistant General Manager:** Dan Lauer. **Receptionist:** Maria Walls.

FIELD STAFF

Manager: Dave Huppert. **Coach:** Nelson Santovenia. **Pitching Coach:** Jorge Cordova. **Trainer:** Jason Schwartzman. **Strength/Conditioning:** Jeff Mathers. **Clubhouse Manager:** Bo Bianco.

GAME INFORMATION

PA Announcer: Unavailable. **Official Scorer:** Ed Luteran.
Stadium Name: Henley Field. **Location:** Exit 32 on I-4 to 98 South, 1.5 miles on left. **Standard Game Times:** 6:30, Sun 1. **Ticket Price Range:** $4-7.
Visiting Club Hotel: Imperial Swan Hotel & Suites, 4141 South Florida Ave. Lakeland, FL 33813. **Telephone:** (863) 647-3000.

PALM BEACH CARDINALS

Address: 4751 Main Street, Jupiter, FL 33458.
Telephone: (561) 775-1818. **Fax:** (561) 691-6886.
E-Mail Address: f.desk@rogerdeanstadium.com. **Website:**www.palmbeachcardinals.com. **Affiliation (first year):** St. Louis
Cardinals (2003). **Years in League:** 2003-

OWNERSHIP/MANAGEMENT

Owned By: St. Louis Cardinals. **Operated By:** Jupiter Stadium LTD. General Manager, **Jupiter Stadium, LTD:** Mike Bauer. **Executive Assistant:** Lynn Besaw. **Assistant GM, Jupiter Stadium LTD/GM Palm Beach Cardinals:** Alex Inman. **Assistant GM, Jupiter Stadium:** Jason Cantone. **Director, Accounting:** John McCahan. **Director, Corporate Partnerships/Marketing:** Katherine Deal. **Director, Ticketing:** Haile Urquhart. **Director, Community Relations/Promotions:** Marissa Korth. **Manager, Event Services:** Alex Inman. **Director, Grounds:** Jordan Treadway. **Assistant Directors, Grounds:** Micah Bennett, Drew Wolcott. **Stadium Building Manager:** Walter Herrera. **Merchandise Manager:** Chelsea Galbraith. **Ticket Manager:** Dustin Davis. **Press Box:** Justin Terry. **Office Manager:** Dianne Detling.

FIELD STAFF

Manager: Oliver Marmol. **Hitting Coach:** Donnie Ecker. **Pitching Coach:** Randy Niemann. **Coach:** Jim Foster. **Athletic Trainer:** Brent Nueharth.

GAME INFORMATION

PA Announcers: John Frost, Dick Sanford, Lou Palmer. **Official Scorer:** Lou Villano. **Stadium Name:** Roger Dean Stadium. **Location:** I-95 to exit 83, east on Donald Ross Road for 1/4 mile. **Standard Game Times:** 6:35 pm, Sat. 5:35pm, Sun. 1:05/5:05 p.m. **Ticket Price Range:** $7- $10. **Visiting Club Hotel:** Fairfield Inn by Marriott, 6748 Indiantown Road, Jupiter, FL 33458. **Telephone:** (561) 748-5252.

ST. LUCIE METS

Address: 525 NW Peacock Blvd., Port St Lucie, FL 34986.
Telephone: (772) 871-2100. **Fax:** (772) 878-9802.
Website: www.stluciemets.com.
Affiliation (first year): New York Mets (1988). **Years in League:** 1988-

OWNERSHIP/MANAGEMENT

Operated by: Sterling Mets LP. **Chairman/CEO:** Fred Wilpon. **President:** Saul Katz. **COO:** Jeff Wilpon. **Executive Director, Minor League Facilities:** Paul Taglieri. **General Manager:** Traer Van Allen. **Assistant General Manager:** Clint Cure. **Executive Assistant:** Cynthia Malaspino. **Staff Accountant:** Shannon Murray. **Manager, Sales/Corporate Partnerships:** Lauren DeAcetis. **Manager, Ticketing/Merchandise:** Kyle Gleockler. **Manager, Food/Beverage Operations:** John Gallagher. **Manager, Media/Broadcast Relations:** Adam MacDonald. **Manager, Group Sales/Community Relations:** Kasey Blair.

FIELD STAFF

Manager: Luis Rojas. **Hitting Coach:** Valentino Pascucci. **Pitching Coach:** Marc Valdes. **Trainer:** Matt Hunter.

Strength Coach: Kory Wan.

GAME INFORMATION

PA Announcer: Evan Nine. **Official Scorer:** Bill Whitehead
Stadium Name: Tradition Field. **Location:** Exit 121 (St Lucie West Blvd) off I-95, east 1/2 mile, left on NW Peacock Blvd. **Standard Game Times:** 6:30 pm, Sun 1pm. **Ticket Price Range:** $6 - $9.
Visiting Club Hotel: Holiday Inn Express, 1601 NW Courtyard Circle, Port St Lucie, FL 34986. **Telephone:** (772) 879-6565.

TAMPA YANKEES

Address: One Steinbrenner Drive, Tampa, FL 33614.
Telephone: (813) 875-7753. **Fax:** (813) 673-3186
E-Mail Address: vsmith@yankees.com. **Website:** tybaseball.com.
Affiliation (first year): New York Yankees (1994). **Years in League:** 1919-27, 1957-1988, 1994-

OWNERSHIP/MANAGEMENT

Operated by: New York Yankees LP. **Principal Owner:** Harold Z Steinbrenner.
General Manager: Vance Smith. **Assistant GM, Sales/Marketing:** Matt Gess. **Operations Coordinator:** AmySue Manzione. **Ticket Operations:** Jennifer Magliocchetti. **Digital Media Coordinator & Community Relations:** Jessica Lack. **Sales Coordinator:** Jeremy Ventura. **Membership Services:** Kate Harvey. **Ticket Sales & Services:** Allison Stortz. **Head Groundskeeper:** Ritchie Anderson.

FIELD STAFF

Manager: Patrick Osborn. **Hitting Coach:** Tom Slater. **Pitching Coach:** Tim Norton. **Coach:** Antonio Pacheco. **Trainer:** Michael Becker. **Strength/Conditioning:** Joe Siara. **Video Coordinator:** Patrick Hafner.

GAME INFORMATION

Radio: www.tybaseball.com.
PA Announcer: Unavailable. **Official Scorer:** Unavailable.
Stadium Name: George M Steinbrenner Field. **Location:** I-275 to Dale Mabry Hwy, North on Dale Mabry Hwy (Facility is at corner of West Martin Luther King Blvd/Dale Mabry Hwy). **Standard Game Times:** 7 pm, Sat. 6, Sun 1. **Ticket Price Range:** $4-6.
Visiting Club Hotel: Unavailable.

MIDWEST LEAGUE

Address: 210 South Michigan Street, 5th Floor-Plaza Building, South Bend, Indiana 46601.
Telephone: (574) 234-3000. **Fax:** (574) 234-4220.
E-Mail Address: mwl@midwestleague.com, dickn@sni-law.com. **Website:** www.mid-westleague.com.

Years League Active: 1947-.
President/**Legal Counsel/Secretary:** Richard A. Nussbaum, II.
Vice President: Dave Walker
President Emeritus: George H. Spelius.
Directors: Andrew Berlin (South Bend), Stuart Katzoff (Bowling Green), Chuck Brockett (Burlington), Lew Chamberlin (West Michigan), Dennis Conerton (Beloit), Paul Davis (Clinton), Tom Dickson (Lansing), Jason Freier (Fort Wayne), David Heller (Quad Cities), Greg Seyfer (Cedar Rapids), Greg Rosenbaum (Dayton), Brad Seymour (Lake County), Paul Barbeau (Great Lakes), Rocky Vonachen (Peoria), Bob Froehlich (Kane County), Rob Zerjav (Wisconsin).
League Administrator: Holly Voss.
Division Structure: East—Bowling Green, Dayton, Fort Wayne, Lake County, Lansing, South Bend, Great Lakes, West Michigan. **West**—Beloit, Burlington, Cedar Rapids, Clinton, Kane County, Peoria, Quad Cities, Wisconsin.
Regular Season: 140 games (split schedule). **Opening Date:** April 7. **Closing Date:** Sept 5.
All-Star Game: June 21 at Cedar Rapids, Iowa.
Playoff Format: Eight teams qualify. First-half and second-half division winners and wild-card teams meet in best of three quarterfinal series. Winners meet in best of three series for division championships. Division champions meet in best-of-five series for league championship.
Roster Limit: 25 active. **Player Eligibility Rule:** No age limit. No more than two players and one player-coach on active list may have more than five years experience.
Brand of Baseball: Rawlings ROM-MID.
Umpires: Unavailable.

Richard Nussbaum

STADIUM INFORMATION

Club	Stadium	Opened	Dimensions LF	CF	RF	Capacity	2015 Att.
Beloit	Pohlman Field	1982	325	380	325	3,500	65,152
Bowling Green	Bowling Green Ballpark	2009	312	401	325	4,559	200,777
Burlington	Community Field	1947	338	403	318	3,200	66,867
Cedar Rapids	Veterans Memorial Stadium	2000	315	400	325	5,300	170,832
Clinton	Ashford University Field	1937	335	390	325	4,000	105,405
Dayton	Fifth Third Field	2000	338	402	338	7,230	574,830
Fort Wayne	Parkview Field	2009	336	400	318	8,100	400,036
Great Lakes	Dow Diamond	2007	332	400	325	5,200	221,749
Kane County	Fifth Third Bank Ballpark	1991	335	400	335	7,400	408,449
Lake County	Classic Park	2003	320	400	320	7,273	221,652
Lansing	Cooley Law School Stadium	1996	305	412	305	11,000	336,752
Peoria	Peoria Chiefs Stadium	2002	310	400	310	7,500	225,089
Quad Cities	Modern Woodmen Park	1931	343	400	318	4,024	250,004
South Bend	Coveleski Regional Stadium	1987	336	405	336	5,000	347,678
West Michigan	Fifth Third Ballpark	1994	317	402	327	10,051	391,055
Wisconsin	Fox Cities Stadium	1995	325	400	325	5,500	247,577

BELOIT SNAPPERS

Office Address: 2301 Skyline Drive, Beloit, WI 53511. **Mailing Address:** PO Box 855, Beloit, WI 53512.
Telephone: (608) 362-2272. **Fax:** (608) 362-0418.
E-Mail Address: snappy@snappersbaseball.com. **Website:** www.snappersbaseball.com.
Affiliation (first year): Oakland Athletics (2013). **Years in League:** 1982-

OWNERSHIP/MANAGEMENT

Operated by: Beloit Professional Baseball Association, Inc. **President:** Dennis Conerton. **General Manager:** Seth Flolid. **Director, Media Relations/Marketing:** Robert Coon. **Director, Tickets/Community Relations/Merchandise:** Crystal Bowen. **Head Groundskeeper:** Dalton Deckert.

FIELD STAFF

Manager: Fran Riordan. **Hitting Coach:** Don Schulze. **Pitching Coach:** Juan Dilone. **Trainer:** Brian Thorson.

GAME INFORMATION
Radio Announcer: TBD. **No. of Games Broadcast:** Home-40. **Flagship Station:**
WADR 103.5 FM. **PA Announcer:** Robert Coon. **Official Scorer:** Unavailable.
Stadium Name: Pohlman Field. **Location:** I-90 to exit 185-A, right at Cranston Road for 1 1/2 miles; I-43 to Wisconsin 81 to Cranston Road, right at Cranston for 1 1/2 miles. **Standard Game Times: 7 pm, 6:**30 (April-May), **Saturdays in April and May are at 4:00 PM, Sundays are at 2:**00 PM. Sun 2. **Ticket Price Range:** $6.50-$10.
Visiting Club Hotel: Rodeway Inn, 2956 Milwaukee Rd, Beloit, WI 53511. **Telephone:** (608) 364-4000.

BOWLING GREEN HOT RODS

Address: Bowling Green Ballpark, 300 8th Avenue, Bowling Green, KY 42101.
Telephone: (270) 901-2121. **Fax:** (270) 901-2165.
E-Mail Address: fun@bghotrods.com. **Website:** www.bghotrods.com.
Affiliation (first year): Tampa Bay Rays (2009). **Years in League:** 2010-

OWNERSHIP/MANAGEMENT
Operated By: Manhattan Capital Sports Acquisition. **President/Managing Partner:** Stuart Katzoff. **Partner:** Jerry Katzoff.
General Manager/COO: Adam Nuse. **Assistant General Manager:** Eric C. Leach. **Director, Creative Services:** Jordan Gracey. **Director, Finance:** Stephanie Morton. **Director, Marketing/Community Relations:** Jennifer Johnson. **Director, Sales:** Matt Ingram. **Manager, Box Office:** Kyle Wolz. **Manager, Broadcast/Media Relations:** Alex Cohen. **Manager, Group Sales:** Daniel "Beans" Langdon. **Head Groundskeeper:** Tyler Lenz. **Account Executives:** Aubrie Luesse, Cole Tynes. **Assistant, Creative Services:** Cate Brown. **Assistant, Merchandise:** Chryssi Attig. **Assistant, Operations:** Kevin Duff.

FIELD STAFF
Manager: Reinaldo Ruiz. **Hitting Coach:** Manny Castillo. **Pitching Coach:** Bill Moloney. **Trainer:** James Ramsdell.

GAME INFORMATION
Radio Announcer: Alex Cohen. **No. of Games Broadcast:** 140. **Flagship Station:** WBGN 1340-AM.
PA Announcer: Unavailable. **Official Scorer:** Unavailable. **Stadium Name:** Bowling Green Ballpark. **Location:** From I-65, take Exit 26 (KY-234/Cemetery Road) into Bowling Green for 3 miles, left onto College Street for .2 miles, right onto 8th Avenue. **Standard Game Times:** 6:**35 pm, Sun 4:**05 pm. **Ticket Price Range:** $7-26. **Visiting Club Hotel:** Jameson Inn & Suites. **Telephone:** (270) 282-7130.

BURLINGTON BEES

Office Address: 2712 Mount Pleasant St, Burlington, IA 52601. **Mailing Address:** PO Box 824, Burlington, IA 52601.
Telephone: (319) 754-5705. **Fax:** (319) 754-5882.
E-Mail Address: staff@gobees.com. **Website:** www.gobees.com.
Affiliation (first year): Los Angeles Angels (2013). **Years in League:** 1962-

OWNERSHIP/MANAGEMENT
Operated By: Burlington Baseball Association Inc.
President: Dave Walker. **General Manager:** Chuck Brockett. Assistant GM/Director, Group Outings, **Tickets, Merchandising:** Kim Parker. **Director of Broadcasting and Media/Community Relations:** Michael Broskowski. **Groundskeeper:** Andrew Raes. **Clubhouse Manager:** Corbin Schindler.

FIELD STAFF
Manager: Adam Melhuse. **Hitting Coach:** Buck Coats. **Pitching Coach:** Jairo Cuevas. **Trainer:** Yusuke Takahashi. **Strength/Conditioning:** Adam Smith.

GAME INFORMATION
Radio Announcer: Michael Broskowski. **No. of Games Broadcast:** 140. **Flagship Station:** KBUR 1490-AM.
PA Announcer: Sean Cockrell . **Official Scorer:** Ted Gutman.
Stadium Name: Community Field. **Location:** From US 34, take US 61 North to Mt. Pleasant Street, east 1/8 mile. **Standard Game Times:** 6:30 pm, Sun 2. April-May Sat. 5:00 pm. **Ticket Price Range:** $4-8. **Visiting Club Hotel:** Pzazz Best Western FunCity, 3001 Winegard Dr., Burlington, IA 52601. **Telephone:** (319) 753-2223.

CEDAR RAPIDS KERNELS

Office Address: 950 Rockford Road SW, Cedar Rapids, IA 52404. **Mailing Address:** PO Box 2001, Cedar Rapids, IA 52406.
Telephone: (319) 363-3887. **Fax:** (319) 363-5631.
E-Mail Address: kernels@kernels.com. **Website:** www.kernels.com.
Affiliation (first year): Minnesota Twins (2013). **Years in League:** 1962-

OWNERSHIP/MANAGEMENT
President: Greg Seyfer. **Chief Executive Officer:** Doug Nelson. **General Manager:** Scott Wilson. **Manager, IT/Communications:** Andrew Pantini. **Sports Turf Manager:** Jesse Roeder. **Director, Ticket/Group Sales:** Andrea Brommelkamp. **Director, Finance:** Tracy Barr. **Director, Broadcasting:** Morgan Hawk. **Manager, Entertainment/Community Relations:** Ryne George. **Director, Corporate Sales/Marketing:** Jessica Fergesen. **Coordinator, History:** Marcia Moran. **Manager, Ticket Office:** Sammy Brzostowski. **Manager, Stadium Operations:** Joe Krumm.

FIELD STAFF
Manager: Jake Mauer. **Hitting Coach:** Brian Dinkelman. **Pitching Coach:** J.P. Martinez. **Trainer:** Steve Taylor.

GAME INFORMATION
Radio Announcer: Morgan Hawk. **No. of Games Broadcast:** 140. **Flagship Station:** KMRY 1450-AM/93.1-FM.
PA Announcers: Bob Hoyt, Josh Paulson. **Official Scorers:** Steve Meyer, Shane Severson.
Stadium Name: Perfect Game Field at Veterans Memorial Stadium. **Location:** From I-380 North, take the Wilson Ave exit, turn left on Wilson Ave, after the railroad tracks, turn right on Rockford Road, proceed .8 miles, stadium is on left; From I-380 South, exit at First Avenue, proceed to Eighth Avenue (first stop sign) and turn left, stadium entrance is on right (before tennis courts). **Standard Game Times:** 6:35 pm, Sun 2:05. **Ticket Price Range:** $8-11 in advance, $9-12 day of game.
Visiting Club Hotel: Best Western Cooper's Mill, 100 F Ave NW, Cedar Rapids, IA 52405. **Telephone:** (319) 366-5323.

CLINTON LUMBERKINGS

Office Address: Ashford University Field, 537 Ball Park Drive, Clinton, IA 52732. **Mailing Address:** PO Box 1295, Clinton, IA 52733.
Telephone: (563) 242-0727. **Fax:** (563) 242-1433.
E-Mail Address: lumberkings@lumberkings.com. **Web site:** www.lumberkings.com.

OWNERSHIP/MANAGEMENT
Operated By: Clinton Baseball Club Inc.
President: Paul Davis. **General Manager:** Ted Tornow. **Director, Broadcasting/Media Relations:** Greg Mroz. **Director, Operations:** Tyler Oehmen. **Director, Concessions:** Alex Swartz. **Manager, Stadium/Sportsturf:** Shaun Thomas. **Accountant:** Ryan Marcum. **Assistant Director, Operations:** Morty Kriner. **Director, Facility Compliance:** Tom Whaley . **Office Procurement Manager:** Les Moore. **Clubhouse Manager:** Cody Eaves. **Community Service Representative:** Tammy Johnson. **Assistant Groundskeeper:** Matt Dunbar. **Special Events Coordinator:** Tom Krogman.

FIELD STAFF
Manager: Mitch Canham. **Hitting Coach:** Cesar Nicolas. **Pitching Coach:** Rich Dorman. **Trainer:** Shane Zdebiak. **Strength/Conditioning:** Paul Howey.

GAME INFORMATION
Radio Announcer: Greg Mroz. **No. of Games Broadcast:** 140. **Flagship Station:** WCCI 100.3 FM. **PA Announcer:** Brad Seward. **Official Scorer:** TBD. **Stadium Name:** Ashford University Field. **Location:** Highway 67 North to Sixth Ave. North, right on Sixth, cross railroad tracks, stadium on right. **Standard Game Times:** 6:30 pm, Sun 2. **Ticket Price Range:** $5-8. **Visiting Club Hotel:** Super 8 Clinton, 1711 Lincoln Way, Clinton, **IA 52732, Telephone:** (563) 242-8870.

DAYTON DRAGONS

Office Address: Fifth Third Field, 220 N Patterson Blvd, Dayton, OH 45402. **Mailing Address:** PO Box 2107, Dayton, OH 45401.
Telephone: (937) 228-2287. **Fax:** (937) 228-2284.
E-Mail Address: dragons@daytondragons.com. **Website:** www.daytondragons.com.
Affiliation (first year): Cincinnati Reds (2000). **Years in League:** 2000-

OWNERSHIP/MANAGEMENT
Operated By: Palisades Arcadia Baseball LLC.

President & General Manager: Robert Murphy.
Executive Vice President: Eric Deutsch. **VP, Accounting/Finance:** Mark Schlein. **VP, Corporate Partnerships:** Jeff Webb, Brad Eaton. **VP, Sponsor Services:** Brandy Guinaugh.
Director, **Media Relations & Broadcasting:** Tom Nichols. **Senior Director, Operations:** John Wallace. **Director, Facility Operations:** Joe Elking. **Senior Director, Entertainment:** Kaitlin Rohrer. **Director, Entertainment:** Katrina Hamilton. **Director, Creative Services:** James Westerheide. **Senior Marketing Manager:** Lindsey Huerter. **Box Office Manager:** Stefanie Mitchell. **Director, Season Ticket Sales:** Trafton Eutsler. **Senior Group Sales Manager:** Carl Hertzberg. **Marketing Managers:** Jacob Coy, Greg Lees, Jason McKendree, Leslie Schmiesing. **Corporate Marketing Managers:** Andrew Hayes, Matt Heithaus, Lauren Merkt, Sam Schneider, Andy Sheets, Kyle Volp, Jacob Welter. **Ticketing & Services Manager:** Mandy Roselli. **Graphic Designer:** Tara McGinnis. **Senior Game Day Operations Manager:** Joe Eaglowski. **Assistant Box Office Manager:** Katelyn Hoover. **Entertainment Assistant:** Samantha Hibbert. **Manager, Retail Operations:** Zack Spencer. **Customer Service Representative:** Amber Mingus. **Office Manager/Executive Assistant to the President:** Leslie Stuck. **Staff Accountant:** Dorothy Day. **Administrative Secretary:** Barbara Van Schaik. **Sports Turf Manager:** Britt Barry.

FIELD STAFF

Manager: Dick Schofield. **Hitting Coach:** Luis Bolivar. **Pitching Coach:** Derrin Ebert. **Coach:** Corky Miller. **Trainer:** Andrew Cleves.

GAME INFORMATION

Radio Announcers: Tom Nichols, Jason Kempf. **No. of Games Broadcast:** 140. **Flagship Station:** WONE 980 AM. **Television Announcer:** Tom Nichols. **No. of Games Broadcast:** Home-25. **Flagship Station:** WHIO 7.2.
PA Announcer: Ben Oburn. **Official Scorers:** Matt Lindsay, Mike Lucas, Matt Zircher.
Stadium Name: Fifth Third Field. **Location:** I-75 South to downtown Dayton, left at First Street; I-75 North, right at First Street exit. **Ticket Price Range:** $9-$17.
Visiting Club Hotel: Courtyard by Marriott, 100 Prestige Place, Miamisburg, OH 45342. **Phone:** 937-433-3131. **Fax:** 937-433-0285.

FORT WAYNE TINCAPS

Address: 1301 Ewing St., Fort Wayne, IN 46802.
Telephone: (260) 482-6400. **Fax:** (260) 471-4678.
E-Mail Address: info@tincaps.com. **Website:** www.tincaps.com.
Affiliation (first year): San Diego Padres (1999). **Years in League:** 1993-Present.

OWNERSHIP/MANAGEMENT

Operated By: Hardball Capital.
Owner: Jason Freier. **President:** Mike Nutter. **Vice President, Corporate Partnerships:** David Lorenz. **VP, Finance:** Brian Schackow. VP, **Marketing & Promotions:** Michael Limmer. **Creative Director:** Tony DesPlaines. **Video Production Manager:** Melissa Darby. **Assistant Video Production Manager:** Tyler Moore. **Broadcasting/Media Relations Manager:** John Nolan. **Group Sales Director:** Jared Parcell. **Group Sales Assistant Director:** Justin Shurley. **Group Sales Assistant Director:** Brent Harring.
Senior Ticket Account Manager: Austin Allen. **Ticket Account Manager:** Dalton McGill.
Ticket Account Manager: Jenn Sylvester. **Ticketing Director:** Pat Ventura. **Reading Program Director/Assistant Director of Ticketing:** Dan Preuett. **Corporate Partnerships Manager:** Tyler Baker. **Special Events Coordinator:** Holly Raney. **Banquet Event Manager:** Katie Read. **Food/Beverage Director:** Bill Lehn. **Executive Chef/Culinary Director:** Scott Kammerer. **VIP Sales Manager:** Bethany Randolph. **Food/Beverage Operations Manager:** Nathan Seaman. **Head Groundskeeper:** Keith Winter. **Assistant Groundskeeper:** Ryan Lehrman. **Facilities Director:** Tim Burkhart. **Accounting Manager/Facilities Manager:** Erik Lose. **Groundskeeping/Ballpark Operations Assistant:** Jake Sperry. **Merchandise Manager:** Jen Klinker. **Human Resources Administrator/Office Manager:** Cathy Tinney.

FIELD STAFF

Manager: Anthony Contreras. **Hitting Coach:** Lance Burkhart. **Pitching Coach:** Burt Hooton. **Coach:** Raul Padron. **Athletic Trainer:** Mitch Mattoon. **Strength/Conditioning Coach:** Drew Heithoff.

GAME INFORMATION

Radio Announcers: John Nolan, Mike Monaco, Mike Maahs. **No. of Radio Games Broadcast:** 140. **Flagship Station:** WKJG 1380-AM/100.9-FM. **TV Announcers:** John Nolan, Dave Doster, Javi DeJesus, Bobby Pierce. **No. of TV Games Broadcast:** Home–70. **Flagship Station:** Comcast Network 81. **PA Announcer:** Jared Parcell. **Official Scorers:** Rich Tavierne, Bill Scott, Dave Coulter. **Stadium Name:** Parkview Field. **Location:** 1301 Ewing St., Fort Wayne, IN, 46802 (Downtown Fort Wayne).
Ticket Price Range: $5-$12.50. **Visiting Club Hotel:** Quality Inn, 1734 West Washington Center Rd., Fort Wayne, IN, 46818 (260-489-5554).

GREAT LAKES LOONS

Address: 825 East Main St, Midland, MI 48640.
Telephone: (989) 837-2255. **Fax:** (989) 837-8780.
E-Mail Address: info@loons.com. **Website:** www.loons.com.
Affiliation (first year): Los Angeles Dodgers (2007). **Years in League:** 2007-

OWNERSHIP/MANAGEMENT

Operated By: Michigan Baseball Operations. **Stadium Ownership:** Michigan Baseball Foundation. **Founder/Foundation President:** William Stavropoulos.
President: Paul Barbeau. **Vice President/General Manager:** Scott Litle. **VP, Facilities/Operations:** Dan Straley. **VP, Finance:** Jana Chotivkova. **VP Marketing/Entertainment:** Chris Mundhenk. **General Manager, Dow Diamond Events:** Dave Gomola. Assistant GM, Corporate Partnerships/Director, Development (MBF): Eric Ramseyer. **VP, Human Resources:** Ann Craig. **Production Manager:** Trent Elliott. **Assistant GM, Ticket Sales:** Tiffany Wardynski. **Director, Accounting:** Jamie Start. **Director, Food/Beverage:** Gary Straight. **Director, Corporate Partnerships:** Kevin Schunk. **Manager, Group Sales:** James Cahilellis, Nick Knieling. **Manager, Communications:** Matt DeVries. **Director, Ticket Sales:** Thom Pepe. **Assistant to MBF President:** Marge Parker. **Accounting Manager:** Hope Wright. **Corporate Account Executive:** Jen Dore. **Manager, Concessions:** Andrew Booms. **Group Sales Coordinator:** Tyler Kring, Steve Horstmann. **Retail Manager:** Jenean Clarkson. **Promotions Manager:** Amber Knieling. **Catering Manager:** Ryan Teeple. **Executive Chef:** Andrea Noonan. **Head Groundskeeper:** Kelly Rensel. **Administrative Assistant:** Melissa Kehoe. **Director, Sales, 100.9-FM:** Jay Arons. **Business Manager, 100.9-FM:** Robin Gover.

FIELD STAFF

Manager: Gil Velazquez. **Hitting Coach:** John Valentin. **Pitching Coach:** Bobby Cuellar. **Coach:** Fumi Ishibashi.

GAME INFORMATION

Play-by-Play Broadcaster: Chris Vosters, Brad Tunney. **No. of Games Broadcast: 140 Flagship Station:** WLUN, ESPN 100.9-FM (ESPN1009.com). **PA Announcer:** Jerry O'Donnell.
Official Scorers: Terry Wilczek, Terry Lynch. **Stadium Name:** Dow Diamond. **Location:** I-75 to US-10 W, Take the M-20/US-10 Business exit on the left toward downtown Midland, Merge onto US-10 W/MI-20 W (also known as Indian Street), Turn left onto State Street, The entrance to the stadium is at the intersection of Ellsworth and State Streets. **Standard Game Times:** 6:05 pm (April), 7:05 (May-Sept), Sun. 2:05. **Ticket Price Range:** $6-9. **Visiting Club Hotel:** Holiday Inn, 810 Cinema Drive, Midland, MI 48642. **Telephone:** (989) 794-8500.

KANE COUNTY COUGARS

Address: 34W002 Cherry Lane, Geneva, IL 60134
Telephone: (630) 232-8811. **Fax:** (630) 232-8815 **E-Mail Address:** info@kanecountycougars.com. **Website:** www.kccougars.com **Affiliation (second year):** Arizona Diamondbacks (2015). **Years in League:** 1991-

OWNERSHIP/MANAGEMENT

Operated By: Cougars Baseball Partnership/American Sports Enterprises, Inc. Chairman/**Chief Executive Officer/President:** Dr. Bob Froehlich. **Owners:** Dr. Bob Froehlich, Cheryl Froehlich. **Board of Directors:** Dr. Bob Froehlich, Cheryl Froehlich, Stephanie Froehlich, Chris Neidhart, Marianne Neidhart.
Vice President/General Manager: Curtis Haug. **Senior Director, Finance/Administration:** Douglas Czurylo. **Finance/Accounting Manager:** Lance Buhmann. **Accounting:** Sally Sullivan. **Senior Director, Ticketing:** R. Michael Patterson. **Senior Ticket Sales Representative:** Alex Miller. **Sales Representatives:** Sean Freed, Alex Boduch, Marty Joyce. **Corporate Sponsorships:** Joe Golota. **Director, Ticket Services/Community Relations:** Amy Mason. **Senior Ticket Operations Representative:** Paul Quillia. **Director, Security:** Dan Klinkhamer. **Promotions Director:** Amy Bromann. **Promotions Assistant:** Julie Brady. **Director, Public Relations:** Shawn Touney. **Design/Graphics:** Emmet Broderick. **Media Placement Coordinator:** Bill Baker.
Video Director: Mike Forrest. **Director, Food/Beverage:** Jon Williams. **Business Manager:** Robin Hull. **Concessions Manager:** Dan McIntosh. **Executive Chef:** Ron Kludac. **Senior Director, Stadium Operations:** Mike Klafehn. **Director, Maintenance:** Jeff Snyder. **Head Groundskeeper:** Sean Ehlert.

FIELD STAFF

Manager: Mike Benjamin. **Hitting Coach:** Jonathan Mathews. **Pitching Coach:** Rich Sauveur. **Coach:** Shawn Roof. **Trainer:** Ryne Eubanks. **Strength/Conditioning Coach:** Skyler Zarndt. **Clubhouse Manager:** Scott Anderson.

GAME INFORMATION

Radio Announcer: Joe Brand. **No. of Games Broadcast:** 140. **Flagship Station:** WBIG 1280-AM.
Official Scorer: Joe Brand.
Stadium Name: Fifth Third Bank Ballpark. **Location:** From east or west, I-88 Ronald Reagan Memorial Tollway) to Farnsworth Ave. North exit, north five miles to Cherry Lane, left into stadium; from northwest, I-90 (Jane Addams Memorial Tollway) to Randall Rd. South exit, south to Fabyan Parkway, east to Kirk Rd., north to Cherry Lane, left into stadium complex. **Standard Game Times:** 6:30 pm, Sun. 1 pm. **Ticket Price Range:** $9-15.

Visiting Club Hotel: Pheasant Run Resort, 4051 E Main St, St. Charles, IL 60174. **Telephone:** (630) 584-6300.

LAKE COUNTY CAPTAINS

Address: Classic Park, 35300 Vine St., Eastlake, OH 44095-3142.
Telephone: (440) 975-8085. **Fax:** (440) 975-8958.
E-Mail Address: bseymour@captainsbaseball.com. **Website:** www.captainsbaseball.com.
Affiliation (first year): Cleveland Indians (2003). **Years in League:** 2010-

OWNERSHIP/MANAGEMENT
Operated By: Cascia LLC. **Owners:** Peter and Rita Carfagna, Ray and Katie Murphy.
Chairman/**Secretary/Treasurer:** Peter Carfagna. **Vice Chairman:** Rita Carfagna. **Vice President:** Ray Murphy. **VP, General Manager:** Brad Seymour.
Assistant GM, Sales: Neil Stein. **Director, Promotions:** Drew LaFollette. **Director, Captains Concessions:** John Klein. **Director, Stadium Operations:** Wayne Loeblein. **Director, Finance:** TBA. **Director, Ticket Operations/Merchandise:** Jen Yorko. **Manager, Turf Operations:** Christo Wallace. **Corporate Sales Executive:** Kevin Shiley. **Ticket Sales Account Executives:** Christy Buchar, Nick Dobrinich, Brian Fisher, Matt Fox, Tim O'Brien (Media Relations Manager), & Brent Pozza. **Office Assistant:** Jim Carfagna.

FIELD STAFF
Manager: Tony Mansolino. **Hitting Coach:** TBA. **Coach:** Junior Betances. **Pitching Coach:** Steve McCatty.

GAME INFORMATION
Radio Announcer: Andrew Luftglass. **No. of Games Broadcast:** 140. Flagship Station: TBA. **PA Announcer:** Tim O'Brien. **Official Scorers:** Glen Blabolil, Mike Mohner.
Stadium Name: Classic Park. **Location:** From Ohio State Route 2 East, exit at Ohio 91, go left and the stadium is 1/4 mile north on your right; From Ohio State Route 90 East, exit at Ohio 91, go right and the stadium in approximately five miles north on your right. **Standard Game Times:** 6:30 pm (April-May), 7 (May-Sept), Sun. 1:30.
Visiting Club Hotel: Red Roof Inn 4166 State Route 306, Willoughby, Ohio 44094. **Telephone:** (440)-946-9872.

LANSING LUGNUTS

Address: 505 E Michigan Ave, Lansing, MI 48912.
Telephone: (517) 485-4500. **Fax:** (517) 485-4518.
E-Mail Address: info@lansinglugnuts.com. **Website:** www.lansinglugnuts.com.
Affiliation (first year): Toronto Blue Jays (2005). **Years in League:** 1996-

OWNERSHIP/MANAGEMENT
Operated By: Take Me Out to the Ballgame LLC. Principal
Owners: Tom Dickson, Sherrie Myers. **General Manager:** Nick Grueser. **Assistant, GM Sales:** Nick Brzezinski. **Community Relations Manager:** Angela Sees. **Director, Business Operations:** Heather Viele. **Corporate Sales Manager:** Kohl Tyrrell. **Corporate Account Executive:** Kyle Benschoter. **Group Sales Representative:** Justin Burkett. **Group Sales Representative:** Eric Pionk. **Box Office/Team Relations Manager:** Josh Calver. **Season Ticket Specialist:** Greg Kruger. **Assistant Retail Director:** Matt Hicks. **Stadium Operations Manager:** Dennis Busse. **Assistant Stadium Operations Manager:** Bill Getschman. **Head Groundskeeper:** Lenny Yoder. **Senior Food/Beverage Director:** Brett Telder. **Assistant Food/Beverage Director:** Andrew Creswell. **Director, Marketing:** Linda Frederickson. **Special Events/Meetings Manager:** Lisa McMahon. **Creative Services/Production Assistant:** Ken Foldenauer. **Corporate Partnerships Manager:** Ashley Loudan.

FIELD STAFF
Manager: John Schneider. **Hitting Coach:** Unavailable. **Pitching Coach:** Jeff Ware.

GAME INFORMATION
Radio Announcer: Jesse Goldberg-Strassler. **No of Games Broadcast:** 140. **Flagship Station:** WQTX 92.1-FM.
PA Announcer: Unavailable. **Official Scorer:** Unavailable. **Stadium Name:** Cooley Law School Stadium. **Location:** I-96 East/West to US 496, exit at Larch Street, north of Larch, stadium on left. **Ticket Price Range:** $8-$23.50. **Visiting Club Hotel:** Radisson Hotel.

PEORIA CHIEFS

Address: 730 SW Jefferson, Peoria, IL 61605.
Telephone: (309) 680-4000. **Fax:** (309) 680-4080.
E-Mail Address: feedback@chiefsnet.com. **Website:** www.peoriachiefs.com.

OWNERSHIP/MANAGEMENT

Operated By: Peoria Chiefs Community Baseball Club LLC. **President:** Rocky Vonachen.
General Manager: Brendan Kelly. **Manager, Box Office:** Ryan Sivori. **Director, Media/Baseball Operations:** Nathan Baliva. **Marketing Manager:** Allison Rhoades. **Manager, Entertainment/Community Relations:** Katie Nichols. **Vice President, Ticket Sales:** Jason Mott. **Account Executives:** Caleb Smith, Matt Szczupakowski, Kate Voss. **Head Groundskeeper:** Mike Reno. **Director, Food/Beverage:** TBA.

FIELD STAFF

Manager: Joe Kruzel. **Hitting Coach:** Jobel Jimenez. **Pitching Coach:** Dernier Orozco. **Coach:** Nathan Sopena. **Trainer:** Dan Martin.

GAME INFORMATION

Radio Announcer: Nathan Baliva. **No. of Games Broadcast:** 140. **Flagship Station:** www.peoriachiefs.com, Peoria Chiefs App in iTunes.
PA Announcer: TBA Official Scorers: Bryan Moore, Nathan Baliva.
Stadium Name: Dozer Park. **Location:** From South/East, I-74 to exit 93 (Jefferson St), continue one mile, stadium is one block on left; From North/West, I-74 to Glen Oak Exit, turn right on Glendale, which turns into Kumpf Blvd, turn right on Jefferson, stadium on left. **Standard Game Times:** 7 pm, 6:30 (April-May, after Aug 18), Sat. 6:30, Sun. 5. **Ticket Price Range:** $7-11.
Visiting Club Hotel: Quality Inn & Suites, 4112 Brandywine Dr, Peoria, IL, 61614. **Telephone:** (309) 685-2556.

QUAD CITIES RIVER BANDITS

Address: 209 S Gaines St, Davenport, IA 52802.
Telephone: (563) 324-3000. **Fax:** (563) 324-3109.
E-Mail Address: bandit@riverbandits.com<mailto:bandit@riverbandits.com>.
Website: www.riverbandits.com.
Affiliation (first year): Houston Astros (2013). **Years in League:** 1960-

OWNERSHIP/MANAGEMENT

Operated by: Main Street Iowa LLC, David Heller, Bob Herrfeldt.
General Manager: Andrew Chesser. **VP, Sales:** Shawn Brown. **Assistant GM, Baseball Operations:** Travis Painter. **Assistant GM, Special Events:** Taylor Satterly. **Assistant GM, Amusements:** Mike Clark. **Finance Manager:** Dustin Miller. **Director, Community Relations:** Denise Clark. **Director, Marketing/Promotions:** Samantha Nicholson. **Director, Media Relations:** Jake Levy. **Director, Sales/Ticketing:** Jacqueline Holm. **Manager, Production:** Trevor Levine. **Manager, Sales:** Paul Kleinhans-Schulz. **Manager, Special Events:** Allie Hudson. **Head Groundskeeper:** Andrew Marking. **Director, Food/Beverage:** Patrick Delaney. **Assistant Director of Food/Beverage:** Hugo Alvarez. **Manager, Concessions:** Kory Gimm. **Executive Chef:** Lamont Tolbert.

FIELD STAFF

Manager: Omar Lopez. **Hitting Coach:** Joel Chimelis. **Pitching Coach:** Chris Holt. **Athletic Trainer:** Corey O'Brien. **Strength/Conditioning Coach:** Joe Bossard.

GAME INFORMATION

Radio Announcer: Jake Levy. **No. of Games Broadcast:** 140. **Flagship Station:** 1170-AM KBOB.
PA Announcer: Scott Werling. **Official Scorer:** Unavailable.
Stadium Name: Modern Woodmen Park. **Location:** From I-74, take Grant Street exit left, west onto River Drive, left on South Gaines Street; from I-80, take Brady Street exit south, right on River Drive, left on S. Gaines Street. **Standard Game Times:** 7 pm; Sat. 6, Sun. 1:15 (April-June/Aug 9), Sun. 5:15 pm (July-Aug 2). **Ticket Price Range:** $5-13.
Visiting Club Hotel: Radisson Quad City Plaza Hotel, 111 E. 2nd St, Davenport, IA 52801. **Telephone:** (563) 322-2200.

SOUTH BEND CUBS

Office Address: 501 W South St, South Bend, IN 46601.
Mailing Address: PO Box 4218, South Bend, IN 46634. **Telephone:** (574) 235-9988.
Fax: (574) 235-9950
E-Mail Address: cubs@southbendcubs.com **Website:** www.southbendcubs.com
Affiliation (second year): Chicago Cubs (2015). **Years in League:** 1988-

OWNERSHIP/MANAGEMENT

Owner: Andrew Berlin. **President:** Joe Hart. **Vice President, Business Development:** Nick Brown. **Assistant GM, Tickets:** Andy Beuster. **Box Office Manager:** Devon Hastings. **Account Executives:** Kevin Drislane, Logan Lee, Mitch McKamey, Alex Withorn. **Office Manager:** Kayla Smith. **Director, Finance/Human Resources:** Cheryl Carlson. **Director, Food/ Beverage:** Nick Barkley. **Catering/Business Manager:** TBD. **Executive Chef:** Josh Farmer. **Director, Creative Services/Promotions/Media Relations:** Chris Hagstrom-Jones. **Production Manager:** Nick Ruthrauff. **Merchandise Manager:** Brandy Beehler. **Assistant GM, Operations:** Peter Argueta. **Head Groundskeeper:** Kyle Jakowitsch. **Groundskeeper:** T.J. Wohlever.

FIELD STAFF

Manager: Jimmy Gonzalez. **Hitting Coach:** Guillermo Martinez. **Pitching Coach:** David Rosario. **Assistant Coach:** Ricardo Medina. **Trainer:** Mike McNulty. **Strength Coach:** Ed Kohl.

GAME INFORMATION

Radio Announcer: Darin Pritchett. **Flagship Station:** 96.1 FM WSBT. **PA Announcer:** Jon Thompson. **Official Scorer:** Peter Yarbro. **Stadium Name:** Four Winds Field. **Location:** I-80/90 toll road to exit 77, take US 31/33 south to South Bend to downtown (Main Street), to Western Ave., right on Western, left on Taylor. **Standard Game Times:** 7:05 pm, Fri. 7:35, Sun. 2:05. **Ticket Price Range:** Advance $10-12, Day of Game $11-13. **Visiting Club Hotel:** DoubleTree by Hilton Hotel South Bend. **Telephone:**(574) 234-2000.

WEST MICHIGAN WHITECAPS

Office Address: 4500 West River Dr, Comstock Park, MI 49321. **Mailing Address:** PO Box 428, Comstock Park, MI 49321.
Telephone: (616) 784-4131. **Fax:** (616) 784-4911.
E-Mail Address: playball@whitecapsbaseball.com. **Website:** www.whitecaps-baseball.com.
Affiliation (first year): Detroit Tigers (1997). **Years in League:** 1994-

OWNERSHIP/MANAGEMENT

Operated By: Whitecaps Professional Baseball Corp. **Principal Owners:** Denny Baxter, Lew Chamberlin. **President:** Scott Lane. **Vice President:** Jim Jarecki. **Vice President, Sales:** Steve McCarthy. **Facility Events Manager:** Mike Klint. **Operations Manager:** Mike Craven. **Director, Food/Beverage:** Matt Timon. **Community Relations Coordinator:** Jessica Muzevuca. **Director, Marketing/Media:** Mickey Graham. **Promotions Manager:** Matt Hoffman. **Multimedia Manager:** Elaine Cunningham. **Box Office Manager:** Shaun Pynnonen. **Groundskeeper:** Chad Gapczynski. **Facility Maintenance Manager:** John Passarelli. **Director, Ticket Sales:** Chad Sayen.

FIELD STAFF

Manager: Andrew Graham. **Coach:** Edgar Alfonzo. **Pitching Coach:** Mark Johnson. **Trainer:** T.J. Obergefell.

GAME INFORMATION

Radio Announcers: Dan Hasty. **No. of Games Broadcast:** 140. **Flagship Station:** WBBL 107.3-FM.
PA Announcers: Mike Newell, Bob Wells. **Official Scorers:** Mike Dean, Don Thomas.
Stadium Name: Fifth Third Ballpark. **Location:** US 131 North from Grand Rapids to exit 91 (West River Drive). **Ticket Price Range:** $6-14.
Visiting Club Hotel: Crowne Plaza 5700 28th Street SE Grand Rapids, MI 49546 **Telephone:** (616) 957-1770.

WISCONSIN TIMBER RATTLERS

Office Address: 2400 N Casaloma Dr, Appleton, WI 54913. **Mailing Address:** PO Box 7464, Appleton, WI 54912.
Telephone: (920) 733-4152. **Fax:** (920) 733-8032.
E-Mail Address: info@timberrattlers.com. **Website:** www.timberrattlers.com.
Affiliation (first year): Milwaukee Brewers (2009). **Years in League:** 1962-

OWNERSHIP/MANAGEMENT

Operated By: Appleton Baseball Club, Inc.
Chairman: Bruce Kornaus. **President/General Manager:** Rob Zerjav. **Vice President/Assistant GM:** Aaron Hahn. **Controller:** Cathy Spanbauer.

MINOR LEAGUES

Director, Food/Beverage: Ryan Grossman. **Director, Stadium Operations/Security:** Ron Kaiser.
Director, Community Relations: Dayna Baitinger. **Director, Media Relations:** Chris Mehring.
Corporate Partnerships: Ryan Cunniff, Jerrad Radocay. **Director, Merchandise:** Jay Gruszznski.
Director, Tickets: Ryan Moede. **Banquet Sales/Events Manager:** Hillary Basten.
Assistant Manager, Banquets/Events: Kim Chonos. **Executive Chef:** Tim Hansen.
Assistant, Food/Beverage Director: Chris Prentice. **Assistant Stadium Operations Manager:** Aaron Johnson.
Director, Group Sales: Seth Merrill. **Group Sales:** Brittany Ezze, Kaitlynn Sablich.
Creative Director: Ann Mollica. **Marketing Coordinator:** Hilary Bauer. **Entertainment Coordinator:** Jacob Jirschele.
Accounting/Human Resources Manager: Sara Mortimer. **Production Manager:** Jerred Drake. **Clubhouse Manager:**
Sam Rosenzweig. **Office Manager:** Mary Robinson. **Groundskeeper:** Jake Hannes.

FIELD STAFF

Manager: Matt Erickson. **Coach:** Al LeBoeuf. **Coach:** Chuckie Caufield. **Pitching Coach:** Gary Lucas. **Trainer:** Jeff
Paxson.

GAME INFORMATION

Radio Announcer: Chris Mehring. **No. of Games Broadcast:** 140. **Flagship Station:** WNAM 1280-AM.
Television Announcers: Bob Brainerd, Dean Leisgang, Ted Stefaniak, Brad Woodall. **No. of Games Broadcast:** 39.
Television Affiliates: Time Warner Cable SportsChannel, WACY-TV. **PA Announcer:** Joey D. **Official Scorer:** Jay
Gruszznski. **Stadium Name:** Neuroscience Group Field at Fox Cities Stadium.
Location: Highway 41 to Highway 15 (00) exit, west to Casaloma Drive, left to stadium.
Standard Game Times: 7:05 pm, 6:35 (April-May), Sat. 6:35, Sun 1:05.
Ticket Price Range: $6-25. **Visiting Club Hotel:** Country Inn & Suites; 355 N Fox River Dr, Appleton, WI 54913.
Telephone: (920) 830-3240.

SOUTH ATLANTIC LEAGUE

EST. 1903
SOUTH ATLANTIC LEAGUE
"THE LEAGUE OF CHOICE"

Address: 13575 58th Street North, Suite 141, Clearwater, FL 33760-3721.
Telephone: (727) 538-4270. **Fax:** (727) 499-6853.
E-Mail Address: office@saloffice.com. **Website:** www.southatlanticleague.com.
Years League Active: 1904-1964, 1979-
President/**Secretary/Treasurer:** Eric Krupa.
First Vice President: Chip Moore (Rome). **Second VP:** Craig Brown (Greenville).
Directors: Don Beaver (Hickory), Cooper Brantley (Greensboro), Craig Brown (Greenville), Brian DeWine (Asheville), Joseph Finley (Lakewood), Jason Freier (Columbia), Marvin Goldklang (Charleston), Chip Moore (Rome), Bruce Quinn (Hagerstown), Brad Smith (Kannapolis), Andy Shea (Lexington), Jeff Eiseman (Augusta), Tom Volpe (Delmarva), Tim Wilcox (West Virginia).
Division Structure: North—Delmarva, Greensboro, Hagerstown, Hickory, Kannapolis, Lakewood, West Virginia. **South**—Asheville, Augusta, Charleston, Columbia, Greenville, Lexington, Rome.
Regular Season: 140 games (split schedule). **2016 Opening Date:** April 7. **Closing Date:** Sept 5.
All-Star Game: June 21 at Lexington.
Playoff Format: First-half and second-half division winners meet in best of three series. Winners meet in best of five series for league championship.
Roster Limit: 25 active. **Player Eligibility Rule:** No age limit. No more than two players and one player-coach on active list may have more than five years of experience.
Brand of Baseball: Rawlings.
Umpires: Justin Anderson (Junction City, OR), Donald Carlyon (Drums, PA), Michael Carroll (Spring, TX), William Clark (Myrtle Beach, SC), David Martinez (Bayonne, NJ), Jose Navas (Barquisimeto, Lara, Venezuela), Anthony Perez (Murrells Inlet, SC), Ryan Powers (Riverside, CA), Brandin Sheeler (Maineville, OH), Donald Smith (Rochester, NY), Jean Velez-Morales (San Juan, PR), Brian Walsh (San Pedro, CA), Thomas West (Scarborough, QLD, Australia), Ronald Whiting (Fairmont, WV).

Eric Krupa

STADIUM INFORMATION

Club	Stadium	Opened	LF	CF	RF	Capacity	2015 Att.
Asheville	McCormick Field	1992	326	373	297	4,000	181,578
Augusta	Lake Olmstead Stadium	1995	330	400	330	4,322	174,382
Charleston	Joseph P. Riley Jr. Ballpark	1997	306	386	336	5,800	292,661
Columbia	Spirit Communications Park	2016	319	400	330	7,501	125,587
Delmarva	Arthur W. Perdue Stadium	1996	309	402	309	5,200	203,520
Greensboro	NewBridge Bank Park	2005	322	400	320	7,599	361,288
Greenville	Fluor Field	2006	310	400	302	5,000	346,828
Hagerstown	Municipal Stadium	1931	335	400	330	4,600	68,688
Hickory	L.P. Frans Stadium	1993	330	401	330	5,062	149,963
Kannapolis	CMC-NorthEast Stadium	1995	330	400	310	4,700	135,727
Lakewood	FirstEnergy Park	2001	325	400	325	6,588	388,718
Lexington	Whitaker Bank Ballpark	2001	320	401	318	6,033	283,873
Rome	State Mutual Stadium	2003	335	400	330	5,100	180,191
West Virginia	Appalachian Power Park	2005	330	400	320	4,300	160,429

ASHEVILLE TOURISTS

Address: McCormick Field, 30 Buchanan Place, Asheville, NC 28801.
Telephone: (828) 258-0428. **Fax:** (828) 258-0320.
E-Mail Address: info@theashevilletourists.com. **Website:** www.theashevilletourists.com.
Affiliation (first year): Colorado Rockies (1994). **Years in League:** 1976-

OWNERSHIP/MANAGEMENT

Operated By: DeWine Seeds Silver Dollar Baseball, LLC. **President:** Brian DeWine.
General Manager: Larry Hawkins. **Assistant General Manager:** Jon Clemmons. **Senior Sales Executive:** Chris Smith. **Box Office Manager:** Megan Lachey. **Business Manager:** Ryan Straney. **Creative Marketing Manager:** Sam Fischer. **Manager, Media Relations/Broadcasting:** Doug Maurer. **Group Sales Associates:** Hannah Martin, Eliot Williams, Kyle Harward. **Outside Sales Associate:** Bob Jones. **Stadium Operations Director:** Brandon Reeves. **Senior Director of Food & Beverage:** Nick Reuter (Pro Sports Catering). **Head Groundskeeper:** Matt Dierdorff. **Publications/Website:** Bill Ballew.

FIELD STAFF

Manager: Warren Schaeffer. **Hitting Coach:** Mike Devereaux. **Pitching Coach:** Mark Brewer. **Development**

Supervisor: Marv Foley.

GAME INFORMATION
Radio Announcer: Doug Maurer. **No. of Games Broadcast:** 140. **Flagship Station:** WRES 100.7-FM.
PA Announcer: Rick Rice. **Official Scorer:** Jim Baker.
Stadium Name: McCormick Field. **Location:** I-240 to Charlotte Street South exit, south one mile on Charlotte, left on McCormick Place. **Ticket Price Range:** $6-13.
Visiting Club Hotel: Ramada, 148 River Ford Parkway, Asheville, NC 28803. **Telephone:** (828) 298-9141.

AUGUSTA GREENJACKETS

Office Address: 78 Milledge Rd, Augusta, GA 30904. **Mailing Address:** PO Box 3746 Hill Station, Augusta, GA 30914.
Telephone: (706) 922-WINS(9467). **Fax:** (706) 736-1122.
E-Mail Address: info@greenjacketsbaseball.com. **Web site:** www.greenjacketsbaseball.com.

OWNERSHIP/MANAGEMENT
Ownership Group: AGON Sports & Entertainment. **Owner:** Chris Schoen. **President:** Jeff Eiseman.
General Manager: Tom Denlinger. **Assistant GM:** Brandon Greene. **Director, Ticket Sales:** Mike Van Hise.
Accounting: Debbie Brown. **Stadium Operations Manager:** David Ryther. **Promotions/Marketing Coordinator:** Caitlyn Smith. **Senior Ticket Sales Account Manager:** Greg Dietz. **Account Executive/Ticket Operations Specialist:** Killian Vallieu. **Account Executive & Community Relations Specialist:** Shannon **Mitchell.Group Sales Executive:** Derek Herron. **Food & Beverage Supervisor:** Johnathan Strabo. **Groundskeeper:** Zach Severns.

FIELD STAFF
Manager: Nestor Rojas. **Hitting Coach:** Doug Clark. **Pitching Coach:** Jerry Cram. **Coach:** Hector Borg.

GAME INFORMATION
PA Announcer: Unavailable.
Stadium Name: Lake Olmstead Stadium. **Location:** I-20 to Washington Road exit, east to Broad Street exit, left on Milledge Road. **Standard Game Times:** 7:05 pm, Sat.. 6:05pm; Sun. 2:05 through May, 5:05 June on. **Ticket Price Range:** $7-15.
Visiting Club Hotel: Comfort Suites, 2911 Riverwest Dr, Augusta, GA. **Telephone:** (706) 434-2540.

CHARLESTON RIVERDOGS

Office Address: 360 Fishburne St, Charleston, SC 29403. **Mailing Address:** PO Box 20849, Charleston, SC 29413.
Telephone: (843) 723-7241. **Fax:** (843) 723-2641.
E-Mail Address: admin@riverdogs.com. **Website:** www.riverdogs.com.
Affiliation (first year): New York Yankees (2005). **Years in League:** 1973-78, 1980-
Affiliation (first year): San Francisco Giants (2005). **Years in League:** 1988-

OWNERSHIP/MANAGEMENT
Operated by: The Goldklang Group/South Carolina Baseball Club LP.
Chairman: Marv Goldklang. **President/General Manager:** Dave Echols. **President Emeritus:** Mike Veeck. **Director, Fun:** Bill Murray. **Co-Owners:** Peter Freund, Gene Budig, Al Phillips. **VP, Corporate Sales:** Andy Lange. **VP, Special Events:** Melissa Azevedo. **Assistant GM:** Ben Abzug. **Director, Promotions:** Nate Kurant. **Director, Broadcasting/Media Relations:** Matt Dean. **Director, Food/Beverage:** Josh Shea. **Director, Merchandise:** Mike DeAntonio. **Director, Community Relations:** Haley Kirchner. **Director, Ticket Sales:** Jake Terrell. **Business Manager:** Dale Stickney. **Box Office Manager:** Morgan Powell. **Special Events Manager:** Kristen Wolfe. **Food/Beverage Manager:** Jay Weekley. **Sales Representative:** Joey Cain, Ryan Gill, Will Senn. **Director, Operations:** Philip Guiry. **Director, Video Production:** Tyler Schwemin Head Groundskeeper:** Mike Williams. **Clubhouse Manager:** Harris Seletsky.

FIELD STAFF
Manager: Luis Dorante. **Hitting Coach:** Greg Colbrunn. **Pitching Coach:** Justin Pope. **Coach:** Travis Chapman.
Coach: Michel Hernandez. **Trainer:** Jimmy Downam. **Strength/Conditioning Coach:** Anthony Velazquez. **Video Manager:** Cody Cockrum.

GAME INFORMATION
Radio Announcer: Matt Dean. **No. of Games Broadcast:** 140. **Flagship Station:** WTMA 1250-AM.
PA Announcer: Unavailable. **Official Scorer:** Mike Hoffman. **Stadium Name:** Joseph Riley Jr. Ballpark. **Location:** 360 Fishburne St, Charleston, SC 29403, From US 17, take Lockwood Dr. North, right on Fishburne St. **Standard Game Times:** 7:05pm, Sat. 6:05pm, Sun. 5:05. **Ticket Price Range:** $5-18. **Visiting Club Hotel:** Unavailable.

COLUMBIA FIREFLIES

Office Address: TBD
Mailing Address: PO Box 8810, Columbia, SC 29210
Telephone: (803) 726-4487. **Fax:** (803) 726-3126
E-Mail Address: info@columbiafireflies.com. **Website:** www.columbiafireflies.com

AFFILIATION: NEW YORK METS. YEARS IN LEAGUE: 1. OWNERSHIP/MANAGEMENT

Operated By: Columbia Fireflies Baseball, LLC. **President:** John Katz. **Executive Vice President:** Brad Shank. Senior Vice President / **Food & Beverage:** Scott Burton. **Vice President of Marketing & Public Relations:** Abby Naas. **Vice President of Partnerships:** Evan Ashton. **Director of Corporate Partnerships:** Blake Buchanan. **Director of Accounting & Baseball Operations:** Jonathan Mercier. **Director of Ticketing:** Joe Shepard. **Director of Group Sales:** Kaylee Swanson. Assistant Director Ticketing / **Reading Program Manager:** Kyle Williamson. **Ticket Account Manager:** Evan Rhoades. **Ticket Account Manager:** Jeff Berger. **Ticket Account Manager:** Dalton Tresvant. **Ticket Account Manager:** Scott Rhodes. Corporate Partnerships / **Activation Manager:** Kate Raaen. Assistant Director of Facilities / **Ticket Account Manager:** Jeremy Keen. **Graphics Manager:** Jak Kerley. **Promotions & Community Relations Manager:** Kyle Martin. **Video Production Manager:** Jared Law. **Merchandise Manager:** Matt Strader. **Food & Beverage Manager:** Josh Andrews. **Head Groundskeeper:** Andy Rock. **Assistant Groundskeeper:** Dalton Workman.

FIELD STAFF

Manager: Jose Leger. **Pitching Coach:** Jonathan Hurst. **Hitting Coach:** Joel Fuentes. **Trainer:** Kiyoshi Tada. **Strength/Conditioning Coach:** Alex Tavarez.

GAME INFORMATION

Radio Announcer: TBD. **No. of Games Broadcast:** TBD. **Flagship Station:** TBD. **PA Announcer:** TBD. **Official Scorer:** TBD. **Stadium Name:** Spirit Communications Park. **Location:** TBD. **Standard Game Times:** 7:05pm, Sun. 2:05 pm or 5:05pm. **Ticket Price Range:** $5-$10. **Visiting Club Hotel:** TBD.

DELMARVA SHOREBIRDS

Office Address: 6400 Hobbs Rd, Salisbury, MD 21804. **Mailing Address:** PO Box 1557, Salisbury, MD 21802.
Telephone: (410) 219-3112. **Fax:** (410) 219-9164.
E-Mail Address: info@theshorebirds.com. **Website:** www.theshorebirds.com.
Affiliation (first year): Baltimore Orioles (1997). **Years in League:** 1996-.

OWNERSHIP/MANAGEMENT

Operated By: 7th Inning Stretch, LLC. **Directors:** Tom Volpe, Pat Filippone. **General Manager:** Chris Bitters. **Assistant GM:** Jimmy Sweet. **Director, Promotions/Community Relations:** Eric Sichau. **Director, Business Development:** Andrew Bryda. **Director, Tickets:** Brandon Harms. **Box Office Manager:** Benjamin Posner. **Ticket Sales Account Executives:** Zac Penman, Skip Krantz, Jaime Cutter, Jason Tremblay. **Director, Stadium Operations:** Joel Chavez. **Head Groundskeeper:** Tim Young. **Director, Broadcasting:** Brendan Gulick. **Communications/Marketing Manager:** Steve Uhlmann. **Accounting Manager:** Gail Potts. **Office Manager:** Audrey Vane.

FIELD STAFF

Manager: Ryan Minor. **Hitting Coach:** Kyle Moore. **Pitching Coach:** Blaine Beatty. **Athletic Trainer:** Trek Schuler.

GAME INFORMATION

Radio Announcer: Brendan Gulick. **No. of Games Broadcast:** 140. **Flagship Station:** 960 WTGM. **PA Announcer:** Tyler Horton. **Official Scorer:** Gary Hicks. **Stadium Name:** Arthur Perdue Stadium. **Location:** From US 50 East, right on Hobbs Rd; From US 50 West, left on Hobbs Road. **Standard Game Time:** 7:05 pm. **Ticket Price Range:** $8-13. **Visiting Club Hotel:** Sleep Inn, 406 Punkin Court, Salisbury, MD 21804. **Telephone:** (410) 572-5516.

GREENSBORO GRASSHOPPERS

Address: 408 Bellemeade St, Greensboro, NC 27401.
Telephone: (336) 268-2255. **Fax:** (336) 273-7350.
E-Mail Address: info@gsohoppers.com. **Website:** www.gsohoppers.com.
Affiliation (first year): Miami Marlins (2003). **Years in League:** 1979-

OWNERSHIP/MANAGEMENT

Operated By: Greensboro Baseball LLC. **Principal Owners:** Cooper Brantley, Wes Elingburg, Len White. **President/General Manager:** Donald Moore. **Vice President, Baseball Operations:** Katie Dannemiller. **CFO:** Benjamin Martin. **Assistant GM/Head Groundskeeper:** Jake Holloway. **Assistant GM, Sales/Marketing:** Tim Vangel.

Director, Ticket Sales: Erich Dietz. **Coordinator, Promotions/Community Relations:** Brooke Robinson. **Director, Production/Entertainment:** Shawn Russell. **Director, Creative Services:** Amanda Williams. **Office Administrator:** Jessica Blake. **Senior Sales Associate:** Todd Olson. **Sales Associate:** Austin Scher. **Sales Associate:** Stephen Johnson. **Director, Stadium Operations:** Tim Hardin. **Assistant Groundskeeper:** Kaid Musgrave.

FIELD STAFF

Manager: Kevin Randel. **Coach:** Rigoberto Silverio. **Pitching Coach:** Brendan Sagara. **Trainer:** Mike Bibbo.

GAME INFORMATION

Radio Announcer: Andy Durham. **No. of Games Broadcast:** 140. **Flagship Station:** WPET 950-AM. **PA Announcer:** TBD. **Official Scorer:** TBD.
Stadium Name: NewBridge Bank Park. **Location:** From I-85, take Highway 220 South (exit 36) to Coliseum Blvd, continue on Edgeworth Street, ballpark at corner of Edgeworth and Bellemeade Streets. **Standard Game Times:** 7 pm, Sun. 4 pm. **Ticket Price Range:** $7-11.00.
Visiting Club Hotel: Days Inn 6102 Landmark Center Boulevard, Greensboro, NC 27407. **Telephone:** (336) 553-2763.

GREENVILLE DRIVE

Address: 945 South Main St, Greenville, SC 29601
Telephone: (864) 240-4500. **Fax:** (864) 240-4501.
E-Mail Address: info@greenvilledrive.com. **Website:** www.greenvilledrive.com.
Affiliation (first year): Boston Red Sox (2005) **Years in League:** 2005-

OWNERSHIP/MANAGEMENT

Operated By: Greenville Drive, LLC. **Owner/President:** Craig Brown.
General Manager: Eric Jarinko. **Executive Vice President:** Nate Lipscomb. **VP, Finance:** Eric Blagg. **VP, Marketing:** Jeff Brown. **VP, Sales:** Kevin Jenko. **Director, Entertainment/Partner Services:** Sam LoBosco. **Director, Events/ Community Relations:** Jennifer Brown. **Director, Food/Beverage:** Matt Weeks. **Director, Inside Sales:** Alex Fiedler. **Sponsorship Events Manager:** Rebecca Ellefson. **Media Relations Manager:** Cameron White. **Creative Services Manager:** James Fowler. **Account Executive:** Thomas Berryhill. **Inside Sales Representative:** Houghton Flanagan. **Inside Sales Representative:** Rhyan Ruf. **Inside Sales Representative:** Matthew Tezza. **Inside Sales Representative:** Andrew Wilber. **Food and Beverage Manager:** Nick Wilcox. **Hospitality Manager:** Jared Peek. **Box Office/ Merchandise Manager:** Steve Seman. **Merchandise Operations Manager:** Corey Brothers. **Box Office Operations Manager:** Katie Cox. **Facilities Manager:** Bob Wagner. **Operations Manager:** John Barnet. **Head Groundskeeper:** Greg Burgess. **Assistant Groundskeeper:** Chris Rinebold. **Accounting Manager:** Tiffany Diemer. **Office Manager:** Amanda Medlin.

FIELD STAFF

Manager: Darren Fenster. **Hitting Coach:** Lee May Jr.. **Pitching Coach:** Walter Miranda. **Head Athletic Trainer:** Nick Faciana.

GAME INFORMATION

Radio Announcer: Ed Jenson. **No. of Games Broadcast:** Home-70, Away-20. **Flagship Station:** www.greenville-drive.com.
PA Announcer: Brian Rushing. **Official Scorer:** Jordan Caskey.
Stadium Name: Fluor Field at the West End. **Location:** From south, I-85N to exit 42 toward downtown Greenville, turn left onto Augusta Road, stadium is two miles on the left; From north, I-85S to I-385 toward Greenville, turn left onto Church Street, turn right onto University Ridge. **Standard Game Times:** 7:05 PM, Sun 4:05 PM. **Ticket Price Range:** $6-9.
Visiting Club Hotel: Baymont Inn and Suites, 246 Congaree Road, Greenville, SC 29607. **Telephone:** (864) 288-1200.

HAGERSTOWN SUNS

Address: 274 E Memorial Blvd, Hagerstown, MD 21740.
Telephone: (301) 791-6266. **Fax:** (301) 791-6066.
E-Mail Address: info@hagerstownsuns.com. **Website:** www.hagerstownsuns.com.
Affiliation (first year): Washington Nationals (2007). **Years in League:** 1993-

OWNERSHIP/MANAGEMENT

Principal Owner/Operated by: Hagerstown Baseball LLC. **President:** Bruce Quinn.
General Manager: N/A. **Assistant GM/Head Groudnskeeper:** Brian Saddler. **Director, Media Relations:** Jordan Nicewarner. **F&B Operations:** Center Plate. **Manager, Promotions/Game Day Production:** Tom Burtman. **Manager, Box Office/Ticket Operations:** Brice Ballentine. **Manager, Group Sales:** Shane Ganley.

FIELD STAFF

Manager: Patrick Anderson. **Hitting Coach:** Amaury Garcia. **Pitching Coach:** Sam Narron. **Trainer:** Don Neidig.

GAME INFORMATION

Radio Announcer: Jordan Nicewarner. **No. of Games Broadcast:** Home-70. **Flagship Station:** Unavailable.
PA Announcer: Rick Reeder. **Official Scorer:** Will Kauffman. **Stadium Name:** Municipal Stadium. **Location:** Exit 32B

(US 40 West) on I-70 West, left at Eastern Boulevard; Exit 6A (US 40 East) on I-81, right at Eastern Boulevard. **Standard Game Times:** 7:05 pm, Sun 2:05. **Ticket Price Range:** $9-12. **Visiting Club Hotel:** Sleep Inn and Suites.

HICKORY CRAWDADS

   Office Address: 2500 Clement Blvd. NW, Hickory, NC 28601. **Mailing Address:** PO Box 1268, Hickory, NC 28603.
   Telephone: (828) 322-3000. **Fax:** (828) 322-6137.
   E-Mail Address: crawdad@hickorycrawdads.com. **Website:** www.hickorycrawdads.com.
   Affiliation (first year): Texas Rangers (2009). **Years in League:** 1952, 1960, 1993-

OWNERSHIP/MANAGEMENT
   Operated by: Hickory Baseball Inc. **Principal Owners:** Don Beaver, Luther Beaver, Charles Young. **President:** Don Beaver. **General Manager:** Mark Seaman. **Assistant GM:** Charlie Downs. **Director, Promotions:** Pete Subsara. **Director, Broadcasting/Media Relations:** Aaron Cox. **Business Manager:** Donna White. **Director, Community Relations/Events:** Megan Meade. **Clubhouse Manager:** Mitch Brasher. **Director, Ticket Operations:** Gian D'Amico. **Director, Creative Services:** Crystal Lin. **Director, Group Sales:** Travis Gortman. **Executive Director, Sales/Merchandise:** Douglas Locascio. **Head Groundskeeper:** Zach Van Voorhees. **Director, Food/Beverage:** Teddy Ingraham. **Group Sales Executives:** Zach Miller, Kyle May.

FIELD STAFF
   Manager: Spike Owen. **Hitting Coach:** Francisco Matos. **Pitching Coach:** Jose Jaimes. **Fourth Coach: Matt Hagen Trainer:** Dustin Vissering. **Strength/Conditioning:** Wade Lamont.

GAME INFORMATION
   Radio Announcer: Aaron Cox. **No. of Games Broadcast:** 140. **Flagship Station:** hickorycrawdads.com.
   PA Announcers: Ralph Mangum, Jason Savage, Steve Jones. **Official Scorers:** Mark Parker, Paul Fogelman.
   Stadium Name: LP Frans Stadium. **Location:** I-40 to exit 123 (Lenoir North), 321 North to Clement Blvd, left for 1/2 mile. **Standard Game Times:** 7 pm, Sun 5.
   Visiting Club Hotel: Crowne Plaza, 1385 Lenior-Rhyne Boulevard SE, Hickory, NC 28602. **Telephone:** (828) 323-1000.

KANNAPOLIS INTIMIDATORS

   Office Address: 2888 Moose Road, Kannapolis, NC 28083. **Mailing Address:** PO Box 64, Kannapolis, NC 28082.
   Telephone: (704) 932-3267. **Fax:** (704) 938-7040.
   E-Mail Address: info@intimidatorsbaseball.com. **Website:** www.intimidatorsbaseball.com.
   Affiliation (first year): Chicago White Sox (2001). **Years in League:** 1995-

OWNERSHIP/MANAGEMENT
   Operated by: Smith Family Baseball Inc. **President:** Brad Smith.
   General Manager: Randy Long. **Head Groundskeeper:** Billy Ball. **Director, Stadium Operations:** Darren Cozart. **Director, Communications:** Josh Feldman. **Assistant Groundskeeper:** Mitchell Hooten.

FIELD STAFF
   Manager: Cole Armstrong. **Hitting Coach:** Justin Jirschele. **Pitching Coach:** Brian Drahman. **Trainer:** Joe Geck. **Strength/Conditioning Coach:** Bret Kelly.

GAME INFORMATION
   Radio Announcer: Josh Feldman. **No. of Games Broadcast:** All 140 games. **Flagship Station:** www.intimidators-baseball.com. **PA Announcer:** Sean Fox.
   Official Scorer: Brent Stastny. **Stadium Name:** Intimidators Stadium supported by Carolinas HealthCare System. **Location:** Exit 63 on I-85, west on Lane Street to Stadium Drive. **Standard Game Times:** 7:05 pm, Sun 5:05pm. **Ticket Price Range:** $6-$10. **Visiting Club Hotel:** Spring Hill Suites. **Address:** 7811 Gateway Lane NW, Concord, NC 28027. **Telephone:** (704) 979-2500.

LAKEWOOD BLUECLAWS

   Address: 2 Stadium Way, Lakewood, NJ 08701.
   Telephone: (732) 901-7000. **Fax:** (732) 901-3967.
   E-Mail Address: info@blueclaws.com. **Website:** www.blueclaws.com
   Affiliation (first year): Philadelphia Phillies (2001). **Years in League:** 2001-

OWNERSHIP/MANAGEMENT
   General Manager: Chris Tafrow. **VP/Events & Operations:** Steve Farago. **VP/Ticket Sales & Service:** Jim McNamara.

VP/Community Relations: Jim DeAngelis. **Director, Sponsorship:** Belinda Wiggins. Director of Media/ **Marketing:** Greg Giombarrese. **Director of Group Sales:** Kevin Fenstermacher. **Director of Food/Beverage:** Mike Barry. **Director, Finance:** Bernadette Miller. **Senior Sales Manager:** Rob McGillick. **Sponsorship Manager:** Wade Johnson. **Sponsorship Managers:** BJ Thomas, Cory Eirich. **Group Sales Managers:** Mike Kasel, Dan Palmeri, Fred Baldwin, Mike Cassidy, Kevin Litus. **Ticket Sales Managers:** Ross Grippin, Michael Ford, Patrick Prendergast, Tommy DeCore. **Box Office Manager:** Garrett Herr. **Ticket Service Coordinator:** Rich Granato. **Marketing Manager:** Jamie Stone. **Sponsorship Services Manager:** Laura Sigle. **Events/Operations Manager:** Kayla Reilly. **Creative/Audiovisual Services Manager:** Kirsten Boye. **Accounting Manager:** Annette Clark. **Front Office Manager:** JoAnne Bell.

FIELD STAFF

Manager: Shawn Williams. **Hitting Coach:** Nelson Prada. **Pitching Coach:** Brian Sweeney.

GAME INFORMATION

Radio Announcers: Greg Giombarrese. **No. of Games Broadcast:** 140. **Flagship Station:** WOBM 1160-AM. **PA Announcers:** Kevin Clark. **Official Scorers:** Joe Bellina. **Stadium Name:** FirstEnergy Park. **Location:** Route 70 to New Hampshire Avenue, North on New Hampshire for 2.5 miles to ballpark. **Standard Game Times:** 7:05 pm, 6:35 pm (April-May); **Sun** 1:05, 5:05 (July-Aug). **Ticket Price Range:** $7-12. **Visiting Team Hotel:** Clarion Hotel Toms River, 815 Route 37 West, Toms River, NJ 08755. **Telephone:** (732) 341-3400.

LEXINGTON LEGENDS

Address: 207 Legends Lane, Lexington, KY 40505.
Telephone: (859) 252-4487. **Fax:** (859) 252-0747.
E-Mail Address: webmaster@lexingtonlegends.com. **Website:** www.lexingtonle-gends.com.
Affiliation (first year): Kansas City Royals (2013). **Years in League:** 2001-

OWNERSHIP/MANAGEMENT

Operated By: STANDS LLC. **Principal Owner:** Susan Martinelli Shea. **CEO:** Andy Shea.
Executive Vice President/General Manager: Gary Durbin. Director, **Stadium Operations/Manager, Human Resources:** Shannon Kidd. **Business Manager:** Tina Wright. **Manager, Box Office:** Mark Costagliola. **Creative Marketing Director:** Ty Cobb. **Director, Broadcasting/Media Relations:** Keith Elkins. **Senior Account Executive:** Ron Borkowski. **Director, Community Relations:** Rebecca Barnes. **Audio Visual Production Manager:** Nick Juhasz. **Head Groundskeeper:** TBA. **Facility Specialist:** Steve Moore.

FIELD STAFF

Manager: Omar Ramirez. **Hitting Coach:** Damon Hollins. **Pitching Coach:** Mitch Stetter. **Bench Coach:** Glenn Hubbard. **Athletic Trainer:** Mark Keiser.

GAME INFORMATION

Radio Announcer: Keith Elkins. **No. of Games Broadcast:** 140. **Flagship Station:** WLXG 1300-AM.
PA Announcer: Ty Cobb. **Official Scorer:** Unavailable. **Stadium Name:** Whitaker Bank Ballpark. **Location:** From I-64/75, take exit 113, right onto North Broadway toward downtown Lexington for 1.2 miles, past New Circle Road (Highway 4), right into stadium, located adjacent to Northland Shopping Center. **Standard Game Times:** 7:05 pm, **Sun** 2:05 (through May 31), 6:05 (June-Aug). **Ticket Price Range:** $4-$24.
Visiting Club Hotel: Ramada Inn and Conference Center, 2143 N Broadway, Lexington, KY 40505. **Telephone:** (859) 299-1261.

ROME BRAVES

Office Address: State Mutual Stadium, 755 Braves Blvd, Rome, GA 30161. **Mailing Address:** PO Box 1915, Rome, GA 30162-1915.
Telephone: (706) 378-5100. **Fax:** (706) 368-6525.
E-Mail Address: rome.braves@braves.com. **Website:** www.romebraves.com.
Affiliation (first year): Atlanta Braves (2003). **Years in League:** 2003-

OWNERSHIP MANAGEMENT

Operated By: Atlanta National League Baseball Club Inc.
General Manager: Michael Dunn. **Assistant GM:** Jim Jones. **Director, Stadium Operations:** Brad Smith. **Director, Ticket Manager:** Jeff Fletcher. **Special Projects Manager:** Erin White. **Administrative Manager:** Christina Shaw. **Account Representatives:** Zach Burke, Katie Aspin. **Head Groundskeeper:** Kevin Schmidt. **Retail Manager:** Starla Roden. **Warehouse Operations Manager:** Morgan McPherson. Neighborhood Outreach / **Digital Manager:** Libby Chambers.

FIELD STAFF

Manager: Randy Ingle. **Coach:** Bobby Moore. **Pitching Coach:** Dan Meyer. **Trainer:** Joe Luat.

GAME INFORMATION

Radio Announcer: Kevin Karel. **No. of Games Broadcast:** 140. **Flagship Station:** 99.5 FM The Jock, RomeBraves.com (home games). **PA Announcer:** Tony McIntosh. **Official Scorers:** Jim O'Hara, Lyndon Huckaby. **Stadium Name:**

GAME INFORMATION

Radio Announcer: Kevin Karel. **No. of Games Broadcast:** 140. **Flagship Station:** 99.5 FM The Jock, RomeBraves. com (home games). **PA Announcer:** Tony McIntosh. **Official Scorers:** Jim O'Hara, Lyndon Huckaby. **Stadium Name:** State Mutual Stadium. **Location:** I-75 North to exit 190 (Rome/Canton), left off exit and follow Highway 411/Highway 20 to Rome, right at intersection on Highway 411 and Highway 1 (Veterans Memorial Highway), stadium is at intersection of Veterans Memorial Highway and Riverside Parkway. **Ticket Price Range:** $5-12. **Visiting Club Hotel:** Days Inn, 840 Turner McCall Blvd, Rome, GA 30161. **Telephone:** (706) 295-0400.

WEST VIRGINIA POWER

Address: 601 Morris St, Suite 201, Charleston, WV 25301.
Telephone: (304) 344-2287. **Fax:** (304) 344-0083.
E-Mail Address: info@wvpower.com. **Website:** www.wvpower.com.
Affiliation (first year): Pittsburgh Pirates (2009). **Years in League:** 1987-

OWNERSHIP MANAGEMENT

Operated By: West Virginia Baseball, LLC. **Managing Partner:** Tim Wilcox. **Executive Vice President:** Ken Fogel. **General Manager:** Tim Mueller. **Assistant GM:** Jeremy Taylor.

Box Office Manager: Hannah Frenchick. **Accountant:** Darren Holstein. **Director, Marketing/Media:** Adam Marco. **Head Groundskeeper:** Chris Mason. **Director, Tickets:** Gary Olson. **Merchandise Manager:** Jenna Plummer. **Director, Food/Beverage:** Aaron Simmons. **Client Services:** Haley Townsend. **Account Executive:** Steven Unser. **Production Manager:** Garrett Weller.

FIELD STAFF

Manager: Brian Esposito. **Coach:** Matt Ford. **Pitching Coach:** Ryan Long.

GAME INFORMATION

Radio Announcer: Adam Marco. **No. of Games Broadcast:** 140. **Flagship Stations:** ESPN 104.5 FM, WSWW 1490-AM. **PA Announcer:** Unavailable. **Official Scorer:** Unavailable.**Stadium Name:** Appalachian Power Park. **Location:** I-77 South to Capitol Street exit, left on Lee Street, left on Brooks Street. **Standard Game Times:** 7:05 pm, Sun 2:05.**Ticket Price Range:** $6-11.**Visiting Club Hotel:** Charleston Capitol Hotel, 1000 Washington Street East, Charleston, WV 25301. **Telephone:** (304) 343-4661.

NEW YORK-PENN LEAGUE

Address: 204 37th Ave. North, #366, St. Petersburg, Florida 33704.
Telephone: (727) 289-7111. **Fax:** (727) 683-9691.
Website: www.newyork-pennleague.com.
Years League Active: 1939-

President: Ben Hayes.
President Emeritus: Robert Julian. **Treasurer:** Jon Dandes (West Virginia). **Secretary:** Doug Estes (Williamsport).
Directors: Tim Bawmann (Lowell), Steve Cohen (Brooklyn), Jon Dandes (West Virginia), Glenn W. Valis (Aberdeen), Mike Voutsinas (Auburn), Bill Gladstone (Tri-City), Marvin Goldklang (Hudson Valley), Chuck Greenberg (State College), Kyle Bostick (Vermont), Michael Savit (Mahoning Valley), Miles Prentice (Connecticut), Naomi Silver (Batavia), Glenn Reicin (Staten Island), Peter Freund (Williamsport).
Office Manager: Laurie Hayes. **League Historian:** Charles Wride. **Media Associate:** Makenzie Burrows.
Division Structure: McNamara—Aberdeen, Brooklyn, Hudson Valley, Staten Island. **Pinckney**—Auburn, Batavia, Mahoning Valley, State College, West Virginia, Williamsport. **Stedler**—Lowell, Connecticut, Tri-City, Vermont.
Regular Season: 76 games. **2016 Opening Date:** June 17. **Closing Date:** Sept 5.
All-Star Game: Aug. 16 at Hudson Valley.
Playoff Format: Division winners and wild-card team meet in best of three series. Winners meet in best of three series for league championship.
Roster Limit: 35 active and eligible to play in any given game. **Player Eligibility Rule:** No more than four players 23 or older; no more than three players on active list may have four or more years of prior service.
Brand of Baseball: Rawlings.
Umpires: Unavailable.

Ben Hayes

STADIUM INFORMATION

Club	Stadium	Opened	Dimensions LF	CF	RF	Capacity	2015 Att.
Aberdeen	Ripken Stadium	2002	310	400	310	6,000	151,758
Auburn	Falcon Park	1995	330	400	330	2,800	50,670
Batavia	Dwyer Stadium	1996	325	400	325	2,600	32,221
Brooklyn	KeySpan Park	2001	315	412	325	7,500	230,658
Connecticut	Dodd Stadium	1995	309	401	309	6,270	78,588
Hudson Valley	Dutchess Stadium	1994	325	400	325	4,494	163,767
Lowell	Edward LeLacheur Park	1998	337	400	301	4,842	140,468
Mahoning Valley	Eastwood Field	1999	335	405	335	6,000	111,079
State College	Medlar Field at Lubrano Park	2006	325	399	320	5,412	127,775
Staten Island	Richmond County Bank Ballpark	2001	325	400	325	6,500	119,195
Tri-City	Joseph L. Bruno Stadium	2002	325	400	325	5,000	153,692
Vermont	Centennial Field	1922	323	405	330	4,000	83,002
West Virginia	WVU Baseball Park	2015	325	400	325	3,500	83,796
Williamsport	Bowman Field	1923	345	405	350	4,200	64,081

ABERDEEN IRONBIRDS

Address: 873 Long Drive, Aberdeen, MD 21001
Telephone: (410) 297-9292. **Fax:** (210)297-6653
E-Mail address: Info@ironbirdsbaseball.com. **Website:** www.ironbirdsbaseball.com
Affiliation (first year): Baltimore Orioles (2002). **Years in league:** 2002-

OWNERSHIP/MANAGEMENT

Operated By: Ripken Professional Baseball LLC.
Principal Owner: Cal Ripken Jr. Co-**Owner/Executive Vice President:** Bill Ripken.
General Manager: Joe Harrington. **Assistant GM:** Brad Cox. **Director, Ticket Sales Manager:** Kevin Heilman **Ticket Operations:** Ian Clark. **Training/Sales Coach:** Lee Greely. **Director, Retail Merchandising:** Don Eney. **Video Production Coordinator:** not available. **Lead Facilities Coordinator:** Larry Gluch. **Head Groundskeeper:** Patrick Coakley.

FIELD STAFF

Manager: Luis Pujols. **Pitching Coach:** Justin Lord. **Hitting Coach:** Scott Beerer. **Trainer:** Marty Brinker. **Strength/Conditioning Coach:** Kevin Clark.

GAME INFORMATION

Radio Announcer: Unavailable. **No. of Games Broadcast:** 76. **Flagship Station:** MiLB.com.
PA Announcer: Danny Mays. **Official Scorer:** Joe Stetka.
Stadium Name: Leidos Field at Ripken Stadium. **Location:** I-95 to exit 85 (route 22), west on 22, right onto long drive. **Ticket Price range:** $9-27.50.
Visiting Club Hotel: Unavailable.

AUBURN DOUBLEDAYS

Address: 130 N Division St, Auburn, NY 13021.
Telephone: (315) 255-2489. **Fax:** (315) 255-2675.
E-Mail Address: info@auburndoubledays.com. **Website:** www.auburndoubledays.com.
Affiliation (first year): Washington Nationals (2011). **Years in League:** 1958-80, 1982-

OWNERSHIP/MANAGEMENT

Owned by: City of Auburn. **Operated by:** Auburn Community Non-Profit Baseball Association Inc. **President:** Doug Selby. **General Manager:** Michael Voutsinas.

FIELD STAFF

Manager: Jerad Head. **Coach:** Mark Harris. **Pitching Coach:** Tim Redding.

GAME INFORMATION

Radio Announcer: Michael Tricarico. **No of Games Broadcast:** 38 (radio), 76 (online). **Flagship Station:** 1590 WAUB.
PA Announcer: Unavailable. **Official Scorer:** Unavailable.
Stadium Name: Falcon Park. **Location:** I-90 to exit 40, right on Route 34 South for 8 miles to York Street, right on York, left on North Division Street. **Standard Game Times:** 7:05 pm (M-Sat), 5:05 pm (Sun). **Ticket Price Range:** $5-9.
Visiting Club Hotel: Unavailable.

BATAVIA MUCKDOGS

Address: Dwyer Stadium, 299 Bank St, Batavia, NY 14020.
Telephone: (585) 343-5454. **Fax:** (585) 343-5620.
E-Mail Address: tsick@muckdogs.com. **Website:** www.muckdogs.com.
Affiliation (first year): Miami Marlins (2013). **Years in League:** 1939-53, 1957-59, 1961-

OWNERSHIP/MANAGEMENT

Operated By: Red Wings Management, LLC.
General Manager: Travis Sick. **Director of Ticket Operations:** Josh Swan. **Director, Stadium Operations:** Don Rock. **Director, Merchandise:** Kathy Bills. **Clubhouse Manager:** John Versage.

FIELD STAFF

Manager: Angel Espada. **Hitting Coach:** Luis Quinones. **Pitching Coach:** TBD. **Trainer:** Eric Reigelsberger.

GAME INFORMATION

Radio Announcer: TBD. **No. of Games Broadcast:** Home-38 Away-10. **Flagship Station:** WBTA 1490-AM/100.1 FM.
PA Announcer: Wayne Fuller. **Official Scorer:** Nicholas Tolle . **Stadium Name:** Dwyer Stadium. **Location:** I-90 to exit 48, left on Route 98 South, left on Richmond Avenue, left on Bank Street. **Standard Game Times:** 7:05 pm, Sun. 1:05/4:05. **Ticket Price Range:** $6.00-8.00. **Visiting Club Hotel:** Days Inn of Batavia, 200 Oak St, Batavia, NY 14020. **Telephone:** (585) 344-6000.

BROOKLYN CYCLONES

Address: 1904 Surf Ave, Brooklyn, NY 11224.
Telephone: (718) 372-5596. **Fax:** (718) 449-6368.
E-Mail Address: info@brooklyncyclones.com. **Website:** www.brooklyncyclones.com.
Affiliation (first year): New York Mets (2001). **Years in League:** 2001-

OWNERSHIP/MANAGEMENT

Chairman, CEO: Fred Wilpon. **President:** Saul Katz. **COO:** Jeff Wilpon.
Vice President: Steve Cohen. **General Manager:** Kevin Mahoney. **Assistant GM:** Gary Perone. **Director, Communications:** Billy Harner. **Manager, Ticket Operations:** Greg Conway. **Graphics Manager:** Kevin Jimenez. **Operations Manager:** Vladimir Lipsman. **Marketing Manager:** Kaitlyn Coufal. . **Community Outreach/Promotions:** King Henry. **Account Executives:** Tom Cox, Tommy Cardona, Nicole Kneessy, Craig Coughlin, Peter Talman, Dan Girard, Brian Kelly, Ricky Viola. **Staff Accountant:** Tatiana Isdith. **Administrative Assistant, Community Relations:** Sharon Lundy.

FIELD STAFF

Manager: TBA. **Coach:** TBA. **Pitching Coach:** TBA.

GAME INFORMATION

Radio Announcer: Stu Johnson. **No. of Games Broadcast:** 76. **Flagship Station:** WKRB 90.3-FM.
PA Announcer: Mark Frotto. **Official Scorer:** TBA.
Stadium Name: MCU Park. **Location:** Belt Parkway to Cropsey Ave South, continue on Cropsey until it becomes West 17th St, continue to Surf Ave, stadium on south side of Surf Ave; By subway, west/south to Stillwell Ave./Coney Island station. **Ticket Price Range:** $8-17.
Visiting Club Hotel: Unavailable.

CONNECTICUT TIGERS

Address: 14 Stott Avenue, Norwich, CT 06360.
Telephone: (860) 887-7962. **Fax:** (860) 886-5996.
E-Mail Address: info@cttigers.com. **Website:** www.cttigers.com.
Affiliation (first year): Detroit Tigers (1999). **Years in League:** 2010-

OWNERSHIP/MANAGEMENT

Operated By: Oneonta Athletic Corp. **President:** Miles Prentice.
Senior Vice President: CJ Knudsen. **VP/General Manager:** Eric Knighton. **Assistant GM:** Dave Schermerhorn.
Director, Concessions/Merchandise: Heather Bartlett. **Director, Sales:** Brent Southworth. **Box Office Manager:** Josh Postler. **Director, Group Sales/Operations:** Jack Kasten. **Head Groundskeeper:** Ryan Lefler.

FIELD STAFF

Manager: Mike Rabelo. **Hitting Coach:** Mike Hessman. **Pitching Coach:** Ace Adams. **Trainer:** Chris Vick.

GAME INFORMATION

PA Announcer: Ed Weyant. **Official Scorer:** Chris Cote.
Stadium Name: Dodd Stadium. **Location:** Exit 14 (old exit 82) off I-395. **Standard Game Times:** 7:05 pm, Sun. 4:05.
Ticket Price Range: $8-20.
Visiting Club Hotel: Unavailable.

HUDSON VALLEY RENEGADES

Office Address: Dutchess Stadium, 1500 Route 9D, Wappingers Falls, NY 12590. **Mailing Address:** PO Box 661, Fishkill, NY 12524.
Telephone: (845) 838-0094. **Fax:** (845) 838-0014.
E-Mail Address: info@hvrenegades.com. **Website:** www.hvrenegades.com.
Affiliation (first year): Tampa Bay Rays (1996). **Years in League:** 1994-

OWNERSHIP/MANAGEMENT

Operated by: Keystone Professional Baseball Club Inc.
Principal Owner: Marv Goldklang. **President:** Jeff Goldklang. **Senior Vice President/General Manager:** Eben Yager.
Vice President: Rick Zolzer. **Assistant GM:** Kristen Huss. Director,
Stadium Operations: Tom Hubmaster. **Director, Baseball Communications:** Joe Ausanio. **Director, Business Operations:** Vicky DeFreese. **Director, Sales:** Sean Kammerer. **Director, Ticket Sales:** Jonathon Basil. **Director, Promotions/Merchandise:** Breven Zimmerman. **Director, Marketing/Communications:** Kasey Commander.
Manager, New Business Development: Dave Neff. Manager, **Director, Food/Beverage:** Teri Bettencourt. **Manager, Stadium Operations:** Chris Lynch. **Head Groundskeeper:** Tim Merante. **Community Relations Specialist:** Bob Outer.
Ticket Sales Associates: Chris Winslow, Dan Horne, Casey Vecchio.

FIELD STAFF

Manager: Tim Parenton. **Hitting Coach:** Craig Albernaz. **Pitching Coach:** Brian Reith. **Trainer:** Brian Newman.
Conditioning Coach: Dan Rousseau.

GAME INFORMATION

Radio Announcer: Unavailable. **No. of Games Broadcast:** Home38. **Flagship Stations:** WKIP 1450-AM. **PA Announcer:** Rick Zolzer. **Official Scorers:** Unavailable.
Stadium Name: Dutchess Stadium. **Location:** I-84 to exit 11 (Route 9D North), north one mile to stadium. **Standard Game Times:** 7:05 pm, Sun. 5:05. **Visiting Club Hotel:** Days Inn, 20 Schuyler Blvd and Route 9, Fishkill, NY 12524.
Telephone: (845) 896-4995.
Visiting Club Hotel: Unavailable.

LOWELL SPINNERS

Address: 450 Aiken St, Lowell, MA 01854.

Telephone: (978) 459-2255. Fax: (978) 459-1674.
E-Mail Address: info@lowellspinners.com. Website: www.lowellspinners.com.
Affiliation (first year): Boston Red Sox (1996). Years in League: 1996-

OWNERSHIP/MANAGEMENT
Operated By: Diamond Action Inc. Owner/CEO: Drew Weber.
President/General Manager: Tim Bawmann. General Manager: Tim Bawmann.
Assistant General Manager: Justin Williams. VP, Finance: Pricilla Harbour. VP, Sales;Food/Beverage Manager: Brian
Lindsay. VP, Facilities: Gareth Markey. VP, Ticket Operations: Jon Healy. Creative Service Manager: Connor Sullivan.
Ticket Office Manager: T.J. Konsant. Director, Game Day Entertainment: Matt Steinberg. Grounds Manager: Jon
Sheehan. Director, Grounds Management: Jack Schmidgall.

FIELD STAFF
Manager: Iggy Suarez. Hitting Coach: Wilton Veras. Pitching Coach: Lance Carter. Athletic Trainer: Scott Gallon.

GAME INFORMATION
Radio Announcer: John Leahy. No. of Games Broadcast: 76. Flagship Station: WCAP 980-AM. PA Announcer:
Mike Riley. Official Scorer: David Rourke. Stadium Name: Edward A LeLacheur Park. Location: From Route 495 and
3, take exit 35C (Lowell Connector), follow connector to exit 5B (Thorndike Street) onto Dutton Street, left onto Father
Morrissette Boulevard, right on Aiken Street. Standard Game Times: 7:05 pm. Ticket Price Range: $7-10 (advance);
$9-12 (day of game). Visiting Club Hotel: Radisson of Chelmsford, 10 Independence Dr, Chelmsford, MA 01879.
Telephone: (978) 356-0800.

MAHONING VALLEY
SCRAPPERS

Address: 111 Eastwood Mall Blvd, Niles, OH 44446.
Telephone: (330) 505-0000. Fax: (303) 505-9696.
E-Mail Address: info@mvscrappers.com. Website: www.mvscrappers.com.
Affiliation (first year): Cleveland Indians (1999). Years in League: 1999-

OWNERSHIP/MANAGEMENT
Operated By: HWS Baseball Group. Managing General Partner: Michael Savit. Vice President, HWS Baseball/
General Manager: Jordan Taylor. Assistant GM, Marketing: Heather Sahli. Assistant GM, Sales: Matt Thompson.
Manager, Box Office: Tyler Adams. Assistant GM, Operations: Brad Hooser. Group Sales Manager: Chris Sumner.
Head Groundskeeper: Ryan Olszewski. Manager, Accounting & Human Resources: Roxanne Herrington. Manager,
Community Relations & Merchandise: Kate Walsh.

FIELD STAFF
Manager: Edwin Rodriguez. Hitting Coach: Kevin Howard. Athletic Trainer: Jake Legan. Pitching Coach: Tighe
Dickinson. Strength/Conditioning Coach: Jake Sankal.

GAME INFORMATION
Radio Announcer: Tim Pozsgai. No. of Games Broadcast: 76. Flagship Station: SportsRadio 1240 AM.
PA Announcer: Unavailable. Official Scorer: Craig Antush.
Stadium Name: Eastwood Field. Location: I-80 to 11 North to 82 West to 46 South; stadium located behind
Eastwood Mall. Ticket Price Range: $8-12.
Visiting Club Hotel: Days Inn & Suites, 1615 Liberty St, Girard, OH 44429. Telephone: (330) 759-9820.

STATE COLLEGE SPIKES

Address: 112 Medlar Field at Lubrano Park, University Park, PA 16802.
Telephone: (814) 272-1711. Fax: (814) 272-1718.
Website: www.statecollegespikes.com.
Affiliation (first year): St. Louis Cardinals (2013). Years in League: 2006-.

OWNERSHIP/MANAGEMENT
Operated By: Spikes Baseball LP. Chairman/Managing Partner: Chuck Greenberg.
President: Jason Dambach. General Manager: Scott Walker. Assistant GM, Operations: Dan Petrazzolo. Manager,
Corporate Partnerships: Chelsea Chidgey. Director, Ticket Sales: Brian DeAngelis. Senior Account Executive: Erik
Hoffman. Ticket Account Executive: Austin Snodgrass. Accounting Manager: Karen Mahon. Manager, Box Office/
Business Ops: Steve Christ. Director, Entertainment/Promotions: Ben Love. Manager of Communications: Joe
Putnam. Director of Food/Beverage: Anthony Sforza. Senior Sports Turf Manager: Matt Neri.

FIELD STAFF
Manager: Johnny Rodriguez. Hitting Coach: Roger LaFrancois. Pitching Coach: Darwin Marrero. Coach: C.J. Beatty.
Trainer: Chris Whitman.

GAME INFORMATION

PA Announcer: Jeff Brown. **Official Scorers:** Dave Baker, John Dixon.

Stadium Name: Medlar Field at Lubrano Park. **Location:** From west, US 322 to Mount Nittany Expressway, I-80 to exit 158 (old exit 23/Milesburg), follow Route 150 South to Route 26 South; From east, I-80 to exit 161 (old exit 24/Bellefonte) to Route 26 South or US 220/I-99 South. **Standard Game Times:** 7:05 pm, Sun. 6:05. **Ticket Price Range:**$8-18.

Visiting Club Hotel: Ramada Conference Center State College, 1450 Atherton St, State College, PA 16801. **Telephone:** (814) 238-3001.

STATEN ISLAND YANKEES

Stadium Address: 75 Richmond Terrace, Staten Island, NY 10301.
Telephone: (718) 720-9265. **Fax:** (718) 273-5763.
Website: www.siyanks.com.
Affiliation (first year): New York Yankees (1999). **Years in League:** 1999-

OWNERSHIP/MANAGEMENT

Principal Owners: Nostalgic Partners.
President/Operating Partner: Will Smith.
General Manager: Jane Rogers. **Director, Corporate Partnerships:** Elizabeth Kasegrande. **Director, Entertainment:** John D'Agostino. **CFO:** Jason Nazzaro. **Vice President, Sales:** TJ Jahn. **Box Office Manager:** Andrew Lupo. **Group Sales Manager:** David Percarpio. **Sales Executives:** Steven Liss, Marc Lopez, Andrew Kane, Peter Warren, Leigh Engle, Danny Goldman. **Senior Director, Marketing/Fan Experience:** Michael Holley. **Marketing Manager:** Ian Fontenot. **Manager, Stadium Operations:** Bobby Brown.

FIELD STAFF

Manager: Dave Bialas. **Hitting Coach:** Eric Duncan. **Pitching Coach:** TBA. **Defensive Coach:** Teuris Olivares.

GAME INFORMATION

Radio Announcer: Unavailable. **No. of Games Broadcast:** 38. **Flagship Station:** WSIA 88.9 FM. **PA Announcer:** Jeff Fromm. **Official Scorer:** Ed Buttle.

Stadium Name: Richmond County Bank Ballpark at St George.

Location: From I-95, take exit 13E (1-278 and Staten Island), cross Goethals Bridge, stay on I-278 East and take last exit before Verrazano Narrows Bridge, north on Father Capodanno Boulevard, which turns into Bay Street, which goes to ferry terminal; ballpark next to Staten Island Ferry Terminal. **Standard Game Times:** 7 pm, Sun. 4pm.

Visiting Club Hotel: Unavailable.

TRI-CITY VALLEYCATS

Office Address: Joseph L Bruno Stadium, 80 Vandenburg Ave, Troy, NY 12180. **Mailing Address:** PO Box 694, Troy, NY 12181.
Telephone: (518) 629-2287. **Fax:** (518) 629-2299.
E-Mail Address: info@tcvalleycats.com. **Website:** www.tcvalleycats.com.
Affiliation (first year): Houston Astros (2002). **Years in League:** 2002 -

OWNERSHIP/MANAGEMENT

Operated By: Tri-City ValleyCats Inc. **Principal Owners:** Martin Barr, John Burton, William Gladstone, Rick Murphy, Alfred Roberts, Stephen Siegel.

President: William Gladstone. **Executive Vice President/Chief Operating Officer:** Rick Murphy. **General Manager:** Matt Callahan. **Assistant GM:** Michelle Skinner. **Stadium Operations Manager:** Keith Sweeney. **Media Relations Manager:** Chris Chenes. **Senior Account Executive:** Chris Dawson. **Box Office Manager:** Jessica Kaszeta. **Account Executive:** Aaron Hodge. **Administrative Assistant:** Elyse Zima.

FIELD STAFF

Manager: Lamarr Rogers. **Hitting Coach:** Dillon Lawson. **Pitching Coach:** Drew French. **Trainer:** John Gregorich.

GAME INFORMATION

Radio Announcer: TBD. **No. of Games Broadcast:** 76. **Flagship Station:** MiLB.com.

PA Announcer: Anthony Pettograsso **Official Scorer:** TBD

Stadium Name: Joseph Bruno Stadium. **Location:** From north, I-87 to exit 7 (Route 7), go east 1 1/2 miles to I-787 South, to Route 378 East, go over bridge to Route 4, right to Route 4South, one mile to Hudson Valley Community College campus on left; From south, I-87 to exit 23 (I-787), I-787 north six miles to exit for Route 378 east, over bridge to Route 4, right to Route 4 South, one mile to campus on left; From east, Massachusetts Turnpike to exit B-1 (I-90), nine miles to Exit 8 (Defreestville), left off ramp to Route 4 North, five miles to campus on right; From west, I-90 to exit 24 (I-90 East), I-90 East for six miles to I-787 North (Troy), 2.2 miles to exit for Route 378 East, over bridge to Route 4, right to Route 4 south for one mile to campus on left.

Standard Game Times: 7pm, Sun. 5pm. **Ticket Price Range:** $5.75-$12.00.

Visiting Club Hotel: Travelodge, 831 New Loudon Road, Latham, NY 12110. **Telephone:** (518) 785-6626.

VERMONT LAKE MONSTERS

Address: 1 King Street Ferry Dock, Burlington, VT 05401.
Telephone: (802) 655-4200. **Fax:** (802) 655-5660.
E-Mail Address: info@vermontlakemonsters.com. **Website:** www.vermontlakemon-sters.com.
Affiliation (first year): Oakland Athletics (2011). **Years in League:** 1994-

OWNERSHIP/MANAGEMENT
Operated by: Vermont Expos Inc. **Principal Owner/President:** Ray Pecor Jr. **Vice President:** Kyle Bostwick. **General Manager:** Joe Doud. **Assistant General Manager:** Adam Matth. Executive Director, **Sales & Marketing:** Nate Cloutier. **Accounts Manager/Merchandise Director:** Kate Echo. Director, **Director, Community Relations:** & Promotions: Zach Betkowski. **Box Office Manager:** Kali Ackerman. **Director, Media Relations:** Paul Stanfield. **Clubhouse Operations:** Curt Echo, Emmitt Ackerman. **Head Groundskeeper:** James Writer.

FIELD STAFF
Manager: Aaron Nieckula. **Hitting Coach:** Lloyd Turner. **Pitching Coach:** Carlos Chavez.

GAME INFORMATION
Radio Announcers: George Commo. **No. of Games Broadcast:** Home-38, Away-12. **Flagship Station:** 960 The Zone.
PA Announcer: Unavailable. **Official Scorer:** Unavailable.
Stadium Name: Centennial Field. **Location:** I-89 to exit 14W, right on East Avenue for one mile, right at Colchester Avenue. **Standard Game Times:** 7:05 pm, Sat. 6:05, Sun. 5:05. **Ticket Price Range:** $5-8.
Visiting Club Hotel: Sheraton Hotel & Conference Center. **Telephone:** (802) 865-6600.

WEST VIRGINIA BLACK BEARS

Office Address: 2040 Jedd Gyorko Drive, Granville, WV 26534
Mailing Address: PO Box 4680 Morgantown, WV 26504.
Telephone: (304)293-7910. **Website:** www.westvirginiablackbears.com.
Affiliation (first year): Pittsburgh Pirates (2015). **Years in League:** 2015-

OWNERSHIP/MANAGEMENT
Operated By: Rich Baseball Operations.
President: Robert Rich Jr. **Chief Operating Officer:** Jonathan Dandes. **General Manager:** Matthew Drayer. **Assistant GM:** John Pogorzelski. **Business Manager:** Jackie Riggleman
Sponsorship and Promotions Manager: Matthew Vullo. **Stadium Manager:** Craig McIntosh.

FIELD STAFF
Manager: Wyatt Toregas. **Hitting Coach:** Jonathan Prieto. **Pitching Coach:** Mark DiFelice

GAME INFORMATION
PA Announcer: Unavailable. **Official Scorer:** Unavailable.
Stadium Name: Monongalia County Ballpark. **Game Times:** 7:05 pm, Sun. 4:05.
Visiting Club Hotel: Lakeview Golf Resort

WILLIAMSPORT CROSSCUTTERS

Office Address: Bowman Field, 1700 W Fourth St, Williamsport, PA 17701. **Mailing Address:** PO Box 3173, Williamsport, PA 17701.
Telephone: (570) 326-3389. **Fax:** (570) 326-3494.
E-Mail Address: mail@crosscutters.com. **Website:** www.crosscutters.com.
Affiliation (first year): Philadelphia Phillies (2007). **Years in League:** 1968-72, 1994-

OWNERSHIP/MANAGEMENT
Operated By: Cutting Edge Baseball, LLC. **Principal Owner:** Peter Freund. **Vice President/General Manager:** Doug Estes. **VP, Marketing/Public Relations:** Gabe Sinicropi. **Director, Concessions:** Bill Gehron. **Director, Ticket Operations/Community Relations:** Sarah Budd. **Director, Partner Services:** TBD.

FIELD STAFF
Manager: Pat Borders. **Coach:** John Mizerock. **Pitching Coach:** Hector Berrios. **Trainer:** Michael Hefta.

GAME INFORMATION
Radio Announcers: Todd Bartley, Ian Catherine. **No. of Games Broadcast:** 76. **Flagship Station:** WLYC 1050-AM.
Stadium Name: Susquehanna Bank Park. **Location:** From south, Route 15 to Maynard Street, right on Maynard, left on Fourth Street for one mile; From north, Route 15 to Fourth Street, left on Fourth. **Ticket Price Range:** $5-$10.
Visiting Club Hotel: Best Western, 1840 E Third St, Williamsport, PA 17701. **Telephone:** (570) 326-1981.

NORTHWEST LEAGUE

Address: 140 N Higgins Ave., No. 211, Missoula, MT, 59802.
Telephone: (406) 541-9301. **Fax:** (406) 543-9463.
E-Mail Address: mellisnwl@aol.com. **Website:** www.northwestleague.com
Years League Active: 1954-
President/Treasurer: Mike Ellis.
Vice President: Jerry Walker (Salem-Keizer). **Corporate Secretary:** Jerry Walker (Salem-Keizer).
Directors: Dave Elmore (Eugene), Bobby Brett (Spokane), Tom Volpe (Everett), Jake Kerr (Vancouver), Mike McMurray (Hillsboro), Brent Miles (Tri-City), Jerry Walker (Salem-Keizer), Jeff Eiseman (Boise).
Administrative Assistant: Judy Ellis.
Division Structure: South—Boise, Hillsboro, Eugene, Salem-Keizer. **North**—Everett, Spokane, Tri-City, Vancouver.
Regular Season: 76 games (split schedule). **2016 Opening Date:** June 17. **Closing Date:** Sept. 5.
All-Star Game: Aug. 2, in Ogden.
Playoff Format: First-half division winners meet second-half division winners in best of three series. Winners meet in best of three series for league championship.
Roster Limit: 35 active, 35 under control. **Player Eligibility Rule:** No more than three players on active list may have four or more years of prior service.
Brand of Baseball: Rawlings.
Umpires: Unavailable.

Mike Ellis

STADIUM INFORMATION

Club	Stadium	Opened	Dimensions LF	CF	RF	Capacity	2015 Att.
Boise	Memorial Stadium	1989	335	400	335	3,426	109,945
Eugene	PK Park	2010	335	400	325	4,000	120,931
Everett	Everett Memorial Stadium	1984	324	380	330	3,682	100,613
Hillsboro	Hillsboro Ballpark	2013	325	400	325	4,500	143,312
Salem-Keizer	Volcanoes Stadium	1997	325	400	325	4,100	85,851
Spokane	Avista Stadium	1958	335	398	335	7,162	188,956
Tri-City	Dust Devils Stadium	1995	335	400	335	3,700	86,022
Vancouver	Nat Bailey Stadium	1951	335	395	335	6,500	215.535

BOISE HAWKS

Address: 5600 N. Glenwood St. Boise, ID 83714.
Telephone: (208) 322-5000. **Fax:** (208) 322-6846.
Website: www.boisehawks.com.
Affiliation: Colorado Rockies (2015).
Years in League: 1975-76, 1978, 1987-

OWNERSHIP/MANAGEMENT

Operated by: Boise Professional Baseball LLC. **Managing Partner:** Jeff Eiseman.
President: Todd Rahr. **General Manager:** Bob Flannery. Dir., Stadium Ops/**Food & Beverage:** Jake Lusk. **Corporate/Group Sales Manager:** Brooke Bedgood. **Ticket Sales Manager: TBD, Marketing:** Joe Kelly. **Manager, Stadium Ops:** Jeff Israel. **Manager, Accounting/Office:** Angela Phillips. **Account Executives:** Stephen Gall, Jon Jensen. Asst., **Media Relations:** Niki DiSera.

FIELD STAFF

Development Supervisor: Fred Nelson. **Manager:** Andy Gonzales. **Hitting Coach:** TBD. **Pitching Coach:** Doug Jones. **Trainer:** Mickey Clarizio

GAME INFORMATION

Radio Announcer: Unavailable. **No. of Games Broadcast:** Unavailable. **Flagship Station:** Unavailable.
PA Announcer: Unavailable. **Official Scorer:** Curtis Haines.
Stadium Name: Memorial Stadium. **Location:** I-84 to Cole Rd., north to Western Idaho Fairgrounds at 5600 North Glenwood St. **Standard Game Time:** 7:15 pm. **Ticket Price Range:** $7-16.
Visiting Club Hotel: Unavailable.

EUGENE EMERALDS

Office Address: 2760 Martin Luther King Jr. Blvd, Eugene, OR 97401. **Mailing Address:** PO Box 10911, Eugene, OR 97440.
Telephone: (541) 342-5367. **Fax:** (541) 342-6089.
E-Mail Address: info@emeraldsbaseball.com. **Website:** www.emeraldsbaseball.com.
Affiliation (first year): Chicago Cubs (2015). **Years in League:** 1955-68, 1974-

OWNERSHIP/MANAGEMENT

Operated By: Elmore Sports Group Ltd. **Principal Owner:** David Elmore.
General Manager: Allan Benavides. **Assistant GM:** Matt Dompe. **Director, Food/Beverage:** Turner Elmore.
Director, Tickets: Peter Billups. **Event Manager:** Chris Bowers. **Group Sales:** Patrick Zajac. **Graphic Designer:** Danny Crowley. **Director, Community Affairs:** Anne Culhane. **Ticket Sales:** Cam LaFerle. **Sponsorship Sales:** Brian Vucovich.

FIELD STAFF

Manager: Jesus Feliciano. **Hitting Coach:** Ty Wright. **Pitching Coach:** Brian Lawrence. **Assistant Coach:** Gary Van Tol. **Trainer:** Logan Severson. **Strength and Conditioning Coach:** Ryan Nordvedt.

GAME INFORMATION

Radio Announcer: Matt Dompe. **No. of Games Broadcast:** 76. **Flagship Station:** 95.3-FM The Score.
PA Announcer: Ted Welker. **Official Scorer:** George McPherson.
Stadium Name: PK Park. **Standard Game Time:** 7:05 pm, Sun. 5:01. **Ticket Price Range:** $7-$13.
Visiting Club Hotel: Candlewood Suites Eugene Springfield.

EVERETT AQUASOX

Mailing Address: 3802 Broadway, Everett, WA 98201.
Telephone: (425) 258-3673. **Fax:** (425) 258-3675.
E-Mail Address: info@aquasox.com. **Website:** www.aquasox.com.
Affiliation (first year): Seattle Mariners (1995). **Years in League:** 1984-

OWNERSHIP/MANAGEMENT

Operated by: 7th Inning Stretch, LLC. **Directors:** Tom Volpe, Pat Filippone.
General Manager: Danny Tetzlaff. **Director, Corporate Partnerships/Broadcasting:** Pat Dillon. **Corporate Partnership Manager:** Duncan Jensen. **Director, Food & Beverage/Finance:** Rick Maddox. **Director, Tickets:** Dustin Coder. **Marketing & Creative Manager:** Cameron Bloch. **Community Relations Manager:** Kellie Howard. **Account Executives:** Kenny Lindberg, Justen Oslund, Alex Clausius.

FIELD STAFF

Manager: Rob Mummau. **Hitting Coach:** Brian Hunter. **Pitching Coach:** Moises Hernandez. **Trainer:** Shane Zdebiak.

GAME INFORMATION

Radio Announcer: Pat Dillon. **No. of Games Broadcast:** 76. **Flagship Station:** KRKO 1380-AM.
PA Announcer: Tom Lafferty. **Official Scorer:** Pat Castro.
Stadium Name: Everett Memorial Stadium. **Location:** I-5, exit 192. **Standard Game Times:** 7:05 pm, Sun. 4:05. **Ticket Price Range:** $8-18.
Visiting Club Hotel: Best Western Cascadia Inn, 2800 Pacific Ave, Everett, WA 98201. **Telephone:** (425) 258-4141.

HILLSBORO HOPS

Address: 4460 NW 229th Ave., Hillsboro, OR, 97124.
Telephone: (503) 640-0887. **E-Mail Address:** info@hillsborohops.com. **Website:** www.hillsborohops.com.
Affiliation (first year): Arizona Diamondbacks (2001). **Years in League:** 2013-

OWNERSHIP/MANAGEMENT

Operated by: Short Season LLC. **Managing Partners:** Mike McMurray, Josh Weinman, Myron Levin. **President:** Mike McMurray.
General Manager: K.L. Wombacher. **Chief Financial Officer:** Laura McMurray. **Director, Ballpark Operations:** Juan Huitron. **Director, Tickets:** Jason Gavigan. **Director, Merchandise:** Lauren Wombacher. **Director, Media Relations/Broadcasting:** Rich Burk.

FIELD STAFF

Manager: Shelley Duncan. **Hitting Coach:** Jose Amado. **Pitching Coach:** Mike Parrott.

GAME INFORMATION

PA Announcer: Brian Rogers. **Official Scorer:** Blair Cash.
Stadium Name: Ron Tonkin Field. **Location:** 4460 NW 229th, Hillsboro, OR, 97124. **Standard Game Times:** 7:05 pm, Sat. 5:03, Sun. 1:05. **Ticket Price Range:** $7-$16.
Visiting Club Hotel: University Place Hotel, Portland, Or. **Telephone:** (503) 221-0140.

SALEM-KEIZER VOLCANOES

Office Address: 6700 Field of Dreams Way, Keizer, OR 97303.
Mailing Address: PO Box 20936, Keizer, OR 97307.
Telephone: (503) 390-2225. **Fax:** (503) 390-2227.
E-Mail Address: Volcanoes@volcanoesbaseball.com. **Website:** www.volcanoesbaseball.com.
Affiliation (first year): San Francisco Giants (1997). **Years in League:** 1997-.

OWNERSHIP/MANAGEMENT

Operated By: Sports Enterprises Inc. **Principal Owners:** Jerry Walker, Lisa Walker.
President/General Manager: Jerry Walker. **President, Stadium Operations: Rick Nelson, Senior Account Executive/Game Day Operations:** Jerry Howard..
Director, Ticket Office Operations: Bea Howard. **Director, Business Development:** Justin Lacche.

FIELD STAFF

Manager: Kyle Haines. **Coach:** Ricky Ward. **Pitching Coach:** Matt Yourkin.

GAME INFORMATION

Radio Announcer: TBA. **No. of Games Broadcast:** 76. Broadcast on www.volcanoesbaseball.com.
PA Announcer: Unavailable. **Official Scorer:** Scott Sepich. **Stadium Name:** Volcanoes Stadium. **Location:** I-5 to exit 260 (Chemawa Road), west one block to Stadium Way NE, north six blocks to stadium. **Standard Game Times:** 6:35 pm, Sun. 5:05. **Ticket Price Range:** $7-30. **Visiting Club Hotel:** Comfort Suites, 630 Hawthorne Ave SE, Salem, OR 97301.
Telephone: (503) 585-9705.

SPOKANE INDIANS

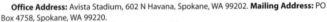

Office Address: Avista Stadium, 602 N Havana, Spokane, WA 99202. **Mailing Address:** PO Box 4758, Spokane, WA 99220.
Telephone: (509) 535-2922. **Fax:** (509) 534-5368.
E-Mail Address: mail@spokaneindians.com. **Website:** www.spokaneindians.com.
Affiliation (first year): Texas Rangers (2003). **Years in League:** 1972, 1983-Present -

OWNERSHIP/MANAGEMENT

Operated By: Longball Inc. **Principal Owner:** Bobby Brett. **Co-Owner/Senior Advisor:** Andrew Billig.
Vice President/General Manager: Chris Duff. **Senior Vice President:** Otto Klein. **VP, Tickets:** Josh Roys. **Director, Business Operations:** Lesley DeHart. **Assistant GM, Sponsorships:** Kyle Day. **Assistant GM, Tickets:** Nick Gaebe.
Director, Concessions/Operations: Justin Stottlemyre. **Sponsorship Coordinators:** Karly Searl, Anthony DeGrazia.
Senior Account Executive: Chris Combo. **Account Executives:** Sean Bozigian, Chelsea Gorman. **Group Sales Manager:** Darby Moore. **Group Sales Coordinator:** Olivia Handwerk. **Personal Account Managers: Jared Baldwin,** Stephanie Guttromson CFO: Greg Sloan. **Controller:** Tim Gittel. **Stadium Operations Manager:** John Tibbett. **Head Groundskeeper:** Unavailable . **Assistant Director, Stadium Operations:** Larry Blummer.

FIELD STAFF

Manager: Tim Hulett. **Hitting Coach:** Kenny Hook. **Pitching Coach:** Brian Shouse. **Assistant Coach:** Jared Goedert.
Strength/Conditioning Coach: Ed Yong. **Trainer:** Unavailable

GAME INFORMATION

Radio Announcer: Mike Boyle. **No. of Games Broadcast:** 76. **Flagship Station:** 1510 KGA.
PA Announcer: Scott Lewis. **Official Scorer:** Todd Gilkey.
Stadium Name: Avista Stadium at the Spokane Fair and Expo Center. **Location:** From west, I-90 to exit 283B (Thor/Freya), east on Third Avenue, left onto Havana; From east, I-90 to Broadway exit, right onto Broadway, left onto Havana. **Standard Game Time:** 6:30 pm, Sun. 3:30 pm. **Ticket Price Range:** $5-13.
Visiting Club Hotel: Mirabeau Park Hotel & Convention Center, N 1100 Sullivan Rd, Spokane, WA 99037. **Telephone:** (509) 924-9000.

TRI-CITY DUST DEVILS

Address: 6200 Burden Blvd, Pasco, WA 99301.
Telephone: (509) 544-8789. **Fax:** (509) 547-9570.
E-Mail Address: info@dustdevilsbaseball.com. **Website:** www.dustdevilsbaseball.com.
Affiliation: San Diego Padres (2015). **Years in League:** 1955-1974, 1983-1986, 2001-

OWNERSHIP/MANAGEMENT

Operated by: Northwest Baseball Ventures. **Principal Owners:** George Brett, Hoshino Dreams Corp, Brent Miles. **President:** Brent Miles.
Vice President/General Manager: Derrel Ebert. **Assistant GM:** Dan O'Neill. **Director of Sponsorships:** Ann Shaffer. **Sponsorships Account Executive:** Kyle Nakama. **Promotions Coordinator:** Samantha Beck. **Group Sales Coordinator:** Joey Edminster. **Ticket Sales Manager:** Trevor Shively. **Account Executive:** Mark Klopping. **Group Sales Coordinator:** Brae Dilley. **Accounting Coordinator:** Jackie Salter. **Head Groundskeeper:** Michael Angel.

FIELD STAFF

Manager: Brandon Wood. **Hitting Coach:** Oscar Bernard. **Coach:** Vinny Lopez. **Pitching Coach:** Unavailable.

GAME INFORMATION

Radio Announcer: Chris King. **No. of Games Broadcast:** 76. **Flagship Station:** 870-AM KFLD.
PA Announcer: Patrick Harvey. **Official Scorers:** Tony Wise, Scott Tylinski.
Stadium Name: Gesa Stadium. **Location:** I-182 to exit 9 (Road 68), north to Burden Blvd, right to stadium. **Standard Game Time:** 7:15 pm. **Ticket Price Range:** $7-10.
Visiting Club Hotel: Red Lion Hotel-Columbia Center, 1101 N Columbia Center Blvd, Kennewick, WA 99336. **Telephone:** (509) 783-0611.

VANCOUVER CANADIANS

Address: Scotiabank Field at Nat Bailey Stadium, 4601 Ontario St, Vancouver, British Columbia V5V 3H4.
Telephone: (604) 872-5232. **Fax:** (604) 872-1714.
E-Mail Address: staff@canadiansbaseball.com. **Website:** www.canadiansbaseball.com.
Affiliation (sixth year): Toronto Blue Jays (2011). **Years in League:** 2000-

OWNERSHIP/MANAGEMENT

Operated by: Vancouver Canadians Professional Baseball LLP. **Managing General Partner:** Jake Kerr. **Partner:** Jeff Mooney. **President:** Andy Dunn.
General Manager: JC Fraser. **Assistant General Manager:** Allan Bailey. **Financial Controller:** Alex Cimiluik. **VP, Sales/Marketing:** Graham Wall. **Director, Communications/Broadcast:** Rob Fai. **Director, Community Relations/Team Operations:** Jeff Holloway. **Manager, Sales/Marketing Services:** Jennifer Jones. **Manager, Group Sales:** Andrew Forsyth. **Manager, Sales/Promotions:** Michael Richardson. **Manager, Ballpark Operations:** Cale Reining. **Coordinator, Sales:** Lindsay Scharf. **Coordinator, Sales:** Stephani Ellis. **Head Groundskeeper:** Matt Horan.

FIELD STAFF

Manager: Unavailable. **Hitting Coach:** Unavailable. **Pitching Coach:** Unavailable. **Trainer:** Unavailable.

GAME INFORMATION

Radio Announcer: Rob Fai. **No. of Games Broadcast:** 76. **Flagship Station:** TSN 1040-AM.
PA Announcer: Don Andrews/John Ashbridge. **Official Scorer:** Mike Hanafin. **Stadium Name:** Scotiabank Field at Nat Bailey Stadium. **Location:** From downtown, take Cambie Street Bridge, left on East 25th Ave./King Edward Ave, right on Main Street, right on 33rd Ave, right on Ontario St to stadium; From south, take Highway 99 to Oak Street, right on 41st Ave, left on Main Street to 33rd Ave, right on Ontario St to stadium. **Standard Game Times:** 7:05 pm, Sun. 1:05. **Ticket Price Range:** $11-25.
Visiting Club Hotel: Accent Inns, 10551 Edwards Dr, Richmond, BC V6X 3L8. **Telephone:** (604) 273-3311.

APPALACHIAN LEAGUE

Mailing Address: 759 182nd Ave. E., Redington Shores, FL 33708. **Telephone:** 704-252-2656. **E-Mail Address:** office@appyleague.net. **Website:** www.appyleague.com.
Years League Active: 1921-25, 1937-55, 1957-
President/Treasurer: Lee Landers. **Corporate Secretary:** David Lane (Greeneville).
Directors: Charlie Wilson (Bluefield), Larry Broadway (Bristol), Ronnie Richardson (Burlington), Jonathan Schuerholz (Danville), Brad Steil (Elizabethton), Allen Rowin (Greeneville), Gary LaRocque (Johnson City), Ian Levin (Kingsport), Mitch Lukevics (Princeton), Eric Schmitt (Pulaski).

Executive Committee: Mike Mains (Elizabethton), David Lane (Greeneville), Dan Moushon (Burlington), Gary La Rocque (St. Louis), Charlie Wilson (Toronto), Larry Broadway (Pittsburgh).
Board of Trustees Representative: Mitch Lukevics (Tampa Bay). **League Administrator:** Bobbi Landers.
Division Structure: East—Bluefield, Burlington, Danville, Princeton, Pulaski. **West**—Bristol, Elizabethton, Greeneville, Johnson City, Kingsport.
Regular Season: 68 games. **2016 Opening Date:** June 23. **Closing Date:** September 1.
All-Star Game: None.
Playoff Format: First- and second-place teams in each division play each other in best of three series. Winners meet in best of three series for league championship.
Roster Limit: 35 active, 35 under control. **Player Eligibility Rule:** No more than three players on the active roster may have three or more years of prior minor league service.
Brand of Baseball: Rawlings. **Umpires:** Unavailable.

Lee Landers

STADIUM INFORMATION

Club	Stadium	Opened	Dimensions LF	CF	RF	Capacity	2015 Att.
Bluefield	Bowen Field	1939	335	400	335	2,250	24,099
Bristol	DeVault Memorial Stadium	1969	325	400	310	2,000	17,849
Burlington	Burlington Athletic Stadium	1960	335	410	335	3,000	46,063
Danville	Dan Daniel Memorial Park	1993	330	400	330	2,588	28,841
Elizabethton	Joe O'Brien Field	1974	335	414	326	1,500	22,069
Greeneville	Pioneer Park	2004	331	400	331	2,400	54,252
Johnson City	Howard Johnson Field	1956	320	410	320	2,500	39,118
Kingsport	Hunter Wright Stadium	1995	330	410	330	2,500	31,086
Princeton	Hunnicutt Field	1988	330	396	330	1,950	27,051
Pulaski	Calfee Park	1935	335	405	310	2,500	57,023

BLUEFIELD BLUE JAYS

Office Address: Stadium Drive, Bluefield, WV 24701. **Mailing Address:** PO Box 356, Bluefield, WV 24701.
Telephone: (304) 324-1326. **Fax:** (304) 324-1318.
E-Mail Address: babybirds1@comcast.net<**mailto:**babybirds1@comcast.net>. **Website:** www.bluefieldjays.com.
Affiliation (first year): Toronto Blue Jays (2011). **Years in League:** 1946-55, 1957-

OWNERSHIP/MANAGEMENT
Director: Charlie Wilson (Toronto Blue Jays).
President: George McGonagle. **Vice President:** David Kersey. **Counsel:** Brian Cochran.

FIELD STAFF
Manager: TBD. **Coach: TBD Pitching Coach:** TBD.

GAME INFORMATION
PA Announcer: Unavailable. **Official Scorer:** Unavailable.
Stadium Name: Bowen Field. **Location:** I-77 to Bluefield exit 1, Route 290 to Route 460 West, fourth light right onto Leatherwood Lane, left at first light, past Hometown Shell station and turn right, stadium quarter-mile on left. **Ticket Price Range:** $6.
Visiting Club Hotel: Quality Inn Bluefield, 3350 Big Laurel Highway/460 West, Bluefield, WV 24701. **Telephone:** (304) 325-6170.

BRISTOL PIRATES

Ballpark Location: 1501 Euclid Ave, Bristol, VA 24201. **Mailing Address:** PO Box 1434, Bristol, VA 24203.
Telephone: (276) 206-9946. **Fax:** (276) 669-7686.
E-Mail Address: gm@bristolpiratesbaseball.com. **Website:** www.bristolpiratesbaseball.com
Affiliation (first year): Pittsburgh Pirates (2014). **Years in League:** 1921-25, 1940-55, 1969-

OWNERSHIP/MANAGEMENT
Owned by: Pittsburgh Pirates. **Operated by:** Bristol Baseball Inc. **Director:** Larry Broadway (Pittsburgh Pirates).
President/General Manager: Mahlon Luttrell. **Vice Presidents:** Lucas Hobbs, Mark Young. **Treasurer:** Jean Luttrell.
Secretary: Perry Hustad.

FIELD STAFF
Manager: Edgar Varela. **Hitting Coach:** Austin McClune. **Pitching Coach:** Tom Filer. **Trainer:** Jorge Islas.

GAME INFORMATION
Radio: milb.com.
PA Announcer: Travis Debusk. **Official Scorer:** Tim Johnston.
Stadium Name: DeVault Memorial Stadium. **Location:** I-81 to exit 3 onto Commonwealth Ave, right on Euclid Ave
for half-mile. **Standard Game Time:** 7 pm, 6 pm Sunday. **Ticket Price Range:** $4-7.
Visiting Club Hotel: Holiday Inn, 3005 Linden Drive Bristol, VA 24202. **Telephone:** (276) 466-4100.

BURLINGTON ROYALS

Office Address: 1450 Graham St, Burlington, NC 27217. **Mailing Address:** PO Box 1143,
Burlington, NC 27216.
Telephone: (336) 222-0223. **Fax:** (336) 226-2498.
E-Mail Address: info@burlingtonroyals.com. **Website:** www.burlingtonroyals.com
Affiliation (first year): Kansas City Royals (2007). **Years in League:** 1986-

OWNERSHIP/MANAGEMENT
Operated by: Burlington Baseball Club Inc. **Director:** Ronnie Richardson (Kansas City). **President:** Miles Wolff. **Vice
President:** Dan Moushon.
General Manager: Ryan Keur. **Assistant GM:** Miranda Ervin. **Director, Stadium Operations:** Mikie Morrison.

FIELD STAFF
Manager: Scott Thorman. **Hitting Coach:** Jesus Azuaje. **Pitching Coach:** Carlos Martinez.

GAME INFORMATION
Radio Announcer: Darren Zaslau. **No. of Games Broadcast:** Home-34, Away-7. **Flagship:** www.burlingtonroyals.
com.
PA Announcer: Tyler Williams. **Official Scorer:** Jon Teich. **Stadium Name:** Burlington Athletic Stadium. **Location:**
I-40/85 to exit 145, north on Route 100 (Maple Avenue) for 1.5 miles, right on Mebane Street for 1.5 miles, right on
Beaumont, left on Graham. **Standard Game Time:** 7 p.m. **Ticket Price Range:** $5-9. **Visiting Club Hotel:** Ramada
Burlington Hotel.

DANVILLE BRAVES

Office Address: Dan Daniel Memorial Park, 302 River Park Dr, Danville, VA 24540.
Mailing Address: PO Box 378, Danville, VA 24543.
Telephone: (434) 797-3792. **Fax:** (434) 797-3799.
E-Mail Address: danvillebraves@braves.com. **Website:** www.dbraves.com.
Affiliation (first year): Atlanta Braves (1993). **Years in League:** 1993-

OWNERSHIP/MANAGEMENT
Operated by: Atlanta National League Baseball Club LLC. **Director:** Jonathan Schuerholz (Atlanta Braves).
General Manager: David Cross. **Assistant GM:** TBA. **Operations Manager:** Tyler Bishop. **Head Groundskeeper:**
Mark Washburn.

FIELD STAFF
Manager: Robinson Cancel. **Coach:** Ivan Cruz. **Pitching Coach:** Gabe Luckert. **Athletic Trainer:** Dave Comeau.
Strength/Conditioning Coach: TBA.

GAME INFORMATION
Radio Announcer: Nick Pierce. **No. of Games Broadcast:** Home-34. **Flagship Station:** www.dbraves.com.
PA Announcer: Jay Stephens. **Official Scorer:** Mark Bowman.
Stadium Name: American Legion Field Post 325 Field at Dan Daniel Memorial Park. **Location:** US 29 Bypass to

River Park Drive/Dan Daniel Memorial Park exit; follow signs to park. **Standard Game Times:** 7 pm, Sun. 4. **Ticket Price Range:** $5-9. **Visiting Club Hotel:** Comfort Inn & Suites, 100 Tower Drive, Danville, VA 24540.

ELIZABETHTON TWINS

Office Address: 300 West Mill St., Elizabethton, TN 37643. **Stadium Address:** 208 N. Holly Lane, Elizabethton, TN 37643. **Mailing Address:** 300 West Mill St., Elizabethton, TN 37643.
Telephone: (423) 547-6441. **Fax:** (423) 547-6442.

OWNERSHIP/MANAGEMENT
Operator: City of Elizabethton. **Director:** Brad Steil. **President:** Harold Mains.
General Manager: Mike Mains. **Clubhouse Operations/Head Groundskeeper:** David McQueen.

FIELD STAFF
Manager: Ray Smith. **Coach:** Jeff Reed. **Pitching Coach:** Luis Ramirez. **Trainer:** Brian Harris.

GAME INFORMATION
Radio Announcer: Evan Ellis. **No. of Games Broadcast:** 34–Home, 6–Away. **Flagship Station:** WBEJ 1240-AM.
PA Announcer: Tom Banks. **Official Scorer:** Gene Renfro. **Stadium Name:** Joe O'Brien Field. **Location:** I-81 to Highway I-26, exit at Highway 321/67, left on Holly Lane. **Standard Game Time:** 7 pm. **Ticket Price Range:** $3-6.
Visiting Club Hotel: Holiday Inn, 101 W Springbrook Dr, Johnson City, TN 37601. **Telephone:** (423) 282-4611.

GREENEVILLE ASTROS

Office Address: 135 Shiloh Road, Greeneville, TN 37743. **Mailing Address:** PO Box 5192, Greeneville, TN 37743.
Telephone: (423) 638-0411. **Fax:** (423) 638-9450.
E-Mail Address: greenevilleoperations@astros.com. **Website:** www.greenevilleastros.com.

OWNERSHIP/MANAGEMENT
Operated by: Houston Astros Baseball Club. **Director:** Allen Rowin (Houston Astros).
General Manager: David Lane. **Assistant GM:** Hunter Reed, Kelsey Thompson. **Director, Stadium Operations:** Ben Spillner, Kelsey Thompson. **Head Groundskeeper:** TBD. **Clubhouse Operations:** Unavailable.

FIELD STAFF
Manager: Josh Bonifay. **Hitting Coach:** Cesar Cedeno. **Pitching Coach:** Pat Murphy.

GAME INFORMATION
Radio Announcer: Steve Wilhoit. **Flagship Station:** greenevilleastros.com.
PA Announcer: TBD. **Official Scorer:** Johnny Painter.
Stadium Name: Pioneer Park. **Location:** On the campus of Tusculum College, 135 Shiloh Rd Greeneville, TN 37743.
Standard Game Time: 7 pm, Sat/Sun 6 pm. **Ticket Price Range:** $6-9.
Visiting Club Hotel: Quality Inn, 3160 E Andrew Johnson Hwy, Greeneville, TN 37745. **Telephone:** (423) 638-7511.

JOHNSON CITY CARDINALS

Office Address: 510 Bert St., Johnson City, TN 37601. **Mailing Address:** PO Box 179, Johnson City, TN 37605.
Telephone: (423) 461-4866. **Fax:** (423) 461-4864. **E-Mail Address:** contact@jccardinals.com. **Website:** www.jccardinals.com.
Affiliation (first year): St. Louis Cardinals (1975). **Years in League:** 1911-13, 1921-24, 1937-55, 1957-61, 1964-

OWNERSHIP/MANAGEMENT
Owned by: St. Louis Cardinals. **Operated by:** Johnson City Sports Foundation Inc. **President:** Lee Sowers. **Director:** John Vuch. **General Manager:** Tyler Parsons. **Assistant GM:** Zac Clark. **Assistant GM, Sales:** Adam Grigsby.

FIELD STAFF
Manager: Chris Swauger. **Hitting Coach:** Robert Espinosa. **Pitching Coach:** Cale Johnson.

GAME INFORMATION
PA Announcer: Unavailable. **Official Scorer:** Unavailable. **Stadium Name:** Howard Johnson Field at Cardinal Park.
Location: I-26 to exit 23, left on East Main, through light onto Legion Street. **Standard Game Time:** 7 pm. **Ticket Price Range:** $5-$7. **Visiting Club Hotel:** Holiday Inn, 101 W Springbrook Dr, Johnson City, TN 37601. **Telephone:** (423) 282-4611.

KINGSPORT METS

Address: 800 Granby Rd, Kingsport, TN 37660.
Telephone: (423) 224-2626. **Fax:** (423) 224-2625.
E-Mail Address: info@kmets.com. **Website:** www.kmets.com
Affiliation (first year): New York Mets (1980). **Years in League:** 1921-25, 1938-52, 1957, 1960-63, 1969-82, 1984-

OWNERSHIP/MANAGEMENT
Operated By: New York Mets. **Director:** Ian Levin.
General Manager: Brian Paupeck. **Staff:** Josh Lawson.

FIELD STAFF
Manager: Luis Rivera. **Hitting Coach:** TBD. **Pitching Coach:** TBD:

GAME INFORMATION
PA Announcer: Brad Jones. **Official Scorer:** TBD.
Stadium Name: Hunter Wright Stadium. **Location:** I-26, Exit 1 (Stone Drive), left on West Stone Drive (US 11W), right on Granby Road. **Game Times:** Mon-Sat: 7 pm, Sun. 4 pm, doubleheaders 5 pm. **Ticket Price Range:** $4-7. **Visiting Club Hotel:** Quality Inn, 3004 Bays Mountain Plaza, Kingsport, TN 37664. **Telephone:** (423) 230-0534.

PRINCETON RAYS

Office Address: 345 Old Bluefield Rd, Princeton, WV 24739. **Mailing Address:** PO Box 5646, Princeton, WV 24740.
Telephone: (304) 487-2000. **Fax:** (304) 487-8762.
E-Mail Address: princetonrays@frontier.com . **Website:** www.princetonrays.net.
Affiliation (first year): Tampa Bay Rays (1997). **Years in League:** 1988-

OWNERSHIP/MANAGEMENT
Operated By: Princeton Baseball Association Inc. **Director:** Mitch Lukevics. **President:** Mori Williams.
General Manager: Nick Carey. **Director, Stadium Operations:** Mick Bayle. **Clubhouse Manager:** Anthony Dunagan. **Administrative Assistant:** Tommy Thomason. **Chaplain:** Craig Stout.

FIELD STAFF
Manager: Danny Sheaffer. **Coach:** Wuarnner Rincones. **Pitching Coach:** Jose Gonzalez. **Athletic Trainer:** Jeremy Spencer.

GAME INFORMATION
Radio Announcer: Kyle Cooper. **No. of Games Broadcast:** 34–Away. **Flagship Station:** WAEY-103.3FM.
PA Announcer: Eric Lester. **Official Scorer:** Bob Redd.
Stadium Name: Hunnicutt Field. **Location:** Exit 9 off I-77, US 460 West to downtown exit, left on Stafford Drive; stadium located behind Mercer County Technical Education Center. **Standard Game Times:** 7 pm, Sun. 5:00. **Ticket Price Range:** $5-7. **Visiting Club Hotel:** Days Inn, I-77 and Ambrose Lane, Princeton, WV 24740. **Telephone:** (304) 425-8100.

PULASKI YANKEES

Office Address: 700 South Washington Ave. Pulaski, VA 24301.
Mailing Address: PO Box 852, Pulaski, VA 24301. **Telephone:** (540) 980-1070.
Email Address: info@pulaskiyankees.net
Affiliation (second season): New York Yankees (2016). **Years in League:** 1942-1951, 1952-55, 1957-58, 1969-77, 1982-92, 1997-2002, 2003-2006, 2008-2014, 2015-

OWNERSHIP/MANAGEMENT
Operated By: Calfee Park Baseball, Inc. **Park Owners:** David Hagan, Larry Shelor. **General Manager:** Blair Hoke. **Assistant Manager:** Jade Campbell.

FIELD STAFF
Manager: Tony Franklin. **Hitting Coach:** Edwar Gonzalez. **Pitching Coach:** Butch Henry. **Defensive Coach:** Hector Rabago. **Trainer:** Josh DiLoreto. **Strength Coach:** Danny Russo. **Video Manager:** Nick Avanzato.

GAME INFORMATION
PA Announcer: Tyler Painter. **Official Scorer:** Unavailable. **Stadium Name:** Historic Calfee Park. **Location:** Interstate 81 to Exit 89-B (Route 11), north to Pulaski, right on
Pierce Avenue. **Ticket Price Range:** $5-10. **Visiting Club Hotel:** Unavailable.

PIONEER LEAGUE

Office Address: 180 S Howard Street, Spokane, WA 99201. **Mailing Address:** PO Box 2564, Spokane, WA 99220.
Telephone: (509) 456-7615. **Fax:** (509) 456-0136.
E-Mail Address: fanmail@pioneerleague.com. **Website:** www.pioneerleague.com.
Years League Active: 1939-42, 1946-

President: Jim McCurdy.
Directors: Dave Baggott (Ogden), Matt Ellis (Missoula), DG Elmore (Helena), Kevin Greene (Idaho Falls), Michael Baker (Grand Junction), Jeff Katofsky (Orem), Vinny Purpura (Great Falls), Bob Herrfeldt (Billings). **League Administrator:** Teryl MacDonald. **Executive Director:** Mary Ann McCurdy.
Division Structure: North-Billings, Great Falls, Helena, Missoula.South-Grand Junction, Idaho Falls, Ogden, Orem.
Regular Season: 76 games (split schedule). **2016 Opening Date:** June 17. **Closing Date:** Sept. 8.
All-Star Game: Pioneer League vs. Northwest League, Aug. 2, Ogden.
Playoff Format: First-half division winners meet second-half division winners in best of three series. Winners meet in best of three series for league championship.
Roster Limit: 35 active, 35 dressed for each game. **Player Eligibility Rule:** No player on active list may have three or more years of prior minor league service.
Brand of Baseball: Rawlings.
Umpires: Unavailable.

Jim McCurdy

STADIUM INFORMATION

Club	Stadium	Opened	Dimensions LF	CF	RF	Capacity	2015 Att.
Billings	Dehler Park	2008	329	410	350	3,071	100,120
Grand Junction	Sam Suplizio Field	1949	302	400	333	7,014	74,794
Great Falls	Centene Stadium at Legion Park	1956	335	414	335	3,800	45,414
Helena	Kindrick Field	1939	335	400	325	1,700	33,841
Idaho Falls	Melaleuca Field	1976	340	400	350	3,400	90,884
Missoula	Ogren Park at Allegiance Field	2004	309	398	287	3,500	77,438
Ogden	Lindquist Field	1997	335	396	334	5,000	125,398
Orem	Home of the Owlz	2005	305	408	312	4,500	85,733

BILLINGS MUSTANGS

Office Address: Dehler Park, 2611 9th Avenue North, Billings, MT 59101.
Mailing Address: PO Box 1553, Billings, MT 59103-1553.
Telephone: (406) 252-1241. **Fax:** (406) 252-2968.
E-Mail Address: mustangs@billingsmustangs.com. **Website:** billingsmustangs.com.
Affiliation (first year): Cincinnati Reds (1974). **Years in League:** 1948-63, 1969-

OWNERSHIP/MANAGEMENT
Operated By: Mustangs Baseball LLC. President / CEO: Dave Heller.
General Manager: Gary Roller. **Senior Director, Corporate Sales/Partnerships:** Chris Marshall. **Senior Director, Stadium Operations:** Matt Schoonover. **Senior Director, Broadcasting/Media Relations:** Kyle Riley. **Senior Director, Food and Beverage Services:** Curt Prchal. **Senior Director, Field Maintenance and Facilities:** John Barta.

FIELD STAFF
Manager: Ray Martinez. **Hitting Coach:** Joe Thurston. **Pitching Coach:** Seth Etherton. **Bench Coach:** Todd Takayoshi. **Strength Coach:** Trey Strickland. **Athletic Trainer:** Jesse Guffey.

GAME INFORMATION
Radio Broadcaster: Kyle Riley. **No. of Games Broadcast:** 76. **Flagship Station:** ESPN 910-AM KBLG.
PA Announcer: Rob Kovatch. **Official Scorer:** George Kimmet. **Stadium Name:** Dehler Park. **Location:** I-90 to Exit 450, north on 27th Street North to 9th Avenue North. **Standard Game Times:** Mon-Fri 7:05 pm, Sat. 6:05 pm, Sun. 1:05 pm. **Ticket Price Range:** $5 - $10.

GRAND JUNCTION ROCKIES

Address: 1315 North Ave. Grand Junction, CO 81501
Telephone: (970) 255-7625. **Fax:** (970) 241-2374
Email: timray@gjrockies.com. **Website:** www.gjrockies.com
Affiliation: Colorado Rockies 2001– . **Years in the Pioneer League:** 2001–.

OWNERSHIP/MANAGEMENT
Principal Owners / **Operated by:** GJR, LLC
President: Joe Kubly, **General Manager:** Tim Ray, **Assistant GM:** Mick Ritter.

FIELD STAFF
Developmental Supervisor: Tony Diaz, **Manager:** Frank Gonzalez, **Hitting Coach:** Unavailable. **Pitching Coach:** Ryan Kibler, **Trainer:** John Duff

GAME INFORMATION
Radio Announcer: Adam Spolane, **Number of Games Broadcast:** Full Schedule (76-Games). **Flagship Station:** KNZZ, 1100-AM. **Television Announcer:** Adam Spolane, **Number of Games Televised:** (All Home games -38). **Flagship:** KGJT – My Network, **Dish Network, Produced by:** Colorado Mesa University. **PA Announcer:** Ryan Bigley, **Official Scorers:** Chris Hanks, Dan Kenyon. **Stadium Name: Suplizio Field, Location:** 1315 North Ave. Grand Junction, CO 81501. **Standard Game Times:** (7:05 pm) **Friday Night Fireworks:** (6:30 pm)
Ticket Price Range: $7 - $10

GREAT FALLS VOYAGERS

Address: 1015 25th St N, Great Falls, MT 59401.
Telephone: (406) 452-5311. **Fax:** (406) 454-0811.
E-Mail Address: voyagers@gfvoyagers.com. **Website:** www.gfvoyagers.com.
Affiliation (first year): Chicago White Sox (2003). **Years in League:** 1948-1963, 1969-

OWNERSHIP/MANAGEMENT
Operated By: Great Falls Baseball Club, Inc. **President:** Vinney Purpura.
General Manager: Scott Reasoner. **Assistant GM:** Matt Coakley. **Sales Manager:** Scott Lettre.

FIELD STAFF
Manager: Tommy Thompson. **Hitting Coach:** Willie Harris. **Pitching Coach:** Matt Zaleski.

GAME INFORMATION
Radio Announcer: N/A. **No. of Games Broadcast:** 76. **Flagship Station:** KXGF-1400 AM.
PA Announcer: Chris Evans. **Official Scorer:** Mike Lewis.
Stadium Name: Centene Stadium. **Location:** From I-15 to exit 281 (10th Ave S), left on 26th, left on Eighth Ave North, right on 25th, ballpark on right, past railroad tracks.
Ticket Price Range: $5-10.
Visiting Club Hotel: Townhouse Inn of Great Falls, 1411 10th Ave S, Great Falls, MT 59405. **Telephone:** (406) 761-4600.

HELENA BREWERS

Office Address: 1300 N. Ewing, Helena, MT 59601. **Mailing Address:** PO Box 6756, Helena, MT 59604.
Telephone: (406) 495-0500. **Fax:** (406) 495-0900.
E-Mail Address: info@helenabrewers.net. **Website:** www.helenabrewers.net.
Affiliation (first year): Milwaukee Brewers (2003). **Years in League:** 1978-2000, 2003-

OWNERSHIP/MANAGEMENT
Operated by: Helena Baseball Club LLC. **Principal Owner:** David Elmore.
General Manager: Paul Fetz. **Director, Operations/Ticketing:** Travis Hawks. **Director, Group Sales/Marketing:** Dylan LaPlante. Radio Announcer/**Director, Broadcasting/Media Relations:** Dustin Daniel. Community Relations/ **Entertainment:** Helen Scholar.

FIELD STAFF
Manager: Tony Diggs. **Hitting Coach:** Jason Dubois. **Pitching Coach:** Rolando Valles.

GAME INFORMATION
Radio Announcer: Dustin Daniel. **No. of Games Broadcast:** 76. **Flagship Station:** Unavailable.
PA Announcer: Kevin Smith. **Official Scorers:** Chris Simonson, Jim Shope.
Stadium Name: Kindrick Field. **Location:** Cedar Street exit off I-15, west to Last Chance Gulch, left at Memorial Park.
Standard Game Time: 7:05 pm, Sun. 1:05. **Ticket Price Range:** $6-10.
Visiting Club Hotel: Red Lion Colonial. **Telephone:** (406) 443-2100.

IDAHO FALLS CHUKARS

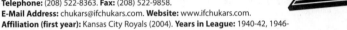

Office Address: 900 Jim Garchow Way, Idaho Falls, ID 83402. **Mailing
Address:** PO 2183, Idaho, ID 83403.
Telephone: (208) 522-8363. **Fax:** (208) 522-9858.
E-Mail Address: chukars@ifchukars.com. **Website:** www.ifchukars.com.
Affiliation (first year): Kansas City Royals (2004). **Years in League:** 1940-42, 1946-

OWNERSHIP/MANAGEMENT
Operated By: The Elmore Sports Group. **Principal Owner:** David Elmore.
President/General Manager: Kevin Greene. **Assistant GM:** Paul Henderson. **Director, Operations:** Alex Groh.
Clubhouse Manager: Patrick Greene. **Head Groundskeeper:** Ryan Coleman.

FIELD STAFF
Manager: Justin Gemoll. **Hitting Coach:** Andre David. **Pitching Coach:** Jeff Suppan.

GAME INFORMATION
Radio Announcer: John Balginy. **No. of Games Broadcast:** 76. **Flagship Station:** KUPI/ESPN 980-AM.
PA Announcer: Unavailable. **Official Scorer:** John Balginy.
Stadium Name: Melaleuca Field. **Location:** I-15 to West Broadway exit, left onto Memorial Drive, right on Mound
Avenue, 1/4 mile to stadium. **Standard Game Times:** 7:15 pm, Sun. 4:00. **Ticket Price Range:** $8-12.
Visiting Club Hotel: Guesthouse Inn & Suites, 850 Lindsay Blvd, Idaho Falls, ID 83402. **Telephone:** (208) 522-6260.

MISSOULA OSPREY

Address: 140 N Higgins, Suite 201, Missoula, MT 59802.
Telephone: (406) 543-3300. **Fax:** (406) 543-9463.
E-Mail Address: info@missoulaosprey.com. **Website:** www.missoulaosprey.com.
Affiliation (first year): Arizona Diamondbacks (1999). **Years in League:** 1956-60, 1999-

OWNERSHIP/MANAGEMENT
Operated By: Mountain Baseball LLC.
President: Mike Ellis. **Executive Vice Presidents:** Judy Ellis, Matt Ellis. **Vice President/General Manager:** Jeff Griffin.
Retail Manager: Kim Klages Johns. **Office Manager/Bookkeeper:** Nola Hunter. **Ticket Sales Executive:** Taylor Rush.

FIELD STAFF
Manager: Joe Mather. **Hitting Coach:** Franklin Stubbs. **Pitching Coach:** Darwin Peguero. **Strength/Conditioning:**
Mike Locasto. **Trainer:** Chris Schepel.

GAME INFORMATION
Radio Announcer: Tyler Geivett. **No. of Games Broadcast:** 76. **Flagship Station:** ESPN 102.9 FM.
PA Announcer: TBD. **Official Scorer:** TBD. **Stadium Name:** Ogren Park Allegiance Field. **Location:** Take Orange
Street to Cregg Lane, west on Cregg Lane, stadium west of McCormick Park past railroad trestle. **Standard Game
Times:** 7:05 pm, Sun. 5:05. **Ticket Price Range:** $6-15. **Visiting Club Hotel:** Comfort Inn-University, 1021 E. Broadway,
Missoula, MT 59802. **Telephone:** (406) 549-7600.

OGDEN RAPTORS

Address: 2330 Lincoln Ave, Ogden, UT 84401.
Telephone: (801) 393-2400. **Fax:** (801) 393-2473.
E-Mail Address: homerun@ogden-raptors.com. **Website:** www.ogden-raptors.com.
Affiliation (first year): Los Angeles Dodgers (2003). **Years in League:** 1939-42, 1946-
55, 1966-74, 1994-

OWNERSHIP/MANAGEMENT
Operated By: Ogden Professional Baseball, Inc. **Principal Owners:** Dave Baggott, John Lindquist.
President/General Manager: Dave Baggott. **Director Media Relations/Broadcaster:** Robbie Bullough. **Director,
Food Services:** Geri Kopinski. **Director, Security:** Scott McGregor. **Director, Ticket Operations:** Trevor Wilson.
Director, Information Technology: Chris Greene. **Public Relations:** Pete Diamond. **Groundskeeper:** Kenny Kopinski.

Assistant Groundkeeper: Bob Richardson.

FIELD STAFF

Manager: Shaun Larkin. **Hitting Coach:** Unavailable. **Pitching Coach:** Unavailable.

GAME INFORMATION

Radio Announcer: Brandon Hart. **No. of Games Broadcast:** 76. **Flagship Station:** 97.5 FM.
PA Announcer: Pete Diamond. **Official Scorer:** Dennis Kunimura.
Stadium Name: Lindquist Field. **Location:** I-15 North to 21th Street exit, east to Lincoln Avenue, south three blocks to park. **Standard Game Times:** 7 pm, Sun. 4. **Ticket Price Range:** $4-10.
Visiting Club Hotel: Unavailable.

OREM OWLZ

Address: 970 W. University Parkway, Orem, UT 84058.
Telephone: (801) 377-2255.
E-Mail Address: brett@oremowlz.com. **Website:** www.oremowlz.com.
Affiliation: Los Angeles Angels (2001). **Years in League:** 2001-.

OWNERSHIP/MANAGEMENT

Operated By: Bery Bery Gud To Me LLC. **Principal Owner:** Jeff Katofsky.
General Manager: Rick Berry. **Assistant GM:** Julie Hatch. **Director of Marketing:** Brett Stevens.

FIELD STAFF

Manager: Dave Stapleton. **Hitting Coach:** Alexis Gomez and Travis Adair. **Pitching Coach:** John Slusarz and Hector Astacio Strength and Conditioning Coach:** Tyler Gniadek.

GAME INFORMATION

Radio Announcer: Dominic Controneo **No. of Games Broadcast:** 76. **Flagship Station:** ESPN 960
PA Announcer: Unavailable. **Official Scorer:** Rachel Hartgrove.
Stadium Name: Home of the Owlz. **Location:** Exit 269 (University Parkway) off I-15 at Utah Valley University campus. **Ticket Price Range:** $5-12.
Visiting Club Hotel: Holiday Inn & Suites, 1290 W. University Parkway, Orem, UT 8405.

ARIZONA LEAGUE

Office Address: 620 W Franklin St., Boise, ID 83702. **Mailing Address:** PO Box 1645, Boise, ID 83701.
Telephone: (208) 429-1511. **Fax:** (208) 429-1525.
E-Mail Address: bobrichmond@qwestoffice.net
Years League Active: 1988-
President/Treasurer: Bob Richmond. **Vice President:** Mike Bell (Diamondbacks). **Corporate Secretary:** Ted
Polakowski (Athletics). **Administrative Assistant:** Rob Richmond.
Divisional Alignment: East—Angels, Athletics, Cubs, Diamondbacks, Giants. **Central**—Brewers, Dodgers, Indians,
Reds, White Sox. **West**—Mariners, Padres, Rangers, Royals.
Regular Season: 56 games (split schedule). **2015 Opening Date:** June 20. **Closing Date:** Aug 29.
Playoff Format: Division champions from the first and second half qualify (six teams). Two teams with best overall
records receive first-round bye. Remaining four teams meet in one-game playoffs. Winners advance to one-game
championship.
All-Star Game: None.
Roster Limit: 35 active. **Player Eligibility Rule:** No player may have three or more years of prior minor league service.

Clubs	Playing Site	Manager	Coach(es)	Pitching Coach
Angels	Angels Complex, Tempe	Elio Sarmiento	B. Betancourth/P. McAnulty	M. Wise/J. Van Eaton
Athletics	Papago Park Baseball Complex, Phoenix	Webster Garrison	Ruben Escalera	Unavailable
Brewers	Maryvale Baseball Complex, Phoenix	Tony Diggs	Hanley Statia	Steve Cline
Cubs	Fitch Park, Mesa	Carmelo Martinez	J. Farrell/C.Valaika	Ron Villone
D-backs	Salt River Fields at Talking Stick	Darrin Garner	Jacob Cruz	Manny Garcia
Dodgers	Camelback Ranch, Glendale	John Shoemaker	A. Bates/R. Fick	G. Sabat/S. Andrade
Giants	Giants complex, Scottsdale	Henry Cotto	Billy Horton	Mario Rodriguez
Indians	Goodyear Ballpark	Anthony Medrano	B.Magallanes/D. Malave	Mark Allen
Mariners	Peoria Sports Complex	Zac Livingston	Andy Bottin	Yoel Monzon
Padres	Peoria Sports Complex	Michael Collins	Doug Banks	Ben Fritz
Rangers	Surprise Recreation Campus	Matt Siegel	Chae Lambin	Joey Seaver
Reds	Goodyear Ballpark	Jose Nieves	Daryle Ward	Elmer Dessens
Royals	Goodyear Ballpark	Darryl Kennedy	Nelson Liriano	Mark Davis
White Sox	Camelback Ranch, Glendale	Mike Gellinger	Gary Ward	Felipe Lira

GULF COAST LEAGUE

Operated By: Minor League Baseball.
Office Address: 9550 16th Street North, St Petersburg, FL 33716.
Telephone: 727-456-1734. **Fax:** 727-456-1745. **Website:** www.milb.com. **Email Address:** gcl@milb.com.
Vice President, Baseball/Business Operations: Tim Brunswick. **Manager, Baseball & Business Operations:** Andy
Shultz.
2016 Opening Date: June 24. **Closing Date:** September 1. **Regular Season:** 56/60 Games.
Divisional Alignment: East—Astros, Cardinals, Marlins, Mets, Nationals. **Northeast**— Braves, Pirates, Tigers East,
Yankees East. **Northwest**—Blue Jays, Phillies, Tigers West, Yankees West. **South**—Orioles, Rays, Red Sox, Twins.
Playoff Format: The division winner with the best record plays the division winner with the lowest record and the
other two division winners meet in a one game semifinals. The winners meet in a best-of-three series for the Gulf Coast
League championship.
All-Star Game: None. **Roster Limit:** 35 active and in uniform and eligible to play in any given game. At least 10
must be pitchers as of July 1. **Player Eligibility Rule:** No player may have three or more years of prior minor league
service. **Brand of Baseball:** Rawlings. **Statistician:** Major League Baseball Advanced Media.

Clubs	Playing Site	Manager	Coach(es)	Pitching Coach
Astros	Astros Complex, Kissimmee	Marty Malloy	Luis Mateo, Wladimir Sutil	Erick Abreu
Blue Jays	Mattick Training Complex, Dunedin	Cesar Martin	Paul Elliott	Unavailable
Braves	Wide World of Sports, Orlando	Nestor Perez Jr.	Rick Albert	Mike Alvarez
Cardinals	Cardinals Complex, Jupiter	Steve Turco	Cody Gabella	Giovanni Carrara
Marlins	Roger Dean Stadium , Jupiter	Julio Bruno	Danny Santin	D. Ambrosini/M. Olivera
Mets	Mets Complex, Port St Lucie	Jose Carreno	Yunir Garcia	Royce Ring
Nationals	Nationals Complex, Viera	Josh Johnson	Jorge Mejia	Michael Tejera
Orioles	Ed Smith Stadium Complex, Sarasota	Orlando Gomez	Milt May, Kevin Bradshaw	Wilson Alvarez
Phillies	Carpenter Complex, Clearwater	Roly deArmas	Rafael DeLima, Eddie Dennis	Hector Mercado
Pirates	Pirate City, Bradenton	Milver Reyes	Kory DeHaan, Jason Erickson	Elvin Nina
Rays	Charlotte Sports Park, Port Charlotte	Jim Morrison	T. Francisco/H. Torres,	R. Valenzuela/M. DeMerritt
Red Sox	Jet Blue Park, Fort Myers	Tom Kotchman	J. Zamora/D. Tomlin	G. Gregorson, D. Such
Tigers 1	Tigertown, Lakeland	Rafael Gil	C. Jaime/R. Zapata	Carlos Bohorquez
Tigers 2	Tigertown, Lakeland	Rafael Martinez	German Geigel, Josman Robles	Nick Avila
Twins	Lee County Sports Complex, Fort Myers	Ramon Borrego	Javier Valentin, Steve Singleton	V. Vasquez, C. Bello
Yankees 1	Himes Complex, Tampa	Raul Dominguez	Kevin Mahoney, Leo Vinas	Elvys Quezada
Yankees 2	Himes Complex, Tampa	Julio Mosquera	Lino Diaz	Armando Galarraga

MINOR LEAGUE SCHEDULES

TRIPLE-A

INTERNATIONAL LEAGUE

BUFFALO BISONS

APRIL
7-10	at Pawtucket
11-13	at Syracuse
14-15	Rochester
16-17	Pawtucket
18-21	at Scranton/WB
22-24	at Rochester
26-28	Rochester
29-30	at Lehigh Valley

MAY
1	at Lehigh Valley
2-4	Scranton/WB
5-8	Syracuse
9-12	at Durham
13-15	at Norfolk
16-18	Toledo
19-22	Pawtucket
24-26	at Columbus
27-29	at Toledo
30-31	Columbus

JUNE
1	Columbus
2-3	Syracuse
4-5	at Syracuse
6-7	at Rochester
8-9	Rochester
10-12	Charlotte
13-15	Durham
17-19	at Lehigh Valley
20-23	Louisville
24-26	at Indianapolis
27-29	at Louisville
30	Scranton/WB

JULY
1-3	Scranton/WB
4-5	at Rochester
6-7	at Scranton/WB
8-10	Lehigh Valley
14-17	at Lehigh Valley
18-20	Norfolk
21-24	Gwinnett
25-27	at Scranton/WB
28-31	Syracuse

AUGUST
2-4	at Syracuse
5-7	at Pawtucket
9-11	Indianapolis
12-14	Pawtucket
15-17	Rochester
18-19	at Rochester
20-22	at Charlotte
23-25	at Gwinnett
26-29	Lehigh Valley
30-31	Scranton/WB

SEPTEMBER
1	Scranton/WB
2-3	at Scranton/WB
4-5	at Pawtucket

CHARLOTTE KNIGHTS

APRIL
7-10	at Durham
11-13	at Norfolk
14-17	Durham
18-20	Norfolk
21-22	Gwinnett
23-25	at Toledo
26-28	at Columbus
29-30	Toledo

MAY
1	Toledo
2-4	Columbus
6-8	at Gwinnett
9-12	at Norfolk
13-15	Durham
16-18	Rochester
19-20	at Gwinnett
21-22	Gwinnett
24-26	at Syracuse
27-29	at Rochester
30-31	Syracuse

JUNE
1	Syracuse
2-5	Lehigh Valley
6-9	at Scranton/WB
10-12	at Buffalo
13-15	Norfolk
17-19	Indianapolis

COLUMBUS CLIPPERS

APRIL
7-10	Indianapolis
20-23	at Durham
24-26	at Gwinnett
27-29	Durham
30	at Lehigh Valley

JULY
1-3	at Lehigh Valley
4-6	Pawtucket
7-10	Gwinnett
14-17	at Pawtucket
18-20	Scranton/WB
21-24	at Indianapolis
25-27	at Louisville
29-31	Columbus

AUGUST
1-4	at Gwinnett
5-7	Norfolk
9-11	Louisville
12-14	at Durham
15-17	Gwinnett
18-19	at Gwinnett
20-22	Buffalo
23-25	Durham
26-28	at Norfolk
29-31	at Louisville

SEPTEMBER
1-3	Norfolk
4-5	Gwinnett

APRIL *(Columbus Clippers continued)*
11-13	Louisville
14-17	at Indianapolis
18-20	at Louisville
21-22	Toledo
23-25	Gwinnett
26-28	Charlotte
29-30	at Gwinnett

MAY
1	at Gwinnett
2-4	at Charlotte
6-8	at Toledo
9-12	Lehigh Valley
13-15	Louisville
16-19	at Indianapolis
20-22	at Louisville
24-26	Buffalo
27-29	Durham
30-31	at Buffalo

JUNE
1	at Buffalo
2-5	at Scranton/WB
6-9	Indianapolis
10-12	Scranton/WB
14-16	at Rochester
17-19	at Syracuse
20-23	Rochester
24-26	Norfolk
27-29	at Lehigh Valley

DURHAM BULLS

APRIL
7-10	Charlotte
11-13	Gwinnett
14-17	at Charlotte
18-20	at Gwinnett
21-23	at Norfolk
24-26	Indianapolis
27-29	Louisville
30	at Louisville

MAY
1	at Louisville
2-4	at Indianapolis
6-8	Norfolk
9-12	Buffalo
13-15	at Charlotte
16-18	at Gwinnett
19-22	Rochester
24-26	at Toledo
27-29	at Columbus
30-31	Scranton/WB

JUNE
1	Scranton/WB
2-5	Gwinnett
6-7	at Norfolk
8-9	Norfolk
10-12	at Lehigh Valley
13-15	at Buffalo
17-19	at Norfolk

JULY *(Durham continued)*
30	at Pawtucket

JULY
1-3	at Pawtucket
4-6	Toledo
7-8	at Louisville
9-10	Indianapolis
14-17	at Toledo
18-20	Louisville
21-24	Pawtucket
26-28	at Norfolk
29-31	at Charlotte

AUGUST
1-4	Indianapolis
5-8	at Louisville
9-11	at Toledo
12-14	Syracuse
15-17	Durham
19-21	Toledo
22-24	at Indianapolis
25-26	at Toledo
27-28	Louisville
29-31	at Durham

SEPTEMBER
1-3	Toledo
4-5	at Toledo

APRIL *(Durham Bulls continued)*
20-23	Charlotte
24-26	Lehigh Valley
27-29	at Charlotte
30	at Norfolk

JULY
1-3	at Norfolk
4-6	Syracuse
7-10	Pawtucket
14-17	at Syracuse
18-20	at Rochester
21-24	at Scranton/WB
25-27	Toledo
29-31	Louisville

AUGUST
1-2	at Norfolk
3-4	Norfolk
5-7	Gwinnett
9-11	at Pawtucket
12-14	Charlotte
15-17	at Columbus
18-20	Norfolk
21-22	at Norfolk
23-25	at Charlotte
26-28	Gwinnett
29-31	Columbus

SEPTEMBER
1-3	at Gwinnett
4-5	Norfolk

GWINNETT BRAVES

APRIL
7-10	at Norfolk
11-13	at Durham
14-17	Norfolk
18-20	Durham
21-22	at Charlotte
23-25	at Columbus
26-28	at Toledo
29-30	Columbus

MAY
1	Columbus
2-4	Toledo
6-8	Charlotte
9-12	at Rochester
13-15	at Pawtucket
16-18	Durham
19-20	Charlotte
21-22	at Charlotte
23-25	at Norfolk

27-29 . . . . Syracuse
30-31 . . . . .Pawtucket

JUNE
1 . . . . .Pawtucket
2-5 . . . . .at Durham
6-9 . . . . Lehigh Valley
10-12 . . . . .Norfolk
14-16 . . . at Lehigh Valley
17-19 . . . at Scranton/WB
20-23 . . . . . .Indianapolis
24-26 . . . . Charlotte
27-29 . . . at Indianapolis
30 . . . . at Louisville

JULY
1-3 . . . . at Louisville
4-6 . . . . .Norfolk
7-10 . . . . at Charlotte
14-17 . . . . . Scranton/WB

18-20 . . . . . . at Syracuse
21-24 . . . . . . at Buffalo
26-28 . . . . . .Indianapolis
29-31 . . . . .at Toledo

AUGUST
1-4 . . . . Charlotte
5-7 . . . . . .at Durham
8-10 . . . . . . at Norfolk
12-14 . . . . Louisville
15-17 . . . . .at Charlotte
18-19 . . . . Charlotte
20-22 . . . . Rochester
23-25 . . . . Buffalo
26-28 . . . . .at Durham
29-31 . . . . .Norfolk

SEPTEMBER
1-3 . . . . Durham
4-5 . . . . . . .at Charlotte

INDIANAPOLIS INDIANS

APRIL
7-10 . . . . . . at Columbus
12-13 . . . . .at Toledo
14-17 . . . . . . .Columbus
18-20 . . . . Toledo
21-23 . . . . . .at Louisville
24-26 . . . . .at Durham
27-28 . . . . at Norfolk
29-30 . . . . .Norfolk

MAY
1 . . . . .Norfolk
2-4 . . . . Durham
6-8 . . . . Louisville
9-12 . . . . at Syracuse
13-15 . . . at Scranton/WB
16-19 . . . . . .Columbus
20-22 . . . . . Scranton/WB
24-26 . . . . . at Rochester
27-29 . . . . . at Pawtucket
30-31 . . . . . . Rochester

JUNE
1-2 . . . . Rochester
3-5 . . . . .at Toledo
6-9 . . . . . . at Columbus
10-12 . . . . . . .Syracuse
14-16 . . . . .Pawtucket
17-19 . . .at Charlotte
20-23 . . . . . .at Gwinnett

24-26 . . . . Buffalo
27-29 . . . . Gwinnett
30 . . . . .at Toledo

JULY
1-3 . . . . .at Toledo
4-6 . . . . Louisville
7-8 . . . . .Toledo
9-10 . . . . . . at Columbus
14-17 . . . . .at Louisville
18-20 . . . . . Lehigh Valley
21-24 . . . . Charlotte
26-28 . . . .at Gwinnett
29-31 . . . . .Norfolk

AUGUST
1-4 . . . . . . at Columbus
5-8 . . . . Toledo
9-11 . . . . at Buffalo
12-14 . . . at Lehigh Valley
15-17 . . . . . . Louisville
19-21 . . . . at Louisville
22-24 . . . . . .Columbus
25-26 . . . . . Louisville
27-28 . . . . .at Toledo
29-31 . . . . Toledo

SEPTEMBER
1-3 . . . . Louisville
4-5 . . . . . . .at Louisville

LEHIGH VALLEY IRONPIGS

APRIL
7-10 . . . . . . at Syracuse
11-13 . . . . at Rochester
14-15 . . . . . .Pawtucket
16-17 . . . . . . Rochester
18-19 . . . . . .Syracuse
20-21 . . . . at Syracuse
22-24 . . . . at Pawtucket
25-27 . . . at Scranton/WB
29-30 . . . . Buffalo

MAY
1 . . . . Buffalo
2-4 . . . . .Pawtucket
5-6 . . . . . . Scranton/WB
7-8 . . . . . at Scranton/WB
9-12 . . . . . at Columbus
13-15 . . . . .at Toledo
16-18 . . . . . .Syracuse
19-22 . . . . Toledo
24-26 . . . at Pawtucket
27-29 . . . . . . Louisville
30-31 . . . . .Norfolk

JUNE
1 . . . . .Norfolk
2-5 . . . . .at Charlotte
6-9 . . . . .at Gwinnett
10-12 . . . . Durham
14-16 . . . . . . Gwinnett
17-19 . . . . Buffalo
20-23 . . . . . at Norfolk
24-26 . . . . .at Durham
27-29 . . . . . .Columbus
30 . . . . Charlotte

JULY
1-3 . . . . Charlotte
4-5 . . . . at Scranton/WB
6-7 . . . . Rochester
8-10 . . . . . . at Buffalo
14-17 . . . . Buffalo
18-20 . . . . at Indianapolis
21-24 . . . . .at Louisville
25-27 . . . . . . .Syracuse
29-31 . . . . . at Rochester

AUGUST
1-4 . . . . Scranton/WB
5-7 . . . . Rochester
9-11 . . . . at Scranton/WB
12-14 . . . . . .Indianapolis
15-17 . . . . . .Pawtucket
18-21 . . . . . . at Syracuse

LOUISVILLE BATS

APRIL
7-10 . . . . .at Toledo
11-13 . . . . . at Columbus
14-17 . . . . Toledo
18-20 . . . . . . .Columbus
21-23 . . . . .Indianapolis
24-26 . . . . . . at Norfolk
27-29 . . . . .at Durham
30 . . . . Durham

MAY
1 . . . . Durham
2-4 . . . . .Norfolk
6-8 . . . .at Indianapolis
9-12 . . . . .at Toledo
13-15 . . . . at Columbus
16-19 . . . . . Scranton/WB
20-22 . . . . . .Columbus
24-26 . . . at Scranton/WB
27-29 . . at Lehigh Valley
30-31 . . . . Toledo

JUNE
1-2 . . . . Toledo
3-5 . . . . Rochester
6-9 . . . . . . at Syracuse
10-12 . . . . at Pawtucket
13-15 . . . . .Syracuse
17-19 . . . . . . .Pawtucket
20-23 . . . . at Buffalo

24-26 . . . . . at Rochester
27-29 . . . . Buffalo
30 . . . . Gwinnett

JULY
1-3 . . . . Gwinnett
4-6 . . . . . . at Indianapolis
7-8 . . . . Columbus
9-10 . . . . .at Toledo
14-17 . . . . .Indianapolis
18-20 . . . . at Columbus
21-24 . . . . . Lehigh Valley
25-27 . . . . Charlotte
29-31 . . . . . .at Durham

AUGUST
1-2 . . . . .at Toledo
3-4 . . . . Toledo
5-8 . . . . .Columbus
9-11 . . . . . . .at Charlotte
12-14 . . . . . at Gwinnett
15-17 . . . . at Indianapolis
19-21 . . . . . .Indianapolis
22-24 . . . . Toledo
25-26 . . . at Indianapolis
27-28 . . . . at Columbus
29-31 . . . . Charlotte

SEPTEMBER
1-3 . . . . . . at Indianapolis
4-5 . . . . .Indianapolis

NORFOLK TIDES

APRIL
7-10 . . . . Gwinnett
11-13 . . . . Charlotte
14-17 . . . . . .at Gwinnett
18-20 . . . . .at Charlotte
21-23 . . . . . . Durham
24-26 . . . . . . Louisville
27-28 . . . . .Indianapolis
29-30 . . . . at Indianapolis

MAY
1 . . . . at Indianapolis
2-4 . . . . . . at Louisville
6-8 . . . . .at Durham
9-12 . . . . Charlotte
13-15 . . . . Buffalo
16-18 . . . . . . at Pawtucket
19-22 . . . . . at Syracuse
23-25 . . . . . . Gwinnett
27-29 . . . . . Scranton/WB
30-31 . . at Lehigh Valley

JUNE
1 . . . . . . at Lehigh Valley
2-5 . . . . .Pawtucket
6-7 . . . . Durham
8-9 . . . . .at Durham
10-12 . . . . . at Gwinnett
13-15 . . . . . .at Charlotte
17-19 . . . . Durham

20-23 . . . . . Lehigh Valley
24-26 . . . . at Columbus
27-29 . . . . . .at Toledo
30 . . . . Durham

JULY
1-3 . . . . Durham
4-6 . . . . .at Gwinnett
7-10 . . . . .Syracuse
14-17 . . . . . at Rochester
18-20 . . . . . . at Buffalo
21-24 . . . . Toledo
26-28 . . . . . . .Columbus
29-31 . . . at Indianapolis

AUGUST
1-2 . . . . Durham
3-4 . . . . .at Durham
5-7 . . . . . . .at Charlotte
8-10 . . . . Gwinnett
12-14 . . . . Toledo
15-17 . . . at Scranton/WB
18-20 . . . . . . .at Durham
21-22 . . . . Durham
23-25 . . . . Rochester
26-28 . . . . Charlotte
29-31 . . . . . . at Gwinnett

SEPTEMBER
1-3 . . . . .at Charlotte
4-5 . . . . .at Durham

PAWTUCKET RED SOX

APRIL
7-10 . . . . Buffalo
11-13 . . . . . Scranton/WB
14-15 . . . . at Lehigh Valley
16-17 . . . . at Buffalo
18-21 . . . . . at Rochester
22-24 . . . . . Lehigh Valley
25-26 . . . . Syracuse
28-30 . . . . at Syracuse

MAY
1 . . . . at Syracuse
2-4 . . . . . at Lehigh Valley
5-8 . . . . Rochester
9-12 . . . . at Scranton/WB
13-15 . . . . Gwinnett
16-18 . . . . .Norfolk
19-22 . . . . . at Buffalo
24-26 . . . . . Lehigh Valley
27-29 . . . . . .Indianapolis
30-31 . . . . . . at Gwinnett

JUNE
1 . . . . at Gwinnett
2-5 . . . . at Norfolk
6-9 . . . . Toledo
10-12 . . . . Louisville
14-16 . . . at Indianapolis
17-19 . . . . . at Louisville

20-23 . . . . Syracuse
24-26 . . . . . . Scranton/WB
27-29 . . . . . at Rochester
30 . . . . Columbus

JULY
1-3 . . . . Columbus
4-6 . . . . .at Charlotte
7-10 . . . . .at Durham
14-17 . . . . Charlotte
18-20 . . . . .at Toledo
21-24 . . . . at Columbus
25-28 . . . . . . Rochester
29-31 . . . . Scranton/WB

AUGUST
2-4 . . . . . . at Rochester
5-7 . . . . Buffalo
9-11 . . . . Durham
12-14 . . . . . . at Buffalo
15-17 . . at Lehigh Valley
18-21 . . at Scranton/WB
22-23 . . . . Syracuse
24-25 . . . . . Lehigh Valley
26-29 . . . . . at Syracuse
30-31 . . . at Lehigh Valley

SEPTEMBER
1-3 . . . . Syracuse
4-5 . . . . Buffalo

ROCHESTER RED WINGS

APRIL
7-8 . . . . . at Scranton/WB
9-10 . . . . . Scranton/WB
11-13 . . . . . Lehigh Valley
14-15 . . . . . . at Buffalo
16-17 . . . . at Lehigh Valley
18-21 . . . . .Pawtucket
22-24 . . . . Buffalo
26-28 . . . . . at Buffalo
29-30 . . . . . Scranton/WB

MAY
1 . . . . Scranton/WB
2-4 . . . . at Syracuse
5-8 . . . . . . at Pawtucket
9-12 . . . . Gwinnett
13-15 . . . . Syracuse
16-18 . . . . . at Charlotte
19-22 . . . . . .at Durham
24-26 . . . . . .Indianapolis
27-29 . . . . . . Charlotte
30-31 . . . . at Indianapolis

JUNE
1-2 . . . . . . at Indianapolis
3-5 . . . . at Louisville
6-7 . . . . Buffalo
8-9 . . . . . . at Buffalo
10-12 . . . . Toledo
14-16 . . . . . .Columbus
17-19 . . . . . .at Toledo
20-23 . . . . . at Columbus

24-26 . . . . Louisville
27-29 . . . . . . .Pawtucket
30 . . . . Syracuse

JULY
1 . . . . Syracuse
2-3 . . . . at Syracuse
4-5 . . . . Buffalo
6-7 . . . . at Lehigh Valley
8-10 . . . at Scranton/WB
14-17 . . . . .Norfolk
18-20 . . . . Durham
21-22 . . . . Syracuse
23-24 . . . . . at Syracuse
25-28 . . . . . at Pawtucket
29-31 . . . . . Lehigh Valley

AUGUST
2-4 . . . . .Pawtucket
5-7 . . . . at Lehigh Valley
9-11 . . . . . . at Syracuse
12-14 . . . . Scranton/WB
15-17 . . . . . . at Buffalo
18-19 . . . . Buffalo
20-22 . . . . . .at Gwinnett
23-25 . . . . at Norfolk
26-27 . . . . at Scranton/WB
28-29 . . . . . Scranton/WB
30-31 . . . . Syracuse

SEPTEMBER
1-2 . . . . . . Lehigh Valley
3-5 . . . . . at Lehigh Valley

SCRANTON/WILKES-BARRE RAILRIDERS

APRIL
7-8 . . . . Rochester
9-10 . . . . . at Rochester
11-13 . . . . . at Pawtucket
14-17 . . . . Syracuse
18-21 . . . . Buffalo
22-24 . . . . at Syracuse
25-27 . . . . . Lehigh Valley

29-30 . . . . . . at Rochester

MAY
1 . . . . at Rochester
2-4 . . . . at Buffalo
5-6 . . . . at Lehigh Valley
7-8 . . . . . Lehigh Valley
9-12 . . . . .Pawtucket
13-15 . . . . . .Indianapolis

16-19 . . . . . .at Louisville
20-22 . . at Indianapolis
24-26 . . . . . . Louisville
27-29 . . . . . at Norfolk
30-31 . . . . . .at Durham

JUNE
1 . . . . .at Durham
2-5 . . . . Columbus
6-9 . . . . Charlotte
10-12 . . . . at Columbus
13-16 . . . . . .at Toledo
17-19 . . . . . Gwinnett
21-23 . . . . Toledo
24-26 . . . at Pawtucket
27-29 . . . . at Syracuse
30 . . . . . . at Buffalo

JULY
1-3 . . . . . . at Buffalo
4-5 . . . . Lehigh Valley
6-7 . . . . Buffalo
8-10 . . . . . Rochester

SYRACUSE CHIEFS

APRIL
7-10 . . . . Lehigh Valley
11-13 . . . . . . Buffalo
14-17 . . . at Scranton/WB
18-19 . . . at Lehigh Valley
20-21 . . . . Lehigh Valley
22-24 . . . . Scranton/WB
25-26 . . . . at Pawtucket
28-30 . . . . . . .Pawtucket

MAY
1 . . . . .Pawtucket
2-4 . . . . Rochester
5-8 . . . . at Buffalo
9-12 . . . . .Indianapolis
13-15 . . . . at Rochester
16-18 . . at Lehigh Valley
19-22 . . . . .Norfolk
24-26 . . . . . Charlotte
27-29 . . .at Gwinnett
30-31 . . . . at Charlotte

JUNE
1 . . . . .at Charlotte
2-3 . . . . at Buffalo
4-5 . . . . Buffalo
6-9 . . . . Louisville
10-12 . . at Indianapolis
13-15 . . . at Louisville
17-19 . . . . Columbus
20-23 . . . . at Pawtucket

24-26 . . . . Toledo
27-29 . . . . Scranton/WB
30 . . . . . at Rochester

JULY
1 . . . . at Rochester
2-3 . . . . Rochester
4-6 . . . . .at Durham
7-10 . . . . . . at Norfolk
14-17 . . . . . . Durham
18-20 . . . . . . Gwinnett
21-22 . . at Rochester
23-24 . . . . . Rochester
25-27 . . at Lehigh Valley
28-31 . . . . . at Buffalo

AUGUST
2-4 . . . . Buffalo
5-7 . . . . at Scranton/WB
9-11 . . . . . Rochester
12-14 . . . at Columbus
15-17 . . . . .at Toledo
18-21 . . . . Lehigh Valley
22-23 . . . . at Pawtucket
24-25 . . . . Scranton/WB
26-29 . . . . . .Pawtucket
30-31 . . . . at Rochester

SEPTEMBER
1-3 . . . . at Pawtucket
4-5 . . . . . at Scranton/WB

TOLEDO MUD HENS

APRIL
7-10 . . . . Louisville
12-13 . . . .Indianapolis
14-17 . . . .at Louisville
18-20 . . . at Indianapolis
21-22 . . . . at Columbus
23-25 . . . . . . Charlotte
26-28 . . . . . . Gwinnett
29-30 . . . . .at Charlotte

MAY
1 . . . . .at Charlotte
2-4 . . . . .at Gwinnett
6-8 . . . . . . Columbus
9-12 . . . . . Louisville
13-15 . . . Lehigh Valley
16-18 . . . . . at Buffalo
19-22 . . at Lehigh Valley
24-26 . . . . Durham

27-29 . . . . Buffalo
30-31 . . . . . .at Louisville

JUNE
1-2 . . . . . . .at Louisville
3-5 . . . . .Indianapolis
6-9 . . . . . . at Pawtucket
10-12 . . . . at Rochester
13-16 . . . . . Scranton/WB
17-19 . . . . . . Rochester
21-23 . . . at Scranton/WB
24-26 . . . . at Syracuse
27-29 . . . . .Norfolk
30 . . . . .Indianapolis

JULY
1-3 . . . . .Indianapolis
4-6 . . . . . at Columbus
7-8 . . at Indianapolis
9-10 . . . . Louisville

14-17 . . . . Columbus
18-20 . . . . Pawtucket
21-24 . . . . at Norfolk
25-27 . . . . . . .at Durham
29-31 . . . . Gwinnett

AUGUST
1-2. . . . . Louisville
3-4. . . . . at Louisville
5-8. . . . . . at Indianapolis
9-11 . . . . Columbus
12-14 . . . . at Norfolk

15-17 . . . . Syracuse
19-21 . . . . . at Columbus
22-24 . . . . . at Louisville
25-26 . . . . Columbus
27-28 . . . . . . .Indianapolis
29-31 . . . . .at Indianapolis

SEPTEMBER
1-3 . . . . at Columbus
4-5 . . . . Columbus
6-7 . . . . at Columbus

PACIFIC COAST LEAGUE

ALBUQUERQUE ISOTOPES

APRIL
7-10 . . . . . . at Tacoma
11-14 . . . . .at Reno
15-18 . . . . .Tacoma
19-22 . . . . Reno
23-26 . . . . . .at Las Vegas
28-30 . . . . .at Reno

MAY
1 . . . . .at Reno
2-5 . . . . Sacramento
6-9 . . . . .Tacoma
10-13 . . . . . at Salt Lake
14-17 . . . . . .Round Rock
19-22 . . . . . New Orleans
23-26 . . . . . . at Omaha
27-30 . . . . .at Iowa
31 . . . . Fresno

JUNE
1-3 . . . . Fresno
4-7 . . . . . . at Sacramento
9-12 . . . . Las Vegas
13-16 . . . . . . at El Paso
17-20 . . . . Reno
21-24 . . . . .at Fresno

25-28 . . . . Salt Lake
30 . . . . . . at Sacramento

JULY
1-3 . . . . . . at Sacramento
4-6. . . . . El Paso
7-9 . . . . .at Las Vegas
14-17 . . . . Memphis
18-21 . . . . .Nashville
22-25 . . . . .at Fresno
26-29 . . . . Salt Lake
30-31 . . . . . . at Tacoma

AUGUST
1-2 . . . . at Tacoma
3-6 . . . . Sacramento
7-10 . . . . Las Vegas
12-15 . . . . . at Col. Springs
16-19 . . . . . .at Okla. City
20-23 . . . . Fresno
24-28 . . . . El Paso
29-31 . . . . . . at Salt Lake

SEPTEMBER
1 . . . . at Salt Lake
2-5 . . . . at El Paso

COLORADO SPRINGS SKY SOX

APRIL
7-10 . . . . . . at Memphis
11-14 . . . . . . at Nashville
15-18 . . . . Memphis
19-22 . . . . .Nashville
23-26 . . . . . . at Omaha
28-30 . . . . at Iowa

MAY
1 . . . . at Iowa
2-5 . . . . .Round Rock
6-9 . . . . Okla. City
10-13 . . . .at New Orleans
14-17 . . . . .Salt Lake
19-22 . . . . . . Las Vegas
23-26 . . . . at Sacramento
27-30 . . . . .at Fresno
31 . . . . Omaha

JUNE
1-3 . . . . Omaha
4-7 . . . . . .at New Orleans
9-12 . . . . . . .at Memphis
13-16 . . . . Iowa
17-20 . . . . Omaha
21-24 . . . . Memphis

25-28 . . . . . at Round Rock
30 . . . . New Orleans

JULY
1-3 . . . . New Orleans
4-6. . . . . . .at Okla. City
7-10 . . . . Iowa
14-17 . . . . .at Tacoma
18-21 . . . . .at Reno
22-25 . . . . . . .Round Rock
26-29 . . . . . at Nashville
30-31 . . . . Okla. City

AUGUST
1-2 . . . . Okla. City
3-6 . . . . .Nashville
7-10 . . . . at Omaha
12-15 . . . . . . Albuquerque
16-19 . . . . El Paso
20-23 . . . . at Round Rock
24-28 . . . . .at Okla. City
29-31 . . . . . New Orleans

SEPTEMBER
1 . . . . New Orleans
2-5 . . . . .at Iowa

EL PASO CHIHUAHUAS

APRIL
7-10 . . . . .at Reno
11-14 . . . . at Tacoma

15-18 . . . . Reno
19-22 . . . . .Tacoma
23-26 . . . . . . at Salt Lake

28-30 . . . . .at Fresno

MAY
1 . . . . .at Fresno
2-5 . . . . Las Vegas
6-9 . . . . Fresno
10-13 . . . .at Las Vegas
14-17 . . . . . New Orleans
19-22 . . . . . .Round Rock
23-26 . . . . .at Iowa
27-30 . . . . . . at Omaha
31 . . . . .Sacramento

JUNE
1-3 . . . . .Sacramento
4-7 . . . . .at Fresno
9-12 . . . . .Sacramento
13-16 . . . . . . Albuquerque
17-20 . . . . at Sacramento
21-24 . . . . .Salt Lake
25-28 . . . . .at Reno
30 . . . . .Reno

FRESNO GRIZZLIES

APRIL
7-10 . . . . . .at Las Vegas
11-14 . . . . at Salt Lake
15-18 . . . . Las Vegas
19-22 . . . . Salt Lake
23-26 . . . . .at Reno
28-30 . . . . El Paso

MAY
1 . . . . El Paso
2-5 . . . . Reno
6-9 . . . . at El Paso
10-13 . . . . .Tacoma
14-17 . . . . . at Nashville
19-22 . . . . . . at Memphis
23-26 . . . . . . Okla. City
27-30 . . . . . .Col. Springs
31 . . . . . at Albuquerque

JUNE
1-3 . . . . . at Albuquerque
4-7 . . . . El Paso
9-12 . . . . .Salt Lake
13-16 . . . . at Sacramento
17-20 . . . . . . .at Tacoma
21-24 . . . . . Albuquerque

25-28 . . . . .Tacoma
30 . . . . at Salt Lake

JULY
1-3 . . . . at Salt Lake
4-6. . . . . .Sacramento
7-10 . . . . Reno
14-17 . . .at New Orleans
18-21 . . . . at Round Rock
22-25 . . . . . Albuquerque
26-29 . . . . . Las Vegas
30-31 . . . . .at Reno

AUGUST
1-2 . . . . at Reno
3-6 . . . . . . .at Las Vegas
7-10 . . . . . . at El Paso
12-15 . . . . Iowa
16-19 . . . . .Omaha
20-23 . . . . at Albuquerque
24-28 . . . . . . Sacramento
29-31 . . . . . . at Tacoma

SEPTEMBER
1 . . . . at Tacoma
2-5 . . . . . . at Sacramento

IOWA CUBS

APRIL
7-10 . . . . .Round Rock
11-14 . . . . . New Orleans
15-18 . . . . at Round Rock
19-22 . . . .at New Orleans
23-26 . . . . . . Okla. City
28-30 . . . . . .Col. Springs

MAY
1 . . . . .Col. Springs
2-5 . . . . . . at Nashville
6-9 . . . . at Omaha
10-13 . . . . .Nashville
14-17 . . . . .at Reno
19-22 . . . . at Tacoma
23-26 . . . . El Paso
27-30 . . . . . . Albuquerque
31 . . . . .at Okla. City

JUNE
1-3 . . . . .at Okla. City
4-7 . . . . Memphis
9-12 . . . . .Round Rock
13-16 . . . . at Col. Springs
17-20 . . . . at Memphis
21-24 . . . . .Nashville

25-28 . . . . . .at Okla. City
30 . . . . . . at Round Rock

JULY
1-3 . . . . at Round Rock
4-6. . . . . .Omaha
7-10 . . . . at Col. Springs
14-17 . . . . . . Las Vegas
18-21 . . . . Salt Lake
22-25 . . . . . .at Memphis
26-29 . . . .at New Orleans
30-31 . . . . . . at Omaha

AUGUST
1-2 . . . . at Omaha
3-6 . . . . New Orleans
7-10 . . . . Okla. City
12-15 . . . . .at Fresno
16-19 . . . . at Sacramento
20-23 . . . . Memphis
25-28 . . . . .Omaha
29-31 . . . . . at Nashville

SEPTEMBER
1 . . . . at Nashville
2-5. . . . . Col. Springs

LAS VEGAS 51S

APRIL	
7-10 . . . . Fresno
11-14 . . . . . . .Sacramento
15-18 . . . . .at Fresno
19-22 . . . . at Sacramento
23-26 . . . . . Albuquerque
28-30 . . . . .Tacoma

MAY	
1 . . . . .Tacoma
2-5 . . . . at El Paso
6-9 . . . . at Sacramento
10-13 . . . . El Paso
14-17 . . . . . .at Okla. City
19-22 . . . . at Col. Springs
23-26 . . . . .Nashville
27-30 . . . . Memphis
31 . . . . .at Reno

JUNE	
1-3 . . . . .at Reno
4-7 . . . . .Tacoma
9-12 . . . . at Albuquerque
13-16 . . . . Reno
17-20 . . . . . at Salt Lake
21-24 . . . . .at Reno

25-28 . . . . . . Sacramento
30 . . . . at Tacoma

JULY	
1-3 . . . . at Tacoma
4-6 . . . . .Salt Lake
7-9 . . . . Albuquerque
14-17 . . . . at Iowa
18-21 . . . . at Omaha
22-25 . . . . Reno
26-29 . . . . .at Fresno
30-31 . . . . El Paso

AUGUST	
1-2 . . . . El Paso
3-6 . . . . Fresno
7-10 . . . . at Albuquerque
12-15 . . . . . New Orleans
16-19 . . . . . .Round Rock
20-23 . . . . at Tacoma
24-27 . . . . . . .Salt Lake
29-31 . . . . at El Paso

SEPTEMBER	
1 . . . . at El Paso
2-5 . . . . at Salt Lake

MEMPHIS REDBIRDS

APRIL	
7-10 . . . . Col. Springs
11-14 . . . . Okla. City
15-18 . . . . at Col. Springs
19-22 . . . . . .at Okla. City
23-26 . . . . . . .Round Rock
28-30 . . . .at New Orleans

MAY	
1 . . . . .at New Orleans
2-5 . . . . .Omaha
6-9 . . . . at Nashville
10-13 . . . . at Omaha
14-17 . . . . . .Sacramento
19-22 . . . . Fresno
23-26 . . . . . at Salt Lake
27-30 . . . . .at Las Vegas
31 . . . . New Orleans

JUNE	
1-3 . . . . New Orleans
4-7 . . . . .at Iowa
9-12 . . . . . . Col. Springs
13-16 . . . . . . at Nashville
17-20 . . . . Iowa
21-24 . . . . at Col. Springs

25-28 . . . . . New Orleans
30 . . . . at Omaha

JULY	
1-3 . . . . at Omaha
4-6 . . . . .Nashville
7-10 . . . . .Round Rock
14-17 . . . . at Albuquerque
18-21 . . . . at El Paso
22-25 . . . . Iowa
26-29 . . . . Okla. City
30-31 . . . . at Round Rock

AUGUST	
1-2 . . . . . at Round Rock
3-6 . . . . .Omaha
7-10 . . . .at New Orleans
12-15 . . . . .Tacoma
16-19 . . . . Reno
20-23 . . . . .at Iowa
24-28 . . . . .Nashville
29-31 . . . . . .at Okla. City

SEPTEMBER	
1 . . . . .at Okla. City
2-5 . . . . . . at Round Rock

NASHVILLE SOUNDS

APRIL	
7-10 . . . . Okla. City
11-14 . . . . . . .Col. Springs
15-18 . . . . .at Okla. City
19-22 . . . . at Col. Springs
23-26 . . . . . New Orleans
28-30 . . . . at Round Rock

MAY	
1 . . . . at Round Rock
2-5 . . . . Iowa
6-9 . . . . Memphis
10-13 . . . . .at Iowa
14-17 . . . . Fresno
19-22 . . . . . .Sacramento
23-26 . . . .at Las Vegas
27-30 . . . . . . at Salt Lake
31 . . . . .Round Rock

JUNE	
1-3 . . . . .Round Rock
4-7 . . . . at Omaha
9-12 . . . . . .at Okla. City
13-16 . . . . Memphis
17-20 . . . . . .Round Rock
21-24 . . . . .at Iowa
25-28 . . . . .Omaha
30 . . . . Okla. City

JULY	
1-3 . . . . Okla. City
4-6 . . . . at Memphis
7-10 . . . . . . New Orleans
14-17 . . . . at El Paso
18-21 . . . . at Albuquerque
22-25 . . . . .Omaha
26-29 . . . . . . Col. Springs

NEW ORLEANS ZEPHYRS

APRIL	
7-10 . . . . at Omaha
11-14 . . . . .at Iowa
15-18 . . . . .Omaha
19-22 . . . . Iowa
23-26 . . . . . at Nashville
28-30 . . . . Memphis

MAY	
1 . . . . Memphis
2-5 . . . . .at Okla. City
6-9 . . . . . at Round Rock
10-13 . . . . . .Col. Springs
14-17 . . . . at El Paso
19-22 . . . . at Albuquerque
23-26 . . . . Reno
27-30 . . . . .Tacoma
31 . . . . at Memphis

JUNE	
1-3 . . . . at Memphis
4-7 . . . . .Col. Springs
9-12 . . . . .Omaha
13-16 . . . . at Round Rock
17-20 . . . . . . Okla. City
21-24 . . . . at Omaha

25-28 . . . . . . .at Memphis
30 . . . . . . at Col. Springs

JULY	
1-3 . . . . . . at Col. Springs
4-6 . . . . .Round Rock
7-10 . . . . at Nashville
14-17 . . . . Fresno
18-21 . . . . .Sacramento
22-25 . . . . . . .at Okla. City
26-29 . . . . Iowa
30-31 . . . . .Nashville

AUGUST	
1-2 . . . . .Nashville
3-6 . . . . .at Iowa
7-10 . . . . Memphis
12-15 . . . . . .at Las Vegas
16-19 . . . . . at Salt Lake
20-23 . . . . Okla. City
24-28 . . . . .Round Rock
29-31 . . . . at Col. Springs

SEPTEMBER	
1 . . . . at Col. Springs
2-5 . . . . .Nashville

OKLAHOMA CITY DODGERS

APRIL	
7-10 . . . . at Nashville
11-14 . . . . . . at Memphis
15-18 . . . . . . .Nashville
19-22 . . . . Memphis
23-26 . . . . . . .at Iowa
28-30 . . . . . . at Omaha

MAY	
1 . . . . at Omaha
2-5 . . . . New Orleans
6-9 . . . . . . at Col. Springs
10-13 . . . . at Round Rock
14-17 . . . . Las Vegas
19-22 . . . . . . .Salt Lake
23-26 . . . . . . .at Fresno
27-30 . . . at Sacramento
31 . . . . Iowa

JUNE	
1-3 . . . . Iowa
4-7 . . . . . at Round Rock
9-12 . . . . .Nashville
13-16 . . . . .Omaha
17-20 . . .at New Orleans
21-24 . . . . . .Round Rock

25-28 . . . . Iowa
30 . . . . at Nashville

JULY	
1-3 . . . . at Nashville
4-6 . . . . Col. Springs
7-10 . . . . .Omaha
14-17 . . . . .at Reno
18-21 . . . . at Tacoma
22-25 . . . . . New Orleans
26-29 . . . . . . .at Memphis
30-31 . . . . at Col. Springs

AUGUST	
1-2 . . . . . at Col. Springs
3-6 . . . . .Round Rock
7-10 . . . . .at Iowa
12-15 . . . . El Paso
16-19 . . . . Albuquerque
20-23 . . . .at New Orleans
24-28 . . . . . Col. Springs
29-31 . . . . Memphis

SEPTEMBER	
1 . . . . Memphis
2-5 . . . . at Omaha

OMAHA STORM CHASERS

APRIL	
7-10 . . . . . . New Orleans
11-14 . . . . . .Round Rock
15-18 . . . .at New Orleans
19-22 . . . . at Round Rock
23-26 . . . . . .Col. Springs
28-30 . . . . . Okla. City

MAY	
1 . . . . Okla. City
2-5 . . . . at Memphis
6-9 . . . . Iowa
10-13 . . . . Memphis
14-17 . . . . at Tacoma
19-22 . . . . .at Reno
23-26 . . . . . Albuquerque
27-30 . . . . El Paso

31 . . . . at Col. Springs

JUNE
1-3 . . . . . . at Col. Springs
4-7 . . . . Nashville
9-12 . . . . . at New Orleans
13-16 . . . . at Okla. City
17-20 . . . . at Col. Springs
21-24 . . . . New Orleans
25-28 . . . . at Nashville
30 . . . . Memphis

JULY
1-3 . . . . Memphis
4-6 . . . . at Iowa
7-10 . . . . . . at Okla. City
14-17 . . . . Salt Lake
18-21 . . . . Las Vegas

RENO ACES

APRIL
7-10 . . . . El Paso
11-14 . . . . . Albuquerque
15-18 . . . . . . at El Paso
19-22 . . . . at Albuquerque
23-26 . . . . Fresno
28-30 . . . . . Albuquerque

MAY
1 . . . . Albuquerque
2-5 . . . . at Fresno
6-9 . . . . at Salt Lake
10-13 . . . . . at Sacramento
14-17 . . . . Iowa
19-22 . . . . Omaha
23-26 . . . at New Orleans
27-30 . . . . at Round Rock
31 . . . . Las Vegas

JUNE
1-3 . . . . Las Vegas
4-7 . . . . Salt Lake
9-12 . . . . at Tacoma
13-16 . . . . . at Las Vegas
17-20 . . . . at Albuquerque
21-24 . . . . Las Vegas

ROUND ROCK EXPRESS

APRIL
7-10 . . . . at Iowa
11-14 . . . . at Omaha
15-18 . . . . Iowa
19-22 . . . . Omaha
23-26 . . . . . . at Memphis
28-30 . . . . Nashville

MAY
1 . . . . Nashville
2-5 . . . . . . at Col. Springs
6-9 . . . . New Orleans
10-13 . . . . Okla. City
14-17 . . . at Albuquerque
19-22 . . . . . . at El Paso
23-26 . . . . Tacoma
27-30 . . . . Reno
31 . . . . at Nashville

JUNE
1-3 . . . . at Nashville
4-7 . . . . Okla. City
9-12 . . . . at Iowa
13-16 . . . . . New Orleans
17-20 . . . . . at Nashville
21-24 . . . . . . at Okla. City

22-25 . . . . . . at Nashville
26-29 . . . . at Round Rock
30-31 . . . . Iowa

AUGUST
1-2 . . . . Iowa
3-6 . . . . at Memphis
7-10 . . . . Col. Springs
12-15 . . . at Sacramento
16-19 . . . . at Fresno
20-23 . . . . Nashville
25-28 . . . . at Iowa
29-31 . . . Round Rock

SEPTEMBER
1 . . . . Round Rock
2-5 . . . . Okla. City

25-28 . . . . El Paso
30 . . . . at El Paso

JULY
1-3 . . . . at El Paso
4-6 . . . . Tacoma
7-10 . . . . at Fresno
14-17 . . . . Okla. City
18-21 . . . . . . Col. Springs
22-25 . . . . . . at Las Vegas
26-29 . . . . . Sacramento
30-31 . . . . Fresno

AUGUST
1-2 . . . . Fresno
3-6 . . . . . . at Salt Lake
7-10 . . . . Salt Lake
12-15 . . . . . at Nashville
16-19 . . . . . at Memphis
20-23 . . . . . Sacramento
24-28 . . . . Tacoma
29-31 . . . at Sacramento

SEPTEMBER
1 . . . . at Sacramento
2-5 . . . . at Tacoma

25-28 . . . . . Col. Springs
30 . . . . Iowa

JULY
1-3 . . . . Iowa
4-6 . . . . . at New Orleans
7-10 . . . . at Memphis
14-17 . . . . . Sacramento
18-21 . . . . Fresno
22-25 . . . . at Col. Springs
26-29 . . . . Omaha
30-31 . . . . Memphis

AUGUST
1-2 . . . . Memphis
3-6 . . . . . . at Okla. City
7-10 . . . . Nashville
12-15 . . . . . . at Salt Lake
16-19 . . . . . at Las Vegas
20-23 . . . . . Col. Springs
24-28 . . . at New Orleans
29-31 . . . . . . at Omaha

SEPTEMBER
1 . . . . at Omaha
2-5 . . . . Memphis

SACRAMENTO RIVER CATS

APRIL
7-10 . . . . . at Salt Lake
11-14 . . . . . at Las Vegas
15-18 . . . . Salt Lake
19-22 . . . . Las Vegas
23-26 . . . . . . at Tacoma
28-30 . . . . at Salt Lake

MAY
1 . . . . at Salt Lake
2-5 . . . . . at Albuquerque
6-9 . . . . Las Vegas
10-13 . . . . Reno
14-17 . . . . . . at Memphis
19-22 . . . . . at Nashville
23-26 . . . . . Col. Springs
27-30 . . . . . . Okla. City
31 . . . . at El Paso

JUNE
1-3 . . . . at El Paso
4-7 . . . . . . Albuquerque
9-12 . . . . at El Paso
13-16 . . . . Fresno
17-20 . . . . El Paso
21-24 . . . . Tacoma

SALT LAKE BEES

APRIL
7-10 . . . . Sacramento
11-14 . . . . Fresno
15-18 . . . . at Sacramento
19-22 . . . . at Fresno
23-26 . . . . El Paso
28-30 . . . . . . Sacramento

MAY
1 . . . . Sacramento
2-5 . . . . at Tacoma
6-9 . . . . Reno
10-13 . . . . . Albuquerque
14-17 . . . at Col. Springs
19-22 . . . . at Okla. City
23-26 . . . . Memphis
27-30 . . . . Nashville
31 . . . . at Tacoma

JUNE
1-3 . . . . at Tacoma
4-7 . . . . at Reno
9-12 . . . . at Fresno
13-16 . . . . Tacoma
17-20 . . . . Las Vegas
21-24 . . . . . . at El Paso

TACOMA RAINIERS

APRIL
7-10 . . . . . . Albuquerque
11-14 . . . . El Paso
15-18 . . . at Albuquerque
19-22 . . . . . at El Paso
23-26 . . . . . Sacramento
28-30 . . . . at Las Vegas

MAY
1 . . . . at Las Vegas
2-5 . . . . Salt Lake
6-9 . . . . at Albuquerque
10-13 . . . . at Fresno
14-17 . . . . Omaha
19-22 . . . . Iowa
23-26 . . . . at Round Rock
27-30 . . . at New Orleans
31 . . . . Salt Lake

25-28 . . . . . at Las Vegas
30 . . . . Albuquerque

JULY
1-3 . . . . Albuquerque
4-6 . . . . at Fresno
7-10 . . . . Tacoma
14-17 . . . . at Round Rock
18-21 . . . at New Orleans
22-24 . . . . El Paso
26-29 . . . . at Reno
30-31 . . . . Salt Lake

AUGUST
1-2 . . . . Salt Lake
3-6 . . . . . at Albuquerque
7-10 . . . . at Tacoma
12-15 . . . . Omaha
16-19 . . . . Iowa
20-23 . . . . at Reno
24-28 . . . . at Fresno
29-31 . . . . Reno

SEPTEMBER
1 . . . . Reno
2-5 . . . . Fresno

25-28 . . . . at Albuquerque
30 . . . . Fresno

JULY
1-3 . . . . Fresno
4-6 . . . . at Las Vegas
7-10 . . . . El Paso
14-17 . . . . at Omaha
18-21 . . . . at Iowa
22-25 . . . . Tacoma
26-29 . . . at Albuquerque
30-31 . . . at Sacramento

AUGUST
1-2 . . . . . at Sacramento
3-6 . . . . Reno
7-10 . . . . at Reno
12-15 . . . . . Round Rock
16-19 . . . . . New Orleans
20-23 . . . . at El Paso
24-27 . . . . . at Las Vegas
29-31 . . . . . Albuquerque

SEPTEMBER
1 . . . . Albuquerque
2-5 . . . . Las Vegas

JUNE
1-3 . . . . Salt Lake
4-7 . . . . at Las Vegas
9-12 . . . . Reno
13-16 . . . . . . at Salt Lake
17-20 . . . . Fresno
21-24 . . . . at Sacramento
25-28 . . . . at Fresno
30 . . . . Las Vegas

JULY
1-3 . . . . Las Vegas
4-6 . . . . at Reno
7-10 . . . . . at Sacramento
14-17 . . . . . Col. Springs
18-21 . . . . . . Okla. City
22-25 . . . . . at Salt Lake
26-29 . . . . El Paso
30-31 . . . . . Albuquerque

AUGUST		
1-2 . . . . Albuquerque	7-10 . . . . Sacramento	20-23 . . . . Las Vegas
3-6 . . . . at El Paso	12-15 . . . . . . at Memphis	24-28 . . . . at Reno
	16-19 . . . . . . at Nashville	29-31 . . . . Fresno

SEPTEMBER	
1 . . . . Fresno	
2-5 . . . . Reno	

DOUBLE-A

EASTERN LEAGUE

AKRON RUBBERDUCKS

APRIL	
7-10 . . . . at Bowie	21-23 . . . . .at Reading
11-13 . . . . . . .at Altoona	24-26 . . . . Trenton
14-17 . . . . .Bowie	27-29 . . . . . at Richmond
18-20 . . . . . . Binghamton	30 . . . . at Erie
21-24 . . . . at Trenton	
25-27 . . . . . .at Reading	JULY
29-30 . . . . Altoona	1-3 . . . . at Erie

MAY	
1 . . . . Altoona	4-7 . . . . Altoona
2-5 . . . . Trenton	8-10 . . . . . at Harrisburg
6-8 . . . . . at Binghamton	14-17 . . . . Erie
9-11 . . . . Erie	18-20 . . . . . at Richmond
12-15 . . . . . at Harrisburg	21-24 . . . . . at Altoona
16-18 . . . . at Hartford	25-27 . . . . Richmond
20-22 . . . . . . Binghamton	28-31 . . . . .Bowie
23-26 . . . . . .at Altoona	
27-30 . . . .Harrisburg	AUGUST
31 . . . . Altoona	2-4 . . . . at New Hampshire

JUNE	
1-2 . . . . Altoona	5-7 . . . . at Portland
3-5 . . . . at Bowie	9-11 . . . . Hartford
7-9 . . . . Reading	12-14 . . . . Portland
10-13 . . . . at Harrisburg	16-18 . . . . . . .at Trenton
14-16 . . . . Erie	19-21 . . . . . . at Bowie
17-19 . . . . New Hampshire	22-24 . . . . Reading
	25-28 . . . . Richmond
	29-31 . . . . at Erie

SEPTEMBER
1 . . . . at Erie
2-5 . . . . .Bowie

ALTOONA CURVE

APRIL	
7-10 . . . . .Harrisburg	21-23 . . . .at Binghamton
11-13 . . . . .Akron	24-26 . . . . . at Bowie
14-17 . . . . . at Richmond	27-29 . . . . . Binghamton
18-20 . . . . at Harrisburg	30 . . . . .Bowie
21-24 . . . . . . Richmond	
25-27 . . . . Erie	JULY
29-30 . . . . . at Akron	1-3 . . . . .Bowie

MAY	
1 . . . . at Akron	4-7 . . . . at Akron
2-5 . . . . at Erie	8-10 . . . . at Erie
6-8 . . . . .Richmond	14-17 . . . . . .Harrisburg
9-11 . . . . Trenton	18-20 . . . . . at Hartford
12-15 . . . . . at Richmond	21-24 . . . . .Akron
17-19 . . .at Binghamton	25-27 . . . . Erie
20-22 . . . . . . Portland	28-31 . . . . . . at Trenton
23-26 . . . . . . .Akron	
27-30 . . . . at Bowie	AUGUST
31 . . . . at Akron	2-4 . . . . Richmond

JUNE	
1-2 . . . . at Akron	5-7 . . . . . . .at Reading
3-5 . . . . Binghamton	9-11 . . . . . . .Harrisburg
6-9 . . . . at Erie	12-14 . . . . Reading
10-12 . . . . . . .at Reading	16-18 . . . . . . at Portland
14-16 . . . . New Hampshire	19-21 . . at New Hampshire
17-19 . . . . Hartford	22-24 . . . . . at Harrisburg
	25-28 . . . . Erie
	29-31 . . . . . Binghamton

SEPTEMBER
1 . . . . Binghamton
2-5 . . . . at Richmond

BINGHAMTON METS

APRIL	
7-10 . . . . New Hampshire	14-17 . . . . at Erie
11-13 . . . . . . .Harrisburg	18-20 . . . . . . .at Akron
	21-24 . . . . Erie

25-27 . . . . Portland	30 . . . . . New Hampshire
29-30 . . at New Hampshire	

MAY	
1 . . . . . at New Hampshire	JULY
2-5 . . . . at Portland	1-3 . . . . . New Hampshire
6-8 . . . . .Akron	4-7 . . . . at Hartford
9-11 . . . . .at Reading	8-10 . . . at New Hampshire
12-15 . . . . . . at Portland	14-17 . . . . Hartford
17-19 . . . . Altoona	18-20 . . . . .Bowie
20-22 . . . . . . at Akron	21-24 . . . . . . at Portland
23-26 . . . . .Richmond	25-27 . . . . .at Reading
27-30 . . . . Trenton	28-31 . . . . Portland
31 . . . . at Erie	

JUNE	AUGUST
1-2 . . . . at Erie	2-4 . . . . .Harrisburg
3-5 . . . . . .at Altoona	5-7 . . . . at Hartford
7-9 . . . . Trenton	9-11 . . . . Reading
10-12 . . . . Hartford	12-14 . . . . . at Harrisburg
14-16 . . . . at Richmond	15-18 . . at New Hampshire
17-19 . . . . . at Trenton	19-21 . . . . Portland
21-23 . . . . Altoona	22-24 . . . . Hartford
24-26 . . . . Richmond	25-28 . . . . . . at Bowie
27-29 . . . . .at Altoona	29-31 . . . . . . .at Altoona

SEPTEMBER
1 . . . . .at Altoona
2-5 . . . . Erie

BOWIE BAYSOX

APRIL	
7-10 . . . . .Akron	21-23 . . . . Trenton
11-13 . . . . at Akron	24-26 . . . . Altoona
14-17 . . . . . . at Akron	27-29 . . . . at Harrisburg
18-20 . . . . . . at Erie	30 . . . . .at Altoona
21-24 . . . . . .Harrisburg	
25-27 . . . . Richmond	JULY
29-30 . . . . . at Harrisburg	1-3 . . . . .at Altoona

MAY	
1 . . . . . . at Harrisburg	4-7 . . . . Trenton
2-5 . . . . . . at Richmond	8-10 . . . . .at Reading
6-8 . . . . Erie	14-17 . . . . Richmond
9-11 . . . . Hartford	18-20 . . . .at Binghamton
12-15 . . . . . . at Erie	21-24 . . . . Erie
17-19 . . . . . . Reading	25-27 . . . . Hartford
20-22 . . . . at Harrisburg	28-31 . . . . . . at Akron
23-26 . . . . at Hartford	
27-30 . . . . . . Altoona	AUGUST
31 . . . . . . at Richmond	1-4 . . . . .at Reading

JUNE	
1-2 . . . . . . at Richmond	5-7 . . . . Richmond
3-5 . . . . .Akron	9-11 . . . . New Hampshire
7-9 . . . . at Portland	12-14 . . . . . at Richmond
10-12 . . at New Hampshire	16-18 . . . . . at Hartford
14-16 . . . . Portland	19-21 . . . . .Akron
17-19 . . . . . . at Erie	22-24 . . . . . . at Trenton
	25-28 . . . . . . Binghamton
	29-31 . . . . . .Harrisburg

SEPTEMBER
1 . . . . .Harrisburg
2-5 . . . . at Akron

ERIE SEAWOLVES

APRIL	
7-10 . . . . .at Trenton	6-8 . . . . at Bowie
11-13 . . . . at Bowie	9-11 . . . . at Akron
14-17 . . . . . . Binghamton	12-15 . . . . .Bowie
18-20 . . . . .Bowie	16-18 . . . . . . .Harrisburg
21-24 . . . .at Binghamton	20-22 . . . . at Richmond
25-27 . . . . . .at Altoona	23-26 . . . . .at Reading
29-30 . . . . Trenton	27-30 . . . . . Richmond
	31 . . . . Binghamton

MAY	JUNE
1 . . . . Trenton	1-2 . . . . Binghamton
2-5 . . . . Altoona	3-5 . . . . .at Trenton

6-9 . . . . Altoona
10-12 . . . . Trenton
14-16 . . . . at Akron
17-19 . . . . .Bowie
20-22 . . . . New Hampshire
24-26 . . . . . at Hartford
27-29 . . . . .at Reading
30 . . . . .Akron

JULY
1-3 . . . . .Akron
4-7 . . . . . . at Harrisburg
8-10 . . . . Altoona
14-17 . . . . at Akron
18-20 . . . . . .Harrisburg
21-24 . . . . at Bowie

HARRISBURG SENATORS

APRIL
7-10 . . . . .at Altoona
11-13 . . . .at Binghamton
14-17 . . . . Reading
18-20 . . . . Altoona
21-24 . . . . at Bowie
25-27 . . . . at Hartford
29-30 . . . . .Bowie

MAY
1 . . . . .Bowie
2-5 . . . . Hartford
6-8 . . . . at Trenton
9-11 . . . . . . at Richmond
12-15 . . . . .Akron
16-18 . . . . at Erie
20-22 . . . . .Bowie
23-26 . . . . Portland
27-30 . . . . . at Akron
31 . . . . . New Hampshire

JUNE
1-2 . . . . . New Hampshire
3-5 . . . . . at Richmond
7-9 . . . . Hartford
10-13 . . . . .Akron
14-16 . . . . . at Trenton
17-19 . . . . Reading

HARTFORD YARD GOATS

APRIL
7-10 . . . . . . at Richmond
11-13 . . at New Hampshire
14-17 . . . . . at Portland
18-20 . . at New Hampshire
21-24 . . . . . . at Portland
25-27 . . . . at Harrisburg
29-30 . . . . . at Richmond

MAY
1 . . . . at Richmond
2-5 . . . . at Harrisburg
6-8 . . . at New Hampshire
9-11 . . . . at Bowie
12-15 . . at New Hampshire
16-18 . . . . at Akron
20-22 . . at New Hampshire
23-26 . . . . . . at Bowie
27-30 . . . . . at Portland
31 . . . . Trenton

JUNE
1-2 . . . . Trenton
3-6 . . . . Portland
7-9 . . . . . at Harrisburg
10-12 . . . .at Binghamton
14-16 . . . . Reading
17-19 . . . . . .at Altoona

25-27 . . . . . . .at Altoona
28-31 . . . . Reading

AUGUST
2-4 . . . . at Portland
5-7 . . . at New Hampshire
9-11 . . . . Portland
12-14 . . . . Hartford
16-18 . . . . at Harrisburg
19-21 . . . . Reading
22-24 . . . . . . Richmond
25-28 . . . .at Altoona
29-31 . . . . .Akron

SEPTEMBER
1 . . . . .Akron
2-5 . . . at Binghamton

21-23 . . . . . . at Portland
24-26 . . at New Hampshire
27-29 . . . . .Bowie
30 . . . . .at Reading

JULY
1-3 . . . . .at Reading
4-7 . . . . Erie
8-10 . . . . .Akron
14-17 . . . . .at Altoona
18-20 . . . . at Erie
21-24 . . . . . . Richmond
25-27 . . . New Hampshire
28-31 . . . . . . at Hartford

AUGUST
2-4 . . . . . .at Binghamton
5-7 . . . . Trenton
9-11 . . . . . . .at Altoona
12-14 . . . . . Binghamton
16-18 . . . . Erie
19-21 . . . . at Richmond
22-24 . . . . . . Altoona
25-28 . . . . at Hartford
29-31 . . . . . at Bowie

SEPTEMBER
1 . . . . at Bowie
2-5 . . . . Hartford

NEW HAMPSHIRE FISHER CATS

APRIL
7-10 . . . . .at Binghamton
11-13 . . . . . at Hartford
14-17 . . . . . . Trenton
18-20 . . . . . . Hartford
22-24 . . . . . .at Reading
25-27 . . . . . at Trenton
29-30 . . . . . Binghamton

MAY
1 . . . . Binghamton
2-5 . . . . Reading
6-8 . . . . . . at Hartford
9-11 . . . . . . Portland
12-15 . . . . . at Hartford
16-18 . . . . . at Hartford
20-22 . . . . . . Hartford
23-26 . . . . . at Trenton
27-30 . . . . . . Reading
31 . . . at Harrisburg

JUNE
1-2 . . . . at Harrisburg
3-6 . . . . . .at Reading
7-9 . . . . . .Richmond
10-12 . . . . .Bowie
14-16 . . . .at Altoona
17-19 . . . . . at Akron

PORTLAND SEA DOGS

APRIL
7-10 . . . . .at Reading
11-13 . . . . . .at Trenton
14-17 . . . . . Hartford
18-20 . . . . . Trenton
21-24 . . . . . at Hartford
25-27 . . .at Binghamton
29-30 . . . . . Reading

MAY
1 . . . . Reading
2-5 . . . . . . Binghamton
6-8 . . . . . .at Reading
9-11 . . . at New Hampshire
12-15 . . . . Binghamton
16-18 . . . New Hampshire
20-22 . . . . . .at Altoona
23-26 . . . at Harrisburg
27-30 . . . . . . Hartford
31 . . . . Reading

JUNE
1-2 . . . . Reading
3-6 . . . . . at Hartford
7-9 . . . . .Bowie
10-12 . . . .Richmond
14-16 . . . . . at Bowie
17-19 . . . at Richmond

READING FIGHTIN PHILS

APRIL
7-10 . . . . Portland
11-13 . . . . . Richmond
14-17 . . at Harrisburg
18-20 . . . . at Binghamton
22-24 . . . New Hampshire
25-27 . . . . . . .Akron
29-30 . . . . . at Portland

MAY
1 . . . . at Portland
2-5 . . . at New Hampshire
6-8 . . . . at Bowie
9-11 . . . . . . Binghamton

20-22 . . . . at Erie
24-26 . . . . . .Harrisburg
27-29 . . . . Hartford
30 . . . . . .at Binghamton

JULY
1-3 . . . . . .at Binghamton
4-7 . . . . Portland
8-10 . . . . . Binghamton
14-17 . . . . at Portland
18-20 . . . . . . Reading
21-24 . . . . . . Trenton
25-27 . . . at Harrisburg
28-31 . . . at Richmond

AUGUST
2-4 . . . . .Akron
5-7 . . . . Erie
9-11 . . . . . . at Bowie
12-14 . . . . . at Trenton
15-18 . . . . Binghamton
19-21 . . . . . Altoona
22-24 . . . . at Portland
25-28 . . . .at Reading
29-31 . . . . . Trenton

SEPTEMBER
1 . . . . Trenton
2-5 . . . . Portland

21-23 . . . . . .Harrisburg
24-26 . . . . . Reading
27-29 . . . . at Trenton
30 . . . . Hartford

JULY
1-3 . . . . Hartford
4-7 . . . at New Hampshire
8-10 . . . . . at Hartford
14-17 . . . New Hampshire
18-20 . . . . at Trenton
21-24 . . . . Binghamton
25-27 . . . . Trenton
28-31 . . . .at Binghamton

AUGUST
2-4 . . . . Erie
5-7 . . . . .Akron
9-11 . . . . . . at Erie
12-14 . . . . . at Akron
16-18 . . . . . Altoona
19-21 . . . .at Binghamton
22-24 . . . New Hampshire
25-28 . . . . . Trenton
29-31 . . . .at Reading

SEPTEMBER
1 . . . . .at Reading
2-5 . . . at New Hampshire

12-15 . . . . . . at Trenton
17-19 . . . . . at Bowie
20-22 . . . . . Trenton
23-26 . . . . Erie
27-30 . . at New Hampshire
31 . . . . at Portland

JUNE
1-2 . . . . at Portland
3-6 . . . . . New Hampshire
7-9 . . . . . . at Akron
10-12 . . . . . Altoona
14-16 . . . . at Hartford
17-19 . . . . at Harrisburg

21-23 . . . . .Akron	**AUGUST**
24-26 . . . . . . at Portland	1-4 . . . . .Bowie
27-29 . . . . Erie	5-7 . . . . Altoona
30 . . . . .Harrisburg	9-11 . . . . .at Binghamton
JULY	12-14 . . . . .at Altoona
1-3 . . . . .Harrisburg	16-18 . . . . .Richmond
4-7 . . . . at Richmond	19-21 . . . . at Erie
8-10 . . . . .Bowie	22-24 . . . . at Akron
14-17 . . . . at Trenton	25-28 . . . New Hampshire
18-20 . . at New Hampshire	29-31 . . . . Portland
21-24 . . . . Hartford	**SEPTEMBER**
25-27 . . . . . Binghamton	1 . . . . Portland
28-31 . . . . at Erie	2-5 . . . . .at Trenton

RICHMOND FLYING SQUIRRELS

APRIL	21-23 . . . . at Hartford
7-10 . . . . at Hartford	24-26 . . . . .at Binghamton
11-13 . . . . . . .at Reading	27-29 . . . . .Akron
14-17 . . . . Altoona	30 . . . . .at Trenton
18-20 . . . . Reading	**JULY**
21-24 . . . . . .at Altoona	1-3 . . . . .at Trenton
25-27 . . . . . at Bowie	4-7 . . . . Reading
29-30 . . . . Hartford	8-10 . . . . Trenton
MAY	14-17 . . . . at Bowie
1 . . . . Hartford	18-20 . . . . .Akron
2-5 . . . . .Bowie	21-24 . . . . . at Harrisburg
6-8 . . . . .at Altoona	25-27 . . . . at Akron
9-11 . . . . . . .Harrisburg	28-31 . . . New Hampshire
12-15 . . . . Altoona	**AUGUST**
17-19 . . . . . .at Trenton	2-4 . . . . .at Altoona
20-22 . . . . Erie	5-7 . . . . at Bowie
23-26 . . . .at Binghamton	8-11 . . . . Trenton
27-30 . . . . . . at Erie	12-14 . . . . .Bowie
31 . . . . .Bowie	16-18 . . . . . .at Reading
JUNE	19-21 . . . . . .Harrisburg
1-2 . . . . .Bowie	22-24 . . . . at Erie
3-5 . . . . .Harrisburg	25-28 . . . . . at Akron
7-9 . . at New Hampshire	29-31 . . . . Hartford
10-12 . . . . . at Portland	**SEPTEMBER**
14-16 . . . . . Binghamton	1 . . . . Hartford
17-19 . . . . . Portland	2-5 . . . . Altoona

TRENTON THUNDER

APRIL	21-23 . . . . at Bowie
7-10 . . . . Erie	24-26 . . . . at Akron
11-13 . . . . Portland	27-29 . . . . Portland
14-17 . . at New Hampshire	30 . . . . Richmond
18-20 . . . . . at Portland	**JULY**
21-24 . . . . .Akron	1-3 . . . . Richmond
25-27 . . . . New Hampshire	4-7 . . . . at Bowie
29-30 . . . . at Erie	8-10 . . . . . . at Richmond
MAY	14-17 . . . . Reading
1 . . . . at Erie	18-20 . . . . Portland
2-5 . . . . at Akron	21-24 . . at New Hampshire
6-8 . . . . .Harrisburg	25-27 . . . . . at Portland
9-11 . . . . .at Altoona	28-31 . . . . Altoona
12-15 . . . . Reading	**AUGUST**
17-19 . . . . . .Richmond	2-4 . . . . Hartford
20-22 . . . . . .at Reading	5-7 . . . . at Harrisburg
23-26 . . . New Hampshire	8-11 . . . . . . at Richmond
27-30 . . . .at Binghamton	12-14 . . . . New Hampshire
31 . . . . at Hartford	16-18 . . . . .Akron
JUNE	19-21 . . . . . at Hartford
1-2 . . . . at Hartford	22-24 . . . . .Bowie
3-5 . . . . Erie	25-28 . . . . . at Portland
7-9 . . . . . .at Binghamton	29-31 . . at New Hampshire
10-12 . . . . at Erie	**SEPTEMBER**
14-16 . . . . . .Harrisburg	1 . . . . at New Hampshire
17-19 . . . . . . Binghamton	2-5 . . . . Reading

SOUTHERN LEAGUE

BILOXI SHUCKERS

APRIL	23-27 . . . . . Montgomery
7-11 . . . . . . Chattanooga	29-30 . . . . .at Birmingham
12-13 . . . . Mobile	**JULY**
14-16 . . . . . . at Mobile	1-3 . . . . . .at Birmingham
17-21 . . . . . . Pensacola	4-8 . . . . Jacksonville
22-26 . . . . .at Mississippi	9-13 . . . . . . at Pensacola
28-30 . . . . . .Tennessee	14-18 . . . . . Birmingham
MAY	20-24 . . . . . . at Pensacola
1-2 . . . . .Tennessee	26-27 . . . . . . at Mobile
4-8 . . . . . . at Pensacola	28-30 . . . . . . Mobile
9-13 . . . . . .Jacksonville	31 . . . . . . at Jacksonville
14-18 . . at Chattanooga	**AUGUST**
19-23 . . . . . at Tennessee	1-4 . . . . at Jacksonville
25-26 . . . . . at Mobile	5-9 . . . . Pensacola
27-29 . . . . . . Mobile	11-15 . . . . . .at Jackson
31 . . . . . .Mississippi	17-18 . . . . Mobile
JUNE	19-21 . . . . . at Mobile
1-4 . . . . .Mississippi	22-26 . . . . . .Mississippi
5-9 . . . . . at Montgomery	27-31 . . . . . . Jackson
10-14 . . . . . Birmingham	**SEPTEMBER**
15-19 . . . . at Jacksonville	1-5 . . . . .at Mississippi

BIRMINGHAM BARONS

APRIL	23-27 . . . . . . at Mobile
7-11 . . . . . at Jacksonville	29-30 . . . . Biloxi
12-16 . . . . . .Tennessee	**JULY**
17-21 . . . . . .at Jackson	1-3 . . . . Biloxi
22-26 . . . at Chattanooga	4-8 . . . . . at Chattanooga
28-30 . . . . . Pensacola	9-13 . . . . .Jacksonville
MAY	14-18 . . . . . at Biloxi
1-2 . . . . Pensacola	20-24 . . . . . Montgomery
4-8 . . . . . at Montgomery	26-30 . . . .at Mississippi
9-13 . . . . . . Jackson	31 . . . . .Tennessee
14-18 . . . . at Tennessee	**AUGUST**
19-23 . . . . . Montgomery	1-4 . . . . .Tennessee
25-29 . . . . at Pensacola	5-9 . . . . . . .at Jackson
31 . . . . . . Chattanooga	11-15 . . . . Chattanooga
JUNE	17-21 . . . . . Jackson
1-4 . . . . Chattanooga	22-26 . . . . at Montgomery
5-9 . . . . Mobile	27-31 . . . . . at Tennessee
10-14 . . . . . . at Biloxi	**SEPTEMBER**
15-19 . . . . . .Mississippi	1-5 . . . . Pensacola

CHATTANOOGA LOOKOUTS

APRIL	29-30 . . . . . at Pensacola
7-11 . . . . at Biloxi	**JULY**
12-16 . . . . Jackson	1-3 . . . . . . at Pensacola
17-21 . . . at Mississippi	4-8 . . . . Birmingham
22-26 . . . . Birmingham	9-13 . . . . . at Tennessee
28-30 . . . . Montgomery	14-18 . . . . Mobile
MAY	20-24 . . . . . .at Jackson
1-2 . . . . . Montgomery	26-30 . . . . .Tennessee
4-8 . . . . at Mobile	31 . . . . . . at Mobile
9-13 . . . . . . Pensacola	**AUGUST**
14-18 . . . . Biloxi	1-4 . . . . at Mobile
19-23 . . . . .at Jackson	5-9 . . . . . . .Jacksonville
25-29 . . . . .Tennessee	11-15 . . . .at Birmingham
31 . . . . . .at Birmingham	17-21 . . . . . Montgomery
JUNE	22-26 . . . at Jacksonville
1-4 . . . .at Birmingham	27-31 . . . . . .Mississippi
5-9 . . . . . .Jacksonville	**SEPTEMBER**
10-14 . . . . . at Tennessee	1-5 . . . . at Jackson
15-19 . . at Montgomery	
23-27 . . . . Jackson	

JACKSON GENERALS

APRIL
7-11 . . . . . . Montgomery
12-16 . . . . at Chattanooga
17-21 . . . . . Birmingham
22-26 . . . . . at Pensacola
28-30 . . . . . . Mobile

MAY
1-2. . . . . Mobile
4-7. . . . . .Jacksonville
9-13 . . . . .at Birmingham
14-18 . . . . at Mobile
19-23 . . . . .Chattanooga
25-29 . . . at Montgomery
31 . . . . at Tennessee

JUNE
1-4. . . . . . at Tennessee
5-9. . . . . Pensacola
10-14 . . . . . at Mississippi
15-19 . . . . . . .Tennessee

23-27 . . . . at Chattanooga
29-30 . . . . . .Mississippi

JULY
1-3 . . . . .Mississippi
4-8. . . . . . . at Tennessee
9-13 . . . . . . Montgomery
14-18 . . . at Mississippi
20-24 . . . . .Chattanooga
26-30 . . . . at Jacksonville
31 . . . . . at Montgomery

AUGUST
1-4. . . . . at Montgomery
5-9. . . . . . . Birmingham
11-15 . . . . Biloxi
17-21 . . . at Birmingham
22-26 . . . . Tennessee
27-31 . . . . . . at Biloxi

SEPTEMBER
1-5 . . . . Chattanooga

JACKSONVILLE SUNS

APRIL
7-11 . . . . . . Birmingham
12-16 . . . . . at Pensacola
17-21 . . . . Mobile
22-26 . . . . at Montgomery
28-30 . . . . . . .Mississippi

MAY
1-2. . . . . . . .Mississippi
4-7. . . . . .at Jackson
9-13 . . . . . . at Biloxi
14-18 . . . . . Montgomery
19-23 . . . . . Pensacola
25-29 . . . . at Mississippi
31 . . . . Montgomery

JUNE
1-4. . . . . . . Montgomery
5-9. . . . at Chattanooga
10-14 . . . . . . at Mobile
15-19 . . . . Biloxi

23-27 . . . . . at Mississippi
29-30 . . . . . Tennessee

JULY
1-3 . . . . .Tennessee
4-8. . . . . at Biloxi
9-13 . . .at Birmingham
14-18 . . . . . . Pensacola
20-24 . . . . . . at Mobile
26-30 . . . . . . Jackson
31 . . . . Biloxi

AUGUST
1-4. . . . . Biloxi
5-9. . . . at Chattanooga
11-15 . . . . . .Mississippi
17-21 . . . . at Tennessee
22-26 . . . . .Chattanooga
27-31 . . . . at Pensacola

SEPTEMBER
1-5 . . . . Mobile

MISSISSIPPI BRAVES

APRIL
7-11 . . . . Pensacola
12-16 . . . . at Montgomery
17-21 . . . . . Chattanooga
22-26 . . . . . . Biloxi
28-30 . . . . at Jacksonville

MAY
1-2. . . . . . at Jacksonville
4-8. . . . . . at Tennessee
9-13 . . . . Mobile
14-18 . . . . at Pensacola
19-23 . . . . at Mobile
25-29 . . . . .Jacksonville
31 . . . . at Biloxi

JUNE
1-4. . . . . at Biloxi
5-9. . . . . . . .Tennessee
10-14 . . . . Jackson
15-19 . . . .at Birmingham

23-27 . . . . . .Jacksonville
29-30 . . . . . . .at Jackson

JULY
1-3 . . . . .at Jackson
4-8. . . . . . . .Montgomery
9-13 . . . . at Mobile
14-18 . . . . .Jackson
20-24 . . . . at Tennessee
26-30 . . . . . Birmingham
31 . . . . . . at Pensacola

AUGUST
1-4. . . . . . at Pensacola
5-9. . . . . Mobile
11-15 . . . . at Jacksonville
17-21 . . . . . . Pensacola
22-26 . . . . . . at Biloxi
27-31 . . at Chattanooga

SEPTEMBER
1-5 . . . . Biloxi

MOBILE BAYBEARS

APRIL
7-11 . . . . . at Tennessee
12-13 . . . . at Biloxi

14-16 . . . . Biloxi
17-21 . . . . at Jacksonville
22-26 . . . . .Tennessee

28-30 . . . . . . .at Jackson

MAY
1-2. . . . . .at Jackson
4-8. . . . . . .Chattanooga
9-13 . . . . . at Mississippi
14-18 . . . . Jackson
19-23 . . . . . . .Mississippi
25-26 . . . . Biloxi
27-29 . . . . at Biloxi
31 . . . . Pensacola

JUNE
1-4. . . . . Pensacola
5-9. . . . .at Birmingham
10-14 . . . .Jacksonville
15-19 . . . . . at Pensacola
23-27 . . . . . Birmingham
29-30 . . . at Montgomery

MONTGOMERY BISCUITS

APRIL
7-11 . . . . .at Jackson
12-16 . . . . . . .Mississippi
17-21 . . . . . . at Tennessee
22-26 . . . . . .Jacksonville
28-30 . . . . at Chattanooga

MAY
1-2. . . . . at Chattanooga
4-8. . . . . . . Birmingham
9-13 . . . . . . .Tennessee
14-18 . . . . at Jacksonville
19-23 . . .at Birmingham
25-29 . . . . Jackson
31 . . . . . . at Jacksonville

JUNE
1-4. . . . . at Jacksonville
5-9. . . . . Biloxi
10-14 . . . . . at Pensacola
15-19 . . . . . Chattanooga

23-27 . . . . at Biloxi
29-30 . . . . Mobile

JULY
1-3 . . . . Mobile
4-8. . . . . . .at Mississippi
9-13 . . . . . .at Jackson
14-18 . . . . . . .Tennessee
20-24 . . . .at Birmingham
26-30 . . . . . Pensacola
31 . . . . Jackson

AUGUST
1-4. . . . . Jackson
5-9. . . . . . at Tennessee
11-15 . . . . Mobile
17-21 . . . . at Chattanooga
22-26 . . . . . Birmingham
27-31 . . . . . . at Mobile

SEPTEMBER
1-5 . . . . .Tennessee

PENSACOLA BLUE WAHOOS

APRIL
7-11 . . . . . . at Mississippi
12-16 . . . . . .Jacksonville
17-21 . . . . at Biloxi
22-26 . . . . Jackson
28-30 . . . .at Birmingham

MAY
1-2. . . . . .at Birmingham
4-8. . . . . Biloxi
9-13 . . . . at Chattanooga
14-18 . . . . . . .Mississippi
19-23 . . . . . .Jacksonville
25-29 . . . . . Birmingham
31 . . . . at Mobile

JUNE
1-4. . . . . at Mobile
5-9. . . . . . . .at Jackson
10-14 . . . . . Montgomery
15-19 . . . . Mobile

23-27 . . . . . at Tennessee
29-30 . . . . . Chattanooga

JULY
1-3 . . . . Chattanooga
4-8. . . . . at Mobile
9-13 . . . . Biloxi
14-18 . . . at Jacksonville
20-24 . . . . Biloxi
26-30 . . . . at Montgomery
31 . . . . .Mississippi

AUGUST
1-4. . . . . .Mississippi
5-9. . . . . at Biloxi
11-15 . . . . . . Tennessee
17-21 . . . . at Mississippi
22-26 . . . . Mobile
27-31 . . . . . .Jacksonville

SEPTEMBER
1-5 . . . . . .at Birmingham

TENNESSEE SMOKIES

APRIL
7-11 . . . . Mobile
12-16 . . . .at Birmingham
17-21 . . . . . Montgomery
22-26 . . . . . at Mobile
28-30 . . . . at Biloxi

MAY
1-2. . . . . at Biloxi
4-8. . . . . .Mississippi
9-13 . . . . at Montgomery
14-18 . . . . . Birmingham
19-23 . . . . Biloxi

25-29 .... at Chattanooga
31 .... Jackson

JUNE
1-4 .... Jackson
5-9 .... at Mississippi
10-14 ..... Chattanooga
15-19 ...... at Jackson
23-27 ...... Pensacola
29-30 ..... at Jacksonville

JULY
1-3 ...... at Jacksonville
4-8 .... Jackson
9-13 ...... Chattanooga

TEXAS LEAGUE
ARKANSAS TRAVELERS

APRIL
7-9 .... Midland
10-12 .... Frisco
14-16 ..... at Midland
17-19 ...... at Frisco
21-24 ...... Springfield
25-28 .... at Tulsa
29-30 ..... at Springfield

MAY
1-2 .... at Springfield
3-6 .... Tulsa
7-10 ...... NW Arkansas
11-14 .... at Tulsa
16-19 .... at NW Arkansas
20-23 ..... Springfield
24-26 ... at Corpus Christi
27-29 .... at San Antonio
31 ...... Corpus Christi

JUNE
1-2 ...... Corpus Christi
3-5 .... San Antonio
7-10 ..... at Springfield
11-14 .... NW Arkansas
15-18 ...... Tulsa
19-22 .... at NW Arkansas

CORPUS CHRISTI HOOKS

APRIL
7-9 .... Tulsa
10-12 ...... Springfield
14-16 ...... at Tulsa
17-19 .... at Springfield
21-24 .... Frisco
25-28 ...... Midland
29-30 .... at Frisco

MAY
1-2 .... at Frisco
3-6 .... at Midland
7-10 ...... San Antonio
12-15 .... Frisco
16-19 .... at San Antonio
20-23 ...... at Midland
24-26 .... Arkansas
27-29 ...... NW Arkansas
31 .... at Arkansas

JUNE
1-2 .... at Arkansas
3-5 ...... at NW Arkansas
7-10 .... Midland
11-14 ..... San Antonio
15-18 ...... at Frisco
19-22 .... at San Antonio

14-18 .... at Montgomery
20-24 .... Mississippi
26-30 .... at Chattanooga
31 ...... at Birmingham

AUGUST
1-4 ...... at Birmingham
5-9 ...... Montgomery
11-15 .... at Pensacola
17-21 ...... Jacksonville
22-26 .... at Jackson
27-31 ..... Birmingham

SEPTEMBER
1-5 ..... at Montgomery

23-26 ..... at Springfield
30 .... Frisco

JULY
1-2 .... Frisco
3-5 ...... Midland
6-8 ...... at Frisco
9-11 ...... at Midland
13-16 ...... Tulsa
17-20 ..... at Springfield
21-24 ...... Tulsa
25-27 .... NW Arkansas
28-31 .... at Tulsa

AUGUST
1-3 ..... at NW Arkansas
4-7 .... Springfield
9-11 ...... at San Antonio
12-14 ..at Corpus Christi
16-18 ...... San Antonio
19-21 ...... Corpus Christi
23-26 .... at Tulsa
27-29 ..... NW Arkansas
30-31 .... Springfield

SEPTEMBER
1-2 ...... Springfield
3-5 ..... at NW Arkansas

23-26 .... at Frisco
30 .... Springfield

JULY
1-2 .... Springfield
3-5 .... Tulsa
6-8 ...... at Springfield
9-11 ...... at Tulsa
13-16 ...... Frisco
17-20 ..... at Midland
21-24 .... Frisco
25-27 .... at San Antonio
28-31 .... Midland

AUGUST
1-3 .... San Antonio
4-7 .... at Midland
9-11 ...... NW Arkansas
12-14 ...... Arkansas
16-18 .... at NW Arkansas
19-21 ...... at Arkansas
23-26 ...... Midland
27-29 ..... San Antonio
30-31 .... at Frisco

SEPTEMBER
1-2 .... at Frisco
3-5 ..... at San Antonio

FRISCO ROUGHRIDERS

APRIL
7-9 ..... at NW Arkansas
10-12 ...... at Arkansas
14-16 .... NW Arkansas
17-19 .... Arkansas
21-24 ...at Corpus Christi
25-28 ...... San Antonio
29-30 ..... Corpus Christi

MAY
1-2 ...... Corpus Christi
3-6 ...... at San Antonio
7-10 .... Midland
12-15 ...at Corpus Christi
16-19 ...... at Midland
20-23 ..... San Antonio
24-26 ...... at Tulsa
27-29 ...at Springfield
31 .... Tulsa

JUNE
1-2 .... Tulsa
3-5 .... Springfield
7-10 .... at San Antonio
11-14 ...... Midland
15-18 ..... Corpus Christi
19-22 ..... at Midland

MIDLAND ROCKHOUNDS

APRIL
7-9 .... at Arkansas
10-12 .... at NW Arkansas
14-16 .... Arkansas
17-19 ..... NW Arkansas
21-24 ..... at San Antonio
25-28 ...at Corpus Christi
29-30 ...... San Antonio

MAY
1-2 .... San Antonio
3-6 ...... Corpus Christi
7-10 ...... at Frisco
12-15 ...at San Antonio
16-19 .... Frisco
20-23 ..... Corpus Christi
24-26 .....at Springfield
27-29 ....at Tulsa
31 .... Springfield

JUNE
1-2 .... Springfield
3-5 .... Tulsa
7-10 ....at Corpus Christi
11-14 ...... at Frisco
15-18 ...... San Antonio
19-22 .... Frisco

NORTHWEST ARKANSAS NATURALS

APRIL
7-9 .... Frisco
10-12 .... Midland
14-16 ...... at Frisco
17-19 ...... at Midland
21-24 .... Tulsa
25-28 ...at Springfield
29-30 ....at Tulsa

MAY
1-2 ....at Tulsa
3-6 .... Springfield
7-10 ..... at Arkansas
12-15 .....at Springfield
16-19 .... Arkansas
20-23 .... Tulsa

23-26 ..... Corpus Christi
30 .... at Arkansas

JULY
1-2 .... at Arkansas
3-5 ..... at NW Arkansas
6-8 .... Arkansas
9-11 ..... NW Arkansas
13-16 ...at Corpus Christi
17-20 ..... San Antonio
21-24 ...at Corpus Christi
25-27 ...... at Midland
28-31 ...... San Antonio

AUGUST
1-3 .... Midland
4-7 ...... at San Antonio
9-11 ......at Springfield
12-14 ....at Tulsa
16-18 ...... Springfield
19-21 .... Tulsa
23-26 .... at San Antonio
27-29 ...... at Midland
30-31 ...... Corpus Christi

SEPTEMBER
1-2 ...... Corpus Christi
3-5 .... Midland

23-26 ...... San Antonio
30 ...... at NW Arkansas

JULY
1-2 ..... at NW Arkansas
3-5 ...... at Arkansas
6-8 .... NW Arkansas
9-11 .... Arkansas
13-16 ...at San Antonio
17-20 .... Corpus Christi
21-24 .... at San Antonio
25-27 .... Frisco
28-31 ...at Corpus Christi

AUGUST
1-3 .... at Frisco
4-7 ...... Corpus Christi
9-11 ....at Tulsa
12-14 ...at Springfield
16-18 ...... Tulsa
19-21 ...... Springfield
23-26 ...at Corpus Christi
27-29 .... Frisco
30-31 ...... San Antonio

SEPTEMBER
1-2 .... San Antonio
3-5 .... at Frisco

24-26 ....at San Antonio
27-29 ....at Corpus Christi
31 .... San Antonio

JUNE
1-2 .... San Antonio
3-5 ...... Corpus Christi
7-10 ....at Tulsa
11-14 .... at Arkansas
15-18 ...... Springfield
19-22 ......Arkansas
23-26 ....at Tulsa
30 .... Midland

JULY
1-2 .... Midland

3-5 . . . . .Frisco	9-11 . . . .at Corpus Christi
6-8 . . . . at Midland	12-14 . . . . at San Antonio
9-11 . . . . at Frisco	16-18 . . . . Corpus Christi
13-16 . . . . . . Springfield	19-21 . . . . . San Antonio
17-20 . . . . .at Tulsa	23-26 . . . . .at Springfield
21-24 . . . . . . Springfield	27-29 . . . . at Arkansas
25-27 . . . . . at Arkansas	30-31 . . . . Tulsa
28-31 . . . .at Springfield	

AUGUST

1-3 . . . . .Arkansas	
4-7 . . . . Tulsa	

SAN ANTONIO MISSIONS

APRIL

7-9 . . . . Springfield	23-26 . . . . . . at Midland
10-12 . . . . Tulsa	30 . . . . Tulsa
14-16 . . . . . .at Springfield	**JULY**
17-19 . . . . .at Tulsa	1-2 . . . . Tulsa
21-24 . . . . Midland	3-5 . . . . Springfield
25-28 . . . . . . at Frisco	6-8 . . . . .at Tulsa
29-30 . . . . . . at Midland	9-11 . . . . . .at Springfield
MAY	13-16 . . . . Midland
1-2 . . . . at Midland	17-20 . . . . at Frisco
3-6 . . . . .Frisco	21-24 . . . . Midland
7-10 . . . .at Corpus Christi	25-27 . . . . Corpus Christi
12-15 . . . . Midland	28-31 . . . . at Frisco
16-19 . . . . Corpus Christi	**AUGUST**
20-23 . . . . at Frisco	1-3 . . . . . .at Corpus Christi
24-26 . . . . . NW Arkansas	4-7 . . . . .Frisco
27-29 . . . . . .Arkansas	9-11 . . . . .Arkansas
31 . . . . . at NW Arkansas	12-14 . . . . NW Arkansas
JUNE	16-18 . . . . . at Arkansas
1-2 . . . . at NW Arkansas	19-21 . . . at NW Arkansas
3-5 . . . . . . at Arkansas	23-26 . . . . .Frisco
7-10 . . . . .Frisco	27-29 . . .at Corpus Christi
11-14 . . . .at Corpus Christi	30-31 . . . . . . at Midland
15-18 . . . . . at Midland	**SEPTEMBER**
19-22 . . . . . Corpus Christi	1-2 . . . . at Midland
	3-5 . . . . . . Corpus Christi

SPRINGFIELD CARDINALS

APRIL

7-9 . . . . . .at San Antonio	25-28 . . . . . NW Arkansas
10-12 . . . .at Corpus Christi	29-30 . . . . . .Arkansas
14-16 . . . . . San Antonio	**MAY**
17-19 . . . . Corpus Christi	1-2 . . . . .Arkansas
21-24 . . . . . . at Arkansas	3-6 . . . . . at NW Arkansas

7-10 . . . . .at Tulsa	9-11 . . . . . . San Antonio
12-15 . . . . . NW Arkansas	13-16 . . . . at NW Arkansas
16-19 . . . . Tulsa	17-20 . . . . .Arkansas
20-23 . . . . . . at Arkansas	21-24 . . . at NW Arkansas
24-26 . . . . Midland	25-27 . . . . .at Tulsa
27-29 . . . . .Frisco	28-31 . . . . NW Arkansas
31 . . . . at Midland	**AUGUST**
JUNE	1-3 . . . . Tulsa
1-2 . . . . at Midland	4-7 . . . . . . at Arkansas
3-5 . . . . at Frisco	9-11 . . . . .Frisco
7-10 . . . . .Arkansas	12-14 . . . . . . Midland
11-14 . . . . Tulsa	16-18 . . . . . . at Frisco
15-18 . . . at NW Arkansas	19-21 . . . . . at Midland
19-22 . . . . . . .at Tulsa	23-26 . . . . NW Arkansas
23-26 . . . . . . .Arkansas	27-29 . . . . Tulsa
30 . . . .at Corpus Christi	30-31 . . . . . at Arkansas
JULY	**SEPTEMBER**
1-2 . . . . .at Corpus Christi	1-2 . . . . at Arkansas
3-5 . . . . .at San Antonio	3-5 . . . . .at Tulsa
6-8 . . . . . . Corpus Christi	

TULSA DRILLERS

APRIL

7-9 . . . . .at Corpus Christi	30 . . . . . .at San Antonio
10-12 . . .at San Antonio	**JULY**
14-16 . . . . Corpus Christi	1-2 . . . . . . at San Antonio
17-19 . . . . . San Antonio	3-5 . . . . .at Corpus Christi
21-24 . . . . at NW Arkansas	6-8 . . . . San Antonio
25-28 . . . . .Arkansas	9-11 . . . . . Corpus Christi
29-30 . . . . . NW Arkansas	13-16 . . . . . . at Arkansas
MAY	17-20 . . . . NW Arkansas
1-2 . . . . . . NW Arkansas	21-24 . . . . at Arkansas
3-6 . . . . at Arkansas	25-27 . . . . . Springfield
7-10 . . . . . . Springfield	28-31 . . . . .Arkansas
11-14 . . . . .Arkansas	**AUGUST**
16-19 . . . .at Springfield	1-3 . . . . .at Springfield
20-23 . . . at NW Arkansas	4-7 . . . . . . at NW Arkansas
24-26 . . . . .Frisco	9-11 . . . . Midland
27-29 . . . . Midland	12-14 . . . . .Frisco
31 . . . . at Frisco	16-18 . . . . . at Midland
JUNE	19-21 . . . . . . at Frisco
1-2 . . . . at Frisco	23-26 . . . . . . .Arkansas
3-5 . . . . at Midland	27-29 . . . . .at Springfield
7-10 . . . . . NW Arkansas	30-31 . . . at NW Arkansas
11-14 . . . .at Springfield	**SEPTEMBER**
15-18 . . . . . at Arkansas	1-2 . . . . . at NW Arkansas
19-22 . . . . . Springfield	3-5 . . . . Springfield
23-26 . . . . NW Arkansas	

HIGH CLASS A

CALIFORNIA LEAGUE

BAKERSFIELD BLAZE

APRIL

7-10 . . . . Visalia	24-26 . Rancho Cucamonga
11-13 . . . . Modesto	27-30 . . . . . Inland Empire
14-17 . . . . at Visalia	**JUNE**
18-20 . . . . . . at Modesto	1-3 . . . . at Stockton
21-24 . . . . . Lake Elsinore	4-7 . . . . at San Jose
26-28 . . . .at Lancaster	9-12 . . . . .Stockton
29-30 . . . .at Inland Empire	13-15 . . . . Visalia
MAY	16-19 . . . . .at Lancaster
1 . . . . . . .at Inland Empire	23-26 . . . . .Modesto
2-5 . .at Rancho Cucamonga	27-29 . . . . . . at San Jose
6-8 . . . . Inland Empire	30 . . . . at Modesto
10-12 . . . . San Jose	**JULY**
13-16 . . . . Stockton	1-3 . . . . at Modesto
17-19 . . . . at High Desert	4-7 . . . . . . .High Desert
20-23 . . . . at Lake Elsinore	8-11 . . . . .at Visalia
	13-15 . . . . .Modesto

16-19 . . . . Visalia	15-18 . . . . San Jose
21-24 . . . . . at Modesto	19-21 . . . . . at Stockton
25-27 . . . . . at San Jose	23-25 . . . . . . .San Jose
28-31 . . . . Lancaster	26-28 . . . . . . .Stockton
AUGUST	30-31 . . . . . . at San Jose
1-3 . . . . San Jose	**SEPTEMBER**
4-7 . . . . . at Lake Elsinore	1 . . . . at San Jose
9-11 . . . . .at Visalia	2-5 . . . . at Stockton
12-14 . . . . . Lake Elsinore	

HIGH DESERT MAVERICKS

APRIL

7-10 . . . . . . Inland Empire	**MAY**
11-13 . . . . . Lake Elsinore	1 . . .at Rancho Cucamonga
14-17 . . . . .at Lancaster	2-5 . . . . Visalia
18-20 . . .at Inland Empire	6-8 . . Rancho Cucamonga
21-24 . . . . . . Lancaster	10-12 . . . . . at Modesto
26-28 . . . . at Lake Elsinore	13-16 . . . . . . .at Visalia
29-30at Rancho Cucamonga	17-19 . . . . . . Bakersfield
	20-23 . . . . Lancaster
	24-26 . . . . . at Modesto

27-30 . . . . . .at Lancaster

JUNE
1-3 . . . . .Modesto
4-7 . . . . at Lake Elsinore
9-12 . . . .at Inland Empire
13-15 . . . . Lake Elsinore
16-19 . . . . . . .Stockton
23-26at Rancho Cucamonga
27-29 . . . . Lancaster
30 . . . . . . Inland Empire

JULY
1-3 . . . . . Inland Empire
4-7 . . . . . .at Bakersfield
8-11 . . Rancho Cucamonga
13-15 . . . . at Stockton
16-19 . . . . San Jose

INLAND EMPIRE 66ERS

APRIL
7-10 . . . . . at High Desert
11-13at Rancho Cucamonga
14-17 . . . . San Jose
18-20 . . . . . .High Desert
21-24 . . . . . at Stockton
26-28 . Rancho Cucamonga
29-30 . . . . . . Bakersfield

MAY
1 . . . . Bakersfield
2-5 . . . . Lancaster
6-8 . . . . . .at Bakersfield
10-12 . . . at Lake Elsinore
13-16 . Rancho Cucamonga
17-19 . . . . . .at Lancaster
20-23 . . . . .Modesto
24-26 . . . . Lake Elsinore
27-30 . . . . .at Bakersfield

JUNE
1-3 . . . . Lancaster
4-7 . .at Rancho Cucamonga
9-12 . . . . . . .High Desert
13-15 . . . . at San Jose
16-19 . . . . . at Modesto
23-26 . . . . Visalia

LAKE ELSINORE STORM

APRIL
7-10 .at Rancho Cucamonga
11-13 . . . . at High Desert
14-17 . Rancho Cucamonga
18-20 . . . . San Jose
21-24 . . . . .at Bakersfield
26-28 . . . . .High Desert
29-30 . . . . . . Lancaster

MAY
1 . . . . Lancaster
2-5 . . . . at Modesto
6-8 . . . . at San Jose
10-12 . . . . . Inland Empire
13-16 . . . .at Lancaster
17-19 . Rancho Cucamonga
20-23 . . . . . . Bakersfield
24-26 . . . .at Inland Empire
27-30 . . . . . .Stockton

JUNE
1-3 . .at Rancho Cucamonga
4-7 . . . . . . .High Desert
9-12 . . Rancho Cucamonga
13-15 . . . at High Desert
16-19 . . . . . . .at Visalia
23-26 . . . .at Lancaster

21-24 . . . . . . .at Lancaster
25-27 . . . . .Stockton
28-31at Rancho Cucamonga

AUGUST
1-3 . . . . .at Inland Empire
4-7 . . Rancho Cucamonga
9-11 . . . . . . at San Jose
12-14 . . . . . . at Stockton
15-18 . . . . Lancaster
19-21 . . . . . Inland Empire
23-25 . . . . . .at Lancaster
26-28 . . . . Lake Elsinore
30-31 . . . . . Inland Empire

SEPTEMBER
1 . . . . Inland Empire
2-5 . . . . . at Lake Elsinore

27-29 . . . . at Lake Elsinore
30 . . . . at High Desert

JULY
1-3 . . . . . . .at High Desert
4-7 . . . Rancho Cucamonga
8-11 . . . . Lancaster
13-15at Rancho Cucamonga
16-19 . . . . . Lake Elsinore
21-24 . . . . . . at San Jose
25-27at Rancho Cucamonga
28-31 . . . . . Lake Elsinore

AUGUST
1-3 . . . . .High Desert
4-7 . . . . .at Visalia
9-11 . . . . Lancaster
12-14 . . . . . . .Modesto
15-18 . . . at Lake Elsinore
19-21 . . . . at High Desert
23-25 . . . . . . .Stockton
26-28 . Rancho Cucamonga
30-31 . . . . at High Desert

SEPTEMBER
1 . . . . at High Desert
2-5 . . . . .at Lancaster

27-29 . . . . Inland Empire
30 . . . . Lancaster

JULY
1-3 . . . . Lancaster
4-7 . . . . at Stockton
8-11 . . . . at Modesto
13-15 . . . . Visalia
16-19 . . .at Inland Empire
21-24 . Rancho Cucamonga
25-27 . . . . . . Lancaster
28-31 . . . .at Inland Empire

AUGUST
1-3 . . . . .at Lancaster
4-7 . . . . Bakersfield
9-11 .at Rancho Cucamonga
12-14 . . . . .at Bakersfield
15-18 . . . . Inland Empire
19-21 . . . . Lancaster
23-25at Rancho Cucamonga
26-28 . . . . at High Desert
30-31 . . . . . . .Modesto

SEPTEMBER
1 . . . . .Modesto
2-5 . . . . .High Desert

LANCASTER JETHAWKS

APRIL
7-10 . . . . at San Jose
11-13 . . . . . . at Stockton
14-17 . . . . . .High Desert
18-20 . Rancho Cucamonga
21-24 . . . . at High Desert
26-28 . . . . . . Bakersfield
29-30 . . . . at Lake Elsinore

MAY
1 . . . . at Lake Elsinore
2-5 . . . . .at Inland Empire
6-8 . . . . Visalia
10-12at Rancho Cucamonga
13-16 . . . . . Lake Elsinore
17-19 . . . . . Inland Empire
20-23 . . . at High Desert
24-26 . . . . .Stockton
27-30 . . . . . . .High Desert

JUNE
1-3 . . . . .at Inland Empire
4-7 . . . . .Modesto
9-12 . . . . at Visalia
13-15at Rancho Cucamonga
16-19 . . . . . . Bakersfield
23-26 . . . Lake Elsinore

MODESTO NUTS

APRIL
7-10 . . . . . . at Stockton
11-13 . . .at Bakersfield
14-17 . . . . . . .Stockton
18-20 . . . . . Bakersfield
21-24 . . . . at San Jose
26-28 . . . . . at Visalia
29-30 . . . . . .Stockton

MAY
1 . . . . at Stockton
2-5 . . . . Lake Elsinore
6-7 . . . . . . at Stockton
8 . . . . .Stockton
10-12 . . . . . .High Desert
13-14 . . . . at San Jose
15-16 . . . . . San Jose
17-19 . . . . Visalia
20-23 . . .at Inland Empire
24-26 . . . . . .High Desert
27-28 . . . . . . San Jose
29-30 . . . . at San Jose

JUNE
1-3 . . . . . at High Desert
4-7 . . . . . . .at Lancaster
9-12 . . . . . . San Jose
13-15 . . . . . . at Stockton

16-19 . . . . Inland Empire
23-26 . . . .at Bakersfield
27-29 . . . . . . .Stockton
30 . . . . Bakersfield

JULY
1-3 . . . . Bakersfield
4-7 . . . . . . at San Jose
8-11 . . . . . . Lake Elsinore
13-15 . . . .at Bakersfield
16-19 . . . . . at Stockton
21-24 . . . . . Bakersfield
25-27 . . . . . at Visalia
28-31 . . . . . San Jose

AUGUST
1-3 . . . . Visalia
4-7 . . . . .at Lancaster
9-11 . . . . .Stockton
12-14 . . . .at Inland Empire
15-18 . Rancho Cucamonga
19-21 . . . . Visalia
23-25 . . . . . at Visalia
26-28 . . . . Lancaster
30-31 . . at Lake Elsinore

SEPTEMBER
1 . . . . . . at Lake Elsinore
2-5 . .at Rancho Cucamonga

RANCHO CUCAMONGA QUAKES

APRIL
7-10 . . . . . Lake Elsinore
11-13 . . . . Inland Empire
14-17 . . . at Lake Elsinore
18-20 . . .at Lancaster
21-24 . . . . Visalia
26-28 . .at Inland Empire
29-30 . . . . .High Desert

MAY
1 . . . . .High Desert
2-5 . . . . Bakersfield
6-8 . . . at High Desert
10-12 . . . . . . Lancaster
13-16 . . . .at Inland Empire
17-19 . . . . at Lake Elsinore
20-23 . . . . San Jose
24-26 . . . .at Bakersfield
27-30 . . . . .at Visalia

JUNE
1-3 . . . . . . Lake Elsinore
4-7 . . . . . . Inland Empire
9-12 . . . . at Lake Elsinore
13-15 . . . . . . Lancaster
16-19 . . . . at San Jose
23-26 . . . . .High Desert
27-29 . . . . . . at Visalia
30 . . . . .Stockton

JULY
1-3 . . . . Stockton
4-7 . . . . . . at Inland Empire
8-11 . . . . . at High Desert
13-15 . . . . Inland Empire
16-19 . . . . . . Lancaster
21-24 . . . . at Lake Elsinore
25-27 . . . . Inland Empire
28-31 . . . . . High Desert

AUGUST
1-3 . . . . at Stockton

SAN JOSE GIANTS

APRIL
7-10 . . . . Lancaster
11-13 . . . . Visalia
14-17 . . . . at Inland Empire
18-20 . . . . at Lake Elsinore
21-24 . . . . Modesto
26-28 . . . . Stockton
29-30 . . . . at Visalia

MAY
1 . . . . at Visalia
2-5 . . . . at Stockton
6-8 . . . . Lake Elsinore
10-12 . . . . . at Bakersfield
13-14 . . . . Modesto
15-16 . . . . . . at Modesto
17-19 . . . . . at Stockton
20-23 at Rancho Cucamonga
24-26 . . . . . . at Visalia
27-28 . . . . . at Modesto
29-30 . . . . Modesto

JUNE
1-3 . . . . Visalia
4-7 . . . . Bakersfield
9-12 . . . . . . at Modesto
13-15 . . . . Inland Empire
16-19 . Rancho Cucamonga

STOCKTON PORTS

APRIL
7-10 . . . . Modesto
11-13 . . . . Lancaster
14-17 . . . . . . at Modesto
18-20 . . . . at Visalia
21-24 . . . . Inland Empire
26-28 . . . . at San Jose
29-30 . . . . . . at Modesto

MAY
1 . . . . Modesto
2-5 . . . . San Jose
6-7 . . . . Modesto
8 . . . . at Modesto
10-12 . . . . . . at Visalia
13-16 . . . . . at Bakersfield
17-19 . . . . San Jose
20-23 . . . . Visalia
24-26 . . . . . . at Lancaster
27-30 . . at Lake Elsinore

JUNE
1-3 . . . . Bakersfield
4-7 . . . . Visalia
9-12 . . . . . at Bakersfield
13-15 . . . . Modesto
16-19 . . . . at High Desert

VISALIA RAWHIDE

APRIL
7-10 . . . . . . at Bakersfield

4-7 . . . . . . at High Desert
9-11 . . . . . . Lake Elsinore
12-14 . . . . Visalia
15-18 . . . . . . at Modesto
19-21 . . . . . at San Jose
23-25 . . . . . Lake Elsinore
26-28 . . . at Inland Empire
30-31 . . . . . . at Lancaster

SEPTEMBER
1 . . . . at Lancaster
2-5 . . . . Modesto

APRIL (cont.)
23-26 . . . . . . at Stockton
27-29 . . . . . . Bakersfield
30 . . . . at Visalia

JULY
1-3 . . . . at Visalia
4-7 . . . . Modesto
8-11 . . . . Stockton
13-15 . . . . . at Lancaster
16-19 . . . . at High Desert
21-24 . . . . Inland Empire
25-27 . . . . . Bakersfield
28-31 . . . . . . at Modesto

AUGUST
1-3 . . . . . . at Bakersfield
4-7 . . . . Stockton
9-11 . . . . . . High Desert
12-14 . . . . . at Lancaster
15-18 . . . . at Bakersfield
19-21 . Rancho Cucamonga
23-25 . . . . at Bakersfield
26-28 . . . . . . at Visalia
30-31 . . . . . Bakersfield

SEPTEMBER
1 . . . . Bakersfield
2-5 . . . . Visalia

JULY (Stockton cont.)
1-3 . at Rancho Cucamonga
4-7 . . . . . . Lake Elsinore
8-11 . . . . . at San Jose
13-15 . . . . . High Desert
16-19 . . . . Modesto
21-24 . . . . . . at Visalia
25-27 . . . . at High Desert
28-31 . . . . Visalia

AUGUST
1-3 . . Rancho Cucamonga
4-7 . . . . . . at San Jose
9-11 . . . . . . at Modesto
12-14 . . . . . High Desert
15-18 . . . . . . at Visalia
19-21 . . . . . . Bakersfield
23-25 . . at Inland Empire
26-28 . . . . at Bakersfield
30-31 . . . . Visalia

SEPTEMBER
1 . . . . Visalia
2-5 . . . . Bakersfield

APRIL (Visalia cont.)
11-13 . . . . . at San Jose
14-17 . . . . . . Bakersfield

18-20 . . . . Stockton
21-24 at Rancho Cucamonga
26-28 . . . . Modesto
29-30 . . . . San Jose

MAY
1 . . . . San Jose
2-5 . . . . at High Desert
6-8 . . . . . . at Lancaster
10-12 . . . . Stockton
13-16 . . . . . High Desert
17-19 . . . . . at Modesto
20-23 . . . . at Stockton
24-26 . . . . . . San Jose
27-30 . Rancho Cucamonga

JUNE
1-3 . . . . at San Jose
4-7 . . . . . . at Stockton
9-12 . . . . Lancaster
13-15 . . . . at Bakersfield
16-19 . . . . . Lake Elsinore
23-26 . . at Inland Empire
27-29 . Rancho Cucamonga
30 . . . . San Jose

CAROLINA LEAGUE

CAROLINA MUDCATS

APRIL
7-10 . . . . at Salem
11-13 . . . . at Wilmington
14-17 . . Myrtle Beach
18-20 . . . . Salem
21-24 . . at Myrtle Beach
26-28 . . . . . Wilmington
29-30 . . . . . . Lynchburg

MAY
1 . . . . Lynchburg
2-4 . . . . at Salem
5-8 . . . . . . at Lynchburg
10-12 . . . . . . Potomac
13-16 . . . . . . Lynchburg
17-19 . . . . . . at Potomac
20-23 . . at Wilmington
24-26 . . Myrtle Beach
27-30 . . . . Frederick

JUNE
1-3 . . . . at Winston-Salem
4-7 . . . . . at Frederick
9-12 . . . . Winston-Salem
13-15 . . . . at Lynchburg
16-19 . . . . Wilmington
23-26 . . . . at Myrtle Beach

FREDERICK KEYS

APRIL
7-10 . . . . at Myrtle Beach
11-13 . . . . Lynchburg
14-17 . . . . . Lynchburg
18-20 . . . . . Wilmington
21-24 . . . . at Lynchburg
26-28 . . . . Salem
29-30 . . . Winston-Salem

MAY
1 . . . . Winston-Salem
2-4 . . . . . at Wilmington
5-8 . . . . . at Potomac
10-12 . . . . Wilmington
13-16 . . . . Myrtle Beach
17-19 . . . . at Wilmington
20-23 . . . . Potomac
24-26 . . at Winston-Salem
27-30 . . . . . at Carolina

27-29 . . . . . at Frederick
30 . . . . Lynchburg

JULY
1-3 . . . . Lynchburg
4-7 . . . . Salem
8-11 . . . . . . at Potomac
13-15 . . . . . . Lynchburg
16-19 . . . . . . Frederick
21-24 . . . at Lynchburg
25-27 . . at Myrtle Beach
28-31 . . . . Potomac

AUGUST
1-3 . . . . . . Winston-Salem
4-7 . . . . . at Myrtle Beach
9-11 . . . . at Winston-Salem
12-14 . . . . Myrtle Beach
15-18 . . . . . . at Salem
19-21 . . . . at Wilmington
23-25 . . . Myrtle Beach
26-28 . . at Winston-Salem
30-31 . . . . . Wilmington

SEPTEMBER
1 . . . . Wilmington
2-5 . . . . . . Winston-Salem

JUNE (Frederick)
1-3 . . . . Potomac
4-7 . . . . Carolina
9-12 . . . . . . at Potomac
13-15 . . . . at Myrtle Beach
16-19 . . . . . Lynchburg
23-26 . . . . . at Salem
27-29 . . . . Carolina
30 . . . . Salem

JULY
1-3 . . . . Salem
4-7 . . . . . . at Lynchburg
8-11 . . . . . Winston-Salem
13-15 . . at Myrtle Beach
16-19 . . . . at Carolina
21-24 . . . . Salem
25-27 . . at Winston-Salem
28-31 . . . at Wilmington

AUGUST
1-3 . . . . . . Myrtle Beach
4-7 . . . . at Winston-Salem
9-11 . . . . . at Wilmington
12-14 . . . . Potomac
15-18 . . . . . . Lynchburg
19-21 . . . . . . at Potomac

23-25 . . . . Winston-Salem
26-28 . . . . at Salem
30-31 . . . . Potomac

SEPTEMBER
1 . . . . Potomac
2-5 . . . . . . Wilmington

LYNCHBURG HILLCATS

APRIL
7-10 . . . . . Winston-Salem
11-13 . . . . Potomac
14-17 . . . . . at Frederick
18-20 . . . . . at Potomac
21-24 . . . . . . Frederick
26-28 . . . at Winston-Salem
29-30 . . . . . . at Carolina

MAY
1 . . . . at Carolina
2-4 . . . . Potomac
5-8 . . . . Carolina
10-12 . . . . . . at Salem
13-16 . . . . . at Carolina
17-19 . . . . Salem
20-23 . . . at Myrtle Beach
24-26 . . . . . . Wilmington
27-30 . . . . Salem

JUNE
1-3 . . . . . at Wilmington
4 . . . . at Salem
5-6 . . . . Salem
7 . . . . at Salem
9-12 . . . . . Myrtle Beach
13-15 . . . . Carolina
16-19 . . . . . at Frederick
23-26 . . . . Potomac
27-29 . . . . at Wilmington
30 . . . . at Carolina

JULY
1-3 . . . . at Carolina
4-7 . . . . Frederick
8-9 . . . . Salem
10-11 . . . . . . at Salem
13-15 . . . . . at Carolina
16-19 . . . . at Wilmington
21-24 . . . . Carolina
25-27 . . . . . Wilmington
28-31 . . . at Winston-Salem

AUGUST
1-3 . . . . Potomac
4-7 . . . . at Salem
9-11 . . . . . . at Potomac
12-14 . . . . Winston-Salem
15-18 . . . . . at Frederick
19-21 . . at Myrtle Beach
23-25 . . . . . . Wilmington
26-28 . . . . Potomac
30-31 . . . at Myrtle Beach

SEPTEMBER
1 . . . . at Myrtle Beach
2-5 . . . . Salem

MYRTLE BEACH PELICANS

APRIL
7-10 . . . . . . Frederick
11-13 . . . . Winston-Salem
14-17 . . . . . at Carolina
18-20 . . . at Winston-Salem
21-24 . . . . . . Carolina
26-28 . . . . at Potomac
29-30 . . . . Salem

MAY
1 . . . . Salem
2-4 . . . at Winston-Salem
5-8 . . . . . at Wilmington
10-12 . . . Winston-Salem
13-16 . . . . at Frederick
17-19 . . . Winston-Salem
20-23 . . . . . Lynchburg
24-26 . . . . at Carolina
27-30 . . . . . Wilmington

JUNE
1-3 . . . . . . at Salem
4-7 . . . . Potomac
9-12 . . . . at Lynchburg
13-15 . . . . . Frederick
16-19 . . . at Potomac
23-26 . . . . . . Carolina
27-29 . . . . . . at Salem
30 . . . . Potomac

JULY
1-3 . . . . Potomac
4-7 . . . at Winston-Salem
8-11 . . . . at Wilmington
13-15 . . . . . Frederick
16-19 . . . at Winston-Salem
21-24 . . . . . Wilmington
25-27 . . . . . Carolina
28-31 . . . . . at Salem

AUGUST
1-3 . . . . at Frederick
4-7 . . . . Carolina
9-11 . . . . Salem
12-14 . . . . at Carolina
15-18 . . . Winston-Salem
19-21 . . . . . Lynchburg
23-25 . . . at Carolina
26-28 . . . at Wilmington
30-31 . . . . . . Lynchburg

SEPTEMBER
1 . . . . . at Myrtle Beach
2-5 . . . . . . at Potomac

POTOMAC NATIONALS

APRIL
7-10 . . . . . at Wilmington
11-13 . . . at Lynchburg
14-17 . . . . . Wilmington
18-20 . . . . . Lynchburg
21-24 . . . . at Wilmington
26-28 . . . . . Myrtle Beach
29-30 . . . . . Wilmington

MAY
1 . . . . Wilmington
2-4 . . . . . . at Lynchburg
5-8 . . . . Frederick
10-12 . . . . . . at Carolina
13-16 . . . at Winston-Salem
17-19 . . . . Carolina
20-23 . . . . . at Frederick
24-26 . . . . Salem
27-30 . . . . Winston-Salem

JUNE
1-3 . . . . . . at Frederick
4-7 . . . . at Myrtle Beach
9-12 . . . . Frederick
13-15 . . . . . . at Salem
16-19 . . . Myrtle Beach
23-26 . . . . at Lynchburg
27-29 . . . . Winston-Salem
30 . . . . . at Myrtle Beach

JULY
1-3 . . . . . at Myrtle Beach
4-7 . . . . Frederick
8-11 . . . . . . at Wilmington
13-15 . . . . . at Carolina
16-19 . . . . at Wilmington
21-24 . . . . . . Carolina
25-27 . . . . . Wilmington
28-31 . . . at Winston-Salem

AUGUST
1-3 . . . . Potomac
4-7 . . . . at Salem
9-11 . . . . . . at Potomac
12-14 . . . . Winston-Salem
15-18 . . . . . at Frederick
19-21 . . at Myrtle Beach
23-25 . . . . . . Wilmington
26-28 . . . . Potomac
30-31 . . . at Myrtle Beach

SEPTEMBER
1 . . . . at Myrtle Beach
2-5 . . . . Salem

SALEM RED SOX

APRIL
7-10 . . . . Carolina
11-13 . . . . . . Frederick
14-17 . . . at Winston-Salem
18-20 . . . . at Carolina
21-24 . . . . Winston-Salem
26-28 . . . . at Frederick
29-30 . . . at Myrtle Beach

MAY
1 . . . . . at Myrtle Beach
2-4 . . . . Carolina
5-8 . . . . at Winston-Salem
10-12 . . . . . Lynchburg
13-16 . . . . . Wilmington
17-19 . . . . at Lynchburg
20-23 . . . Winston-Salem
24-26 . . . at Potomac
27-30 . . . . at Lynchburg

JUNE
1-3 . . . . . Myrtle Beach
4 . . . . Lynchburg
5-6 . . . . . at Lynchburg
7 . . . . Lynchburg
9-12 . . . . . at Wilmington
13-15 . . . . Potomac
16-19 . . . at Winston-Salem
23-26 . . . . Frederick
27-29 . . . . . Myrtle Beach
30 . . . . at Frederick

JULY
1-3 . . . . . . at Frederick
4-7 . . . . at Carolina
8-9 . . . . . at Lynchburg
10-11 . . . . . Lynchburg
13-15 . . . . . Wilmington
16-19 . . . . . . at Frederick
21-24 . . . . . at Frederick
25-27 . . . . at Potomac
28-31 . . . . Myrtle Beach

AUGUST
1-3 . . . . . at Wilmington
4-7 . . . . Lynchburg
9-11 . . . . at Myrtle Beach
12-14 . . . . . Wilmington
15-18 . . . . Carolina
19-21 . . . at Winston-Salem
23-25 . . . at Potomac
26-28 . . . . . Frederick
30-31 . . . Winston-Salem

SEPTEMBER
1 . . . . . . Winston-Salem
2-5 . . . . at Lynchburg

WILMINGTON BLUE ROCKS

APRIL
7-10 . . . . Potomac
11-13 . . . . Carolina
14-17 . . . . . . at Potomac
18-20 . . . . . at Frederick
21-24 . . . . Potomac
26-28 . . . . . at Carolina
29-30 . . . . . . at Potomac

MAY
1 . . . . at Potomac
2-4 . . . . Frederick
5-8 . . . . . . Myrtle Beach
10-12 . . . . . at Frederick
13-16 . . . . at Salem
17-19 . . . . Frederick
20-23 . . . . . . Lynchburg
24-26 . . . at Lynchburg
27-30 . . . at Myrtle Beach

JUNE
1-3 . . . . Lynchburg
4-7 . . . . at Winston-Salem
9-12 . . . . Salem
13-15 . . . . Winston-Salem
16-19 . . . . . . at Carolina
23-26 . . . at Winston-Salem
27-29 . . . . . Lynchburg
30 . . . . . . Winston-Salem

JULY
1-3 . . . . . Winston-Salem
4-7 . . . . at Potomac
8-11 . . . . . . Myrtle Beach
13-15 . . . . . . at Salem
16-19 . . . . . . at Carolina
21-24 . . . at Myrtle Beach
25-27 . . . at Lynchburg
28-31 . . . . Frederick

AUGUST
1-3 . . . . Salem
4-7 . . . . . . at Potomac
9-11 . . . . Frederick
12-14 . . . . . . at Salem
15-18 . . . . Potomac
19-21 . . . . Carolina
23-25 . . . at Lynchburg
26-28 . . . Myrtle Beach
30-31 . . . . . at Carolina

SEPTEMBER
1 . . . . .at Carolina

WINSTON-SALEM DASH

APRIL
7-10 . . . . . . at Lynchburg
11-13 . . . . at Myrtle Beach
14-17 . . . . .Salem
18-20 . . . . . Myrtle Beach
21-24 . . . . at Salem
26-28 . . . . . . .Lynchburg
29-30 . . . . . . at Frederick

MAY
1 . . . . at Frederick
2-4 . . . . Myrtle Beach
5-8 . . . . .Salem
10-12 . . . at Myrtle Beach
13-16 . . . . .Potomac
17-19 . . . at Myrtle Beach
20-23 . . . . at Salem
24-26 . . . . . . .Frederick
27-30 . . . . . . at Potomac

JUNE
1-3 . . . . Carolina
4-7 . . . . .Wilmington
9-12 . . . . .at Carolina
13-15 . . . . at Wilmington
16-19 . . . . .Salem
23-26 . . . . . . Wilmington

FLORIDA STATE LEAGUE

BRADENTON MARAUDERS

APRIL
7-8 . . . . . . at Fort Myers
9-10 . . . . . . .Fort Myers
11-14 . . . . .at Tampa
15-18 . . . . .Lakeland
19-21 . . . . at Palm Beach
22-24 . . . . . . at St. Lucie
26-28 . . . . . Palm Beach
29-30 . . . . . . at Jupiter

MAY
1 . . . . at Jupiter
2-4 . . . . St. Lucie
5-7 . . . . Charlotte
9 . . . . .Fort Myers
10 . . . . . . at Fort Myers
11 . . . . .Fort Myers
12 . . . . . . at Fort Myers
13-15 . . . at Palm Beach
16-19 . . .at Brevard County
20-23 . . . . Dunedin
24-26 . . . . at Jupiter
27-29 . . . . St. Lucie
31 . . . . Palm Beach

JUNE
1-2 . . . . Palm Beach
3-6 . . . . . . at Lakeland
8-11 . . . . Tampa
12-15 . . . . .at Clearwater
16 . . . . .Fort Myers
20-22 . . . . Jupiter

BREVARD COUNTY MANATEES

APRIL
7 . . . . at Daytona
8 . . . . Daytona
9 . . . . at Daytona
10 . . . . Daytona
11-14 . . . . . at Fort Myers
15-16 . . . . St. Lucie
17-18 . . . . at St. Lucie
19-21 . . . . . at Lakeland
22-24 . . . . .at Clearwater

2-5 . . . . at Frederick

27-29 . . . . . . at Potomac
30 . . . . . . at Wilmington

JULY
1-3 . . . . . . at Wilmington
4-7 . . . . . . Myrtle Beach
8-11 . . . . at Frederick
13-15 . . . . .Potomac
16-19 . . . . . Myrtle Beach
21-24 . . . . . at Potomac
25-27 . . . . . . .Frederick
28-31 . . . . . . .Lynchburg

AUGUST
1-3 . . . . .at Carolina
4-7 . . . . .Frederick
9-11 . . . . Carolina
12-14 . . . .at Lynchburg
15-18 . . . at Myrtle Beach
19-21 . . . . .Salem
23-25 . . . . . . at Frederick
26-28 . . . . Carolina
30-31 . . . . . . at Salem

SEPTEMBER
1 . . . . at Salem
2-5 . . . . .at Carolina

23 . . . . Charlotte
24-25 . . . . . at Charlotte
26 . . . . . at Fort Myers
27 . . . . .Fort Myers
28-30 . . . . Jupiter

JULY
1-2 . . . . Charlotte
3-6 . . . . at Charlotte
7 . . . . at Fort Myers
8-11 . . . . Brevard County
13-16 . . . . . . at Dunedin
17-20 . . . . . . Clearwater
21-24 . . . . Daytona
26-28 . . . . . at St. Lucie
29-31 . . . . . . at Daytona

AUGUST
1 . . . . at Daytona
3-4 . . . . .Fort Myers
5-7 . . . . at St. Lucie
8-10 . . . . Palm Beach
11-13 . . . . St. Lucie
14-15 . . . . . . .Fort Myers
16-18 . . . . at Palm Beach
19-21 . . . . . .at Charlotte
23-25 . . . . at Jupiter
26-28 . . . . Charlotte
29-31 . . . . Jupiter

SEPTEMBER
1-4 . . . . . . at Fort Myers

26-28 . . . . .Lakeland
29-30 . . . . .at Tampa

MAY
1 . . . . .at Tampa
2-4 . . . . .Dunedin
5-7 . . . . .Lakeland
9 . . . . at Daytona
10 . . . . Daytona
11-12 . . . . . . at Daytona
13-15 . . . . . at Dunedin
16-19 . . . . . . .Bradenton
20-23 . . . . at Jupiter
24-26 . . . . . . Clearwater
27-29 . . . . Tampa
31 . . . . at Lakeland

JUNE
1-2 . . . . at Lakeland
3-4 . . . . at St. Lucie
5-6 . . . . St. Lucie
8-11 . . . . . . .Fort Myers
12-15 . . . Palm Beach
16 . . . . at Daytona
20-22 . . . . at Dunedin
23-25 . . . . . . Clearwater
26-28 . . . . . . .at Tampa
29 . . . . Daytona
30 . . . . . . at Daytona

CHARLOTTE STONE CRABS

APRIL
7-8 . . . . . . at Palm Beach
9-10 . . . . Palm Beach
11-14 . . . . . .at Clearwater
15-18 . . . . Tampa
19-21 . . . . . . at St. Lucie
22-24 . . . . at Fort Myers
26-28 . . . . St. Lucie
29-30 . . . . . . .Fort Myers

MAY
1 . . . . .Fort Myers
2-4 . . . . Jupiter
5-7 . . . . . at Bradenton
8-10 . . . . at Palm Beach
11-12 . . . . Palm Beach
13-15 . . . . Jupiter
16-19 . . . . Daytona
20-23 . . . . at Lakeland
24-26 . . . . at St. Lucie
27-29 . . . . . . .Fort Myers
31 . . . . at Jupiter

JUNE
1-2 . . . . at Jupiter
3-6 . . . . .at Tampa
8-11 . . . . . . Clearwater
12-15 . . . . Dunedin
20-22 . . . at Fort Myers
23 . . . . at Bradenton

CLEARWATER THRESHERS

APRIL
7 . . . . at Dunedin
8 . . . . at Dunedin
9-10 . . . . at Dunedin
11-14 . . . . Charlotte
15-18 . . . . . . at Jupiter
19-21 . . . . Daytona
22-24 . . . . Brevard County
26-28 . . . . . at Daytona
29-30 . . . . .Lakeland

MAY
1 . . . . .Lakeland
2 . . . . .at Tampa

JULY
1-3 . . . . at Clearwater
4-6 . . . . Dunedin
7 . . . . Daytona
8-11 . . . . . . at Bradenton
13-16 . . . . Jupiter
17-20 . . . at Palm Beach
21-24 . . . . .at Charlotte
26-28 . . . . Tampa
29-31 . . . . Charlotte

AUGUST
1 . . . . Charlotte
3 . . . . at Daytona
4 . . . . Daytona
5-7 . . . . Dunedin
8-10 . . . . . at Lakeland
11-13 . . . . . at Dunedin
14 . . . . Daytona
15 . . . . at Daytona
16-18 . . . . .Lakeland
19-21 . . . . Tampa
23-25 . . . .at Clearwater
26-28 . . . . . . .at Tampa
29-31 . . . . . Clearwater

SEPTEMBER
1 . . . . at Daytona
2-4 . . . . Daytona

24-25 . . . . . . .Bradenton
26-27 . . . . . Palm Beach
28-30 . . . . St. Lucie

JULY
1-2 . . . . at Bradenton
3-6 . . . . .Bradenton
7 . . . . Palm Beach
8-11 . . . . . . at Daytona
13-16 . . . . .Lakeland
17-20 . . . . . . at Dunedin
21-24 . . . . Brevard County
26-28 . . . . . . at Jupiter
29-31 . . .at Brevard County

AUGUST
1 . . . . .at Brevard County
3-4 . . . . Palm Beach
5-7 . . . . .Fort Myers
8-10 . . . . at Jupiter
11-13 . . . at Fort Myers
14-15 . . . . at Palm Beach
16-18 . . . . Jupiter
19-21 . . . . . . .Bradenton
23-25 . . . . . . at St. Lucie
26-28 . . . . at Bradenton
29-31 . . . . St. Lucie

SEPTEMBER
1 . . . . Palm Beach
2-4 . . . . . . at Palm Beach

3-4 . . . . Tampa
5-7 . . . . .at Tampa
9 . . . . at Dunedin
10 . . . . Dunedin
11 . . . . . . at Dunedin
12 . . . . Dunedin
13-14 . . . . . .at Tampa
15 . . . . Tampa
16-19 . . . . . at St. Lucie
20-23 . . . . . Palm Beach
24-26 . . .at Brevard County
27-29 . . . . at Lakeland
31 . . . . Tampa

JUNE
1 . . . . Tampa
3-6. . . . . Jupiter
7 . . . . Tampa
8-11 . . . . . . .at Charlotte
12-15 . . . . . . .Bradenton
16 . . . . Dunedin
20-22 . . . . .Lakeland
23-25 . . .at Brevard County
26-28 . . . . Daytona
29-30 . . . . Dunedin

JULY
1-3 . . . . . Brevard County
4 . . . . at Lakeland
5 . . . . .Lakeland
6 . . . . at Lakeland
7 . . . . at Dunedin
8-11 . . . . St. Lucie
13-16 . . . . . at Palm Beach
17-20 . . . . at Bradenton
21-24 . . . . .Fort Myers

26-28 . . . . . . at Daytona
29-31 . . . . . at Fort Myers

AUGUST
1 . . . . at Fort Myers
3 . . . . at Dunedin
4 . . . . Dunedin
5-6. . . . . .Lakeland
7 . . . . at Lakeland
8-10 . . . . Tampa
11-13 . . . . . . at Lakeland
14 . . . . at Dunedin
15 . . . . Dunedin
16-18 . . . . . . .at Tampa
19-21 . . . . Daytona
23-25 . . . . Brevard County
26-28 . . . . . . at Daytona
29-31 . . .at Brevard County

SEPTEMBER
1 . . . . at Dunedin
2-3. . . . . Dunedin
4 . . . . at Dunedin

DAYTONA TORTUGAS

APRIL
7 . . . . . . Brevard County
8 . . . . .at Brevard County
9 . . . . . Brevard County
10 . . . .at Brevard County
11-14 . . . . at Palm Beach
15-18 . . . . . . .Fort Myers
19-21 . . .at Clearwater
22-24 . . . . . . .at Tampa
26-28 . . . . . Clearwater
29-30 . . . . Dunedin

MAY
2-4. . . . . at Lakeland
5-8. . . . . at Dunedin
9 . . . . . . Brevard County
10 . . . .at Brevard County
11-12 . . . Brevard County
13-15 . . . . . . .Lakeland
16-19 . . . . .at Charlotte
20-23 . . . . . St. Lucie
24-26 . . . . Tampa
27-28 . . . . at Dunedin
29-31 . . . . Dunedin

JUNE
1 . . . . Dunedin
3-6. . . . . . . at Fort Myers
8-11 . . . . Palm Beach
12-15 . . . . . . at Jupiter
16 . . . . . Brevard County
20-22 . . . . Tampa
23 . . . . at Lakeland
24-25 . . . . .Lakeland

26-28 . . . . .at Clearwater
29 . . . .at Brevard County
30 . . . . . Brevard County

JULY
1-2 . . . . at Lakeland
3 . . . . .Lakeland
4-6 . . . . .at Tampa
7 . . . .at Brevard County
8-11 . . . . Charlotte
13-16 . . . . . at St. Lucie
17-20 . . . . Jupiter
21-24 . . . . at Bradenton
26-28 . . . . . Clearwater
29-31 . . . . . . .Bradenton

AUGUST
1 . . . . .Bradenton
3 . . . . . . Brevard County
4 . . . .at Brevard County
5-7 . . . . .at Tampa
8-10 . . . . .Dunedin
11-13 . . . . Tampa
14 . . . .at Brevard County
15 . . . . . Brevard County
16-18 . . . . . at Dunedin
19-21 . . . .at Clearwater
23-25 . . . . .Lakeland
26-28 . . . . . Clearwater
29-31 . . . . at Lakeland

SEPTEMBER
1 . . . . . . Brevard County
2-4. . . . .at Brevard County

DUNEDIN BLUE JAYS

APRIL
7 . . . . Clearwater
8 . . . . .at Clearwater
9-10 . . . . Clearwater
11-14 . . . . at St. Lucie
15-18 . . . . Palm Beach
19-21 . . . . . . .at Tampa
22-24 . . . . at Lakeland
26-28 . . . . Tampa
29-30 . . . . . . at Daytona

MAY
2-4. . . . .at Brevard County
5-8. . . . . Daytona
9 . . . . Clearwater
10 . . . . . . .at Clearwater

11 . . . . Clearwater
12 . . . . . . .at Clearwater
13-15 . . . Brevard County
16-19 . . . . . . .Fort Myers
20-23 . . . . . at Bradenton
24-26 . . . . . .Lakeland
27-28 . . . . . Daytona
29-31 . . . . . at Daytona

JUNE
1 . . . . at Daytona
3-6. . . . . at Palm Beach
8-11 . . . . St. Lucie
12-15 . . . .at Charlotte
16 . . . . . .at Clearwater
20-22 . . . . Brevard County

FORT MYERS MIRACLE

APRIL
7-8. . . . . .Bradenton
9-10 . . . . . . at Bradenton
11-14 . . . Brevard County
15-18 . . . . . . at Daytona
19-21 . . . . Jupiter
22-24 . . . . . . Charlotte
26-28 . . . . at Jupiter
29-30 . . . . .at Charlotte

MAY
1 . . . . at Charlotte
2-4. . . . . at Palm Beach
5-7 . . . . St. Lucie
9 . . . . at Bradenton
10 . . . . .Bradenton
11 . . . . at Bradenton
12 . . . . .Bradenton
13-15 . . . . . at St. Lucie
16-19 . . . . . at Dunedin
20-23 . . . . Tampa
24-26 . . . . . Palm Beach
27-29 . . . . .at Charlotte
31 . . . . St. Lucie

JUNE
1-2 . . . . St. Lucie
3-6. . . . . Daytona
8-11 . . . .at Brevard County
12-15 . . . . . . at Bradenton
16 . . . . . at Bradenton

23-25 . . . . .at Tampa
26-28 . . . . at Lakeland
29-30 . . . . .at Clearwater

JULY
1-3 . . . . Tampa
4-6 . . . .at Brevard County
7 . . . . Clearwater
8-11 . . . . . . at Fort Myers
13-16 . . . . . . .Bradenton
17-20 . . . . . . Charlotte
21-24 . . . . . at Jupiter
26-28 . . . . . . .Lakeland
29-31 . . . . Jupiter

AUGUST
1 . . . . Jupiter

3 . . . . Clearwater
4 . . . . . . .at Clearwater
5-7. . . .at Brevard County
8-10 . . . . at Daytona
11-13 . . . Brevard County
14 . . . . Clearwater
15 . . . . . . .at Clearwater
16-18 . . . . Daytona
19-21 . . . . . at Lakeland
23-25 . . . . . . .at Tampa
26-28 . . . . . . .Lakeland
29-31 . . . . Tampa

SEPTEMBER
1 . . . . Clearwater
2-3. . . . . . .at Clearwater
4 . . . . Clearwater

20-22 . . . . Charlotte
23-25 . . . . . . at Jupiter
26 . . . . .Bradenton
27 . . . . . . at Bradenton
28-30 . . . at Palm Beach

JULY
1-3 . . . . Jupiter
4-6 . . . . at St. Lucie
7 . . . . .Bradenton
8-11 . . . . Dunedin
13-16 . . . . . .at Tampa
17-20 . . . . .Lakeland
21-24 . . . .at Clearwater
25-27 . . . . Palm Beach
29-31 . . . . . Clearwater

AUGUST
1 . . . . Clearwater
3-4. . . . . . at Bradenton
5-7. . . . . . .at Charlotte
8-10 . . . . St. Lucie
11-13 . . . . . . Charlotte
14-15 . . . . at Bradenton
16-18 . . . . . at St. Lucie
19-21 . . . . Jupiter
23-25 . . . . Palm Beach
26-28 . . . . . at Jupiter
29-31 . . . . at Palm Beach

SEPTEMBER
1-4. . . . . .Bradenton

JUPITER HAMMERHEADS

APRIL
7-8. . . . . at St. Lucie
9-10 . . . . St. Lucie
11-14 . . . . . .at Lakeland
15-18 . . . . Clearwater
19-21 . . . . . at Fort Myers
22 . . . . Palm Beach
23 . . . . . . at Palm Beach
24 . . . . Palm Beach
26-28 . . . . . . .Fort Myers
29-30 . . . . . . .Bradenton

MAY
1 . . . . .Bradenton
2-4. . . . . .at Charlotte
5 . . . . . . at Palm Beach
6 . . . . Palm Beach
7 . . . . Palm Beach
9-10 . . . . . at St. Lucie
11-12 . . . . . . St. Lucie
13-15 . . . . .at Charlotte
16-19 . . . . . . .at Tampa
20-23 . . . Brevard County
24-26 . . . . . . .Bradenton

27 . . . . . . at Palm Beach
28 . . . . Palm Beach
29 . . . . . at Palm Beach
31 . . . . Charlotte

JUNE
1-2 . . . . Charlotte
3-6. . . . . . .at Clearwater
8-11 . . . . .Lakeland
12-15 . . . . Daytona
16 . . . . at St. Lucie
20-22 . . . . at Bradenton
23-25 . . . . . .Fort Myers
26-27 . . . . . St. Lucie
28-30 . . . at Bradenton

JULY
1-3 . . . . at Fort Myers
4-6 . . . . Palm Beach
7 . . . . St. Lucie
8-11 . . . . Tampa
13-16 . . .at Brevard County
17-20 . . . . at Daytona
21-24 . . . . . . .Dunedin
26-28 . . . . . Charlotte

29-31 . . . . at Dunedin

AUGUST
1 . . . . at Dunedin
3-4 . . . . St. Lucie
5-6 . . . . . . at Palm Beach
7 . . . . Palm Beach
8-10 . . . . Charlotte
11-12 . . . . . at Palm Beach
13 . . . . Palm Beach

LAKELAND FLYING TIGERS

APRIL
7 . . . . Tampa
8 . . . . .at Tampa
9-10 . . . . Tampa
11-14 . . . . Jupiter
15-18 . . . . at Bradenton
19-21 . . . . Brevard County
22-24 . . . . Dunedin
26-28 . .at Brevard County
29-30 . . . . at Clearwater

MAY
1 . . . . .at Clearwater
2-4 . . . . Daytona
5-7 . . . . .at Brevard County
9-10 . . . . .at Tampa
11-12 . . . . Tampa
13-15 . . . . . at Daytona
16-19 . . . . at Palm Beach
20-23 . . . . . . Charlotte
24-26 . . . . . at Dunedin
27-29 . . . . . Clearwater
31 . . . . . Brevard County

JUNE
1-2 . . . . . Brevard County
3-6 . . . . .Bradenton
8-11 . . . . . . at Jupiter
12-15 . . . . . . .Fort Myers
16 . . . . Tampa
20-22 . . . .at Clearwater
23 . . . . Daytona
24-25 . . . . at Daytona
26-28 . . . . Dunedin

PALM BEACH CARDINALS

APRIL
7-8 . . . . Charlotte
9-10 . . . . . . .at Charlotte
11-14 . . . . Daytona
15-18 . . . . . at Dunedin
19-21 . . . . . .Bradenton
22 . . . . at Jupiter
23 . . . . Jupiter
24 . . . . at Jupiter
26-28 . . . . . at Bradenton
29-30 . . . . . . at St. Lucie

MAY
1 . . . . at St. Lucie
2-4 . . . . .Fort Myers
5 . . . . Jupiter
6 . . . . at Jupiter
7 . . . . Jupiter
8-10 . . . . Charlotte
11-12 . . . .at Charlotte
13-15 . . . . . . .Bradenton
16-19 . . . . . . .Lakeland
20-23 . . . .at Clearwater
24-26 . . . . at Fort Myers
27 . . . . Jupiter
28 . . . . at Jupiter
29 . . . . Jupiter
31 . . . . at Bradenton

14-15 . . . . . . at St. Lucie
16-18 . . . . . . .at Charlotte
19-21 . . . . . at Fort Myers
23-25 . . . . . . .Bradenton
26-28 . . . . . . .Fort Myers
29-31 . . . . . at Bradenton

SEPTEMBER
1 . . . . St. Lucie
2-4 . . . . at St. Lucie

29-30 . . . . .at Tampa

JULY
1-2 . . . . Daytona
3 . . . . at Daytona
4 . . . . Clearwater
5 . . . . . . .at Clearwater
6 . . . . Clearwater
7 . . . . .at Tampa
8-11 . . . . . . Palm Beach
13-16 . . . . . .at Charlotte
17-20 . . . . at Fort Myers
21-24 . . . . St. Lucie
26-28 . . . . . at Dunedin
29-31 . . . . . at St. Lucie

AUGUST
1 . . . . at St. Lucie
3-4 . . . . Tampa
5-6 . . . . . . .at Clearwater
7 . . . . Clearwater
8-10 . . . . Brevard County
11-13 . . . . . Clearwater
14-15 . . . . . .at Tampa
16-18 . .at Brevard County
19-21 . . . . . . .Dunedin
23-25 . . . . . at Daytona
26-28 . . . . . at Dunedin
29-31 . . . . . Daytona

SEPTEMBER
1 . . . . .at Tampa
2-3 . . . . Tampa
4 . . . . .at Tampa

JUNE
1-2 . . . . . . at Bradenton
3-6 . . . . .Dunedin
8-11 . . . . at Daytona
12-15 . .at Brevard County
20-22 . . . . St. Lucie
23-25 . . . . . at St. Lucie
26-27 . . . . .at Charlotte
28-30 . . . . . . .Fort Myers

JULY
1-3 . . . . St. Lucie
4-6 . . . . at Jupiter
7 . . . . . . .at Charlotte
8-11 . . . . . . at Lakeland
13-16 . . . . . Clearwater
17-20 . . . . Brevard County
21-24 . . . . . . .at Tampa
25-27 . . . at Fort Myers
29-31 . . . . Tampa

AUGUST
1 . . . . Tampa
3-4 . . . . . . .at Charlotte
5-6 . . . . Jupiter
7 . . . . at Jupiter
8-10 . . . . . at Bradenton
11-12 . . . . Jupiter
13 . . . . at Jupiter

14-15 . . . . Charlotte
16-18 . . . . . . .Bradenton
19-21 . . . . St. Lucie
23-25 . . . . . at Fort Myers
26-28 . . . . . . at St. Lucie

ST. LUCIE METS

APRIL
7-8 . . . . Jupiter
9-10 . . . . at Jupiter
11-14 . . . . .Dunedin
15-16 . . .at Brevard County
17-18 . . . Brevard County
19-21 . . . . Charlotte
22-24 . . . . . . .Bradenton
26-28 . . . . .at Charlotte
29-30 . . . . . Palm Beach

MAY
1 . . . . Palm Beach
2-4 . . . . . . at Bradenton
5-7 . . . . . at Fort Myers
9-10 . . . . Jupiter
11-12 . . . . . . at Jupiter
13-15 . . . . . . .Fort Myers
16-19 . . . . . Clearwater
20-23 . . . . . at Daytona
24-26 . . . . . Charlotte
27-29 . . . at Bradenton
31 . . . . . . at Fort Myers

JUNE
1-2 . . . . . at Fort Myers
3-4 . . . . . Brevard County
5-6 . . .at Brevard County
8-11 . . . . . . at Dunedin
12-15 . . . . . . .at Tampa
16 . . . . Jupiter

TAMPA YANKEES

APRIL
7 . . . . at Lakeland
8 . . . . at Lakeland
9-10 . . . . . . at Lakeland
11-14 . . . . . . .Bradenton
15-18 . . . . . at Charlotte
19-21 . . . . . . .Dunedin
22-24 . . . . . Daytona
26-28 . . . . at Dunedin
29-30 . . . Brevard County

MAY
1 . . . . . Brevard County
2 . . . . Clearwater
3-4 . . . . . . .at Clearwater
5-7 . . . . Clearwater
9-10 . . . . .Lakeland
11-12 . . . . at Lakeland
13-14 . . . . . Clearwater
15 . . . . . . .at Clearwater
16-19 . . . . Jupiter
20-23 . . . at Fort Myers
24-26 . . . . at Daytona
27-29 . .at Brevard County
31 . . . . . . .at Clearwater

JUNE
1 . . . . .at Clearwater
3-6 . . . . Charlotte
7 . . . . .at Clearwater
8-11 . . . . at Bradenton
12-15 . . . . . . St. Lucie
16 . . . . at Lakeland

29-31 . . . . .Fort Myers

SEPTEMBER
1 . . . . .at Charlotte
2-4 . . . . Charlotte

20-22 . . . . . at Palm Beach
23-25 . . . . . Palm Beach
26-27 . . . . . . at Jupiter
28-30 . . . . .at Charlotte

JULY
1-3 . . . . . . at Palm Beach
4-6 . . . . .Fort Myers
7 . . . . at Jupiter
8-11 . . . . . .at Clearwater
13-16 . . . . . . Daytona
17-20 . . . . Tampa
21-24 . . . . . at Lakeland
26-28 . . . . . .Bradenton
29-31 . . . . . . .Lakeland

AUGUST
1 . . . . .Lakeland
3-4 . . . . at Jupiter
5-7 . . . . .Bradenton
8-10 . . . . . at Fort Myers
11-13 . . . . . at Bradenton
14-15 . . . . Jupiter
16-18 . . . . . . .Fort Myers
19-21 . . . . at Palm Beach
23-25 . . . . Charlotte
26-28 . . . . . Palm Beach
29-31 . . . . . .at Charlotte

SEPTEMBER
1 . . . . at Jupiter
2-4 . . . . Jupiter

20-22 . . . . . . at Daytona
23-25 . . . . . . .Dunedin
26-28 . . . . Brevard County
29-30 . . . . .Lakeland

JULY
1-3 . . . . at Dunedin
4-6 . . . . Daytona
7 . . . . .Lakeland
8-11 . . . . at Jupiter
13-16 . . . . . . .Fort Myers
17-20 . . . . . at St. Lucie
21-24 . . . . . Palm Beach
26-28 . . .at Brevard County
29-31 . . . at Palm Beach

AUGUST
1 . . . . at Palm Beach
3-4 . . . . at Lakeland
5-7 . . . . Daytona
8-10 . . . . .at Clearwater
11-13 . . . . at Daytona
14-15 . . . . . . .Lakeland
16-18 . . . . . Clearwater
19-21 . .at Brevard County
23-25 . . . . . . .Dunedin
26-28 . . . . Brevard County
29-31 . . . . . at Dunedin

SEPTEMBER
1 . . . . .Lakeland
2-3 . . . . at Lakeland
4 . . . . .Lakeland

LOW CLASS A

MIDWEST LEAGUE

BELOIT SNAPPERS

APRIL
7-8 . . . . Wisconsin
9-10 . . . . . . at Wisconsin
11-13 . . . . at Clinton
14-17 . . . . .Burlington
18-20 . . . at Kane County
21-24 . . . . at Burlington
26-28 . . . . Lansing
29-30 . . . . . . Great Lakes

MAY
1 . . . . Great Lakes
2-4 . . . . at West Michigan
5-7 . . . . . . at South Bend
9-11 . . . . Peoria
12-15 . . . . . . Quad Cities
17-19 . . . at Cedar Rapids
20-23 . . . . at Peoria
24-26 . . . . . Quad Cities
27-30 . . . . at Kane County
31 . . . . . . Cedar Rapids

JUNE
1-2 . . . . . . Cedar Rapids
3-5 . . . . .Clinton
7-9 . . . . . . at Quad Cities
10-12 . . . . . . at Clinton
13-15 . . . . . Kane County

16-19 . . . . Wisconsin
23-26 . . . . at Cedar Rapids
27-30 . . . . Peoria

JULY
1-3 . . . . . . Cedar Rapids
4-7 . . . . . at Quad Cities
8-11 . . . . .Burlington
13-15 . . . . . . at Dayton
16-18 . . at Bowling Green
20-22 . . . . Lake County
23-25 . . . . . . Fort Wayne
27-29 . . . . at Burlington
30-31 . . . . . . Quad Cities

AUGUST
1-2 . . . . Quad Cities
3-5 . . . . . . Kane County
6-9 . . . . . . at Clinton
11-14 . . . . Wisconsin
15-18 . . at Burlington
19-21 . . at Wisconsin
22-25 . . . . .Clinton
26-29 . . . . at Kane County
31 . . . . .at Peoria

SEPTEMBER
1-2 . . . . .at Peoria
3-5 . . . . Wisconsin

BOWLING GREEN HOT RODS

APRIL
7-8 . . . . .Dayton
9-10 . . . . at Dayton
11-13 . . . . at South Bend
14-17 . . . . Lansing
18-20 . . . . at South Bend
21-24 . . . . at Great Lakes
26-28 . . . . .Clinton
29-30 . . . . . Kane County

MAY
1 . . . . Kane County
2-4 . . . . .at Peoria
5-7 . . . . at Burlington
9-11 . . . . Lansing
12-15 . . . . . Lake County
17-19 . . . at West Michigan
20-23 . . . . at Dayton
24-26 . . . . . West Michigan
27-30 . . . . . . Great Lakes
31 . . . . . . at Lake County

JUNE
1-2 . . . . . .at Lake County
3-5 . . . . .at Lansing
7-9 . . . . Fort Wayne
10-12 . . . . . . South Bend
13-15 . . . . . Lake County

16-19 . . . . .at Fort Wayne
23-26 . . . . . . Fort Wayne
27-30 . . at West Michigan

JULY
1-3 . . . . . . at Great Lakes
4-7 . . . . . . Lake County
8-11 . . . at South Bend
13-15 . . . . . . Wisconsin
16-18 . . . . Beloit
20-22 . . at Cedar Rapids
23-25 . . . . at Quad Cities
27-29 . . . . . . Lansing
30-31 . . . . at Dayton

AUGUST
1-2 . . . . at Dayton
3-5 . . . . .at Lansing
6-9 . . . . . West Michigan
11-14 . . at Fort Wayne
15-18 . . . . . South Bend
19-21 . . . . . Great Lakes
22-25 . . . .at Lake County
26-29 . . . . .Dayton
31 . . . . .at Lansing

SEPTEMBER
1-2 . . . . .at Lansing
3-5 . . . . Fort Wayne

BURLINGTON BEES

APRIL
7-8 . . . . Peoria
9-10 . . . . .at Peoria
11-13 . . . . . Wisconsin
14-17 . . . . at Beloit
18-20 . . . . . Cedar Rapids
21-24 . . . . Beloit

9-11 . . . . . at Quad Cities
12-15 . . . . . Kane County
17-19 . . . . at Wisconsin
20-23 . . . . at Clinton
24-26 . . . . Cedar Rapids
27-30 . . . . .Clinton
31 . . . . . . at Kane County

JUNE
1-2 . . . . . at Kane County
3-5 . . . . . at Quad Cities
7-9 . . . . Peoria
10-12 . . . . Quad Cities
13-15 . . at Cedar Rapids
16-19 . . . . . .at Peoria
23-26 . . . . Peoria
27-30 . . at Kane County

JULY
1-3 . . . . Wisconsin
4-7 . . . . at Clinton
8-11 . . . . . . at Beloit

CEDAR RAPIDS KERNELS

APRIL
7-8 . . . . . . Quad Cities
9-10 . . . . . at Quad Cities
11-13 . . . at Kane County
14-17 . . . . .Clinton
18-20 . . . . . at Burlington
21-24 . . . . . at Clinton
26-28 . . . .West Michigan
29-30 . . . . . . South Bend

MAY
1 . . . . South Bend
2-4 . . . . .at Lansing
5-7 . . . . at Great Lakes
9-11 . . . . . Kane County
12-15 . . . at Wisconsin
17-19 . . . . .Beloit
20-23 . . . . . Quad Cities
24-26 . . . at Burlington
27-30 . . . . . Wisconsin
31 . . . . at Beloit

JUNE
1-2 . . . . at Beloit
3-5 . . . . Peoria
7-9 . . . . . . Kane County
10-12 . . . . . .at Peoria
13-15 . . . . .Burlington

16-19 . . . . at Quad Cities
23-26 . . . . .Beloit
27-30 . . . . at Quad Cities

JULY
1-3 . . . . at Beloit
4-7 . . . . Wisconsin
8-11 . . . . . . Kane County
13-15 . . . . at Lake County
16-18 . . . . .at Fort Wayne
20-22 . . . . Bowling Green
23-25 . . . . .Dayton
27-29 . . . at Kane County
30-31 . . . . . at Burlington

AUGUST
1-2 . . . . . . at Burlington
3-5 . . . . .Clinton
6-9 . . . . Peoria
11-14 . . . at Kane County
15-18 . . . . . . .at Peoria
19-21 . . . . . . .Burlington
22-25 . . . . . . Quad Cities
26-29 . . . . . at Clinton
31 . . . . at Wisconsin

SEPTEMBER
1-2 . . . . at Wisconsin
3-5 . . . . .Clinton

CLINTON LUMBERKINGS

APRIL
7-8 . . . . . at Kane County
9-10 . . . . . . Kane County
11-13 . . . . .Beloit
14-17 . . . at Cedar Rapids
18-20 . . . . .at Peoria
21-24 . . . . Cedar Rapids
26-28 . . at Bowling Green
29-30 . . . . at Dayton

MAY
1 . . . . at Dayton
2-4 . . . . Fort Wayne
5-7 . . . . Lake County
9-11 . . . . . . at Wisconsin
12-15 . . . . Peoria
17-19 . . . . at Quad Cities
20-23 . . . . . . .Burlington
24-26 . . . . Wisconsin

26-28 . . . .at Lake County
29-30 . . . . .at Fort Wayne

MAY
1 . . . . .at Fort Wayne
2-4 . . . . .Dayton
5-7 . . . . Bowling Green

27-30 . . . . . . at Burlington
31 . . . . Quad Cities

JUNE
1-2 . . . . Quad Cities
3-5 . . . . at Beloit
7-9 . . . . at Wisconsin
10-12 . . . . .Beloit
13-15 . . . . Peoria
16-19 . . . at Kane County
23-26 . . . . . Kane County
27-30 . . . . . at Wisconsin

JULY
1-3 . . . . .at Peoria
4-7 . . . . .Burlington
8-11 . . . . at Quad Cities
13-15 . . . . . South Bend
16-18 . . . .West Michigan
20-22 . . . . . . .at Lansing

23-25 . . . . . at Great Lakes
27-29 . . . . Wisconsin
30-31 . . . . at Kane County

AUGUST
1-2. . . . . at Kane County
3-5. . . . . at Cedar Rapids
6-9. . . . . Beloit
11-14 . . . . . at Burlington

DAYTON DRAGONS

APRIL
7-8. . . . . at Bowling Green
9-10 . . . . . Bowling Green
11-13 . . . . .at Lansing
14-17 . . . . West Michigan
18-20 . . . . at Great Lakes
21-24 . . . at West Michigan
26-28 . . . . . . Kane County
29-30 . . . . Clinton

MAY
1 . . . . Clinton
2-4. . . . . . . at Burlington
5-7. . . . . at Peoria
9-11 . . . . South Bend
12-15 . . . . . . Great Lakes
17-19 . . . .at Lake County
20-23 . . . . Bowling Green
24-26 . . . . . Lake County
27-30 . . at West Michigan
31 . . . . Lansing

JUNE
1-2. . . . . Lansing
3-5. . . . . . . .at Fort Wayne
7-9. . . . . . . at South Bend
10-12 . . . . . . Fort Wayne
13-15 . . . . . . South Bend

FORT WAYNE TINCAPS

APRIL
7-8. . . . . .at Lake County
9-10 . . . . . . Lake County
11-13 . . . . at Great Lakes
14-17 . . . . . . South Bend
18-20 . . . . at Lansing
21-24 . . . . at South Bend
26-28 . . . . Peoria
29-30 . . . . . . .Burlington

MAY
1 . . . . .Burlington
2-4. . . . . at Clinton
5-7. . . . at Kane County
9-11 . . . . Great Lakes
12-15 . . . at West Michigan
17-19 . . . . Lansing
20-23 . . . . . West Michigan
24-26 . . . . at Lansing
27-30 . . . .at Lake County
31 . . . . South Bend

JUNE
1-2. . . . . South Bend
3-5. . . . . .Dayton
7-9. . . . at Bowling Green
10-12 . . . . at Dayton
13-15 . . . . . West Michigan

GREAT LAKES LOONS

APRIL
7-8. . . . . .at Lansing
9-10 . . . . Lansing

15-18 . . . . . . Quad Cities
19-21 . . . . Peoria
22-25 . . . . at Beloit
26-29 . . . . . Cedar Rapids
31 . . . . .Burlington

SEPTEMBER
1-2. . . . . Burlington
3-5. . . . . at Cedar Rapids

16-19 . . . . at Great Lakes
23-26 . . . . . . South Bend
27-30 . . . . .at Fort Wayne

JULY
1-3. . . . . . . West Michigan
4-7. . . . . at Lansing
8-11 . . . . . at Great Lakes
13-15 . . . . Beloit
16-18 . . . . Wisconsin
20-22 . . . . at Quad Cities
23-25 . . . at Cedar Rapids
27-29 . . . . . . Great Lakes
30-31 . . . . Bowling Green

AUGUST
1-2. . . . . . . Bowling Green
3-5. . . . . at West Michigan
6-9. . . . . .at Lake County
11-14 . . . . . . South Bend
15-18 . . . . . . Fort Wayne
19-21 . . . at West Michigan
22-25 . . . . Lansing
26-29 . . at Bowling Green
31 . . . . Lake County

SEPTEMBER
1-2. . . . . . . Lake County
3-5. . . . . . at South Bend

16-19 . . . .Bowling Green
23-26 . . . at Bowling Green
27-30 . . . . .Dayton

JULY
1-3. . . . . . .at Lake County
4-7. . . . . South Bend
8-11 . . . . at West Michigan
13-15 . . . . . Quad Cities
16-18 . . . . . Cedar Rapids
20-22 . . . . . at Wisconsin
23-25 . . . . at Beloit
27-29 . . . . West Michigan
30-31 . . . . Lansing

AUGUST
1-2. . . . . Lansing
3-5. . . . . . at South Bend
6-9. . . . . .at Lansing
11-14 . . . . . Bowling Green
15-18 . . . . at Dayton
19-21 . . . . . Lake County
22-25 . . . . at Great Lakes
26-29 . . . . West Michigan
31 . . . . Great Lakes

SEPTEMBER
1-2. . . . . . . Great Lakes
3-5. . . . at Bowling Green

11-13 . . . . . . Fort Wayne
14-17 . . . .at Lake County
18-20 . . . . .Dayton
21-24 . . . . Bowling Green

26-28 . . . . . . at Wisconsin
29-30 . . . . at Beloit

MAY
1 . . . . at Beloit
2-4. . . . . Quad Cities
5-7. . . . Cedar Rapids
9-11 . . .at Fort Wayne
12-15 . . . . . . at Dayton
17-19 . . . . . . South Bend
20-23 . . . . Lansing
24-26 . . . . at South Bend
27-30 . . at Bowling Green
31 . . . . . . West Michigan

JUNE
1-2. . . . . . . West Michigan
3-5. . . . . Lake County
7-9. . . . at West Michigan
10-12 . . .at Lake County
13-15 . . . . . .at Lansing
16-19 . . . . .Dayton
23-26 . . .at Lake County
27-30 . . . . Lansing

KANE COUNTY COUGARS

APRIL
7-8. . . . . Clinton
9-10 . . . . at Clinton
11-13 . . . . . Cedar Rapids
14-17 . . . . at Quad Cities
18-20 . . . . Beloit
21-24 . . . . . Quad Cities
26-28 . . . . at Dayton
29-30 . . . at Bowling Green

MAY
1 . . . . . at Bowling Green
2-4. . . . . . . Lake County
5-7. . . . . . . Fort Wayne
9-11 . . . . at Cedar Rapids
12-15 . . . . . at Burlington
17-19 . . . . Peoria
20-23 . . . . . at Wisconsin
24-26 . . . . . . at Peoria
27-30 . . . . Beloit
31 . . . . .Burlington

JUNE
1-2. . . . . .Burlington
3-5. . . . . at Wisconsin
7-9. . . . . at Cedar Rapids
10-12 . . . . . . Wisconsin
13-15 . . . . . at Beloit

LAKE COUNTY CAPTAINS

APRIL
7-8. . . . . . . Fort Wayne
9-10 . . . .at Fort Wayne
11-13 . . . at West Michigan
14-17 . . . . . Great Lakes
18-20 . . . at West Michigan
21-24 . . . . . . .at Lansing
26-28 . . . . .Burlington
29-30 . . . . Peoria

MAY
1 . . . . Peoria
2-4. . . . . at Kane County
5-7. . . . . . at Clinton
9-11 . . . . . West Michigan
12-15 . . .at Bowling Green
17-19 . . . . .Dayton
20-23 . . . . . . South Bend
24-26 . . . . . at Dayton
27-30 . . . . Fort Wayne

JULY
1-3. . . . . . Bowling Green
4-7. . . . at West Michigan
8-11 . . . . .Dayton
13-15 . . . . at Burlington
16-18 . . . . at Peoria
20-22 . . . . . Kane County
23-25 . . . . .Clinton
27-29 . . . . . . at Dayton
30-31 . . . . . . South Bend

AUGUST
1-2. . . . . South Bend
3-5. . . . . . . Lake County
6-9. . . . . . at South Bend
11-14 . . . . . Lake County
15-18 . . . . . . .at Lansing
19-21 . . at Bowling Green
22-25 . . . . . . Fort Wayne
26-29 . . . . at South Bend
31 . . . . . . .at Fort Wayne

SEPTEMBER
1-2. . . . . . . .at Fort Wayne
3-5. . . . . . West Michigan

16-19 . . . . .Clinton
23-26 . . . . . . at Clinton
27-30 . . . . . . .Burlington

JULY
1-3. . . . . Quad Cities
4-7. . . . . .at Peoria
8-11 . . . . at Cedar Rapids
13-15 . . . West Michigan
16-18 . . . . South Bend
20-22 . . . . at Great Lakes
23-25 . . . . . .at Lansing
27-29 . . . . . Cedar Rapids
30-31 . . . . .Clinton

AUGUST
1-2. . . . . .Clinton
3-5. . . . . at Beloit
6-9. . . . . . . at Wisconsin
11-14 . . . . . Cedar Rapids
15-18 . . . . Wisconsin
19-21 . . . . at Quad Cities
22-25 . . . . . at Burlington
26-29 . . . . .Beloit
31 . . . . at Quad Cities

SEPTEMBER
1-2. . . . . . . at Quad Cities
3-5. . . . . Peoria

31 . . . . . . Bowling Green

JUNE
1-2. . . . . . Bowling Green
3-5. . . . . at Great Lakes
7-9. . . . . Lansing
10-12 . . . . . Great Lakes
13-15 . . at Bowling Green
16-19 . . . . at South Bend
23-26 . . . . . Great Lakes
27-30 . . at South Bend

JULY
1-3. . . . . Fort Wayne
4-7. . . . at Bowling Green
8-11 . . . . .at Lansing
13-15 . . . . . Cedar Rapids
16-17 . . . . . Quad Cities
20-22 . . . . . . at Beloit
23-25 . . . . . at Wisconsin

27-29 . . . . . . South Bend
30-31 . . at West Michigan

AUGUST
1-2. . . . at West Michigan
3-5. . . . . . at Great Lakes
6-9. . . . . Dayton
11-14 . . . . at Great Lakes
15-18 . . . . . West Michigan

LANSING LUGNUTS

APRIL
7-8. . . . . . . Great Lakes
9-10. . . . at Great Lakes
11-13 . . . . Dayton
14-17 . . at Bowling Green
18-20 . . . . . Fort Wayne
21-24 . . . . . Lake County
26-28 . . . . . . at Beloit
29-30 . . . . at Wisconsin

MAY
1 . . . . at Wisconsin
2-4. . . . . Cedar Rapids
5-7. . . . . . Quad Cities
9-11. . . . at Bowling Green
12-15 . . . . . South Bend
17-19 . . . . at Fort Wayne
20-23 . . . at Great Lakes
24-26 . . . . . Fort Wayne
27-30 . . . . at South Bend
31 . . . . at Dayton

JUNE
1-2. . . . . at Dayton
3-5. . . . . Bowling Green
7-9. . . . . .at Lake County
10-12 . . at West Michigan
13-15 . . . . . . Great Lakes

PEORIA CHIEFS

APRIL
7-8. . . . . . at Burlington
9-10. . . . . . .Burlington
11-13 . . . . . Quad Cities
14-17 . . . . at Wisconsin
18-20 . . . . Clinton
21-24 . . . . . . Wisconsin
26-28 . . . .at Fort Wayne
29-30 . . . .at Lake County

MAY
1 . . . . . .at Lake County
2-4. . . . . Bowling Green
5-7. . . . . Dayton
9-11 . . . . at Beloit
12-15 . . . . . at Clinton
17-19 . . . at Kane County
20-23 . . . . Beloit
24-26 . . . Kane County
27-30 . . . . at Quad Cities
31 . . . . Wisconsin

JUNE
1-2. . . . . Wisconsin
3-5. . . . . at Cedar Rapids
7-9. . . . . . at Burlington
10-12 . . . Cedar Rapids
13-15 . . . . at Clinton

QUAD CITIES RIVER BANDITS

APRIL
7-8. . . . . at Cedar Rapids
9-10. . . . . . Cedar Rapids
11-13 . . . . . .at Peoria
14-17 . . . Kane County

19-21 . . . . . .at Fort Wayne
22-25 . . . . Bowling Green
26-29 . . . . Lansing
31 . . . . at Dayton

SEPTEMBER
1-2. . . . . at Dayton
3-5. . . . . Lansing

16-19 . . . . West Michigan
23-26 . . . . West Michigan
27-30 . . . . at Great Lakes

JULY
1-3. . . . . at South Bend
4-7. . . . . Dayton
8-11 . . . . . Lake County
13-15 . . . . .at Peoria
16-18 . . . . at Burlington
20-22 . . . . Clinton
23-25 . . . . . Kane County
27-29 . . at Bowling Green
30-31 . . . .at Fort Wayne

AUGUST
1-2. . . . . . .at Fort Wayne
3-5. . . . . . Bowling Green
6-9. . . . . Fort Wayne
11-14 . . at West Michigan
15-18 . . . . . Great Lakes
19-21 . . . . . South Bend
22-25 . . . . at Dayton
26-29 . . .at Lake County
31 . . . . . . Bowling Green

SEPTEMBER
1-2. . . . . . Bowling Green
3-5. . . . . . .at Lake County

16-19 . . . . . .Burlington
23-26 . . . . at Burlington
27-30 . . . . at Beloit

JULY
1-3. . . . . Clinton
4-7. . . . . . Kane County
8-11 . . . . . at Wisconsin
13-15 . . . . Lansing
16-18 . . . . Great Lakes
20-22 . . at West Michigan
23-25 . . . . at South Bend
27-29 . . . at Quad Cities
30-31 . . . . Wisconsin

AUGUST
1-2. . . . . Wisconsin
3-5. . . . . Quad Cities
6-9. . . . . at Cedar Rapids
11-14 . . . . . Quad Cities
15-18 . . . . . Cedar Rapids
19-21 . . . . . . at Clinton
22-25 . . . . at Wisconsin
26-29 . . . . . .Burlington
31 . . . . Beloit

SEPTEMBER
1-2. . . . . Beloit
3-5. . . . . at Kane County

18-20 . . . . . at Wisconsin
21-24 . . . at Kane County
26-28 . . . . . South Bend
29-30 . . . . West Michigan

MAY
1 . . . . West Michigan
2-4. . . . . . at Great Lakes
5-7. . . . . at Lansing
9-11 . . . . .Burlington
12-15 . . . . at Beloit
17-19 . . . . Clinton
20-23 . . . at Cedar Rapids
24-26 . . . . at Beloit
27-30 . . . . Peoria
31 . . . . at Clinton

JUNE
1-2. . . . . at Clinton
3-5. . . . . .Burlington
7-9. . . . . Beloit
10-12 . . . . at Burlington
13-15 . . . . . Wisconsin
16-19 . . . Cedar Rapids
23-26 . . . . at Wisconsin
27-30 . . . Cedar Rapids

JULY
1-3. . . . . . at Kane County

SOUTH BEND CUBS

APRIL
7-8. . . . . West Michigan
9-10. . . at West Michigan
11-13 . . . .Bowling Green
14-17 . . . .at Fort Wayne
18-20 . . . .Bowling Green
21-24 . . . . . Fort Wayne
26-28 . . . at Quad Cities
29-30 . . . at Cedar Rapids

MAY
1 . . . . . . at Cedar Rapids
2-4. . . . . Wisconsin
5-7. . . . . Beloit
9-11 . . . . at Dayton
12-15 . . . . . .at Lansing
17-19 . . . at Great Lakes
20-23 . . .at Lake County
24-26 . . . . . Great Lakes
27-30 . . . . Lansing
31 . . . . . .at Fort Wayne

JUNE
1-2. . . . . . .at Fort Wayne
3-5. . . . . . West Michigan
7-9. . . . . Dayton
10-12 . . . at Bowling Green
13-15 . . . . at Dayton

4-7. . . . . Beloit
8-11 . . . . Clinton
13-15 . . . .at Fort Wayne
16-17 . . . .at Lake County
20-22 . . . . Dayton
23-25 . . . Bowling Green
27-29 . . . . Peoria
30-31 . . . . at Beloit

AUGUST
1-2. . . . . at Beloit
3-5. . . . . .at Peoria
6-9. . . . . .Burlington
11-14 . . . . . . .at Peoria
15-18 . . . . at Clinton
19-21 . . . . Kane County
22-25 . . . at Cedar Rapids
26-29 . . . . . Wisconsin
31 . . . . Kane County

SEPTEMBER
1-2. . . . . . Kane County
3-5. . . . . . . at Burlington

16-19 . . . . . Lake County
23-26 . . . . at Dayton
27-30 . . . . Lake County

JULY
1-3. . . . . Lansing
4-7. . . . . . .at Fort Wayne
8-11 . . . . .Bowling Green
13-15 . . . . . at Clinton
16-18 . . . at Kane County
20-22 . . . . . . .Burlington
23-25 . . . . . . Peoria
27-29 . . .at Lake County
30-31 . . . at Great Lakes

AUGUST
1-2. . . . . at Great Lakes
3-5. . . . . . Fort Wayne
6-9. . . . . . . Great Lakes
11-14 . . . . . . at Dayton
15-18 . . at Bowling Green
19-21 . . . . . . .at Lansing
22-25 . . . . . West Michigan
26-29 . . . . . Great Lakes
31 . . . . at West Michigan

SEPTEMBER
1-2. . . . . at West Michigan
3-5. . . . . Dayton

WEST MICHIGAN WHITECAPS

APRIL
7-8. . . . . . at South Bend
9-10. . . . . . South Bend
11-13 . . . . Lake County
14-17 . . . . . . at Dayton
18-20 . . . . Lake County
21-24 . . . . Dayton
26-28 . . . at Cedar Rapids
29-30 . . . at Quad Cities

MAY
1 . . . . at Quad Cities
2-4. . . . . Beloit
5-7. . . . . Wisconsin
9-11 . . . .at Lake County
12-15 . . . . . Fort Wayne
17-19 . . . Bowling Green
20-23 . . .at Fort Wayne
24-26 . . at Bowling Green
27-30 . . . . Dayton
31 . . . . . . at Great Lakes

JUNE
1-2. . . . . . at Great Lakes
3-5. . . . . . at South Bend
7-9. . . . . . Great Lakes
10-12 . . . . Lansing
13-15 . . . .at Fort Wayne
16-19 . . . . . at Lansing
23-26 . . . . . at Lansing
27-30 . . . . Bowling Green

JULY
1-3. . . . . at Dayton
4-7. . . . . . . Great Lakes
8-11 . . . . . . Fort Wayne
13-15 . . at Kane County
16-18 . . . . . at Clinton
20-22 . . . . . . Peoria
23-25 . . . . . .Burlington
27-29 . . .at Fort Wayne
30-31 . . . Lake County

AUGUST
1-2 . . . . Lake County
3-5 . . . . Dayton
6-9 . . . . at Bowling Green
11-14 . . . . Lansing
15-18 . . . . at Lake County
19-21 . . . . Dayton
22-25 . . . . . at South Bend
26-29 . . . . . at Fort Wayne
31 . . . . South Bend
SEPTEMBER
1-2 . . . . South Bend
3-5 . . . . at Great Lakes

WISCONSIN TIMBER RATTLERS

APRIL
7-8 . . . . at Beloit
9-10 . . . . Beloit
11-13 . . . . . at Burlington
14-17 . . . . Peoria
18-20 . . . . . . Quad Cities
21-24 . . . . at Peoria
26-28 . . . . . . Great Lakes
29-30 . . . . Lansing
MAY
1 . . . . Lansing
2-4 . . . . . at South Bend
5-7 . . . . at West Michigan
9-11 . . . . Clinton
12-15 . . . . . Cedar Rapids
17-19 . . . . Burlington
20-23 . . . . . Kane County
24-26 . . . . . . at Clinton
27-30 . . . at Cedar Rapids
31 . . . . at Peoria
JUNE
1-2 . . . . at Peoria
3-5 . . . . . . Kane County
7-9 . . . . Clinton
10-12 . . . at Kane County
13-15 . . . . at Quad Cities
16-19 . . . . at Beloit
23-26 . . . . . . Quad Cities
27-30 . . . . Clinton
JULY
1-3 . . . . at Burlington
4-7 . . . . . at Cedar Rapids
8-11 . . . . Peoria
13-15 . . . at Bowling Green
16-18 . . . . at Dayton
20-22 . . . . . . Fort Wayne
23-25 . . . . . Lake County
27-29 . . . . . . at Clinton
30-31 . . . . at Peoria
AUGUST
1-2 . . . . at Peoria
3-5 . . . . Burlington
6-9 . . . . . . Kane County
11-14 . . . . at Beloit
15-18 . . . . at Kane County
19-21 . . . . Beloit
22-25 . . . . Peoria
26-29 . . . . at Quad Cities
31 . . . . Cedar Rapids
SEPTEMBER
1-2 . . . . Cedar Rapids
3-5 . . . . at Beloit

SOUTH ATLANTIC LEAGUE

ASHEVILLE TOURISTS

APRIL
7-10 . . . . . . at Greenville
11-13 . . . . . at Charleston
14-17 . . . . Rome
18-20 . . . . Lexington
21-24 . . . . at Rome
26-28 . . . . . . Hagerstown
29-30 . . . at West Virginia
23-26 . . . . . West Virginia
27-29 . . . . . . at Augusta
30 . . . . at Greenville
MAY
1-2 . . . . . at West Virginia
4-6 . . . . Lakewood
7-10 . . . . Delmarva
12-15 . . . . . . at Columbia
16-18 . . . . . . at Augusta
19-22 . . . . . . Kannapolis
23-25 . . . . Greenville
26-29 . . . . . at Kannapolis
30-31 . . . . at Hagerstown
JUNE
1 . . . . at Hagerstown
2-4 . . . . Greenville
6-8 . . . . Hagerstown
9-12 . . . . . . at Charleston
13-15 . . . . at Greensboro
16-19 . . . . Columbia
JULY
1-3 . . . . at Greenville
4-6 . . . . Lexington
7-10 . . . . Charleston
12-14 . . . . at Hagerstown
15-18 . . . . . at Lexington
20-22 . . . . Augusta
23-26 . . . . Greenville
28-31 . . . . . . at Columbia
AUGUST
1-3 . . . . at Greenville
4-7 . . . . Augusta
8-10 . . . . . . at Lexington
11-14 . . . . at Hagerstown
16-18 . . . . Columbia
19-22 . . . . Rome
23-25 . . . . at Hickory
26-28 . . . . . at Greenville
30-31 . . . . Hickory
SEPTEMBER
1 . . . . Hickory
2-5 . . . . Hagerstown

AUGUSTA GREENJACKETS

APRIL
7-10 . . . . at Rome
11-13 . . . . . at Lexington
14-17 . . . . . . Charleston
18-20 . . . . Rome
21-24 . . . . . at Charleston

CHARLESTON RIVERDOGS

APRIL
7-10 . . . . Columbia
11-13 . . . . Asheville
14-17 . . . . . at Augusta
18-20 . . . . . at Columbia
21-24 . . . . Augusta
26-28 . . . . . at Lakewood
29-30 . . . . . at Delmarva
26-28 . . . . . . Kannapolis
29-30 . . . . . . Greensboro
MAY
1-2 . . . . at Delmarva
4-6 . . . . . . West Virginia
7-10 . . . . Hickory
12-15 . . . . . at Lexington
16-18 . . . . . at Greenville
19-22 . . . . Columbia
23-25 . . . . . West Virginia
26-29 . . . . . . at Augusta
30-31 . . . . . at Greenville
1-2 . . . . Greensboro
4-6 . . . . . . at Greenville
7-10 . . . . at Rome
12-15 . . . . Greenville
16-18 . . . . Asheville
19-22 . . . . at Rome
23-25 . . . . . . at Columbia
26-29 . . . . . . Charleston
30-31 . . . . at Kannapolis
JUNE
1 . . . . at Greenville
2-4 . . . . Kannapolis
6-8 . . . . at Rome
9-12 . . . . Asheville
13-15 . . . . Augusta
16-19 . . . at West Virginia
1 . . . . at Kannapolis
2-4 . . . . West Virginia
6-8 . . . . Columbia
9-12 . . . . Asheville
13-15 . . . . . at Charleston
16-19 . . . . Lexington
23-26 . . . . . . at Columbia
27-29 . . . . Asheville
30 . . . . at Charleston
JULY
1-3 . . . . Augusta
4-6 . . . . at Columbia
7-10 . . . . at Asheville
12-14 . . . . Rome
15-18 . . . . Lakewood
20-22 . . . at West Virginia
23-26 . . . . at Hagerstown
28-31 . . . . Lexington
AUGUST
1-3 . . . . . . at Kannapolis
4-7 . . . . Greenville
8-10 . . . . Rome
11-14 . . . . . at Greenville
16-18 . . . . at Augusta
19-22 . . . . Greenville
23-25 . . . . Columbia
26-28 . . . . . . at Hickory
30-31 . . . . . . Hagerstown
SEPTEMBER
1 . . . . Hagerstown
2-5 . . . . at Columbia

COLUMBIA FIREFLIES

APRIL
7-10 . . . . . at Charleston
11-13 . . . . at Rome
14-17 . . . . Greenville
18-20 . . . . . . Charleston
21-24 . . . . . at Greenville
26-28 . . . . . . Lexington
29-30 . . . . . . Kannapolis
2-4 . . . . Hagerstown
6-8 . . . . at Augusta
9-12 . . . . . West Virginia
13-15 . . . . Rome
16-19 . . . . . . at Asheville
23-26 . . . . Augusta
27-29 . . . . . . at Hickory
30 . . . . . at West Virginia
MAY
1-2 . . . . Kannapolis
4-6 . . . . . at Greensboro
7-10 . . . . . at Greenville
12-15 . . . . Asheville
16-18 . . . . Rome
19-22 . . . . . at Charleston
23-25 . . . . Augusta
26-29 . . . at West Virginia
30-31 . . . . at Rome
JUNE
1 . . . . at Rome
JULY
1-3 . . . . . at West Virginia
4-6 . . . . Charleston
7-10 . . . . at Augusta
12-14 . . . . Delmarva
15-18 . . . . Rome
20-22 . . . . at Hagerstown
23-26 . . . . . at Lexington
28-31 . . . . Asheville
AUGUST
1-3 . . . . at Augusta
4-7 . . . . at Rome

8-10 . . . . Greenville
11-14 . . . . . . Greensboro
16-18 . . . . . at Asheville
19-22 . . . . Augusta
23-25 . . . . . at Charleston

26-28 . . . . . at Kannapolis
30-31 . . . . . West Virginia
SEPTEMBER
1 . . . . West Virginia
2-5 . . . . Charleston

DELMARVA SHOREBIRDS

APRIL
7-10 . . . . . at Hagerstown
11-13 . . . . .at Kannapolis
14-17 . . . . . .Hagerstown
18-20 . . . . . Greensboro
21-24 . . . . at Kannapolis
26-28 . . . . . Greenville
29-30 . . . . . . Charleston
MAY
1-2 . . . . Charleston
4-6 . . . . at Lexington
7-10 . . . . . . at Asheville
12-15 . . . . . Greensboro
16-18 . . . . . West Virginia
19-22 . . . . at Lakewood
23-25 . . . at Greensboro
26-29 . . . . . Lakewood
30-31 . . . . .Hickory
JUNE
1 . . . . .Hickory
2-4 . . . . . at Greensboro
6-8 . . . . . at West Virginia
9-12 . . . . . . Lakewood
13-15 . . . . . Kannapolis
16-19 . . . . . . at Hickory

23-26 . . . . .at Kannapolis
27-29 . . . . . Greensboro
30 . . . . . . at Hagerstown
JULY
1-3 . . . . . . at Hagerstown
4-6 . . . . .Lakewood
7-10 . . . . . . .Hagerstown
12-14 . . . . .at Columbia
15-18 . . . . at Augusta
20-22 . . . . .Hickory
23-26 . . . . . Kannapolis
28-31 . . . at West Virginia
AUGUST
1-3 . . . . at Hickory
4-7 . . . . . West Virginia
8-10 . . . . Lakewood
11-14 . . . at West Virginia
16-18 . . . at Greensboro
19-22 . . . . . . Lakewood
23-25 . . . at Hagerstown
26-28 . . . . . Lexington
30-31 . . . at Greensboro
SEPTEMBER
1 . . . . at Greensboro
2-5 . . . . Kannapolis

GREENSBORO GRASSHOPPERS

APRIL
7-10 . . . . . West Virginia
11-13 . . . . .Hickory
14-17 . . . . . at Lakewood
18-20 . . . . .at Delmarva
21-24 . . . . .Lakewood
26-28 . . . . . at Hickory
29-30 . . . . . at Augusta
MAY
1-2 . . . . at Augusta
4-6 . . . . Columbia
7-10 . . . . Lexington
12-15 . . . . . .at Delmarva
16-18 . . . . .at Kannapolis
19-22 . . . . .Hagerstown
23-25 . . . . . Delmarva
26-29 . . . . at Hickory
30-31 . . . at Lexington
JUNE
1 . . . . at Lexington
2-4 . . . . Delmarva
6-8 . . . . at Hickory
9-12 . . . . Rome
13-15 . . . . . .Asheville
16-19 . . . . . at Rome

23-26 . . . . .Hickory
27-29 . . . . .at Delmarva
30 . . . . at Lakewood
JULY
1-3 . . . . . . at Lakewood
4-6 . . . . . West Virginia
7-10 . . . . . Kannapolis
12-14 . . . . at Greenville
15-18 . . . .at Kannapolis
20-22 . . . . . . Greenville
23-26 . . . . . . Augusta
28-31 . . . . .at Kannapolis
AUGUST
1-3 . . . . .Lakewood
4-7 . . . . Kannapolis
8-10 . . . at West Virginia
11-14 . . . .at Columbia
16-18 . . . . . Delmarva
19-22 . . . . .Hickory
23-25 . . at Lakewood
26-28 . . . . at Hagerstown
30-31 . . . . . Delmarva
SEPTEMBER
1 . . . . Delmarva
2-5 . . . . at Lakewood

GREENVILLE DRIVE

APRIL
7-10 . . . . .Asheville
11-13 . . . . . West Virginia
14-17 . . . .at Columbia
18-20 . . . . . at Hickory
21-24 . . . . . Columbia
26-28 . . . .at Delmarva
29-30 . . . . at Lakewood

MAY
1-2 . . . . . . at Lakewood
4-6 . . . . Augusta
7-10 . . . . Columbia
12-15 . . . . at Augusta
16-18 . . . . . Charleston
19-22 . . . . . Lexington
23-25 . . . . at Asheville
26-29 . . . . at Rome

30-31 . . . . . . Charleston
JUNE
1 . . . . Charleston
2-4 . . . . at Asheville
6-8 . . . . . . .at Kannapolis
9-12 . . . . Augusta
13-15 . . . . .Hickory
16-19 . . . at Hagerstown
23-26 . . . . . . Lakewood
27-29 . . . . at Charleston
30 . . . . .Asheville
JULY
1-3 . . . . .Asheville
4-6 . . . . at Rome
7-10 . . . . at Lexington
12-14 . . . . . Greensboro
15-18 . . . .Hagerstown

HAGERSTOWN SUNS

APRIL
7-10 . . . . Delmarva
11-13 . . . . .Lakewood
14-17 . . . .at Delmarva
18-20 . . . . at Lakewood
21-24 . . . . .Hickory
26-28 . . . . at Asheville
29-30 . . . . .Rome
MAY
1-2 . . . . .Rome
4-6 . . . . . .at Kannapolis
7-10 . . . at West Virginia
12-15 . . . . . Kannapolis
16-18 . . . . . .Lakewood
19-22 . . . at Greensboro
23-25 . . . at Lakewood
26-29 . . . . . Lexington
30-31 . . . . .Asheville
JUNE
1 . . . . .Asheville
2-4 . . . . .at Columbia
6-8 . . . . at Asheville
9-12 . . . . Lexington
13-15 . . . . at Lakewood
16-19 . . . . . Greenville

23-26 . . . . . at Lexington
27-29 . . . . . . Lakewood
30 . . . . Delmarva
JULY
1-3 . . . . Delmarva
4-6 . . . . . .at Kannapolis
7-10 . . . . . .at Delmarva
12-14 . . . . . .Asheville
15-18 . . . . at Greenville
20-22 . . . . . . Columbia
23-26 . . . . . Charleston
28-31 . . . . . at Hickory
AUGUST
1-3 . . . . West Virginia
4-7 . . . . at Lakewood
8-10 . . . . . Kannapolis
11-14 . . . . . .Asheville
16-18 . . . . . . at Rome
19-22 . . . . at Lexington
23-25 . . . . . Delmarva
26-28 . . . . . Greensboro
30-31 . . . . .at Charleston
SEPTEMBER
1 . . . . .at Charleston
2-5 . . . . at Asheville

HICKORY CRAWDADS

APRIL
7-10 . . . . . .at Kannapolis
11-13 . . . at Greensboro
14-17 . . . . . . Kannapolis
18-20 . . . . . Greenville
21-24 . . . . at Hagerstown
26-28 . . . . . Greensboro
29-30 . . . . . Lexington
MAY
1-2 . . . . Lexington
4-6 . . . . at Rome
7-10 . . . . at Charleston
12-15 . . . . .Rome
16-18 . . . . at Lexington
19-22 . . . at West Virginia
23-25 . . . . .Rome
26-29 . . . . . Greensboro
30-31 . . . .at Delmarva
JUNE
1 . . . . . . .at Greensboro
2-4 . . . . . . at Lakewood
6-8 . . . . Greensboro
9-12 . . . . .at Kannapolis
13-15 . . . . at Greenville
16-19 . . . . . Delmarva

23-26 . . . . at Greensboro
27-29 . . . . . . Columbia
30 . . . . Kannapolis
JULY
1-3 . . . . Kannapolis
4-6 . . . . at Augusta
7-10 . . . . at Rome
12-14 . . . . . .Lakewood
15-18 . . . . . West Virginia
20-22 . . . .at Delmarva
23-26 . . . . at Lakewood
28-31 . . . . . .Hagerstown
AUGUST
1-3 . . . . Delmarva
4-7 . . . . at Lexington
8-10 . . . . Augusta
11-14 . . . . .Rome
16-18 . . . . at Lakewood
19-22 . . . . at Greensboro
23-25 . . . . .Asheville
26-28 . . . . . Charleston
30-31 . . . . at Asheville
SEPTEMBER
1 . . . . at Asheville
2-5 . . . . Lexington

30-31 . . . . Charleston
JUNE
1 . . . . Charleston
2-4 . . . . at Asheville
6-8 . . . . . . .at Kannapolis
9-12 . . . . Augusta
13-15 . . . . .Hickory
16-19 . . . at Hagerstown
23-26 . . . . . . Lakewood
27-29 . . . . at Charleston
30 . . . . .Asheville
JULY
1-3 . . . . .Asheville
4-6 . . . . at Rome
7-10 . . . . at Lexington
12-14 . . . . . Greensboro
15-18 . . . .Hagerstown

20-22 . . . . at Greensboro
23-26 . . . . . . at Asheville
28-31 . . . . .Rome
AUGUST
1-3 . . . . .Asheville
4-7 . . . . . . at Charleston
8-10 . . . .at Columbia
11-14 . . . . . . Charleston
16-18 . . . . . Kannapolis
19-22 . . . . at Charleston
23-25 . . . . at Augusta
26-28 . . . . .Asheville
30-31 . . . . .Rome
SEPTEMBER
1 . . . . .Rome
2-5 . . . . . at West Virginia

KANNAPOLIS INTIMIDATORS

APRIL
7-10 . . . . .Hickory
11-13 . . . . Delmarva
14-17 . . . . at Hickory
18-20 . . . . at West Virginia
21-24 . . . . Delmarva
26-28 . . . . . . at Augusta
29-30 . . . . . .at Columbia

MAY
1-2 . . . . .at Columbia
4-6 . . . . .Hagerstown
7-10 . . . . .Lakewood
12-15 . . . at Hagerstown
16-18 . . . . . .Greensboro
19-22 . . . . . at Asheville
23-25 . . . . at Lexington
26-29 . . . . . . .Asheville
30-31 . . . . Augusta

JUNE
1 . . . . Augusta
2-4 . . . . . . .at Charleston
6-8 . . . . Greenville
9-12 . . . . .Hickory
13-15 . . . . .at Delmarva
16-19 . . . . . at Lakewood

LAKEWOOD BLUECLAWS

APRIL
7-10 . . . . . . at Lexington
11-13 . . . . at Hagerstown
14-17 . . . . . .Greensboro
18-20 . . . . .Hagerstown
21-24 . . . . at Greensboro
26-28 . . . . . . Charleston
29-30 . . . . . Greenville

MAY
1-2 . . . . Greenville
4-6 . . . . at Asheville
7-10 . . . . . .at Kannapolis
12-15 . . . . . West Virginia
16-18 . . . . at Hagerstown
19-22 . . . . . Delmarva
23-25 . . . . .Hagerstown
26-29 . . . . . .at Delmarva
30-31 . . . . at West Virginia

JUNE
1 . . . . . . at West Virginia
2-4 . . . . .Hickory
6-8 . . . . Lexington
9-12 . . . . . .at Delmarva
13-15 . . . . . .Hagerstown
16-19 . . . . . Kannapolis

LEXINGTON LEGENDS

APRIL
7-10 . . . . .Lakewood
11-13 . . . . Augusta
14-17 . . . at West Virginia
18-20 . . . . . at Asheville
21-24 . . . . . West Virginia
26-28 . . . . .at Columbia
29-30 . . . . . . at Hickory

MAY
1-2 . . . . at Hickory
4-6 . . . . Delmarva
7-10 . . . . . at Greensboro
12-15 . . . . . Charleston
16-18 . . . . .Hickory
19-22 . . . . . at Greenville

23-26 . . . . Delmarva
27-29 . . . . .Rome
30 . . . . at Hickory

JULY
1-3 . . . . .at Hickory
4-6 . . . . .Hagerstown
7-10 . . . . . at Greensboro
12-14 . . . . Lexington
15-18 . . . . Greensboro
20-22 . . . . . at Lakewood
23-26 . . . . . .at Delmarva
28-31 . . . . Greensboro

AUGUST
1-3 . . . . Charleston
4-7 . . . . . . at Greensboro
8-10 . . . . at Hagerstown
11-14 . . . . Lakewood
16-18 . . . . at Greenville
19-22 . . . . . West Virginia
23-25 . . . . . . at Rome
26-28 . . . . Columbia
30-31 . . . . at Lakewood

SEPTEMBER
1 . . . . at Lakewood
2-5 . . . . .at Delmarva

23-26 . . . . . at Greenville
27-29 . . . . at Hagerstown
30 . . . . Greensboro

JULY
1-3 . . . . Greensboro
4-6 . . . . . . .at Delmarva
7-10 . . . . . . West Virginia
12-14 . . . . . . at Hickory
15-18 . . . . at Charleston
20-22 . . . . . Kannapolis
23-26 . . . . . . .Hickory
28-31 . . . . at Augusta

AUGUST
1-3 . . . . . . at Greensboro
4-7 . . . . . . .Hagerstown
8-10 . . . . .at Delmarva
11-14 . . . .at Kannapolis
16-18 . . . . .Hickory
19-22 . . . .at Delmarva
23-25 . . . . . Greensboro
26-28 . . . . at West Virginia
30-31 . . . . . Kannapolis

SEPTEMBER
1 . . . . Kannapolis
2-5 . . . . Greensboro

23-25 . . . . . . Kannapolis
26-29 . . . . at Hagerstown
30-31 . . . . . Greensboro

JUNE
1 . . . . Greensboro
2-4 . . . . .Rome
6-8 . . . . . . at Lakewood
9-12 . . . . at Hagerstown
13-15 . . . . . West Virginia
16-19 . . . . . at Augusta
23-26 . . . . . .Hagerstown
27-29 . . . . at West Virginia
30 . . . . .Rome

ROME BRAVES

APRIL
7-10 . . . . Augusta
11-13 . . . . . . Columbia
14-17 . . . . . at Asheville
18-20 . . . . . at Augusta
21-24 . . . . . .Asheville
26-28 . . . at West Virginia
29-30 . . . at Hagerstown

MAY
1-2 . . . at Hagerstown
4-6 . . . . .Hickory
7-10 . . . . Augusta
12-15 . . . . at Hickory
16-18 . . . . . .at Columbia
19-22 . . . . . . Augusta
23-25 . . . . at Hickory
26-29 . . . . . . Greenville
30-31 . . . . Columbia

JUNE
1 . . . . Columbia
2-4 . . . . . . at Lexington
6-8 . . . . Charleston
9-12 . . . at Greensboro
13-15 . . . . .at Columbia
16-19 . . . . . . Greensboro

JULY
1-3 . . . . .Rome
4-6 . . . . at Asheville
7-10 . . . . Greenville
12-14 . . . .at Kannapolis
15-18 . . . . .Asheville
20-22 . . . . . . at Rome
23-26 . . . . . Columbia
28-31 . . . at Charleston

AUGUST
1-3 . . . . at Rome

WEST VIRGINIA POWER

APRIL
7-10 . . . . . at Greensboro
11-13 . . . . . at Greenville
14-17 . . . . Lexington
18-20 . . . . . . Kannapolis
21-24 . . . . . at Lexington
26-28 . . . . .Rome
29-30 . . . . .Asheville

MAY
1-2 . . . . .Asheville
4-6 . . . . . .at Charleston
7-10 . . . . . . .Hagerstown
12-15 . . . . . at Lakewood
16-18 . . . . .at Delmarva
19-22 . . . . .Hickory
23-25 . . . . .at Charleston
26-29 . . . . Columbia
30-31 . . . . . . .Lakewood

JUNE
1 . . . . .Lakewood
2-4 . . . . at Augusta
6-8 . . . . Delmarva
9-12 . . . . . . .at Columbia
13-15 . . . . at Lexington
16-19 . . . . . . Charleston

4-7 . . . . .Hickory
8-10 . . . . .Asheville
11-14 . . . . . at Augusta
16-18 . . . . . West Virginia
19-22 . . . .Hagerstown
23-25 . . . at West Virginia
26-28 . . . . .at Delmarva
30-31 . . . . . . Augusta

SEPTEMBER
1 . . . . Augusta
2-5 . . . . at Hickory

23-26 . . . . . . Charleston
27-29 . . . . .at Kannapolis
30 . . . . at Lexington

JULY
1-3 . . . . at Lexington
4-6 . . . . Greenville
7-10 . . . . .Hickory
12-14 . . . at Charleston
15-18 . . . .at Columbia
20-22 . . . . . Lexington
23-26 . . . . West Virginia
28-31 . . . at Greenville

AUGUST
1-3 . . . . Lexington
4-7 . . . . Columbia
8-10 . . . .at Charleston
11-14 . . . . . at Hickory
16-18 . . . . . .Hagerstown
19-22 . . . . . at Asheville
23-25 . . . . . Kannapolis
26-28 . . . . . Augusta
30-31 . . . . at Greenville

SEPTEMBER
1 . . . . at Greenville
2-5 . . . . at Augusta

23-26 . . . . . at Asheville
27-29 . . . . . Lexington
30 . . . . Columbia

JULY
1-3 . . . . Columbia
4-6 . . . . . . at Greensboro
7-10 . . . . . . at Lakewood
12-14 . . . . Augusta
15-18 . . . . . .at Hickory
20-22 . . . . . Charleston
23-26 . . . . . at Rome
28-31 . . . . . Delmarva

AUGUST
1-3 . . . . . at Hagerstown
4-7 . . . . .at Delmarva
8-10 . . . . . . Greensboro
11-14 . . . . . . Delmarva
16-18 . . . . at Lexington
19-22 . . . .at Kannapolis
23-25 . . . . . Lexington
26-28 . . . . . Lakewood
30-31 . . . . .at Columbia

SEPTEMBER
1 . . . . .at Columbia
2-5 . . . . Greenville

SHORT SEASON

NEW YORK-PENN LEAGUE

ABERDEEN IRONBIRDS

JUNE
17-18 . . . .at Hudson Valley
19-21 . . . at Staten Island
22-24 . . . . .Auburn
25-27 . . . . . .Connecticut
28-30 . . . . at Vermont

JULY
1-3. . . . . .at Lowell
4-6. . . . . . . West Virginia
8-10 . . .at Williamsport
11-13 . . . . .Brooklyn
14-16 . . . . . . at Batavia
17-19 . . . . . Staten Island
21-23 . . . . at Brooklyn
24-26 . . .at Hudson Valley
28-30 . . .Mahoning Valley

31 . . . . at Brooklyn

AUGUST
1-2. . . . . at Brooklyn
3-5. . . . . .Tri-City
6-8. . . . . . . at Connecticut
9-11 . . . . . . Staten Island
12-14 . . . . Lowell
17-19 . . . . . . at Tri-City
20-22 . . . . Vermont
23-25 . . . at Staten Island
26-28 . . . . . Hudson Valley
29-31 . . . at State College

SEPTEMBER
1-3. . . . . .Brooklyn
4-5. . . . . . Hudson Valley

AUBURN DOUBLEDAYS

JUNE
17-18 . . . . .Batavia
19-21 . . . .Mahoning Valley
22-24 . . . . . at Aberdeen
25-27 . . . . . Williamsport
28-30 . . at Mahoning Valley

JULY
1-3. . . . . at West Virginia
4-6. . . . . Lowell
8-10 . . . . . at State College
11-13 . . . . .Vermont
14-16 . . . . at West Virginia
17-19 . . .Mahoning Valley
21-23 . . . at State College
24-26 . . .at Williamsport
28-30 . . . . . West Virginia

31 . . . . . . at Staten Island

AUGUST
1-2. . . . . at Staten Island
3-5. . . . . . . State College
6-8. . . . . at Batavia
9-11 . . . . . . .Connecticut
12-14 . . . . .Batavia
17-19 . . .at Hudson Valley
20-22 . . .at Williamsport
23-25 . . . . .Tri-City
26-28 . . . . . State College
29-31 . . . . . at Brooklyn

SEPTEMBER
1-3. . . . . . . West Virginia
4-5. . . . . at Batavia

BATAVIA MUCKDOGS

JUNE
17-18 . . . . at Auburn
19-21 . . . at West Virginia
22-24 . . . . . State College
25-27 . . at Mahoning Valley
28-30 . . . . . West Virginia

JULY
1-3. . . . . .at Williamsport
4-6. . . . . .Brooklyn
8-10 . . . . at Vermont
11-13 . . .at Williamsport
14-16 . . . . . . Aberdeen
17-19 . . . . . . at Tri-City
21-23 . . . . . Williamsport
24-26 . . . . . State College
28-30 . . . . . .at Lowell

31 . . . . . . Hudson Valley

AUGUST
1-2. . . . . . Hudson Valley
3-5. . . . . . at Connecticut
6-8. . . . . .Auburn
9-11 . . at Mahoning Valley
12-14 . . . . at Auburn
17-19 . . .Mahoning Valley
20-22 . . . . West Virginia
23-25 . . . at State College
26-28 . . . . . Staten Island
29-31 . . . at West Virginia

SEPTEMBER
1-3. . . . . . . Williamsport
4-5. . . . . .Auburn

BROOKLYN CYCLONES

JUNE
17 . . . . . . Staten Island
18 . . . . . at Staten Island
19-21 . . . . .Tri-City
22-24 . . . . at Connecticut
25-27 . . . . Hudson Valley
28-30 . . . . at State College

JULY
1-3. . . . . . . .Connecticut
4-6. . . . . at Batavia
8-10 . . . . Hudson Valley
11-13 . . . . at Aberdeen
14-16 . . . . Lowell
17-19 . . .at Hudson Valley
21-23 . . . . Aberdeen

24-26 . . . . . Staten Island
28-30 . . . . . . at Vermont
31 . . . . Aberdeen

AUGUST
1-2. . . . . Aberdeen
3-5. . . .at Hudson Valley
6-8. . . . . at Tri-City
9-11 . . . . .Vermont
12-14 . . . . West Virginia

CONNECTICUT TIGERS

JUNE
17-18 . . . . . . at Tri-City
19-21 . . . . at Vermont
22-24 . . . . .Brooklyn
25-27 . . . at Aberdeen
28-30 . . . . . . Lowell

JULY
1-3. . . . . . . at Brooklyn
4-6. . . . . . . Williamsport
8-10 . . . . .at Lowell
11-13 . . . State College
14-16 . . . . at Tri-City
17-19 . . . . . . Vermont
21-23 . . . at West Virginia
24-26 . . at Mahoning Valley
28-30 . . . . Tri-City

31 . . . . . . at Vermont

AUGUST
1-2. . . . . at Vermont
3-5. . . . . .Batavia
6-8. . . . . . . at Aberdeen
9-11 . . . . .at Auburn
12-14 . . . . Hudson Valley
17-19 . . . . . .at Lowell
20-22 . . . . . Staten Island
23-25 . . .at Hudson Valley
26-28 . . . . . . Vermont
29-31 . . . at Staten Island

SEPTEMBER
1-3. . . . . Lowell
4-5. . . . . .Tri-City

HUDSON VALLEY RENEGADES

JUNE
17-18 . . . . . Aberdeen
19-21 . . . . at State College
22-24 . . . . Lowell
25-27 . . . . at Brooklyn
28 . . . . Staten Island
29 . . . . . at Staten Island
30 . . . . . . Staten Island

JULY
1-3. . . . . .Tri-City
4 . . . . . at Staten Island
5 . . . . . . Staten Island
6 . . . . . at Staten Island
8-10 . . . . at Brooklyn
11-13 . . . . West Virginia
14 . . . . at Staten Island
15 . . . . . . Staten Island
16 . . . . at Staten Island
17-19 . . . . . . .Brooklyn
21-23 . . . . . . at Vermont

24-26 . . . . Aberdeen
28 . . . . Staten Island
29 . . . . at Staten Island
30 . . . . . . Staten Island
31 . . . . at Batavia

AUGUST
1-2. . . . . at Batavia
3-5. . . . . .Brooklyn
6-8. . . . .Mahoning Valley
9-11 . . .at Williamsport
12-14 . . . . . at Connecticut
17-19 . . . . .Auburn
20-22 . . . . . at Tri-City
23-25 . . . . . .Connecticut
26-28 . . . at Aberdeen
29-31 . . . . . . .at Lowell

SEPTEMBER
1-3. . . . . Vermont
4-5. . . . . . . at Aberdeen

LOWELL SPINNERS

JUNE
17-18 . . . . .Vermont
19-21 . . . . . Williamsport
22-24 . . .at Hudson Valley
25-27 . . . . .Tri-City
28-30 . . . at Connecticut

JULY
1-3. . . . . Aberdeen
4-6. . . . . at Auburn
8-10 . . . . . .Connecticut
11-13 . . . . . Staten Island
14-16 . . . . at Brooklyn
17-19 . . . . State College
21-23 . . at Mahoning Valley
24-26 . . . at West Virginia
28-30 . . . . Batavia

31 . . . . at Tri-City

AUGUST
1-2. . . . . at Tri-City
3-5. . . . . .Vermont
6-8. . . . . at Staten Island
9-11 . . . . .Tri-City
12-14 . . . . . at Aberdeen
17-19 . . . . . .Connecticut
20-22 . . . . . . .Brooklyn
23-25 . . . . . at Vermont
26-28 . . . . . at Tri-City
29-31 . . . . Hudson Valley

SEPTEMBER
1-3. . . . .at Connecticut
4-5. . . . . at Vermont

MAHONING VALLEY SCRAPPERS

JUNE
17-18 . . . . . . West Virginia
19-21 . . . . at Auburn
22-24 . . . .at Williamsport
25-27 . . . . Batavia
28-30 . . . . .Auburn

JULY
1-3 . . . . . at State College
4-6 . . . . Vermont
8-10 . . . . . at Staten Island
11-13 . . . . Tri-City
14-16 . . . at State College
17-19 . . . . at Auburn
21-23 . . . . Lowell
24-26 . . . . . .Connecticut
28-30 . . . . at Aberdeen

31 . . . . Williamsport
AUGUST
1-2 . . . . Williamsport
3-5 . . . . . at West Virginia
6-8 . . . . . .at Hudson Valley
9-11 . . . . Batavia
12-14 . . . . . Williamsport
17-19 . . . . . . at Batavia
20-22 . . . . . State College
23-25 . . . . . at Brooklyn
26-28 . . . . West Virginia
29-31 . . . .at Williamsport
SEPTEMBER
1-3 . . . . State College
4-5 . . . . at West Virginia

STATE COLLEGE SPIKES

JUNE
17 . . . . . .at Williamsport
18 . . . . Williamsport
19-21 . . . . Hudson Valley
22-24 . . . . . at Batavia
25-27 . . . at West Virginia
28-30 . . . . .Brooklyn

JULY
1-3 . . . . .Mahoning Valley
4-6 . . . . at Tri-City
8-10 . . . . .Auburn
11-13 . . . at Connecticut
14-16 . . .Mahoning Valley
17-19 . . . . .at Lowell
21-23 . . . . .Auburn
24-26 . . . . at Batavia
28 . . . . . .at Williamsport
29-30 . . . . . Williamsport

31 . . . . West Virginia
AUGUST
1-2 . . . . West Virginia
3-5 . . . . at Auburn
6-8 . . . . at Vermont
9-11 . . . . . . West Virginia
12-14 . . . . . Staten Island
17 . . . . Williamsport
18-19 . . . .at Williamsport
20-22 . . at Mahoning Valley
23-25 . . . . .Batavia
26-28 . . . . . . at Auburn
29-31 . . . . Aberdeen
SEPTEMBER
1-3 . . . . at Mahoning Valley
4 . . . . Williamsport
5 . . . . .at Williamsport

STATEN ISLAND YANKEES

JUNE
17 . . . . at Brooklyn
18 . . . . .Brooklyn
19-21 . . . . Aberdeen
22-24 . . . . . West Virginia
25-27 . . . . . . at Vermont
28 . . . . .at Hudson Valley
29 . . . . . Hudson Valley
30 . . . . .at Hudson Valley

JULY
1-3 . . . . Vermont
4 . . . . .Hudson Valley
5 . . . . . . .at Hudson Valley
6 . . . . Hudson Valley
8-10 . . . .Mahoning Valley
11-13 . . . . .at Lowell
14 . . . . . Hudson Valley
15 . . . . .at Hudson Valley
16 . . . . . . Hudson Valley
17-19 . . . . at Aberdeen
21-23 . . . . Tri-City

24-26 . . . . . at Brooklyn
28 . . . . .at Hudson Valley
29 . . . . . . Hudson Valley
30 . . . . .at Hudson Valley
31 . . . . .Auburn
AUGUST
1-2 . . . . .Auburn
3-5 . . . . .at Williamsport
6-8 . . . . Lowell
9-11 . . . . . . at Aberdeen
12-14 . . . at State College
17-19 . . . . .Brooklyn
20-22 . . . . at Connecticut
23-25 . . . . . Aberdeen
26-28 . . . . . at Batavia
29-31 . . . . . .Connecticut
SEPTEMBER
1-3 . . . . at Tri-City
4 . . . . at Brooklyn
5 . . . . .Brooklyn

TRI-CITY VALLEYCATS

JUNE
17-18 . . . . . .Connecticut
19-21 . . . . . . at Brooklyn
22-24 . . . . Vermont
25-27 . . . . .at Lowell
28-30 . . . . . . Williamsport

JULY
1-3 . . . . .at Hudson Valley
4-6 . . . . State College
8-10 . . . at West Virginia
11-13 . . at Mahoning Valley
14-16 . . . . . .Connecticut
17-19 . . . . Batavia

JUNE
21-23 . . . . at Staten Island
24-26 . . . . Vermont
28-30 . . . . .at Connecticut
31 . . . . Lowell
AUGUST
1-2 . . . . Lowell
3-5 . . . . at Aberdeen
6-8 . . . . .Brooklyn
9-11 . . . . .at Lowell

12-14 . . . . at Vermont
17-19 . . . . Aberdeen
20-22 . . . . . Hudson Valley
23-25 . . . . at Auburn
26-28 . . . . Lowell
29-31 . . . . . . at Vermont
SEPTEMBER
1-3 . . . . Staten Island
4-5 . . . . . .at Connecticut

VERMONT LAKE MONSTERS

JUNE
17-18 . . . . .at Lowell
19-21 . . . . . .Connecticut
22-24 . . . . at Tri-City
25-27 . . . Staten Island
28-30 . . . . Aberdeen

JULY
1-3 . . . . . at Staten Island
4-6 . . . . at Mahoning Valley
8-10 . . . . Batavia
11-13 . . . . at Auburn
14-16 . . . . . Williamsport
17-19 . . . at Connecticut
21-23 . . . . Hudson Valley
24-26 . . . . . . at Tri-City
28-30 . . . . . . .Brooklyn

31 . . . . .Connecticut
AUGUST
1-2 . . . . .Connecticut
3-5 . . . . .at Lowell
6-8 . . . . State College
9-11 . . . . . . at Brooklyn
12-14 . . . . Tri-City
17-19 . . . . at West Virginia
20-22 . . . . at Aberdeen
23-25 . . . . Lowell
26-28 . . . . .at Connecticut
29-31 . . . . Tri-City
SEPTEMBER
1-3 . . . . . .at Hudson Valley
4-5 . . . . Lowell

WEST VIRGINIA BLACK BEARS

JUNE
17-18 . . at Mahoning Valley
19-21 . . . . .Batavia
22-24 . . . . at Staten Island
25-27 . . . . State College
28-30 . . . . . at Batavia

JULY
1-3 . . . . .Auburn
4-6 . . . . at Aberdeen
8-10 . . . . .Tri-City
11-13 . . . .at Hudson Valley
14-16 . . . . .Auburn
17-19 . . . .at Williamsport
21-23 . . . . .Connecticut
24-26 . . . . Lowell
28-30 . . . . . at Auburn

31 . . . . . at State College
AUGUST
1-2 . . . . . at State College
3-5 . . . . .Mahoning Valley
6-8 . . . . . . Williamsport
9-11 . . . . at State College
12-14 . . . . . . at Brooklyn
17-19 . . . . .Vermont
20-22 . . . . . at Batavia
23-25 . . . . Williamsport
26-28 . . at Mahoning Valley
29-31 . . . . .Batavia
SEPTEMBER
1-3 . . . . at Auburn
4-5 . . . . .Mahoning Valley

WILLIAMSPORT CROSSCUTTERS

JUNE
17 . . . . State College
18 . . . . . at State College
19-21 . . . . .at Lowell
22-24 . . .Mahoning Valley
25-27 . . . . . . at Auburn
28-30 . . . . . . at Tri-City

JULY
1-3 . . . . .Batavia
4-6 . . . . . .at Connecticut
8-10 . . . . Aberdeen
11-13 . . . . .Batavia
14-16 . . . . . . at Vermont
17-19 . . . . . West Virginia
21-23 . . . . . . at Batavia
24-26 . . . . .Auburn
28 . . . . State College
29-30 . . . . at State College

31 . . . . at Mahoning Valley
AUGUST
1-2 . . . . at Mahoning Valley
3-5 . . . . Staten Island
6-8 . . . . . at West Virginia
9-11 . . . . . Hudson Valley
12-14 . . at Mahoning Valley
17 . . . . . at State College
18-19 . . . . . State College
20-22 . . . . .Auburn
23-25 . . . at West Virginia
26-28 . . . . .Brooklyn
29-31 . . . .Mahoning Valley
SEPTEMBER
1-3 . . . . at Batavia
4 . . . . at State College
5 . . . . State College

NORTHWEST LEAGUE

BOISE HAWKS

JUNE	
17-19 . . . . at Eugene	29-31 . . . . .Eugene
20-22 . . . . . Salem-Keizer	**AUGUST**
23-27 . . . . at Everett	4-8. . . . . at Tri-City
28-30 . . . . .Eugene	9-11 . . . . .Hillsboro
JULY	12-16 . . . . Tri-City
1-3. . . . . .Hillsboro	17-19 . . . . .at Eugene
4-8. . . . . at Spokane	20-24 . . . . . at Vancouver
9-11 . . . . Salem-Keizer	26-28 . . . . . . at Hillsboro
13-17 . . . . . . .Vancouver	29-31 . . . . Everett
18-20 . . . at Salem-Keizer	**SEPTEMBER**
21-25 . . . . .Spokane	1-2. . . . . Everett
26-28 . . . . . . at Hillsboro	3-5. . . . . at Salem-Keizer

EUGENE EMERALDS

JUNE	
17-19 . . . . Boise	29-31 . . . . at Boise
20-22 . . . . . at Hillsboro	**AUGUST**
23-27 . . . . .Spokane	4-8. . . . . .Vancouver
28-30 . . . . at Boise	9-11 . . . . at Salem-Keizer
JULY	12-16 . . . . . . at Spokane
1-3. . . . . . . Salem-Keizer	17-19 . . . . Boise
4-8. . . . . at Everett	20-24 . . . . Everett
9-11 . . . . .Hillsboro	26-28 . . . . at Salem-Keizer
13-17 . . . . at Tri-City	29-31 . . . . Tri-City
18-20 . . . . . . .Hillsboro	**SEPTEMBER**
21-25 . . . . . at Vancouver	1-2. . . . . Tri-City
26-28 . . . . . Salem-Keizer	3-5. . . . . at Hillsboro

EVERETT AQUASOX

JUNE	
17-19 . . . . at Tri-City	29-31 . . . . . . at Spokane
20-22 . . . . . at Vancouver	**AUGUST**
23-27 . . . . Boise	4-8. . . . . .Hillsboro
28-30 . . . . . . at Spokane	9-11 . . . . . at Vancouver
JULY	12-16 . . . . . . Salem-Keizer
1-3. . . . . at Tri-City	17-19 . . . . Tri-City
4-8. . . . . .Eugene	20-24 . . . . . . at Eugene
9-11 . . . . .Spokane	26-28 . . . . . .Vancouver
13-17 . . . . . . at Hillsboro	29-31 . . . . at Boise
18-20 . . . . .Tri-City	**SEPTEMBER**
21-25 . . . at Salem-Keizer	1-2. . . . . at Boise
26-28 . . . . . . .Vancouver	3-5. . . . . .Spokane

HILLSBORO HOPS

JUNE	
17-19 . . . . at Salem-Keizer	29-31 . . . . . Salem-Keizer
20-22 . . . . .Eugene	**AUGUST**
23-27 . . . . . at Vancouver	4-8. . . . . at Everett
28-30 . . . . . Salem-Keizer	9-11 . . . . at Boise
JULY	12-16 . . . . . . .Vancouver
1-3. . . . . at Boise	17-19 . . . . at Salem-Keizer
4-8. . . . . Tri-City	20-24 . . . . .Spokane
9-11 . . . . at Eugene	26-28 . . . . Boise
13-17 . . . . Everett	29-31 . . . . at Spokane
18-20 . . . . at Eugene	**SEPTEMBER**
21-25 . . . . . . at Tri-City	1-2. . . . . at Spokane
26-28 . . . . Boise	3-5. . . . . .Eugene

SALEM-KEIZER VOLCANOES

JUNE	
17-19 . . . . .Hillsboro	29-31 . . . . . . at Hillsboro
20-22 . . . . at Boise	**AUGUST**
23-27 . . . . Tri-City	4-8. . . . . .Spokane
28-30 . . . . . at Hillsboro	9-11 . . . . .Eugene
JULY	12-16 . . . . . . at Everett
1-3. . . . . at Eugene	17-19 . . . . .Hillsboro
4-8. . . . . .Vancouver	20-24 . . . . . . at Tri-City
9-11 . . . . at Boise	26-28 . . . . .Eugene
12-16 . . . . at Spokane	29-31 . . . . . at Vancouver
18-20 . . . . Boise	**SEPTEMBER**
21-25 . . . . Everett	1-2. . . . . . . at Vancouver
26-28 . . . . . . at Eugene	3-5. . . . . Boise

SPOKANE INDIANS

JUNE	
17-19 . . . . . . .Vancouver	29-31 . . . . Everett
20-22 . . . . . at Tri-City	**AUGUST**
23-27 . . . . . at Eugene	4-8. . . . at Salem-Keizer
28-30 . . . . . Everett	9-11 . . . . . . at Tri-City
JULY	12-16 . . . . .Eugene
1-3. . . . . . . at Vancouver	17-19 . . . . at Vancouver
4-8. . . . . Boise	20-24 . . . . . . at Hillsboro
9-11 . . . . . . at Everett	26-28 . . . . Tri-City
12-16 . . . . Salem-Keizer	29-31 . . . . .Hillsboro
18-20 . . . . . .Vancouver	**SEPTEMBER**
21-25 . . . . . . at Boise	1-2. . . . . .Hillsboro
26-28 . . . . Tri-City	3-5. . . . . at Everett

TRI-CITY DUST DEVILS

JUNE	
17-19 . . . . Everett	29-31 . . . . . at Vancouver
20-22 . . . . .Spokane	**AUGUST**
23-27 . . . . at Salem-Keizer	4-8. . . . . Boise
28-30 . . . . .Vancouver	9-11 . . . . .Spokane
JULY	12-16 . . . . at Boise
1-3. . . . . Everett	17-19 . . . . at Everett
4-8. . . . . at Hillsboro	20-24 . . . . . Salem-Keizer
9-11 . . . . . at Vancouver	26-28 . . . . . . at Spokane
13-17 . . . . .Eugene	29-31 . . . . . . at Eugene
18-20 . . . . . . at Everett	**SEPTEMBER**
21-25 . . . . .Hillsboro	1-2. . . . . at Eugene
26-28 . . . . . at Spokane	3-5. . . . . .Vancouver

VANCOUVER CANADIANS

JUNE	
17-19 . . . . . . at Spokane	29-31 . . . . Tri-City
20-22 . . . . Everett	**AUGUST**
23-27 . . . . .Hillsboro	4-8. . . . . at Eugene
28-30 . . . . at Tri-City	9-11 . . . . Everett
JULY	12-16 . . . . . . at Hillsboro
1-3. . . . . .Spokane	17-19 . . . . .Spokane
4-8. . . . . at Salem-Keizer	20-24 . . . . Boise
9-11 . . . . Tri-City	26-28 . . . . at Everett
13-17 . . . . at Boise	29-31 . . . . . . Salem-Keizer
18-20 . . . . . at Spokane	**SEPTEMBER**
21-25 . . . . .Eugene	1-2. . . . . . . Salem-Keizer
26-28 . . . . . . at Everett	3-5. . . . . at Tri-City

ROOKIE

APPALACHIAN LEAGUE

BLUEFIELD BLUE JAYS

JUNE
23-25 . . . Bristol
26-28 . . . at Burlington
29-30 . . . Kingsport

JULY
1 . . . Kingsport
2-4 . . . at Elizabethton
5 . . . Princeton
6-8 . . . Danville
9-11 . . . at Johnson City
13-15 . . . Princeton
16-18 . . . at Greeneville
19-21 . . . at Bristol
22-24 . . . Burlington
25-27 . . . at Kingsport
28-30 . . . Greeneville
31 . . . at Burlington

AUGUST
1-2 . . . at Burlington
4-6 . . . Danville
7-9 . . . at Princeton
10-12 . . . Pulaski
13-15 . . . Elizabethton
16 . . . at Princeton
18-20 . . . at Pulaski
21-23 . . . at Danville
24-26 . . . Pulaski
27-29 . . . Johnson City
30-31 . . . at Princeton

SEPTEMBER
1 . . . at Princeton

BRISTOL PIRATES

JUNE
23-25 . . . at Bluefield
26-28 . . . Greeneville
29-30 . . . Burlington

JULY
1 . . . Burlington
2-5 . . . at Pulaski
6-8 . . . Elizabethton
9-11 . . . at Princeton
13-15 . . . at Kingsport
16-18 . . . Danville
19-21 . . . Bluefield
22-24 . . . at Greeneville
25-27 . . . at Burlington
28-29 . . . Elizabethton
30 . . . at Elizabethton
31 . . . Johnson City

AUGUST
1-2 . . . Johnson City
4-6 . . . at Greeneville
7-9 . . . Kingsport
10-12 . . . at Danville
13-16 . . . Pulaski
18-20 . . . Johnson City
21-22 . . . at Elizabethton
23 . . . Elizabethton
24-26 . . . at Johnson City
27-29 . . . Princeton
30-31 . . . at Kingsport

SEPTEMBER
1 . . . at Kingsport

BURLINGTON ROYALS

JUNE
23-25 . . . Princeton
26-28 . . . Bluefield
29-30 . . . at Bristol

JULY
1 . . . at Bristol
2-3 . . . at Danville
4-5 . . . Danville
6-8 . . . at Greeneville
9-11 . . . at Pulaski
13-15 . . . Johnson City
16-18 . . . Kingsport
19-21 . . . at Princeton
22-24 . . . at Bluefield
25-27 . . . Bristol
28-30 . . . Pulaski
31 . . . Bluefield

AUGUST
1-2 . . . Bluefield
4-6 . . . at Kingsport
7-9 . . . at Johnson City
10-12 . . . Princeton
13-14 . . . Danville
15-16 . . . at Danville
18-20 . . . Elizabethton
21-23 . . . Greeneville
24-26 . . . at Elizabethton
27-29 . . . at Pulaski
30-31 . . . at Danville

SEPTEMBER
1 . . . at Danville

DANVILLE BRAVES

JUNE
23-25 . . . at Pulaski
26-28 . . . at Princeton
29-30 . . . Johnson City

JULY
1 . . . Johnson City
2-3 . . . Burlington
4-5 . . . at Burlington
6-8 . . . at Bluefield
9-11 . . . Kingsport
13-15 . . . Elizabethton
16-18 . . . at Bristol
19-21 . . . Pulaski
22-24 . . . Princeton
25-27 . . . at Johnson City
28-30 . . . at Princeton
31 . . . Pulaski

AUGUST
1-2 . . . Pulaski
4-6 . . . at Bluefield
7-9 . . . at Elizabethton
10-12 . . . Bristol
13-14 . . . at Burlington
15-16 . . . Burlington
18-20 . . . Greeneville
21-23 . . . Bluefield
24-26 . . . at Greeneville
27-29 . . . at Kingsport
30-31 . . . Burlington

SEPTEMBER
1 . . . Burlington

ELIZABETHTON TWINS

JUNE
23-25 . . . at Kingsport
26-28 . . . at Johnson City
29-30 . . . Pulaski

JULY
1 . . . Pulaski
2-4 . . . Bluefield
5 . . . at Johnson City
6-8 . . . at Bristol
9-11 . . . Greeneville
13-15 . . . at Danville
16-18 . . . at Princeton
19-21 . . . Kingsport
22-24 . . . Johnson City
25-27 . . . at Pulaski
28-29 . . . at Bristol
30 . . . Bristol
31 . . . Princeton

AUGUST
1-2 . . . Princeton
4-6 . . . at Johnson City
7-9 . . . Danville
10-12 . . . Kingsport
13-15 . . . at Bluefield
16 . . . Johnson City
18-20 . . . at Burlington
21-22 . . . Bristol
23 . . . at Bristol
24-26 . . . Burlington
27-29 . . . at Greeneville
30-31 . . . Greeneville

SEPTEMBER
1 . . . Greeneville

GREENEVILLE ASTROS

JUNE
23-25 . . . Johnson City
26-28 . . . at Bristol
29-30 . . . at Princeton

JULY
1 . . . at Princeton
2-4 . . . Kingsport
5 . . . at Kingsport
6-8 . . . Burlington
9-11 . . . at Elizabethton
13-15 . . . Pulaski
16-18 . . . Bluefield
19-21 . . . at Johnson City
22-24 . . . Bristol
25-27 . . . Princeton
28-30 . . . at Bluefield
31 . . . at Kingsport

AUGUST
1-2 . . . at Kingsport
4-6 . . . Bristol
7-9 . . . at Pulaski
10-12 . . . Johnson City
13-15 . . . at Kingsport
16 . . . Kingsport
18-20 . . . at Danville
21-23 . . . at Burlington
24-26 . . . Danville
27-29 . . . Elizabethton
30-31 . . . at Elizabethton

SEPTEMBER
1 . . . at Elizabethton

JOHNSON CITY CARDINALS

JUNE
23-25 . . . at Greeneville
26-28 . . . Elizabethton
29-30 . . . at Danville

JULY
1 . . . at Danville
2-4 . . . Princeton
5 . . . Elizabethton
6-8 . . . at Kingsport
9-11 . . . Bluefield
13-15 . . . at Burlington
16-18 . . . at Pulaski
19-21 . . . Greeneville
22-24 . . . at Elizabethton
25-27 . . . Danville
28-30 . . . Kingsport
31 . . . at Bristol

AUGUST
1-2 . . . at Bristol
4-6 . . . Elizabethton
7-9 . . . Burlington
10-12 . . . at Greeneville
13-15 . . . at Princeton
16 . . . at Elizabethton
18-20 . . . at Bristol
21-23 . . . Kingsport
24-26 . . . Bristol
27-29 . . . at Bluefield
30-31 . . . Pulaski

SEPTEMBER
1 . . . Pulaski

KINGSPORT METS

JUNE
23-25 . . . . . Elizabethton
26-28 . . . . Pulaski
29-30 . . . . . . at Bluefield

JULY
1 . . . . at Bluefield
2-4 . . . . . . at Greeneville
5 . . . . Greeneville
6-8 . . . . . . Johnson City
9-11 . . . . . . .at Danville
13-15 . . . . Bristol
16-18 . . . . at Burlington
19-21 . . .at Elizabethton
22-24 . . . . . . at Pulaski
25-27 . . . . .Bluefield
28-30 . . at Johnson City

31 . . . . Greeneville
AUGUST
1-2 . . . . Greeneville
4-6 . . . . .Burlington
7-9 . . . . .at Bristol
10-12 . .at Elizabethton
13-15 . . . . . Greeneville
16 . . . .at Greeneville
18-20 . . .at Princeton
21-23 . . at Johnson City
24-26 . . . . . . Princeton
27-29 . . . . Danville
30-31 . . . . Bristol

SEPTEMBER
1 . . . . Bristol

PRINCETON RAYS

JUNE
23-25 . . . . . at Burlington
26-28 . . . . Danville
29-30 . . . . . . Greeneville

JULY
1 . . . . Greeneville
2-4 . . . . at Johnson City
5 . . . . at Bluefield
6-8 . . . . Pulaski
9-11 . . . . Bristol
13-15 . . . . at Bluefield
16-18 . . . . . Elizabethton
19-21 . . . . .Burlington
22-24 . . . . . .at Danville
25-27 . . . .at Greeneville
28-30 . . . . . . Danville

31 . . . . . .at Elizabethton
AUGUST
1-2 . . . . . .at Elizabethton
4-6 . . . . . . at Pulaski
7-9 . . . . Bluefield
10-12 . . . at Burlington
13-15 . . . Johnson City
16 . . . . Bluefield
18-20 . . . . . Kingsport
21-23 . . . . . at Pulaski
24-26 . . . . at Kingsport
27-29 . . . . . at Bristol
30-31 . . . . . . Bluefield

SEPTEMBER
1 . . . . Bluefield

PULASKI YANKEES

JUNE
23-25 . . . . . . Danville
26-28 . . . . . at Kingsport
29-30 . . .at Elizabethton

JULY
1 . . . . . . .at Elizabethton
2-5 . . . . Bristol
6-8 . . . . . .at Princeton
9-11 . . . . . .Burlington
13-15 . . . . .at Greeneville
16-18 . . . . Johnson City
19-21 . . . .at Danville
22-24 . . . . Kingsport
25-27 . . . . . Elizabethton
28-30 . . . . . at Burlington

31 . . . . . . .at Danville
AUGUST
1-2 . . . . .at Danville
4-6 . . . . Princeton
7-9 . . . . . . Greeneville
10-12 . . . at Bluefield
13-16 . . . at Bristol
18-20 . . . . Bluefield
21-23 . . . . . Princeton
24-26 . . . . at Bluefield
27-29 . . . . .Burlington
30-31 . . . at Johnson City

SEPTEMBER
1 . . . . at Johnson City

PIONEER LEAGUE

BILLINGS MUSTANGS

JUNE
17-20 . . . . Missoula
21-22 . . . . Helena
23-26 . . . . . at Missoula
27-29 . . . . . at Great Falls
30 . . . . Great Falls

JULY
1-2 . . . . Great Falls
4-6 . . . . Helena
7-8 . . . . . at Great Falls
9-11 . . . . . . at Helena
13-15 . . . . Grand Junction

16-19 . . . . Orem
21-24 . . . at Grand Junction
25-27 . . . . . at Orem
29-31 . . . . . .Great Falls

AUGUST
4-7 . . . . Ogden
8-10 . . . . .Idaho Falls
12-14 . . . . . . at Ogden
15-18 . . . . at Idaho Falls
19-22 . . . . Missoula
23-26 . . . . at Missoula
27-28 . . . . . at Helena
29-31 . . . . . at Great Falls

GRAND JUNCTION ROCKIES

JUNE
17-18 . . . . Orem
20-23 . . . . at Ogden
24-27 . . . . . . .Idaho Falls
28-29 . . . . . . at Orem
30 . . . . at Idaho Falls

JULY
1-3 . . . . . . at Idaho Falls
4-5 . . . . Orem
6-7 . . . . at Orem
8-11 . . . . Ogden
13-15 . . . . at Billings
16-19 . . . at Great Falls
21-24 . . . . Billings

25-27 . . . . . .Great Falls
28-31 . . . . . at Idaho Falls
AUGUST
4-7 . . . . Missoula
8-10 . . . . Helena
12-14 . . . . . at Missoula
15-18 . . . . . at Helena
20-23 . . . . . . .Idaho Falls
24-27 . . . . . at Ogden
28-31 . . . . Orem

SEPTEMBER
1-4 . . . . at Orem
5-8 . . . . Ogden

GREAT FALLS VOYAGERS

JUNE
17-20 . . . . at Helena
21-22 . . . . . at Missoula
23-26 . . . . Helena
27-29 . . . . Billings
30 . . . . . . at Billings

JULY
1-2 . . . . . . at Billings
4-6 . . . . Missoula
7-8 . . . . Billings
9-11 . . . . . at Missoula
13-15 . . . . Orem
16-19 . . . . Grand Junction
21-24 . . . . . at Orem
25-27 . . .at Grand Junction
29-31 . . . . . at Billings

AUGUST
4-7 . . . . .Idaho Falls
8-10 . . . . Ogden
12-14 . . . at Idaho Falls
15-18 . . . . at Ogden
19-20 . . . . Helena
21-22 . . . . . at Helena
23-24 . . . . Helena
25-26 . . . . . at Helena
27-28 . . . . Missoula
29-31 . . . . Billings

SEPTEMBER
1-2 . . . . at Billings
3-5 . . . . Missoula
6-8 . . . . at Missoula

HELENA BREWERS

JUNE
17-20 . . . . . . .Great Falls
21-22 . . . . . . at Billings
23-26 . . . . at Great Falls
27-29 . . . . Missoula
30 . . . . at Missoula

JULY
1-2 . . . . . . at Missoula
4-6 . . . . at Billings
7-8 . . . . Missoula
9-11 . . . . Billings
13-15 . . . .at Idaho Falls
16-19 . . . . . at Ogden
21-24 . . . . .Idaho Falls
25-27 . . . . . . Ogden
29-31 . . . . at Missoula

AUGUST
4-7 . . . . at Orem
8-10 . . . .at Grand Junction
12-14 . . . . Orem
15-18 . . . . Grand Junction
19-20 . . . . at Great Falls
21-22 . . . . . . .Great Falls
23-24 . . . . . . .Great Falls
25-26 . . . . . .Great Falls
27-28 . . . . Billings
29-31 . . . . Missoula

SEPTEMBER
1-2 . . . . at Missoula
3-5 . . . . at Billings
6-8 . . . . Billings

IDAHO FALLS CHUKARS

JUNE
17-18 . . . . Ogden
20-23 . . . . Orem
24-27 . . .at Grand Junction
28-29 . . . . . . at Ogden
30 . . . . Grand Junction

JULY
1-3 . . . . . . Grand Junction
4-5 . . . . Ogden
6-7 . . . . . . at Ogden
8-11 . . . . . . at Orem
13-15 . . . . Helena
16-19 . . . . Missoula

21-24 . . . . at Helena
25-27 . . . . . at Missoula
28-31 . . . Grand Junction
AUGUST
4-7 . . . . at Great Falls
8-10 . . . . at Billings
12-14 . . . . . .Great Falls
15-18 . . . . Billings
20-23 . . .at Grand Junction
24-25 . . . . . at Orem
26-27 . . . . Orem
28-31 . . . . Ogden

SEPTEMBER
1-4 . . . . at Ogden

MISSOULA OSPREY

JUNE
17-20 . . . . at Billings
21-22 . . . . . . .Great Falls
23-26 . . . . Billings
27-29 . . . . at Helena
30 . . . . Helena

JULY
1-2 . . . . Helena
4-6 . . . . at Great Falls
7-8 . . . . at Helena
9-11 . . . . .Great Falls
13-15 . . . . at Ogden
16-19 . . . . . at Idaho Falls
21-24 . . . . Ogden
25-27 . . . . . . .Idaho Falls

OGDEN RAPTORS

JUNE
17-18 . . . . . at Idaho Falls
20-23 . . . . Grand Junction
24-25 . . . . at Orem
26-27 . . . . .Orem
28-29 . . . . . .Idaho Falls
30 . . . . Orem

JULY
1 . . . . Orem
2-3 . . . . at Orem
4-5 . . . . at Idaho Falls
6-7 . . . . .Idaho Falls
8-11 . . . . at Grand Junction
13-15 . . . . Missoula
16-19 . . . . Helena

OREM OWLZ

JUNE
17-18 . . . at Grand Junction
20-23 . . . . . at Idaho Falls
24-25 . . . . Ogden
26-27 . . . . at Ogden
28-29 . . . . Grand Junction
30 . . . . at Ogden

JULY
1 . . . . at Ogden
2-3 . . . . Ogden
4-5 . . . .at Grand Junction
6-7 . . . . . Grand Junction
8-11 . . . . .Idaho Falls
13-15 . . . . . at Great Falls
16-19 . . . . at Billings
21-24 . . . . . . .Great Falls

ARIZONA LEAGUE   *HOME GAMES ONLY

AZL ANGELS

JUNE
20 . . . . .Athletics
22 . . . . Brewers
25 . . . . Cubs
26 . . . . Royals
29 . . . . Padres

JULY
2 . . . . White Sox
4 . . . . .Athletics
6 . . . . Giants

5-6 . . . . at Orem
7-8 . . . . Orem

29-31 . . . . Helena
AUGUST
4-7 . . . .at Grand Junction
8-10 . . . . at Orem
12-14 . . . Grand Junction
15-18 . . . . Orem
19-22 . . . . at Billings
23-26 . . . . Billings
27-28 . . . . at Great Falls
29-31 . . . . at Helena
SEPTEMBER
1-2 . . . . Helena
3-5 . . . . . at Great Falls
6-8 . . . . Great Falls

21-24 . . . . . . at Missoula
25-27 . . . . at Helena
28-31 . . . . Orem
AUGUST
4-7 . . . . at Billings
8-10 . . . . . at Great Falls
12-14 . . . . Billings
15-18 . . . . . . .Great Falls
19-23 . . . . at Orem
24-27 . . . . Grand Junction
28-31 . . . . at Idaho Falls
SEPTEMBER
1-4 . . . . .Idaho Falls
5-8 . . . . .at Grand Junction

25-27 . . . . Billings
28-31 . . . . at Ogden
AUGUST
4-7 . . . . Helena
8-10 . . . . .Missoula
12-14 . . . . . at Helena
15-18 . . . . . at Missoula
19-23 . . . . Ogden
24-25 . . . . . .Idaho Falls
26-27 . . . . at Idaho Falls
28-31 . . .at Grand Junction
SEPTEMBER
1-4 . . . . . Grand Junction
5-6 . . . . .Idaho Falls
7-8 . . . . . at Idaho Falls

9 . . . . Mariners
10 . . . . D-backs
16 . . . . Giants
17 . . . . Reds
21 . . . . D-backs
22 . . . . Rangers
26 . . . . .Athletics
27 . . . . Brewers
31 . . . . Cubs

AUGUST
1 . . . . Indians
4 . . . . Rangers
6 . . . . Royals
9 . . . . .Athletics
11 . . . . Giants

AZL ATHLETICS

JUNE
22 . . . . Giants
24 . . . . Mariners
27 . . . . D-backs
29 . . . . Brewers

JULY
3 . . . . Cubs
5 . . . . Angels
7 . . . . Dodgers
8 . . . . Cubs
13 . . . . D-backs
15 . . . . Rangers
19 . . . . White Sox
21 . . . . Giants
23 . . . . Angels

AZL BREWERS

JUNE
21 . . . . Angels
24 . . . . Padres
26 . . . . Rangers
30 . . . . .Athletics

JULY
1 . . . . Dodgers
4 . . . . Reds
7 . . . . White Sox
10 . . . . Indians
13 . . . . Mariners
15 . . . . Indians
16 . . . . White Sox
20 . . . . Royals
21 . . . . Dodgers

AZL CUBS

JUNE
20 . . . . Brewers
23 . . . . D-backs
24 . . . . Angels
28 . . . . Giants
30 . . . . Mariners

JULY
2 . . . . .Athletics
4 . . . . Indians
7 . . . . Padres
10 . . . . Giants
14 . . . . Royals
16 . . . . D-backs
18 . . . . .Athletics
20 . . . . Angels

AZL D-BACKS

JUNE
20 . . . . Giants
22 . . . . Cubs
25 . . . . White Sox
28 . . . . .Athletics
30 . . . . Dodgers

15 . . . . D-backs
17 . . . . Dodgers
20 . . . . Giants
22 . . . . Dodgers
25 . . . . Cubs
27 . . . . White Sox

24 . . . . Cubs
28 . . . . Giants
30 . . . . Royals
AUGUST
2 . . . . D-backs
5 . . . . Padres
8 . . . . Cubs
10 . . . . Angels
12 . . . . Dodgers
14 . . . . Angels
17 . . . . Brewers
18 . . . . Indians
23 . . . . Reds
25 . . . . D-backs
27 . . . . Rangers
28 . . . . Cubs

25 . . . . Cubs
28 . . . . Padres
31 . . . . D-backs
AUGUST
2 . . . . Rangers
4 . . . . Reds
6 . . . . Dodgers
9 . . . . Reds
12 . . . . White Sox
15 . . . . Indians
16 . . . . Giants
19 . . . . Royals
20 . . . . White Sox
25 . . . . Dodgers
27 . . . . Mariners
29 . . . . Indians

23 . . . . White Sox
26 . . . . Brewers
29 . . . . D-backs
30 . . . . Angels
AUGUST
3 . . . . Giants
5 . . . . Dodgers
7 . . . . White Sox
10 . . . . Padres
12 . . . . Rangers
13 . . . . Giants
18 . . . . Reds
20 . . . . D-backs
22 . . . . .Athletics
24 . . . . Angels
29 . . . . .Athletics

JULY
1 . . . . Royals
5 . . . . Cubs
6 . . . . Reds
11 . . . . Angels
14 . . . . Rangers
18 . . . . Giants
19 . . . . Padres

22 . . . . Indians
24 . . . . Mariners
26 . . . . Giants
28 . . . . Cubs
AUGUST
1 . . . . Brewers
3 . . . . Athletics
5 . . . . Angels

7 . . . . Athletics
11 . . . . Reds
13 . . . . Athletics
16 . . . . Angels
18 . . . . Royals
22 . . . . Giants
23 . . . . Padres
26 . . . . Angels
27 . . . . Cubs

7 . . . . Royals
10 . . . . Padres
15 . . . . Angels
16 . . . . Indians
18 . . . . Brewers
21 . . . . Padres
23 . . . . D-backs
25 . . . . Royals
28 . . . . Dodgers
29 . . . . Reds
AUGUST
2 . . . . Padres

3 . . . . Indians
7 . . . . Rangers
10 . . . . D-backs
12 . . . . Royals
15 . . . . Padres
17 . . . . Giants
20 . . . . Reds
22 . . . . White Sox
23 . . . . Rangers
28 . . . . Rangers
29 . . . . Royals

AZL DODGERS

JUNE
20 . . . . White Sox
22 . . . . Padres
25 . . . . Reds
27 . . . . Mariners
JULY
2 . . . . Brewers
3 . . . . D-backs
5 . . . . White Sox
8 . . . . Indians
10 . . . . Reds
13 . . . . Angels
16 . . . . Athletics
19 . . . . Cubs
22 . . . . Brewers
24 . . . . Royals

26 . . . . White Sox
29 . . . . Rangers
31 . . . . Reds
AUGUST
2 . . . . Angels
7 . . . . Brewers
8 . . . . Giants
10 . . . . White Sox
13 . . . . Indians
15 . . . . Reds
18 . . . . Rangers
20 . . . . Athletics
21 . . . . Indians
26 . . . . Brewers
28 . . . . Giants

AZL GIANTS

JUNE
21 . . . . D-backs
23 . . . . Athletics
26 . . . . Indians
27 . . . . Cubs
30 . . . . Reds
JULY
2 . . . . D-backs
7 . . . . Angels
8 . . . . Rangers
13 . . . . Royals
14 . . . . Athletics
17 . . . . Dodgers
19 . . . . Mariners
23 . . . . Brewers

24 . . . . Padres
27 . . . . D-backs
29 . . . . Athletics
AUGUST
1 . . . . Royals
2 . . . . Cubs
5 . . . . Mariners
7 . . . . Angels
10 . . . . Indians
12 . . . . Angels
15 . . . . Cubs
18 . . . . White Sox
21 . . . . Angels
23 . . . . Cubs
25 . . . . Padres
27 . . . . Dodgers

AZL INDIANS

JUNE
20 . . . . Reds
24 . . . . Rangers
25 . . . . Giants
29 . . . . Royals
JULY
1 . . . . White Sox
5 . . . . Padres
6 . . . . Dodgers
9 . . . . Brewers
11 . . . . Dodgers
14 . . . . White Sox
17 . . . . D-backs
19 . . . . Rangers
21 . . . . Cubs

24 . . . . Reds
26 . . . . Reds
30 . . . . Brewers
31 . . . . Athletics
AUGUST
4 . . . . Mariners
6 . . . . White Sox
9 . . . . Cubs
11 . . . . Dodgers
14 . . . . Brewers
16 . . . . Dodgers
19 . . . . Angels
20 . . . . Padres
24 . . . . Royals
25 . . . . Mariners
28 . . . . Reds

AZL MARINERS

JUNE
22 . . . . White Sox
25 . . . . Athletics
28 . . . . Dodgers

29 . . . . Cubs
JULY
2 . . . . Rangers
5 . . . . Giants

AZL PADRES

JUNE
20 . . . . Mariners
23 . . . . Dodgers
25 . . . . Brewers
27 . . . . White Sox
30 . . . . Angels
JULY
3 . . . . Royals
4 . . . . Rangers
8 . . . . D-backs
9 . . . . Royals
14 . . . . Mariners
15 . . . . Reds
18 . . . . Rangers
20 . . . . Indians

25 . . . . Athletics
26 . . . . Mariners
29 . . . . Indians
31 . . . . Giants
AUGUST
3 . . . . Reds
4 . . . . Cubs
8 . . . . Royals
9 . . . . Rangers
12 . . . . D-backs
14 . . . . Royals
18 . . . . Mariners
19 . . . . Cubs
22 . . . . Rangers
24 . . . . Brewers
28 . . . . White Sox

AZL RANGERS

JUNE
22 . . . . Royals
23 . . . . Indians
27 . . . . Brewers
29 . . . . Reds
JULY
1 . . . . Angels
3 . . . . Mariners
7 . . . . D-backs
9 . . . . Cubs
11 . . . . Giants
13 . . . . Padres
17 . . . . Royals
20 . . . . Athletics
23 . . . . Dodgers

25 . . . . Indians
28 . . . . Royals
30 . . . . Mariners
AUGUST
1 . . . . White Sox
3 . . . . Dodgers
6 . . . . Giants
8 . . . . Mariners
13 . . . . Padres
14 . . . . Mariners
17 . . . . Padres
19 . . . . Mariners
21 . . . . Royals
24 . . . . Athletics
26 . . . . Royals
29 . . . . Padres

AZL REDS

JUNE
21 . . . . Indians
23 . . . . Royals
26 . . . . Dodgers
28 . . . . Rangers
JULY
1 . . . . Giants
3 . . . . Indians
5 . . . . Brewers
9 . . . . Athletics
11 . . . . White Sox
14 . . . . Dodgers
16 . . . . Padres
20 . . . . Mariners
22 . . . . White Sox

25 . . . . Angels
27 . . . . Indians
30 . . . . Padres
AUGUST
1 . . . . Dodgers
5 . . . . Brewers
6 . . . . D-backs
8 . . . . Indians
10 . . . . Brewers
14 . . . . Cubs
16 . . . . White Sox
19 . . . . Athletics
21 . . . . D-backs
24 . . . . Mariners
26 . . . . Giants
29 . . . . Angels

AZL ROYALS

JUNE
21 . . . . Rangers
24 . . . . Reds
27 . . . . Angels
28 . . . . Indians

JULY
2 . . . . Padres
4 . . . . Mariners
6 . . . . Rangers
8 . . . . Mariners
11 . . . . Brewers
15 . . . . Cubs
18 . . . . Dodgers
19 . . . . Reds
22 . . . . Giants

23 . . . . Padres
27 . . . . Rangers
29 . . . . White Sox

AUGUST
3 . . . . White Sox
4 . . . . Athletics
7 . . . . Padres
9 . . . . Mariners
11 . . . . Rangers
13 . . . . Mariners
16 . . . . Rangers
17 . . . . D-backs
22 . . . . Brewers
23 . . . . Indians
27 . . . . Padres
28 . . . . D-backs

AZL WHITE SOX

JUNE
21 . . . . Dodgers
23 . . . . Mariners
26 . . . . D-backs
28 . . . . Padres
30 . . . . Indians

JULY
3 . . . . Giants
6 . . . . Brewers
8 . . . . Reds
10 . . . . Athletics
13 . . . . Cubs
17 . . . . Brewers
18 . . . . Angels
21 . . . . Reds

24 . . . . Rangers
27 . . . . Dodgers
28 . . . . Angels
31 . . . . Mariners

AUGUST
2 . . . . Royals
5 . . . . Indians
8 . . . . D-backs
11 . . . . Brewers
13 . . . . Reds
15 . . . . Athletics
17 . . . . Cubs
21 . . . . Brewers
23 . . . . Dodgers
25 . . . . Reds
26 . . . . Indians

GULF COAST LEAGUE   *HOME GAMES ONLY

ASTROS

JUNE
26 . . . . Mets
28 . . . . Cardinals
30 . . . . Nationals

JULY
6 . . . . Mets
8 . . . . Cardinals
10 . . . . Nationals
12 . . . . Marlins
18 . . . . Cardinals
20 . . . . Nationals
22 . . . . Marlins
26 . . . . Mets

28 . . . . Cardinals

AUGUST
1 . . . . Marlins
5 . . . . Mets
7 . . . . Cardinals
9 . . . . Nationals
11 . . . . Marlins
15 . . . . Mets
17 . . . . Cardinals
19 . . . . Nationals
21 . . . . Marlins
25 . . . . Mets
29 . . . . Nationals
31 . . . . Marlins

BLUE JAYS

JUNE
24 . . . . Tigers West
27 . . . . Yankees West
29 . . . . Tigers East

JULY
5 . . . . Braves
7 . . . . Yankees East
8 . . . . Yankees West
12 . . . . Tigers West
13 . . . . Phillies
18 . . . . Pirates
20 . . . . Braves
22 . . . . Yankees East
26 . . . . Yankees West

27 . . . . Tigers West

AUGUST
1 . . . . Tigers East
4 . . . . Pirates
9 . . . . Yankees East
10 . . . . Yankees West
15 . . . . Phillies
18 . . . . Tigers East
19 . . . . Pirates
22 . . . . Braves
25 . . . . Phillies
29 . . . . Tigers West
31 . . . . Phillies

BRAVES

JUNE
24 . . . . . . Yankees East
27 . . . . Pirates
29 . . . . . . Yankees West

JULY
4 . . . . Blue Jays
7 . . . . Tigers West
12 . . . . . . Yankees East
14 . . . . Tigers East
18 . . . . Phillies
21 . . . . Blue Jays
22 . . . . Tigers West
25 . . . . Pirates
27 . . . . . . Yankees East
29 . . . . Tigers East

AUGUST
1 . . . . Yankees West
4 . . . . Phillies
5 . . . . Blue Jays
9 . . . . Tigers West
11 . . . . Pirates
16 . . . . Tigers East
18 . . . . . Yankees West
19 . . . . Phillies
23 . . . . Blue Jays
24 . . . . Tigers East
26 . . . . Pirates
29 . . . . . Yankees East

SEPTEMBER
1 . . . . Tigers East

GCL CARDINALS

JUNE
27 . . . . Nationals
29 . . . . Marlins

JULY
3 . . . . Astros
5 . . . . Mets
7 . . . . Nationals
13 . . . . Astros
15 . . . . Mets
17 . . . . Nationals
19 . . . . Marlins
25 . . . . Mets
27 . . . . Nationals
29 . . . . Marlins

AUGUST
2 . . . . Astros
4 . . . . Mets
8 . . . . Marlins
12 . . . . Astros
14 . . . . Mets
16 . . . . Nationals
18 . . . . Marlins
24 . . . . Mets
26 . . . . Nationals
28 . . . . Marlins

SEPTEMBER
1 . . . . Astros

GCL MARLINS

JUNE
24 . . . . Cardinals
27 . . . . Astros
28 . . . . Mets

JULY
1 . . . . Nationals
4 . . . . Cardinals
7 . . . . Astros
8 . . . . Mets
11 . . . . . . Nationals
14 . . . . . . Cardinals
17 . . . . Astros
18 . . . . Mets

21 . . . . Nationals
24 . . . . . . Cardinals
27 . . . . Astros
28 . . . . Mets
31 . . . . . . Nationals

AUGUST
3 . . . . . . Cardinals
7 . . . . Mets
10 . . . . . . Nationals
17 . . . . Mets
23 . . . . . . Cardinals
26 . . . . Astros
30 . . . . . . Nationals

GCL METS

JUNE
24 . . . . Nationals
30 . . . . . . Cardinals

JULY
1 . . . . Astros
3 . . . . Marlins
4 . . . . Nationals
10 . . . . . . Cardinals
11 . . . . Astros
13 . . . . . . Marlins
14 . . . . . . Nationals
20 . . . . . Cardinals
21 . . . . Astros
24 . . . . . . Nationals

31 . . . . Astros

AUGUST
2 . . . . Marlins
3 . . . . . . Nationals
9 . . . . . . Cardinals
10 . . . . Astros
12 . . . . . . Marlins
19 . . . . . Cardinals
22 . . . . . . Marlins
23 . . . . . Nationals
29 . . . . . Cardinals
30 . . . . . . Astros

SEPTEMBER
1 . . . . . . Marlins

GCL NATIONALS

JUNE	
26 . . . . .Marlins	
29 . . . . Mets	
JULY	
5 . . . . .Astros	
6 . . . . .Marlins	
12 . . . . .Cardinals	
15 . . . . .Astros	
19 . . . . Mets	
22 . . . . .Cardinals	
25 . . . . .Astros	
26 . . . . .Marlins	
29 . . . . Mets	

AUGUST	
1 . . . . .Cardinals	
4 . . . . .Astros	
5 . . . . .Marlins	
8 . . . . Mets	
11 . . . . .Cardinals	
14 . . . . .Astros	
15 . . . . .Marlins	
18 . . . . Mets	
21 . . . . .Cardinals	
24 . . . . .Astros	
25 . . . . .Marlins	
28 . . . . Mets	
31 . . . . .Cardinals	

GCL ORIOLES

JUNE	
24 . . . . .Rays	
27-29 . . . . Twins	
JULY	
4-6 . . . . Red Sox	
8 . . . . .Rays	
12-14 . . . . Twins	
19-21 . . . . Red Sox	
22 . . . . .Rays	

25-27 . . . . Twins	
AUGUST	
1-3 . . . . Red Sox	
5 . . . . .Rays	
9-11 . . . . .Twins	
16-18 . . . . Red Sox	
19 . . . . .Rays	
22-24 . . . . Twins	
29-31 . . . . Red Sox	

GCL PHILLIES

JUNE	
28 . . . . Tigers West	
30 . . . . Yankees East	
JULY	
1 . . . . Braves	
4 . . . . Pirates	
6 . . . . .Tigers East	
11 . . . . . . .Yankees West	
14 . . . . .Blue Jays	
15 . . . . Yankees East	
19 . . . . Braves	
21 . . . . Pirates	
25 . . . . Tigers West	
28 . . . . . . .Yankees West	
29 . . . . .Blue Jays	

AUGUST	
2 . . . . Yankees East	
3 . . . . Braves	
5 . . . . Pirates	
8 . . . . .Tigers East	
11 . . . . Tigers West	
12 . . . . . . .Yankees West	
16 . . . . .Blue Jays	
17 . . . . Yankees East	
23 . . . . Pirates	
24 . . . . .Blue Jays	
26 . . . . Tigers West	
30 . . . . . . .Yankees West	
SEPTEMBER	
1 . . . . .Blue Jays	

GCL PIRATES

JUNE	
28 . . . . Braves	
30 . . . . Tigers West	
JULY	
1 . . . . .Blue Jays	
5 . . . . Phillies	
6 . . . . . . .Yankees West	
8 . . . . Braves	
11 . . . . .Tigers East	
13 . . . . Yankees East	
15 . . . . Tigers West	
19 . . . . .Blue Jays	
20 . . . . Phillies	

26 . . . . Braves	
28 . . . . .Tigers East	
AUGUST	
2 . . . . Tigers West	
3 . . . . .Blue Jays	
8 . . . . . . .Yankees West	
10 . . . . Braves	
12 . . . . .Tigers East	
15 . . . . Yankees East	
17 . . . . Tigers West	
22 . . . . Phillies	
25 . . . . Yankees East	
30 . . . . .Tigers East	
31 . . . . Yankees East	

GCL RAYS

JUNE	
28-30 . . . . Red Sox	
JULY	
1 . . . . Orioles	
5-7 . . . . Twins	
11-13 . . . . Red Sox	

15 . . . . Orioles	
18-20 . . . . Twins	
26-28 . . . . Red Sox	
29 . . . . Orioles	
AUGUST	
2-4 . . . . Twins	

8-10 . . . . Red Sox	
12 . . . . Orioles	
15-17 . . . . Twins	
23-25 . . . . Red Sox	

26 . . . . Orioles	
30 . . . . Twins	
SEPTEMBER	
1 . . . . Twins	

GCL RED SOX

JUNE	
24 . . . . Twins	
27 . . . . Rays	
29 . . . . Rays	
JULY	
5-7 . . . . Orioles	
8 . . . . Twins	
12-14 . . . . Rays	
14 . . . . Rays	
18-20 . . . . Orioles	
20 . . . . Orioles	
22 . . . . Twins	
25-27 . . . . Rays	
27 . . . . Rays	

AUGUST	
2-4 . . . . Orioles	
4 . . . . Orioles	
5 . . . . Twins	
9-11 . . . . .Rays	
11 . . . . .Rays	
15-17 . . . . Orioles	
17 . . . . Orioles	
19 . . . . Twins	
22 . . . . .Rays	
24 . . . . .Rays	
30 . . . . Orioles	
SEPTEMBER	
1 . . . . Orioles	

GCL TIGERS EAST

JUNE	
24 . . . . Pirates	
28 . . . . . . Yankees East	
30 . . . . .Blue Jays	
JULY	
5 . . . . .Yankees West	
7 . . . . Phillies	
12 . . . . Pirates	
13 . . . . Braves	
15 . . . . .Blue Jays	
18 . . . . Tigers West	
20 . . . . . . .Yankees West	
22 . . . . Phillies	
25 . . . . . . Yankees East	

27 . . . . Pirates	
AUGUST	
2 . . . . .Blue Jays	
4 . . . . Tigers West	
9 . . . . Phillies	
11 . . . . Yankees East	
15 . . . . Braves	
17 . . . . .Blue Jays	
19 . . . . Tigers West	
22 . . . . . .Yankees East	
25 . . . . Braves	
26 . . . . . . Yankees East	
29 . . . . Pirates	
31 . . . . Braves	

GCL TIGERS WEST

JUNE	
27 . . . . Phillies	
29 . . . . Pirates	
JULY	
1 . . . . .Tigers East	
4 . . . . Yankees East	
6 . . . . Braves	
8 . . . . Phillies	
11 . . . . .Blue Jays	
14 . . . . . . .Yankees West	
19 . . . . .Tigers East	
21 . . . . Yankees East	
26 . . . . Phillies	

28 . . . . .Blue Jays	
29 . . . . . . .Yankees West	
AUGUST	
1 . . . . Pirates	
3 . . . . .Tigers East	
5 . . . . Yankees East	
8 . . . . Braves	
10 . . . . Phillies	
12 . . . . .Blue Jays	
16 . . . . . . .Yankees West	
18 . . . . Pirates	
23 . . . . Yankees East	
24 . . . . . . .Yankees West	
30 . . . . .Blue Jays	

GCL TWINS

JUNE	
28-30 . . . . Orioles	
JULY	
1 . . . . Red Sox	
4-6 . . . . .Rays	
11-13 . . . . Orioles	
15 . . . . Red Sox	
19-21 . . . . .Rays	
26-28 . . . . Orioles	
29 . . . . Red Sox	

AUGUST	
1-3 . . . . .Rays	
8-10 . . . . Orioles	
12 . . . . Red Sox	
16-18 . . . . .Rays	
23-25 . . . . Orioles	
26 . . . . Red Sox	
29-31 . . . . .Rays	

GCL YANKEES EAST

JUNE	
27	Tigers East
29	Phillies

JULY	
1	Yankees West
5	Tigers West
6	Blue Jays
8	Tigers East
11	Braves
14	Pirates
19	Yankees West
20	Tigers West
26	Tigers East
28	Braves

29	Pirates

AUGUST	
1	Phillies
3	Yankees West
8	Blue Jays
10	Tigers East
12	Braves
16	Pirates
18	Phillies
22	Tigers West
24	Pirates
30	Braves

SEPTEMBER	
1	Pirates

GCL YANKEES WEST

JUNE	
24	Phillies
28	Blue Jays
30	Braves

JULY	
4	Tigers East
7	Pirates
12	Phillies
13	Tigers West
15	Braves
18	Yankees East
21	Tigers East
22	Pirates
25	Blue Jays

27	Phillies

AUGUST	
2	Braves
4	Yankees East
5	Tigers East
9	Pirates
11	Blue Jays
15	Tigers West
17	Braves
19	Yankees East
23	Tigers East
25	Tigers West
26	Blue Jays
29	Phillies
31	Tigers West

INDEPENDENT

AMERICAN ASSOCIATION

FARGO-MOORHEAD REDHAWKS

MAY	
27-29	Wichita
30-31	Sioux City

JUNE	
1	Sioux City
9-12	Winnipeg
14-16	Lincoln
21-23	Sioux Falls
28-30	Sioux City

JULY	
7-10	St. Paul

11-14	Gary Southshore
22-24	Sioux City
25-27	Winnipeg

AUGUST	
8-10	Wichita
11-14	Gary Southshore
19-21	St. Paul
26-28	Sioux Falls
29-31	Kansas City

SEPTEMBER	
1	Kansas City

GARY SOUTHSHORE RAILCATS

MAY	
27-29	Joplin
30-31	Kansas City

JUNE	
1-2	Kansas City
6-8	Fargo-Moorhead
10-12	Sioux City
24-26	Laredo

JULY	
4-6	Winnipeg

7-10	Wichita
19-21	Laredo
22-24	Lincoln

AUGUST	
4-7	Winnipeg
8-10	St. Paul
15-18	Sioux Falls
19-21	Wichita
26-28	Kansas City

SEPTEMBER	
2-5	Joplin

JOPLIN BLASTERS

MAY	
19-22	Winnipeg
24-26	Wichita
30-31	St. Paul

JUNE	
1-2	St. Paul
3-5	Texas
14-16	Laredo
17-19	Sioux Falls
28-30	Laredo

JULY	
1-3	Wichita
7-10	Lincoln
15-17	Kansas City
25-27	Texas
28-31	Fargo-Moorhead

AUGUST	
8-10	Sioux City
15-18	Lincoln
26-28	Laredo

KANSAS CITY T-BONES

MAY	
19-22	Texas
23-26	Lincoln

JUNE	
6-8	Wichita
10-13	Joplin
21-23	Joplin
24-27	Fargo-Moorhead

JULY	
1-3	St. Paul
7-9	Sioux City
22-24	Winnipeg
25-27	Gary Southshore

AUGUST	
8-10	Lincoln

11-14	Laredo
19-21	Texas
23-25	Laredo

SEPTEMBER	
2-5	Sioux Falls

LAREDO LEMURS

MAY	
19-22	Fargo-Moorhead
23-25	Winnipeg

JUNE	
3-5	St. Paul
6-8	Joplin
17-19	Kansas City
20-22	Wichita

JULY	
1-3	Texas
11-14	Kansas City

15-17	Lincoln
29-31	Wichita

AUGUST	
4-7	Joplin
15-17	Texas
19-21	Joplin
29-31	Texas

SEPTEMBER	
1	Texas
2-5	Wichita

TEXAS AIRHOGS

MAY	
23-25	Fargo-Moorhead*
27-29	Laredo*

JUNE	
6-8	St. Paul@
9-12	Wichita@
20-22	Gary Southshore*
24-26	Joplin*

JULY	
4-6	Lincoln@
7-10	Laredo@

19-21	Wichita*
22-24	Sioux Falls*
28-31	Gary Southshore@

AUGUST	
8-10	Laredo*
11-14	Joplin
22-24	Joplin@

SEPTEMBER	
1-5	Sioux City@

* At Grand Prarie
@ At Amarillo

ST. PAUL SAINTS

MAY	
19-22	Gary Southshore
26-29	Kansas City

JUNE	
13-15	Sioux City
24-27	Winnipeg
28-30	Sioux Falls

JULY	
4-6	Joplin
12-14	Sioux Falls
15-17	Fargo-Moorhead

22-24	Laredo
25-27	Sioux City

AUGUST	
4-6	Fargo-Moorhead
11-14	Sioux Falls
22-24	Wichita
30-31	Winnipeg

SEPTEMBER	
1	Winnipeg
2-5	Lincoln

SIOUX CITY EXPLORERS

MAY	
19 . . . . Sioux Falls	4-6 . . . . . Fargo-Moorhead
23-26 . . . Gary Southshore	15-17 . . . . Texas
JUNE	19-21 . . . . Joplin
3-5 . . . . . Fargo-Moorhead	30-31 . . . . Sioux Falls
9-12 . . . . St. Paul	**AUGUST**
14-16 . . . Gary Southshore	4-7 . . . . Kansas City
24-25 . . . . Laredo	16-18 . . . Fargo-Moorhead
JULY	19-21 . . . . Winnipeg
1-3 . . . . . Gary Southshore	29-31 . . . . Lincoln
	SEPTEMBER
	1 . . . . Lincoln

SIOUX FALLS CANARIES

MAY	
20-21 . . . . Sioux City	19-21 . . . Fargo-Moorhead
23-25 . . . . St. Paul	25-27 . . . . Laredo
JUNE	28-29 . . . . Sioux City
3-5 . . . . . Fargo-Moorhead	**AUGUST**
9-12 . . . . St. Paul	3 . . . . Sioux City
14-16 . . . Gary Southshore	4-7 . . . . Texas
24-25 . . . . Laredo	8-10 . . . . Winnipeg
JULY	19-21 . . . . Lincoln
4-6 . . . . Kansas City	23-25 . . . . Sioux City
7-10 . . . . Winnipeg	30-31 . . . Gary Southshore
	SEPTEMBER
	1 . . . . . . Gary Southshore

WICHITA WINGNUTS

MAY	
19-22 . . . . Lincoln	12-14 . . . . Joplin
30-31 . . . . Laredo	15-18 . . . . . . Sioux Falls
JUNE	22-24 . . . . Joplin
1-2 . . . . Laredo	25-27 . . . . Lincoln
3-5 . . . Gary Southshore	**AUGUST**
14-16 . . . . Kansas City	16-18 . . . . . Kansas City
17-19 . . . Fargo-Moorhead	26-28 . . . . Texas
23-25 . . . . . . Sioux City	30-31 . . . . Joplin
27-30 . . . . Texas	**SEPTEMBER**
JULY	1 . . . . Joplin
4-6 . . . . Laredo	

WINNIPEG GOLDEYES

MAY	
30-31 . . . . Sioux Falls	15-17 . . . Gary Southshore
JUNE	18-20 . . . . St. Paul
1-2 . . . . Sioux Falls	29-31 . . . . . . Kansas City
3-5 . . . . Lincoln	**AUGUST**
14-16 . . . . Texas	11-14 . . . . Wichita
17-19 . . . . St. Paul	15-18 . . . . St. Paul
29-30 . . Gary Southshore	22-25 . . Fargo-Moorhead
JULY	26-28 . . . . . . Sioux City
1-3 . . . . Sioux Falls	**SEPTEMBER**
12-14 . . . . Sioux City	2-5 . . . . Fargo-Moorhead

ATLANTIC LEAGUE

BRIDGEPORT BLUEFISH

APRIL	
28-30 . . . . . . New Britain	31 . . . . York
MAY	**JUNE**
1 . . . . New Britain	1-2 . . . . York
6-8 . . . . Long Island	7-9 . . . . Lancaster
17-19 . . . . Somerset	10-12 . . . . . New Britain
27-30 . . Southern Maryland	20-22 . . . . . . Lancaster
	23-26 . . . . . . Long Island

JULY / AUGUST / SEPTEMBER (continued Sioux City?)

JULY	
4-6 . . . . York	9-11 . . . . Sugar Land
15-18 . . . . Sugar Land	19-21 . . . . Somerset
22-24 . . . . . . New Britain	29-31 . . . . York
25-27 . . Southern Maryland	**SEPTEMBER**
AUGUST	1 . . . . York
2-4 . . . . Sugar Land	2-4 . . . Southern Maryland
5-7 . . . . Long Island	13-14 . . . . Somerset
	15-18 . . . . . . Lancaster

NEW BRITAIN BEES

APRIL	JULY
21-24 . . . . York	1-3 . . . Southern Maryland
25-27 . . . . . . Long Island	7-10 . . . . . . Bridgeport
MAY	19-21 . . . . . . Lancaster
2-5 . . . . Sugar Land	28-31 . . . . Maryland
13-15 . . . . . . Bridgeport	**AUGUST**
20-22 . . . . York	2-4 . . . . York
24-26 . . . . Lancaster	5-7 . . . . Lancaster
JUNE	12-14 . . . . . . Sugar Land
3-5 . . . Southern Maryland	15-18 . . . Long Island
7-9 . . . . Somerset	23-25 . . . . . . Bridgeport
17-19 . . . . . . Sugarland	**SEPTEMBER**
20-22 . . . . Somerset	2-4 . . . . Long Island
	15-18 . . . . . . Somerset

LANCASTER BARNSTORMERS

APRIL	JULY
28-30 . . . . Somerset	4-5 . . . . Long Island
1 . . . . Somerset	15-18 . . Southern Maryland
6-8 . . . . New Britain	22-24 . . . . . . Somerset
10-12 . Southern Maryland	25-27 . . . . . . Sugar Land
15-19 . . . . York	**AUGUST**
27-30 . . . . . Sugar Land	9-11 . . Southern Maryland
31 . . . . Long Island	19-21 . . . . York
JUNE	26-28 . . . . . Bridgeport
1-2 . . . . Long Island	29-31 . . . . . Long Island
11-13 . . . . Somerset	**SEPTEMBER**
14-16 . . . . . Sugar Land	1 . . . . Long Island
23-26 . . . . . New Britain	6-8 . . . . New Britain
27-30 . . . . . . Bridgeport	9-11 . . . . . . Bridgeport
	12-14 . . . . York

LONG ISLAND DUCKS

APRIL	JULY
28-30 . Southern Maryland	1-3 . . . . Sugar Land
MAY	15-17 . . . . Somerset
1 . . . . Southern Maryland	19-21 . . . . . . Bridgeport
3-5 . . . . Lancaster	25-27 . . . . . New Britain
10-12 . . . . . . Somerset	28-31 . . . . . Sugar Land
13-15 . Southern Maryland	**AUGUST**
24-26 . . . . . Bridgeport	8-11 . . . . . . Springfield
27-29 . . . . . New Britain	12-14 . . . . . . Lancaster
JUNE	23-25 . . . . . . Maryland
3-5 . . . . Sugar Land	26-28 . . . . York
14-16 . . . . . New Britain	**SEPTEMBER**
17-19 . . . . . . Lancaster	5-8 . . . . Bridgeport
27-30 . . . . York	9-11 . . . . York

SOMERSET PATRIOTS

APRIL	24-26 . . . . . . Sugar Land
21-24 . . . . . . Long Island	**JUNE**
26-27 . . . . York	3-5 . . . . Bridgeport
MAY	14-16 . . . . York
3-5 . . Southern Maryland	17-19 . . Southern Maryland
13-15 . . . . . . Lancaster	27-30 . . . . . New Britain
20-22 . . . . . . Long Island	

JULY
1-3 . . . . Bridgeport
7-10 . . . . Lancaster
19-21 . . . . . . Sugar Land
28-31 . . . . Bridgeport

AUGUST
2-4 . . . . Long Island

12-14 . . Southern Maryland
15-18 . . . . York
23-25 . . . . Lancaster
26-28 . . . . . . New Britain

SEPTEMBER
5-7 . . . . Sugar Land
9-11 . . . . New Britain

SOUTHERN MARYLAND BLUE CRABS

APRIL
21-23 . . . . Lancaster
26-27 . . . . . . Bridgeport

MAY
6-8 . . . . York
17-19 . . . . . New Britain
20-22 . . . . Lancaster
31 . . . . Somerset

JUNE
1-2 . . . . Somerset
10-12 . . . . . Long Island
14-16 . . . . . Bridgeport
23-26 . . . . York
27-30 . . . . . . Sugar Land

JULY
4-6 . . . . Somerset
7-10 . . . . . . Long Island
22-24 . . . . . Long Island

AUGUST
2-4 . . . . Lancaster
5-7 . . . . York
15-18 . . . . . . Bridgeport
19-21 . . . . . New Britain
26-28 . . . . . Sugar Land
29-31 . . . . . . Somerset

SEPTEMBER
1 . . . . Somerset
9-11 . . . . . . Sugar Land
12-14 . . . . . New Britain

YORK REVOLUTION

APRIL
28-30 . . . . . . Sugar Land

MAY
1 . . . . Sugar Land
2-4 . . . . Bridgeport
10-12 . . . . . New Britain
13-15 . . . . . Sugar Land
24-26 . Southern Maryland
27-30 . . . . . . Somerset

JUNE
3-5 . . . . Lancaster
7-9 . . . . Long Island
17-19 . . . . . Bridgeport
20-22 . . . . . Long Island

JULY
1-3 . . . . Lancaster
15-17 . . . . . New Britain
19-21 . Southern Maryland
25-27 . . . . . . Somerset
28-31 . . . . . . Lancaster

AUGUST
8-11 . . . . . . New Britain
12-14 . . . . . Bridgeport
23-25 . . . . Sugar Land

SEPTEMBER
2-4 . . . . Somerset
5-8 . . Southern Maryland
15-18 . . . . Long Island
19-21 . Southern Maryland

NEW JERSEY JACKALS

MAY
27-29 . . . . Trois Rivieres
30 . . . . Quebec

JUNE
1 . . . . Quebec
9-12 . . . . Rockland
14-16 . . . . Japan
21-23 . . . . . . Rockland
24-26 . . . . . . Ottawa
28-30 . . . . Cuba

JULY
5-7 . . . . Ottawa

8-11 . . . . Quebec
19-21 . . . . Trois Rivieres
22-24 . . . . Sussex County
28-31 . . . . . . Rockland

AUGUST
12-14 . . . . . . Ottawa
15-17 . . . . . Quebec
26-28 . . . Trois Rivieres
30-31 . . . . Sussex County

SEPTEMBER
1 . . . . Sussex County

OTTAWA CHAMPIONS

MAY
19-23 . . . . . New Jersey
30-31 . . . . . . Rockland

JUNE
1 . . . . Rockland
2-5 . . . . Rockland
14-16 . . . . . . Quebec
17-19 . . . . Cuba
21-23 . . . Trois Rivieres
28-30 . . . . . Japan

JULY
1-3 . . . . . Sussex County
12-14 . . . . Trois Rivieres
15-17 . . . . . . Rockland
25-27 . . . . . Quebec

AUGUST
4-7 . . . . . . New Jersey
8-11 . . . . . Sussex County
19-21 . . . . Trois Rivieres
22-24 . . . . . Rockland

SEPTEMBER
2-5 . . . . Quebec

QUEBEC CAPITALES

MAY
20, 22 . . . . . Trois Rivieres
24-26 . . . . . New Jersey
27-29 . . . . . . Rockland

JUNE
6-8 . . . . Ottawa
9-12 . . . . Cuba
17-19 . . . . Sussex County
21-23 . . . . Japan

JULY
1-3 . . . . New Jersey
5-7 . . . . Rockland

12-14 . . . . . Sussex County
19-21 . . . . Ottawa
22-24 . . . Trois Rivieres

AUGUST
4-7 . . . . Rockland
8-11 . . . . . New Jersey
19-21 . . . Sussex County
25-28 . . . . . . Ottawa
31 . . . . . . Trois Rivieres

SEPTEMBER
1 . . . . Trois Rivieres

ROCKLAND BOULDERS

MAY
19,21 . . . . Sussex County
24-26 . . . . . . Ottawa

JUNE
2-5 . . . . Quebec
6-8 . . . . . Trois Rivieres
14-16 . . Sussex County
17-19 . . . . . . Japan
24-26 . . . . . . Cuba

JULY
1-4 . . . . . Trois Rivieres

12-14 . . . . . New Jersey
20 . . . . . Sussex County
22-23 . . . . . . Ottawa
25,27 . . . Sussex County

AUGUST
8-11 . . . Trois Rivieres
19-21 . . . . New Jersey
26,28 . . . Sussex County
30-31 . . . . . Ottawa

SEPTEMBER
1 . . . . Ottawa
2-5 . . . . . . New Jersey

SUSSEX COUNTY MINERS

MAY
20,22 . . . . . . Rockland
27-29 . . . . . Ottawa
30-31 . . . . Trois Rivieres

JUNE
6-8 . . . . . . New Jersey
14-16 . . . . Sussex County
17-19 . . . . . . Japan
24-26 . . . . . . Cuba
28-30 . . . . . Rockland

JULY
8-11 . . . . Ottawa
15-17 . . . New Jersey
19,21 . . . . . Rockland
26 . . . . . . Rockland
28-31 . . . . . Quebec

AUGUST
4-7 . . . . . Trois Rivieres
12-14 . . . Trois Rivieres
16-17 . . . . . Ottawa
23-24 . . . . New Jersey
25,27 . . . . Rockland

TROIS RIVIERES AIGLES

MAY
19,21 . . . . . Quebec
24-26 . . . . Sussex County

JUNE
2-4 . . . . . . New Jersey
9-12 . . . . . . Ottawa
14-16 . . . . . Cuba
17-19 . . . . New Jersey
24-26 . . . . . Japan
28-30 . . . . . Quebec

JULY
4-7 . . . . . . Sussex County

8-10 . . . . . Rockland
15-17 . . . . . Quebec
25-27 . . . . New JERSEY
28-31 . . . . . Ottawa

AUGUST
3 . . . . Quebec
15-18 . . . . . Rockland
22-24 . . . . . Quebec
30 . . . . Quebec

SEPTEMBER
2-5 . . . . . Sussex County

FRONTIER LEAGUE

EVANSVILLE OTTERS

MAY		JULY	
13-15 . . . . . Schaumburg		5-7 . . . . River City	
20-22 . . . . Florence		8-9 . . . . Gateway	
31 . . . . Joliet		19-21 . . . . . . Lake Erie	
JUNE		29-31 . . . . . Traverse City	
1-2 . . . . Joliet		**AUGUST**	
8-9 . . . . Normal		19-21 . . . . . . Florence	
14-16 . . . . . . Gateway		23-25 . . . . Normal	
17-18 . . . . . River City		26-28 . . . . Southern Illinois	

FLORENCE FREEDOM

MAY		22-24 . . . . Joliet	
13-15 . . . . . . Windy City		29-31 . . . . . . Washington	
18-19 . . . . . . River City		**AUGUST**	
25-26 . . . Southern Illinois		17-18 . . . . Normal	
JUNE		26-28 . . . . Gateway	
3-5 . . . . Traverse City		30-31 . . . . . . River City	
10-12 . . . . . . Evansville		**SEPTEMBER**	
22-23 . . . . . . Evansville		1 . . . . River City	
JULY			
4-7 . . . . . Southern Illinois			

GATEWAY GRIZZLIES

MAY		15-17 . . . . Lake Erie	
13-15 . . . . . . Washington		26-28 . . . . . Schaumburg	
24-26 . . . . Normal		29-31 . . . . . Windy City	
27-29 . . . . Florence		**AUGUST**	
30 . . . . Evansville		19-21 . . . . Joliet	
JUNE		24-25 . . . . . River City	
7-9 . . . Southern Illinois		30-31 . . . . Southern Illinois	
10-12 . . . . . . Normal		**SEPTEMBER**	
17-19 . . . . . Florence		1 . . . . . Southern Illinois	
JULY		2-4 . . . . Evansville	
1-4 . . . . River City			

JOLIET SLAMMERS

MAY		5-7 . . . . Washington	
17-19 . . . . . Washington		15-17 . . . . Florence	
24-25 . . . . . Schaumburg		19-21 . . . Southern Illinois	
JUNE		26-28 . . . . . . Evansville	
3-5 . . . . Gateway		29-31 . . . . . . River City	
7-9 . . . . Lake Erie		**AUGUST**	
17-19 . . . . Schaumburg		23-25 . . . . . . Windy City	
JULY		**SEPTEMBER**	
1-3 . . . . . . Windy City		2-4 . . . . . . Traverse City	

LAKE ERIE CRUSHERS

MAY		JULY	
12-14 . . . . . . River City		1-3 . . . . Evansville	
17-19 . . . . . Schaumburg		8-10 . . . . Joliet	
24-26 . . . . . Windy City		22-24 . . . . Normal	
31 . . . . Gateway		**AUGUST**	
JUNE		16-18 . . . . . Windy City	
1-2 . . . . Gateway		16-18 . . . . . Washington	
10-12 . . . . . Washington		19-21 . . . . Traverse City	
14-16 . . . . . Windy City		30-31 . . . . Joliet	
17-19 . . . . Traverse City		**SEPTEMBER**	
		1 . . . . Joliet	
		2-4 . . . . Washington	

NORMAL CORNBELTERS

MAY		JULY	
13-15 . . . . Joliet		5-7 . . . . Gateway	
17-19 . . . . . . Evansville		8-10 . . . . Florence	
20-22 . . . Southern Illinois		19-21 . . . . Schaumburg	
31 . . . . Washington		29-31 . . . . . Lake Erie	
JUNE		**AUGUST**	
1-2 . . . . Washington		19-21 . . . Southern Illinois	
3-5 . . . . Windy City		30-31 . . . . . . Evansville	
14-16 . . . . . . River City		**SEPTEMBER**	
21-23 . . . . Gateway		1 . . . . Evansville	
		2-4 . . . . Florence	

RIVER CITY RASCALS

MAY		22-24 . . . . . Traverse City	
20-22 . . . . Gateway		26-28 . . . . Lake Erie	
25-26 . . . . Evansville		**AUGUST**	
27-29 . . . . Normal		16-18 . . . . . . Evansville	
JUNE		19-21 . . . . . Windy City	
7-9 . . . . Florence		26-28 . . . . Normal	
10-12 . . . Southern Illinois		**SEPTEMBER**	
22-23 . . . Southern Illinois			
JULY			
15-17 . . . . . Schaumburg			

SCHAUMBURG BOOMERS

MAY		JULY	
20-22 . . . . Windy City		1-3 . . . . Normal	
24 . . . . Joliet		4 . . . . Joliet	
27-29 . . . . . Washington		5-7 . . . . . Traverse City	
31 . . . . Florence		22-24 . . . . . Evansville	
JUNE		29-31 . . . Southern Illinois	
1-2 . . . . Florence		**AUGUST**	
3-5 . . . . River City		17-18 . . . . Joliet	
14-16 . . . . Traverse City		23-25 . . . . . Lake Erie	
21-23 . . . . . Lake Erie		**SEPTEMBER**	
		2-4 . . . . Windy City	

SOUTHERN ILLINOIS MINERS

MAY		JULY	
13-15 . . . . Traverse City		8-10 . . . . River City	
17-19 . . . . Gateway		22-24 . . . . . Washington	
27-29 . . . . . . Evansville		26-28 . . . . . Windy City	
JUNE		**AUGUST**	
3-5 . . . . Lake Erie		16-18 . . . . Gateway	
14-16 . . . . . . Florence		23-25 . . . . Florence	
17-19 . . . . Normal		**SEPTEMBER**	
		2-4 . . . . River City	

TRAVERSE CITY BEACH BUMS

MAY		JULY	
2 . . . . River City		1-3 . . . . Southern Illinois	
20-22 . . . . Joliet		8-10 . . . . . Windy City	
27-29 . . . . Lake Erie		15-17 . . . . Evansville	
31 . . . . River City		19-21 . . . . . . Gateway	
JUNE		26-28 . . . . Florence	
1 . . . . River City		**AUGUST**	
7-9 . . . . Schaumburg		26-28 . . . . Lake Erie	
10-12 . . . . Joliet		30-31 . . . Schaumburg	
21-23 . . . . . Washington		**SEPTEMBER**	
		1 . . . . Schaumburg	

WASHINGTON WILD THINGS

MAY
9 . . . . Windy City
20-22 . . . . .Lake Erie
25-26 . . . . . Traverse City

JUNE
3-5. . . . . Evansville
8 . . . . Windy City
14-16 . . . . Joliet
17-19 . . . . . . Windy City

JULY
1-3. . . . . Florence

8-10 . . . . . . Schaumburg
15-17 . . . . Southern Illinois
20-21 . . . . River City
26-28 . . . . .Normal

AUGUST
19-21 . . . . . . Schaumburg
24-25 . . . . . Traverse City
26-28 . . . . Joliet

SEPTEMBER

WINDY CITY THUNDERBOLTS

MAY
17-18 . . . . . Traverse City
27-29 . . . . Joliet
31 . . . . . Southern Illinois

JUNE
1-2. . . . . Southern Illinois
10-12 . . . . . Schaumburg
22-23 . . . . Joliet

JULY
6-7. . . . . .Lake Erie
15-17 . . . . .Normal

18-20 . . . . Florence
22-24 . . . . Gateway

AUGUST
26-28 . . . . . Schaumburg
30-31 . . . . . . .Washington

SEPTEMBER
1 . . . . .Washington

SPRING TRAINING SCHEDULES

CACTUS LEAGUE

ARIZONA DIAMONDBACKS

MARCH	
2	at Colorado
3	Colorado
4	Oakland
5	at Los Angeles (NL)
6	Chicago (NL)
7	at Seattle
8	Los Angeles (AL)
8	at San Diego
9	San Diego
10	at Los Angeles (AL)
11	at Kansas City
12	at San Francisco
12	Kansas City
13	at Chicago (AL)
14	Seattle
16	Cincinnati
17	at Chicago (NL)
18	Los Angeles (NL)
19	Texas
19	at Seattle
20	at Cincinnati
21	Milwaukee
22-23	San Francisco
24	at San Diego
25	Cleveland
26	at Milwaukee
27	at Texas
27	Colorado
28	at San Francisco
29	Colorado
30	at Oakland
31	at Colorado
APRIL	
1-2	Kansas City

CHICAGO CUBS

MARCH	
3	at Milwaukee
4	Los Angeles (AL)
5	Cincinnati
6	at Arizona
7	Kansas City
7	at Colorado
8	Los Angeles (NL)
9	Cleveland
10	at Seattle
11	Cincinnati
12	Chicago (AL)
12	at Los Angeles (NL)
13	at Oakland
14	San Diego
15	at San Diego
16	at Kansas City
17	Arizona
18	at Chicago (AL)
19	at Cleveland
20	Kansas City
22	at Cincinnati
23	at Texas
24	at San Francisco
25	Milwaukee
26	San Francisco
27	Seattle
28	at Los Angeles (AL)
29	Oakland
30	Colorado
31	New York (NL)
APRIL	
1	New York (NL)
3	at Los Angeles (AL)

CHICAGO WHITE SOX

MARCH	
3	at Los Angeles (NL)
4	Cleveland
5	at Kansas City
6	San Diego
7	at Los Angeles (AL)
8	Milwaukee
9	Oakland
10	at Texas
10	Kansas City
11	at San Diego
12	at Chicago (NL)
13	Arizona
14	at Kansas City
15	Los Angeles (NL)
16	at Milwaukee
18	Chicago (NL)
19	Los Angeles (NL)
20	at Oakland
21	at Cleveland
22	San Francisco
23	San Diego
24	Los Angeles (AL)
25	at Seattle
26	Cincinnati
26	at Los Angeles (NL)
27	at San Francisco
28	at Colorado
29	Texas
30	at Cincinnati
APRIL	
1-2	at San Diego

CINCINNATI REDS

MARCH	
1	at Cleveland
2	Cleveland
3	at Cleveland
4	San Francisco
5	at Chicago (NL)
6	Colorado
7	Los Angeles (AL)
8	at San Francisco
9	Texas
10	at Colorado
11	at Chicago (NL)
11	Oakland
12	Seattle
13	at Seattle
14	at Los Angeles (AL)
15	Kansas City
16	at Arizona
17	Cleveland
18	at Milwaukee
19	at Oakland
20	Arizona
21	at San Diego
22	Chicago (NL)
24	at Texas
25	Colorado
26	at Chicago (AL)
26	Cleveland
27	at Los Angeles (NL)
28	Milwaukee
29	at Milwaukee
30	Chicago (AL)
31	at Cleveland
APRIL	
2	at Pittsburgh

CLEVELAND INDIANS

MARCH	
1	Cincinnati
2	at Cincinnati
3	Cincinnati
4	at Chicago (AL)
5	San Francisco
6	at Milwaukee
7	at Los Angeles (NL)
8	Seattle
9	at Chicago (NL)
10	San Diego
11	at Colorado
12	at San Diego
13	at Kansas City
13	Milwaukee
14	Texas
15	at Texas
16	Los Angeles (AL)
17	at Cincinnati
18	Oakland
19	Chicago (NL)
20	at Seattle
21	Chicago (AL)
23	Kansas City
24	Los Angeles (NL)
25	at Arizona
26	at Cincinnati
27	Milwaukee
28	at Oakland
29	at Los Angeles (AL)
29	Seattle
30	at Los Angeles (NL)
31	Cincinnati
APRIL	
1-2	at Texas

COLORADO ROCKIES

MARCH	
2	Arizona
3	at Arizona
4	at Oakland
5	San Diego
6	at Cincinnati
7	Chicago (NL)
8	at Kansas City
9	at San Francisco
10	Cincinnati
11	Cleveland
12	at Milwaukee
13	Los Angeles (NL)
14	at Seattle
15	Oakland
16	at Los Angeles (NL)
17	Los Angeles (AL)
18	at Los Angeles (AL)
19	at San Diego
20	San Francisco
21	at Texas
22	Milwaukee
24	Seattle
25	at Cincinnati
26	Texas
27	at Arizona
28	Chicago (AL)
29	at Arizona
30	at Chicago (NL)
30	Milwaukee
31	Arizona
APRIL	
1	at Seattle
2	Seattle

KANSAS CITY ROYALS

MARCH	
2-3	Texas
4	at San Diego
5	Chicago (AL)
6	at Los Angeles (AL)
7	at Chicago (NL)
7	at Oakland
8	Colorado
9	Milwaukee
9	at Seattle
10	at Chicago (AL)
11	Arizona
12	at Arizona
13	Cleveland
14	Chicago (AL)
15	at Cincinnati
16	Chicago (NL)
17	at Los Angeles (AL)
18	Los Angeles (AL)
18-19	at Texas
19	Seattle
20	at Chicago (NL)
22	Los Angeles (NL)
23	at Cleveland
24	at Milwaukee
25	at San Francisco
26	Oakland
27	at Oakland

28 . . . . San Diego
28 . . . . at Seattle
29 . . . . . . .San Francisco

30 . . . . at Texas

APRIL
1-2. . . . . at Arizona

12 . . . . at Texas
13 . . . . Chicago (NL)
14 . . . . .San Francisco
15 . . . . at Colorado
17 . . . . Seattle
18 . . . . at Cleveland
19 . . . . Cincinnati
19 . . . . . at San Francisco
20 . . . . Chicago (AL)
21 . . . . at San Francisco
22 . . . at Los Angeles (AL)
23 . . . . at Seattle

24 . . . . Texas
25 . . . . .Los Angeles (AL)
26 . . . . . at Kansas City
27 . . . . Kansas City
28 . . . . Cleveland
29 . . . .at Chicago (NL)
30 . . . . .Arizona
31 . . . . . at San Francisco

APRIL
1 . . . . at San Francisco
2 . . . . .San Francisco

LOS ANGELES ANGELS OF ANAHEIM

MARCH	
2 . . . . . . at San Francisco	18 . . . . . . at Kansas City
3 . . . . Oakland	18 . . . . .Colorado
4 . . . . . .at Chicago (NL)	19 . . . . Milwaukee
5 . . . . at Seattle	20 . . . . at Texas
6 . . . . Kansas City	21 . . . . . .at Milwaukee
7 . . . . at Cincinnati	22 . . . . Oakland
7 . . . . Chicago (AL)	24 . . . . .at Chicago (AL)
8 . . . . at Arizona	25 . . . . . . at Oakland
9 . . . . .Los Angeles (NL)	26 . . . . . . .San Diego
10 . . . . .Arizona	27 . . . . . at San Diego
11 . . at Los Angeles (NL)	28 . . . . . . Chicago (NL)
12 . . . . . .San Francisco	29 . . . . Cleveland
13 . . . . Texas	31 . . . at Los Angeles (NL)
14 . . . . Cincinnati	**APRIL**
15 . . . . Seattle	1 . . . . at Los Angeles (NL)
16 . . . . . . at Cleveland	2 . . . . .Los Angeles (NL)
17 . . . . . . at Colorado	3 . . . . Chicago (NL)

LOS ANGELES DODGERS

MARCH	
3 . . . . Chicago (AL)	19 . . . . .at Chicago (AL)
4 . . . . at Texas	20 . . . . . .at Milwaukee
5 . . . . .Arizona	20 . . . . San Diego
6 . . . . at San Francisco	21 . . . . Seattle
7 . . . . Cleveland	22 . . . . . at Kansas City
8 . . . .at Chicago (NL)	24 . . . . . . at Cleveland
9 . . . at Los Angeles (AL)	25 . . . . .San Francisco
10 . . . . . . at Oakland	26 . . . . at Seattle
11 . . . .Los Angeles (AL)	26 . . . . . Chicago (AL)
12 . . . . . Chicago (NL)	27 . . . . . Cincinnati
12 . . . . . at Seattle	28 . . . . Texas
13 . . . . . at Colorado	29 . . . . at San Diego
14 . . . . Milwaukee	30 . . . . Cleveland
15 . . . .at Chicago (AL)	31 . . . . .Los Angeles (AL)
16 . . . . . . .Colorado	**APRIL**
17 . . . . . . Kansas City	1 . . . . . .Los Angeles (AL)
18 . . . . at Arizona	2 . . . . at Los Angeles (AL)

MILWAUKEE BREWERS

MARCH	
3 . . . . Chicago (NL)	18 . . . . Cincinnati
3 . . . . . at San Francisco	19 . . . at Los Angeles (AL)
4 . . . . Seattle	20 . . . .Los Angeles (NL)
5 . . . . at Oakland	21 . . . .Los Angeles (AL)
6 . . . . Cleveland	21 . . . . at Arizona
7 . . . . . San Diego	22 . . . . . at Colorado
8 . . . .at Chicago (AL)	24 . . . . . . Kansas City
9 . . . . at Kansas City	25 . . . . .at Chicago (NL)
10 . . . . . .San Francisco	26 . . . . .Arizona
11 . . . . Texas	27 . . . . . . at Cleveland
12 . . . . . . .Colorado	28 . . . . . at Cincinnati
13 . . . . . at Cleveland	29 . . . . . . Cincinnati
14 . . . at Los Angeles (NL)	30 . . . . . at Colorado
16 . . . . . Chicago (AL)	31 . . . . at Houston
17 . . . . at Texas	**APRIL**
	1 . . . . at Houston

OAKLAND ATHLETICS

MARCH	
3 . . . . at Los Angeles (AL)	6 . . . . at San Diego
4 . . . . .Colorado	7 . . . . Kansas City
4 . . . . at Arizona	8 . . . . Texas
5 . . . . Milwaukee	9 . . . . .at Chicago (AL)
	10 . . . . .Los Angeles (NL)
	11 . . . . . at Cincinnati

SAN DIEGO PADRES

MARCH	
2 . . . . at Seattle	19 . . . . .Colorado
3 . . . . Seattle	20 . . . at Los Angeles (NL)
4 . . . . Kansas City	21 . . . . Cincinnati
5 . . . . at Colorado	22 . . . . Texas
6 . . . .at Chicago (AL)	23 . . . .at Chicago (AL)
6 . . . . Oakland	24 . . . . .Arizona
7 . . . .at Milwaukee	25 . . . . . . at Texas
8 . . . . . . .Arizona	26 . . . . Houston
9 . . . . . at Arizona	26 . . . at Los Angeles (AL)
10 . . . . . at Cleveland	27 . . . . Houston
11 . . . . . Chicago (AL)	27 . . . .Los Angeles (AL)
12 . . . . . Cleveland	28 . . . . at Kansas City
13 . . . at San Francisco	29 . . . .Los Angeles (NL)
14 . . . . .at Chicago (NL)	30 . . . . at Seattle
15 . . . . Chicago (NL)	**APRIL**
17 . . . . .San Francisco	1 . . . . Chicago (AL)
18 . . . at San Francisco	2 . . . . Chicago (AL)

SAN FRANCISCO GIANTS

MARCH	
2 . . . . .Los Angeles (AL)	18 . . . . San Diego
3 . . . . Milwaukee	19 . . . . Oakland
4 . . . . . at Cincinnati	20 . . . . . . at Colorado
5 . . . . . at Cleveland	21 . . . . Oakland
5 . . . . Texas	22 . . . .at Chicago (AL)
6 . . . .Los Angeles (NL)	22-23 . . . . . . at Arizona
7 . . . . at Texas	24 . . . . . Chicago (NL)
8 . . . . . Cincinnati	25 . . . . . Kansas City
9 . . . . . . .Colorado	25 . . . at Los Angeles (NL)
10 . . . .at Milwaukee	26 . . . .at Chicago (NL)
11 . . . . Seattle	27 . . . . . Chicago (AL)
12 . . . . . . .Arizona	28 . . . . . . .Arizona
12 . . . at Los Angeles (AL)	29 . . . . at Kansas City
13 . . . . . San Diego	31 . . . . Oakland
14 . . . . . . at Oakland	**APRIL**
16 . . . . . . at Seattle	1 . . . . Oakland
17 . . . . . at San Diego	2 . . . . at Oakland

SEATTLE MARINERS

MARCH	
2 . . . . San Diego	17 . . . . at Oakland
3 . . . . at San Diego	18 . . . . Texas
4 . . . . . .at Milwaukee	19 . . . . . at Kansas City
5 . . . .Los Angeles (AL)	19 . . . . .Arizona
6 . . . . at Texas	20 . . . . Cleveland
7 . . . . .Arizona	21 . . . at Los Angeles (NL)
8 . . . . . at Cleveland	23 . . . . Oakland
9 . . . . Kansas City	24 . . . . . . at Colorado
10 . . . . . Chicago (NL)	25 . . . . . Chicago (AL)
11 . . . at San Francisco	26 . . . .Los Angeles (NL)
12 . . . . . at Cincinnati	27 . . . .at Chicago (NL)
12 . . . .Los Angeles (NL)	28 . . . . . Kansas City
13 . . . . . Cincinnati	29 . . . . . . at Cleveland
14 . . . . .Colorado	30 . . . . San Diego
14 . . . . at Arizona	**APRIL**
15 . . at Los Angeles (AL)	1 . . . . .Colorado
16 . . . . . . .San Francisco	2 . . . . at Colorado

TEXAS RANGERS

MARCH
2-3 . . . . . at Kansas City
4 . . . . . .Los Angeles (NL)
5 . . . . . . at San Francisco
6 . . . . Seattle
7 . . . . .San Francisco
8 . . . . at Oakland
9 . . . . at Cincinnati
10 . . . . . . Chicago (AL)
11 . . . . . . at Milwaukee
12 . . . . Oakland
13 . . . . at Los Angeles (AL)
14 . . . . . . at Cleveland
15 . . . . Cleveland
17 . . . . Milwaukee
18 . . . . at Seattle

18-19 . . . . . . Kansas City
19 . . . . at Arizona
20 . . . . .Los Angeles (AL)
21 . . . . .Colorado
22 . . . . . . at San Diego
23 . . . . Chicago (NL)
24 . . . . Cincinnati
24 . . . . at Oakland
25 . . . . San Diego
26 . . . . at Colorado
27 . . . . .Arizona
28 . . at Los Angeles (NL)
29 . . . . . .at Chicago (AL)
30 . . . . Kansas City

APRIL
1-2 . . . . Cleveland

GRAPEFRUIT LEAGUE

ATLANTA BRAVES

MARCH
1 . . . . Baltimore
2 . . . . at Baltimore
3 . . . . Detroit
4 . . . . . . .at Philadelphia
5 . . . . .Pittsburgh
6 . . . . .at New York (NL)
7 . . . . at Toronto
8 . . . . . New York (NL)
9 . . . . at Houston
10 . . . . at Miami
11 . . . . . . at St. Louis
11 . . . . Philadelphia
12 . . . . . . .Washington
13 . . . . at Houston
14 . . . . Tampa Bay
15 . . . . at Detroit
16 . . . . St. Louis
17 . . . . . . at Washington

17 . . . . Houston
18 . . . . Miami
19 . . . . .at New York (AL)
20 . . . . Detroit
21 . . . . . at Tampa Bay
22 . . . . at Houston
24 . . . . Philadelphia
25 . . . . at Detroit
25 . . . . Houston
26 . . . . . . New York (NL)
27 . . . . at Washington
28 . . . . Houston
29 . . . . . . .at Baltimore
30 . . . . . New York (AL)
31 . . . . . . .at Baltimore

APRIL
1 . . . . Tampa Bay
2 . . . . Detroit

BALTIMORE ORIOLES

MARCH
1 . . . . at Atlanta
2 . . . . Atlanta
3 . . . . at Tampa Bay
4 . . . . at Toronto
5 . . . . . . at Minnesota
5 . . . . Tampa Bay
6 . . . . at Boston
7 . . . . .Minnesota
8 . . . . Boston
9 . . . .at Philadelphia
10 . . . . . New York (AL)
11 . . . .at New York (AL)
12 . . . . .Minnesota
13 . . . . . . at Minnesota
14 . . . . Philadelphia
15 . . . . at Toronto
16 . . . . .Pittsburgh

17 . . . . at Boston
17 . . . . .Minnesota
18 . . . . .at New York (AL)
19 . . . . . .at Tampa Bay
20 . . . . Tampa Bay
22 . . . . . . at Minnesota
23 . . . . . . at Pittsburgh
24 . . . . .Pittsburgh
25 . . . . . New York (AL)
26 . . . . Boston
27 . . . . . . at Pittsburgh
28 . . . . at Boston
29 . . . . .Atlanta
30 . . . . Detroit
31 . . . . Atlanta

APRIL
1 . . . . . . .at Philadelphia

BOSTON RED SOX

MARCH
2 . . . . .Minnesota
3 . . . . at Minnesota
4 . . . . Tampa Bay
5 . . . .at New York (AL)
6 . . . . Baltimore
7 . . . . Tampa Bay

8 . . . . .at Baltimore
9 . . . . at Pittsburgh
10 . . . . .Minnesota
11 . . . . .at Toronto
12 . . . . Miami
13 . . . .at Tampa Bay
14 . . . . .Pittsburgh

---

15 . . . . . . New York (AL)
16 . . . . at Minnesota
17 . . . . Baltimore
18 . . . . at Tampa Bay
18 . . . . .Minnesota
19 . . . . St. Louis
20 . . . .at New York (NL)
21 . . . . at St. Louis
22 . . . . at Miami
24 . . . . . New York (NL)

25 . . . . .Pittsburgh
26 . . . . . . .at Baltimore
27 . . . . Philadelphia
28 . . . . Baltimore
29 . . . . . . at Minnesota
30 . . . . . . at Pittsburgh
31 . . . . . . at Minnesota

APRIL
1-2 . . . . at Toronto

DETROIT TIGERS

MARCH
1 . . . . .Pittsburgh
2 . . . .at New York (AL)
2 . . . . at Pittsburgh
3 . . . . at Atlanta
4 . . . . . New York (AL)
5 . . . . . . at Washington
6 . . . . Miami
7 . . . .at New York (NL)
8 . . . . Tampa Bay
9 . . . . .Washington
10 . . . .at Philadelphia
11 . . . . at Houston
12 . . . . .Pittsburgh
13 . . . . . at Pittsburgh
14 . . . . . New York (NL)
15 . . . . .Atlanta
16 . . . . . . at Houston

17 . . . . St. Louis
18 . . . . at St. Louis
19 . . . . .at Miami
20 . . . . at Atlanta
20 . . . . . . .Washington
21 . . . . Philadelphia
22 . . . . Toronto
24 . . . . at Toronto
25 . . . . .Atlanta
26 . . . . . .at Philadelphia
27 . . . . Houston
28 . . at New York (AL)
29 . . . . Toronto
30 . . . . . . .at Baltimore
31 . . . . . New York (AL)

APRIL
1 . . . . Tampa Bay
2 . . . . at Atlanta

HOUSTON ASTROS

MARCH
3 . . . . . .at Philadelphia
4 . . . . St. Louis
5 . . . . . New York (NL)
6 . . . . . at Pittsburgh
6 . . . . Toronto
7 . . . .at New York (AL)
8 . . . . .Washington
9 . . . . Atlanta
10 . . . . . at Washington
11 . . . . Detroit
12 . . . . . at St. Louis
13 . . . . .Atlanta
14 . . . . at Washington
15 . . . . . . .Washington
16 . . . . Detroit
17 . . . . at Atlanta

17 . . . . Toronto
18 . . . . at Toronto
20 . . . . .at Philadelphia
21 . . . . . . at Washington
22 . . . . Atlanta
23 . . . . Philadelphia
24 . . . .at New York (NL)
25 . . . . at Atlanta
26 . . . . . at San Diego
26 . . . . Miami
27 . . . . at San Diego
27 . . . . at Detroit
28 . . . . at Atlanta
30 . . . .at Philadelphia
31 . . . . Milwaukee

APRIL
1 . . . . Milwaukee

MIAMI MARLINS

MARCH
3 . . . . at St. Louis
4 . . . . .Washington
4 . . . .at New York (NL)
5 . . . . St. Louis
6 . . . . at Detroit
7 . . . . . . at Washington
8 . . . . . New York (AL)
9 . . . . . . at St. Louis
10 . . . . .Atlanta
11 . . . . . at Minnesota
12 . . . . at Boston
13 . . . . . New York (NL)
15 . . . . . New York (NL)
16 . . . . . . .Washington
17 . . . . . New York (NL)

18 . . . . at Atlanta
19 . . . . Detroit
20 . . . . . . at St. Louis
21 . . . . .at New York (NL)
22 . . . . Boston
23 . . . . . . at St. Louis
24 . . . . .Minnesota
25 . . . . . . .Washington
26 . . . . . . at Houston
27 . . . . St. Louis
28 . . . . at Washington
29 . . . .at New York (NL)
30 . . . . St. Louis

APRIL
1 . . . . . . New York (AL)
2 . . . . . . New York (AL)

MINNESOTA TWINS

MARCH
2 . . . . at Boston
3 . . . . Boston
4 . . . . at Pittsburgh
5 . . . . Baltimore
6 . . . . . . at Tampa Bay
7 . . . .at Baltimore
8 . . . . St. Louis
8 . . . . at Toronto
9 . . . . . . Philadelphia
10 . . . . . . at Boston
11 . . . . Miami
12 . . .at Baltimore
13 . . . . . . Baltimore
14 . . . . . at St. Louis
16 . . . . Boston
17 . . . . . . .at Baltimore

18 . . . . at Boston
19 . . . . at Pittsburgh
20 . . . . . . New York (AL)
21 . . . . . . .Pittsburgh
22 . . . . Baltimore
22 . . . . . at Philadelphia
23 . . . . Tampa Bay
24 . . . . at Miami
25 . . . . . at Tampa Bay
26 . . . . .Pittsburgh
27 . . . . at New York (AL)
28 . . . . . . at Pittsburgh
29 . . . . Boston
30 . . . . Toronto
31 . . . . Boston

APRIL
1-2 . . . . . . at Washington

NEW YORK METS

MARCH
3 . . . . . . at Washington
4 . . . . Miami
5 . . . . . . at Houston
6 . . . . .Atlanta
7 . . . . at St. Louis
7 . . . . Detroit
8 . . . . . . at Atlanta
9 . . . . . New York (AL)
10 . . . . St. Louis
11 . . at Washington
12 . . . . . . St. Louis
13 . . . . . at Miami
14 . . . . . at Detroit
15-17 . . . . at Miami
18 . . . . . . .Washington

19 . . . . . at Washington
20 . . . . Boston
21 . . . . Miami
22 . . . at New York (AL)
23 . . . . at Toronto
24 . . . . at Boston
24 . . . . Houston
25 . . . . St. Louis
26 . . . . . . at Atlanta
27 . . . . . . .Washington
28 . . . . . . at St. Louis
29 . . . . Miami
30 . . . . . . .Washington
31 . . . . .at Chicago (NL)

APRIL
1 . . . . . . .at Chicago (NL)

NEW YORK YANKEES

MARCH
2 . . . . Detroit
3 . . . . Philadelphia
4 . . . . at Detroit
5 . . . . Boston
6 . . .at Philadelphia
7 . . . . Houston
8 . . . . at Miami
9 . . . . .at New York (NL)
10 . . . .at Baltimore
10 . . . . . . Toronto
11 . . . . . . Baltimore
12 . . . . . at Tampa Bay
13 . . . . . Philadelphia
15 . . . . . at Boston
16 . . . . . . Toronto
17 . . . . . . at Pittsburgh

18 . . . . Baltimore
19 . . . . .Atlanta
20 . . . . . . at Minnesota
22 . . . . . New York (NL)
23 . . . . at Washington
24 . . . . . . Tampa Bay
25 . . . . . .at Baltimore
26 . . . . . . at Toronto
27 . . . . . . .Minnesota
28 . . . . Detroit
29 . . .at Philadelphia
29 . . . . . . .Pittsburgh
30 . . . . . at Atlanta
31 . . . . . . at Detroit
31 . . . . . . St. Louis

APRIL
1-2 . . . . .at Miami

PHILADELPHIA PHILLIES

MARCH
1 . . . . Toronto
2 . . . . at Toronto
3 . . . . Houston
3 . . . . .at New York (AL)
4 . . . . .Atlanta
5 . . . . at Toronto
6 . . . . . New York (AL)
7 . . . . . at Pittsburgh
8 . . . . . . .Pittsburgh
9 . . . . Baltimore
9 . . . . . . at Minnesota

10 . . . . Detroit
11 . . . . . . at Atlanta
12 . . . . Toronto
13 . . . . at New York (AL)
14 . . . . . . .at Baltimore
15 . . . . . at Tampa Bay
17 . . . . . . Tampa Bay
18 . . . . . . .Pittsburgh
19 . . . . at Toronto
20 . . . . . . Houston
21 . . . . . at Detroit
22 . . . . .Minnesota

PITTSBURGH PIRATES

MARCH
1 . . . . at Detroit
2 . . . . Detroit
3 . . . . Toronto
4 . . . . . .Minnesota
5 . . . . . at Atlanta
6 . . . . Houston
7 . . . . . Philadelphia
8 . .at Philadelphia
9 . . . . Boston
10 . . . . at Tampa Bay
11 . . . . . Tampa Bay
12 . . . . . at Detroit
13 . . . . Detroit
14 . . . . . at Boston
16 . . . .at Baltimore
17 . . . . New York (AL)

18 . . . . .at Philadelphia
19 . . . . . .Minnesota
20 . . . . . at Toronto
21 . . . at Minnesota
23 . . . . . . Baltimore
24 . . . . .at Baltimore
25 . . . . . at Boston
26 . . . . at Minnesota
26 . . . . . . Tampa Bay
27 . . . . . . Baltimore
28 . . . . . .Minnesota
29 . . at New York (AL)
30 . . . . Boston
31 . . . . at Tampa Bay

APRIL
2 . . . . Cincinnati

ST. LOUIS CARDINALS

MARCH
3 . . . . Miami
4 . . . . . . at Houston
5 . . . . .at Miami
6 . . . . . .Washington
7 . . . . New York (NL)
8 . . . at Minnesota
9 . . . . Miami
10 . . . .at New York (NL)
11 . . . . . . .Atlanta
12 . . . . Houston
12 . . .at New York (NL)
13 . . . . at Washington
14 . . . . . .Minnesota
16 . . . . . . at Atlanta

17 . . . . at Detroit
18 . . . . Detroit
19 . . . . . at Boston
20 . . . . Miami
21 . . . . Boston
23 . . . . Miami
24 . . . . at Washington
25 . . . .at New York (NL)
26 . . . . . .Washington
27 . . . . . at Miami
28 . . . . New York (NL)
29 . . . . . .Washington
30 . . . . . . at Miami
31 . . at New York (AL)

TAMPA BAY RAYS

MARCH
2 . . . . .Washington
3 . . . . Baltimore
4 . . . . . . at Boston
5 . . . .at Baltimore
6 . . . . .Minnesota
7 . . . . . at Boston
8 . . . . at Detroit
9 . . . . . . Toronto
10 . . . . .Pittsburgh
11 . . at Pittsburgh
12 . . . . New York (AL)
13 . . . . Boston
13 . . . . .at Toronto
14 . . . . . at Atlanta

15 . . . . . . Philadelphia
17 . . . . .at Philadelphia
18 . . . . Boston
19 . . . . Baltimore
20 . . . .at Baltimore
21 . . . . . . .Atlanta
23 . . . . at Minnesota
24 . . . at New York (AL)
25 . . . . . .Minnesota
26 . . . at Pittsburgh
27 . . . . . . Toronto
31 . . . . . .Pittsburgh

APRIL
1 . . . . at Atlanta
1 . . . . at Detroit

(top right, Minnesota Twins continued)
23 . . . . at Houston
24 . . . . . . at Atlanta
25 . . . . Toronto
26 . . . . Detroit
27 . . . . . at Boston

28 . . . . .at Toronto
29 . . . . . New York (AL)
30 . . . . Houston

APRIL
1 . . . . Baltimore

TORONTO BLUE JAYS

MARCH
1 . . . . at Philadelphia
2 . . . . Philadelphia
3 . . . . at Pittsburgh
4 . . . . Baltimore
5 . . . . Philadelphia
6 . . . . at Houston
7 . . . . Atlanta
8 . . . . Minnesota
9 . . . . at Tampa Bay
10 . . . . . at New York (AL)
11 . . . . Boston
12 . . . . . . at Philadelphia
13 . . . . Tampa Bay
15 . . . . Baltimore
16 . . . . . at New York (AL)

17 . . . . at Houston
18 . . . . Houston
19 . . . . Philadelphia
20 . . . . Pittsburgh
22 . . . . at Detroit
23 . . . . . New York (NL)
24 . . . . Detroit
25 . . . . . . at Philadelphia
26 . . . . . New York (AL)
27 . . . . . . at Tampa Bay
28 . . . . Philadelphia
29 . . . . at Detroit
30 . . . . at Minnesota

APRIL
1-2 . . . . Boston

WASHINGTON NATIONALS

2 . . . . at Tampa Bay
3 . . . . New York (NL)
4 . . . . at Miami
5 . . . . Detroit
6 . . . . at St. Louis
7 . . . . Miami
8 . . . . at Houston
9 . . . . at Detroit
10 . . . . Houston
11 . . . . . New York (NL)
12 . . . . at Atlanta
13 . . . . St. Louis
14 . . . . Houston
15 . . . . at Houston
16 . . . . at Miami
17 . . . . Atlanta

18 . . . . . at New York (NL)
19 . . . . . New York (NL)
20 . . . . at Detroit
21 . . . . Houston
23 . . . . . New York (AL)
24 . . . . St. Louis
25 . . . . at Miami
26 . . . . . at St. Louis
27 . . . . Atlanta
27 . . . . at New York (NL)
29 . . . . at St. Louis
30 . . . . . at New York (NL)

APRIL
1-2 . . . . Minnesota

INDEPENDENT LEAGUES

AMERICAN ASSOCIATION

Office Address: 1415 Hwy 54 West, Suite 210, Durham, NC 27707.
Telephone: (919) 401-8150. **Fax:** (919) 401-8152. **Website:** www.americanassociationbaseball.com.
Year Founded: 2006.
Commissioner: Miles Wolff. **President:** Dan Moushon.
Director, Umpires: Kevin Winn.
Division Structure - North Division: Fargo-Moorhead RedHawks, St. Paul Saints, Sioux Falls Canaries, Winnipeg Goldeyes.
Central Division: Gary SouthShore RailCats, Kansas City T-Bones, Lincoln Saltdogs, Sioux City Explorers.
South Division: Joplin Blasters, Laredo Lemurs, Texas AirHogs, Wichita Wingnuts.
Regular Season: 100 games.
2015 Opening Date: May 19. **Closing Date:** Sept. 5.
Playoff Format: Three division winners and one wild card play in best-of-five series. Winners play for best-of-five American Association championship.
Roster Limit: 22.
Eligibility Rule: Minimum of four first-year players; maximum of five veterans (at least six or more years of professional service).
Brand of Baseball: Rawlings.
Statistician: Pointstreak.com, 602-1595 16th Avenue, Richmond Hill, ON Canada L4B 3N9.

STADIUM INFORMATION

Club	Stadium	Opened	LF	CF	RF	Capacity	2015 Att.
Amarillo (Texas)	National Bank Stadium	1949	355	429	355	7,500	52,472
Fargo-Moorhead	Newman Outdoor Field	1996	318	408	314	4,513	187,099
Gary SouthShore	U.S. Steel Yard	2002	320	400	335	6,139	165,036
Joplin	Joe Becker Stadium	1913	330	400	330	4,200	67,975
Kansas City	CommunityAmerica Ballpark	2003	300	396	328	6,537	232,068
Laredo	Uni-Trade Stadium	2012	335	405	335	6,000	62,517
Lincoln	Haymarket Park	2001	335	395	325	4,500	171,605
St. Paul	CHS Field	2015	330	396	320	7,140	404,528
Sioux City	Lewis and Clark Park	1993	330	400	330	3,630	77,429
Sioux Falls	Sioux Falls Stadium	1964	312	410	312	4,656	132,280
Texas	AirHogs Stadium	2008	330	400	330	5,445	52,072
Wichita	Lawrence-Dumont Stadium	1934	344	401	312	6,055	141,837
Winnipeg	Shaw Park	1999	325	400	325	7,481	141,837

Dimensions (spanning LF, CF, RF)

FARGO-MOORHEAD
REDHAWKS

Office Address: 1515 15th Ave N, Fargo, ND 58102.
Telephone: (701) 235-6161. **Fax:** (701) 297-9247.
Email Address: redhawks@fmredhawks.com. **Website:** www.fmredhawks.com.
Operated by: Fargo Baseball LLC.
Chairman of the Board: Bruce Thom. **President:** Brad Thom.
VP/General Manager: Josh Buchholz. **Director, Accounting:** Rick Larson. **Assistant General Manager/Director, Ticket Operations:** Michael Larson. **Director, Promotions/Merchandise:** Karl Hoium. **Director, Group Sales:** Corey Eidem. **Director, Field/Stadium Operations:** Tim Jallen. **Director, Stadium Operations:** Michael Stark. **Director, Food/Beverage:** Sean Kiernan.
Manager/Director, Player Procurement: Doug Simunic. **Player Procurement Consultant:** Jeff Bittiger. **Pitching Coach:** Michael Schlact. **Coaches:** Bucky Burgau, Kole Zimmerman, Robbie Lopez. **Trainer:** Matt McManus. **Clubhouse Manager:** Chris Krick.

GAME INFORMATION

Radio Announcer: Scott Miller. **No. of Games Broadcast:** 100. **Flagship Station:** 740-AM The FAN.
Stadium Name: Newman Outdoor Field. **Location:** I-29 North to exit 67, east on 19th Ave North, right on Albrecht Boulevard. **Standard Game Times:** 7:02 pm, Sat 6, Sun 1.

GARY SOUTHSHORE RAILCATS

Office Address: One Stadium Plaza, Gary, IN 46402.
Telephone: (219) 882-2255. **Fax:** (219) 882-2259.

Email Address: info@railcatsbaseball.com. **Website:** www.railcatsbaseball.com.
Operated by: Salvi Sports Enterprises.
Owner/CEO: Pat Salvi. **Owner:** Lindy Salvi.
President, Salvi Sports Enterprises: Pete Laven. **General Manager:** Brian Lyter. **Assistant GM/Director, Tickets:** David Kay. **Director, Marketing/Promotions:** David Kerr. **Business Manager:** Brooke Stelter. **Manager, Community Relations/Merchandise:** Crystal Torres. **Marketing Consultant:** Renee Connelly. **Head Groundskeeper/Operations:** Noah Simmons.
Manager: Greg Tagert.

GAME INFORMATION
Broadcaster: Dan Vaughan. **No. of Games Broadcast:** 100. **Flagship Station:** WEFM 95.9-FM.
Stadium Name: US Steel Yard. **Location:** Take I-65 North to end of highway at U.S. 12/20 [Dunes Highway]. Turn left on U.S. 12/20 heading west for 1.5 miles (three stoplights). Stadium is on left side. **Standard Game Times:** 7:10 p.m., Sat 6:10, Sun 2:10.

JOPLIN BLASTERS

Office Address: 131 South High Avenue, Joplin, MO 64801.
Telephone: (417) 622-4838. **Fax:** (417) 622-4848.
E-mail address: info@joplinblasters.com.
Website: www.joplinblasters.com.
CEO: Gabriel Suarez.
Manager: TBA.
Stadium Name: Joe Becker Stadium. **Standard Game Times:** May 19-June 18 Mon-Sat 6:35 p.m., Sun 2:05; June 19-September 5 Mon-Sat 7:05, Sun 5:05.

KANSAS CITY T-BONES

Office Address: 1800 Village West Parkway, Kansas City, KS 66111.
Telephone: (913) 328-5618. **Fax:** (913) 328-5674.
Email Address: tickets@tbonesbaseball.com.
Website: www.tbonesbaseball.com.
Operated By: T-Bones Baseball Club, LLC; Ehlert Development.
Owner: John Ehlert. **President:** Adam Ehlert.
VP/General Manager: Chris Browne. **Senior Director, Corporate Sales/Assistant General Manager:** Jeff Husted. **Senior Director, Broadcasting/Media Relations:** Matt Fulks. **Assistant Director, Group Sales:** Stephen Hardwick. **Director, Ticket Sales/Merchandise:** Kacy Muller. **Manager, Promotions:** Joe Goll. **Account Executive:** Connor Terry. **Group Sales Associates:** Scott Hull and Nick Restivo. **Coordinator, Stadium Operations:** Kyle Disney. **Head Groundskeeper:** Caleb Adams. **Bookkeeper:** Karen Slaughter.
Manager: John Massarelli. **Coaches:** Frank White, Bill Sobbe, Dave Schaub.

GAME INFORMATION
Radio Announcer: Nathan Moore. **No. of Games Broadcast:** 100. **Flagship Station:** KMBZ 1660-AM.
Stadium Name: CommunityAmerica Ballpark. **Location:** State Avenue West off I-435 and State Avenue. **Standard Game Times:** 7:05 p.m., 1:05 p.m. (Sun).

LAREDO LEMURS

Office Address: 6320 Sinatra Drive, Laredo, TX 78045.
Telephone: (956) 753-6877. **Fax:** (956) 791-0672.
Website: www.laredolemurs.com.
CEO: Ariana Torres. **President:** Marcus Holliman.
GM/Director, Marketing: Ana Rivera Soto. **Sales Manager:** Stephanie Gonzalez. **Box Office Manager:** Krystal Gil. **Events, Sales & Rentals:** Lizette Sanchez. **Digital Integration/Game-Day Production Manager:** Jacob Patiño.
Manager: Pete Incaviglia. **Coaches:** Lance Brown, Joe Urtuzuastegui.

GAME INFORMATION
Announcer: Bill Harrington. **No. of Games Broadcast:** 100. **Webcast:** www.laredolemurs.com.
Stadium Name: Uni-Trade Stadium. **Location: From North:** I-35 to Exit 9 turn left onto Loop 20/Bob Bullock Blvd, south on Loop 20 for 3 miles, make right onto Sinatra Blvd, stadium on left; **From South:** I-35 to Exit 2 turn right onto Hwy 59 for 4 miles, turn left onto Loop 20 North for 2 miles, turn left onto Sinatra Drive, stadium on left.
Standard Game Times: 7:05 p.m.

LINCOLN SALTDOGS

Office Address: 403 Line Drive Circle, Suite A, Lincoln, NE 68508.
Telephone: (402) 474-2255. **Fax:** (402) 474-2254.
Email Address: info@saltdogs.com. **Website:** www.saltdogs.com.
Chairman: Jim Abel. **President/GM:** Charlie Meyer.
Director, Marketing: Bret Beer. **Director, Broadcasting/Communications:**
Drew Bontadelli. **Director, Stadium Operations:** Dave Aschwege. **Director, Sales:** Steve Zoucha. **Director, Video Production:** Cade McFadden. **Assistant Director, Stadium Operations:** Dan Busch. **Manager, Ticket Sales:** Colter Clarke. **Athletic Turf Manager:** Josh Klute. **Assistant Athletic Turf Managers:** Jeremy Johnson, Jen Roeber. **Office Manager:** Shelby Meier.
Manager: Bobby Brown. **Coaches:** Tom Carcione, Jim Haller. **Trainers:** Corey Courtney, Ryan Pederson, Matt Honerman.

GAME INFORMATION
Radio Announcer: Drew Bontadelli. **No. of Games Broadcast:** 100. **Flagship Station:** KFOR 1240-AM. **Webcast Address:** www.kfor1240.com.
Stadium Name: Haymarket Park. **Location:** I-80 to Cornhusker Highway West, left on First Street, right on Sun Valley Boulevard, left on Line Drive.
Standard Game Times: 6:35 p.m., Sunday 5:05.

ST. PAUL SAINTS

Office Address: 360 Broadway Street, St. Paul, MN 55101.
Telephone: (651) 644-3517. **Fax:** (651) 644-1627.
Email Address: funisgood@saintsbaseball.com.
Website: www.saintsbaseball.com.
Principal Owners: Marv Goldklang, Bill Murray, Mike Veeck. **Chairman:** Marv Goldklang. **President:** Mike Veeck. **Vice-President/Owner:** Jeff Goldklang.
Executive Vice President/General Manager: Derek Sharrer. **Executive VP:** Tom Whaley. **Assistant GM:** Chris Schwab. **Director, Broadcast/Media Relations:** Sean Aronson. **Manager, Box Office:** Alex Harkaway. **Manager, Promotions:** Sierra Bailey. **Manager, Ticket Sales:** Tyson Jeffers. **Manager, Marketing Services:** Kelly Hagenson. **Manager, Fan Services & Community Relations:** Emily Vickers. **Events Manager:** Jillian Beard.
Account Executives: Mark Jeffrey, Zane Heinselman, Mike Hobbs, Cameron Koopman. **Marketing Associate:** Jordan Lynn. **Manager, Events:** Anna Gutknecht. **Business Manager:** Krista Schnelle. **Director, Operations:** Curtis Nachtsheim. **Office Manager:** Gina Kray. **Director, Food/Beverage:** Justin Grandstaff. **Head Groundskeeper:** Nick Baker.
Manager: George Tsamis. **Coaches:** Kerry Ligtenberg, Ole Sheldon. **Trainer:** Jason Ellenbecker. **Clubhouse Manager:** Ed Luka.

GAME INFORMATION
Radio Announcer: Sean Aronson. **No. of Games Broadcast:** 100. **Flagship Station:** Club 1220 AM. **Webcast Address:** www.saintsbaseball.com.
Stadium Name: CHS Field. **Location:** From the west take I-94 to the 7th St. Exit and head south to 5th & Broadway. From the east take I-94 to the Mounds Blvd/US-61N exit. Turn left on Kellogg and a right on Broadway until you reach 5th St.
Standard Game Times: 7:05 pm, Sun 5:05.

SIOUX CITY EXPLORERS

Office Address: 3400 Line Drive, Sioux City, IA 51106.
Telephone: (712) 277-9467. **Fax:** (712) 277-9406.
Email Address: promotions@xsbaseball.com. **Website:** www.xsbaseball.com.
President: Matt Adamski.
VP/General Manager: Shane M Tritz. **Manager, Season Ticket/Group Sales:** Connor Ryan. **Groundskeeper/Manager, Stadium Operations:** Brent Recker. **Assistant, Media Relations:** Michael Moos.
Field Manager: Steve Montgomery. **Coaches:** Bobby Post, Matt Passerelle. **Clubhouse Manager:** Mike Ward.

GAME INFORMATION
Radio Announcer: Dave Nitz. **No. of Games Broadcast:** 100. **Flagship Station:** KSCJ 1360-AM. **Webcast Address:** www.xsbaseball.com.
Stadium Name: Lewis and Clark Park. **Location:** I-29 to Singing Hills Blvd, North, right on Line Drive.
Standard Game Times: 7 p.m., Sun 2.

SIOUX FALLS CANARIES

Office Address: 1001 N West Ave, Sioux Falls, SD 57104.
Telephone: (605) 333-0179. **Fax:** (605) 333-0139.
Email Address: info@sfcanaries.com. **Website:** www.sfcanaries.com.
Operated by: Sioux Falls Canaries, LLC.
CEO/Managing Partner: Tom Garrity.
Director, Business Development: Scott Ogren. **General Manager, Baseball Operations:** Duell Higbe. **Director, Sales:** Greg Weis. **Director, Game Operations & Merchandise:** Anthony Hegstrom.
Manager: Chris Paterson. **Trainer:** Derek West.

GAME INFORMATION

Radio Announcer: JJ Hartigan. **No. of Games Broadcast:** 100. **Flagship Station:** KWSN 1230-AM. **Webcast Address:** www.kwsn.com.
Stadium Name: Sioux Falls Stadium. **Location:** I-29 to Russell Street, east one mile, south on West Avenue.
Standard Game Times: 7:05 p.m., Sat 6:05, Sun 4:05.

TEXAS AIRHOGS

Office Address: 1600 Lone Star Parkway, Grand Prairie, TX 75050.
Telephone: (972) 504-9383. **Fax:** (972) 504-2288.
Website: www.airhogsbaseball.com.
Operated By: Southern Independent Baseball, LLC.
Owner: Gary Elliston. **Vice President/General Manager:** John Bilbow.
Manager: James Frisbie.

GAME INFORMATION

No of Games Broadcast: 100. **Webcast:** www.airhogsbaseball.com.
Stadium Name: AirHogs Stadium - Grand Prairie (25 home games). **Location:** From I-30, take Beltline Road exit going north, take Lone Star Park entrance towards the stadium.
Potter County Stadium - Amarillo (25 home games). **Location:** Take Grand Street exit and proceed north on Grand Street; turn left onto SE 3rd Ave.
Standard Game Times - Grand Prairie: 7:05 p.m., Sun 6:05. **Amarillo:** 7:05 p.m., Sat 6:05, Sun 6:05.

WICHITA WINGNUTS

Office Address: 300 South Sycamore, Wichita, KS 67213.
Telephone: (316) 264-6887. **Fax:** (316) 264-2129.
Website: www.wichitawingnuts.com.
Owners: Steve Ruud, Gary Austerman, Nate Robertson.
President/General Manager: Josh Robertson. **Assistant GM/Director, Corporate Sales:** Brian Turner. **Manager, Ticket Sales:** Robert Slaughter. **Director, Stadium Operations:** Jeff Kline.. **Manager, Merchandise/Game Day Staff:** Ashley Binder. **Manager, Group Sales/Community Relations:** Stepheny Frederiksen. **Director, Food and Beverage:** Greg Read. **Finance/Office Manager:** Aaron McMullin. **Manager, Game Operations:** Tim Pile
Manager: TBA. **Coaches:** Paul Sanagorski, Luke Robertson, Jim Foltz.

GAME INFORMATION

Broadcaster: TBA. **No. of Games Broadcast:** 100. **Flagship Station:** TBA.
Webcast Address: www.wichitawingnuts.com.
Stadium Name: Lawrence-Dumont Stadium. **Location:** 135 North to Kellogg (54) West, Take Seneca Street exit North to Maple, Go East on Maple to Sycamore, Stadium is located on corner of Maple and Sycamore.
Standard Game Times: 7:05 p.m., Sun 1:05.

WINNIPEG GOLDEYES

Office Address: One Portage Ave E, Winnipeg, Manitoba R3B 3N3.
Telephone: (204) 982-2273. **Fax:** (204) 982-2274.
Email Address: goldeyes@goldeyes.com. **Website:** www.goldeyes.com.
Operated by: Winnipeg Goldeyes Baseball Club, Inc.
Principal Owner/President: Sam Katz.
General Manager: Andrew Collier. **Assistant GM:** Regan Katz. **CFO:** Jason McRae-King. **Director, Sales/Marketing:** Dan Chase. **Manager, Box Office:** Kevin Arnst. **Coordinator, Food/Beverage:** Melissa Schlichting. **Account Executive:**

INDEPENDENT LEAGUES

Steve Schuster. **Consultant, Media Relations:** Scott Taylor. **Suite Manager/Sales & Marketing:** Angela Sanche. **Manager, Promotions:** Tara Maslowsky. **Manager, Retail:** Kendra Gibson. **Controller:** Judy Jones. **Facility Manager:** Don Ferguson. **Executive Assistant:** Sherri Rheubottom. **Administrative Assistant:** Bonnie Benson.
  Manager/Director, Player Procurement: Rick Forney. **Coaches:** Jamie Vermilyea, Tom Vaeth. **Trainer:** Stephen Wady.
  Clubhouse Manager: Jamie Samson.

GAME INFORMATION
  Radio Announcer: Steve Schuster. **No. of Games Broadcast:** 100. **Flagship Station:** CJNU 93.7 FM. **Television Announcers:** Scott Taylor. **No. of Games Telecast:** Home-10, Away-0. **Station:** Shaw TV/Shaw Direct.
  Stadium Name: Shaw Park. **Location:** North on Pembina Highway to Broadway, East on Broadway to Main Street, North on Main Street to Water Avenue, East on Water Avenue to Westbrook Street, North on Westbrook Street to Lombard Avenue, East on Lombard Avenue to Mill Street, South on Mill Street to ballpark.
  Standard Game Times: 7 p.m., Sat 6, Sun 1.

ATLANTIC LEAGUE

  Mailing Address: PO Box 5190, Lancaster, Pa., 17606.
  Telephone: (720) 389-6992 or (978) 790-5421
  Email Address: info@atlanticleague.com. **Website:** www.atlanticleague.com.
  Year Founded: 1998.
  Senior Vice President/Founder: Frank Boulton. **Sr. Vice President:** Jon Danos. **Senior Vice President:** Josh Kalafer. **Senior Vice President:** Peter Kirk. **Senior Vice President:** Seth Waugh.
  President: Rick White. **Executive Director, Baseball Operations:** Joe Klein. **League Administrator:** Emily Merrill.
  Division Structure: Liberty Division—Bridgeport, Long Island, New Britain, Somerset. **Freedom Division**—Lancaster, Southern Maryland, Sugar Land, York.
  Regular Season: 140 games (split-schedule).
  2016 Opening Date: April 21. **Closing Date:** Sept 18.
  All-Star Game: July 13 in Lancaster.
  Playoff Format: First-half division winners meet second-half winners in best of five series. Winners meet in best-of-five final for league championship.
  Roster Limit: 25. Teams may keep 27 players from start of season until May 31.
  Eligibility Rule: No restrictions.
  Brand of Baseball: Rawlings.
  Statistician: Statistician: Pointstreak.com, 602 - 1595 16th Avenue, Richmond Hill, ON, Canada L4B 3N9.

STADIUM INFORMATION

			Dimensions				
Club	Stadium	Opened	LF	CF	RF	Capacity	2015 Att.
Bridgeport	The Ballpark at Harbor Yard	1998	325	405	325	5,300	192,466
Lancaster	Clipper Magazine Stadium	2005	372	400	300	6,000	276,975
Long Island	Citibank Park	2000	325	400	325	6,002	358,317
New Britain	New Britain Stadium	1996	330	400	300	6,146	N/A
Somerset	Commerce Bank Ballpark	1999	317	402	315	6,100	347,770
So. Maryland	Regency Stadium	2008	305	400	320	6,000	222,611
Sugar Land	Constellation Field	2012	348	405	325	7,500	301,860
York	Sovereign Bank Stadium	2007	300	400	325	5,000	259,989

BRIDGEPORT BLUEFISH

  Office Address: 500 Main St, Bridgeport, CT 06604. **Telephone:** (203) 345-4800.
  Fax: (203) 345-4830. **Website:** www.bridgeportbluefish.com.
  Operated by: Past Time Partners, LLC.
  Principal Owner/CEO, Past Time Partners: Frank Boulton. **Senior VP, Past Time Partners:** Mike Pfaff. **Partners, Past Time Partners:** Tony Rosenthal, Fred Heyman, Jeffrey Serkes.
  General Manager: Jamie Toole. **Assistant General Manager:** Gregory Hodges. **Senior Director, Public Relations/Baseball Operations:** Paul Herrmann. **Director, Ticket Operations & Operations:** Drew LaBov. **Senior Director, Stadium Operations:** Dan Gregory. **Executive Director, Business Development:** Jody Sellers. **Group Sales Manager:** Jeff Gabriel. **Head Groundskeeper, Promotions Coordinator:** Geremy Grate. **Coordinator, Community Relations/Marketing:** Chelsea Merritt..
  Manager: Luis Rodriguez. **Trainer:** Ericka Ventura.

GAME INFORMATION
  Radio Announcer: Michael Mohr. **No. of Games Broadcast:** 140 (webcast).

Flagship Station: webcast, www.bridgeportbluefish.com. **PA Announcer:** Bill Jensen. **Official Scorer:** Chuck Sadowski.

Stadium Name: The Ballpark at Harbor Yard. **Location:** I-95 to exit 27, Route 8/25 to exit 1. **Standard Game Times:** 7:12 pm, Sat 6:12, Sun 1:12. **Visiting Club Hotel:** Holiday Inn Bridgeport, 1070 Main St, Bridgeport, CT 06604. **Telephone:** (203) 334-1234.

LANCASTER BARNSTORMERS

Office Address: 650 North Prince St, Lancaster, PA 17603.
Telephone: (717) 509-4487. **Fax:** (717) 509-4486.
Email Address: info@lancasterbarnstormers.com. **Website:** www.lancasterbarn stormers.com.
Operated by: Lancaster Barnstormers Baseball Club, LLC. **Principal Owners:** Dakota Baseball.
Partner: Robert Liss. **Vice President, Business Development:** Vince Bulik. **Vice President, Fan Experience:** Anthony DeMarco. **Vice President:** Kristen Simon. **Director, Business Development:** Bob Ford. **Director, IT/Digital:** Chris Kurtz. **Director, Stadium Operations:** Don Pryer. **Director, Sky Boxes & Ticket Services:** Maureen Wheeler. **Accounting Manager:** Leanne Beaghan. **Box Office Manager:** Holly Shelton. **Stadium Operations Manager:** Andrew Wurst. **Business Development Representatives:** John Brennan, Quinton Collins, Zachary Cunningham, Matt Dombrowski, Dawn Rissmiller, Melissa Tucker. **Administrator, Community Partnerships:** Debra MacDonald. **Community Partnerships Representative:** Derek Sharp. **Client Services Representative:** Amber Guinther. **Client Services Representative:** Liz Welch. **Experience Sales Representative:** Alex Einhorn. **Radio Announcer:** Dave Collins. **Head Groundskeeper:** Patrick Hilton. **Assistant Groundskeeper:** Joe Morgan. **Suites and Catering Manager:** Jay Lero. **Legends Executive Chef:** Matt DiGuglielmo. **General Manager, Legends Hospitality:** Tyler Kramlick. **Merchandise Manager:** Sarah Nicosia.
Manager: Butch Hobson. **Clubhouse Manager:** Demetrius Ortiz.

GAME INFORMATION

Radio Announcer: Dave Collins. **No. of Games Broadcast:** Home-70, Away-70. **Flagship Stations:** TBA. **PA Announcer:** John Witwer. **Official Scorer:** Joel Schreiner.

Stadium Name: Clipper Magazine Stadium. **Location:** From Route 30, take Fruitville Pike or Harrisburg Pike toward downtown Lancaster, stadium on North Prince between Clay Street and Frederick Street. **Standard Game Times:** 7 p.m., Sun 1 p.m.

LONG ISLAND DUCKS

Mailing Address: 3 Court House Dr, Central Islip, NY 11722
Telephone: (631) 940-3825. **Fax:** (631) 940-3800.
Email Address: info@liducks.com. **Website:** www.liducks.com
Operated by: Long Island Ducks Professional Baseball, LLC.
Founder/CEO: Frank Boulton. **Owner/Chairman:** Seth Waugh. **Owner/Senior VP,**
Baseball Operations: Bud Harrelson.
President/General Manager: Michael Pfaff. **Assistant GM/Senior VP, Sales:** Doug Cohen. **Director, Administration:** Gerry Anderson. **Director, Group Sales:** John Wolff. **Director, Season Sales:** Brad Kallman. **Manager, Box Office:** Ben arper. **Director, Merchandise & Client Relations:** Jason Randall. **Director, Media Relations & Broadcasting:** Michael Polak. **Director, Marketing & Promotions:** Jordan Schiff. **Head Groundskeeper:** Isaiah Lienau, **Staff Accountant:** Annmarie DeMasi. **Group Sales Manager:** Anthony Rubino. **Coordinator, Facilities Maintenance:** Ryan Reeves. **Coordinator, Administration:** Michelle Jensen. **Account Executive:** Sean Smith. **Assistants, Group Sales:** Michelle Leto, Phil Mastrogiacomo. **Assistant, Tickets:** Matt Snider.
Manager: Kevin Baez. **Coaches:** Bud Harrelson, Marty Janzen. **Trainers:** Tony Amin, Dorothy Pitchford, Adam Lewis

GAME INFORMATION

Radio Announcers: Michael Polak, Chris King, David Weiss. **No. of Games Broadcast:** 140 on www.liducks.com. **Flagship Station:** 103.9-FM LI News Radio. **PA Announcer:** Bob Ottone. **Official Scorer:** Michael Polak.

NEW BRITAIN BEES

Office Address: 230 John Karbonic Way, New Britain, CT 06051
Telephone: (860) 826-2337.
Email Address: info@nbbees.com. **Website:** www.nbbees.com.
Operated by: Hard Hittin' Professional Baseball, LLC.
Principal Owner: Frank Boulton. **Partner:** Michael Pfaff. **General Manager:** Patrick Day. **Assistant General Manager:** Scott Henrichsen. **Operations Manager:** Sean O'Brien. **Business Manager:** John McKenna. **Promotions and Community Relations Coordinator:** Katie Force.
Manager: Stan Clinburn

GAME INFORMATION

Stadium Name: New Britain Stadium. **Location:** 230 John Karbonic Way New Britain, CT 06051. **Directions:** From Route 9, take the ramp left towards New Britain, Merge onto CT-571 via exit 24 on left towards CT-71/CT-371/Kensington. Take the CT-71 ramp toward Kensington, and then make slight left onto John Karbonic Way. **Standard Game Times:** Monday-Saturday 6:35 p.m., Sunday 1:35 p.m.

SOMERSET PATRIOTS

Office Address: One Patriots Park, Bridgewater, NJ 08807.
Telephone: (908) 252-0700. **Fax:** (908) 252-0776.
Website: www.somersetpatriots.com.
Operated by: Somerset Baseball Partners, LLC.
Principal Owners: Steve Kalafer, Josh Kalafer, Jonathan Kalafer.
Chairman: Steve Kalafer.
President/General Manager: Patrick McVerry. **Senior Vice President, Marketing:** Dave Marek. **VP, Public Relations:** Marc Russinoff. **VP, Operations:** Bryan Iwicki. **VP, Ticket Operations:** Matt Kopas. **Senior Director, Merchandise:** Rob Crossman. **Director of Sales/Marketing:** Kevin Fleming. **Director of Operations:** Tom McCartney. **Director of Promotions:** Deanna Liotard. **Media Relations Manager:** Marc Schwartz. **Ticket Office Manager:** Nick Cherrillo. **Group Sales Managers:** Chris Kornmann, Justin Keating. **Executive Assistant to GM:** Michele DaCosta. **Senior Vice President/Treasurer:** Ron Schulz. **Accountant:** Stephanie DePass. **Receptionist:** Lorraine Ott. **GM, Centerplate:** Mike McDermott. **Head Groundskeeper:** Dan Purner.
Manager: Brett Jodie. **Hitting/3B Coach:** TBD. **Pitching Coach:** Cory Domel. **Director of Player Personnel:** Jon Hunton. **Trainer:** Ryan McMahon. **Manager Emeritus:** Sparky Lyle.

GAME INFORMATION

Radio Announcer: Justin Antweil. **No. of Games Broadcast:** Home-70, Away-70. **Flagship Station:** WCTC 1450-AM. **Live Video Streams:** Home-20 (SPN.tv). **PA Announcer:** Paul Spychala.
Official Scorer: John Nolan.
Ballpark Name: TD Bank Ballpark. **Location:** Route 287 North to exit 13B/Route 287 South to exit 13 (Somerville Route 28 West); follow signs to ballpark. **Standard Game Times:** 7:05 pm, Sun 1:35/5:05.
Visiting Club Hotel: TBD.

SOUTHERN MARYLAND
BLUE CRABS

Office Address: 11765 St Linus Dr, Waldorf, MD 20602.
Telephone: 301-638-9788. **Fax:** 301-638-9788.
Email address: info@somdbluecrabs.com. **Website:** www.somdbluecrabs.com.
Principal Owners: Opening Day Partners LLC, Brooks Robinson.
General Manager: Courtney Knichel. **Assistant GM:** Theresa Coffey. **Box Office Manager:** Carlton Silvestro. **Marketing Manager:** Austin Gore. **Accounting Coordinator:** Samantha Slovik. **Sales Account Executives:** Kenney Aicher, Sara Mackie. **Lead Broadcaster:** Jim Tarabocchia. **Senior Director of Business Development:** Bill Snitcher. **Corporate Sales Executive:** Tim Lills. **Creative Services:** Josh Owens. **Stadium Operations:** Greg Wilkes. **Centerplate Concessions/Merchandise:** Magen Dilworth.
Manager: Jeremy Owens. **Hitting Coach:** Jake Optiz. **Pitching Coach:** TBD

GAME INFORMATION

Radio: All home games, www.somdbluecrabs.com.
Stadium: Regency Furniture Stadium. **Standard Game Times:** 7:05 p.m., Sat 6:35, Sun 2:05.

SUGAR LAND SKEETERS

Office Address: 1 Stadium Drive, Sugar Land, Texas, 77498.
Telephone: (281) 240-4487.
Owners: Marcie & Bob Zlotnik. **Special Advisor:** Deacon Jones.
President: Jay Miller. **Assistant GM- Operations & Finance:** JT Onyett. **AGM-Community:** Kyle Dawson. **Vice President- Marketing and Public Relations:** Jay Lucas.
Human Resources: Kimberly Ciszewski. **Accounting:** Tina Gately. **Accounting Assistant:** Isabel Perez. **Box Office Mgr.:** Jennifer Schwarz. **Sr. Dir. Stadium Ops:** Donnie Moore.
Ballpark Ops: Clayton Lemke. **Head Groundskeeper:** Brad Detmore. **Senior Director of Broadcasting and Sales:** Ira Liebman. **Video Production Coord.:** Troy Young.
Senior Director Special Events: Matt Thompson. **Special Events Manager:** Ryan Derr. **Special Events Manager:** Samantha Ferriera. **Senior Director Sales:** Scott Podsim. **Senior Sales Manager:** Tyler Stamm. **Customer Service Mgr.:** Adam Mettler. **Group Services Mgr.:** Chris Parsons. **Sales Manager:** Garrett Sampson. **Senior Sales Manager:** Soleil

Thon. **Senior Sales Manager:** Sunny Okpon. **Senior Sales Manager:** Teneisha Hall. **Sales Manager:** Drew Maulsby. **Marketing Manager:** Molly Onyett. **Community Relations Manager:** Sallie Weir. **Mascot Coordinator:** Zach Bohls. **Reception:** Rachel Fort. **Legends General Manager:** Greg Hernandez. **Legends Events Manager:** Jessica Anderson. **Legends Staffing Coordinator/Buzz Shop Manager:** Abbey Stevens. **Legends Accountant:** Andrea Jennings. **Executive Chef:** Tait Guthrie. **Warehouse Supervisor:** Denzil Pitts.

    Manager: Gary Gaetti. **Pitching Coach:** Jeff Scott. **Team Doctor:** Dr. Bhojani. **Team Trainer:** Max Mahaffey.

GAME INFORMATION

    Radio Announcer: Ira Liebman. **No. of Games Broadcast:** 140. **Flagship Station:** ESPN3. **Standard Game Times:** 7:05 p.m., **Sat:** 6:05 Sun: 2:05/6:05. **Directions to Ballpark:** Southbound HWY 59-Take the exit toward Corporate Dr/ US-90/Stafford/Sugar Land. Turn right onto HWY 6. Travel northbound to Imperial Blvd. Turn right onto Imperial Blvd from HWY 6. **Visiting Club Hotel:** Sugar Land Marriott Town Square.

YORK REVOLUTION

    Office Address: 5 Brooks Robinson Way, York, PA 17401.
    Telephone: (717) 801-4487. **Fax:** (717) 801-4499.
    Email Address: info@yorkrevolution.com. **Website:** www.yorkrevolution.com.
    Operated by: York Professional Baseball Club, LLC. **Principal Owners:** York Professional Baseball Club, LLC.
    President: Eric Menzer. **General Manager/Vice President of Operations:** John Gibson. **Vice President, Business Development:** Nate Tile. **Vice President, Finance:** Lori Brunson. **Director, Ticketing:** Cindy Brown. **Box Office Manager:** Bob Gibson. **Director, Marketing/Communications:** Paul Braverman. **Marketing Manager:** Mark Serratore. **Creative Director:** Corey Shaud. **Coordinator, Mutli-media:** Scott Parker. **Director, Group Sales/Hospitality:** Reed Gunderson. **Senior Account Executive:** Mike Coleman. **Senior Account Executive:** Brandon Tesluk. **Account Executives:** Tylor Toll, Whitney Goulish, Cameron Lipnicky. **Coordinator, Client Services:** Quinn Ney. **Director, Special Events:** Adam Nugent. **Stadium Operations Manager:** Jackson Federle. **Baseball Operations Manager:** Nate Sterner. **Head Groundskeeper:** Mike Urich. **Legends Hospitality GM, Concessions/Merchandise/Catering:** Brett Herman. **Legends Hospitality Catering Manager:** Lou Rivera. **Legends Hospitality Chef:** Tiffany Livering. **Legends Hospitality Concessions Manager:** Amanda Shusko.
    Manager: Mark Mason. **Pitching Coach:** Paul Fletcher. **Bench/Third-Base Coach:** Enohel Polanco.

GAME INFORMATION

    Radio Announcer: Darrell Henry. **No. of Games Broadcast:** 140. **Flagship Station:** WOYK 1350 AM. **PA Announcer:** Ray Jensen. **Official Scorer:** Brian Wisler.
    Stadium Name: PeoplesBank Park. **Location:** Take Route 30 West to North George Street. **Directions:** Turn left onto North George Street; follow that straight for four lights, Santander Stadium is on left. **Standard Game Times:** 6:30 p.m., Sun, 1 p.m. **Visiting Club Hotel:** The Yorktowne Hotel, 48 E Market Street, York, PA 17401. **Telephone:** (717) 848-1111.

CAN-AM LEAGUE

Office Address: 1415 Hwy 54 West, Suite 210, Durham, NC 27707.
Telephone: (919) 401-8150. **Fax:** (919) 401-8152. **Website:** www.canamleague.com.
Year Founded: 2005.
Commissioner: Miles Wolff. **President:** Dan Moushon. **Director, Umpires:** Kevin Winn.
Regular Season: 100 games. **2015 Opening Date:** May 19. **Closing Date:** Sept. 5. **Playoff Format:** Top four teams meet in best-of-five semifinals; winners meet in best-of-five finals. **Roster Limit:** 22. **Eligibility Rule:** Minimum of five and maximum of eight first-year players; minimum of five players must be an LS-4 or higher; a maximum of four may be veterans. **Brand of Baseball:** Rawlings. **Statistician:** Pointstreak.com.

STADIUM INFORMATION

Club	Stadium	Opened	Dimensions LF	CF	RF	Capacity	2015 Att.
New Jersey	Yogi Berra Stadium	1998	308	398	308	3,784	78,913
Ottawa	Raymond Chabot Grant Thornton Park	1993	325	404	325	10,332	115,880
Quebec	Stade Municipal	1938	315	385	315	4,500	130,510
Rockland	Provident Bank Park	2011	323	403	313	4,750	161,796
Sussex County	Skylands Stadium	1994	330	392	330	4,200	56,988
Trois-Rivieres	Stade Fernand-Bedard	1938	342	372	342	4,500	96,997

NEW JERSEY JACKALS

Office Address: One Hall Dr, Little Falls, NJ 07424. **Telephone:** (973) 746-7434. **Fax:** (973) 655-8006. **Email Address:** info@jackals.com. **Website:** www.jackals.com.
Operated by: Floyd Hall Enterprises, LLC. **Chairman:** Floyd Hall.
President: Greg Lockard. **Executive Vice President:** Larry Hall. **Vice President, Finance/Operations:** Jennifer Fertig. **Senior Vice President, Marketing:** John Fabian.
Corporate Partnership & Advertising Sales: Joseph Redmon. **Group Sales & Ticket Operations:** Jeff Palladino. **Group Sales & Operations:** Jarrett Schack, Crystal Borbonus. **Group Sales/Director, Social Media:** Kimberly Herve. **Facilities Manager:** Aldo Licitra. **Concessions Manager:** Eric McConnell.
Manager: Joe Calfapietra. **Coaches:** Anthony Claggett, Jerod Edmondson, Ani Ramos. **Trainer:** Xavier Alzate. **Clubhouse Manager:** Dan DiTommasso.

GAME INFORMATION
Webcast Announcer: Michael Cohen. **No. of Games Broadcast:** 100. **Webcast Address:** www.jackals.com. **Stadium Name:** Yogi Berra Stadium. **Location:** On the campus of Montclair State University; Route 80 or Garden State Parkway to Route 46, take Valley Road exit to Montclair State University. **Standard Game Times:** 7:05 p.m., Sat 6:35, Sun 2:05.

OTTAWA CHAMPIONS

Office Address: 300 Coventry Road, Ottawa, ON K1K 4P5. **Telephone:** (613) 745-2255. **Fax:** (613) 745-3289. **Email address:** info@ottawachampions.com. **Website:** www.ottawachampions.com.
Owner: Miles Wolff. **President:** David Gourlay. **CFO:** Scott Gibeault. **General Manager:** Ben Hodge. **Assistant General Manager:** Davyd Balloch. **Director, Marketing & Communications:** Craig Richenback. **Director, Business Operations and Ticketing:** Ian Hooper. **Manager, Game Operations and Community Outreach:** Erica Dubowski. **Account Manager:** Mike Massel. **Account Executive:** Andy Desilets.
Manager: Hal Lanier. **Coaches:** Sebastien Boucher, Bily Horn, Jared Lemieux, Stephane Petronzio. **Director, Player Personnel:** Nick Belmonte.

GAME INFORMATION
Broadcaster - English: Mike Nellis. **Broadcaster - French:** Jadrino Huot. **Flagship Station - English:** CKDJ 107.9-FM. **Flagship Station - French:** CHUO 89.1-FM. **Webcast address:** www.ottawachampions.com. **Stadium Name:** Raymond Chabot Grant Thornton Park. **Location:** From Hwy #417 (Queensway), take Vanier Parkway (Exit #117). Turn right on to Coventry Road. Raymond Chabot Grant Thornton Park is at your immediate right. **Standard Game Times:** Mon-Sat 7:05 p.m., Sun 1:35.

QUEBEC CAPITALES

Office Address: 100 Rue du Cardinal Maurice-Roy, Quebec City, QC G1K 8Z1.
Telephone: (418) 521-2255. **Fax:** (418) 521-2266. **Email Address:** info@capitalesdequebec.com. **Website:** www.capitalesdequebec.com.

Owner: Jean Tremblay. **President/GM:** Michel Laplante. **Assistant General Manager:** Anne-Marie Nappert. **Administrative Director:** Julie Lefrançois. **Director, Communications:** Maxime Aubry. **Representative, Group Sales:** Jean Marois. **Representatives, Corporate Sales:** Bobby Baril, Frédéric Munger. **Group Sales/Box Office Supervisor:** Jean-Philippe Otis. **Coordinator, Community and Promotions:** Annie-Pier Couture. **Coordinator, Promotions and Marketing:** Charles Demers.

Manager: Patrick Scalabrini. **Coaches:** TJ Stanton, Mike Provencher. **Trainer:** Jean-François Brochu.

GAME INFORMATION

Broadcaster: François Paquet. **Stadium Name:** Stade Municipal de Québec. **Location:** Highway 40 to Highway 173 (Centre-Ville) exit 2 to Parc Victoria. **Standard Game Times:** 7:05 p.m., Sat 6:05, Sun 1:05.

ROCKLAND BOULDERS

Office Address: 1 Provident Bank Park Drive, Pomona, NY 10970. **Telephone:** (845) 364-0009. **Fax:** (845) 364-0001. **E-Mail Address:** info@rocklandboulders.com. **Website:** www.rocklandboulders.com.

President: Ken Lehner. **Executive Vice President/General Manager:** Shawn Reilly. **Assistant General Manager:** Seth Cantor. **Director of Finance:** David Wenner. **Manager, Facility Operations:** Nick Barbalato. **Manager, Promotions and Public Relations:** Christian Heimall. **Manager, Box Office:** Mira Patel. **Manager, Retail Store:** Deidra Verona. **Ticket Sales Manager:** Karen McCombs. **Account Executives:** Tom Triglia, Courtney Vardi, Nolan Ouellette, Matt Kosciolek, Brian Napier. **Promotions/Operations Assistant:** Steph Stierle. **Manager, Concessions:** George McElroy. **Manager, Suites/Catering:** Kathy Paras. **Director, Security:** Jeff Rinaldi. **Audio/Visual Specialist:** Jim Houston. **Bookkeeper:** Michele Almash.

Manager: Jamie Keefe. **Coach:** Carlos Mirabal. **Trainer:** Lori Rahaim. **Clubhouse Manager:** Anthony Cervone.

GAME INFORMATION

Broadcasters: Seth Cantor, Dan Arndt, Christian Heimall. **No. of Games Broadcast:** 70. **Flagship Station:** WBNR 1260-AM. **TV** – Verizon FIOS1, Optimum (select games). **Webcast Address:** www.rocklandboulders.com. **Stadium Name:** Provident Bank Park. **Location:** Take Palisades Parkway Exit 12 towards Route 45, make left at stop sign on Conklin Road, make left on Route 45, turn right on Pomona Road, take 1st right on Fireman's Memorial Drive. **Standard Game Times:** Mon-Fri, 7 p.m.; Sat 6:30 p.m.; Sun (May-Jun), 2 p.m., 5 p.m. (Jul-Sep).

SUSSEX COUNTY MINERS

Office Address: 94 Championship Place, Suite 11, Augusta, NJ 07822. **Telephone:** (973) 383-7644. **Fax :** (973) 383-7522. **Email Address :** contact@scminers.com. **Website:** www.scminers.com

Owner, President: Al Dorso, Sr. **Vice President, Operations:** Al Dorso, Jr. **Vice President, Marketing:** Mike Dorso. **General Manager:** Dave Chase. **Assistant General Manager:** Tyler Borkowski. **Director, Creative Services:** Dennis Mark. **Director, Broadcasting and Media Relations:** Andrew Luftglass. **Manager, Corporate Partnerships:** Joann Ciancitto. **Manager, Corporate Partnerships and Group Sales:** Bill Lorenzo. **Manager, Concessions:** Mark Wilman. **Manager, Box Office:** Kathleen Florich. **Manager, Events:** Nick Savva. **Manager, Facilities:** Shane White.

Manager: Bobby Jones.

GAME INFORMATION

Broadcaster: Andrew Luftglass. **No. of Games Broadcast:** 100. **Webcast Address:** www.scminers.com. **Stadium Name:** Skylands Stadium. **Location:** In New Jersey, I-80 to exit 34B (Route 15 North) to Route 565 North; From Pennsylvania, I-84 to Route 6 (Matamoras) to Route 206 North to Route 565 North. **Standard Game Times:** 7:05 p.m., Sunday 5:05.

TROIS-RIVIÈRES AIGLES

Office Address: 1760 Avenue Gilles-Villeneuve, Trois-Rivières, QC G9A 5K8. **Telephone:** (819) 379-0404. **Fax:** (819) 379-5087. **Email Address:** info@lesaiglestr.com. **Website:** www.lesaiglestr.com

President: Marc-André Bergeron. **General Manager:** René Martin. **Assistant General Manager:** Richard Lahaie. **Director, Communications/Marketing:** Simon Laliberté. **Assistant, Communications/Marketing:** Hugues Marcil. **Director, Stadium Operations:** Real Lajoie. **Bookkeepers:** Gabrielle Côté, Audrey Hayes.

Manager: Pierre-Luc Laforest. **Coaches:** Maxime Poulin, Matt Rusch. **Director, Player Personnel:** John Harris.

GAME INFORMATION

Broadcaster: Simon Laliberté. **No. of Games Broadcast:** 65. **Webcast address:** http://www.cfou.ca/direct.php

Stadium Name: Stade Fernand-Bedard. **Location:** Take Hwy 40 West, exit Boul. des Forges/Centre-ville, keep right, turn right at light, turn right at stop sign.

Standard Game Times: 7:05 p.m., Sat 6:05, Sun 1:05.

FRONTIER LEAGUE

Office Address: 2041 Goose Lake Rd Suite 2A, Sauget, IL 62206.
Telephone: (618) 215-4134. **Fax:** (618) 332-2115.
Email Address: office@frontierleague.com. **Website:** www.frontierleague.com.
Year Founded: 1993.
Commissioner: Bill Lee.
Deputy Commissioner: Steve Tahsler.
President: Rich Sauget (Gateway). **Executive Committee:** Clint Brown (Florence), Steve Malliet (Normal/River City), Nick Semaca (Joliet), Leslye Wuerfel (Traverse City).
Board of Directors: Chad Brigham (Southern Illinois), Bill Bussing (Evansville), Tom Kramig (Lake Erie), Al Oremus (Windy City), Pat Salvi (Schaumburg), Stu Williams (Washington).
Division Structure: East—Joliet, Lake Erie, Schaumburg, Traverse City, Washington, Windy City. **West**—Evansville, Florence, Gateway, Normal, River City, Southern Illinois.
Regular Season: 96 games. **2016 Opening Date:** May 12. **Closing Date:** Sept 4.
All-Star Game: July 13 at Florence.
Playoff Format: Two division winners and next two best records; two best-of-five rounds.
Roster Limit: 24. **Eligibility Rule:** Minimum of eleven Rookie 1/Rookie 2 players. No player may be 27 prior to Jan. 1 of current season with the exception of one player that may not be 30 years of age prior to Jan. 1 of the current season.
Brand of Baseball: Rawlings.
Statistician: Pointstreak, 602-1595 16th Avenue, Richmond Hill, ONT L4B 3N9.

STADIUM INFORMATION

Club	Stadium	Opened	Dimensions LF	CF	RF	Capacity	2015 Att.
Evansville	Bosse Field	1915	315	415	315	5,110	114,787
Florence	UC Health Stadium	2004	325	395	325	4,200	104,578
Gateway	GCS Ballpark	2002	318	395	325	5,500	149,319
Joliet	Silver Cross Field	2002	330	400	327	6,229	95,673
Lake Erie	All-Pro Freight	2009	325	400	325	5,000	86,155
Normal	The Corn Crib	2010	356	400	344	7,000	102,290
River City	T.R. Hughes Ballpark	1999	320	382	299	4,989	91,354
Schaumburg	Schaumburg Stadium	1999	355	400	353	8,107	162,210
So. Illinois	Rent One Park	2007	325	400	330	4,500	151,503
Traverse City	Wuerfel Park	2006	320	400	320	4,600	132,404
Washington	CONSOL Energy Park	2002	325	400	325	3,200	83,087
Windy City	Standard Bank Stadium	1999	335	390	335	2,598	76,550

EVANSVILLE OTTERS

Mailing Address: 23 Don Mattingly Way, Evansville, IN 47711.
Telephone: (812) 435-8686.
Operated by: Evansville Baseball, LLC.
President: Bill Bussing. **Senior Vice President:** Bix Branson. **General Manager:** Joel Padfield. **Director, Operations:** Jake Riffert. **Controller:** Casie Williams. **Sports Turf Manager:** Lance Adler.
Manager: Andy McCauley.

GAME INFORMATION
No. of Games Broadcast: Home-51, Away-45. **Flagship Station:** WUEV 91.5-FM. **PA Announcer:** Zane Clodfelter.
Stadium Name: Bosse Field. **Location:** US 41 to Lloyd Expressway West (IN-62), Main St Exit, Right on Main St, ahead 1 mile to Bosse Field. **Standard Game Times:** 6:35 p.m., Sun 5:05; **Doubleheaders:** 5:35 p.m.
Visiting Club Hotel: Comfort Inn & Suites, 3901 Hwy 41 N, Evansville, IN 47711.

FLORENCE FREEDOM

Office Address: 7950 Freedom Way, Florence, KY, 41042.
Telephone: (859) 594-4487. **Fax:** (859) 594-3194.
Email Address: info@florencefreedom.com.
Operated by: Canterbury Baseball, LLC.
President: Clint Brown. **General Manager:** Josh Anderson. **Assistant GM, Operations:** Kim Brown. **Director, Ticket Sales:** Zach Ziler. **Groups Sales Manager:** Amanda Sipple. **Director, Food/Beverage:** Joel Bogart. **Director, Business Manager:** Shelli Bitter. **Director, Amateur Baseball:** Greg Ashcraft. **Box Office Manager:** Chanel Lessing. **Stadium Maintenance Director:** Mike Conrad. **Director, Marketing & Promotions:** Knicko Hartung.

Manager: Dennis Pelfrey. **Pitching Coach:** Chad Rhoades. **Hitting Coach:** AJ Cicconi.

GAME INFORMATION
Official Scorer: Joe Gall.
Stadium: UC Health Stadium. **Location:** I71/75 South to exit 180, left onto US 42, right on Freedom Way; I-71/75 North to exit 180. **Standard Game Times:** 6:35 p.m., Fri 7:05, Sat-Sun 6:05.
Visiting Club Hotel: Rodeway Inn, Florence, KY

GATEWAY GRIZZLIES

Telephone: (618) 337-3000. **Fax:** (618) 332-3625.
Email Address: info@gatewaygrizzlies.com. **Website:** www.gatewaygrizzlies.com
Operated by: Gateway Baseball, LLC. **Managing Officer:** Richard Sauget.
General Manager: Steven Gomric. **Assistant General Manager:** Alex Wilson.
Director of Stadium Operations and Events: Kurt Ringkamp. **Director of Corporate Partnerships:** James Caldwell. **Director of Media Relations and Marketing:** Mike Rains. **Radio Broadcaster:** Sam Levitt. **Director of New Media and In-Game Entertainment:** Joe Masterson. **Director of Community Relations:** Shannon Lacker. **Director of Promotions:** Taylor Glueck. **Box Office Manager:** Carly Ketsenburg
Manager: Phil Warren. **Pitching Coach:** Randy Martz. **Trainer:** Geof Manzo.

GAME INFORMATION
Radio Announcer: Sam Levitt. **No of Games Broadcast:** Home-50, Away-48.
PA Announcer: Tom Calhoun. **Stadium Name:** GCS Ballpark. **Location:** I-255 at exit 15 (Mousette Lane). **Standard Game Times:** 7:05 p.m., Sun 6:05 p.m.

JOLIET SLAMMERS

Office Address: 1 Mayor Art Schultz Dr, Joliet, IL 60432
Telephone: (815) 722-2287
E-Mail Address: info@jolietslammers.com. **Website:** www.jolietslammers.com
Owner: Joliet Community Baseball & Entertainment, LLC.
Assistant General Manager: Heather Mills. **Director of Food/Beverage:** Tom Fremarek. **Director, Community Relations:** Ken Miller. **Manager, Corporate Sales:** Porscha Johnson. **Manager, Ticket Sales:** Shawn Hardy. **Manager, Marketing:** Megan Becker.
Manager: Jeff Isom.

GAME INFORMATION
No. of Games Broadcast: 96. **Flagship Station:** www.jolietslammers.com. **Official Scorer:** Dave Laketa. **Stadium Name:** Silver Cross Field. **Location:** 1 Mayor Art Schultz Drive, Joliet, IL 60432. **Standard Game Times:** 7:05 p.m.; Sat 6:05 p.m.; Sun 1:05 p.m. **Visiting Club Hotel:** TBD.

LAKE ERIE CRUSHERS

Address: 2009 Baseball Boulevard. Avon, Ohio 44011.
Telephone: 440-934-3636. **Website:** www.lakeeriecrushers.com.
Operated by: Avon Pro Baseball LLC.
Managing Officer: Tom Kramig. **VP Operations:** Paul Siegwarth. **Accountant:** Unavailable. **Box Office Manager:** Collin DeJong. **Director, Concessions/Catering:** Greg Kobunski. **Director, Marketing & Promotions:** Catie Graf. **Director of Ticketing:** Mike Kalchik. **Account Executive:** Matt Moos, Mike Mays. **Director, Broadcasting:** Andy Barch.
Manager: Chris Mongiardo.

GAME INFORMATION
Stadium Name: All Pro Freight Stadium. **Location:** Intersection of I-90 and Colorado Ave in Avon, OH. **Standard Game Times:** 7:05 p.m., Sun 5:05.

NORMAL CORNBELTERS

Mailing Address: 1000 West Raab Road, Normal, IL 61761.
Telephone: 309-454-2255 (BALL). **Fax:** 309- 454-2287 (BATS).
Ownership: Normal Baseball Group.
President/General Manager: Steve Malliet. **Assistant General Manager:** Jeff Holtke. **Assistant General Manager** Mike Petrini. **Senior Ticket Executive** Brendan O'Neill. **Business Manager:** Deana Roberts. **Director of Community Relations:** Jeff Hager. **Box Office Manager:** Sean

Mendyk. **Public Address Announcer:** Keith Blakenship.
  Field Manager: Brooks Carey.

GAME INFORMATION

  Radio Announcer: Greg Halbleib. **Flagship Station:** Online only at www.Normalbaseball.com **No. of Games Broadcast:** All games streaming online at www.normalbaseball.com
  Stadium Name: The Corn Crib. **Location:** From I-55 North, go south on I-55 and take the 165 exit, turn left at light, turn right on Raab Road to ballpark on right; From I-55 South, go north on I-55 and take the 165 exit, merge onto Route 51 (Main Street), turn right on Raab Road to ballpark on right. **Standard Game Times:** 6:35 p.m., Sun 3:05.

RIVER CITY RASCALS

  Office Address: 900 TR Hughes Blvd, O'Fallon, MO 63366.
  Telephone: (636) 240-2287. **Fax:** (636) 240-7313.
  Email Address: info@rivercityrascals.com. **Website:** www.rivercityrascals.com.
  Operated by: PS and J Professional Baseball Club LLC.
  Owners: Tim Hoeksema, Jan Hoeksema, Fred Stratton, Anne Stratton, Pam Malliet, Steve Malliet, Michael Veeck, Greg Wendt.
  President/General Manager: Dan Dial. **Assistant GM:** Lisa Ferreira. **Senior Director, Ticket Operations:** Tim McConkey. **Director, Stadium Operations:** Tom Bauer. **Director, Food/Beverage:** Maureen Stranz. **Business Manager:** Carrie Green. **Account Executive:** Courtney Adams.
  Manager: Steve Brook.

GAME INFORMATION

  No. of Games Broadcast: Home-48, Away-48. **PA Announcer:** Randy Moehlman.
  Stadium Name: TR Hughes Ballpark. **Location:** I-70 to exit 219, north on TR Hughes Road, follow signs to ballpark. **Standard Game Times:** 6:35 p.m., Sun 4:05.
  Visiting Club Hotel: America's Best Value Inn 1310 Bass Pro Drive St Charles, MO. **Telephone:** (636) 947-5900.

SCHAUMBURG BOOMERS

  Office Address: 1999 Springinsguth Road, Schaumburg, IL 60193
  Email Address: info@boomersbaseball.com **Website:** www.boomersbaseball.com
Owned by: Pat and Lindy Salvi.
  President / General Manager: Pete Laven. **Assistant General Manager Director, Sales:** Mike Kline. **Business Manager:** Todd Fulk. **Director of Facilities:** Mike Tlusty.
Director Food/Beverage: Rich Essegian. **Broadcaster:** Tim Calderwood. **Director of Tickets:** Ryan Kukla. **Director of Entertainment:** Murphy Row. **Director of Community Relations:** Kelsey Gilbert. **Director of Corporate Alliances:** Gerry Clarke. **Director of Stadium Operations:** Nick Hanson. **Account Executive:** Peter Long
  Manager: Jamie Bennett.

GAME INFORMATION

  Broadcaster: Tim Calderwood. **No. of Games Broadcast:** Home-48, Away-48.
  Flagship Station: WRMN 1410 AM Elgin. **Official Scorer:** Ken Trendel.
  Stadium: Schaumburg Boomers Stadium. **Location:** I-290 to Thorndale Ave Exit, head West on Elgin-O'Hare Expressway until Springinsguth Road Exit, second left at Springinsguth Road (shared parking lot with Schaumburg Metra Station). **Visiting Club Hotel:** AmericInn Hotel & Suites, 1300 East Higgins Road, Schaumburg IL 60173.

SOUTHERN ILLINOIS MINERS

  Office Address: Rent One Park, 1000 Miners Drive, Marion, IL 62959.
  Telephone: (618) 998-8499. **Fax:** (618) 969-8550.
  Email Address: info@southernillinoisminers.com. **Website:** www.southernillinoismin-ers.com.
  Operated by: Southern Illinois Baseball Group. **Owner:** Jayne Simmons.
  Chief Operating Officer: Mike Pinto. **Assistant General Manager/Director of Finance;** Cathy Perry. **Director, Ticket Operations:** Jake Holtkamp. **Director, Sponsorships/Promotions:** Jon Brownfield. **Director, Video Production/Creative Services:** Heath Hooker. **Director, Radio Broadcasting/Media Relations:** Jason Guerette . **Account Executive:** Dane Eubanks. **Client Service and DiamondClub Manager,** Rachel Stroud
  Manager: Mike Pinto. **Hitting Coach:** Pat O'Sullivan. **Pitching Coach:** Preston Vancil. **Instructor:** Ralph Santana. **Coach/Advance Scout:** John Lakin. **Advance Scout:** Chris Colwell. **Strength/Conditioning Coordinator:** Chris Stone.

GAME INFORMATION

  No. of Games Broadcast: 96. **Flagship Station:** 97.7 WHET-FM.
  Stadium Name: Rent One Park. **Location:** US 57 to Route 13 East, right at Halfway Road to Fairmont Drive. **Standard Game Times:** 7:05 p.m., Sat 6:05, Sun 5:05.

Visiting Club Hotel: EconoLodge, 1806 Bittle Place, Marion, IL 62959 618-993-1644

TRAVERSE CITY BEACH BUMS

Office Address: 333 Stadium Dr, Traverse City, MI 49685.
Telephone: (231) 943-0100. **Fax:** (231) 943-0900.
Email Address: info@tcbeachbums.com. **Website:** www.tcbeachbums.com.
Operated by: Traverse City Beach Bums, LLC.
Managing Member/President/COO: John Wuerfel. **Member/GM:** Leslye Wuerfel.
Vice President/Director, Baseball Operations: Jason Wuerfel. **Assistant General Manager/Director, Food/Beverage:** Tom Goethel. **Director, Ticketing:** Tony Burch. **Director, Promotion/Community Events:** Jessica Mason. **Manager, Food & Beverage:** Kameron Hollenbeck. **Bookkeeping:** Gretchen Bensinger.
Field Manager: Dan Rohn. **Infield/Hitting Coach:** Jose Vargas. **Pitching Coach:** TBA

GAME INFORMATION
No. of Games Broadcast: 96. **PA Announcer:** Bill Froelich.
Stadium Name: Wuerfel Park. **Location:** Three miles south of the Grand Traverse Mall just off US-31 and M-37 in Chums Village. Stadium is visible from the highway. **Standard Game Times:** 7:05 p.m., Sun 5:05.

WASHINGTON WILD THINGS

Office Address: One Washington Federal Way, Washington, PA 15301.
Telephone: (724) 250-9555. **Fax:** (724) 250-2333.
Email Address: info@washingtonwildthings.com. **Website:** www.washingtonwildthings.com.
Owned by: Sports Facility, LLC. **Operated by:** Washington Frontier League Baseball, LLC.
President/Chief Executive Officer: Stuart Williams. **Managing Partner:** Francine W. Williams. **General Manager:** Steven Zavacky. **Director, Marketing/Communications/Corporate Relations:** Christine Blaine. **Corporate Partnership Account Executives:** Zack Kaminski. **Ticket Manager:** Brian King. **Account Executive:** Easton Le-Mon. **Special Events/Operations:** Wayne Herrod. **Controller:** JJ Heider. **Assistant Controller:** Jordan Millorino. **Creative Services:** Bryan Leones.
Manager: Gregg Langbehn.

GAME INFORMATION
Stadium Name: CONSOL Energy Park. **Location:** I-70 to exit 15 (Chestnut. Street), right on Chestnut Street to Washington Crown Center Mall, right at mall entrance, right on to Mall Drive to stadium. **Standard Game Times:** 7:05 p.m., Sunday 5:05.
Visiting Club Hotel: Red Roof Inn.

WINDY CITY THUNDERBOLTS

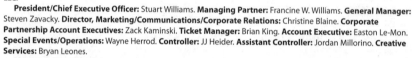

Office Address: 14011 South Kenton Avenue, Crestwood, IL 60445-2252.
Telephone: (708) 489-2255. **Fax:** (708) 489-2999.
Email Address: info@wcthunderbolts.com. **Website:** www.wcthunderbolts.com.
Owned by: Crestwood Professional Baseball, LLC.
General Manager: Mike Lucas. **Assistant GM:** Mike VerSchave. **Director, Community Relations:** Marissa Miller. **Senior Sales Executive:** Bill Waliewski.
Field Manager: Ron Biga. **Pitching Coach:** Will Flynt.

GAME INFORMATION
Radio Announcer: Terry Bonadonna. **No. of Games Broadcast:** 96. **Flagship Station:** WXAV, 88.3 FM. **Official Scorer:** Chris Gbur
Stadium Name: Standard Bank Stadium. **Location:** I-294 to South Cicero Ave, exit (Route 50), south for 1 1/2 miles, left at Midlothian Turnpike, right on Kenton Ave; I-57 to 147th Street, west on 147th to Cicero, north on Cicero, right on Midlothian Turnpike, right on Kenton. **Standard Game Times:** 7:05 pm, Sat 6:05, Sun 2:05/5:05.
Visiting Club Hotel: Georgioís Comfort Inn, 8800 W 159th St, Orland Park, IL 60462. **Telephone:** (708) 403-1100.

ADDITIONAL LEAGUES

PACIFIC ASSOCIATION OF PROFESSIONAL BASEBALL CLUBS

Mailing address: 1379 Canyon Road, Geyserville CA 95441.
Telephone: (707) 857-1780 or (925) 588-3047
Year Founded: 2013.
Ownership Group: Wholly owned by its teams and operators.
Teams: San Rafael Pacifics, Sonoma Stompers, Vallejo Admirals and Pittsburg Diamonds.
Roster Limit: 22. **Eligibility Rules:** None.
2016 Start Date: June 1
Playoff Format: First-half winner plays second half winner (if different teams win each half), play one-game playoff.
Playoff Start Date: Aug. 31.
Brand of Baseball: Rawlings.
Statistician: Pointstreak.

PECOS LEAGUE

Website: http://www.PecosLeague.com.
Address: PO Box 271489, Houston, Tx 77277. **Telephone:** 575-680-2212.
E-mail: info@pecosleague.com
Divisions: Kansas Division-Topeka Train Robbers (Topeka, Kan.); Garden City Wind (Garden City, Kan.); Salina Stockade (Salina Kan.); Great Benders (Great Bend, Kan.).
   South Divison-Alpine Cowboys (Alpine, Texas);Las Cruces Vaqueros (Las Cruces, N.M.); Roswell Invaders (Roswell N.M.); White Sands Pupfish (Alamogordo, N.M.), Santa Fe Fuego (Santa Fe, N.M.) Tucson Saguaros (Tucson Ariz.).
Year Founded: 2010.
Regular Season: 70 games. **Start Date:** May 19. **Playoff Format:** Best of 5 in first round, best of 3 in finals.
Roster Limit: 22.
Eligibility Rules: 25 and under.
Brand of Baseball: National League.

UNITED SHORE PROFESSIONAL BASEBALL LEAGUE

Mailing address: 400 Water Street, Suite 250, Rochester, MI 48307.
Telephone: 248-601-2400.
Email: info@uspbl.com.
Website: www.uspbl.com.
Year Founded: 2016
Ownership Group: General Sports & Entertainment.
Teams: Beavers/Unicorns/Diamond Hoppers.
Roster Limit: 23-25.
Eligibility Rules: 18-25.
2016 Start Date: May 30th.
No of Games: 75.
Playoff Format: Single Game elimination.

INTERNATIONAL

AMERICAS

MEXICO

MEXICAN LEAGUE

MEMBER, NATIONAL ASSOCIATION

NOTE: The Mexican League is a member of the National Association of Professional Baseball Leagues and has a Triple-A classification. However, its member clubs operate largely independent of the 30 major league teams, and for that reason the league is listed in the international section.

Address: Av Insurgentes Sur #797 3er. piso. Col. Napoles. C.P. 03810, Benito Juarez, Mexico, D.F. **Telephone:** 52-55-5557-1007. **Fax:** 52-55-5395-2454. **E-Mail Address:** oficina@lmb.com.mx. **Website:** www.lmb.com.mx.

Years League Active: 1955-.

President: Plinio Escalante Bolio. **Operations Manager:** Nestor Alba Brito.

Division Structure: North—Aguascalientes, Laguna, Mexico City, Monclova, Monterrey, Reynosa, Saltillo, Tijuana. **South**—Campeche, Ciudad del Carmen, Oaxaca, Puebla, Quintana Roo, Tabasco, Veracruz, Yucatan.

Regular Season: 110 games (split-schedule). **2016 Opening Date:** April 1. **Closing Date:** Aug 12.

All-Star Game: May 27-29, Monterrey, Nuevo Leon.

Playoff Format: Eight teams qualify, including first- and second-half division winners plus wild-card teams with best overall records; Quarterfinals, semifinals and finals are all best-of-seven series.

Roster Limit: 28. **Roster Limit, Imports:** 6.

AGUASCALIENTES RAILROADMEN

Office Address: López Mateos # 101 Torre "A" Int 214 y 215, Plaza Cristal, Colonia San Luis, CP 20250. **Telephone:** (52) 449-915-1596. **Fax:** (52) 614-459-0336. **E-Mail Address:** Not available. **Website:** www.rielerosags.com.

President: Mario Rodriguez. **General Manager:** Iram Campos Lara.

Manager: Marco Romero.

CAMPECHE PIRATES

Office Address: Calle Filiberto Qui Farfan No. 2, Col. Camino Real, CP 24020, Campeche, Campeche. **Telephone:** (52) 981-827-4759. **Fax:** (52) 981-827-4767. **E-Mail Address:** piratas@prodigy.net.mx. **Website:** www.piratasdecampeche.mx.

President: Gabriel Escalante Castillo. **General Manager:** Gabriel Lozano Berron.

Manager: Lino Rivera.

CIUDAD DEL CARMEN DOLPHINS

Telephone: (52) 938-286-1627. **E-Mail Address:** contacto@delfinesbeisbol.com.mx. **Website:** http://www.delfinesbeisbol.com.mx

President: Carlos Mejía Berrio.

Manager: Jose Offerman.

LAGUNA COWBOYS

Office Address: Juan Gutenberg s/n, Col Centro, CP 27000, Torreon, Coahuila. **Telephone:** (52) 871-718-5515. **Fax:** (52) 871-717-4335. **E-Mail Address:** Not available. **Website:** www.clubvaqueroslaguna.com.

President: Ricardo Martin Bringas. **General Manager:** Luis Dovalina Flores.

Manager: Mario Mendoza.

MEXICO CITY RED DEVILS

Office Address: Av Cuauhtemoc #451-101, Col Narvarte, CP 03020, Mexico DF. **Telephone:** (52) 555-639-8722. **Fax:** (52) 555-639-9722. **E-Mail Address:** diablos@sportsya.com. **Website:** www.diablos.com.mx.

President: Roberto Mansur Galán. **General Manager:** Roberto Castellon.

Manager: Miguel Ojeda.

MONCLOVA STEELERS

Office Address: Cuauhtemoc #299, Col Ciudad Deportiva, CP 25750, Monclova, Coahuila. **Telephone:** (52) 866-636-2650. **Fax:** (52) 866-636-2688. **E-Mail Address:** acererosdelnorte@prodigy.net.mx. **Website:** www.acereros.com.mx.

General Manager: Donaciano Garza Gutierrez.

Manager: Homar Rojas.

MONTERREY SULTANS

Office Address: Av Manuel Barragan s/n, Estadio Monterrey, Apartado Postal 870, Monterrey, Nuevo Leon, CP 66460. **Telephone:** (52) 81-8351-0209. **Fax:** (52) 81-8351-8022. **E-Mail Address:** sultanes@sultanes.com.mx. **Website:** www.sultanes.com.mx.

President: José Maiz Garcia. **General Manager:** Leobardo Figueroa.

Manager: Felix Fermin.

OAXACA WARRIORS

Office Address: M Bravo 417 Col Centro 68000, Oaxaca, Oaxaca. **Telephone:** (52) 951-515-5522. **Fax:** (52) 951-515-4966. **E-Mail Address:** oaxacaguerreros@gmail.com. **Website:** www.guerreros.mx.

President: Lorenzo Peón Escalante. **General Manager:** Guillermo Spindola Morales.

Manager: Enrique Reyes.

PUEBLA PARROTS

Office Address: Calz Zaragoza S/N, Unidad Deportiva 5 de Mayo, Col Maravillas, CP 72220, Puebla, Puebla. **Telephone:** (52) 222-222-2116. **Fax:** (52) 222-222-2117. **E-Mail Address:** oficina@pericosdepuebla.com.mx. **Website:** www.pericosdepuebla.com.mx.

President: Juan Villareal. **General Manager:** Jose Raul Melendez Habib.

Manager: Matias Carrillo.

QUINTANA ROO TIGERS

Office Address: Av Mayapan Mz 4 Lt 1 Super Mz 21, CP 77500, Cancun, Quintana Roo. **Telephone:** (52) 998-887-3108. **Fax:** (52) 998-887-1313. **E-Mail Address:** tigres@tigrescapitalinos.com.mx. **Website:** www.tigresqr.mx.

President: Cuauhtémoc Rodriguez. **General Manager:** Francisco Minjarez Garcia.

Manager: Jerry Royster.

REYNOSA BRONCOS

Office Address: Paris 511, Esq c/ Tiburcio Garza Zamora Altos, Locales 6 y 7, Col Beatty, Reynosa, Tamps. **Telephone:** (52) 922-3462. **Fax:** (52) 925-7118. **E-Mail Address:** broncosdereynosa@gmail.com. **Website:** www.broncosdereynosa.com.mx.

President: Eliud Villarreal Garza. **General Manager:** Leonardo Clayton Rodríguez.

Manager: Rafael Castaneda.

SALTILLO SARAPE MAKERS

Office Address: Blvd Nazario Ortiz Esquina con Blvd Jesus Sanchez, CP 25280, Saltillo, Coahuila. **Telephone:** (52) 844-416-9455. **Fax:** (52) 844-439-1330. **E-Mail Address:** aley@grupoley.com. **Website:** www.saraperos.com.mx.

President: Alvaro Ley Lopez. **General Manager:** Eduardo Valenzuela Guajardo.

Manager: Juan Rodriguez.

TABASCO OLMECS
Office Address: Av Circuito Deportiva S/N, Col Atasta, Villahermosa, Tabasco, CP 86100. **Telephone:** (52) 993-352-2787. **Fax:** (52) 993-352-2788. **E-Mail Address:** club@olmecastabasco.com. **Website:** www.olmecastabasco.com.
President: Raul Gonzalez Rodriguez. **General Manager:** Luis Guzman Ramos.
Manager: Francisco Estrada.

TIJUANA BULLS
Office Address: Blvd Agua Caliente #11720, Col Hipodromo 22020, Tijuana, BC. **Telephone:** (52) 664-633-3195. **E-Mail Address:** Not available. **Website:** www.torosdetijuana.com.
General Manager: Antonio Cano.
Manager: Juan Castro.

VERACRUZ RED EAGLES
Office Address: Av Jacarandas S/N, Esquina España, Fraccionamiento Virginia, CP 94294, Boca del Rio, Veracruz. **Telephone:** (52) 229-935-5004. **Fax:** (229) 935-5008. **E-Mail Address:** rojosdelaguila@terra.com.mx. **Website:** www.aguiladeveracruz.com.
President: Jose Antonio Mansur Beltran. **General Manager:** Grimaldo Martinez Gonzalez.
Manager: Mark Weidemaier.

YUCATAN LIONS
Office Address: Calle 50 #406-B, Entre 35 y 37, Col Jesus Carranza, CP 97109, Merida, Yucatán. **Telephone:** (52) 999-926-3022. **Fax:** (52) 999-926-3631. **E-Mail Addresses:** mserrano@leones.mx. **Website:** www.leones.mx.
President: Erick Ernesto Arellano Hernández. **General Manager:** Juan Carlos Canizales Castillo.
Manager: Wilfredo Romero.

MEXICAN ACADEMY

Rookie Classification
Mailing Address: Angel Pola No 16, Col Periodista, CP 11220, Mexico, DF Telephone: (52) 555-557-1007. **Fax:** (52) 555-395-2454. **E-Mail Address:** mbl@prodigy.net.mx. **Website:** www.lmbacademia.com.mx.
President: C.P. Plinio Escalante Bolio. **Director General:** Raul Martinez Salazar.
Regular Season: 50 games. **Opening Date:** Not available. **Closing Date:** Not available.

DOMINICAN REPUBLIC
DOMINICAN SUMMER LEAGUE

Member, National Association
Rookie Classification
Mailing Address: Calle Segunda No 64, Reparto Antilla, Santo Domingo, Dominican Republic. **Telephone/Fax:** (809) 532-3619. **Website:** www.dominicansummerleague.com. **E-Mail Address:** ligadeverano@codetel.net.do.
Years League Active: 1985-.
President: Orlando Diaz.
Member Clubs/Division Structure: Boca Chica North—Angels, Astros Orange, Cardinals, Mariners 2, Nationals, Rangers 1. **Boca Chica South**—Dodgers, Giants, Mariners 1, Mets 1, Orioles 2, Red Sox 1, Reds/Diamondbacks, Rockies, Twins, Yankees 1. **Boca Chica Northwest**—Astros Blue, Athletics, Indians, Phillies, Rays, Royals. **Boca Chica Baseball City**—Blue Jays, Diamondbacks, Orioles 1, Padres, Reds, White Sox. **San Pedro de Macoris**—Blue Jays, Braves, Brewers, Marlins, Mets 2, Pirates, Rangers 2, Red Sox 2, Tigers, Yankees 2.
Regular Season: 72 games. **Opening Date:** Unavailable. **Closing Date:** Unavailable.
Playoff Format: Six teams qualify for playoffs, including four division winners and two wild-card teams. Teams with two best records receive a bye to the semifinals; four other playoff teams play best-of-three series. Winners advance to best-of-three semifinals. Winners advance to best-of-five championship series.
Roster Limit: 35 active. **Player Eligibility Rule:** No player may have four or more years of prior minor league service. No draft-eligible player from the U.S. or Canada (not including players from Puerto Rico) may participate in the DSL. No age limits apply.

CHINA
CHINA BASEBALL LEAGUE

Mailing Address: 5, Tiyuguan Road, Beijing 100763, China. **Telephone:** (86) 10-6716-9082. **Fax:** (86) 10-6716-2993. **Website:** baseball.sport.org.cn.
Years League Active: 2002-
Chairman: Hu Jian Guo. **Vice Chairmen:** Tom McCarthy, Shen Wei. **Executive Director:** Yang Jie. **General Manager, Marketing/Promotion:** Lin Xiao Wu.
Member Clubs: Beijing Tigers, Guangdong Leopards, Jiangsu Pegasus, Shanghai Golden Eagles, Sichuan Dragons, Tianjin Lions.

Regular Season: 15 games.
Playoff Format: Top two teams meet in a best-of-three championship.

JAPAN
NIPPON PROFESSIONAL BASEBALL

Mailing Address: Mita Bellju Building, 11th Floor, 5-36-7 Shiba, Minato-ku, Tokyo 108-0014. **Telephone:** 03-6400-1189. **Fax:** 03-6400-1190.
Website: www.npb.or.jp, www.npb.or.jp/eng
Commissioner: Katsuhiko Kumazaki.
Executive Secretary: Atsushi Ihara. **Executive**

Director, Baseball Operations: Minoru Hata. **Executive Director, NPB Rules & Labor:** Nobuhisa "Nobby" Ito.

Executive Director, Central League Operations: Kazuhide Kinefuchi. **Executive Director, Pacific League Operations:** Kazuo Nakano.

Nippon Series: Best-of-seven series between Central and Pacific League champions, begins Oct 22.

All-Star Series: July 15 at Fukuoka Dome; July 16 at Yokohama Stadium.

Roster Limit: 70 per organization (one major league club, one minor league club). Major league club is permitted to register 28 players at a time, though just 25 may be available for each game.

Roster Limit, Imports: Four in majors (no more than three position players or pitchers); unlimited in minors.

CENTRAL LEAGUE

Regular Season: 143 games.

2016 Opening Date: March 25. **Closing Date:** Sept. 27.

Playoff Format: Second-place team meets third-place team in best-of-three series. Winner meets first-place team in best-of-seven series to determine representative in Japan Series (first-place team has one-game advantage to begin series).

CHUNICHI DRAGONS

Mailing Address: Chunichi Bldg 6F, 4-1-1 Sakae, Naka-ku, Nagoya 460-0008. **Telephone:** 052-261-8811. **Fax:** 052-263-7696.

Chairman: Bungo Shirai. **President:** Takao Sasaki. **General Manager:** Hiromitsu Ochiai. **Field Manager:** Motonobu Tanishige.

2016 Foreign Players: Anderson Hernandez, Juan Jaime, Ricardo Nanita, Drew Naylor, Jordan Norberto, Raul Valdes, Dayan Viciedo.

HANSHIN TIGERS

Mailing Address: 2-33 Koshien-cho, Nishinomiya-shi, Hyogo-ken 663-8152. **Telephone:** 0798-46-1515. **Fax:** 0798-46-3555.

Chairman: Shinya Sakai. **President:** Keiichiro Yotsufuji. **Field Manager:** Tomoaki Kanemoto.

2016 Foreign Players: Rafael Dolis, Mauro Gomez, Matt Hague, Marcos Mateo, Randy Messenger, Nelson Perez, Tom O'Malley (Coach).

HIROSHIMA TOYO CARP

Mailing Address: 2-3-1 Minami Kaniya, Minami-ku, Hiroshima 732-8501. **Telephone:** 082-554-1000. **Fax:** 082-568-1190.

President: Hajime Matsuda. **General Manager:** Kiyoaki Suzuki. **Field Manager:** Koichi Ogata.

2016 Foreign Players: Brad Eldred, Bradin Hagens, Jay Jackson, Kris Johnson, Hector Luna, Jason Pridie.

TOKYO YAKULT SWALLOWS

Mailing Address: Seizan Bldg, 4F, 2-12-28 Kita Aoyama, Minato-ku, Tokyo 107-0061. **Telephone:** 03-3405-8960. **Fax:** 03-3405-8961.

Chairman: Sumiya Hori. **President:** Tsuyoshi Kinugasa. **Senior Director:** Junji Ogawa. **Field Manager:** Mitsuru Manaka.

2016 Foreign Players: Wladimir Balentien, Kyle Davies, Josh Lueke, Logan Ondrusek, Luis Perez.

YOKOHAMA DENA BAYSTARS

Mailing Address: Kannai Arai Bldg, 7F, 1-8 Onoe-cho, Naka-ku, Yokohama 231-0015. **Telephone:** 045-681-0811. **Fax:** 045-661-2500.

Chairman: Makoto Haruta. **President:** Jun Ikeda. **General Manager:** Shigeru Takada. **Field Manager:** Alex Ramirez.

2016 Foreign Players: Yoslan Herrera, Jose Lopez,

Guillermo Moscoso, Zach Petrick, Jamie Romak.

YOMIURI GIANTS

Mailing Address: Yomiuri Shimbun Bldg, 26F, 1-7-1 Otemachi, Chiyoda-ku, Tokyo 100-8151. **Telephone:** 03-3246-7733. **Fax:** 03-3246-2726.

Chairman: Kojiro Shiraishi. **President:** Hiroshi Kubo. **General Manager:** Tatsuyoshi Tsutsumi. **Field Manager:** Yoshinobu Takahashi.

2016 Foreign Players: Leslie Anderson, Luis Cruz, Garrett Jones, Scott Mathieson, Hector Mendoza, Miles Mikolas, Aaron Poreda, John Turney (Coach).

PACIFIC LEAGUE

Regular Season: 143 games.

2016 Opening Date: March 25. **Closing Date:** Sept. 28.

Playoff Format: Second-place team meets third-place team in best-of-three series. Winner meets first-place team in best-of-seven series to determine league's representative in Japan Series (first-place team has one-game advantage to begin series).

CHIBA LOTTE MARINES

Mailing Address: 1 Mihama, Mihama-ku, Chiba-shi, Chiba-ken 261-8587. **Telephone:** 03-5682-6341.

Chairman: Takeo Shigemitsu. **President:** Shinya Yamamuro. **Field Manager:** Tsutomu Ito.

2016 Foreign Players: Kuan-Yu Chen, Alfredo Despaigne, Yamaico Navarro, Dae-Eun Rhee, Jason Standridge.

FUKUOKA SOFTBANK HAWKS

Mailing Address: Fukuoka Yahuoku Japan Dome, Hawks Town, 2-2-2 Jigyohama, Chuo-ku, Fukuoka 810-0065. **Telephone:** 092-847-1006. **Fax:** 092-844-4600.

Owner: Masayoshi Son. **Chairman:** Sadaharu Oh. **President:** Yoshimitsu Goto. **Field Manager:** Kimiyasu Kudo.

2015 Foreign Players: Edison Barrios, Barbaro Canizares, Dennis Sarfate, Robert Suarez, Rick VandenHurk.

HOKKAIDO NIPPON HAM FIGHTERS

Mailing Address: 1 Hitsujigaoka, Toyohira-ku, Sapporo 062-8655. **Telephone:** 011-857-3939. **Fax:** 011-857-3900.

Chairman: Juichi Suezawa. **President:** Kenso Takeda. **General Manager:** Hiroshi Yoshimura. **Field Manager:** Hideki Kuriyama.

2016 Foreign Players: Anthony Bass, Brandon Laird, Chris Martin, Luis Mendoza.

ORIX BUFFALOES

Mailing Address: 3-Kita-2-30 Chiyozaki, Nishi-ku, Osaka 550-0023. **Telephone:** 06-6586-0221. **Fax:** 06-6586-0240.

Chairman: Yoshihiko Miyauchi. **President:** Hiroaki Nishina. **General Manager:** Ryuzo Setoyama. **Field Manager:** Junichi Fukura.

2016 Foreign Players: Tony Blanco, Brian Bogusevic, Erik Cordier, Brandon Dickson, Brent Morel.

SAITAMA SEIBU LIONS

Mailing Address: 2135 Kami-Yamaguchi, Tokorozawa-shi, Saitama-ken 359-1189. **Telephone:** 04-2924-1155. **Fax:** 04-2928-1919.

President: Hajime Igo. **Field Manager:** Norio Tanabe.

2016 Foreign Players: Shun-rin Kaku, C.C. Lee, Ernesto Mejia, Andy Van Hekken, Esmerling Vasquez.

TOHOKU RAKUTEN GOLDEN EAGLES

Mailing Address: 2-11-6 Miyagino, Miyagino-ku, Sendai-shi, Miyagi-ken 983-0045. **Telephone:** 022-298-5300. **Fax:** 022-298-5360.

Chairman: Hiroshi Mikitani. **President:** Yozo Tachibana. **Field Manager:** Masataka Nashida.

2016 Foreign Players: Japhet Amador, Jake Brigham, Radhames Liz, Kam Mickolio, Kenny Ray, Zelous Wheeler.

KOREA
KOREA BASEBALL ORGANIZATION

Mailing Address: 946-16 Dokokdong, Kangnam-gu, Seoul, Korea. **Telephone:** (02) 3460-4600. **Fax:** (02) 3460-4639.
Years League Active: 1982-.
Website: www.koreabaseball.com.
Commissioner: Koo Bon-Neung. **Secretary General:** Yang Hae-Young.
Member Clubs: Doosan Bears, Hanwha Eagles, Kia Tigers, KT Wiz, LG Twins, Lotte Giants, NC Dinos, Nexen Heroes, Samsung Lions, SK Wyverns.
Regular Season: 128 games. **2016 Opening Date:** April 1.
Playoffs: Third- and fourth-place teams meet in best-of-three series; winner advances to meet second-place team in best-of-five series; winner meets first-place team in best-of-seven Korean Series for league championship.
Roster Limit: 26 active through Sept 1, when rosters expand to 31. **Imports:** Two active.

TAIWAN
CHINESE PROFESSIONAL BASEBALL LEAGUE

Mailing Address: 2F, No 32, Pateh Road, Sec 3, Taipei, Taiwan 10559. **Telephone:** 886-2-2577-6992. **Fax:** 886-2-2577-2606. **Website:** www.cpbl.com.tw.
Years League Active: 1990-.
Commissioner: Jenn-Tai Hwang. **Deputy Secretary General:** Hueimin Wang. **E-Mail Address:** richard.wang@cpbl.com.tw.
Member Clubs: Chinatrust Brothers, EDA Rhinos, Lamigo Monkeys, Uni-President 7-Eleven Lions.
Regular Season: 120 games. **2016 Opening Date:** Not available. **Playoffs:** Half-season winners are eligible for the postseason. If a non-half-season winner team possesses a higher overall winning percentage than any other half-season winner, then this team gains a wild-card and will play a best-of-five series against the half-season winner with lower winner percentage.
The winner of the playoff series advances to Taiwan Series (best-of-seven).

EUROPE

NETHERLANDS
DUTCH MAJOR LEAGUE

Mailing Address: Koninklijke Nederlandse Baseball en Softball Bond (Royal Dutch Baseball and Softball Association), Postbus 2650, 3430 GB Nieuwegein, Holland. **Telephone:** 31-30-751-3650. **Fax:** 31-30-751-3651. **Website:** www.knbsb.nl.
Member Clubs: Corendon Kinheim, DSS, Curacao Neptunus, L&D Amsterdam, Mampaey Hawks, HCAW, UVV, Vaessen Pioniers.
President: Bob Bergkamp.

ITALY
ITALIAN BASEBALL LEAGUE

Mailing Address: Federazione Italiana Baseball Softball, Viale Tiziano 74, 00196 Roma, Italy. **Telephone:** 39-06-32297201. **Fax:** 39-06-36858201. **Website:** www.fibs.it.
Member Clubs: Bologna, Godo, Nettuno, Nettuno 2, Parma, Rimini, San Marino, Tomassin.
President: Riccardo Fraccari.

WINTER BASEBALL

CARIBBEAN BASEBALL CONFEDERATION
Mailing Address: Frank Feliz Miranda No 1 Naco, Santo Domingo, Dominican Republic. **Telephone:** (809) 381-2643. **Fax:** (809) 565-4654.
Commissioner: Juan Francisco Puello. **Secretary:** Benny Agosto.
Member Countries: Colombia, Dominican Republic, Mexico, Nicaragua, Puerto Rico, Venezuela (Colombia and Nicaragua do not play in the Caribbean Series).
2017 Caribbean Series: Culiacan, Mexico, February.

DOMINICAN LEAGUE

Office Address: Ave. Tiradentes, Ensanche La Fé, Estadio Quisqueya, Santo Domingo, Dominican Republic. **Telephone:** (809) 567-6371. **Fax:** (809) 567-5720. **E-Mail Address:** ligadom@hotmail.com. **Website:** www.lidom.com.

Years League Active: 1951-.
President: Leonardo Matos Berrido. **Vice President:** Jose Manuel Mallen. **Vice President, Operations:** Don Winston Llenas Davila.
Member Clubs: Aguilas Cibaenas, Estrellas de Oriente, Gigantes del Cibao, Leones del Escogido, Tigres del Licey, Toros del Este.
Regular Season: 50 games. **2016 Opening Date:** Unavailable.
Playoff Format: Top four teams meet in 18-game round-robin. Top two teams advance to best-of-nine series for league championship. Winner advances to Caribbean Series.
Roster Limit: 30. **Imports:** 7.

MEXICAN PACIFIC LEAGUE

Mailing Address: Blvd Solidaridad No 335, Plaza las Palmas, Edificio A, Nivel 1, Local 4, Hermosillo, Sonora, Mexico CP 83246. **Telephone:** (52) 662-310-9714. **Fax:** (52) 662-310-9715. **E-Mail Address:** medios@lmp.mx. **Website:** www.ligadelpacifico.com.mx.
Years League Active: 1958-.
President: Omar Canizales Soto. **Administration:** Remigio Valencia. **General Manager:** Christian O. Valencia Veliz. **Media Manager:** Ramon Ruiz Meyemberg.
Member Clubs: Culiacan Tomateros, Hermosillo Naranjeros, Jalisco Charros, Los Mochis Caneros, Mazatlan Venados, Mexicali Aguilas, Navojoa Mayos, Obregon Yaquis.
Regular Season: 68 games. **2016 Opening Date:** Unavailable.
Playoff Format: Six teams advance to best-of-seven quarterfinals. Three winners and losing team with best record advance to best-of-seven semifinals. Winners meet in best-of-seven series for league championship. Winner advances to Caribbean Series.
Roster Limit: 30. **Imports:** 5.

PUERTO RICAN LEAGUE

Office Address: Avenida Munoz Rivera 1056, Edificio First Federal, Suite 501, Rio Piedras, PR 00925. **Mailing Address:** PO Box 191852, San Juan, PR 00019. **Telephone:** (787) 765-6285, 765-7285. **Fax:** (787) 767-3028. **Website:** www.ligapr.com.
Years League Active: 1938-2007; 2008-
President: Hector Rivera. **Vice President:** Raul Villalobos.
Member Clubs: Caguas Criollos, Carolina Gigantes, Mayaguez Indios, Santurce Canjrejeros.
Regular Season: 40 games. **2016 Opening Date:** Unavailable.
Playoff Format: Top three teams meet in round robin series, with top two teams advancing to best-of-seven final. Winner advances to Caribbean Series.
Roster Limit: 30. **Imports:** 5.

VENEZUELAN LEAGUE

Mailing Address: Avenida Casanova, Centro Comercial "El Recreo," Torre Sur, Piso 3, Oficinas 6 y 7, Sabana Grande, Caracas, Venezuela. **Telephone:** (58) 212-761-6408. **Fax:** (58) 212-761-7661. **Website:** www.lvbp.com.
Years League Active: 1946-.
President: Oscar Prieto Párraga. **Vice Presidents:** Humberto Angrisano, Domingo Santander. **General Manager:** Domingo Alvarez.
Member Clubs: Anzoategui Caribes, Aragua Tigres, Caracas Leones, La Guaira Tiburones, Lara Cardenales, Magallanes Navegantes, Margarita Bravos, Zulia Aguilas.
Regular Season: 64 games. **2016 Opening Date:** Unavailable.
Playoff Format: Top two teams in each division, plus a wild-card team, meet in 16-game round-robin series. Top two finishers meet in best-of-seven series for league

championship. Winner advances to Caribbean Series.
Roster Limit: 26. **Imports:** 7.

COLOMBIAN LEAGUE

Office/Mailing Address: Cra54 No 47-01 Estadio Tomas Arrieta, Baranquilla, Colombia. **Telephone:** 370-5083. **E-mail Address:** ligadebeisbolprocol@hotmail.com. **Website:** www.lcbp.com.co.
President: Edinson Renteria. **Vice Presidents:** Edgar Perez, George Baladi, Orlando Covo.
Member Clubs: Barranquilla Caimanes, Cartegena Tigres, Monteria Leones, Sincelejo Toros.
Regular season: 65 games. **2016 Opening Date:** Unavailable.
Playoff Format: Top two teams meet in best-of-seven finals for league championship.

AUSTRALIA
AUSTRALIAN BASEBALL LEAGUE

Mailing Address: Suite 203/46 Market St, Sydney NSW 2000, Australia. **Telephone:** (61) 2-8226-0225. **Fax:** (61)-2-8226-0293. **E-Mail Address:** admin@theABL.com.au. **Website:** www.theabl.com.
CEO: Peter Wermuth. **General Manager:** Ben Foster.
Teams: Adelaide Bite, Brisbane Bandits, Canberra Cavalry, Melbourne Aces, Perth Heat, Sydney Blue Sox.
Playoff Format: First-place team plays second-place team in major semifinal; third-place team plays fourth-place team in minor semifinal, both best of three series. Loser of major semifinal plays winner of minor semifinal in best of three series. Winner of that series plays winner of major semifinal in best of three series for league championship.

DOMESTIC LEAGUE
ARIZONA FALL LEAGUE

Mailing Address: 2415 E Camelback Road, Suite 850, Phoenix, AZ 85016. **Telephone:** (602) 281-7250. **Fax:** (602) 281-7313. **E-Mail Address:** afl@mlb.com. **Website:** http://mlb.mlb.com/mlb/events/afl/.
Years League Active: 1992-.
Operated by: Major League Baseball.
Executive Director: Steve Cobb. **Administrator:** Darlene Emert. **Communications:** Paul Jensen.
Teams: Glendale Desert Dogs, Mesa Solar Sox, Peoria Javelinas, Salt River Rafters, Scottsdale Scorpions, Surprise Saguaros.
2016 Opening Date: Unavailable. Play usually opens in mid-October. **Playoff Format:** Division champions meet in one-game championship.
Roster Limit: 30. Players with less than one year of major league service are eligible, with one foreign player and one player below the Double-A level allowed per team.

COLLEGES

COLLEGE ORGANIZATIONS

NATIONAL COLLEGIATE ATHLETIC ASSOCIATION

Mailing Address: 700 W. Washington Street, PO Box 6222, Indianapolis, IN 46206. **Telephone:** (317) 917-6222. **Fax:** (317) 917-6826 (championships), (317) 917-6710 (baseball).

E-mail Addresses: Division I Championship: rprettyman@ncaa.org (Ron Prettyman), rlburhr@ncaa.org (Randy Buhr), ctolliver@ncaa.org (Chad Tolliver), thalpin@ncaa.org (Ty Halpin), jhamilton@ncaa.org (JD Hamilton), kgiles@ncaa.org (Kim Giles). **Division II Championship:** ebreece@ncaa.org (Eric Breece). **Division III:** jpwilliams@ncaa.org (J.P. Williams).

Websites: www.ncaa.org, www.ncaa.com.
President: Dr. Mark Emmert. **Managing director, Division I Championships/Alliances:** Ron Prettyman. **Director, Division I Championships/Alliances:** Randy Buhr. **Assistant Director, Championships/Alliances:** Chad Tolliver. **Division II Assistant Director, Championshps/Alliances:** Eric Breece. **Division III Assistant Director, Championships/Alliances:** J.P. Williams. **Media Contact, Division I Championships, Alliances/College World Series:** J.D. Hamilton. **Playing Rules Contact:** Ty Halpin. **Statistics Contacts:** Jeff Williams (Division I and RPI); Mark Bedics (Division II); Sean Straziscar (Division III).

Chairman, Division I Baseball Committee: Joel Erdmann (Director, Athletics, South Alabama). **Division I Baseball Committee:** Kevin Anderson (Director of Athletics, Maryland); Michael Bobinski (Director of Athletics, Georgia Tech); Patrick Chun (Director of Athletics, Florida Atlantic); Christopher Del Conte (Director of Athletics, Texas Christian); Robert Goodman (Senior Associate Commissioner, Colonial Athletic Association); Shawn Heilbron (Director of Athletics, Stony Brook): Scott Sidwell (Director, Athletics, University of San Francisco); Ray Tanner (Director of Athletics, South Carolina). **Chairman, Division II Baseball Committee:** Doug Jones (Head Baseball Coach, Tusculum). **Chairman, Division III Baseball Committee:** Jim Peeples (Head Baseball Coach, Piedmont College).

2017 National Convention: Jan. 18-21 at Nashville, Tenn.

2016 CHAMPIONSHIP TOURNAMENTS

NCAA DIVISION I
College World Series: Omaha, Neb., June 18-28/29
Super Regionals (8): Campus sites, June 10-13
Regionals (16): Campus sites, June 3-6

NCAA DIVISION II
World Series: USA Baseball National Training Complex, Cary, N.C., May 28-June 4
Regionals (8): Campus sites, May 19-22

NCAA DIVISION III
World Series: Fox Cities Stadium, Appleton, Wis., May27-31
Regionals (8): Campus sites, May 18-22

NATIONAL JUNIOR COLLEGE ATHLETIC ASSOCIATION

Mailing Address: 1631 Mesa Ave., Suite B, Colorado Springs, CO 80906. **Telephone:** (719) 590-9788. **Fax:** (719) 590-7324. **E-mail Address:** mkrug@njcaa.org. **Website:**

www.njcaa.org.
Executive Director: Mary Ellen Leicht. **Director, Division I Baseball Tournament:** Jamie Hamilton. **Director, Division II Baseball Tournament:** Billy Mayberry. **Director, Division III Baseball Tournament:** Bill Ellis. **Director Media Relations:** Mark Krug.

2016 CHAMPIONSHIP TOURNAMENTS

DIVISION I
World Series: Grand Junction, CO, May 28-June 4

DIVISION II
World Series: Enid, OK, May 28-June 4

DIVISION III
World Series: Kinston, NC, May 28-June 4

CALIFORNIA COMMUNITY COLLEGE ATHLETIC ASSOCIATION

Mailing Address: 2017 O St., Sacramento, CA 95811. **Telephone:** (916) 444-1600. **Fax:** (916) 444-2616. **E-Mail Addresses:** ccarter@cccaasports.org, jboggs@cccaasports.org. **Website:** www.cccaasports.org.

Executive Director: Carlyle Carter. **Director, Membership Services:** Jennifer Cardone. **Director, Championships:** George Mategakis. **Assistant Director, Sports Information/Communications:** Jason Boggs. **Director, Membership Services:** Jennifer Cardone, jcardone@cccaasports.org. **Buisness Operations Specialist:** Rina Kasim, rkasim@cccaasports.org. **Administrative Assistant:** Rima Trotter, rtrotter@cccaasports.org.

2016 CHAMPIONSHIP TOURNAMENT

State Championship: Fresno, CA, May 28-30.

NORTHWEST ATHLETIC CONFERENCE

Mailing Address: Clark College TGB 121, 1933 Fort Vancouver Way, Vancouver, WA 98663. **Telephone:** (360) 992-2833. **Fax:** (360) 696-6210. **E-Mail Address:** nwaacc@clark.edu. **Website:** wwww.nwacsports.org.

Executive Director: Marco Azurdia. **Executive Assistant:** Carol Hardin. **Sports Information Director:** Tracy Swisher. **Director, Operations:** Garet Studer. **Compliance Manager:** Jim Jackson.

2016 CHAMPIONSHIP TOURNAMENT

NWAC Championship: Lower Columbia College, Longview, WA, May 26-30.

AMERICAN BASEBALL COACHES ASSOCIATION

Office Address: 4101 Piedmont Parkway, Suite C, Greensboro, NC 27410. **Telephone:** (336) 821-3140. **Fax:** (336) 886-0000. **E-Mail Address:** abca@abca.org. **Website:** www.abca.org.

Executive Director: Craig Keilitz. **Director, Exhibits/Branding:** Juahn Clark. **Communications/Business Coordinator:** Jon Litchfield. **Membership/Convention Coordinator:** Zach Haile.

Chairman: Mark Johnson. **President:** John Casey (Tufts).

2017 National Convention: Jan. 5-8 in Anaheim, Calif.

NCAA DIVISION I CONFERENCES

AMERICA EAST CONFERENCE

Mailing Address: 451 D Street, Suite 702, Boston, MA 02127. **Telephone:** (617) 695-6369. **Fax:** (617) 695-6380.
E-Mail Address: hager@americaeast.com.
Website: www.americaeast.com.
Baseball Members (First Year): Albany (2002), Binghamton (2002), Hartford (1990), Maine (1990), Maryland-Baltimore County (2004), Massachusetts-Lowell (2014), Stony Brook (2002). **Director, Strategic Media/ Baseball Contact:** Jared Hager. **2016 Tournament:** Four teams, double-elimination, May 21-24 at LeLacheur Park, Lowell, Mass.

AMERICAN ATHLETIC CONFERENCE

Mailing Address: 15 Park Row West, Providence, RI 02903. **Telephone:** (401) 453-0660. **Fax:** (401) 751-8540.
E-Mail Address: csullivan@theamerican.org.
Website: www.theamerican.org.
Baseball Members (First Year): UCF (2014), Cincinnati (2014), Connecticut (2014), East Carolina (2015), Houston (2014), Memphis (2014), USF (2014), Tulane (2015). **Director, Communications:** Chuck Sullivan. **2016 Tournament:** Eight teams, double-elimination until the final, May 24-29 at Clearwater, Fla.

ATLANTIC COAST CONFERENCE

Mailing Address: 4512 Weybridge Ln., Greensboro, NC 27407. **Telephone:** (336) 851-6062. **Fax:** (336) 854-8797.
E-Mail Address: sphillips@theacc.org.
Website: www.theacc.com.
Baseball Members (First Year): Boston College (2006), Clemson (1954), Duke (1954), Florida State (1992), Georgia Tech (1980), Maryland (1954), Miami (2005), North Carolina (1954), North Carolina State (1954), Notre Dame (2014), Pittsburgh (2014), Virginia (1955), Virginia Tech (2005), Wake Forest (1954). **Associate Director, Communications:** Steve Phillips. **2016 Tournament:** Eight teams, group play. May 24-29 at Durham Bulls Athletic Park, Durham, NC.

ATLANTIC SUN CONFERENCE

Mailing Address: 3370 Vineville Ave., Suite 108-B, Macon, GA 31204. **Telephone:** (478) 474-3394. **Fax:** (478) 474-4272.
E-Mail Addresses: pmccoy@atlanticsun.org.
Website: www.atlanticsun.org.
Baseball Members (First Year): East Tennessee State (2006), Florida Gulf Coast (2008), Jacksonville (1999), Kennesaw State (2006), Lipscomb (2004), Mercer (1979), North Florida (2006), Northern Kentucky (2013), South Carolina-Upstate (2008), Stetson (1986). **Director, Sports Information:** Patrick McCoy. **2016 Tournament:** Eight teams, double-elimination. May 25-28 at Lipscomb, Tenn.

ATLANTIC 10 CONFERENCE

Mailing Address: 11827 Canon Blvd., Suite 200, Newport News, VA 23606. **Telephone:** (757) 706-3059. **Fax:** (757) 706-3042.
E-Mail Address: ckilcoyne@atlantic10 .org.
Website: www.atlantic10.com.
Baseball Members (First Year): Davidson (2015), Dayton (1996), Fordham (1996), George Mason (2014), George Washington (1977), La Salle (1996), Massachusetts (1977), Rhode Island (1981), Richmond (2002), St. Bonaventure (1980), Saint Joseph's (1983), Saint Louis

(2006), Virginia Commonwealth (2013). **Commissioner:** Bernadette V. McGlade. **Director, Communications:** Drew Dickerson. **Assistant Director, Communications/ Baseball Contact:** Chris Kilcoyne. **2015 Tournament:** Seven teams, double elimination. May 25-28 at Houlihan Park, Bronx, N.Y.

BIG EAST CONFERENCE

Mailing Address: BIG EAST Conference, 655 3rd Avenue, 7th Floor, New York, NY 10017. **Telephone:** (212) 969-3181. **Fax:** (212) 969-2900.
E-Mail Address: kquinn@bigeast.com.
Website: www.bigeast.com.
Baseball Members (First Year): Butler (2014), Creighton (2014), Georgetown (1985), St. John's (1985), Seton Hall (1985), Villanova (1985), Xavier (2014). **Assistant Commissioner, Olympic Sports/Marketing Communications:** Kristin Quinn. **2015 Tournament:** Four teams, modified double-elimination. May 26-29 at Ripken Field, Aberdeen, Md.

BIG SOUTH CONFERENCE

Mailing Address: 7233 Pineville-Matthews Rd., Suite 100, Charlotte, NC 28226. **Telephone:** (704) 341-7990. **Fax:** (704) 341-7991.
E-Mail Address: brianv@bigsouth.org.
Website: www.bigsouthsports.com.
Baseball Members (First Year): Campbell (2012), Charleston Southern (1983), Coastal Carolina (1983), Gardner-Webb (2009), High Point (1999), Liberty (1991), Longwood (2013), UNC Asheville (1985), Presbyterian (2009), Radford (1983), Winthrop (1983). **Assistant Director, Public Relations/Baseball Contact:** Brian Verdi. **2016 Tournament:** Eight teams, double-elimination. May 24-28, Site TBD.

BIG TEN CONFERENCE

Mailing Address: 5440 Park Place, Rosemont, IL 60018. **Telephone:** (847) 696-1010. **Fax:** (847) 696-1110.
E-Mail Addresses: kkane@bigten.org.
Website: www.bigten.org.
Baseball Members (First Year): Illinois (1896), Indiana (1906), Iowa (1906), Maryland (1893), Michigan (1896), Michigan State (1950), Minnesota (1906), Nebraska (2012), Northwestern (1898), Ohio State (1913), Penn State (1992), Purdue (1906), Rutgers (1870). **2016 Tournament:** Eight teams, double-elimination. May 25-29 at TD Ameritrade Park, Omaha.

BIG 12 CONFERENCE

Mailing Address: 400 E. John Carpenter Freeway, Irving, TX 75062. **Telephone:** (469) 524-1009.
E-Mail Address: lrasmussen@big12sports.com.
Website: www.big12sports.com.
Baseball Members (First Year): Baylor (1997), Kansas (1997), Kansas State (1997), Oklahoma (1997), Oklahoma State (1997), Texas Christian (2013), Texas (1997), Texas Tech (1997), West Virginia (2013). **Director, Communications:** Rob Carolla. **2016 Tournament:** Double-elimination division play. May 25-29 at Chickasaw Bricktown Ballpark, Oklahoma City.

BIG WEST CONFERENCE

Mailing Address: 2 Corporate Park, Suite 206, Irvine, CA 92606. **Telephone:** (949) 261-2525. **Fax:** (949) 261-2528.
E-Mail Address: jstcyr@bigwest.org.

Website: www.bigwest.org.
Baseball Members (First Year): Cal Poly (1997), UC Davis (2008), UC Irvine (2002), UC Riverside (2002), UC Santa Barbara (1970), Cal State Fullerton (1975), Cal State Northridge (2001), Hawaii (2013), Long Beach State (1970). **Director, Communications:** Julie St. Cyr. **2016 Tournament:** None.

COLONIAL ATHLETIC ASSOCIATION

Mailing Address: 8625 Patterson Ave., Richmond, VA 23229. **Telephone:** (804) 754-1616. **Fax:** (804) 754-1973.
E-Mail Address: rwashburn@caasports.com.
Website: www.caasports.com.
Baseball Members (First Year): College of Charleston (2014), Delaware (2002), Elon (2015), Hofstra (2002), James Madison (1986), UNC Wilmington (1986), North-eastern (2006), Towson (2002), William & Mary (1986).
Associate Commissioner/Communications: Rob Washburn. **2016 Tournament:** Six teams, double-elimination. May 25-28 at Charleston, S.C. (College of Charleston).

CONFERENCE USA

Mailing Address: 5201 N. O'Connor Blvd., Suite 300, Irving, TX 75039. **Telephone:** (214) 774-1300. **Fax:** (214) 496-0055.
E-Mail Address: rdanderson@c-usa.org.
Website: www.conferenceusa.com.
Baseball Members (First Year): Alabama-Birmingham (1996), Charlotte (2014), East Carolina (2002), Florida Atlantic (2014), Florida International (2014), Louisiana Tech (2014), Marshall (2006), Middle Tennessee State (2014), Old Dominion (2014), Rice (2006), Southern Mississippi (1996), Tulane (1996), Texas-San Antonio (2014). **Assistant Commissioner, Baseball Operations:** Russell Anderson. **2016 Tournament:** Eight teams, double-elimination. May 25-29 Pete Taylor Park at Hattiesburg, Miss. (Southern Miss).

HORIZON LEAGUE

Mailing Address: 201 S. Capitol Ave., Suite 500, Indianapolis, IN 46225. **Telephone:** (317) 237-5604. **Fax:** (317) 237-5620.
E-Mail Address: bpotter@horizonleague.org.
Website: www.horizonleague.org.
Baseball Members (First Year): Illinois-Chicago (1994), Oakland (2014), Valparaiso (2008), Wright State (1994), Wisconsin-Milwaukee (1994), Youngstown State (2002). **Assistant Commissioner, Messaging and Media:** Bill Potter. **2016 Tournament:** Six teams, modified double-elimination. Hosted by No. 1 seed.

IVY LEAGUE

Mailing Address: 228 Alexander Rd., Second Floor, Princeton, NJ 08544. **Telephone:** (609) 258-6426. **Fax:** (609) 258-1690.
E-Mail Address: trevor@ivyleaguesports.com.
Website: www.ivyleaguesports.com.
Baseball Members (First Year): Rolfe—Brown (1948), Dartmouth (1930), Harvard (1948), Yale (1930). Gehrig—Columbia (1930), Cornell (1930), Pennsylvania (1930), Princeton (1930). **Assistant Executive Director, Communications/Championships:** Trevor Rutledge-Leverenz. **2016 Tournament:** Best-of-three series between division champions. Team with best Ivy League record hosts. Dates unavailable.

METRO ATLANTIC ATHLETIC CONFERENCE

Mailing Address: 712 Amboy Ave., Edison, NJ 08837. **Telephone:** (732) 738-5455.
E-Mail Address: sean.radu@maac.org.
Website: www.maacsports.com.
Baseball Members (First Year): Canisius (1990), Fairfield (1982), Iona (1982), Manhattan (1982), Marist (1998), Monmouth (2014), Niagara (1990), Quinnipiac (2014), Rider (1998), Saint Peter's (1982), Siena (1990). **Assistant Commissioner, New Media:** Lily Rodriguez. **Director, New Media (Baseball Contact):** Ruben Perez Jr. **2016 Tournament:** Six teams, double-elimination. May 25-29 at Dutchess Stadium, Fishkill, N.Y.

MID-AMERICAN CONFERENCE

Mailing Address: 24 Public Square, 15th Floor, Cleveland, OH 44113. **Telephone:** (216) 566-4622. **Fax:** (216) 858-9622.
E-Mail Address: jguy@mac-sports.com.
Website: www.mac-sports.com.
Baseball Members (First Year): Akron (1992), Ball State (1973), Bowling Green State (1952), Buffalo (2001), Central Michigan (1971), Eastern Michigan (1971), Kent State (1951), Miami (1947), Northern Illinois (1997), Ohio (1946), Toledo (1950), Western Michigan (1947). **Director, Communications:** Jeremy Guy. **2016 Tournament:** Eight teams (regardless of division), double-elimination. May 25-29 at All Pro Freight Stadium (Avon, Ohio).

MID-EASTERN ATHLETIC CONFERENCE

Mailing Address: 2730 Ellsmere Ave., Norfolk, VA 23513. **Telephone:** (757) 951-2055. **Fax:** (757) 951-2077.
E-Mail Address: brian.howard@themeac.com; porterp@themeac.com.
Website: www.meacsports.com.
Baseball Members (First Year): Bethune-Cookman (1979), Coppin State (1985), Delaware State (1970), Florida A&M (1979), Maryland Eastern Shore (1970), Norfolk State (1998), North Carolina A&T (1970), North Carolina Central (2012), Savannah State (2012). **Assistant Director, Media Relations/Baseball Contact:** Brian Howard. **2016 Tournament:** six-teams, double-elimination. May 19-22 at Perdue Stadium in Salisbury, Md.

MISSOURI VALLEY CONFERENCE

Mailing Address: 1818 Chouteau Ave., St. Louis, MO 63103. **Telephone:** (314) 444-4300. **Fax:** (314) 444-4333.
E-Mail Address: kbriscoe@mvc.org.
Website: www.mvc-sports.com.
Baseball Members (First Year): Bradley (1955), Dallas Baptist (2014), Evansville (1994), Illinois State (1980), Indiana State (1976), Missouri State (1990), Southern Illinois (1974), Wichita State (1945). **Assistant Commissioner, Communications:** Ashley Dickerson. **2016 Tournament:** Eight-team tournament with two four-team brackets mirroring the format of the College World Series, with the winners of each four-team bracket meeting in a single championship game. May 25-28 at Bob Warn Field at Sycamore Stadium in Terre Haute, Ind.

MOUNTAIN WEST CONFERENCE

Mailing Address: 10807 New Allegiance Dr., Suite 250, Colorado Springs, CO 80921. **Telephone:** (719) 488-4052. **Fax:** (719) 487-7241.
E-Mail Address: jwillson@themw.com.
Website: www.themw.com.
Baseball Members (First Year): Air Force (2000),

Fresno State (2013), Nevada (2013), Nevada-Las Vegas (2000), New Mexico (2000), San Diego State (2000), San Jose State (2014). **Associate Director, Communications:** Judy Willson. **2016 Tournament:** Seven teams; play-in game, followed by six-team double-elimination. May 25-29 at New Mexico.

NORTHEAST CONFERENCE

Mailing Address: 200 Cottontail Lane, Vantage Court South, Somerset, NJ 08873. **Telephone:** (732) 469-0440. **Fax:** (732) 469-0744.
E-Mail Address: rventre@northeast conference.org.
Website: www.northeastconference.org.
Baseball Members (First Year): Bryant (2010), Central Connecticut State (1999), Fairleigh Dickinson (1981), Long Island (1981), Mount St. Mary's (1989), Sacred Heart (2000), Wagner (1981). **Director, Communications/Social Media:** Ralph Ventre. **2016 Tournament:** Four teams, double-elimination. May 26-29 at Dodd Stadium, Norwich, Conn.

OHIO VALLEY CONFERENCE

Mailing Address: 215 Centerview Dr., Suite 115, Brentwood, TN 37027. **Telephone:** (615) 371-1698. **Fax:** (615) 891-1682.
E-Mail Address: kschwartz@ovc.org.
Website: www.ovcsports.com.
Baseball Members (First Year): Austin Peay State (1962), Belmont (2013), Eastern Illinois (1996), Eastern Kentucky (1948), Jacksonville State (2003), Morehead State (1948), Murray State (1948), Southeast Missouri State (1991), Southern Illinois Edwardsville (2012), Tennessee-Martin (1992), Tennessee Tech (1949). **Assistant Commissioner:** Kyle Schwartz. **2016 Tournament:** Six teams, double-elimination. May 25-29 at Jackson, Tenn.

PAC-12 CONFERENCE

Mailing Address: Pac-12 Conference 360 3rd Street, 3rd Floor San Francisco, CA 94107. **Telephone:** (415) 580-4200. **Fax:** (415)549-2828.
E-Mail Address: jolivero@pac-12.org.
Website: www.pac-12.com.
Baseball Members (First Year): Arizona (1979), Arizona State (1979), California (1916), UCLA (1928), Oregon (2009) Oregon State (1916), Southern California (1923), Stanford (1918), Utah (2012), Washington (1916), Washington State (1919). **Public Relations Contact:** Jon Olivero. **2016 Tournament:** None.

PATRIOT LEAGUE

Mailing Address: 3773 Corporate Pkwy., Suite 190, Center Valley, PA 18034. **Telephone:** (610) 289-1950. **Fax:** (610) 289-1951.
E-Mail Address: mdougherty@patriotleague.com.
Website: www.patriotleague.com.
Baseball Members (First Year): Army (1993), Bucknell (1991), Holy Cross (1991), Lafayette (1991), Lehigh (1991), Navy (1993). **Assistant Executive Director, Communications:** Matt Dougherty. **2015 Tournament:** Four teams, May 14-15 and May 21-22 at higher seeds.

SOUTHEASTERN CONFERENCE

Mailing Address: 2201 Richard Arrington Blvd. N., Birmingham, AL 35203. **Telephone:** (205) 458-3000. **Fax:** (205) 458-3030.
E-Mail Address: scartell@sec.org.
Website: www.secsports.com.
Baseball Members (First Year): East—Florida (1933),

Georgia (1933), Kentucky (1933), Missouri (2013), South Carolina (1992), Tennessee (1933), Vanderbilt (1933). **West**—Alabama (1933), Arkansas (1992), Auburn (1933), Louisiana State (1933), Mississippi (1933), Mississippi State (1933), Texas A&M (2013). **Director, Communications:** Chuck Dunlap. **2016 Tournament:** 12 teams, modified single/double-elimination. May 24-29 at Hoover, Ala.

SOUTHERN CONFERENCE

Mailing Address: 702 N. Pine St., Spartanburg, SC 29303. **Telephone:** (864) 591-5100. **Fax:** (864) 591-3448.
E-Mail Address: pperry@socon.org.
Website: www.soconsports.com.
Baseball Members (First Year): The Citadel (1937), ETSU (1979-2005, 2015), Furman (1937), Mercer (2015), UNCG (1998), Samford (2009), VMI (1925-2003, 2015), Western Carolina (1977), Wofford (1998). **Media Relations:** Phil Perry. **2016 Tournament:** Nine teams, single-game play-in for bottom two seeds, then double-elimination followed by a single-elimination championship game. May 19-24 at Fluor Field, Greenville, S.C.

SOUTHLAND CONFERENCE

Mailing Address: 2600 Network Blvd, Suite 150, Frisco, Texas 75034. **Telephone:** (972) 422-9500. **Fax:** (972) 422-9225.
E-Mail Address: mcebold@southland.org
Website: southland.org.
Baseball Members (First Year): Abilene Christian (2014), Central Arkansas (2007), Houston Baptist (2014), Incarnate Word (2014), Lamar (1999), McNeese State (1973), New Orleans (2014), Nicholls (1992), Northwestern State (1988), Sam Houston State (1988), Southeastern Louisiana (1998), Stephen F. Austin State (2006), Texas A&M-Corpus Christi (2007). **Baseball Contact/Assistant Director:** Melissa Cebold. **2016 Tournament:** Two four-team brackets, double-elimination. May 25-28 at Constellation Field, Sugar Land, Texas (Neutral Site).

SOUTHWESTERN ATHLETIC CONFERENCE

Mailing Address: 2101 6th Ave. North, Suite 700, Birmingham, AL 35203. **Telephone:** (205) 251-7573. **Fax:** (205) 297-9820.
E-Mail Address: j.jones@swac.org.
Website: www.swac.org.
Baseball Members (First Year): East Division—Alabama A&M (2000), Alabama State (1982), Alcorn State (1962), Jackson State (1958), Mississippi Valley State (1968). **West Division**—Arkansas-Pine Bluff (1999), Grambling State (1958), Prairie View A&M (1920), Southern (1934), Texas Southern (1954). **Director, Communications:** Bridgette Robles. **2016 Tournament:** Eight teams, double-elimination. May 18-22 at Wesley Barrow Stadium in New Orleans, La.

SUMMIT LEAGUE

Mailing Address: 340 W. Butterfield Rd., Suite 3D, Elmhurst, IL 60126. **Telephone:** (630) 516-0661. **Fax:** (630) 516-0673.
E-Mail Address: mette@thesummitleague.org.
Website: www.thesummitleague.org.
Baseball Members (First Year): IPFW (2008), Omaha (2013), North Dakota State (2008), Oral Roberts (1998), South Dakota State (2008), Western Illinois (1984). **Associate Director, Communications (Baseball Contact):** Greg Mette. **2016 Tournament:** Four teams, double-elimination. May 25-28 at J.L. Johnson Stadium, Tulsa, Okla. (Oral Roberts).

COLLEGE

SUN BELT CONFERENCE

Mailing Address: 1500 Sugar Bowl Dr., New Orleans, LA 70112. **Telephone:** (504) 556-0884. **Fax:** (504) 299-9068.
E-Mail Address: nunez@sunbeltsports.org.
Website: www.sunbeltsports.org.
Baseball Members (First Year): Appalachian State (2015), UALR (1991), Arkansas State (1991), Georgia Southern, (2015), Georgia State (2014), UL Lafayette (1991), UL Monroe (2007), South Alabama (1976), UT Arlington (2014), Texas State (2014), Troy (2006). **Assistant Director, Communications:** Keith Nunez. **2016 Tournament:** Eight teams, double-elimination. May 25-29 at San Marcos, Texas, Bobcat Ballpark (Texas State.)

WESTERN ATHLETIC CONFERENCE

Mailing Address: 9250 East Costilla Ave., Suite 300, Englewood, CO 80112. **Telephone:** (303) 799-9221. **Fax:** (303) 799-3888.
E-Mail Address: cthompson@wac.org.
Website: www.wacsports.com.
Baseball Members (First Year): Cal State Bakersfield (2013), Chicago State (2014), Grand Canyon (2014), New Mexico State (2006), North Dakota (2014), Northern Colorado (2014), Sacramento State (2006), Seattle (2013), Texas-Pan American (2014), Utah Valley (2014). **Commissioner:** Jeff Hurd. **Associate Commissioner:** Dave Chaffin. **Director, Media Relations:** Chris Thompson. **2016 Tournament:** Six teams, double-elimination, May 25-29 at Hohokam Stadium, Mesa, Ariz.

WEST COAST CONFERENCE

Mailing Address: 1111 Bayhill Dr., Suite 405, San Bruno, CA 94066. **Telephone:** (650) 873-8622. **Fax:** (650) 873-7846. **E-Mail Addresses:** rmccrary@westcoast.org (primary), jtourial@westcoast.org (secondary).
Website: www.wccsports.com.
Baseball Members (First Year): Brigham Young (2012), Gonzaga (1996), Loyola Marymount (1968), Pacific (2014), Pepperdine (1968), Portland (1996), Saint Mary's (1968), San Diego (1979), San Francisco (1968), Santa Clara (1968). **Senior Director, Communications:** Ryan McCrary. **Associate Commissioner, Broadcast Administration/Strategic Communications:** Jeff Tourial. **2016 Tournament:** Four teams, May 26-28 at Banner Island Ballpark, Stockton, Calif.

NCAA DIVISION I TEAMS
* Denotes recruiting coordinator

ABILENE CHRISTIAN WILDCATS

Conference: Southland.
Mailing Address: ACU Box 27916 Abilene, TX 79699.
Website: www.acusports.com.
Head Coach: Britt Bonneau. **Telephone:** (325) 668-1983. **Baseball SID:** Lance Fleming. **Telephone:** (325) 674-2693. **Fax:** (325) 674-6798. **Assistant Coaches:** Brad Flanders, *Brandon Stover. **Telephone:** (325) 674-2817.
Home Field: Crutcher Scott Field. **Seating Capacity:** 4,000. **Outfield Dimension:** LF—334, CF—400, RF—334.

AIR FORCE FALCONS

Conference: Mountain West.
Mailing Address: 2169 Field House Drive, USAF Academy, CO 80840.
Website: www.goairforcefalcons.com.
Head Coach: Mike Kazlausky (Maj. retired). **Tele-**

phone: (719) 333-0835. **Baseball SID:** Nick Arseniak. **Telephone:** (719) 333-9251. **Assistant Coaches:** Blake Miller. **Telephone:** (719) 333-7539.
Home Field: Falcon Field. **Seating Capacity:** 1,000.
Outfield Dimension: LF—349, CF— 400, RF— 315.

ALABAMA CRIMSON TIDE

Conference: Southeastern.
Mailing Address: 1201 Coliseum Drive, Tuscaloosa, AL 35401.
Website: www.RollTide.com.
Head Coach: Mitch Gaspard. **Telephone:** (205) 348-4029. **Baseball SID:** Alex Thompson. **Telephone:** (205) 348-6084. **Assistant Coaches:** *Dax Norris, Andy Phillips. **Telephone:** (205) 348-4029.
Home Field: Sewell-Thomas Stadium. **Seating Capacity:** 8,500. **Outfield Dimension:** LF—325, CF—390, RF—320.

ALABAMA A&M BULLDOGS

Conference: Southwestern Athletic.
Mailing Address: 4900 Meridian Street, P.O. Box 1597, Normal, AL 35762.
Website: www.aamusports.com.
Head Coach: Mitch Hill. **Telephone:** (256) 372-4004. **Baseball SID:** Bud McLaughlin. **Telephone:** (256) 372-4005. **Assistant Coaches:** Manny Lora. **Telephone:** (305) 726-9060.
Home Field: Bulldog Baseball Field. **Seating Capacity:** 500. **Outfield Dimension:** LF— 330, CF— 402, RF— 318.

ALABAMA STATE HORNETS

Conference: Southwestern Athletic.
Mailing Address: 915 South Jackson Street, Montgomery, AL 36104.
Website: www.bamastatesports.com.
Head Coach: Mervyl Melendez. **Telephone:** (334) 229-5600. **Baseball SID:** Duane Lewis. **Telephone:** (334) 229-5230. **Assistant Coaches:** *Jose Vazquez, Drew Clark. **Telephone:** (334) 229-5607.
Home Field: Wheeler- Watkins Complex. **Seating Capacity:** 1,000. **Outfield Dimension:** LF—330, CF—400, RF—330.

ALABAMA-BIRMINGHAM BLAZERS

Conference: Conference USA.
Mailing Address: 236 Ullman Building, 1212 University Blvd., Birmingham, AL 35294.
Website: www.uabsports.com.
Head Coach: Brian Shoop. **Telephone:** (205) 934-5181. **Baseball SID:** Andrew Elaimy. **Telephone:** (205) 934-0725. **Assistant Coaches:** Josh Hopper, *Perry Roth. **Telephone:** (205) 934-5184.
Home Field: Regions Field. **Seating Capacity:** 8,500.
Outfield Dimension: LF—320, CF—400, RF—325.

ALBANY GREAT DANES

Conference: America East.
Mailing Address: 1400 Washington Avenue, Albany, NY 12222.
Website: www.UAlbanySports.com.
Head Coach: Jon Mueller. **Telephone:** (548) 442-3014. **Baseball SID:** Lizzie Barlow. **Telephone:** (518) 442-3359. **Assistant Coaches:** Jeff Kaier, *Drew Pearce. **Telephone:** (518) 442-3337.
Home Field: Varsity Field. **Outfield Dimension:** LF—330, CF—400, RF—330.

ALCORN STATE BRAVES

Conference: Southwestern Athletic.
Mailing Address: 1000 ASU Drive #510, Lorman, MS.
Website: www.alcornsports.com.
Head Coach: Bretton Richardson. **Telephone:** (601) 877-4090. **Baseball SID:** Herman Shelton. **Telephone:** (713) 540-3606. **Assistant Coaches:** Oscar Reed, Frank Schaeffer.
Home Field: McGowan Stadium.

APPALACHIAN STATE MOUNTAINEERS

Conference: Sun Belt.
Mailing Address: Appalachian State Box 32025, Boone, NC 28608.
Website: www.appstatesports.com.
Head Coach: Billy Jones. **Telephone:** (828) 262-6097. **Baseball SID:** Mike Flynn. **Telephone:** (828) 262-2845. **Assistant Coaches:** Justin Aspegren, Matt Payne. **Telephone:** (828) 262-8664.
Home Field: Smith Stadium. **Seating Capacity:** 1,000. **Outfield Dimension: LF**—330, **CF**—400, **RF**—330.

ARIZONA WILDCATS

Conference: Pacific-12.
Mailing Address: 1 National Championship Dr., Tucson, AZ, 85721.
Website: www.arizonawildcats.com.
Head Coach: Jay Johnson. **Telephone:** (520) 621-4102. **Baseball SID:** Derrick Fazenidn. **Telephone:** (520) 626-9395. **Fax:** (520) 621-2681. **Assistant Coaches:** *Sergio Brown, David Lawn. **Telephone:** (520) 621-4714.
Home Field: Hi Corbett Field. **Seating Capacity:** 9,500. **Outfield Dimension: LF**—366, **CF**—392, **RF**—349.

ARIZONA STATE SUN DEVILS

Conference: Pacific-12.
Mailing Address: 5999 E. Van Buren; Phoenix, AZ 85008.
Website: www.thesundevils.com.
Head Coach: Tracy Smith. **Telephone:** (480) 965-1904. **Baseball SID:** Thomas Lenneberg. **Telephone:** (480) 965-6594. **Assistant Coaches:** *Ben Greenspan, Brandon Higelin. **Telephone:** (480) 965-3920.
Home Field: Phoenix Municipal Stadium. **Seating Capacity:** 8,775. **Outfield Dimension: LF**—345, **CF**—410, **RF**—345.

ARKANSAS RAZORBACKS

Conference: Southeastern.
Mailing Address: 228 Broyles Center, PO Box 7777, Fayetteville, AR 72701.
Website: www.arkansasrazor backs.com.
Head Coach: Dave Van Horn. **Telephone:** (479) 575-3655. **Assistant Coaches:** Dave Jorn, *Tony Vitello. **Telephone:** (479) 575-3552.
Home Field: Baum Stadium. **Seating Capacity:** 10,737. **Outfield Dimension: LF**—320, **CF**—400, **RF**—320.

ARKANSAS STATE RED WOLVES

Conference: Sun Belt.
Mailing Address: Arkansas State Athletic Department, 217 Olympic Drive, Jonesboro, AR 72401.
Website: www.astateredwolves.com.
Head Coach: Tommy Raffo. **Telephone:** (870) 972-2700. **Baseball SID:** Dennen Cuthbertson. **Telephone:** (870) 972-3383. **Assistant Coaches:** Caleb Longshore,

*Noah Sanders. **Telephone:** (972) 680-4339.
Home Field: Tomlinson Stadium/Kell Field. **Seating Capacity:** 1,200. **Outfield Dimension: LF**—335, **CF**—400, **RF**—335.

ARKANSAS-LITTLE ROCK TROJANS

Conference: Sun Belt.
Mailing Address: 2801 S. University Ave., Little Rock, AR 72204.
Website: www.lrtrojans.com.
Head Coach: Chris Curry. **Telephone:** (501) 663-8095. **Baseball SID:** Tyler Morrison. **Telephone:** (501) 683-7003. **Fax:** (501) 683-7002. **Assistant Coaches:** *Roland Fanning, Russell Raley. **Telephone:** (501) 664-5443.
Home Field: Gary Hogan Field. **Seating Capacity:** 1,000. **Outfield Dimension: LF**—325, **CF**—390, **RF**—305.

ARKANSAS-PINE BLUFF GOLDEN LIONS

Conference: Southwestern Athletic.
Mailing Address: 1200 North University Drive, Pine Bluff, AR 71601.
Website: www.uapblionsroar.com.
Head Coach: Carlos James. **Telephone:** (870) 575-8995. **Baseball SID:** Cameo Stokes. **Telephone:** (870) 575-7949. **Assistant Coaches:** *Joe Tatum, Chris Kirkscey. **Telephone:** (870) 575-8995.
Home Field: Torii Hunter Baseball Complex. **Seating Capacity:** 1,500. **Outfield Dimension: LF**—330, **CF**—400, **RF**—330.

ARMY BLACK KNIGHTS

Conference: Patriot.
Mailing Address: 639 Howard Road, West Point, NY 10996.
Website: www.goarmywestpoint.com.
Head Coach: Matt Reid. **Telephone:** (845) 938-4938. **Baseball SID:** Mark Mohrman. **Telephone:** (845) 938-6929. **Fax:** (845) 938-1725. **Assistant Coaches:** Tyler Cannon, *Anthony DeCicco. **Telephone:** (845) 938-5877.
Home Field: Johnson Stadium at Doubleday Field. **Seating Capacity:** 1,000. **Outfield Dimension: LF**—327, **CF**—400, **RF**—327.

AUBURN TIGERS

Conference: Southeastern.
Mailing Address: Plainsman Park, 351 S Donahue Drive, Auburn, AL 36849.
Website: www.auburntigers.com.
Head Coach: Butch Thompson. **Telephone:** (334) 844-4990. **Baseball SID:** Taylor Bryan. **Telephone:** (334) 750-3862. **Assistant Coaches:** *Brad Bohannon, Doug Sisson. **Telephone:** (334) 844-4990.
Home Field: Plainsman Park. **Seating Capacity:** 4,096. **Outfield Dimension: LF**—310, **CF**—380, **RF**—330.

AUSTIN PEAY STATE GOVERNORS

Conference: Ohio Valley.
Mailing Address: 601 College St. P.O.Box 4515 Clarksville, TN 37044.
Website: www.letsgopeay.com.
Head Coach: Travis Janssen. **Telephone:** (931) 221-6266. **Baseball SID:** Cody Bush. **Telephone:** (931) 221-7561. **Fax:** (931) 221-7562. **Assistant Coaches:** Greg Byron, *Derrick Dunbar. **Telephone:** (931) 221-6392.
Home Field: Raymond C Hand Park. **Seating Capacity:** 777. **Outfield Dimension: LF**—319, **CF**—392, **RF**—329.

BALL STATE CARDINALS

Conference: Mid-American.
Mailing Address: Ball State University HP 386, Muncie, IN 47306.
Website: www.ballstatesports.com.
Head Coach: Rich Maloney. **Telephone:** (765) 285-8911. **Baseball SID:** Michael Clark. **Telephone:** (765) 285-8904. **Assistant Coaches:** *Scott French, Chris Fetter. **Telephone:** (765) 285-2862.
Home Field: First Merchants Ball Park. **Seating Capacity:** 1,000. **Outfield Dimension: LF**—325, **CF**—394, **RF**—325.

BAYLOR BEARS

Conference: Big 12.
Mailing Address: 1612 S. University Parks Dr., Waco, TX 76706.
Website: www.baylorbears.com.
Head Coach: Steve Rodriguez. **Telephone:** (254) 710-3029. **Baseball SID:** Zach Peters. **Telephone:** (254) 710-3784. **Fax:** (254) 710-1369. **Assistant Coaches:** Jon Strauss, *Mike Taylor. **Telephone:** (254) 710-3044.
Home Field: Baylor Ballpark. **Seating Capacity:** 5,000. **Outfield Dimension: LF**—330, **CF**—400, **RF**—330.

BELMONT BRUINS

Conference: Ohio Valley.
Mailing Address: 1900 Belmont Blvd., Nashville, TN 37212.
Website: www.belmontbruins.com.
Head Coach: Dave Jarvis. **Telephone:** (615) 460-6166. **Baseball SID:** Sam Stolte. **Telephone:** (615) 460-8023. **Assistant Coaches:** Matt Barnett, *Aaron Smith. **Telephone:** (615) 460-5586.
Home Field: Rose Park. **Seating Capacity:** 800. **Outfield Dimension: LF**—330, **CF**—400, **RF**—330.

BETHUNE-COOKMAN WILDCATS

Conference: Mid-Eastern Athletic.
Mailing Address: 640 Dr. Mary McLeod Blvd, Daytona Beach FL 32114.
Website: www.bcuathletics.com.
Head Coach: Jason Beverlin. **Telephone:** (386) 481-2224. **Baseball SID:** Bryan Harvey. **Telephone:** (386) 481-2206. **Assistant Coaches:** *Barrett Shaft, Jason Bell. **Telephone:** (386) 481-2241.
Home Field: Jackie Robinson Ballpark. **Seating Capacity:** 6,500. **Outfield Dimension: LF**—317, **CF**—400, **RF**—325.

BINGHAMTON BEARCATS

Conference: America East.
Mailing Address: Binghamton University, Events Center Office #110, Binghamton, NY, 13902.
Website: www.bubearcats.com.
Head Coach: Tim Sinicki. **Telephone:** (607) 777-2525. **Baseball SID:** John Hartrick. **Telephone:** (607) 777-6800. **Assistant Coaches:** *Ryan Hu6rba, Dan Jurik. **Telephone:** (607) 777-4552.
Home Field: Bearcats Sports Complex. **Seating Capacity:** 500. **Outfield Dimension: LF**—325, **CF**—390, **RF**—325.

BOSTON COLLEGE EAGLES

Conference: Atlantic Coast.
Mailing Address: 140 Commonwealth Ave., Chestnut Hill, MA 02467.
Website: www.bceagles.com.
Head Coach: Mike Gambino. **Telephone:** (617) 552-2674. **Baseball SID:** Zanna Ollove. **Telephone:** (617) 552-2004. **Fax:** (617) 552-4903. **Assistant Coaches:** *Jim Foster, Greg Sullivan. **Telephone:** (617) 552-3092.
Home Field: Eddie Pellagrini Diamond at Commander Shea Field. **Seating Capacity:** 1,000. **Outfield Dimension: LF**—330, **CF**—400, **RF**—320.

BOWLING GREEN STATE FALCONS

Conference: Mid-American.
Mailing Address: 1610 Stadium Drive, Bowling Green, Ohio 43403.
Website: www.bgsufalcons.com.
Head Coach: Danny Schmitz. **Telephone:** (419) 372-7065. **Baseball SID:** James Nahikian. **Telephone:** (419) 372-7105. **Assistant Coaches:** *Rick Blanc, Ryan Shay. **Telephone:** (419) 372-7641.
Home Field: Warren E. Steller. **Seating Capacity:** 1,100. **Outfield Dimension: LF**—345, **CF**—400, **RF**—345.

BRADLEY BRAVES

Conference: Missouri Valley.
Mailing Address: 1501 W. Bradley Avenue, Peoria, IL 61625.
Website: www.bradleybraves.com.
Head Coach: Elvis Dominguez. **Telephone:** (309) 677-2684. **Baseball SID:** Bobby Parker. **Telephone:** (309) 677-2624. **Fax:** (309) 677-2626. **Assistant Coaches:** *Sean Lyons, Larry Scully. **Telephone:** (309) 677-4996.
Home Field: Dozer Park. **Seating Capacity:** 7,500. **Outfield Dimension: LF**—310, **CF**—400, **RF**—310.

BRIGHAM YOUNG COUGARS

Conference: West Coast.
Mailing Address: 111 Miller Park, Provo, UT 84062.
Website: www.byucougars.com.
Head Coach: Mike Littlewood. **Telephone:** (801) 422-5049. **Baseball SID:** Ralph Zobell. **Telephone:** (801) 422-9769. **Assistant Coaches:** *Brent Haring, Trent Pratt. **Telephone:** (801) 422-5064.
Home Field: Miller Park. **Seating Capacity:** 2,500. **Outfield Dimension: LF**—330, **CF**—400, **RF**—330.

BROWN BEARS

Conference: Ivy League.
Website: www.brownbears.com.
Head Coach: Grant Achilles. **Telephone:** (434) 221-9652. **Baseball SID:** Christopher Humm. **Telephone:** (401) 863-1095. **Assistant Coaches:** *Mike McCormick, Bill Murphy. **Telephone:** (401) 863-2032.
Home Field: Murray Stadium. **Seating Capacity:** 1,500. **Outfield Dimension: LF**—330, **CF**—415, **RF**—320.

BRYANT BULLDOGS

Conference: Northeast.
Mailing Address: 1150 Douglas Pike, Smithfield, RI 02917.
Website: www.bryantbulldogs.com.
Head Coach: Steve Owens. **Telephone:** (401) 232-6397. **Baseball SID:** Tristan Hobbes. **Telephone:** (401) 232-6558 (ext. 2). **Fax:** (401) 319-5158. **Assistant Coaches:** *Ryan Fecteau, Kyle Pettoruto. **Telephone:** (401) 319-5148.
Home Field: Conaty Park. **Seating Capacity:** 500. **Outfield Dimension: LF**—330, **CF**—400, **RF**—330.

BUCKNELL BISON

Conference: Patriot.
Mailing Address: 701 Moore Avenue, Lewisburg, PA 17837.
Website: www.bucknellbison.com.
Head Coach: Scott Heather. **Telephone:** (570) 577-3593. **Baseball SID:** Todd Merriett. **Telephone:** (570) 577-3488. **Fax:** (570) 577-1660. **Assistant Coaches:** Matt Busch, *Jason Neitz. **Telephone:** (570) 577-1059.
Home Field: Depew Field. **Seating Capacity:** 500.
Outfield Dimension: LF—330, **CF**—400, **RF**—330.

BUFFALO BULLS

Conference: Mid-American.
Mailing Address: 21 Alumni Arena, Buffalo, NY 14150.
Website: www.ubbulls.com.
Head Coach: Ron Torgalski. **Telephone:** (716) 645-6834. **Baseball SID:** Louie Spina. **Telephone:** (716) 645-6837. **Assistant Coaches:** Brad Cochrane, *Steve Ziroli. **Telephone:** (716) 645-6192.
Home Field: Audubon Field. **Seating Capacity:** 500.
Outfield Dimension: LF—330, **CF**—400, **RF**—330.

BUTLER BULLDOGS

Conference: Big East.
Mailing Address: 510 W. 49th Street, Indianapolis, IN 46208.
Website: www.butlersports.com.
Head Coach: Steve Farley. **Telephone:** (317) 940-9721. **Baseball SID:** Kit Stezel. **Telephone:** (317) 940-9994. **Assistant Coaches:** Andy Judkins, *Miles Miller. **Telephone:** (317) 940-6536.
Home Field: Bulldog Park. **Seating Capacity:** 500.
Outfield Dimension: LF—330, **CF**—400, **RF**—330.

CAL POLY MUSTANGS

Conference: Big West.
Mailing Address: Cal Poly Baseball, 1 Grand Avenue, San Luis Obispo, CA 93407.
Website: www.gopoly.com.
Head Coach: Larry Lee. **Telephone:** (805) 756-6367. **Baseball SID:** Eric Burdick. **Telephone:** (805) 756-6550. **Fax:** (805) 756-2650. **Assistant Coaches:** Chal Fanning, *Teddy Warrecker. **Telephone:** (805) 756-2462.
Home Field: Baggett Stadium. **Seating Capacity:** 2,800. **Outfield Dimension: LF**—335, **CF**—405, **RF**—335.

CAL STATE BAKERSFIELD ROADRUNNERS

Conference: Western Athletic.
Mailing Address: 9000 Stockdale Highway, Bakersfield, CA 93311.
Website: www.gorunners.com.
Head Coach: Bob Macluso. **Telephone:** (661) 654-2678. **Baseball SID:** Matt Turk. **Telephone:** (661) 654-3071. **Fax:** (661) 654-6978. **Assistant Coaches:** Jeremy Beard, *Alex Hoover. **Telephone:** (661) 654-2678.
Home Field: Hardt Field. **Seating Capacity:** 2,000.
Outfield Dimension: LF—325, **CF**—390, **RF**—325.

CAL STATE FULLERTON TITANS

Conference: Big West.
Mailing Address: 800 N. State College Blvd., Fullerton, CA 92831.
Website: www.fullertontitans.com.
Head Coach: Rick Vanderhook. **Telephone:** (657) 278-3780. **Baseball SID:** Rafael Guerrero. **Telephone:** (657) 278-7547. **Assistant Coaches:** Chad Baum, *Jason Dietrich. **Telephone:** (657) 278-8449.
Home Field: Goodwin Field. **Seating Capacity:** 3,500.
Outfield Dimension: LF—330, **CF**—400, **RF**—330.

CAL STATE NORTHRIDGE MATADORS

Conference: Big West.
Mailing Address: 18111 Nordhoff St., Northridge, CA 91330.
Website: www.gomatadors.com.
Head Coach: Greg Moore. **Telephone:** (818) 677-7055. **Baseball SID:** Nick Bocanegra. **Telephone:** (818) 677-7188. **Assistant Coaches:** *Jordon Twohig, Chris Hom. **Telephone:** (818) 677-6652.
Home Field: Matador Field. **Seating Capacity:** 1,000.
Outfield Dimension: LF—325, **CF**—390, **RF**—325.

CALIFORNIA GOLDEN BEARS

Conference: Pacific-12.
Mailing Address: Haas Pavilion #4422, Berkley, CA 94720.
Website: www.calbears.com.
Head Coach: David Esquer. **Telephone:** (510) 642-9026. **Baseball SID:** Jordan Stepp. **Telephone:** (510) 642-6895. **Fax:** (510) 643-7778. **Assistant Coaches:** Thomas Eager, *Brad Sanfilippo. **Telephone:** (510) 643-6006.
Home Field: Evans Diamond. **Seating Capacity:** 2,500.
Outfield Dimension: LF—320, **CF**—395, **RF**—320.

CAMPBELL CAMELS

Conference: Big South.
Mailing Address: P.O Box 10, Buies Creek, NC 27506.
Website: www.gocamels.com.
Head Coach: Justin Haire. **Telephone:** (910) 893-1338. **Baseball SID:** Jason Williams. **Telephone:** (910) 814-4367. **Assistant Coaches:** *Chris Marx, Jeff Steele. **Telephone:** (910) 814-4335.
Home Field: Perry Stadium. **Seating Capacity:** 1,500.
Outfield Dimension: LF—337, **CF**—395, **RF**—328.

CANISIUS GOLDEN GRIFFINS

Conference: Metro Atlantic Athletic.
Mailing Address: 2001 Main St., Buffalo, NY 14216.
Website: www.gogriffs.com.
Head Coach: Mike McRae. **Telephone:** (716) 888-8485. **Baseball SID:** Christopher HIll. **Telephone:** (716) 888-8266. **Assistant Coaches:** *Matt Mazurek, Paul Panik. **Telephone:** (716) 888-8478.
Home Field: Demske Sports Complex. **Seating Capacity:** 500. **Outfield Dimension: LF**—327, **CF**—350, **RF**—315.

CENTRAL ARKANSAS BEARS

Conference: Southland.
Mailing Address: PO Box 5004, Conway, AR 72035.
Website: www.ucasports.com.
Head Coach: Allen Gum. **Telephone:** (501) 450-3407. **Baseball SID:** Steve East. **Telephone:** (501) 450-5743. **Assistant Coaches:** Nick Harlan, Trent Kline. **Telephone:** (501) 450-3407.
Home Field: Bear Stadium. **Seating Capacity:** 1,000.
Outfield Dimension: LF—320, **CF**—400, **RF**—320.

CENTRAL CONNECTICUT STATE BLUE DEVILS

Conference: Northeast.
Mailing Address: 1615 Stanley Street, New Britain, CT 06050.
Website: www.ccsubluedevils.com.

COLLEGE

Head Coach: Charlie Hickey. **Telephone:** (860) 832-3074. **Baseball SID:** Jeff Mead. **Telephone:** (860) 832-3057. **Assistant Coaches:** *Pat Hall, Jim Ziogas. **Telephone:** (860) 832-3075.
Home Field: CCSU Baseball Field.

CENTRAL FLORIDA KNIGHTS

Conference: American Athletic.
Mailing Address: 4000 Central Florida Blvd., Orlando, FL 32816.
Website: www.ucfknights.com.
Head Coach: Terry Rooney. **Telephone:** (407) 823-0140. **Baseball SID:** Nate Blythe. **Telephone:** (407) 823-6489. **Fax:** (407) 823-4296. **Assistant Coaches:** *Ryan Klosterman, Brandon Romans. **Telephone:** (407) 823-3260.
Home Field: UCF Baseball Complex. **Seating Capacity:** 3,600. **Outfield Dimension: LF**—325, **CF**—405, **RF**—325.

CENTRAL MICHIGAN CHIPPEWAS

Conference: Mid-American.
Mailing Address: 120 Rose Center, Mount Pleasant, MI 48859.
Website: www.cmuchippewas.com.
Head Coach: Steve Jaksa. **Telephone:** (989) 774-2051. **Baseball SID:** Andy Sneddon. **Telephone:** (989) 774-3277. **Assistant Coaches:** *Jeff Opalewski, Doug Sanders. **Telephone:** (989) 774-1580.
Home Field: Theunissen Stadium. **Seating Capacity:** 2,046. **Outfield Dimension: LF**—330, **CF**—400, **RF**—330.

CHARLESTON SOUTHERN BUCCANEERS

Conference: Big South.
Mailing Address: 9200 University Blvd, North Charleston, SC 29406.
Website: www.csusports.com.
Head Coach: Stuart Lake. **Telephone:** (843) 863-7591. **Baseball SID:** Zeke Beam. **Telephone:** (843) 863-7687. **Assistant Coaches:** Chris Brown, *Adam Ward. **Telephone:** (843) 863-7832.
Home Field: CSU Ballpark. **Seating Capacity:** 1,500. **Outfield Dimension: LF**—320, **CF**—395, **RF**—325.

CHARLOTTE 49ERS

Conference: Conference USA.
Mailing Address: 9201 University City Boulevard, Charlotte, NC 28223.
Website: www.charlotte49ers.com.
Head Coach: Loren Hibbs. **Telephone:** (704) 687-0726. **Baseball SID:** Sean Fox. **Telephone:** (704) 687-1023. **Fax:** (704) 687-4918. **Assistant Coaches:** *Brandon Hall, Bo Robinson. **Telephone:** (704) 687-0728.
Home Field: Hayes Stadium. **Seating Capacity:** 3,200. **Outfield Dimension: LF**—335, **CF**—390, **RF**—335.

CHICAGO STATE COUGARS

Conference: Western Athletic.
Mailing Address: 9501 S King Dr., Chicago, IL 60628.
Website: www.gocsucougars.com.
Head Coach: Steve Joslyn. **Telephone:** (773) 995-3637. **Baseball SID:** Corey Miggins. **Telephone:** (773) 995-2217. **Assistant Coaches:** John Ely, *Dan Pirillo. **Telephone:** (773) 821-4962.
Home Field: Cougar Stadium. **Seating Capacity:** 200. **Outfield Dimension: LF**—330, **CF**—400, **RF**—330.

CINCINNATI BEARCATS

Conference: American Athletic.
Mailing Address: 2741 O'Varsity Way, Richard E. Lindner Center, Cincinnati, OH 45221.
Website: www.gobearcats.com.
Head Coach: Ty Neal. **Telephone:** (513) 556-1577. **Baseball SID:** Alex Lange. **Telephone:** (513) 556-5145. **Assistant Coaches:** *John Lackaff, Ted Tom. **Telephone:** (513) 556-1577.
Home Field: Marge Schott Stadium. **Seating Capacity:** 3,085. **Outfield Dimension: LF**—325, **CF**—400, **RF**—325.

CITADEL BULLDOGS

Conference: Southern.
Mailing Address: McAlister Field House, 171 Moultrie Street, Charleston, SC 29409.
Website: www.citadel sports.com.
Head Coach: Fred Jordan. **Telephone:** (843) 708-9631. **Baseball SID:** Haley Shotwell. **Telephone:** (843) 953-5120. **Assistant Coaches:** *Ryan Mattocks, Daniel Willis. **Telephone:** (843) 953-5905.
Home Field: Riley Park. **Seating Capacity:** 6,000. **Outfield Dimension: LF**—305, **CF**—398, **RF**—337.

CLEMSON TIGERS

Conference: Atlantic Coast.
Mailing Address: 100 Perimeter Road; Clemson, SC 29633.
Website: www.clemsontigers.com.
Head Coach: Monte Lee. **Telephone:** (864) 656-1947. **Baseball SID:** Brian Hennessy. **Telephone:** (864) 656-1921. **Fax:** (864) 656-0299. **Assistant Coaches:** *Bradley LeCroy, Andrew See. **Telephone:** (864) 656-1948.
Home Field: Doug Kingsmore Stadium. **Seating Capacity:** 6,272. **Outfield Dimension: LF**—310, **CF**—390, **RF**—320.

COASTAL CAROLINA CHANTICLEERS

Conference: Big South.
Mailing Address: P.O. Box 261954 Conway, SC 29528.
Head Coach: Gary Gilmore. **Telephone:** (843) 349-2524. **Baseball SID:** Mike Cawood. **Telephone:** (843) 349-2822. **Fax:** (843) 349-2819. **Assistant Coaches:** *Kevin Schnall, Drew Thomas. **Telephone:** (843) 349-2524.
Home Field: Springs Brooks Stadium. **Seating Capacity:** 5,500. **Outfield Dimension: LF**—320, **CF**—390, **RF**—320.

COLLEGE OF CHARLESTON COUGARS

Conference: Colonial Athletic.
Mailing Address: 66 George Street, Charleston, SC 29424.
Website: www.cofcsports.com.
Head Coach: Matt Heath. **Telephone:** (843) 953-5916. **Baseball SID:** Wes Johnson. **Telephone:** (843) 953-3683. **Assistant Coaches:** Austin Morgan, *Jeff Whitfield. **Telephone:** (843) 953-7013.
Home Field: The Ball Park at Patriots Point. **Seating Capacity:** 2,000. **Outfield Dimension: LF**—300, **CF**—400, **RF**—330.

COLUMBIA LIONS

Conference: Ivy.
Mailing Address: 3030 Broadway, New York, NY 10027.

Website: www.gocolumbialions.com.
Head Coach: Bret Boretti. **Telephone:** (212) 854-8448.
Baseball SID: Mike Kowalsky. **Telephone:** (212) 854-7064. **Assistant Coaches:** Erik Supplee, *Dan Tischler.
Telephone: (212) 851-0105.
Home Field: Robertson Field at Satow Stadium. **Seating Capacity:** 600.

CONNECTICUT HUSKIES

Conference: American Athletic.
Mailing Address: 2095 Hillside Road Unit 1173, Storrs, CT 06269.
Website: www.uconnhuskies.com.
Head Coach: Jim Penders. **Telephone:** (860) 208-9140.
Baseball SID: Jeffrey Piascik. **Telephone:** (860) 486-4707.
Assistant Coaches: *Jeffrey Hourigan, Joshua MacDonald. **Telephone:** (860) 465-6088.
Home Field: J.O. Christian Field. **Seating Capacity:** 2,000. **Outfield Dimension: LF**—337, **CF**—400, **RF**—325.

COPPIN STATE EAGLES

Conference: Mid-Eastern Athletic.
Mailing Address: 2523 Gwynns Falls Parkway, Baltimore, MD 21216.
Website: www.coppinstatesports.com.
Head Coach: Sherman Reed. **Telephone:** (410) 951-3723. **Baseball SID:** Jason Pompey. **Telephone:** (410) 951-3729. **Assistant Coaches:** Greg Beckman, *Geoff Kimmel. **Telephone:** (410) 951-6941.
Home Field: Joe Cannon Stadium. **Seating Capacity:** 2,000. **Outfield Dimension: LF**—325, **CF**—425, **RF**—325.

CORNELL BIG RED

Conference: Ivy.
Mailing Address: Teagle Hall, Ithaca, NY 14853.
Website: www.cornellbigred.com.
Head Coach: Dan Pepicelli. **Telephone:** (607) 255-3812. **Baseball SID:** Brandon Thomas. **Telephone:** (607) 255-5627. **Fax:** (607) 255-9791. **Assistant Coaches:** Tom Ford, *Scott Marsh. **Telephone:** (607) 255-6604.
Home Field: Hoy Field. **Seating Capacity:** 830. **Outfield Dimension: LF**—315, **CF**—400, **RF**—325.

CREIGHTON BLUEJAYS

Conference: Big East.
Mailing Address: 2500 California Plaza, Omaha, NE 68178.
Website: www.gocreighton.com.
Head Coach: Ed Servais. **Telephone:** (402) 280-2720.
Baseball SID: Glen Sisk. **Telephone:** (402) 280-2433.
Assistant Coaches: Brian Furlong, *Rich Wallace. **Telephone:** (402) 280-2720.
Home Field: TD Ameritrade Park Omaha. **Seating Capacity:** 24,000. **Outfield Dimension: LF**—335, **CF**—408, **RF**—335.

DALLAS BAPTIST PATRIOTS

Conference: Missouri Valley.
Mailing Address: 3000 Mountain Creek Parkway, Dallas, TX 75211.
Website: www.dbupatriots.com.
Head Coach: Dan Heefner. **Telephone:** (214) 333-5942. **Baseball SID:** Reagan Ratcliff. **Telephone:** (214) 333-5942. **Fax:** (214) 333-5306. **Assistant Coaches:** *Dan Fitzgerald, Rick McCarty. **Telephone:** (214) 333-5942.
Home Field: Horner Ballpark. **Seating Capacity:** 2,000. **Outfield Dimension: LF**—330, **CF**—390, **RF**—330.

DARTMOUTH BIG GREEN

Conference: Ivy.
Mailing Address: 6083 Alumni Gym, Hanover, NH 03755.
Website: www.dartmouthsports.com.
Head Coach: Bob Whalen. **Telephone:** (603) 646-2477.
Baseball SID: Rick Bender. **Telephone:** (603) 646-1030.
Fax: (603) 646-3348. **Assistant Coaches:** *Jonathan Anderson, Evan Wells. **Telephone:** (603) 646-9775.
Home Field: Red Rolfe Field at Biondi Park. **Seating Capacity:** 2,000. **Outfield Dimension: LF**—324, **CF**—403, **RF**—342.

DAVIDSON WILDCATS

Conference: Atlantic 10.
Mailing Address: Box 7158, Davidson, NC 28035.
Website: www.davidsonwildcats.com.
Head Coach: Dick Cooke. **Telephone:** (704) 894-2368.
Baseball SID: Kelly Shuman. **Telephone:** (704) 894-2931.
Fax: (704) 894-2636. **Assistant Coaches:** Ryan Munger, Rucker Taylor. **Telephone:** (704) 894-2772.
Home Field: Wilson Field. **Seating Capacity:** 700.
Outfield Dimension: LF—320, **CF**—385, **RF**—325.

DAYTON FLYERS

Conference: Atlantic 10.
Mailing Address: 300 College Park, Dayton, OH 45469.
Website: www.daytonflyers.com.
Head Coach: Tony Vittorio. **Telephone:** (937) 229-4456. **Baseball SID:** Ross Bagienski. **Telephone:** (937) 229-4491. **Fax:** (937) 877-0948. **Assistant Coaches:** Ryan Cypret, Ryne Romick. **Telephone:** (937) 229-4633.
Home Field: Woerner Field at Time Warner Cable Stadium. **Seating Capacity:** 2,000. **Outfield Dimension: LF**—330, **CF**—400, **RF**—330.

DELAWARE FIGHTIN' BLUE HENS

Conference: Colonial Athletic.
Mailing Address: 631 South College Avenue, Bob Carpenter Center, Newark, DE 19716.
Website: www.bluehens.com.
Head Coach: Jim Sherman. **Telephone:** (302) 831-8596. **Baseball SID:** Scott Selheimer. **Telephone:** (302) 831-8007. **Assistant Coaches:** Dan Hammer, *Brian Walker. **Telephone:** (302) 831-2723.
Home Field: Bob Hannah Stadium. **Seating Capacity:** 2,000. **Outfield Dimension: LF**—320, **CF**—400, **RF**—330.

DELAWARE STATE HORNETS

Conference: Mid-Eastern Athletic.
Mailing Address: 1200 North DuPont Highway, Dover, DE 19901.
Website: www.dsuhornets.com.
Head Coach: J.P. Blandin. **Telephone:** (302) 857-6035.
Baseball SID: Dennis Jones. **Telephone:** (302) 857-6068.
Assistant Coach: Tony Gatto.
Home Field: Solider Field. **Seating Capacity:** 500.
Outfield Dimension: LF—320, **CF**—380, **RF**—320.

DUKE BLUE DEVILS

Conference: Atlantic Coast.
Mailing Address: PO Box 90555, Durham, NC 27708.
Website: www.goduke.com.
Head Coach: Chris Pollard. **Telephone:** (919) 668-0255. **Baseball SID:** Ashley Wolf. **Telephone:** (919) 668-4393. **Fax:** (919) 681-2583. **Assistant Coaches:** *Josh

Jordan, Pete Maki. **Telephone:** (919) 668-5735. **Home Field:** Durham Bulls Athletic Park. **Seating Capacity:** 10,000. **Outfield Dimension: LF**—305, **CF**—400, **RF**—325.

EAST CAROLINA PIRATES

Conference: American Athletic.
Mailing Address: 102 Clark-LeClair Stadium, Greenville, NC 27858.
Website: www.ecupirates.com.
Head Coach: Cliff Godwin. **Telephone:** (252) 737-1985. **Baseball SID:** Malcolm Gray. **Telephone:** (252) 737-4523. **Fax:** (252) 737-4528. **Assistant Coaches:** *Jeff Palumbo, Dan Roszel. **Telephone:** (252) 737-1467.
Home Field: Lewis Field at Clark-LeClair Stadium. **Seating Capacity:** 5,000. **Outfield Dimension: LF**—320, **CF**—400, **RF**—320.

EAST TENNESSEE STATE BUCCANEERS

Conference: Southern.
Mailing Address: 1276 Gilbreath Dr., Box 70300, Johnson City, TN 37614.
Website: www.etsubucs.com.
Head Coach: Tony Skole. **Telephone:** (423) 439-4496. **Baseball SID:** Mitchell Miegel. **Telephone:** (423) 439-8212. **Assistant Coaches:** Chris Gordon. **Telephone:** (423) 736-6591.
Home Field: Thomas Stadium. **Seating Capacity:** 1,000. **Outfield Dimension: LF**—325, **CF**—400, **RF**—325.

EASTERN ILLINOIS PANTHERS

Conference: Ohio Valley.
Mailing Address: 600 Lincoln Avenue, Charleston, IL 61920.
Website: www.eiupanthers.com.
Head Coach: Jason Anderson. **Telephone:** (217) 581-7283. **Baseball SID:** Rich Moser. **Telephone:** (217) 581-7480. **Assistant Coaches:** *Blake Beemer, Julio Godinez. **Telephone:** (217) 581-8510.
Home Field: Coaches Stadium. **Seating Capacity:** 400. **Outfield Dimension: LF**—340, **CF**—390, **RF**—340.

EASTERN KENTUCKY COLONELS

Conference: Ohio Valley.
Mailing Address: 115 Alumni Coliseum, 521 Lancaster Avenue, Richmond, KY 40475.
Website: www.ekusports.com.
Head Coach: Edwin Thompson. **Telephone:** (859) 622-2128. **Baseball SID:** Kevin Britton. **Telephone:** (859) 622-2006. **Fax:** (859) 622-5108. **Assistant Coaches:** *Tyler Hanson, Adam Revelette. **Telephone:** (859) 622-4996.
Home Field: Turkey Hughes Field. **Seating Capacity:** 500. **Outfield Dimension: LF**—340, **CF**—410, **RF**—330.

EASTERN MICHIGAN EAGLES

Conference: Mid-American.
Mailing Address: 206 Bowen Field House, Ypsilanti, MI 48197.
Website: www.emueagles.com.
Head Coach: Mark Van Ameyde. **Telephone:** (734) 487-0315. **Baseball SID:** Dan Whitaker. **Telephone:** (734) 487-0317. **Assistant Coaches:** Eric Roof, *Spencer Schmitz. **Telephone:** (734) 487-1985.
Home Field: Oestrike Stadium. **Seating Capacity:** 1,200. **Outfield Dimension: LF**—330, **CF**—390, **RF**—330.

ELON PHOENIX

Conference: Colonial Athletic.
Mailing Address: 100 Campus Drive, Elon, NC 27244.
Website: www.elonphoenix.com.
Head Coach: Mike Kennedy. **Telephone:** (336) 278-6741. **Baseball SID:** Chris Rash. **Telephone:** (336) 278-6712. **Fax:** (336) 278-6767. **Assistant Coaches:** *Robbie Huffstetler, Micah Posey. **Telephone:** (336) 278-6708.
Home Field: Latham Park. **Seating Capacity:** 2,000. **Outfield Dimension: LF**—328, **CF**—385, **RF**—328.

EVANSVILLE PURPLE ACES

Conference: Missouri Valley.
Mailing Address: 1800 Lincoln Ave. Evansville, IN 47722.
Website: www.gopurpleaces.com.
Head Coach: Wes Carroll. **Telephone:** (812) 488-2059. **Baseball SID:** Clay Trainum. **Telephone:** (812) 488-2394. **Fax:** (812) 488-2199. **Assistant Coaches:** *Cody Fick, Jake Mahon. **Telephone:** (812) 488-2764.
Home Field: Charles H. Braun Stadium. **Seating Capacity:** 1,200. **Outfield Dimension: LF**—330, **CF**—400, **RF**—330.

FAIRFIELD STAGS

Conference: Metro Atlantic Athletic.
Mailing Address: 1073 North Benson Road, Fairfield, CT 06824.
Website: www.fairfieldstags.com.
Head Coach: Bill Currier. **Telephone:** (203) 254-4000 (ext. 2605). **Baseball SID:** Ivey Speight. **Telephone:** (203) 254-4000 (ext. 2878). **Assistant Coaches:** *Mike Cole, Ted Hurvul.
Home Field: Alumni Diamond. **Seating Capacity:** 1,000. **Outfield Dimension: LF**—330, **CF**—400, **RF**—330.

FAIRLEIGH DICKINSON KNIGHTS

Conference: Northeast.
Mailing Address: 1000 River Road, Teaneck, NJ 07666.
Website: www.fduknights.com.
Head Coach: Gary Puccio. **Telephone:** (201) 692-2245. **Baseball SID:** Tom Meade. **Telephone:** (201) 692-2149. **Fax:** (201) 692-9361. **Assistant Coaches:** *Justin McKay. **Telephone:** (201) 692-2245.
Home Field: Naimoli Family Baseball Complex. **Seating Capacity:** 500. **Outfield Dimension: LF**—321, **CF**—370, **RF**—321.

FLORIDA GATORS

Conference: Southeastern.
Mailing Address: University Athletic Association, P.O. Box 14485, Gainesville, FL 32604.
Website: www.florida gators.com.
Head Coach: Kevin OSullivan. **Telephone:** (352) 375-4457. **Baseball SID:** John Hines. **Telephone:** (352) 375-6130. **Fax:** (352) 375-4809. **Assistant Coaches:** *Craig Bell, Brad Weitzel. **Telephone:** (352) 375-4457.
Home Field: Alfred A. McKethan Stadium at Perry Field. **Seating Capacity:** 5,500. **Outfield Dimension: LF**—326, **CF**—400, **RF**—321.

FLORIDA A&M RATTLERS

Conference: Mid-Eastern Athletic.
Mailing Address: 1800 Wahnish Way, Tallahassee, FL 32307.
Website: www.famuathletics.com.

Head Coach: Jamey Shouppe. **Telephone:** (850) 599-3202. **Baseball SID:** Mike Morrell. **Telephone:** (850) 599-3200. **Fax:** (850) 599-3206. **Assistant Coaches:** *Bryan Henry, Anthony Robinson. **Telephone:** (850) 412-7391. **Home Field:** Moore-Kittles Field. **Seating Capacity:** 500. **Outfield Dimension: LF**—330, **CF**—410, **RF**—330.

FLORIDA ATLANTIC OWLS

Conference: Conference USA.
Mailing Address: 777 Glades Road, Boca Raton, FL 33431.
Website: www.fausports.com.
Head Coach: John McCormack. **Telephone:** (561) 297-1055. **Baseball SID:** Brandon Goodwin. **Telephone:** (561) 756-0653. **Fax:** (561) 297-3963. **Assistant Coaches:** *Jason Jackson, Greg Mamula. **Telephone:** (561) 297-3956. **Home Field:** FAU Baseball Stadium. **Seating Capacity:** 2,000. **Outfield Dimension: LF**—330, **CF**—400, **RF**—330.

FLORIDA GULF COAST EAGLES

Conference: Atlantic Sun.
Mailing Address: 10501 FGCU Blvd. S., Fort Myers, FL 33965.
Website: www.fgcuathletics.com.
Head Coach: Dave Tollett. **Telephone:** (239) 590-7051. **Baseball SID:** George Nunnelley. **Telephone:** (239) 590-7064. **Assistant Coaches:** *Rusty McKee, Pete Woodworth. **Telephone:** (239) 590-7059. **Home Field:** Swanson Stadium. **Seating Capacity:** 1,500. **Outfield Dimension: LF**—330, **CF**—400, **RF**—330.

FLORIDA INTERNATIONAL GOLDEN PANTHERS

Conference: Conference USA.
Mailing Address: 11200 SW 8th Street, Miami, FL 33199.
Website: www.fiusports.com.
Head Coach: Turtle Thomas. **Telephone:** (305) 348-3166. **Baseball SID:** Pete Pelegrin. **Telephone:** (305) 348-1357. **Assistant Coaches:** *Mark Kertenian, Dean Stiles. **Telephone:** (305) 348-1048. **Home Field:** FIU Baseball Stadium. **Seating Capacity:** 2,000. **Outfield Dimension: LF**—325, **CF**—400, **RF**—325.

FLORIDA STATE SEMINOLES

Conference: Atlantic Coast.
Mailing Address: PO Box 2195, Tallahassee, FL 32316.
Website: www.seminoles.com.
Head Coach: Mike Martin. **Telephone:** (850) 644-1068. **Baseball SID:** Jon Cole. **Telephone:** (850) 644-5656. **Fax:** (850) 644-3820. **Assistant Coaches:** Mike Bell, *Mike Martin, Jr. **Telephone:** (850) 644-1068. **Home Field:** Mike Martin Field at Dick Howser Stadium. **Seating Capacity:** 6,700. **Outfield Dimension: LF**—340, **CF**—400, **RF**—320.

FORDHAM RAMS

Conference: Atlantic 10.
Mailing Address: 441 East Fordham Road, Bronx, NY 10458.
Website: www.fordhamsports.com.
Head Coach: Kevin Leighton. **Telephone:** (718) 817-4292. **Baseball SID:** Scott Kwiatkowski. **Telephone:** (718) 817-4219. **Fax:** (718) 817-4244. **Assistant Coaches:** *Rob DiToma, Pat Pinkman. **Telephone:** (718) 817-4290. **Home Field:** Houlihan Park. **Seating Capacity:** 1,000. **Outfield Dimension: LF**—338, **CF**—399, **RF**—328.

FRESNO STATE BULLDOGS

Conference: Mountain West.
Mailing Address: 1620 E Bulldog Lane, Fresno, CA 93740.
Website: www.gobulldogs.com.
Head Coach: Mike Batesole. **Telephone:** (559) 278-2178. **Baseball SID:** Travis Blanshan. **Telephone:** (559) 278-4647. **Assistant Coaches:** *Ryan Overland, Steve Rousey. **Telephone:** (559) 278-2178. **Home Field:** Beiden Field. **Seating Capacity:** 5,500. **Outfield Dimension: LF**—330, **CF**—400, **RF**—330.

FURMAN PALADINS

Conference: Southern.
Mailing Address: 3300 Poinsett Highway, Greenville, SC 29613.
Website: www.furmanpaladins.com.
Head Coach: Ron Smith. **Telephone:** (864) 294-2146. **Baseball SID:** Hunter Reid. **Telephone:** (864) 294-2061. **Fax:** (864) 294-3061. **Assistant Coaches:** Taylor Harbin, *Brett Harker. **Telephone:** (864) 294-2243. **Home Field:** Latham Stadium. **Seating Capacity:** 2,000. **Outfield Dimension: LF**—330, **CF**—393, **RF**—330.

GARDNER-WEBB RUNNIN' BULLDOGS

Conference: Big South.
Mailing Address: PO Box 877 Boiling Springs, NC 28017.
Website: www.gwusports.com.
Head Coach: Rusty Stroupe. **Telephone:** (704) 406-4421. **Baseball SID:** Marc Rabb. **Telephone:** (704) 406-4355. **Assistant Coaches:** Ray Greene, Ross Steedley. **Telephone:** (704) 406-3557. **Home Field:** John Henry Moss Stadium/Bill Masters Field. **Seating Capacity:** 750. **Outfield Dimension: LF**—330, **CF**—390, **RF**—330.

GEORGE MASON PATRIOTS

Conference: Atlantic 10.
Mailing Address: 4400 University Drive, Fairfax, VA 22030.
Website: www.gomason.com.
Head Coach: Bill Brown. **Telephone:** (703) 993-3282. **Baseball SID:** Steve Kolbe. **Telephone:** (703) 993-3264. **Fax:** (703) 993-3259. **Assistant Coaches:** *Tag Montague, Brian Pugh. **Telephone:** (703) 993-3328. **Home Field:** Raymond Spuhler Field. **Seating Capacity:** 1,000. **Outfield Dimension: LF**—320, **CF**—400, **RF**—320.

GEORGE WASHINGTON COLONIALS

Conference: Atlantic 10.
Mailing Address: 600 22nd St NW, Washington, DC 20052.
Website: www.gwsports.com.
Head Coach: Gregg Ritchie. **Telephone:** (202) 994-7399. **Baseball SID:** Dan DiVeglio. **Telephone:** (202) 994-0339. **Assistant Coaches:** *Dave Lorber, Tyler McCarthy. **Telephone:** (202) 994-5933. **Home Field:** Tucker Field at Barcroft Park. **Seating Capacity:** 500. **Outfield Dimension: LF**—330, **CF**—380, **RF**—330.

GEORGETOWN HOYAS

Conference: Big East.
Mailing Address: McDonough Arena, Washington, DC 20057.

Website: www.guhoyas.com.
Head Coach: Pete Wilk. Telephone: (202) 687-2462.
Baseball SID: Brendan Thomas. Telephone: (207) 400-2840. Assistant Coaches: Alex Swenson, *Ryan Wood.
Telephone: (202) 687-6406.
Home Field: Shirley Povich Field. Seating Capacity: 1,500. Outfield Dimension: LF—330, CF—375, RF—330.

GEORGIA BULLDOGS

Conference: Southeastern.
Mailing Address: P.O. Box 1472, Athens, GA 30603-1472.
Website: www.georgiadogs.com.
Head Coach: Scott Stricklin. Telephone: (706) 542-7971. Baseball SID: Christopher Lakos. Telephone: (706) 542-7994. Fax: (706) 542-9339. Assistant Coaches: Fred Corral, *Scott Daeley. Telephone: (706) 542-7971.
Home Field: Foley Field. Seating Capacity: 2760. Outfield Dimension: LF—350, CF—404, RF—314.

GEORGIA SOUTHERN EAGLES

Conference: Sun Belt.
Mailing Address: P.O. Box 8086, Statesboro, GA 30460.
Website: www.gseagles.com.
Head Coach: Rodney Hennon. Telephone: (912) 478-7360. Baseball SID: A.J. Henderson. Telephone: (912) 478-5071. Assistant Coaches: Alan Beck, B.J. Green.
Telephone: (912) 478-5188.
Home Field: J.J. Clements Stadium. Seating Capacity: 3,000. Outfield Dimension: LF—330, CF—385, RF—330.

GEORGIA STATE PANTHERS

Conference: Sun Belt.
Mailing Address: P.O. Box 3975, Atlanta, GA 30302.
Website: www.georgiastatesports.com.
Head Coach: Greg Frady. Telephone: (404) 413-4153.
Baseball SID: Allison George. Telephone: (404) 413-4032. Assistant Coaches: *Adam Pavkovich, Adam Scott.
Telephone: (404) 413-4077.
Home Field: GSU Baseball Complex. Seating Capacity: 1,100. Outfield Dimension: LF—334, CF—385, RF—338.

GEORGIA TECH YELLOW JACKETS

Conference: Atlantic Coast.
Mailing Address: 150 Bobby Dodd Way NW, Atlanta, GA 30332.
Website: www.ramblinwreck.com.
Head Coach: Danny Hall. Telephone: (404) 894-5471.
Baseball SID: Mike DeGeorge. Telephone: (404) 894-5467. Assistant Coaches: Jason Howell, *Bryan Prince.
Telephone: (404) 894-5081.
Home Field: Russ Chandler Stadium. Seating Capacity: 4,157. Outfield Dimension: LF—329, CF—390, RF—334.

GONZAGA BULLDOGS

Conference: West Coast.
Mailing Address: 502 E Boone Ave, Spokane, WA 99202.
Website: www.gozags.com.
Head Coach: Mark Machtolf. Telephone: (509) 3134209. Baseball SID: Kyle Scholzen. Telephone: (509) 313-4227. Fax: (509) 313-5730. Assistant Coaches: *Danny Evans, Brandon Harmon. Telephone: (509) 313-4078.
Home Field: Patterson Baseball Complex and Wash-

ington Trust Field. Seating Capacity: 1,500. Outfield Dimension: LF—328, CF—398, RF—328.

GRAMBLING STATE TIGERS

Conference: Southwestern Athletic.
Mailing Address: 403 Main Street, PO Box 4252, Grambling, LA 71245.
Website: www.gsutigers.com.
Head Coach: James Cooper. Telephone: (318) 274-6224. Baseball SID: Robert Vogel. Telephone: (318) 274-6562. Assistant Coaches: Davin Pierre. Telephone: (318) 274-2416.
Home Field: R.W.E. Jones Park.

GRAND CANYON ANTELOPES

Conference: Western Athletic.
Mailing Address: 3300 W. Camelback Road, Phoenix, AZ 85017.
Website: www.gculopes.com.
Head Coach: Andy Stankiewicz. Telephone: (602) 639-6042. Baseball SID: Steven Gonzalez. Telephone: (602) 639-6126 Assistant Coaches: *Nathan Choate, Gregg Wallis. Telephone: (602) 639-7467.
Home Field: Brazell Stadium. Seating Capacity: 1,500. Outfield Dimension: LF—320, CF—385, RF—328.

HARTFORD HAWKS

Conference: America East.
Mailing Address: 200 Bloomfield Ave, West Hartford, CT 06117.
Website: www.hartfordhawks.com.
Head Coach: Justin Blood. Telephone: (860) 768-5760.
Baseball SID: Michael Sivo. Telephone: (860) 768-4620.
Fax: (860) 768-5047. Assistant Coaches: *Steve , Elliot Glynn. Telephone: (860) 768-4972.
Home Field: Fiondella Field. Seating Capacity: 1,500. Outfield Dimension: LF—325, CF—400, RF—325.

HARVARD CRIMSON

Conference: Ivy.
Mailing Address: 65 North Harvard Street, Boston MA 02163.
Website: www.gocrimson.com.
Head Coach: William Decker. Telephone: (617) 495-2629. Baseball SID: Zach Reynolds. Telephone: (617) 495-2206. Assistant Coaches: Bryan Stark, *Mike Zandler. Telephone: (617) 495-3465.
Home Field: O'Donnell Field. Seating Capacity: 1,600. Outfield Dimension: LF—340, CF—415, RF—340.

HAWAII RAINBOW WARRIORS

Conference: Big West.
Mailing Address: 1337 Lower Campus Rd. Honolulu, HI 96822.
Website: www.hawaiiathletics.com.
Head Coach: Mike Trapasso. Telephone: (808) 956-6247. Baseball SID: Michael Stambaugh. Telephone: (808) 968-7505. Assistant Coaches: Carl Fraticelli, *Rusty McNamara. Telephone: (808) 956-6247.
Home Field: Les Murakami Stadium. Seating Capacity: 4,312. Outfield Dimension: LF—325, CF—385, RF—325.

HIGH POINT PANTHERS

Conference: Big South.
Mailing Address: 833 Montlieu Avenue, High Point, NC 27267.

Website: www.highpointpanthers.com. **Head Coach:** Craig Cozart. **Telephone:** (336) 841-9190. **Baseball SID:** Joe Arancio. **Telephone:** (336) 841-4638. **Assistant Coaches:** Jason Laws, *Kenny Smith. **Telephone:** (336) 841-4628. **Home Field:** Williard Stadium. **Seating Capacity:** 550. **Outfield Dimension: LF**—325, **CF**—400, **RF**—330.

HOFSTRA PRIDE

Conference: Colonial Athletic. **Mailing Address:** 230 Hofstra University, PEC Room 233, Hempstead, NY 11549. **Website:** www.gohofstra.com. **Head Coach:** John Russo. **Telephone:** (516) 463-3759. **Baseball SID:** Len Skoros. **Telephone:** (516) 463-4602. **Fax:** (516) 463-7514. **Assistant Coaches:** John Habyan, *Tyler Kavanaugh. **Telephone:** (516) 463-5065. **Home Field:** University Field. **Seating Capacity:** 600. **Outfield Dimension: LF**—322, **CF**—382, **RF**—337.

HOLY CROSS CRUSADERS

Conference: Patriot. **Mailing Address:** One College Street, Worcester, MA 01610. **Website:** www.goholycross.com. **Head Coach:** Greg DiCenzo. **Telephone:** (508) 793-2753. **Baseball SID:** Jim Sarkisian. **Telephone:** (508) 793-2583. **Assistant Coaches:** Jason Falcon, *Ron Rakowski. **Telephone:** (508) 793-2753. **Home Field:** Fitton Field. **Seating Capacity:** 3,000. **Outfield Dimension: LF**—332, **CF**—385, **RF**—313.

HOUSTON COUGARS

Conference: American Athletic. **Mailing Address:** 3204 Cullen Blvd. Houston, Texas 77204. **Website:** www.uhcougars.com. **Head Coach:** Todd Whitting. **Telephone:** (713) 743-9396. **Baseball SID:** Allison McClain. **Telephone:** (713) 743-9404. **Fax:** (713) 743-9411. **Assistant Coaches:** Frank Anderson, Trip Couch. **Telephone:** (713) 743-9404. **Home Field:** Cougar Field. **Seating Capacity:** 3,500. **Outfield Dimension: LF**—330, **CF**—390, **RF**—330.

HOUSTON BAPTIST HUSKIES

Conference: Southland. **Mailing Address:** 7502 Fondren Road, Houston, TX 77074. **Website:** www.hbuhuskies.com. **Head Coach:** Jared Moon. **Telephone:** (281) 649-3332. **Baseball SID:** Russ Reneau. **Telephone:** (281) 649-3098. **Fax:** (281) 649-3496. **Assistant Coaches:** Xavier Hernandez, Russell Stockton. **Telephone:** (281) 649-3262. **Home Field:** Husky Field. **Seating Capacity:** 500. **Outfield Dimension: LF**—330, **CF**—400, **RF**—330.

ILLINOIS FIGHTING ILLINI

Conference: Big Ten. **Mailing Address:** 1700 S. Fourth Street, Champaign, IL 61820. **Website:** www.fightingillini.com. **Head Coach:** Dan Hartleb. **Telephone:** (217) 244-8144. **Baseball SID:** Brett Moore. **Telephone:** (217) 244-2092. **Assistant Coaches:** Adam Christ, *Drew Dickinson. **Telephone:** (217) 244-5539. **Home Field:** Illinois Field. **Seating Capacity:** 1,500. **Outfield Dimension: LF**—330, **CF**—400, **RF**—330.

ILLINOIS STATE REDBIRDS

Conference: Missouri Valley. **Mailing Address:** 207 Horton Field House; Normal, IL 61790. **Website:** www.goredbirds.com. **Head Coach:** Bo Durkac. **Telephone:** (309) 438-4458. **Baseball SID:** Matt Wing. **Telephone:** (309) 438-3249. **Fax:** (309) 438-5634. **Assistant Coaches:** Michael Kellar, *Mike Stalowy. **Telephone:** (309) 438-5151. **Home Field:** Duffy Bass Field. **Seating Capacity:** 1,500. **Outfield Dimension: LF**—330, **CF**—400, **RF**—330.

ILLINOIS-CHICAGO FLAMES

Conference: Horizon. **Mailing Address:** 839 West Roosevelt Rd, Chicago, IL 60608. **Website:** www.uicflames.com. **Head Coach:** Mike Dee. **Telephone:** (312) 996-8645. **Baseball SID:** Eric Phillips. **Telephone:** (312) 355-0716. **Fax:** (312) 996-8349. **Assistant Coaches:** *John Flood, Sean McDermott. **Telephone:** (312) 355-1757. **Home Field:** Les Miller Field at Curtis Granderson Stadium. **Seating Capacity:** 2,000. **Outfield Dimension: LF**—320, **CF**—396, **RF**—324.

INCARNATE WORD CARDINALS

Conference: Southland. **Mailing Address:** 4301 Broadway, San Antonio, TX 78209. **Website:** wwww.uiwcardinals.com. **Head Coach:** Danny Heep. **Telephone:** (210) 829-3830. **Baseball SID:** Daniel Yancelson. **Telephone:** (210) 535-4877. **Assistant Coaches:** Ryan Aguayo, Chase Tidwell. **Telephone:** (210) 805-3025. **Home Field:** Sullivan Field. **Seating Capacity:** 1,000. **Outfield Dimension: LF**—335, **CF**—405, **RF**—335.

INDIANA HOOSIERS

Conference: Big Ten. **Mailing Address:** Assembly Hall, 1001 East 17th Street, Bloomington, IN 47408. **Website:** www.iuhoosiers.com. **Head Coach:** Chris Lemonis. **Telephone:** (812) 855-8240. **Baseball SID:** Greg Kincaid. **Telephone:** (786) 972-1299. **Fax:** (812) 855-9401. **Assistant Coaches:** Kyle Bunn, *Kyle Cheesebrough. **Telephone:** (812) 855-8240. **Home Field:** Bart Kaufman Field. **Seating Capacity:** 2,500. **Outfield Dimension: LF**—330, **CF**—400, **RF**—330.

INDIANA STATE SYCAMORES

Conference: Missouri Valley. **Mailing Address:** 401 N. 4th Street, Arena 104 Terre Haute, IN 47809. **Website:** www.gosycamores.com. **Head Coach:** Mitch Hannahs. **Telephone:** (812) 237-4051. **Baseball SID:** Dan Wacker. **Telephone:** (812) 237-4145. **Fax:** (812) 237-4913. **Assistant Coaches:** *Brian Smiley, Jordan Tiegs. **Telephone:** (812) 237-4090. **Home Field:** Bob Warn Field. **Seating Capacity:** 2,000. **Outfield Dimension: LF**—335, **CF**—395, **RF**—335.

IONA GAELS

Conference: Metro Atlantic Athletic. **Mailing Address:** Hynes Center, 715 North Avenue, New Rochelle, NY 10801. **Website:** www.icgaels.com.

Head Coach: Pat Carey. **Telephone:** (914) 633-2319. **Baseball SID:** Brian Beyrer. **Telephone:** (914) 633-2334. **Assistant Coaches:** Matt Perper, George Schaefer. **Telephone:** (914) 633-2319.
Home Field: City Park.

IOWA HAWKEYES

Conference: Big Ten.
Mailing Address: N411 Carver-Hawkeye Arena, Iowa City, IA 52242.
Website: www.hawkeyesports.com.
Head Coach: Rick Heller. **Telephone:** (319) 335-9257. **Baseball SID:** James Allan. **Telephone:** (319) 335-6439. **Assistant Coaches:** Scott Brickman, *Marty Sutherland. **Telephone:** (319) 335-9257.
Home Field: Duane Banks Field. **Seating Capacity:** 3,000. **Outfield Dimension: LF**—329, **CF**—395, **RF**—329.

IPFW MASTODONS

Conference: Summit.
Mailing Address: 2101 E. Coliseum Blvd., Fort Wayne, IN 46805.
Website: www.gomastodons.com.
Head Coach: Bobby Pierce. **Telephone:** (260) 481-5480. **Baseball SID:** Greg Prouty. **Telephone:** (260) 481-0729. **Assistant Coaches:** *Grant Birely, Connor Lawhead. **Telephone:** (260) 481-5455.
Home Field: Mastodon Field. **Seating Capacity:** 1,000. **Outfield Dimension: LF**—330, **CF**—405, **RF**—330.

JACKSON STATE TIGERS

Conference: Southwestern Athletic.
Mailing Address: 1400 JR Lynch Street Jackson, MS 39203.
Website: www.jsutigers.com.
Head Coach: Omar Johnson. **Telephone:** (601) 979-3930. **Baseball SID:** Wesley Peterson. **Telephone:** (601) 979-5899. **Assistant Coaches:** *Christopher Crenshaw, Frank Solis. **Telephone:** (601) 979-3928.
Home Field: Bob Braddy Field. **Seating Capacity:** 8,000. **Outfield Dimension: LF**—325, **CF**—401, **RF**—325.

JACKSONVILLE DOLPHINS

Conference: Atlantic Sun.
Mailing Address: 2800 University Blvd. N. Jacksonville, FL 32211.
Website: www.judolphins.com.
Head Coach: Tim Montez. **Telephone:** (904) 256-7414. **Baseball SID:** Nolan Alexander. **Telephone:** (904) 256-7444. **Assistant Coaches:** Chris Hayes, *Chuck Jeroloman. **Telephone:** (904) 256-7476.
Home Field: Sessions Stadium. **Seating Capacity:** 3,000. **Outfield Dimension: LF**—340, **CF**—405, **RF**—340.

JACKSONVILLE STATE GAMECOCKS

Conference: Ohio Valley.
Mailing Address: 700 Pelham Road North, Jacksonville, AL 36265.
Website: www.jsugamecock sports.com.
Head Coach: Jim Case. **Telephone:** (256) 782-5367. **Baseball SID:** Tony Schmidt. **Telephone:** (256) 782-5377. **Fax:** (256) 782-5958. **Assistant Coaches:** Evan Bush, Mike Murphree. **Telephone:** (256) 782-8141.
Home Field: Rudy Abbott Field. **Seating Capacity:** 1,500. **Outfield Dimension: LF**—330, **CF**—400, **RF**—335.

JAMES MADISON DUKES

Conference: Colonial Athletic.
Mailing Address: Memorial Hall 1150, 395 South High Street, Baseball Office, Harrisonburg, VA 22807.
Website: www.jmusports.com.
Head Coach: Marlin Ikenberry. **Telephone:** (540) 568-3932. **Baseball SID:** Jason Krech. **Telephone:** (540) 568-7910. **Assistant Coaches:** *Alex Guerra, Jimmy Jackson. **Telephone:** (540) 568-3630.
Home Field: Eagle Field at Veterans Memorial Park. **Seating Capacity:** 1,200. **Outfield Dimension: LF**—340, **CF**—400, **RF**—320.

KANSAS JAYHAWKS

Conference: Big 12.
Mailing Address: 1651 Naismith Drive, Lawrence, KS 66045.
Website: www.kuathletics.com.
Head Coach: Ritch Price. **Telephone:** (785) 864-7907. **Baseball SID:** D.J. Haurin. **Telephone:** (785) 864-3575. **Fax:** (785) 864-7944. **Assistant Coaches:** Ryan Graves, *Ritchie Price. **Telephone:** (785) 864-7907.
Home Field: Hoglund Ballpark. **Seating Capacity:** 2,500. **Outfield Dimension: LF**—330, **CF**—400, **RF**—330.

KANSAS STATE WILDCATS

Conference: Big 12.
Mailing Address: Tointon Family Stadium, 1700 College Ave., Manhattan, KS 66503.
Website: www.kstatesports.com.
Head Coach: Brad Hill. **Telephone:** (785) 532-5723. **Baseball SID:** Chris Kutz. **Telephone:** (785) 532-7976. **Assistant Coaches:** *Tyler Kincaid, Andy Sawyers. **Telephone:** (785) 532-7714.
Home Field: Tointon Family Stadium. **Seating Capacity:** 2,331. **Outfield Dimension: LF**—340, **CF**—400, **RF**—325.

KENNESAW STATE OWLS

Conference: Atlantic Sun.
Mailing Address: 590 Cobb Avenue, Mailbox 0201, Kennesaw, GA 30144.
Website: www.ksuowls.com.
Head Coach: Mike Sansing. **Telephone:** (470) 578-6264. **Baseball SID:** Jake Dorow. **Telephone:** (470) 578-2562. **Assistant Coaches:** Kevin Erminio, *Derek Simmons. **Telephone:** (470) 578-2098.
Home Field: Stillwell Stadium. **Seating Capacity:** 1,200. **Outfield Dimension: LF**—331, **CF**—400, **RF**—330.

KENT STATE GOLDEN FLASHES

Conference: Mid-American.
Mailing Address: MAC Center, PO Box 5190, Kent, OH 44242.
Website: www.kentstatesports.com.
Head Coach: Jeff Duncan. **Telephone:** (330) 672-8432. **Baseball SID:** Mollie Radzinski. **Telephone:** (330) 672-8419. **Assistant Coaches:** Mike Birkbeck, *Alex Marconi. **Telephone:** (330) 672-8433.
Home Field: Schoonover Stadium. **Seating Capacity:** 2,000. **Outfield Dimension: LF**—320, **CF**—415, **RF**—320.

KENTUCKY WILDCATS

Conference: Southeastern.
Mailing Address: 338 Lexington Ave., Lexington, KY 40506.

Website: www.ukathletics.com.
Head Coach: Gary Henderson. **Telephone:** (859) 257-8052. **Baseball SID:** Brent Ingram. **Telephone:** (859) 257-8052. **Assistant Coaches:** *Toby Bicknell, Rick Eckstein. **Telephone:** (859) 257-8000.
Home Field: Cliff Hagan Stadium. **Seating Capacity:** 3,000. **Outfield Dimension: LF**—340, **CF**—390, **RF**—310.

LA SALLE EXPLORERS

Conference: Atlantic 10.
Mailing Address: Hayman Center, 1900 West Olney Avenue, Philadelphia, PA 19141.
Website: www.go explorers.com.
Head Coach: Mike Lake. **Telephone:** (215) 951-1995.
Baseball SID: Mike Adleman. **Telephone:** (215) 951-1637.
Assistant Coaches: Scott Grimes, Michael McCarry.
Telephone: (215) 951-1995.
Home Field: DeVincent Field. **Seating Capacity:** 1,000. **Outfield Dimension: LF**—305, **CF**—410, **RF**—321.

LAFAYETTE LEOPARDS

Conference: Patriot.
Mailing Address: Lafayette College, Alan P. Kirby Sports Center, 420 Hamilton Street, Easton, PA 18042.
Website: www.goleopards.com.
Head Coach: Joe Kinney. **Telephone:** (610) 330-5476.
Baseball SID: Erik Pedersen. **Telephone:** (610) 330-5518.
Fax: (610) 330-5519. **Assistant Coaches:** *Tanner Biagini, Gregg Durrah. **Telephone:** (610) 330-5476.
Home Field: Hilton Rahn '51 Field at Kamine Stadium. **Seating Capacity:** 500. **Outfield Dimension: LF**—332, **CF**—403, **RF**—335.

LAMAR CARDINALS

Conference: Southland.
Mailing Address: Jim Gilligan Way, Beaumont, TX 77705.
Website: www.lamarcardinals.com.
Head Coach: Jim. **Telephone:** (409) 880-8315. **Baseball SID:** Matthew Fowler. **Telephone:** (409) 880-7845.
Assistant Coaches: Scott Hatten, *Jimmy Ricklefsen.
Telephone: (409) 880-8135.
Home Field: Vincent-Beck Stadium. **Seating Capacity:** 3,500. **Outfield Dimension: LF**—325, **CF**—380, **RF**—325.

LEHIGH MOUNTAIN HAWKS

Conference: Patriot.
Mailing Address: 641 Taylor St, Bethlehem, PA 18015.
Website: www.lehighsports.com.
Head Coach: Sean Leary. **Telephone:** (610) 758-4315.
Baseball SID: Chelsea Vielhauer. **Telephone:** (610) 758-5101. **Fax:** (610) 758-6629. **Assistant Coaches:** John Bisco, *John Fugett. **Telephone:** (610) 758-3152.
Home Field: Legacy Park. **Seating Capacity:** 350.
Outfield Dimension: LF—320, **CF**—400, **RF**—320.

LIBERTY FLAMES

Conference: Big South.
Mailing Address: 1971 University Blvd., Lynchburg, VA 24515.
Website: www.libertyflames.com.
Head Coach: Jim Toman. **Telephone:** (434) 582-2305.
Baseball SID: Ryan Bomberger. **Telephone:** (434) 582-2605. **Fax:** (434) 582-2076. **Assistant Coaches:** *Jason Murray, Garrett Quinn. **Telephone:** (434) 582-2119.
Home Field: Liberty Baseball Stadium. **Seating Capacity:** 2,500. **Outfield Dimension: LF**—325, **CF**—371, **RF**—325.

LIPSCOMB BISONS

Conference: Atlantic Sun.
Mailing Address: One University Park Dr, Nashville, TN 37204.
Website: www.lipscombsports.com.
Head Coach: Jeff Forehand. **Telephone:** (615) 966-5716. **Baseball SID:** Kirk Downs. **Telephone:** (615) 966-5457. **Assistant Coaches:** Brad Coon, *Brian Ryman.
Telephone: (615) 966-5149.
Home Field: Ken Dugan Field at Stephen L. Marsh Stadium. **Seating Capacity:** 750. **Outfield Dimension: LF**—330, **CF**—405, **RF**—330.

LONG BEACH STATE DIRTBAGS

Conference: Big West.
Mailing Address: 1250 Bellflower Blvd. Long Beach, CA 90840.
Website: www.longbeachstate.com.
Head Coach: Troy Buckley. **Telephone:** (562) 985-8215. **Baseball SID:** Tyler Hendrickson. **Telephone:** (562) 985-7797. **Assistant Coaches:** Greg Bergeron, Mike Steele. **Telephone:** (562) 985-2125.
Home Field: Blair Field. **Seating Capacity:** 3,000.
Outfield Dimension: LF—348, **CF**—400, **RF**—348.

LONG ISLAND–BROOKLYN BLACKBIRDS

Conference: Northeast.
Mailing Address: 1 University Plaza, Brooklyn, NY 11201.
Website: www.liuathletics.com.
Head Coach: Alex Trezza. **Telephone:** (718) 488-1538. **Baseball SID:** Casey Snedecor. **Telephone:** (718) 488-1307. **Assistant Coaches:** Matt Grosso, Al Sontag.
Telephone: (718) 400-1000 (ext. 3034).
Home Field: LIU Field. **Seating Capacity:** 500. **Outfield Dimension: LF**—300, **CF**—401, **RF**—300.

LONGWOOD LANCERS

Conference: Big South.
Mailing Address: 201 High St. Farmville, VA 23909.
Website: www.longwoodlancers.com.
Head Coach: Ryan Mau. **Telephone:** (434) 395-2843.
Baseball SID: Darius Thigpen. **Telephone:** (434) 395-2345. **Assistant Coaches:** *Chad Oxendine, Daniel Wood.
Telephone: (434) 395-2351.
Home Field: Buddy Bolding Stadium. **Seating Capacity:** 500. **Outfield Dimension: LF**—335, **CF**—400, **RF**—335.

LOUISIANA STATE TIGERS

Conference: Southeastern.
Mailing Address: LSU Athletics Administration Building, Baton Rouge, LA 70803.
Website: www.lsu sports.net.
Head Coach: Paul Mainieri. **Telephone:** (225) 578-4148. **Baseball SID:** Bill Franques. **Telephone:** (225) 578-2527. **Assistant Coaches:** *Andy Cannizaro, Alan Dunn.
Telephone: (225) 578-4148.
Home Field: Alex Box Stadium. **Seating Capacity:** 10,800. **Outfield Dimension: LF**—330, **CF**—400, **RF**—330.

LOUISIANA TECH BULLDOGS

Conference: Conference USA.
Mailing Address: 305 Wisteria St, Ruston, LA 71272.
Website: www.latechsports.com.

Head Coach: Greg Goff. **Telephone:** (318) 257-3314. **Baseball SID:** Anna Claire Thomas. **Telephone:** (318) 257-5314. **Fax:** (318) 257-3757. **Assistant Coaches:** Christian Ostrander, *Jake Wells. **Telephone:** (318) 257-3314. **Home Field:** J.C. Love Field at Pat Patterson Park. **Seating Capacity:** 3,000. **Outfield Dimension: LF**—315, **CF**—385, **RF**—325.

LOUISIANA-LAFAYETTE RAGIN' CAJUNS

Conference: Sun Belt.
Mailing Address: 201 Reinhardt Drive, Lafayette, LA 70506.
Website: www.ragincajuns.com.
Head Coach: Tony Robichaux. **Telephone:** (337) 262-5189. **Baseball SID:** Jeff Schneider. **Telephone:** (337) 482-6332. **Assistant Coaches:** Anthony Babineaux, *Jeremy Talbot. **Telephone:** (337) 262-5189.
Home Field: M.L. Tigue Moore Field. **Seating Capacity:** 4,000. **Outfield Dimension: LF**—330, **CF**—400, **RF**—330.

LOUISIANA-MONROE WARHAWKS

Conference: Sun Belt.
Mailing Address: 308 Warhawk Way Monroe, LA 71209.
Website: www.ulmwarhawks.com.
Head Coach: Bruce Peddie. **Telephone:** (318) 342-3591. **Baseball SID:** Alex Edwards. **Telephone:** (318) 342-5463. **Assistant Coaches:** *Eric Folmar, Chris Smith. **Telephone:** (318) 342-5396.
Home Field: Warhawk Field. **Seating Capacity:** 1,800. **Outfield Dimension: LF**—330, **CF**—405, **RF**—330.

LOUISVILLE CARDINALS

Conference: Atlantic Coast.
Mailing Address: Athletics Department SAC Building, University of Louisville, 2100 South Floyd Street, Louisville, KY 40292.
Website: www.gocards.com.
Head Coach: Dan McDonnell. **Telephone:** (502) 852-0103. **Baseball SID:** Garett Wall. **Telephone:** (502) 852-3088. **Fax:** (502) 852-7401. **Assistant Coaches:** *Eric Snider, Roger Williams. **Telephone:** (502) 852-3929.
Home Field: Jim Patterson Stadium. **Seating Capacity:** 4,000. **Outfield Dimension: LF**—330, **CF**—402, **RF**—330.

LOYOLA MARYMOUNT LIONS

Conference: West Coast.
Mailing Address: 1 LMU Drive, Los Angeles, CA 90045.
Website: www.lmulions.com.
Head Coach: Jason Gill. **Telephone:** (310) 338-2949. **Baseball SID:** Tyler Geivett. **Telephone:** (310) 338-7638. **Assistant Coaches:** Ronnie Prettyman, *Danny Ricabal. **Telephone:** (310) 338-4533.
Home Field: Page Stadium. **Seating Capacity:** 600. **Outfield Dimension: LF**—326, **CF**—406, **RF**—321.

MAINE BLACK BEARS

Conference: America East.
Mailing Address: The University of Maine Orono, ME 04469.
Website: www.goblackbears.com.
Head Coach: Steve Trimper. **Telephone:** (207) 581-1090. **Baseball SID:** Shawn Berry. **Telephone:** (207) 581-4158. **Assistant Coaches:** Conor Burke, *Nick Derba. **Telephone:** (207) 581-1096.

Home Field: Mahaney Diamond. **Seating Capacity:** 4,400. **Outfield Dimension: LF**—330, **CF**—400, **RF**—330.

MANHATTAN JASPERS

Conference: Metro Atlantic Athletic.
Mailing Address: 4513 Manhattan College Parkway, Riverdale, NY 10471.
Website: www.gojaspers.com.
Head Coach: Jim Duffy. **Telephone:** (718) 862-7821. **Baseball SID:** Kevin Ross. **Telephone:** (718) 862-7228. **Fax:** (718) 862-8020. **Assistant Coaches:** Kevin Flynn, *Brian McCullough. **Telephone:** (718) 862-7218.
Home Field: Dutchess Stadium. **Seating Capacity:** 4494. **Outfield Dimension: LF**—325, **CF**—400, **RF**—325.

MARIST RED FOXES

Conference: Metro Atlantic Athletic.
Mailing Address: McCann Center, 3399 North Road, Poughkeepsie, NY 12601.
Website: www.goredfoxes.com.
Head Coach: Chris Tracz. **Telephone:** (845) 575-3000 (ext. 2570). **Baseball SID:** Sam Rathbun. **Telephone:** (845) 575-3000 (ext. 2150). **Assistant Coaches:** Jesse Marsh, Eric Pelletier. **Telephone:** (845) 575-3000 (ext. 7583).
Home Field: McCann Baseball Field. **Seating Capacity:** 350. **Outfield Dimension: LF**—317, **CF**—390, **RF**—317.

MARSHALL THUNDERING HERD

Conference: Conference USA.
Mailing Address: PO box 1360, Huntington, WV 25703.
Website: www.herdzone.com.
Head Coach: Jeff Waggoner. **Telephone:** (304) 696-5277. **Baseball SID:** Corey Dieteman. **Telephone:** (304) 696-5276. **Assistant Coaches:** *Tim Donnelly, Josh Newman. **Telephone:** (304) 696-7146.
Home Field: Appalachian Power Park. **Seating Capacity:** 4,500. **Outfield Dimension: LF**— 330, **CF**— 400, **RF**— 320.

MARYLAND TERRAPINS

Conference: Big Ten.
Mailing Address: University of Maryland, College Park, MD 20742.
Website: www.umterps.com.
Head Coach: John Szefc. **Telephone:** (301) 314-1845. **Baseball SID:** Taylor Smyth. **Telephone:** (301) 314-8052. **Assistant Coaches:** Jim Belanger, *Rob Vaughn. **Telephone:** (301) 314-9772.
Home Field: Bob "Turtle" Smith Stadium. **Seating Capacity:** 2,500. **Outfield Dimension: LF**—320, **CF**—380, **RF**—325.

MARYLAND-BALTIMORE COUNTY RETRIEVERS

Conference: America East.
Mailing Address: 1000 Hilltop Circle, Baltimore, MD 21250.
Website: www.umbcretrievers.com.
Head Coach: Bob Mumma. **Telephone:** (410) 459-2239. **Baseball SID:** David Castellanos. **Telephone:** (410) 459-1530. **Fax:** (410) 455-1536. **Assistant Coaches:** *Liam Bowen, Larry Williams. **Telephone:** (410) 459-2239.
Home Field: Alumni Field. **Seating Capacity:** 1,000. **Outfield Dimension: LF**—330, **CF**—360, **RF**—340.

MARYLAND-EASTERN SHORE HAWKS

Conference: Mid-Eastern Athletic.
Mailing Address: 1 College Backbone Road. Princess Anne, MD 21853.
Website: www.umeshawks.com.
Head Coach: John O'Neil. **Telephone:** (410) 651-8158.
Baseball SID: Matt McCann. **Telephone:** (410) 651-3358.
Assistant Coaches: Jason Bell. **Telephone:** (410) 651-8908.
Home Field: Hawk Stadium. **Seating Capacity:** 1,000.
Outfield Dimension: LF—340, **CF**—400, **RF**—340.

MASSACHUSETTS MINUTEMEN

Conference: Atlantic 10.
Mailing Address: 200 Commonwealth Avenue, 3rd Floor, Amherst, MA 01003.
Website: www.umassathletics.com.
Head Coach: Mike Stone. **Telephone:** (413) 545-3120.
Baseball SID: Jillian Jakuba. **Telephone:** (413) 420-3116.
Assistant Coaches: Nate Cole, Rich Graef. **Telephone:** (413) 545-3766.
Home Field: Lorden Field. **Seating Capacity:** 1,400.
Outfield Dimension: LF—330, **CF**—400, **RF**—330.

MASSACHUSETTS-LOWELL RIVER HAWKS

Conference: America East.
Mailing Address: 1 University Ave, Lowell, MA 01854.
Website: www.goriverhawks.com.
Head Coach: Ken Harring. **Telephone:** (978) 934-2344.
Baseball SID: Tommy Coyle. **Telephone:** (978) 934-6748.
Fax: (978) 934-4001. **Assistant Coaches:** Jerod Edmondson, *Brendan Monaghan. **Telephone:** (978) 934-2564.
Home Field: LeLacheur Park. **Seating Capacity:** 7,800.
Outfield Dimension: LF—337, **CF**—400, **RF**—301.

MCNEESE STATE COWBOYS

Conference: Southland.
Mailing Address: 615 Bienville St., Lake Charles, LA 70609.
Website: www.mcneesesports.com.
Head Coach: Justin Hill. **Telephone:** (337) 475-5484.
Baseball SID: Hunter Bower. **Telephone:** (337) 475-5941.
Fax: (337) 475-5202. **Assistant Coaches:** *Cory Barton, Nick Zaleski. **Telephone:** (337) 475-5904.
Home Field: Cowboy Diamond. **Seating Capacity:** 2,000. **Outfield Dimension: LF**—330, **CF**—400, **RF**—330.

MEMPHIS TIGERS

Conference: Conference USA.
Mailing Address: 570 Normal St., Memphis, TN 38152.
Website: www.gotigersgo.com.
Head Coach: Daron Schoenrock. **Telephone:** (901) 678-4137. **Baseball SID:** Kevin J Rodriguez. **Telephone:** (901) 678-5108. **Assistant Coaches:** *Clay Greene, Russ McNickle. **Telephone:** (901) 678-4139.
Home Field: FedExPark. **Seating Capacity:** 2,000.
Outfield Dimension: LF—318, **CF**—379, **RF**—317.

MERCER BEARS

Conference: Southern.
Mailing Address: 1501 Coleman Ave., Macon, GA 31207.
Website: www.mercerbears.com.
Head Coach: Craig Gibson. **Telephone:** (478) 301-2396. **Baseball SID:** Jordon Bruner. **Telephone:** (478) 301-5209. **Fax:** (478) 301-5350. **Assistant Coaches:** *Brent

Shade, Willie Stewart. **Telephone:** (478) 301-2738.
Home Field: Claude Smith Field. **Seating Capacity:** 500. **Outfield Dimension: LF**—330, **CF**—400, **RF**—320.

MIAMI HURRICANES

Conference: Atlantic Coast.
Mailing Address: Mark Light Field, 6201 San Amaro Drive, Coral Gables, FL 33146.
Website: www.hurricanesports.com.
Head Coach: Jim Morris. **Telephone:** (305) 284-4171.
Baseball SID: Camron Ghorbi. **Telephone:** (305) 284-3230. **Assistant Coaches:** J.D. Arteaga, *Gino DiMare. **Telephone:** (305) 284-4171.
Home Field: Alex Rodriguez Park at Mark Light Field.
Seating Capacity: 4,999. **Outfield Dimension: LF**—330, **CF**—400, **RF**—330.

MIAMI (OHIO) REDHAWKS

Conference: Mid-American.
Mailing Address: 550 East Withrow St., Oxford, OH 45056.
Website: www.muredhawks.com.
Head Coach: Danny Hayden. **Telephone:** (513) 529-6631. **Baseball SID:** Caleb Saunders. **Telephone:** (513) 529-0901. **Assistant Coaches:** Matt Davis, *Jeremy Ison. **Telephone:** (513) 529-6746.
Home Field: McKie Field at Hayden Park. **Seating Capacity:** 1,000. **Outfield Dimension: LF**—336, **CF**—400, **RF**—343.

MICHIGAN WOLVERINES

Conference: Big Ten.
Mailing Address: 1000 S. State St. Ann Arbor, Mich. 48109.
Website: www.mgoblue.com.
Head Coach: Erik Bakich. **Telephone:** (734) 647-4550.
Baseball SID: Katie Gwinn. **Telephone:** (734) 763-4423.
Fax: (734) 647-1188. **Assistant Coaches:** Sean Kenny, *Nick Schnabel. **Telephone:** (734) 647-4550.
Home Field: Ray Fisher Stadium. **Seating Capacity:** 4,000. **Outfield Dimension: LF**—330, **CF**—400, **RF**—330.

MICHIGAN STATE SPARTANS

Conference: Big Ten.
Mailing Address: 223 Kalamazoo St., East Lansing, MI 48824.
Website: www.msuspartans.com.
Head Coach: Jake Boss. **Telephone:** (517) 355-4486.
Baseball SID: Jeff Barnes. **Telephone:** (517) 355-2271.
Assistant Coaches: Skylar Meade, *Graham Sikes. **Telephone:** (517) 355-0259.
Home Field: Kobs Field. **Seating Capacity:** 3,000.
Outfield Dimension: LF—340, **CF**—402, **RF**—302.

MIDDLE TENNESSEE STATE BLUE RAIDERS

Conference: Conference USA.
Mailing Address: MTSU Box 90, 1500 Greenland Drive, Murfreesboro, TN 37132.
Website: www.goblueraiders.com.
Head Coach: Jim McGuire. **Telephone:** (615) 898-2961. **Baseball SID:** Eric Beovich. **Telephone:** (615) 904-2378. **Fax:** (615) 898-5626. **Assistant Coaches:** JP Davis, *Scott Hall. **Telephone:** (615) 494-8796.
Home Field: Reese Smith Jr. Field. **Seating Capacity:** 2,100. **Outfield Dimension: LF**—330, **CF**—390, **RF**—330.

MINNESOTA GOLDEN GOPHERS

Conference: Big Ten.
Mailing Address: 516 15th Ave. SE, Minneapolis, MN 55455.
Website: www.gophersports.com.
Head Coach: John Anderson. **Telephone:** (612) 625-1060. **Baseball SID:** Cody Voga. **Telephone:** (612) 624-4345. **Assistant Coaches:** *Rob Fornasiere, Todd Oakes. **Telephone:** (612) 625-3568.
Home Field: Siebert Field. **Seating Capacity:** 1,420.
Outfield Dimension: LF—330, **CF**—390, **RF**—330.

MISSISSIPPI REBELS

Conference: Southeastern.
Mailing Address: 400 University Place, Oxford, MS 38677.
Website: www.olemisssports.com.
Head Coach: Mike Bianco. **Telephone:** (662) 915-6643. **Baseball SID:** Adam Kuffner. **Telephone:** (662) 915-7031. **Fax:** (662) 915-7006. **Assistant Coaches:** Mike Clement, *Carl Lafferty. **Telephone:** (662) 915-7556.
Home Field: Oxford University Stadium - Swayze Field. **Seating Capacity:** 10,323. **Outfield Dimension: LF**—330, **CF**—390, **RF**—330.

MISSISSIPPI STATE BULLDOGS

Conference: Southeastern.
Mailing Address: 288 Lakeview Dr., Bryan Building, Mississippi State, MS 39762.
Website: www.hailstate.com.
Head Coach: John Cohen. **Telephone:** (662) 325-3597. **Baseball SID:** Kyle Niblett. **Telephone:** (662) 325-8040. **Fax:** (662) 325-2563. **Assistant Coaches:** Wes Johnson, *Nick Mingione. **Telephone:** (662) 325-3597.
Home Field: Dudy Noble Field. **Seating Capacity:** 15,000. **Outfield Dimension: LF**—330, **CF**—390, **RF**—326.

MISSISSIPPI VALLEY STATE DEVILS

Conference: Southwestern Athletic.
Mailing Address: 14000 Highway 82 West, Box 7246, Itta Bena, MS 38941.
Website: www.mvsusports.com.
Head Coach: Aaron Stevens. **Telephone:** (662) 254-3834. **Baseball SID:** LaMonica Scott. **Assistant Coaches:** Luke Walker. **Telephone:** (662) 254-3834.
Home Field: Magnolia Field.

MISSOURI TIGERS

Conference: Southeastern.
Mailing Address: 100 MATC Columbia, MO 65211.
Website: www.mutigers.com.
Head Coach: Tim Jamieson. **Telephone:** (573) 882-1917. **Baseball SID:** Shawn Davis. **Telephone:** (573) 882-0711. **Fax:** (573) 882-2332. **Assistant Coaches:** Hunter Mense, *Jerry Zulli. **Telephone:** (573) 882-1917.
Home Field: Simmons Field. **Seating Capacity:** 3,031. **Outfield Dimension: LF**—333, **CF**—390, **RF**—339.

MISSOURI STATE BEARS

Conference: Missouri Valley.
Mailing Address: 901 S. National Ave., Springfield, MO 65897.
Website: www.missouristatebears.com.
Head Coach: Keith Guttin. **Telephone:** (417) 836-5242. **Baseball SID:** Eric Doennig. **Telephone:** (417) 836-4586.

Assistant Coaches: Paul Evans, *Nate Thompson. **Telephone:** (417) 836-4496.
Home Field: Hammons Field. **Seating Capacity:** 8,000. **Outfield Dimension: LF**—315, **CF**—400, **RF**—330.

MONMOUTH HAWKS

Conference: Metro Atlantic Athletic.
Mailing Address: 400 Cedar Avenue, West Long Branch, NJ 07764.
Website: www.monmouthhawks.com.
Head Coach: Dean Ehehalt. **Telephone:** (732) 263-5186. **Baseball SID:** Gary Kowal. **Telephone:** (732) 263-5557. **Fax:** (732) 571-3535. **Assistant Coaches:** Chris Collazo, *Rick Oliveri. **Telephone:** (732) 263-5347.
Home Field: Monmouth University Baseball Field. **Seating Capacity:** 2,100. **Outfield Dimension: LF**—320, **CF**—390, **RF**—320.

MOREHEAD STATE EAGLES

Conference: Ohio Valley.
Mailing Address: 195 Academic-Athletic Center, Morehead, KY 40351.
Website: www.msueagles.com.
Head Coach: Mike McGuire. **Telephone:** (606) 783-2882. **Baseball SID:** Matt Schabert. **Telephone:** (606) 783-2556. **Assistant Coaches:** *Adam Brown, Graham Johnson. **Telephone:** (606) 783-2881.
Home Field: Allen Field. **Seating Capacity:** 1,000. **Outfield Dimension: LF**—320, **CF**—380, **RF**—320.

MOUNT ST. MARY'S MOUNTAINEERS

Conference: Northeast.
Mailing Address: 16300 Old Emmitsburg Road, Emmitsburg, MD 21727.
Website: www.mountathletics.com.
Head Coach: Scott Thompson. **Telephone:** (301) 447-3806. **Baseball SID:** Evan Roeser. **Telephone:** (301) 447-5384. **Assistant Coaches:** Ben Leonard. **Telephone:** (301) 447-3806.
Home Field: E.T. Straw Family Stadium.

MURRAY STATE RACERS

Conference: Ohio Valley.
Mailing Address: 217 Stewart Stadium, Murray, KY 42071.
Website: www.goracers.com.
Head Coach: Kevin Moulder. **Telephone:** (270) 809-4892. **Baseball SID:** Kevin DeVries. **Telephone:** (270) 809-7044. **Assistant Coaches:** Daniel Dulin, *Andy Morgan. **Telephone:** (270) 809-4192.
Home Field: Reagan Field. **Seating Capacity:** 800. **Outfield Dimension: LF**—330, **CF**—400, **RF**—330.

NAVY MIDSHIPMEN

Conference: Patriot.
Mailing Address: Ricketts Hall, 566 Brownson Rd., Annapolis, MD 21402.
Website: www.navysports.com.
Head Coach: Paul Kostacopoulos. **Telephone:** (410) 293-5571. **Baseball SID:** Alex Lumb. **Telephone:** (410) 293-8771. **Fax:** (410) 293-8954. **Assistant Coaches:** Bobby Applegate, *Jeff Kane. **Telephone:** (410) 293-8946.
Home Field: Terwilliger Brothers Field at Max Bishop Stadium. **Seating Capacity:** 1,500. **Outfield Dimension: LF**—323, **CF**—397, **RF**—304.

NEBRASKA CORNHUSKERS

Conference: Big Ten.
Mailing Address: 403 Line Drive Circle, Suite B Lincoln, NE 68588.
Website: www.huskers.com.
Head Coach: Darin Erstad. **Telephone:** (402) 472-9166.
Baseball SID: Jeremy Foote. **Telephone:** (402) 472-7778.
Assistant Coaches: Mike Kirby, *Ted Silva. **Telephone:** (402) 472-1445.
Home Field: Hawks Field. **Seating Capacity:** 8,486.
Outfield Dimension: LF—335, **CF**—395, **RF**—325.

NEBRASKA-OMAHA MAVERICKS

Conference: Summit.
Mailing Address: Sapp Fieldhouse, 6001 Dodge Street, Omaha, NE 68182.
Website: www.omavs.com.
Head Coach: Bob Herold. **Telephone:** (402) 554-3388.
Baseball SID: Bonnie Ryan. **Telephone:** (402) 554-3267.
Assistant Coaches: Chris Gadsden, Evan Porter. **Telephone:** (402) 554-2141.
Home Field: Ballpark at Boys Town. **Outfield Dimension: LF**—335, **CF**—410, **RF**—335.

NEVADA WOLFPACK

Conference: Mountain West.
Mailing Address: 1664 N. Virginia Street, Legacy Hall, MS 264, Reno, NV 89557.
Website: www.nevadawolfpack.com.
Head Coach: T.J. Bruce. **Telephone:** (775) 682-6978.
Baseball SID: Brady Johnson. **Telephone:** (775) 682-6985. **Fax:** (775) 784-4386. **Assistant Coaches:** Steve Bennett, Jake Silverman. **Telephone:** (775) 682-6979.
Home Field: Peccole Park. **Seating Capacity:** 3,000.
Outfield Dimension: LF—340, **CF**—401, **RF**—340.

NEVADA-LAS VEGAS REBELS

Conference: Mountain West.
Mailing Address: 4505 S. Maryland Parkway, Box 74, Las Vegas, NV 89154.
Website: www.unlvrebels.com.
Head Coach: Stan Stolte. **Telephone:** (702) 895-3802.
Baseball SID: Jeffrey Seals. **Telephone:** (702) 895-3134.
Assistant Coaches: Kevin Higgins. **Telephone:** (702) 895-3802.
Home Field: Earl E. Wilson Stadium. **Seating Capacity:** 3,000. **Outfield Dimension: LF**—335, **CF**—400, **RF**—335.

NEW JERSEY TECH HIGHLANDERS

Conference: Atlantic Sun.
Mailing Address: 80 Lock St. Newark, NJ 07102.
Website: www.njithighlanders.com.
Head Coach: Brian Guiliana. **Telephone:** (973) 596-5827. **Baseball SID:** Stephanie Pillari. **Telephone:** (973) 596-8324. **Assistant Coaches:** *Robbie Mcclellan, Grant Neary. **Telephone:** (973) 596-8396.
Home Field: Bears and Eagles Riverfront Stadium. **Seating Capacity:** 6,500. **Outfield Dimension: LF**—306, **CF**—390, **RF**—335.

NEW MEXICO LOBOS

Conference: Mountain West.
Mailing Address: Colleen J. Maloof Administration Building, 1 University of New Mexico, MSC04 2680, Albuquerque, NM 87131.
Website: www.golobos.com.

Head Coach: Ray Birmingham. **Telephone:** (505) 925-5721. **Baseball SID:** Terry Kelly. **Telephone:** (505) 925-5520. **Assistant Coaches:** *Buddy Gouldsmith, Ken Jacome. **Telephone:** (505) 925-5721.
Home Field: Lobo Field. **Seating Capacity:** 1,000.
Outfield Dimension: LF—338, **CF**—413, **RF**—338.

NEW MEXICO STATE AGGIES

Conference: Western Athletic.
Mailing Address: P.O. Box 3001, Las Cruces, NM 88003.
Website: www.nmstatesports.com.
Head Coach: Brian Green. **Telephone:** (575) 646-7693.
Baseball SID: Jake Hudspeth. **Telephone:** (575) 646-1885. **Assistant Coaches:** Mike Brown, *Joel Mangrum. **Telephone:** (575) 646-5813.
Home Field: Pressley Askew Field. **Seating Capacity:** 1,000. **Outfield Dimension: LF**—330, **CF**—410, **RF**—330.

NEW ORLEANS PRIVATEERS

Conference: Southland.
Mailing Address: 2000 Lakeshore Drive, New Orleans, LA 70148.
Website: www.unoprivateers.com.
Head Coach: Blake Dean. **Telephone:** (504) 280-3879.
Baseball SID: Emmanuel Pepis. **Telephone:** (504) 280-7039. **Assistant Coaches:** Lee Bryant, Brett Stewart. **Telephone:** (504) 280-3879.
Home Field: Maestri Field at First NBC Ballpark.
Seating Capacity: 2,900. **Outfield Dimension: LF**—330, **CF**—405, **RF**—330.

NEW YORK TECH BEARS

Conference: Independent.
Mailing Address: Northern Blvd. PO Box 8000 Old Westbury, NY 11568.
Website: www.nyitbears.com.
Head Coach: Bob Malvagna. **Telephone:** (516) 686-7513. **Baseball SID:** Emily Dorko. **Telephone:** (516) 686-7522. **Assistant Coaches:** Steve Malvagna, Vinny Rubino. **Telephone:** (516) 686-1315.
Home Field: Angelo Lorenzo Memorial Field. **Seating Capacity:** 500. **Outfield Dimension: LF**—312, **CF**—395, **RF**—311.

NIAGARA PURPLE EAGLES

Conference: Metro Atlantic Athletic.
Mailing Address: Upper Level Gallagher Center, PO Box 2009, Niagara University, NY 14109.
Website: www.purpleeagles.com.
Head Coach: Rob McCoy. **Telephone:** (716) 286-7361.
Baseball SID: Brenna Jacobs. **Telephone:** (7160286-8586.
Assistant Coaches: Ronnie Bernick, *Matt Spatafora. **Telephone:** (716) 286-8264.
Home Field: Bobo Field.

NICHOLLS STATE COLONELS

Conference: Southland.
Mailing Address: 906 East 1st Street, Thibodaux, LA 70310.
Website: www.gocolonels.com.
Head Coach: Seth Thibodeaux. **Telephone:** (985) 449-7149. **Baseball SID:** Zach Carlton. **Telephone:** (985) 448-4282. **Fax:** (985) 448-4490. **Assistant Coaches:** *Walt Jones, Zach Butler. **Telephone:** (985) 448-4882.
Home Field: Ray E. Didier Field. **Seating Capacity:** 3,200. **Outfield Dimension: LF**—330, **CF**—400, **RF**—330.

NORFOLK STATE SPARTANS

Conference: Mid-Eastern Athletic.
Mailing Address: 700 Park Ave., Norfolk, VA 23504.
Website: www.nsuspartans.com.
Head Coach: Claudell Clark. **Telephone:** (757) 676-3082. **Baseball SID:** Matthew Michalec. **Telephone:** (757) 823-2628. **Fax:** (757) 823-8218. **Assistant Coaches:** Wiley Lee, *Joey Seal. **Telephone:** (757) 823-8196.
Home Field: Marty L. Miller Field. **Seating Capacity:** 1,500. **Outfield Dimension: LF**—330, **CF**—404, **RF**—318.

NORTH CAROLINA TAR HEELS

Conference: Atlantic Coast.
Mailing Address: PO Box 2126, Chapel Hill, NC 27515.
Website: www.goheels.com.
Head Coach: Mike Fox. **Telephone:** (919) 962-2351.
Baseball SID: Bobby Hundley. **Telephone:** (919) 843-5678. **Assistant Coaches:** Scott Forbes, *Scott Jackson. **Telephone:** (919) 962-5451.
Home Field: Boshamer Stadium. **Seating Capacity:** 5,100. **Outfield Dimension: LF**—335, **CF**—400, **RF**—340.

NORTH CAROLINA A&T AGGIES

Conference: Mid-Eastern Athletic.
Mailing Address: 1601 E. Market Street, Greensboro, NC 27411.
Website: www.ncataggies.com.
Head Coach: Ben Hall. **Telephone:** (336) 285-4272.
Baseball SID: Brian Holloway. **Telephone:** (336) 285-3608. **Assistant Coaches:** Tyrone Dawson, Jamie Serber. **Telephone:** (336) 285-3608.
Home Field: War Memorial Stadium. **Seating Capacity:** 2,000. **Outfield Dimension: LF**—370, **CF**—401, **RF**—336.

NORTH CAROLINA CENTRAL EAGLES

Conference: Mid-Eastern Athletic.
Mailing Address: McDougald-McLendon Arena, 1801 Fayetteville Street, Durham, NC 27707.
Website: www.nccueaglepride.com.
Head Coach: Jim Koerner. **Telephone:** (919) 530-6723. **Baseball SID:** Jonathan Duren. **Telephone:** (919) 530-6892. **Assistant Coaches:** A.J. Battisto, Neal Henry. **Telephone:** (919) 530-5439.
Home Field: Durham Athletic Park. **Seating Capacity:** 2,000. **Outfield Dimension: LF**—327, **CF**—398, **RF**—290.

NORTH CAROLINA STATE WOLFPACK

Conference: Atlantic Coast.
Mailing Address: 2500 Warren Carroll Drive, Campus Box 8505, Raleigh, NC 27695.
Website: www.gopack.com.
Head Coach: Elliott Avent. **Telephone:** (919) 515-3613. **Baseball SID:** Cavan Fosnes. **Telephone:** (919) 896-1863. **Assistant Coaches:** Scott Foxhall, *Chris Hart. **Telephone:** (919) 515-3613.
Home Field: Doak Field at Dail Park. **Seating Capacity:** 3,100. **Outfield Dimension: LF**—325, **CF**—400, **RF**—330.

NORTH DAKOTA FIGHTING HAWKS

Conference: Western Athletic.
Mailing Address: 2751 2nd Avenue, N Stop 9013, Grand Forks, ND 58202.
Website: www.undsports.com.
Head Coach: Jeff Dodson. **Telephone:** (701) 777-4038.

Baseball SID: Mitch Wigness. **Telephone:** (701) 777-4210.
Fax: (701) 777-4352. **Assistant Coaches:** *Brian DeVillers, Mitch Mormann. **Telephone:** (701) 777-2937.
Home Field: Kraft Field. **Seating Capacity:** 2,000.
Outfield Dimension: LF—330, **CF**—410, **RF**—330.

NORTH DAKOTA STATE BISON

Conference: Summit.
Mailing Address: NDSU Dept. 1200, PO Box 6050, Fargo, ND 58108.
Website: www.gobison.com.
Head Coach: Tod Brown. **Telephone:** (701) 231-8853.
Baseball SID: Ryan Anderson. **Telephone:** (701) 231-5591. **Assistant Coaches:** Tyler Oakes, *David Pearson. **Telephone:** (701) 231-7817.
Home Field: Newman Outdoor Field. **Seating Capacity:** 4,419. **Outfield Dimension: LF**—318, **CF**—408, **RF**—314.

NORTH FLORIDA OSPREYS

Conference: Atlantic Sun.
Mailing Address: 1 UNF Drive, Jacksonville, FL 32224.
Website: www.unfospreys.com.
Head Coach: Smoke Laval. **Telephone:** (904) 620-1556. **Baseball SID:** Scott Fitzgerald. **Telephone:** (904) 620-4029. **Assistant Coaches:** Andrew Hannon, *Judd Loveland. **Telephone:** (904) 620-2586.
Home Field: Harmon Stadium. **Seating Capacity:** 1,000. **Outfield Dimension: LF**—325, **CF**—400, **RF**—325.

NORTHEASTERN HUSKIES

Conference: Colonial Athletic.
Mailing Address: 360 Huntington Avenue, 219 Cabot Center, Boston, MA 02115.
Website: www.gonu.com.
Head Coach: Mike Glavine. **Telephone:** (617) 373-3657. **Baseball SID:** Mike Skovan. **Telephone:** (617) 373-4154. **Fax:** (617) 373-8988. **Assistant Coaches:** Kevin Casey, *Kevin Cobb. **Telephone:** (617) 373-5256.
Home Field: Friedman Diamond. **Seating Capacity:** 2,000. **Outfield Dimension: LF**—326, **CF**—415, **RF**—342.

NORTHERN COLORADO BEARS

Conference: Western Athletic.
Mailing Address: 270 D Butler-Hancock Athletic Center, Greeley, CO 80639.
Website: www.uncbears.com.
Head Coach: Carl Iwasaki. **Telephone:** (970) 351-1714.
Baseball SID: Ryan Pfeifer. **Telephone:** (970) 351-3645.
Assistant Coaches: R.D. Spiehs, Kainoa Correa. **Telephone:** (970) 351-1203.
Home Field: Jackson Field. **Seating Capacity:** 1,500.
Outfield Dimension: LF—345, **CF**—407, **RF**—356.

NORTHERN ILLINOIS HUSKIES

Conference: Mid-American.
Mailing Address: Convocation Center, DeKalb, IL 60115.
Website: www.niuhuskies.com.
Head Coach: Mike Kunigonis. **Telephone:** (815) 753-0147. **Baseball SID:** Matt Scheerer. **Telephone:** (815) 753-1708. **Assistant Coaches:** *Andrew Maki, Luke Stewart. **Telephone:** (815) 753-0147.
Home Field: Ralph McKinzie Field. **Seating Capacity:** 1,500. **Outfield Dimension: LF**—312, **CF**—395, **RF**—322.

NORTHERN KENTUCKY NORSE

Conference: Horizon.
Mailing Address: 500 Nunn Dr. Highland Heights, KY 41099.
Website: www.nkunorse.com.
Head Coach: Todd Asalon. **Telephone:** (859) 572-6474. **Baseball SID:** Melissa Powell. **Telephone:** (859) 572-7850. **Assistant Coaches:** Brad Gschwind, *Dizzy Peyton. **Telephone:** (859) 572-1525.
Home Field: Bill Aker Baseball Complex. **Seating Capacity:** 500. **Outfield Dimension: LF**—320, **CF**—365, **RF**—320.

NORTHWESTERN WILDCATS

Conference: Big Ten.
Mailing Address: 1501 Central St., Evanston, IL 60208.
Website: www.nusports.com.
Head Coach: Spencer Allen. **Telephone:** (847) 491-4652. **Baseball SID:** Mallory Majcher. **Telephone:** (847) 467-3274. **Assistant Coaches:** Dusty Napoleon, *Josh Reynolds. **Telephone:** (847) 467-1211.
Home Field: Rocky and Bernice Miller Park. **Seating Capacity:** 1,000. **Outfield Dimension: LF**—310, **CF**—400, **RF**—330.

NORTHWESTERN STATE DEMONS

Conference: Southland.
Mailing Address: 220 South Jefferson Street, Natchitoches, LA 71497.
Website: www.nsudemons.com.
Head Coach: Lane Burroughs. **Telephone:** (318) 357-4139. **Baseball SID:** Jason Pugh. **Telephone:** (318) 357-6469. **Fax:** (318) 357-4515. **Assistant Coaches:** *Bobby Barbier, G.T. McCullough. **Telephone:** (318) 357-4176.
Home Field: Brown-Stroud Field. **Seating Capacity:** 1,200. **Outfield Dimension: LF**—320, **CF**—405, **RF**—340.

NOTRE DAME FIGHTING IRISH

Conference: Atlantic Coast.
Mailing Address: University of Notre Dame Notre Dame, IN 46556.
Website: www.und.com.
Head Coach: Mik Aoki. **Telephone:** (574) 631-4840. **Baseball SID:** Russ Dorn. **Telephone:** (574) 673-4780. **Assistant Coaches:** Chuck Ristano, *Jesse Woods. **Telephone:** (574) 631-4840.
Home Field: Frank Eck Stadium. **Seating Capacity:** 2,500. **Outfield Dimension: LF**—330, **CF**—400, **RF**—330.

OAKLAND GOLDEN GRIZZLIES

Conference: Horizon.
Mailing Address: 2200 N. Squirrel Road, Rochester, MI 48309.
Website: www.goldengrizzlies.com.
Head Coach: John Musachio. **Telephone:** (248) 370-4059. **Baseball SID:** Daniel Gliot. **Telephone:** (248) 370-3201. **Assistant Coaches:** Kyle Dean, *Jacke Healey. **Telephone:** (258) 370-4228.
Home Field: Oakland Baseball Field. **Seating Capacity:** 500. **Outfield Dimension: LF**—333, **CF**—380, **RF**—320.

OHIO BOBCATS

Conference: Mid-American.
Mailing Address: Ohio University, Intercollegiate Athletics, Convocation Center, Athens, OH 45701.
Website: www.ohiobobcats.com.
Head Coach: Rob Smith. **Telephone:** (740) 593-1180. **Baseball SID:** Mike Ashcraft. **Telephone:** (740) 593-1299. **Fax:** (740) 593-2420. **Assistant Coaches:** Craig Moore, *C.J. Wamsley. **Telephone:** (740) 593-1954.
Home Field: Bob Wren Stadium. **Seating Capacity:** 4,000. **Outfield Dimension: LF**—340, **CF**—405, **RF**—340.

OHIO STATE BUCKEYES

Conference: Big Ten.
Mailing Address: 250 Bill Davis Stadium, 650 Borror Dr., Columbus, OH 43210
Website: www.ohiostatebuck eyes.com.
Head Coach: Greg Beals. **Telephone:** (614) 292-1075. **Baseball SID:** Alex Morando. **Telephone:** (614) 292-1389. **Fax:** (614) 292-8547. **Assistant Coaches:** *Chris Holick, Mike Stafford. **Telephone:** (614) 292-1075.
Home Field: Nick Swisher Field at Bill Davis Stadium. **Seating Capacity:** 4,450. **Outfield Dimension: LF**—330, **CF**—400, **RF**—330.

OKLAHOMA SOONERS

Conference: Big 12.
Mailing Address: McClendon Center for Intercollegiate Athletics, 180 W. Brooks, Norman, OK 73019.
Website: www.soonersports.com.
Head Coach: Pete Hughes. **Telephone:** (405) 325-8354. **Baseball SID:** Brendan Flynn. **Telephone:** (405) 325-6449. **Assistant Coaches:** Mike Anderson, *Rudy Darrow. **Telephone:** (405) 325-8354.
Home Field: L. Dale Mitchell Park. **Seating Capacity:** 3,180. **Outfield Dimension: LF**—335, **CF**—411, **RF**—335.

OKLAHOMA STATE COWBOYS

Conference: Big 12.
Mailing Address: Allie P. Reynolds Stadium, Stillwater, OK 74078.
Website: www.okstate.com.
Head Coach: Josh Holliday. **Telephone:** (405) 744-5849. **Baseball SID:** Wade McWhorter. **Telephone:** (405) 744-7853. **Fax:** (405) 744-7754. **Assistant Coaches:** *James Vilade, Rob Walton. **Telephone:** (405) 744-5849.
Home Field: Allie P. Reynolds Stadium. **Seating Capacity:** 4,000. **Outfield Dimension: LF**—330, **CF**—398, **RF**—330.

OLD DOMINION MONARCHS

Conference: Conference USA.
Mailing Address: Jim Jarrett Athletic Admin. Building, Norfolk, VA 23529.
Website: www.odusports.com.
Head Coach: Chris Finwood. **Telephone:** (757) 683-4230. **Baseball SID:** Maggie Bonner. **Telephone:** (757) 683-5581. **Assistant Coaches:** Mike Marron, *Karl Nonemaker. **Telephone:** (757) 683-4331.
Home Field: Bud Metheny Baseball Complex. **Seating Capacity:** 2,500. **Outfield Dimension: LF**—325, **CF**—395, **RF**—325.

ORAL ROBERTS GOLDEN EAGLES

Conference: Summit.
Mailing Address: 7777 S. Lewis Ave. Tulsa, OK 74171.
Website: www.oruathletics.com.
Head Coach: Ryan Folmar. **Telephone:** (918) 495-7639. **Baseball SID:** Tim McCaughan. **Telephone:** (918) 459-6646. **Assistant Coaches:** Ryan Neill, Sean Snedeker.

Telephone: (918) 495-7132.
Home Field: J.L Johnson Stadium. **Seating Capacity:** 2,418. **Outfield Dimension: LF**—330, **CF**—400, **RF**—330.

OREGON DUCKS

Conference: Pacific-12.
Mailing Address: Len Casanova Center, 2727 Leo Harris Parkway, Eugene, OR 97401.
Website: www.goducks.com.
Head Coach: George Horton. **Telephone:** (541) 646-5235. **Baseball SID:** Todd Miles. **Telephone:** (541) 346-0962. **Fax:** (541) 346-5449. **Assistant Coaches:** *Jay Uhlman, Mark Wasikowski. **Telephone:** (541) 346-5768.
Home Field: PK Park. **Seating Capacity:** 4,000. **Outfield Dimension:** LF-—335, **CF**—400, **RF**—325.

OREGON STATE BEAVERS

Conference: Pacific-12.
Mailing Address: 114 Gill Coliseum, Corvallis, OR 97331.
Website: www.osubeavers.com.
Head Coach: Pat Casey. **Telephone:** (541) 737-0598.
Baseball SID: Hank Hager. **Telephone:** (541) 737-7472.
Assistant Coaches: Pat Bailey, *Nate Yeskie. **Telephone:** (541) 737-0598.
Home Field: Goss Stadium at Coleman Field. **Seating Capacity:** 3,248. **Outfield Dimension: LF**—330, **CF**—400, **RF**—330.

PACIFIC TIGERS

Conference: West Coast.
Mailing Address: 3601 Pacific Ave. Stockton, CA 95219.
Website: www.pacifictigers.com.
Head Coach: Mike Neu. **Telephone:** (209) 946-2709.
Baseball SID: Ben Laskey. **Telephone:** (209) 932-3217.
Assistant Coaches: *Noah Jackson, Mike Reuvekamp. **Telephone:** (209) 946-2163.
Home Field: Klein Family Field. **Seating Capacity:** 2,500. **Outfield Dimension: LF**—317, **CF**—405, **RF**—325.

PENN STATE NITTANY LIONS

Conference: Big Ten.
Mailing Address: Medlar Field at Lubrano Park, Suite 230, University Park, PA 16802.
Website: www.gopsusports.com.
Head Coach: Rob Cooper. **Telephone:** (814) 863-0239.
Baseball SID: Mark Brumbaugh. **Telephone:** (814) 865-1757. **Assistant Coaches:** Brian Anderson, Ross Oeder. **Telephone:** (814) 863-0230.
Home Field: Medlar Field at Lubrano Park. **Seating Capacity:** 5,406. **Outfield Dimension: LF**—325, **CF**—399, **RF**—320.

PENNSYLVANIA QUAKERS

Conference: Ivy.
Mailing Address: 233 South 33rd Street, Philadelphia, PA 19104.
Website: www.pennathletics.com.
Head Coach: John Yurkow. **Telephone:** (215) 898-6282. **Baseball SID:** Daniel Kurish. **Telephone:** (215) 898-1748. **Assistant Coaches:** *Mike Santello, Josh Schwartz. **Telephone:** (215) 746-2325.
Home Field: Mieklejohn Stadium. **Seating Capacity:** 850. **Outfield Dimension: LF**—330, **CF**—380, **RF**—330.

PEPPERDINE WAVES

Conference: West Coast.
Mailing Address: 24255 PCH, Malibu, CA 90263.
Website: www.pepperdinesports.com.
Head Coach: Rick Hirtensteiner. **Telephone:** (310) 506-4404. **Baseball SID:** Jacob Breems. **Telephone:** (310) 506-4333. **Assistant Coaches:** *Cooper Fouts, Rolando Garza. **Telephone:** (310) 506-4371.
Home Field: Eddy D. Field Stadium. **Seating Capacity:** 1,800. **Outfield Dimension: LF**—330, **CF**—400, **RF**—330.

PITTSBURGH PANTHERS

Conference: Atlantic Coast.
Mailing Address: Fitzgerald Field House, Allequippa St., Pittsburgh, PA 15261.
Website: www.pittsburghpanthers.com.
Head Coach: Joe Jordano. **Telephone:** (412) 648-8208.
Baseball SID: Ryan Sheets. **Telephone:** (412) 648-9807.
Assistant Coaches: Jerry Oakes, *Bryan Peters. **Telephone:** (412) 648-3825.
Home Field: Charles L. Cost Field. **Seating Capacity:** 900. **Outfield Dimension: LF**—330, **CF**—405, **RF**—330.

PORTLAND PILOTS

Conference: West Coast.
Mailing Address: 5000 North Willamette Blvd., Portland, OR 97203.
Website: www.portlandpilots.com.
Head Coach: Geoff Loomis. **Telephone:** (503) 943-7707. **Baseball SID:** Adam Linnman. **Telephone:** (503) 943-7731. **Assistant Coaches:** *Greg Swenson, Jake Valentine. **Telephone:** (503) 943-7732.
Home Field: Joe Etzel Field. **Seating Capacity:** 1,000.
Outfield Dimension: LF—325, **CF**—390, **RF**—325.

PRAIRIE VIEW A&M PANTHERS

Conference: Southwestern Athletic.
Mailing Address: PVAMU Athletics Department, PO Box 519, MS 1500, Prairie View, TX 77446.
Website: www.pvpanthers.com.
Head Coach: Auntwan Riggins. **Telephone:** (936) 261-9121. **Baseball SID:** Alan Wiederhold. **Telephone:** (936) 261-9106. Assistant Coache: Brian White. **Telephone:** (936) 261-9115.
Home Field: Tankersley Field. **Seating Capacity:** 512.

PRESBYTERIAN BLUE HOSE

Conference: Big South.
Mailing Address: 105 Ashland Avenue, Clinton, SC 29325.
Website: www.gobluehose.com.
Head Coach: Elton Pollock. **Telephone:** (864) 833-8236. **Baseball SID:** Simon Whitaker. **Telephone:** (864) 833-8252. **Fax:** (864) 833-8323. **Assistant Coaches:** Parker Bangs, *Mark Crocco. **Telephone:** (864) 833-7134.
Home Field: Presbyterian College Baseball Complex. **Seating Capacity:** 500. **Outfield Dimension: LF**—325, **CF**—400, **RF**—325.

PRINCETON TIGERS

Conference: Ivy.
Mailing Address: Princeton University, Jadwin Gym, Princeton, NJ 08544.
Website: www.goprincetontigers.com.
Head Coach: Scott Bradley. **Telephone:** (609) 258-5059. **Baseball SID:** Ben Badua. **Telephone:** (609)

258-2630. **Assistant Coaches:** *Lloyd Brewer, Mike Russo. **Telephone:** (609) 258-5684.
　　Home Field: Clarke Field. **Seating Capacity:** 1,000. **Outfield Dimension: LF**—335, **CF**—400, **RF**—320.

PURDUE BOILERMAKERS

　　Conference: Big Ten.
　　Mailing Address: Ross-Ade Pavilion, Room 6031, 850 Beering Drive, West Lafayette, IN 47907.
　　Website: www.purduesports.com.
　　Head Coach: Doug Schreiber. **Telephone:** (765) 494-3998. **Baseball SID:** Ben Turner. **Telephone:** (765) 494-3198. **Fax:** (765) 494-5447. **Assistant Coaches:** Wally Crancer, *Tristan McIntyre. **Telephone:** (765) 494-9360.
　　Home Field: Alexander Field. **Seating Capacity:** 2,000. **Outfield Dimension: LF**—340, **CF**—408, **RF**—330.

QUINNIPIAC BOBCATS

　　Conference: Metro Atlantic Athletic.
　　Mailing Address: 275 Mount Carmel Ave., Hamden, CT 06518.
　　Website: www.quinnipiacbobcats.com.
　　Head Coach: John Delaney. **Telephone:** (203) 582-6546. **Baseball SID:** Kevin Noonan. **Telephone:** (203) 582-5387. **Assistant Coaches:** *Patrick Egan, Kyle Nisson. **Telephone:** (203) 582-7774.
　　Home Field: QU Baseball Field. **Seating Capacity:** 1,000. **Outfield Dimension: LF**—340, **CF**—400, **RF**—325.

RADFORD HIGHLANDERS

　　Conference: Big South.
　　Mailing Address: PO Box 6913, Radford, VA 24142.
　　Website: www.radfordhighlanders.com.
　　Head Coach: Joe Raccuia. **Telephone:** (540) 831-5881. **Baseball SID:** Brian Cox. **Telephone:** (540) 831-5726. **Assistant Coaches:** Mark McQueen, *Jason Walck. **Telephone:** (540) 831-6513.
　　Home Field: RU Baseball Stadium. **Seating Capacity:** 800. **Outfield Dimension: LF**—330, **CF**—400, **RF**—330.

RHODE ISLAND RAMS

　　Conference: Atlantic 10.
　　Mailing Address: 45 Upper College Rd, Kingston, RI 02881.
　　Website: www.gorhody.com.
　　Head Coach: Raphael Cerrato. **Telephone:** (401) 874-4550. **Baseball SID:** Jodi Pontbriand. **Telephone:** (401) 481-6648. **Fax:** (401) 874-4935. **Assistant Coaches:** *Jim Martin, Sean O'Brien. **Telephone:** (401) 874-4888.
　　Home Field: Bill Beck Field. **Seating Capacity:** 500. **Outfield Dimension: LF**—330, **CF**—400, **RF**—330.

RICE OWLS

　　Conference: Conference USA.
　　Mailing Address: 6100 Main St., MS 548, Houston, TX 77005.
　　Website: www.riceowls.com.
　　Head Coach: Wayne Graham. **Telephone:** (713) 348-8864. **Baseball SID:** John Sullivan. **Telephone:** (713) 348-5636. **Assistant Coaches:** *Pat Hallmark, Clay Van. **Telephone:** (713) 348-8859.
　　Home Field: Reckling Park. **Seating Capacity:** 6,193. **Outfield Dimension: LF**—330, **CF**—400, **RF**—330.

RICHMOND SPIDERS

　　Conference: Atlantic 10.
　　Mailing Address: University of Richmond, VA 23173.

　　Website: www.richmondspiders.com.
　　Head Coach: Tracy Woodson. **Telephone:** (804) 289-8391. **Baseball SID:** TBA. **Telephone:** (804) 289-8365. **Fax:** (804) 289-8820. **Assistant Coaches:** Josh Davis, *Matt Tyner. **Telephone:** (804) 289-8391.
　　Home Field: Pitt Field. **Seating Capacity:** 600. **Outfield Dimension: LF**—328, **CF**—390, **RF**—328.

RIDER BRONCS

　　Conference: Metro Atlantic Athletic.
　　Mailing Address: 2083 Lawrenceville Road, Lawrenceville, NJ 08648.
　　Website: www.gobroncs.com.
　　Head Coach: Barry Davis. **Telephone:** (609) 896-5054. **Baseball SID:** Bud Focht. **Telephone:** (609) 896-5138. **Fax:** (609) 896-0341. **Assistant Coaches:** John Crane, *Barry Davis. **Telephone:** (609) 895-5703.
　　Home Field: Sonny Pittaro Field. **Seating Capacity:** 2,000. **Outfield Dimension: LF**—330, **CF**—405, **RF**—330.

RUTGERS SCARLET KNIGHTS

　　Conference: Big Ten.
　　Mailing Address: 83 Rockafeller Road, Piscataway, NJ 08854.
　　Website: www.scarletknights.com.
　　Head Coach: Joe Litterio. **Telephone:** (732) 445-7834. **Baseball SID:** Jimmy Gill. **Telephone:** (732) 445-8103. **Assistant Coaches:** Casey Gaynor, *Tim Reilly. **Telephone:** (732) 445-7882.
　　Home Field: Bainton Field. **Seating Capacity:** 1,500. **Outfield Dimension: LF**—330, **CF**—410, **RF**—320.

SACRAMENTO STATE HORNETS

　　Conference: Western Athletic.
　　Mailing Address: 6000 J St., Sacramento, CA 95819.
　　Website: www.hornetsports.com.
　　Head Coach: Reggie Christiansen. **Telephone:** (916) 278-4036. **Baseball SID:** Andrew Tomsky. **Telephone:** (916) 278-6896. **Assistant Coaches:** *Jake Angier, Steve Holm. **Telephone:** (916) 278-4036.
　　Home Field: John Smith Field. **Seating Capacity:** 1,500. **Outfield Dimension: LF**—330, **CF**—400, **RF**—330.

SACRED HEART PIONEERS

　　Conference: Northeast.
　　Mailing Address: 5151 Park Ave. Fairfield, CT 06825.
　　Website: www.sacredheartpioneers.com.
　　Head Coach: Nick Giaquinto. **Telephone:** (203) 365-7632. **Baseball SID:** Zachary Durham. **Telephone:** (203) 365-4813. **Assistant Coaches:** Wayne Mazzoni, *Nick Restaino. **Telephone:** (203) 365-4469.
　　Home Field: The Ballpark at Harbor Yard. **Seating Capacity:** 5,300. **Outfield Dimension: LF**—325, **CF**—405, **RF**—325.

SAINT LOUIS BILLIKENS

　　Conference: Atlantic 10.
　　Mailing Address: 3330 Laclede Ave., St. Louis, MO 63103.
　　Website: www.slubillikens.com.
　　Head Coach: Darin Hendrickson. **Telephone:** (314) 977-3172. **Baseball SID:** Jake Gossage. **Telephone:** (314) 977-2524. **Fax:** (314) 977-3178. **Assistant Coaches:** *Will Bradley, Connor Gandossy. **Telephone:** (314) 977-3260.
　　Home Field: Billiken Sports Center. **Seating Capacity:** 500. **Outfield Dimension: LF**—330, **CF**—403, **RF**—330.

SAM HOUSTON STATE BEARKATS

Conference: Southland.
Mailing Address: 1806 Avenue J, Huntsville, TX 77340.
Website: www.gobearkats.com. **Head Coach:** Matt Deggs. **Telephone:** (936) 294-1731.
Baseball SID: Andrew Pate. **Telephone:** (936) 294-2692.
Assistant Coaches: *Lance Harvell, Jay Sirianni. **Telephone:** (936) 294-4435.
Home Field: Don Sanders Stadium. **Seating Capacity:** 1,164. **Outfield Dimension: LF**—330, **CF**—400, **RF**—330.

SAMFORD BULLDOGS

Conference: Southern.
Mailing Address: 800 Lakeshore Drive, Birmingham, AL 35229.
Website: www.samfordsports.com.
Head Coach: Casey Dunn. **Telephone:** (205) 726-2134.
Baseball SID: Zac Schrieber. **Telephone:** (205) 726-2802.
Assistant Coaches: Tony David, Tyler Shrout. **Telephone:** (205) 726-4294.
Home Field: Joe Lee Griffin Field. **Seating Capacity:** 1,000. **Outfield Dimension: LF**—330, **CF**—390, **RF**—335.

SAN DIEGO TOREROS

Conference: West Coast.
Mailing Address: 5998 Alcala Park, San Diego, CA 92110.
Website: www.usdtoreros.com.
Head Coach: Rich Hill. **Telephone:** (619) 260-5953.
Baseball SID: Chris Loucks. **Telephone:** (619) 260-7930.
Assistant Coaches: Brad Marcelino, *Ramon Orozco. **Telephone:** (619) 260-7486.
Home Field: Fowler Park. **Seating Capacity:** 1,700. **Outfield Dimension: LF**—312, **CF**—391, **RF**—327.

SAN DIEGO STATE AZTECS

Conference: Mountain West.
Mailing Address: 5500 Campanile Rd., San Diego, CA 92182.
Website: www.goaztecs.com.
Head Coach: Mark Martinez. **Telephone:** (619) 594-3357. **Baseball SID:** Dave Kuhn. **Telephone:** (619) 594-5242. **Assistant Coaches:** *Joe Oliveira, Sam Peraza. **Telephone:** (619) 594-6582.
Home Field: Tony Gwynn Stadium. **Seating Capacity:** 3,500. **Outfield Dimension: LF**—340, **CF**—410, **RF**—340.

SAN FRANCISCO DONS

Conference: West Coast.
Mailing Address: 2130 Fulton Street, San Francisco, CA 94117.
Website: www.usfdons.com.
Head Coach: Nino Giarratano. **Telephone:** (415) 422-2934. **Baseball SID:** Adam Hicks. **Telephone:** (415) 422-3222. **Fax:** (415) 422-2510. **Assistant Coaches:** Matt Hiserman, *Troy Nakamura. **Telephone:** (415) 422-6881.
Home Field: Benedetti Diamond. **Seating Capacity:** 1,000. **Outfield Dimension: LF**—330, **CF**—410, **RF**—330.

SAN JOSE STATE SPARTANS

Conference: Mountain West.
Mailing Address: 1 Washington Square San Jose, CA 95192.
Website: www.sjsuspartans.com.

Head Coach: Dave Nakama. **Telephone:** (408) 924-1255. **Baseball SID:** Nathan Edwards. **Telephone:** (408) 924-1217. **Fax:** (408) 924-1291. **Assistant Coaches:** *Nicholas Enriquez, Jimmy Meuel. **Telephone:** (408) 924-1262.
Home Field: Municipal Stadium. **Seating Capacity:** 5,200. **Outfield Dimension: LF**—320, **CF**—390, **RF**—320.

SANTA CLARA BRONCOS

Conference: West Coast.
Mailing Address: 500 El Camino Real, Santa Clara, CA 95053.
Website: www.santaclarabroncos.com.
Head Coach: Dan O'Brien. **Telephone:** (408) 554-4882.
Baseball SID: David Gentile. **Telephone:** (408) 554-4661.
Fax: (408) 554-6969. **Assistant Coaches:** Keith Beauregard, *Gabe Ribas. **Telephone:** (408) 554-4151.
Home Field: Stephen Schott Stadium. **Seating Capacity:** 1,500. **Outfield Dimension: LF**—340, **CF**—402, **RF**—335.

SAVANNAH STATE TIGERS

Conference: Mid-Eastern Athletic.
Mailing Address: Savannah State University, Attn: Baseball Office, PO Box 20271, Savannah, GA 31404.
Website: www.ssuathletics.com.
Head Coach: Carlton Hardy. **Telephone:** (912) 358-3082. **Baseball SID:** Opio Mashariki. **Telephone:** (912) 358-3430. **Fax:** (912) 358-3583. **Assistant Coaches:** Anthony Macon, *Eric McCombie. **Telephone:** (912) 358-3155.
Home Field: Tiger Field. **Seating Capacity:** 800. **Outfield Dimension: LF**—330 - 375, **CF**—400, **RF**—330 - 375.

SEATTLE REDHAWKS

Conference: Western Athletic.
Mailing Address: 901 12th Street, PO Box 222000, Seattle, WA 98122.
Website: www.goseattleu.com.
Head Coach: Danny Harrel. **Telephone:** (206) 398-4399. **Baseball SID:** Jason Behenna. **Telephone:** (206) 296-5915. **Assistant Coaches:** Elliott Cribby, Mike Nadeau. **Telephone:** (206) 398-4396.
Home Field: Bannerwood Park. **Seating Capacity:** 1,500. **Outfield Dimension: LF**—325, **CF**—400, **RF**—325.

SETON HALL PIRATES

Conference: Big East.
Mailing Address: 400 South Orange Ave, South Orange, NJ 07079.
Website: www.shupirates.com.
Head Coach: Robert Sheppard. **Telephone:** (973) 761-9557. **Baseball SID:** Matthew Sweeney. **Telephone:** (973) 761-9493. **Assistant Coaches:** *Phil Cundari, Mark Pappas. **Telephone:** (973) 275-6437.
Home Field: Owen T. Carrol Field. **Seating Capacity:** 1,800. **Outfield Dimension: LF**—315, **CF**—398, **RF**—320.

SIENA SAINTS

Conference: Metro Atlantic Athletic.
Mailing Address: 515 Loudon Rd., Loudonville, NY 12211.
Website: www.sienasaints.com.
Head Coach: Tony Rossi. **Telephone:** (518) 786-5044.
Baseball SID: Jason Rich. **Telephone:** (518) 783-2411.
Fax: (518) 783-2992. **Assistant Coaches:** *Pat Carroll, Joe Migliaccio. **Telephone:** (518) 782-6875.
Home Field: Siena Field. **Seating Capacity:** 1,000.

Outfield Dimension: LF—300, CF—400, RF—325.

SOUTH ALABAMA JAGUARS

Conference: Sun Belt.
Mailing Address: 6001 USA Drive South, Suite 35, Mobile, AL 36688.
Website: www.usajaguars.com.
Head Coach: Mark Calvi. Telephone: (251) 414-8243.
Baseball SID: Charlie Nichols. Telephone: (251) 414-8017. Assistant Coaches: Bob Keller, *Chris Prothro. Telephone: (251) 414-8209.
Home Field: Stanky Field. Seating Capacity: 3,775.
Outfield Dimension: LF—330, CF—400, RF—330.

SOUTH CAROLINA GAMECOCKS

Conference: Southeastern.
Mailing Address: 431 Williams Street, Columbia, SC 29201.
Website: www.gamecocksonline.com.
Head Coach: Chad Holbrook. Telephone: (803) 777-0116. Baseball SID: Andrew Kitick. Telephone: (803) 777-5257. Fax: (803) 777-2967. Assistant Coaches: *Sammy Esposito, Jerry Meyers. Telephone: (803) 777-7913.
Home Field: Founders Park. Seating Capacity: 8,242.
Outfield Dimension: LF—325, CF—400, RF—325.

SOUTH CAROLINA-UPSTATE SPARTANS

Conference: Atlantic Sun.
Mailing Address: 800 University Way, Spartanburg, SC 29303.
Website: www.upstatespartans.com.
Head Coach: Dr. Matt Fincher. Telephone: (864) 503-5135. Baseball SID: Steve Grandy. Telephone: (864) 503-5129. Assistant Coaches: Tyler Cook, *Ethan Guevin. Telephone: (864) 503-5164.
Home Field: Cleveland S. Harley Park. Seating Capacity: 500. Outfield Dimension: LF—330, CF—402, RF—330.

SOUTH DAKOTA STATE JACKRABBITS

Conference: Summit.
Mailing Address: 2820 HPER Center Brookings, SD 57006.
Website: www.gojacks.com.
Head Coach: David Schrage. Telephone: (605) 688-5027. Baseball SID: Jason Hove. Telephone: (605) 688-4623. Fax: (605) 688-5999. Assistant Coaches: *Brian Grunzke, Ben Norton. Telephone: (605) 688-5778.
Home Field: Erv Huether Field. Seating Capacity: 700.
Outfield Dimension: LF—330, CF—390, RF—320.

SOUTH FLORIDA BULLS

Conference: American Athletic.
Mailing Address: 4202 E. Fowler Ave. ATH 100 Tampa, FL 33620.
Website: www.gousfbulls.com.
Head Coach: Mark Kingston. Telephone: (813) 974-2504. Baseball SID: Mike Radomski. Telephone: (813) 974-7099. Assistant Coaches: *Mike Current, Billy Mohl. Telephone: (813) 974-2507.
Home Field: USF Baseball Stadium. Seating Capacity: 3,211. Outfield Dimension: LF—325, CF—400, RF—330.

SOUTHEAST MISSOURI STATE REDHAWKS

Conference: Ohio Valley.
Mailing Address: One University Plaza, Cape Girardeau, MO 63701.

Website: www.gosoutheast.com.
Head Coach: Steve Bieser. Telephone: (573) 986-6002.
Baseball SID: Sean Stevenson. Telephone: (573) 651-2294. Fax: (573) 651-2810. Assistant Coaches: Dillon Lawson, *Lance Rhodes. Telephone: (573) 986-6002.
Home Field: Capaha Field. Seating Capacity: 2,000.
Outfield Dimension: LF—330, CF—400, RF—330.

SOUTHEASTERN LOUISIANA LIONS

Conference: Southland.
Mailing Address: Southeastern Louisiana University Athletics, SLU 10309, Hammond, LA 70402.
Website: www.lionsports.com.
Head Coach: Matt Riser. Telephone: (985) 549-3566.
Baseball SID: Damon Sunde. Telephone: (985) 549-3774. Fax: (985) 549-3495. Assistant Coaches: *Andrew Gipson, Daniel Latham. Telephone: (985) 549-2896.
Home Field: Pat Kenelly Diamond at Alumni Field. Seating Capacity: 2,500. Outfield Dimension: LF—330, CF—400, RF—330.

SOUTHERN JAGUARS

Conference: Southwestern Athletic.
Mailing Address: 801 Harding Boulevard, Baton Rouge, LA 70813.
Website: www.gojagsports.com.
Head Coach: Roger Cador. Telephone: (225) 771-3172. Baseball SID: Christopher Jones. Telephone: (225) 771-3791. Assistant Coaches: Dan Canevari, Elliot Jones.
Home Field: Lee-Hines Field. Seating Capacity: 1,500.
Outfield Dimension: LF—360, CF—395, RF—320.

SOUTHERN CALIFORNIA TROJANS

Conference: Pacific-12.
Mailing Address: 3501 Watt Way, HER 103A Los Angeles, CA 90089.
Website: www.usctrojans.com.
Head Coach: Dan Hubbs. Telephone: (213) 740-8446.
Baseball SID: Rachel Caton. Telephone: (213) 740-3809.
Assistant Coaches: *Gabe Alvarez, Matt Curtis. Telephone: (213) 740-8447.
Home Field: Dedeaux Field. Seating Capacity: 2,500.
Outfield Dimension: LF—335, CF—395, RF—335.

SOUTHERN ILLINOIS SALUKIS

Conference: Missouri Valley.
Mailing Address: 425 Saluki Drive Carbondale, IL 62901.
Website: www.siusalukis.com.
Head Coach: Ken Henderson. Telephone: (618) 453-3794. Baseball SID: Rico Cruz. Telephone: (618) 453-7236. Assistant Coaches: *P.J. Finigan, Ryan Strain. Telephone: (618) 453-7646.
Home Field: Itchy Jones Stadium. Seating Capacity: 2,000. Outfield Dimension: LF—330, CF—390, RF—330.

SOUTHERN ILLINOIS-EDWARDSVILLE COUGARS

Conference: Ohio Valley.
Mailing Address: 35 Circle Drive Edwardsville, IL 62026.
Website: www.siuecougars.com.
Head Coach: Tony Stoecklin. Telephone: (618) 650-2032. Baseball SID: Joe Pott. Telephone: (618) 650-2860. Fax: (618) 650-2545. Assistant Coaches: Chase Green, *Danny Jackson. Telephone: (618) 650-2032.
Home Field: Simmons Complex. Seating Capacity: 1,300. Outfield Dimension: LF—330, CF—390, RF—330.

SOUTHERN MISSISSIPPI GOLDEN EAGLES

Conference: Conference USA.
Mailing Address: 118 College Dr., #5017, Hattiesburg, MS 39406.
Website: www.southernmiss.com.
Head Coach: Scott Berry. **Telephone:** (601) 255-6542.
Baseball SID: Jack Duggan. **Telephone:** (601) 266-4503.
Fax: (601) 277-4507. **Assistant Coaches:** *Chad Caillet, Michael Federico. **Telephone:** (601) 266-6542.
Home Field: Pete Taylor Park. **Seating Capacity:** 6,600. **Outfield Dimension:** LF—340, CF—400, RF—340.

ST. BONAVENTURE BONNIES

Conference: Atlantic 10.
Mailing Address: PO Box G, Reilly Center, St. Bonaventure, NY 14778.
Website: www.gobonnies.sbu.edu.
Head Coach: Larry Sudbrook. **Telephone:** (716) 375-2641. **Baseball SID:** Scott Eddy. **Telephone:** (716) 375-4019. Assistant Coache: B.J. Salerno. **Telephone:** (716) 375-2699.
Home Field: Fred Handler Park. **Seating Capacity:** 500. **Outfield Dimension:** LF—330, CF—403, RF—330.

ST. JOHN'S RED STORM

Conference: Big East.
Mailing Address: 8000 Utopia Parkway, Queens, NY 11439.
Website: www.redstormsports.com.
Head Coach: Ed Blankmeyer. **Telephone:** (718) 990-6148. **Baseball SID:** Tim Brown. **Telephone:** (718) 990-1521. **Assistant Coaches:** *Mike Hampton, Corey Muscara. **Telephone:** (718) 990-7523.
Home Field: Jack Kaiser Stadium. **Seating Capacity:** 3,500. **Outfield Dimension:** LF—325, CF—390, RF—325.

ST. JOSEPH'S HAWKS

Conference: Atlantic 10.
Mailing Address: 5600 City Ave. Philadelphia, PA 19131.
Website: www.sjuhawks.com.
Head Coach: Fritz Hamburg. **Telephone:** (610) 660-1718. **Baseball SID:** Joe Greenwich. **Telephone:** (610) 660-1738. **Fax:** (610) 660-1724. **Assistant Coaches:** Matt Allison, *Ryan Wheeler. **Telephone:** (610) 660-1704.
Home Field: Smithson Field. **Seating Capacity:** 400. **Outfield Dimension:** LF—327, CF—400, RF—331.

ST. MARY'S GAELS

Conference: West Coast.
Mailing Address: 1928 St. Marys Road, Moraga, CA 94575.
Website: www.smcgaels.com.
Head Coach: Eric Valenzuela. **Telephone:** (925) 631-4637. **Baseball SID:** Mark Rivera. **Telephone:** (925) 631-4950. **Assistant Coaches:** Greg Bordes, *Matt Fonteno. **Telephone:** (925) 631-8150.
Home Field: Louis Guisto Field. **Seating Capacity:** 500. **Outfield Dimension:** LF—330, CF—400, RF—330.

ST. PETER'S PEACOCKS

Conference: Metro Atlantic Athletic.
Mailing Address: 2641 Kennedy Boulevard, Jersey City, NJ 07306.
Website: www.stpeterspeacocks.com.
Head Coach: T.J. Baxter. **Telephone:** (201) 761-7319.
Baseball SID: Dave Musil. **Telephone:** (201) 761-7316.

Assistant Coaches: Ed Moskal, Matt Owens. **Telephone:** (201) 761-6362.
Home Field: Jaroshack Field. **Outfield Dimension:** LF—318, CF—405, RF—310.

STANFORD CARDINAL

Conference: Pacific-12.
Mailing Address: Arrillaga Family Sports Center, 641 E. Campus Drive, Stanford, CA 94305.
Website: www.gostanford.com.
Head Coach: Mark Marquess. **Telephone:** (650) 723-4528. **Baseball SID:** Eric Dolan. **Assistant Coaches:** *Rusty Filter, Brock Ungricht. **Telephone:** (650) 725-2373.
Home Field: Klein Field at Sunken Diamond. **Seating Capacity:** 4,000. **Outfield Dimension:** LF—335, CF—400, RF—335.

STEPHEN F. AUSTIN STATE LUMBERJACKS

Conference: Southland.
Mailing Address: SFA Athletics, PO Box 13010, SFA Station, Nacogdoches, TX 75962.
Website: www.sfajacks.com.
Head Coach: Johnny Cardenas. **Telephone:** (936) 468-5982. **Baseball SID:** Charlie Hurley. **Telephone:** 468-5800. **Fax:** (936) 468-4593. **Assistant Coaches:** *Matt Collins, Mike Haynes. **Telephone:** (936) 468-7796.
Home Field: Jaycees Field. **Seating Capacity:** 1,000. **Outfield Dimension:** LF—320, CF—390, RF—320.

STETSON HATTERS

Conference: Atlantic Sun.
Mailing Address: 421 N. Woodland Blvd., Unit 8359, DeLand, FL 32723.
Website: www.gohatters.com.
Head Coach: Pete Dunn. **Telephone:** (386) 822-8106.
Baseball SID: Ricky Hazel. **Telephone:** (386) 822-8130.
Assistant Coaches: *Mark Leavitt, Dave Therneau. **Telephone:** (386) 822-8733.
Home Field: Melching Field at Conrad Park. **Seating Capacity:** 2,500. **Outfield Dimension:** LF—335, CF—403, RF—335.

STONY BROOK SEAWOLVES

Conference: America East.
Mailing Address: Indoor Sports Complex, Stony Brook, NY 11794.
Website: www.stonybrookathletics.com.
Head Coach: Matt Senk. **Telephone:** (631) 632-9226.
Baseball SID: Brian Miller. **Telephone:** (631) 632-4318.
Assistant Coaches: George Brown, *Joe Pennucci. **Telephone:** (631) 632-4755.
Home Field: Joe Nathan Field. **Seating Capacity:** 1,000. **Outfield Dimension:** LF—330, CF—390, RF—330.

TENNESSEE VOLUNTEERS

Conference: Southeastern.
Mailing Address: 1511 Pat Head Summitt St., Knoxville, TN 37996.
Website: www.utsports.com.
Head Coach: Dave Serrano. **Telephone:** (865) 974-2057. **Baseball SID:** MJ Burns. **Telephone:** (865) 974-8876. **Assistant Coaches:** Larry Simcox, *Aric Thomas. **Telephone:** (865) 974-2057.
Home Field: Lindsey Nelson Stadium. **Seating Capacity:** 4,283. **Outfield Dimension:** LF—320, CF—390, RF—320.

TENNESSEE TECH GOLDEN EAGLES.

Conference: Ohio Valley.
Mailing Address: 1100 McGee Ave., Cookeville, TN 38505.
Website: www.ttusports.com.
Head Coach: Matt Bragga. **Telephone:** (931) 372-3925. **Baseball SID:** Mike Lehman. **Telephone:** (931) 372-6139. **Assistant Coaches:** *Justin Holmes, Derek Weldon. **Telephone:** (931) 372-6546.
Home Field: Quillen Field. **Seating Capacity:** 500.
Outfield Dimension: LF—330, **CF**—405, **RF**—330.

TENNESSEE-MARTIN SKYHAWKS

Conference: Ohio Valley.
Mailing Address: 1022 Elam Center, Martin, TN 38238.
Website: www.utmsports.com.
Head Coach: Rick Robinson. **Telephone:** (731) 881-7337. **Baseball SID:** Ryne Rickman. **Telephone:** (731) 881-7632. **Assistant Coaches:** Seth Cutler-Voltz, *Rick Guarno. **Telephone:** (731) 881-3691.
Home Field: Skyhawk Park. **Seating Capacity:** 300.
Outfield Dimension: LF—330, **CF**—385, **RF**—330.

TEXAS LONGHORNS

Conference: Big 12.
Mailing Address: Intercollegiate Athletics, The University of Texas at Austin, PO Box 7399, Austin, TX 78713.
Website: www.texassports.com.
Head Coach: Augie Garrido. **Telephone:** (512) 471-5732. **Assistant Coaches:** Skip Johnson, *Tommy Nicholson. **Telephone:** (512) 471-5732.
Home Field: UFCU- Disch Falk Field. **Seating Capacity:** 6,649. **Outfield Dimension: LF**—340, **CF**—400, **RF**—325.

TEXAS A&M AGGIES

Conference: Southeastern.
Mailing Address: Texas A&M Athletics, 1228 TAMU, College Station, TX 77843.
Website: www.12thman.com.
Head Coach: Rob Childress. **Telephone:** (979) 845-4810. **Baseball SID:** Thomas Dick. **Telephone:** (512) 784-2153. **Assistant Coaches:** Will Bolt, *Justin Seely. **Telephone:** (979) 845-4810.
Home Field: Olsen Field at Blue Bell Park. **Seating Capacity:** 6,100. **Outfield Dimension: LF**—330 - 375, **CF**—400, **RF**—330 - 375.

TEXAS A&M-CORPUS CHRISTI ISLANDERS

Conference: Southland.
Mailing Address: 6300 Ocean Drive, Unit 5719, Corpus Christi, TX 78412.
Website: www.goislanders.com.
Head Coach: Scott Malone. **Telephone:** (361) 825-3413. **Baseball SID:** Jacob Bell. **Telephone:** (361) 825-2831. **Fax:** (361) 825-3737. **Assistant Coaches:** *Brett Gips, Marty Smith. **Telephone:** (361) 825-3720.
Home Field: Chapman Field. **Seating Capacity:** 700.
Outfield Dimension: LF—330, **CF**—404, **RF**—330.

TEXAS CHRISTIAN HORNED FROGS

Conference: Big 12.
Mailing Address: 2800 Stadium Dr. Fort Worth, TX 76129.
Website: www.gofrogs.com.
Head Coach: Jim Schlossnagle. **Telephone:** (817) 257-

5354. **Baseball SID:** Brandie Davidson. **Telephone:** (817) 257-7479. **Fax:** (817) 257-7964. **Assistant Coaches:** Bill Mosiello, *Kirk Saarloos. **Telephone:** (817) 257-5588.
Home Field: Lupton Stadium. **Seating Capacity:** 4,500. **Outfield Dimension: LF**—375, **CF**—395, **RF**—370.

TEXAS SOUTHERN TIGERS

Conference: Southwestern Athletic.
Mailing Address: 3100 Cleburne St, Houston, TX 77004.
Website: www.tsuball.com.
Head Coach: Michael Robertson. **Telephone:** (713) 313-4315. **Baseball SID:** Andrew Roberts. **Telephone:** (713) 313-6829. **Fax:** (713) 313-1045. **Assistant Coaches:** Ehren Moreno. **Telephone:** (713) 313-7993.
Home Field: MacGregor Park. **Outfield Dimension: LF**—315, **CF**—395, **RF**—315.

TEXAS STATE BOBCATS

Conference: Sun Belt.
Mailing Address: 601 University Drive, San Marcos, Texas 78666.
Website: www.txstatebobcats.com.
Head Coach: Ty Harrington. **Telephone:** (512) 245-3383. **Baseball SID:** Joshua Flanagan. **Telephone:** (512) 245-4692. **Fax:** (512) 245-2967. **Assistant Coaches:** *Jeremy Fikac, Steven Trout. **Telephone:** (512) 245-3383.
Home Field: Bobcat Ballpark. **Seating Capacity:** 2,500.
Outfield Dimension: LF—330, **CF**—405, **RF**—330.

TEXAS TECH RED RAIDERS

Conference: Big 12.
Mailing Address: 2526 6th St., Lubbock, TX 79409.
Website: www.texastech.com.
Head Coach: Tim Tadlock. **Telephone:** (806) 834-4836. **Baseball SID:** Matt Dowdy. **Telephone:** (806) 834-4529. **Assistant Coaches:** Ray Hayward, *J-Bob Thomas. **Telephone:** (806) 834-4836.
Home Field: Dan Law Field at Rip Griffin Park. **Seating Capacity:** 4,368. **Outfield Dimension: LF**—330, **CF**—404, **RF**—330.

TEXAS-ARLINGTON MAVERICKS

Conference: Sun Belt.
Mailing Address: College Park Center, 601 Spaniolo Dr., Arlington, TX 76019.
Website: www.utamavs.com.
Head Coach: Darin Thomas. **Telephone:** (817) 272-2542. **Baseball SID:** Ben Rikard. **Telephone:** (817) 272-2212. **Assistant Coaches:** Fuller Smith, *Jon Wente. **Telephone:** (817) 272-0111.
Home Field: Clay Gould Ballpark. **Seating Capacity:** 1,600. **Outfield Dimension: LF**—330, **CF**—400, **RF**—300.

TEXAS-RIO GRANDE VALLEY VAQUEROS

Conference: Western Athletic.
Mailing Address: UTRGV Department of Intercollegiate Athletics, 1201 West University Drive, Edinburg, TX 78539.
Website: www.goutrgv.com.
Head Coach: Manny Mantrana. **Telephone:** (956) 665-2235. **Baseball SID:** Jonah Goldberg. **Telephone:** (956) 665-2240. **Assistant Coaches:** Jordan Banfield, Brian Nelson. **Telephone:** (956) 665-2891.
Home Field: Edinburg Baseball Stadium. **Seating Capacity:** 4,000. **Outfield Dimension: LF**—325, **CF**—410, **RF**—325.

TEXAS-SAN ANTONIO ROADRUNNERS

Conference: Conference USA.
Mailing Address: Department of Intercollegiate Athletics, Physical Education Building, One UTSA Circle, San Antonio, TX 798249.
Website: www.utsa.com.
Head Coach: Jason Marshall. **Telephone:** (210) 458-4811. **Baseball SID:** Zena Rex. **Telephone:** (956) 739-4878. **Assistant Coaches:** Jim Blair, Brett Lawler. **Telephone:** (210) 458-4805.
Home Field: Roadrunner Field. **Seating Capacity:** 800. **Outfield Dimension: LF**—335, **CF**—405, **RF**—340.

TOLEDO ROCKETS

Conference: Mid-American.
Mailing Address: 2801 West Bancroft St., MS-408, Toledo, OH 43606.
Website: www.utrockets.com.
Head Coach: Cory Mee. **Telephone:** (419) 530-6263. **Baseball SID:** Michael Scholze. **Telephone:** (419) 530-4926. **Fax:** (419) 530-4428. **Assistant Coaches:** *Josh Bradford, Nick McIntyre. **Telephone:** (419) 530-3097.
Home Field: Scott Park. **Seating Capacity:** 1,000. **Outfield Dimension: LF**—330, **CF**—400, **RF**—330.

TOWSON TIGERS

Conference: Colonial Athletic.
Mailing Address: 8000 York Road Towson, MD 21252.
Website: www.towsontigers.com.
Head Coach: Mike Gottlieb. **Telephone:** (410) 704-3773. **Baseball SID:** John Brush. **Telephone:** (410) 704-3102. **Fax:** (410) 704-3861. **Assistant Coaches:** Scott Roane. **Telephone:** (410) 704-4587.
Home Field: Schuerholz Park. **Seating Capacity:** 500. **Outfield Dimension: LF**—312, **CF**—424, **RF**—301.

TROY TROJANS

Conference: Sun Belt.
Mailing Address: Troy University Athletics, Tine Davis Field House, Troy, AL 36082.
Website: www.troytrojans.com.
Head Coach: Mark Smartt. **Telephone:** (334) 670-3333. **Baseball SID:** Adam Predergast. **Telephone:** (334) 670-3832. **Assistant Coaches:** *Shane Gierke, Brad Phillips. **Telephone:** (334) 670-5705.
Home Field: Riddle-Pace Field. **Seating Capacity:** 2,000. **Outfield Dimension: LF**—345, **CF**—400, **RF**—310.

TULANE GREEN WAVE

Conference: American Athletic.
Mailing Address: 333 James W. Wilson Jr. Center, Ben Weiner Drive, New Orleans, LA 70118.
Website: www.tulanegreenwave.com.
Head Coach: David Pierce. **Telephone:** (504) 862-8216. **Baseball SID:** Curtis Akey. **Telephone:** (504) 314-7271. **Assistant Coaches:** *Sean Allen, Philip Miller. **Telephone:** (504) 314-7203.
Home Field: Greer Field at Turchin Stadium. **Seating Capacity:** 5,000. **Outfield Dimension: LF**—325, **CF**—400, **RF**—325.

UC DAVIS AGGIES

Conference: Big West.
Mailing Address: Hickey Gym 264, One Shields Ave, Davis, CA 95616.
Website: www.ucdavisaggies.com.

Head Coach: Matt Vaughn. **Telephone:** (530) 752-7513. **Baseball SID:** Jason Spencer. **Telephone:** (530) 752-2663. **Assistant Coaches:** *Lloyd Acosta, Brett Lindgren. **Telephone:** (530) 752-7513.
Home Field: Dobbins Baseball Complex. **Seating Capacity:** 3,500. **Outfield Dimension: LF**—310, **CF**—410, **RF**—310.

UC IRVINE ANTEATERS

Conference: Big West.
Mailing Address: UC Irvine; Intercollegiate Athletics Building; 625 Humanities Quad; Irvine, CA 92697.
Website: www.ucirvinesports.com.
Head Coach: Mike Gillespie. **Telephone:** (949) 824-4292. **Baseball SID:** Fumi Kimura. **Telephone:** (949) 824-9474. **Assistant Coaches:** Daniel Bibona, *Ben Orloff. **Telephone:** (949) 824-1154.
Home Field: Anteater Ballpark. **Seating Capacity:** 3,200. **Outfield Dimension: LF**—335, **CF**—405, **RF**—335.

UC RIVERSIDE HIGHLANDERS

Conference: Big West.
Mailing Address: 900 University Ave., Riverside, CA 92521.
Head Coach: Troy Percival. **Telephone:** (951) 827-5441. **Baseball SID:** John Maxwell. **Telephone:** (951) 827-5438. **Fax:** (951) 827-3569. **Assistant Coaches:** *Bryson LeBlanc, Curt Smith. **Telephone:** (951) 827-5441.
Home Field: The Plex. **Seating Capacity:** 2,227. **Outfield Dimension: LF**—330, **CF**—400, **RF**—330.

UC SANTA BARBARA GAUCHOS

Conference: Big West.
Mailing Address: ICA Building, UC Santa Barbara, Santa Barbara, CA 93106.
Website: www.ucsbgauchos.com.
Head Coach: Andrew Checketts. **Telephone:** (805) 893-3690. **Baseball SID:** Andrew Wagner. **Telephone:** (805) 893-8603. **Fax:** (805) 893-5477. **Assistant Coaches:** *Eddie Cornejo, Neil Walton. **Telephone:** (805) 893-2021.
Home Field: Caesar Uyesaka Stadium. **Seating Capacity:** 1,000. **Outfield Dimension: LF**—335, **CF**—400, **RF**—335.

UCLA BRUINS

Conference: Pacific-12.
Mailing Address: 325 Westwood Plaza, Los Angeles, CA 90095.
Website: www.uclabruins.com.
Head Coach: John Savage. **Telephone:** (310) 794-8210. **Baseball SID:** Evan Kaplan. **Telephone:** (310) 206-7870. **Fax:** (310) 825-8664. **Assistant Coaches:** Rex Peters, Bryant Ward. **Telephone:** (310) 794-8210.
Home Field: Jackie Robinson Stadium. **Seating Capacity:** 1,250. **Outfield Dimension: LF**—330, **CF**—395, **RF**—330.

UNC ASHEVILLE BULLDOGS

Conference: Big South.
Mailing Address: One University Heights CPO #2600 Asheville, NC 28804.
Website: www.uncabulldogs.com.
Head Coach: Scott Friedholm. **Telephone:** (828) 251-6903. **Baseball SID:** Nick Phillips. **Telephone:** (828) 251-6931. **Assistant Coaches:** Chris Bresnahan, *Jonathan Johnston. **Telephone:** (828) 250-2309.
Home Field: Greenwood Field. **Seating Capacity:** 400.

Outfield Dimension: LF—330, CF—400, RF—330.

UNC GREENSBORO SPARTANS

Conference: Southern.
Mailing Address: 1509 Walker Ave. Greensboro, NC 27410.
Website: www.uncgspartans.com.
Head Coach: Link Jarrett. Telephone: (336) 334-3247.
Baseball SID: Matt McCollester. Telephone: (336) 334-5615. Assistant Coaches: Jerry Edwards, *Joey Holcomb. Telephone: (336) 334-3247.
Home Field: UNCG Baseball Stadium. Seating Capacity: 3,500. Outfield Dimension: LF—340, CF—410, RF—340.

UNC WILMINGTON SEAHAWKS

Conference: Colonial Athletic.
Mailing Address: 601 S. College Road, Wilmington, NC 28403.
Website: www.uncwsports.com.
Head Coach: Mark Scalf. Telephone: (910) 962-3570.
Baseball SID: Tom Riordan. Telephone: (910) 962-4099.
Assistant Coaches: *Randy Hood, Matt Williams. Telephone: (910) 962-7471.
Home Field: Brooks Field. Seating Capacity: 3,500.
Outfield Dimension: LF—340, CF—380, RF—340.

UTAH UTES

Conference: Pacific-12.
Mailing Address: 1825 E. South Campus Dr., Salt Lake City, UT 84112.
Website: www.utahutes.com.
Head Coach: Bill Kinneberg. Telephone: (801) 581-3526. Baseball SID: Brooke Frederickson. Telephone: (801) 581-8302. Assistant Coaches: *Mike Crawford, Jason Hawkins. Telephone: (801) 581-3024.
Home Field: Smith's Ballpark. Seating Capacity: 15,500.
Outfield Dimension: LF—345, CF—420, RF—315.

UTAH VALLEY WOLVERINES

Conference: Western Athletic.
Mailing Address: 800 W University Parkway, Orem, UT 84058.
Website: www.wolverinegreen.com.
Head Coach: Eric Madsen. Telephone: (801) 863-6509.
Baseball SID: Clint Burgi. Telephone: (801) 863-8644.
Fax: (801) 863-8813. Assistant Coaches: *Derek Amicone, Dave Carter. Telephone: (801) 863-8467.
Home Field: Brent Brown Ballpark. Seating Capacity: 5,000. Outfield Dimension: LF—305, CF—408, RF—312.

VALPARAISO CRUSADERS

Conference: Horizon.
Mailing Address: 1009 Union Street Valparaiso, IN 46393.
Website: www.valpoathletics.com.
Head Coach: Brian Schmack. Telephone: (219) 464-6117. Baseball SID: Brad Collignon. Telephone: (219) 464-6953. Assistant Coaches: Nic Mishler, *Ben Wolgamot. Telephone: .
Home Field: Emory G. Bauer. Seating Capacity: 500.
Outfield Dimension: LF—340, CF—400, RF—340.

VANDERBILT COMMODORES

Conference: Southeastern.
Mailing Address: 2601 Jess Neely Drive, Nashville, TN 37212.

Website: www.vucommodores.com.
Head Coach: Tim Corbin. Telephone: (615) 322-3716.
Baseball SID: Kyle Parkinson. Telephone: (615) 343-0020. Assistant Coaches: Scott Brown, *Travis Jewett. Telephone: (615) 322-3074.
Home Field: Hawkins Field. Seating Capacity: 3,626.
Outfield Dimension: LF—310, CF—400, RF—330.

VILLANOVA WILDCATS

Conference: Big East.
Mailing Address: 800 East Lancaster Avenue, Jake Nevin Field House, Villanova, PA 19085.
Website: www.villaova.com.
Head Coach: Joe Godri. Telephone: (610) 519-4529.
Baseball SID: David Berman. Telephone: (610) 519-4122.
Assistant Coaches: *Kevin Mulvey, Adah White. Telephone: (610) 519-4529.
Home Field: Villanova Ballpark at Plymouth. Seating Capacity: 750. Outfield Dimension: LF—330, CF—405, RF—330.

VIRGINIA CAVALIERS

Conference: Atlantic Coast.
Mailing Address: University Hall, PO Box 400839, Charlottesville, VA 22904.
Website: www.virginiasports.com.
Head Coach: Brian O'Connor. Telephone: (434) 982-4932. Baseball SID: Andy Fledderjohann. Telephone: (434) 982-5131. Assistant Coaches: Karl Kuhn, *Kevin McMullan. Telephone: (434) 982-5776.
Home Field: Davenport Field. Seating Capacity: 5,025. Outfield Dimension: LF—332, CF—404, RF—332.

VIRGINIA COMMONWEALTH RAMS

Conference: Atlantic 10.
Mailing Address: 1300 W. Broad St., Richmond, VA 23284.
Website: www.vcuathletics.com.
Head Coach: Shawn Stiffler. Telephone: (804) 828-4822. Baseball SID: Dan Sherman. Telephone: (804) 828-3440. Fax: (804) 828-4938. Assistant Coaches: *Kurt Elbin, Steve Hay. Telephone: (804) 828-4821.
Home Field: The Diamond. Seating Capacity: 9,560.
Outfield Dimension: LF—330, CF—402, RF—330.

VIRGINIA MILITARY INSTITUTE KEYDETS

Conference: Southern.
Mailing Address: Cameron Hall, Lexington, VA 24450.
Website: www.vmikeydets.com.
Head Coach: Jonathan Hadra. Telephone: (540) 464-7601. Baseball SID: Brad Salois. Telephone: (540) 464-7015. Assistant Coaches: Travis Beazley, *Casey Dykes. Telephone: (540) 464-7605.
Home Field: Gray-Minor Stadium. Seating Capacity: 1,400. Outfield Dimension: LF—330, CF—390, RF—335.

VIRGINIA TECH HOKIES

Conference: Atlantic Coast.
Mailing Address: Cassell Coliseum, Suite 204 (0502), 675 Washington St. SW, Blacksburg, VA 24061.
Website: www.hokiesports.com.
Head Coach: Patrick Mason. Telephone: (540) 231-3671. Baseball SID: Marc Mullen. Telephone: (540) 231-1894. Assistant Coaches: Ryan Connolly, *Robert Woodard. Telephone: (540) 231-3098.
Home Field: English Field. Seating Capacity: 3,500.
Outfield Dimension: LF—330, CF—400, RF—330.

WAGNER SEAHAWKS

Conference: Northeast.
Mailing Address: One Campus Road, Staten Island, NY 10301.
Website: www.wagnerathletics.com.
Head Coach: Jim Carone. **Telephone:** (718) 390-3154. **Baseball SID:** Brian Morales. **Telephone:** (718) 390-3215. **Assistant Coaches:** *Eddie Brown, Dan Wasilick. **Telephone:** (718) 390-4081.
Home Field: Richmond County Bank Ballpark. **Seating Capacity:** 7,171. **Outfield Dimension: LF**—320, **CF**—390, **RF**—318.

WAKE FOREST DEMON DEACONS

Conference: Atlantic Coast.
Mailing Address: PO Box 7265, Winston-Salem, NC 27109.
Website: www.wakeforestsports.com.
Head Coach: Tom Walter. **Telephone:** (336) 758-5570. **Baseball SID:** Jay Garneau. **Telephone:** (336) 758-3229. **Assistant Coaches:** *Bill Cilento, Matt Hobbs. **Telephone:** (336) 758-4208.
Home Field: Wake Forest Baseball Park. **Seating Capacity:** 5,298. **Outfield Dimension: LF**—310, **CF**—400, **RF**—300.

WASHINGTON HUSKIES

Conference: Pacific-12.
Mailing Address: Department of Intercollegiate Athletics, University of Washington, Box 354070, Graves Building, Seattle, WA 98195.
Website: www.gohuskies.com.
Head Coach: Lindsay Meggs. **Telephone:** (206) 616-4335. **Baseball SID:** Brian Tom. **Telephone:** (206) 897-1742. **Assistant Coaches:** Donegal Fergus, *Jason Kelly. **Telephone:** (206) 685-7016.
Home Field: Husky Ballpark. **Seating Capacity:** 2,200. **Outfield Dimension: LF**—327, **CF**—395, **RF**—317.

WASHINGTON STATE COUGARS

Conference: Pacific-12.
Mailing Address: P.O. Box 641602, Pullman, WA 99164.
Website: www.wsucougars.com.
Head Coach: Marty Lees. **Telephone:** (509) 335-0332. **Baseball SID:** Bobby Alworth. **Telephone:** (509) 335-5785. **Fax:** (509) 335-5197. **Assistant Coaches:** Jim Horner, *Dan Spencer. **Telephone:** (509) 335-0211.
Home Field: Bailey-Brayton Field. **Seating Capacity:** 3,500. **Outfield Dimension: LF**—330, **CF**—400, **RF**—330.

WEST VIRGINIA MOUNTAINEERS

Conference: Big 12.
Mailing Address: PO Box 0877, Morgantown, WV 26507.
Website: www.wvusports.com.
Head Coach: Randy Mazey. **Telephone:** (304) 293-2300. **Baseball SID:** Charlie Healy. **Telephone:** (304) 293-2821. **Assistant Coaches:** Derek Matlock, Steve Sabins. **Telephone:** (304) 293-9880.
Home Field: Monongalia County Ballpark. **Seating Capacity:** 2,500. **Outfield Dimension: LF**—325, **CF**—400, **RF**—325.

WESTERN CAROLINA CATAMOUNTS

Conference: Southern.
Mailing Address: 92 Catamount Road, Ramsey Center – Athletics, Cullowhee, NC 28723.
Website: www.catamountsports.com.
Head Coach: Bobby Moranda. **Telephone:** (828) 227-2021. **Baseball SID:** Daniel Hooker. **Telephone:** (828) 227-2339. **Assistant Coaches:** *Nate Cocolin, Todd Guilliams. **Telephone:** (828) 227-7338.
Home Field: Hennon Stadium. **Seating Capacity:** 1,500. **Outfield Dimension: LF**—325, **CF**—395, **RF**—325.

WESTERN ILLINOIS LEATHERNECKS

Conference: Summit.
Mailing Address: 1 University Circle Macomb, IL 61455.
Website: www.goleathernecks.com.
Head Coach: Ryan Brownlee. **Telephone:** (309) 298-1521. **Baseball SID:** Patrick Osterman. **Telephone:** (309) 298-1133. **Assistant Coaches:** *Shane Davis, Matt Igara. **Telephone:** (309) 298-1521.
Home Field: Alfred Boyer Stadium. **Seating Capacity:** 502. **Outfield Dimension: LF**—325, **CF**—395, **RF**—330.

WESTERN KENTUCKY HILLTOPPERS

Conference: Conference USA.
Mailing Address: 1605 Avenue of Champions, Bowling Green, KY 42101.
Website: www.wkusports.com.
Head Coach: John Pawlowski. **Telephone:** (270) 745-2277. **Baseball SID:** Brett Pund. **Telephone:** (270) 745-5388. **Assistant Coaches:** *Ty Megahee, Rob Reinstetle. **Telephone:** (270) 745-2274.
Home Field: Nick Denes Field. **Seating Capacity:** 1,800. **Outfield Dimension: LF**—330, **CF**—390, **RF**—330.

WESTERN MICHIGAN BRONCOS

Conference: Mid-American.
Mailing Address: 1903 W. Michigan Avenue, Kalamazoo, MI, 49008.
Website: www.wmubroncos.com.
Head Coach: Billy Gernon. **Telephone:** (269) 276-3205. **Baseball SID:** Kristin Keirns. **Telephone:** (269) 387-4123. **Fax:** (269) 387-4139. **Assistant Coaches:** JP Maracani, *Adam Piotrowicz. **Telephone:** (269) 276-3208.
Home Field: Robert J. Bobb Stadium at Hyames Field. **Seating Capacity:** 1,500. **Outfield Dimension: LF**—310, **CF**—395, **RF**—335.

WICHITA STATE SHOCKERS

Conference: Missouri Valley.
Mailing Address: 1845 Fairmount, Box 18, Wichita, KS 67260-0018.
Website: www.goshockers.com.
Head Coach: Todd Butler. **Telephone:** (316) 978-3636. **Baseball SID:** Tami Cutler. **Telephone:** (316) 978-5559. **Fax:** (316) 978-3336. **Assistant Coaches:** Brent Kemnitz, *Brian Walker. **Telephone:** (316) 978-3636.
Home Field: Eck Stadium. **Seating Capacity:** 8,103. **Outfield Dimension: LF**—330, **CF**—390, **RF**—330.

WILLIAM & MARY TRIBE

Conference: Colonial Athletic.
Mailing Address: 751 Ukrop Way, Williamsburg, VA 23185.
Website: www.tribeathletics.com.
Head Coach: Brian Murphy. **Telephone:** (757) 221-3492. **Baseball SID:** Andrew Phillips. **Telephone:** (757) 221-3344. **Assistant Coaches:** *Brian Casey, Andy Kiriakedes. **Telephone:** (757) 221-3399.

Home Field: Plumeri Park. **Seating Capacity:** 1,100. **Outfield Dimension: LF**—325, **CF**—400, **RF**—325.

WINTHROP EAGLES

Conference: Big South.
Mailing Address: Winthrop Baseball, 1162 Eden Terrace, Rock Hill, SC 29733.
Website: www.winthropeagles.com.
Head Coach: Tom Riginos. **Telephone:** (864) 903-9796.
Baseball SID: Jack Frost. **Telephone:** (803) 323-6245. **Fax:** (803) 323-5676. **Assistant Coaches:** *Clint Chrysler, Rich Witten. **Telephone:** (859) 319-1398.
Home Field: Winthrop Ball Park. **Seating Capacity:** 1,900. **Outfield Dimension: LF**—325, **CF**—400, **RF**—325.

WISCONSIN-MILWAUKEE PANTHERS

Conference: Horizon.
Mailing Address: PO Box 413, The Pavilion – Room 150, Milwaukee, WI 53201.
Website: www.mkepanthers.com.
Head Coach: Scott Doffek. **Telephone:** (414) 229-5670. **Baseball SID:** Chris Zills. **Telephone:** (414) 229-4593. **Fax:** (414) 229-5749. **Assistant Coaches:** Cory Bigler, Cole Kraft. **Telephone:** (414) 229-2433.
Home Field: Henry Aaron Field. **Seating Capacity:** 500. **Outfield Dimension: LF**—320, **CF**—390, **RF**—320.

WOFFORD TERRIERS

Conference: Southern.
Mailing Address: 429 N. Church Street, Spartanburg, SC 29303.
Website: www.woffordterriers.com.
Head Coach: Todd Interdonato. **Telephone:** (864) 597-4497. **Baseball SID:** Brent Williamson. **Telephone:** (864) 597-4093. **Fax:** (864) 597-4112. **Assistant Coaches:** *Jason Burke, J.J. Edwards. **Telephone:** (864) 597-4499.
Home Field: Russell C. King Field. **Seating Capacity:** 2,500. **Outfield Dimension: LF**—325, **CF**—395, **RF**—325.

WRIGHT STATE RAIDERS

Conference: Horizon.
Mailing Address: 3640 Colonel Glenn Hwy., Dayton, OH 45435.
Website: www.wsuraiders.com.
Head Coach: Greg Lovelady. **Telephone:** (937) 775-3668. **Baseball SID:** Matt Zircher. **Telephone:** (937) 775-2831. **Assistant Coaches:** *Jeff Mercer, Justin Parker. **Telephone:** (937) 775-4188.
Home Field: Nischwitz Stadium. **Seating Capacity:** 750. **Outfield Dimension: LF**—330, **CF**—400, **RF**—330.

XAVIER MUSKETEERS

Conference: Big East.
Mailing Address: 3800 Victory Parkway, Cincinnati, OH 45207.
Website: www.goxavier.com.
Head Coach: Scott Googins. **Telephone:** (513) 745-2891. **Baseball SID:** Brendan Bergen. **Telephone:** (513) 745-3388. **Assistant Coaches:** *Billy O'Conner, Nick Otte. **Telephone:** (513) 745-1962.
Home Field: Hayden Field. **Seating Capacity:** 500. **Outfield Dimension: LF**—310, **CF**—380, **RF**—310.

YALE BULLDOGS

Conference: Ivy.
Mailing Address: PO Box 208216, New Haven, CT 06520.
Website: www.yalebulldogs.com.
Head Coach: John Stuper. **Telephone:** (203) 432-1466. **Baseball SID:** Steve Lewis. **Telephone:** (203) 432-1448. **Fax:** (203) 432-1454. **Assistant Coaches:** Tucker Frawley, Ray Guario. **Telephone:** (203) 432-1467.
Home Field: Yale Field. **Seating Capacity:** 5,000. **Outfield Dimension: LF**—330, **CF**—405, **RF**—315.

YOUNGSTOWN STATE PENGUINS

Conference: Horizon.
Mailing Address: 1 University Plaza, Youngstown, OH, 44555.
Website: www.ysusports.com.
Head Coach: Steve Gillispie. **Baseball SID:** John Vogel. **Telephone:** (330) 941-1480. **Fax:** (330) 941-3191. **Assistant Coaches:** *Jason Neal, Kevin Smallcomb.
Home Field: Eastwood Field. **Seating Capacity:** 6,000. **Outfield Dimension: LF**—335, **CF**—405, **RF**—335.

AMATEUR & YOUTH

INTERNATIONAL ORGANIZATIONS

WORLD BASEBALL SOFTBALL CONFEDERATION

Headquarters: Maison du Sport International—54, Avenue de Rhodanie, 1007 Lausanne, Switzerland. **Telephone:** (+41-21) 318-82-40. **Fax:** (41-21) 318-82-41. **Website:** www.wbsc.org. **E-Mail:** office@ibaf.org. **Year Founded:** 1938.
President: Riccardo Fraccari.
1st Vice President: Alonso Perez Gonzalez. **2nd Vice President:** Tom Peng. **3rd Vice President:** Antonio Castro. **Secretary General:** Israel Roldan. **Treasurer:** Angelo Vicini. **Members at Large:** Masaaki Nagino, Paul Seiler, Luis Melero. **Continental VP, Africa:** Sabeur Jlajla. **Continental VP, Americas:** Nemesio Guillermo Porras Lopez. **Continental VP, Asia:** Byung-Suk Lee. **Continental VP, Europe:** Jan Esselman. **Continental VP, Oceania:** Laurent Cassier. **Executive Director:** Michael Schmidt.
Assistant to the President: Victor Isola. **Marketing/Tournament Manager:** Masaru Yokoo. **Public Relations Officer:** Oscar Lopez. **National Federation Relations:** Francesca Fabretto. **Antidoping Officer:** Victor Isola. **Administration/Finance:** Sandrine Pennone.

CONTINENTAL ASSOCIATIONS

CONFEDERATION PAN AMERICANA DE BEISBOL (COPABE)

Mailing Address: Calle 3, Francisco Filos, Vista Hermosa, Edificio 74, Planta Baja Local No. 1, Panama City, Panama. **Telephone:** (507) 229-8684. **Fax:** Unavailable. **Website:** www.copabe.net. **E-Mail:** copabe@sinfo.net.
Chairman: Eduardo De Bello (Panama). **Secretary General:** Hector Pereyra (Dominican Republic).

AFRICA BASEBALL SOFTBALL ASSOCIATION (ABSA)

Office Address: Paiko Road, Chanchaga, Minna, Niger State, Nigeria.
Mailing Address: P.M.B. 150, Minna, Niger State, Nigeria.
Telephone: (234) 8037188491. **E-mail:** absasecretariat@yahoo.com
President: Sabeur Jlajla. **Vice President Baseball:** Etienne N'Guessan. **Vice President Softball:** Fridah Shiroya. **Secretary General:** Ibrahim N'Diaye. **Treasurer:** Moira Dempsey. **Executive Director:** Lieutenant Colonel (rtd) Friday Ichide. **Deputy Executive Director:** Francoise Kameni-Lele.

BASEBALL FEDERATION OF ASIA

Mailing Address: 9F. -3, No. 288, Sec 6 Civic Blvd.,Xinyi Dist., Taipei City, Taiwan (R.O.C.). **Telephone:** 886-2-27473368. **E-Mail Address:** bfa@baseballasia.org
President: Tom Peng. **Vice Presidents:** Suzuki Yoshinobu, Kim Jong-Up, Shen Wei (China). **Secretary General:** Hua-Wei Lin. **Executive Director, West Asia:** Syed Khawar Shah. **Members At Large:** Allan Mak, Tom Navasero, Vutichai Udomkarnjananan.

EUROPEAN BASEBALL CONFEDERATION

Mailing Address: Savska cesta 137, 10 000 Zagreb, Croatia. **Telephone/Fax:** +385 1 561 5227. **E-Mail Address:** office@baseballeurope.com. **Website:** baseballeurope.com.
President: Jan Esselman (Netherlands). **1st Vice President:** Peter Kurz (Israel). **2nd Vice President:** Jürgen Elsishans (Germany). **3rd Vice President:** Petr Ditrich (Czech Republic). **Secretary General:** Krunoslav Karin (Croatia) **Treasurer:** Rene Laforce (Belgium). **Vocals:** Mick Manning (Ireland), Mats Fransson (Sweden), Monique Schmitt (Switzerland), Valentinas Bubulis (Lithuania).

BASEBALL CONFEDERATION OF OCEANIA

Mailing Address: 48 Partridge Way, Mooroolbark, Victoria 3138, Australia. **Telephone:** 613 9727 1779. **Fax:** 613 9727 5959. **E-Mail Address:** bcosecgeneral@baseballoceania.com. **Website:** www.baseballoceania.com.
President: Bob Steffy (Guam). **1st Vice President:** Laurent Cassier (New Caledonia). **2nd Vice President:** Victor Langkilde (American Samoa). **Secretary General:** Chet Gray (Australia). **Executive Committee:** Rose Igitol (CNMI), Temmy Shmull (Palau), Innoke Niubalavu (Fiji).

INTERNATIONAL GOODWILL SERIES, INC.

Mailing Address: 982 Slate Drive, Santa Rosa, CA 95405. **Telephone:** (707) 538-0777. **E-Mail Address:** rwilliams@goodwillseries.org. **Website:** www.goodwillseries.org.
President, Goodwill Series, Inc.: Bob Williams.

INTERNATIONAL SPORTS GROUP

Mailing Address: 3829 S Oakbrook Dr. Greenfield, WI 53228. **Telephone:** (541) 882-4293. **E-Mail Address:** isgbaseball14@gmail.com. **Website:** www.isgbaseball.com.
President: Tom O'Connell. **Vice President:** Peter Caliendo.
Secretary/Treasurer: Randy Town. **Board Members:** Jim Jones, Rick Steen, Bill Mathews, Pat Doyle, John Vodenlich. **Founder/Senior Consultant:** Bill Arce.

NATIONAL ORGANIZATIONS

USA BASEBALL

Mailing Address, Corporate Headquarters: 403 Blackwell St., Durham, NC 27701. **Telephone:** (919) 474-8721. **Fax:** (919) 474-8822. **E-mail Address:** info@usabaseball.com. **Website:** www.usabaseball.com.
President: Mike Gaski. **Treasurer:** Jason Dobis.
Board of Directors: Jenny Dalton-Hill, John McHale, Jr. (Major League Baseball), Wes Skelton (Dixie Baseball), Steve Keener (Little League), Steve Tellefsen (Babe Ruth), Damani Leech (NCAA), George Grande (At Large).
Executive Director/Chief Executive Officer: Paul Seiler. **Director, National Team Development Programs/Women's National Team:** Ashley Bratcher. **General Manager, National Teams:** Eric Campbell. **Chief Financial Officer:** Ray Darwin. **Director, Travel Services:** Jocelyn Fern. **Assistant Director, Operations:** Tom Gottlieb. **Director, Digital/Social Media:** Kevin

Jones. **Assistant Director, Accounting/Finance:** Cicely Lopez. **Chief Operating Officer:** David Perkins. **Director, Development:** Rick Riccobono. **Director, Community Relations:** Kevin Kelly.

National Members: Amateur Athletic Union (AAU), American Amateur Baseball Congress (AABC), American Baseball Coaches Association (ABCA), American Legion Baseball, Babe Ruth Baseball, Dixie Baseball, Little LeagueBaseball, National Amateur Baseball Federation (NABF), National Association of Intercollegiate Athletics (NAIA), National Baseball Congress (NBC), National Collegiate Athletic Association (NCAA), National Federation of State High School Athletic Associations, National High School Baseball Coaches Association (BCA), National Junior College Athletic Association (NJCAA), Police Athletic League (PAL), PONY Baseball, T-Ball USA, United States Specialty Sports Association (USSSA).
Events: www.usabaseball.com/events/schedule.jsp.

BASEBALL CANADA

Mailing Address: 2212 Gladwin Cres., Suite A7, Ottawa, Ontario K1B 5N1. **Telephone:** (613) 748-5606. **Fax:** (613) 748-5767. **E-mail Address:** info@baseball.ca. **Website:** www.baseball.ca.

Director General: Jim Baba. **Head Coach/Director, National Teams:** Greg Hamilton. **Manager, Baseball Operations:** Andre Lachance. **Program Coordinator:** Kelsey McIntosh. **Manager, Media/Public Relations:** Adam Morissette. **Administrative Coordinator:** Denise Thomas. **Administrative Assistant:** Penny Baba.

NATIONAL BASEBALL CONGRESS

Mailing Address: 111 S. Main, Suite 600, Wichita, KS 67202. **Telephone:** (316) 977-9400. **Fax:** (316) 462-4506. **Website:** www.nbcbaseball.com.
Year Founded: 1931.

ATHLETES IN ACTION

Mailing Address: 651 Taylor Dr., Xenia, OH 45385. **Telephone:** (937) 352-1000. **Fax:** (937) 352-1245. **E-mail Address:** baseball@athletesinaction.org. **Website:** www.aiabaseball.org.
Director, AIA Baseball: Chris Beck. **General Manager, Alaska:** Chris Beck. **General Manager, Great Lakes:** John Henschen. **General Manager, New York Collegiate League:** Chris Rainwater. **International Teams Director:** John McLaughlin. **Youth Baseball Director:** Matt Richter.

SUMMER COLLEGE LEAGUES

NATIONAL ALLIANCE OF COLLEGE SUMMER BASEBALL

Telephone: (321) 206-9714 **E-Mail Address:** RSitz@FloridaLeague.com **Website:** www.nacsb.org
Executive Director: Rob Sitz (Florida League) **Assistant Executive Director:** Bobby Bennett (Sunbelt Baseball League), Jeff Carter (Southern Collegiate Baseball League). **Treasurer:** Larry Tremitiere (Southern Collegiate Baseball League). **Director, Public Relations/Secretary:** Stefano Foggi (Florida Collegiate Summer League). **Compliance Officer:** Paul Galop (Cape Cod Baseball League).

Member Leagues: Atlantic Collegiate Baseball League, California Collegiate League, Cal Ripken Collegiate Baseball League, Cape Cod Baseball League, Florida Collegiate Summer League, Great Lakes Summer Collegiate League, New England Collegiate Baseball League, New York Collegiate Baseball League, Southern Collegiate Baseball League, Sunbelt Baseball League, Valley Baseball League, Hamptons Collegiate Baseball League.

ALASKA BASEBALL LEAGUE

Mailing Address: P.O. Box 2690, Palmer, AK 99645. **Telephone:** (907) 745-6401. **Fax:** (907) 746-5068. **E-Mail Address:** mikebaxter@acsalaska.net.
Year Founded: 1974 (reunited, 1998).
President, Marketing & Umpire Payroll: Pete Christopher (Mat-Su Miners). **1st VP, Secretary:** Mike Hinshaw (Anchorage Glacier Pilots). **2nd VP, Umpires & Scheduling:** Shawn Maltby (Anchorage Bucs). **3rd VP, Bylaws:** Mike Baxter (Peninsula Oilers). **4th VP, Rules & Bylaws:** Chric Beck (Chugiak-Eagle River Chinooks).
Regular Season: 44 league games and approximately 5 non-league games. **2016 Opening Date:** June 9. **Closing Date:** August 3.
Playoff Format: Regular season league champion qualifies for National Baseball Congress World Series if desired. Also, a round robin end-of-season tournament

with a best of three final determines playoff champion.
Roster Limit: 26 plus exemption for Alaska residents.
Player Eligibility: Open except drafted college seniors.

ANCHORAGE BUCS

Mailing Address: PO Box 240061, Anchorage, AK 99524-0061. **Telephone:** (907) 561-2827. **Fax:** (907) 561-2920. **E-Mail Address:** gm@anchoragebucs.com. **Website:** anchoragebucs.com. **General Manager:** Shawn Maltby. **Head Coach:** Mike Grahovac. **Field:** Mulcahy Field—turf infield, grass outfield, lights.

ANCHORAGE GLACIER PILOTS

Mailing Address: 435 West 10th Avenue, Suite A, Anchorage, AK 99501. **Telephone:** (907) 274-3627. **Fax:** (907) 274-3628. **E-Mail Address:** gpilots@alaska.net. **Website:** glacierpilots.com. **General Manager:** Mike Hinshaw. **Head Coach:** Darren Westergard (Skagit Valley CC, Wash.). **Field:** Mulcahy Field—turf infield, grass outfield, lights.

CHUGIAK-EAGLE RIVER CHINOOKS

Mailing Address: 651 Taylor Dr, Xenia, OH 45385. **Telephone:** (937) 352-1237. **Fax:** (937) 352-1245. **E-Mail Address:** chris.beck@athletesinaction.org. **Website:** www.aiabaseball.org. **Additional Website:** www.cerchinooks.com. **General Manager:** Chris Beck. **Head Coach:** Jon Groth (Tyler, Texas, CC). **Field:** Lee Jordan Field—turf infield, grass outfield, no lights.

MAT-SU MINERS

Mailing Address: PO Box 2690, Palmer, AK 99645-2690. **Telephone:** (907) 746-4914; (907) 745-6401. **Fax:** (907) 746-5068. **E-Mail Address:** generalmanager@matsuminers.org. **Website:** matsuminers.org. **General Manager:** Pete Christopher. **Head Coach:** Ben Taylor

(Chandler-Gilbert, CC). **Field:** Hermon Brothers Field—grass, no lights.

PENINSULA OILERS

Mailing Address: 601 S Main St, Kenai, AK 99611. **Telephone:** (907) 283-7133. **Fax:** (907) 283-3390. **E-Mail Address:** gm@oilersbaseball.com. **Website:** oilersbaseball.com. **General Manager:** Mike Baxter. **Head Coach:** TBA. **Field:** Coral Seymour Memorial Park—grass, no lights.

ALL AMERICAN COLLEGIATE BASEBALL LEAGUE
Mailing Address: 8442 Sandowne Ln, Huntersville NC 28078. **Website:** www.allamericanleague.com. **VP/CFO:** Joseph Finch. **Telephone:** 304-685-3532. **Telephone:** 617-543-4247.
Founded: 2013.
Teams: Mooresville All Americans (Mooresville, NC), Carolina Freedom (Morganton, NC), North Carolina Liberty (Salisbury, NC), Rowan Patriots (Spencer, NC), Stanly Pioneers (Oakboro, NC), Mt Pleasant Militia (Mt Pleasant, NC), Caldwell Warriors (Lenoir, NC).

ATLANTIC COLLEGIATE BASEBALL LEAGUE
Mailing Address: 1760 Joanne Drive, Quakertown, PA 18951. **Telephone:** (215) 536-5777. **Fax:** (215) 536-5777. **E-Mail:** tbonekemper@verizon.net. **Website:** www.acbl-online.com.
Year Founded: 1967.
Commissioner: Ralph Addonizio. **President/Acting Secretary:** Tom Bonekemper. **Assistant Commissioner:** Doug Cinella. **Vice Presidents:** Brian Casey. **Treasurer:** Bob Hoffman.
Regular Season: 40 games. **2016 Opening Date:** June 4. **Closing Date:** August 7. **All-Star Game:** July 21 at Provident Bank Park, Pomona, NY. **Roster Limit:** 26.

ALLENTOWN RAILERS
Mailing Address: Suite 202, 1801 Union Blvd, Allentown, PA 18109. **E-Mail Address:** ddando@lehighvalleybaseballacademy.com. **Field Manager:** Dylan Dando.

JERSEY PILOTS
Mailing Address: 11 Danemar Drive, Middletown, NJ 07748. **Telephone:** (732) 939-0627. **E-Mail Address:** baseball@jerseypilots.com. **General Manager:** Mike Kalb. **Field Manager:** Aaron Kalb.

LEHIGH VALLEY CATZ
Mailing Address: 103 Logan Dr, Easton, PA 18045. **Telephone:** (610) 533-9349. **Website:** www.lvcatz.com. **General Manager:** Tom Lisinicchia. **Field Manager:** Dennis Morgan.

NORTH JERSEY EAGLES
Mailing Address: 107 Pleasant Avenue, Upper Saddle River, NJ 07458. **General Manager:** Brian Casey. **Field Manager:** Doug Cinnella.

QUAKERTOWN BLAZERS
Telephone: (215) 679-5072. **E-Mail Address:** quakertownblazers@outlook.com. **Website:** www.quakertownblazers.com. **General Manager:** George Bonekemper. **Field Manager:** Dewey Oriente.

SOUTH JERSEY GIANTS
Website: www.southjerseygiants.com. **Field Manager:** Greg Manco (gmanco@sju.edu).

STATEN ISLAND TIDE
Website: www.statenislandtide.com. **General Manager:** Mike O'Brien. **Field Manager:** Greg Delgeorge.

TRENTON GENERALS
E-Mail Address: lmaher5@verizon.net. **General Manager:** Jim Maher. **Field Manager:** TBA.

CALIFORNIA COLLEGIATE LEAGUE
Mailing Address: 806 W Pedregosa St, Santa Barbara, CA 93101. **Telephone:** (805) 680-1047. **Fax:** (805) 684-8596. **E-Mail Address:** burns@calsummerball.com. **Website:** www.calsummerball.com.
Founded: 1993.
Commissioner: Pat Burns.
Division Structure: North Division—Healdsburg Prune Packers, Menlo Park Legends, Neptune Beach Pearl, Walnut Creek Crawdads. **Central**—Conejo Oaks, San Luis Obispo Blues, Santa Barbara Foresters, Ventura Halos. **South**—Academy Barons, Long Beach Legends, Orange County Riptide, Southern California Catch.
Regular Season: 36 games (24 divisional games, 12 inter-divisional games). **2016 Opening Date:** June 1. **Closing Date:** July 31. **Playoff Format:** Divisional champions and wild card team play double-elimination championship tournament. **Roster Limit:** 33.

ACADEMY BARONS
Address: 901 E. Artesia Blvd, Compton, CA 90221. **Telephone:** (310) 635-2967. **Website:** www.academybarons.org. **E-Mail Address:** charles.dickerson@mlb.com. **Contact:** Charles Dickerson, director.

CONEJO OAKS
Address: 1710 N. Moorpark Rd., #106, Thousand Oaks, CA 91360. **Telephone:** (805) 797-7889. **Website:** www.oaksbaseball.org. **E-Mail Address:** oaksbaseball@yahoo.com. **Contact:** David Soliz, field manager.

HEALDSBURG PRUNE PACKERS
Address: 230 Pheasant Dr., Healdsburg, CA 95448. **Telephone:** 707-280-6693. **Website:** prunepackers.org. **Email:** jgg1@aol.com. **Contact:** Joey Gomes, field manager.

LONG BEACH LEGENDS
Address: 9732 Skylark Blvd, Garden Grove, CA 92841. **Telephone:** 714-322-7306. **Website:** lblegends.com. **E-Mail:** jrodlbcc@gmail.com. **Contact:** Johnathan Rodriguez, general manager.

MENLO PARK LEGENDS

Address: PO Box 280, Menlo Park, CA 94026-0280. **Telephone:** (650) 387-4427. **Website:** www.menlopark legends.com. **E-Mail Address:** mplegends@gmail.com. **Contact:** David Klein, general manager.

NEPTUNE BEACH PEARL

Address: PO Box 2602, Alameda, CA 94501. **Telephone:** (510) 590-3139. **Website:** www.neptune beachpearl.com. **E-Mail Address:** bcummings@neptune beachpearl.com. **Contact:** Brant Cummings, field manager.

ORANGE COUNTY RIPTIDE

Address: 14 Calendula Rancho, Santa Margarita, CA 92688. **Telephone:** 949-228-7676. **Website:** ocriptide .com. **E-Mail Address:** ocriptidebaseball@gmail.com. **Contact:** Moe Geohagen, general manager.

SAN LUIS OBISPO BLUES

Address: 241-B Prado Rd., San Luis Obispo, CA 93401. **Telephone:** (805) 704-4388. **Website:** www.bluesbaseball .com. **E-Mail Address:** adam@bluesbaseball.com. **Contact:** Adam Stowe, general manager.

SANTA BARBARA FORESTERS

Address: 4299 Carpinteria Ave., Suite 201, Carpinteria, CA 93013. **Telephone:** (805) 684-0657. **Website:** www.sb foresters.org. **E-Mail Address:** pintard@earthlink.net. **Contact:** Bill Pintard, field manager.

VENTURA HALOS

Address: 722 West Santa Paula St., Santa Paula, CA 93060. **Telephone:** (805) 207-3565. **Website:** www. venturahalos.com. **E-Mail Address:** c_t_gomez@hotmail .com. **Contact:** Chris Gomez, general manager.

SOUTHERN CALIFORNIA CATCH

Address: 14830 Grayville Drive, La Mirada, CA 90638. **Telephone:** (562) 686-8262. **Website:** www.socalcatch .com. **E-Mail Address:** borr@fca.org. **Contact:** Ben Orr, general manager.

WALNUT CREEK CRAWDADS

Address: 1630 Challenge Dr., Concord, CA 94520. **Telephone:** (925) 354-7315. **Website:** www.walnutcreek crawdads.com. **E-Mail Address:** mnisco@gmail.com. **Contact:** Mike Nisco, general manager.

CAL RIPKEN COLLEGIATE LEAGUE

Address: 4006 Broadstone St, Frederick, MD 21704. **Telephone:** (301) 693-2577. **E-Mail:** jwoodward@cal ripkenleague.org or brifkin@calripkenleague.org. **Website:** www.calripkenleague.org.

Year Founded: 2005.

Commissioner: Jason Woodward. **League President:** Brad Rifkin. **Deputy Commissioner:** Jerry Wargo.

Regular Season: 40 games. **Playoff Format:** Top two teams from each division plus two remaining teams with best records qualify. Teams play best of three series, winners advance to best of three series for league cham-

pionship. **Roster Limit:** 30 (college-eligible players 22 and under).

ALEXANDRIA ACES

Address: 600 14th Street NW, Suite 400, Washington, DC 20005. **Telephone:** (202) 255-1683. **E-Mail:** dondinan @gmail.com. **Website:** www.alexandriaaces.org. **Chairman/CEO:** Donald Dinan. **General Manager:** Lou Nolan. **Head Coach:** David DeSilva. **Ballpark:** Frank Mann Field at Four Mile Run Park.

BALTIMORE DODGERS

Address: 131 Sunnydale Way, Reisterstown, MD 21136. **Telephone:** (443) 834-3500. **Email:** juan.waters@ verizon.net. **Website:** www.baltimoredodgers.org. **President:** Juan Waters. **Head Coach:** Derek Brown. **Ballpark:** Joe Cannon Stadium at Harmans Park.

BALTIMORE REDBIRDS

Address: 2208 Pine Hill Farms Lane, Cockeysville, MD 21030. **Telephone:** (410) 802-2220. **Fax:** (410) 785-6138. **E-Mail:** johntcarey@hotmail.com. **Website:** www. baltimoreredbirds.org. **President:** John Carey. **Head Coach:** Larry Sheets. **Ballpark:** Carlo Crispino Stadium at Calvert Hall High School.

BETHESDA BIG TRAIN

Address: 5420 Butler Road, Bethesda, MD 20816. **Telephone:** 301-983-1006. **Fax:** 301- 229-8362. **E-Mail:** faninfo@bigtrain.org. **Website:** www.bigtrain.org. **General Manager:** Eddie Herndon. **Head Coach:** Sal Colangelo. **Ballpark:** Shirley Povich Field.

D.C. GRAYS

Address: 1800 M Street NW, 500 South Tower, Washington, DC 20036. **Telephone:** (202) 492-6226. **Website:** www.dcgrays.com. **E-Mail Address:** barbera@ acg-consultants.com. **President:** Michael Barbera. **General Manager:** Antonio Scott. **Head Coach:** Reggie Terry. **Ballpark:** Washington Nationals Youth Academy.

GAITHERSBURG GIANTS

Address: 10 Brookes Avenue, Gaithersburg, MD 20877. **Telephone:** (240) 888-6810. **Fax:** (301) 355-5006. **E-Mail:** alriley13@gmail.com. **Website:** www.gaithersburg giants.org. **General Manager:** Alfie Riley. **Head Coach:** Jeff Rabberman. **Ballpark:** Criswell Automotive Field at Kelley Park.

FCA HERNDON BRAVES

Address: 1305 Kelly Court, Herndon, VA 20170-2605. **Telephone:** (702) 909-2750. **Fax:** (703) 783-1319. **E-Mail:** fcaherndonbraves@yahoo.com. **Website:** www.herndon braves.com. **President/General Manager:** Todd Burger. **Head Coach:** Chris Warren. **Ballpark:** Alan McCullock Field at Herndon High School.

ROCKVILLE EXPRESS

Address: PO Box 10188, Rockville, MD 20849. **Telephone:** 301-367-9435. **E-Mail:** info@rockvilleexpress .org. **Website:** www.rockvilleexpress.org. **President/GM:** Jim Kazunas. **Email:** jameskazunas@rockvilleexpress. org. **Head Coach:** Rick Price. **Ballpark:** Knights Field at Montgomery College-Rockville.

SILVER SPRING-TAKOMA T-BOLTS

Address: 906 Glaizewood Court, Takoma Park, MD 20912. **Telephone:** (301) 270-0794. **E-Mail:** tboltsbaseball @gmail.com. **Website:** www.tbolts.org. **General Manager:** David Stinson. **Head Coach:** Doug Remer. **Ballpark:** Blair Stadium at Montgomery Blair High School.

VIENNA RIVER DOGS

Address: 12703 Hitchcock Ct, Reston, VA 20191. **Telephone:** (703) 615-4396. **E-Mail Address:** tickets@ brucehallsports.com. **Website:** www.viennariverdogs.org. **President/General Manager/Head Coach:** Bruce Hall. **Ballpark:** James Madison High School.

CAPE COD BASEBALL LEAGUE

Mailing Address: PO Box 266, Harwich Port, MA 02646. **Telephone:** (508) 432-6909. **E-Mail:** info@capecod baseball.org. **Website:** www.capecodbaseball.org.
Year Founded: 1885.
Commissioner: Paul Galop. **President:** Chuck Sturtevant. **Treasurer/Webmaster:** Steven Wilson. **Secretary:** Kim Wolfe. **Senior Vice President:** Jim Higgins. **VP/Deputy Commissioner:** Bill Bussiere. **VP:** Peter Ford. **Senior Deputy Commissioner/Director of Officiating:** Sol Yas. **Deputy Commissioner, West:** Mike Carrier. **Deputy Commissioner, East:** Peter Hall.
Director, Public Relations/Broadcasting: John Garner Jr. **Director, Communications:** Jim McGonigle. **Director, Publications:** Sean Sullivan. **Director, Memorabilia:** Dan Dunn. **Editor, Publications:** Rich Plante. **Assistant to the Officers:** Bill Watson. **Assistants, Marketing:** Melissa Ellis, Sue Pina. **Director, Social Media:** Elizabeth Cohen. **Website Editor:** Victoria Martin.
Division Structure: East—Brewster, Chatham, Harwich, Orleans, Yarmouth-Dennis. **West**—Bourne, Cotuit, Falmouth, Hyannis, Wareham. **Regular Season:** 44 games. **2016 Opening Date:** June 10. **Closing Date:** August 13. **All-Star Game:** July 23. **Playoff Format:** Top four teams in each division qualify for three rounds of best-of-three series.
Roster Limit: 30 (college-eligible players only).

BOURNE BRAVES

Mailing Address: PO Box 895, Monument Beach, MA 02553. **Telephone:** (508) 868-8378. **E-Mail Address:** nnorkevicius@yahoo.com. **Website:** www.bournebraves .org. **President:** Nicole Norkevicius. **General Manager:** Mike Carrier. **Head Coach:** Harvey Shapiro.

BREWSTER WHITECAPS

Mailing Address: PO Box 2349, Brewster, MA 02631. **Telephone:** (508) 896-8500, ext. 147. **Fax:** (508) 896-9845. **E-Mail Address:** cagradone@comcast.net. **Website:** www.brewsterwhitecaps.com. **President:** Chris Kenney. **General Manager:** Ned Monthie. **Head Coach:** Jamie Shevchick.

CHATHAM ANGLERS

Mailing Address: PO Box 428, Chatham, MA 02633. **Telephone:** (508) 348-1607. **Website:** www.chathamas .com. **President:** Steve West. **General Manager:** Mike Geylin. **Head Coach:** John Schiffner.

COTUIT KETTLEERS

Mailing Address: PO Box 411, Cotuit, MA 02635. **Telephone:** (508) 428-3358. **Fax:** (508) 420-5584. **E-Mail Address:** info@kettleers.org. **Website:** www.kettleers.org. **President:** Paul Logan. **General Manager:** Bruce Murphy. **Head Coach:** Mike Roberts.

FALMOUTH COMMODORES

Mailing Address: PO Box 808 Falmouth, MA 02541. **Telephone:** (508) 566-4988. **Website:** www.falmouth commodores.org. **President:** Mark Kasprzyk. **General Manager:** Eric Zmuda. **Head Coach:** Jeff Trundy.

HARWICH MARINERS

Mailing Address: PO Box 201, Harwich Port, MA 02646. **Telephone:** (508) 432-2000. **Fax:** (508) 432-5357. **E-Mail Address:** mehendy@comcast.net. **Website:** www.harwich mariners.org. **President:** Mary Henderson. **General Manager:** Ben Layton. **Head Coach:** Steve Englert.

HYANNIS HARBOR HAWKS

Mailing Address: PO Box 852, Hyannis, MA 02601. **Telephone:** (508) 737-5890. **Fax:** (877) 822-2703. **E-Mail Address:** brpfeifer@aol.com. **Website:** www.harborhawks .org. **President:** Brad Pfeifer. **General Manager:** Tino DiGiovanni. **Head Coach:** Chad Gassman.

ORLEANS FIREBIRDS

Mailing Address: PO Box 504, Orleans, MA 02653. **Telephone:** (508) 255-0793. **Fax:** (508) 255-2237. **E-Mail Address:** gene.hornsby@outlook.com. **Website:** www. orleansfirebirds.com. **President:** Gene Hornsby. **General Manager:** Sue Horton. **Head Coach:** Kelly Nicholson.

WAREHAM GATEMEN

Mailing Address: PO Box 287, Wareham, MA 02571. **Telephone:** (508) 748-0287. **Fax:** (508) 880-2602. **E-Mail Address:** paulatufts4gatemen@comcast.net. **Website:** www.gatemen.org. **President:** Tom Gay. **General Manager:** Andrew Lang. **Head Coach:** Jerry Weinstein.

YARMOUTH-DENNIS RED SOX

Mailing Address: PO Box 78 Yarmouth Port, MA 02675. **Telephone:** (508) 889-8721. **E-Mail Address:** sfaucher64@gmail.com. **Website:** www.ydredsox.org. **President:** Ed Pereira. **General Manager:** Steve Faucher. **Head Coach:** Scott Pickler.

CENTENNIAL STATE LEAGUE

Mailing Address: 543 Saturn Drive, Fort Collins, CO 80525. **Telephone:** (970) 225-9564. **Commissioner:** Kurt Colicchio. **Director of Umpires:** Gary Weibert.
Regular Season: 34 games (June 1-July 17). **Playoff Format:** Second-place team plays best of three series against first-place team for league championship. **All-Star Game:** None. **Roster limit:** 23 active (college-eligible players only). **Participating teams:** Fort Collins Foxes, Loveland Blue Jays, Windsor Beavers.

CENTRAL VALLEY COLLEGIATE LEAGUE

Mailing Address: P.O. Box 561, Fowler, CA 93625.

E-mail: j_scot25@hotmail.com, jcederquist@aol.com.
Website: www.cvclbaseball.webs.com. Twitter: @CVCL1.
Year Founded: 2013. President: Jamie Cederquist.
Vice-President: Jon Scott. Regular Season: 30 games.
2015 Opening Date: June 2. Closing Date: July 26. All-
Star Game: July 15, Kingsburg, Calif. Roster Limit: 35
(college-eligible players only).

BAKERSFIELD BRAVES

Mailing Address: PO Box 20760, Bakersfield, CA,
93390. Website: eteamz.com/bakersfieldbraves. Field
Manager: Bobby Maitia.

CALIFORNIA EXPOS

Mailing Address: P.O. Box 561, Fowler, CA 93625.
E-mail: exposcv@aol.com. Website: www.californiaexpos
.webs.com. Twitter: @cvexpos. Field Manager: Thomas
Raymundo.

CALIFORNIA PILOTS

Mailing Address: PO Box 561 Fowler, CA 93625.
E-mail: valleystormbaseball@aol.com. Website: valley
stormbaseball.webs.com. Twitter: @calistorm1. Field
Manager: Kolton Carbal

LIGHTNING BASEBALL

Mailing Address: Visalia, CA. E-mail: d.dominguez@
att.net. Website: Unavailable. General Manager: Dereck
Dominguez. Field Manager: Dereck Dominguez.

MERCED VOLUNTEERS

Mailing Address: 472 Grogan Avenue Merced, CA
95341 E-mail: rollo@allprojanitorialservices.com Field
Manager: Rollo Adams

SOUTH COUNTY VIPERS

Mailing Address: P.O Box 144, Kingsburg, CA 93631.
E-mail: j_scot25@hotmail.com. Website: www.cvipers.
webs.com. Twitter: @SouthcountryV. Field Manager:
Jon Scott.

COASTAL PLAIN LEAGUE

Mailing Address: 102 Hyannis Drive, Holly Springs,
NC 27540. Telephone: (919) 852-1960. Fax: (919) 516-
0852. Email Address: justins@coastalplain.com. Website:
www.coastalplain.com.
Year Founded: 1997.
Chairman/CEO: Jerry Petitt. President: Pete Bock.
Commissioner: Justin Sellers. Director, On-Field
Operations: Jeff Bock.
Division Structure: East—Edenton, Fayetteville, Holly
Springs, Morehead City, Peninsula, Petersburg, Wilmington,
Wilson. West—Asheboro, Florence, Forest City, Gastonia,
High Point-Thomaville, Lexington, Martinsville.
Regular Season: 56 games (split schedule). 2015
Opening Date: May 26. Closing Date: August 15. All-
Star Game: July 13. Playoff Format: Three rounds of
best of three series.
Roster Limit: 30 (college-eligible players only).

ASHEBORO COPPERHEADS

Mailing Address: PO Box 4006, Asheboro, NC 27204.
Telephone: (336) 460-7018. Fax: (336) 629-2651. E-Mail
Address: info@teamcopperhead.com. Website: www.
teamcopperhead.com. Owners: Ronnie Pugh, Steve
Pugh, Doug Pugh, Mike Pugh. General Manager: David
Camp. Head Coach: Keith Ritsche (Winston-Salem State).

EDENTON STEAMERS

Mailing Address: PO Box 86, Edenton, NC 27932.
Telephone: (252) 482-4080. Fax: (252) 482-1717. E-Mail
Address: edentonsteamers@hotmail.com. Website:
www.edentonsteamers.com. Owners: Edenton Steamers
Inc. President: Wallace Evans. General Manager: Tyler
Russell. Head Coach: Bryan Hill (Chowan University).

FAYETTEVILLE SWAMPDOGS

Mailing Address: PO Box 64691, Fayetteville, NC
28306.Telephone: (910) 426-5900. Fax: (910) 426-3544.
E-Mail Address: info@goswampdogs.com. Website: www.
goswampdogs.com. Owners: Lew Handelsman. General
Manager: Jeremy Aagard. Head Coach: Zach Brown

FLORENCE REDWOLVES

Mailing Address: PO Box 809, Florence, SC 29503.
Telephone: (843) 629-0700. Fax: (843) 629-0703. E-Mail
Address: barbara@florenceredwolves.com. Website:
www.florenceredwolves.com. Owners: Kevin Barth,
Donna Barth. General Manager: Barbara Osborne.
Head Coach: Blake Maxwell.

FOREST CITY OWLS

Mailing Address: PO Box 1062, Forest City, NC 28043.
Telephone: (828) 245-0000. Fax: (828) 245-6666. E-Mail
Address: info@forestcitybaseball.com. Website: www.
forestcitybaseball.com. Owner/President: Ken Silver.
Managing Partner: Jesse Cole. General Manager: Kiva
Fuller. Head Coach: JT Maguire (Wofford College).

GASTONIA GRIZZLIES

Mailing Address: PO Box 177, Gastonia, NC 28053.
Telephone: (704) 866-8622. Fax: (704) 864-6122. E-Mail
Address: jesse@gastoniagrizzlies.com. Website: www.
gastoniagrizzlies.com. Owner: Jesse Cole. Assistant
General Manager: David McDonald. Head Coach: Evan
Wise (Lenoir-Rhyne).

HIGH POINT-THOMASVILLE HI-TOMS

Mailing Address: PO Box 3035, Thomasville, NC
27361. Telephone: (336) 472-8667. Fax: (336) 472-7198.
E-Mail Address: info@hitoms.com. Website: www.
hitoms.com. Owner: Richard Holland. President: Greg
Suire. General Manager: Brian Roundtree.

HOLLY SPRINGS SALAMANDERS

Mailing Address: PO Box 1208, Holly Springs, NC
27540. Telephone: 919-249-7322. Email Address:
tommya@salamandersbaseball.com. Website: www.
salamandersbaseball.com. Owner: Jerry Petitt and Pete
Bock. General Manager: Tommy Atkinson. Head Coach:
Andrew Ciencin.

LEXINGTON COUNTY BLOWFISH

Mailing Address: PO Box 2018, Lexington, SC. **Telephone:** (803) 254-3474. **Fax:** (803) 254-4482. **E-Mail Address:** info@blowfishbaseball.com. **Website:** www.blowfishbaseball.com. **Owner:** HWS Baseball V (Michael Savit, Bill Shanahan). **General Manager:** Kelly Evans **Head Coach:** Jonathan Johnson

MARTINSVILLE MUSTANGS

Mailing Address: PO Box 1112, Martinsville, VA 24114. **Telephone:** (276) 403-5250. **Fax:** (276) 403-5387. **E-Mail Address:** shea@martinsvillemustangs.com. **Website:** www.martinsvillemustangs.com. **Owner:** City of Martinsville. **General Manager:** Shea Maple. **Head Coach:** Sean West.

MOREHEAD CITY MARLINS

Mailing Address: 1921 Oglesby Road, Morehead City, NC 28557. **Telephone:** (252) 269-9767. **Fax:** (252) 727-9402. **E-Mail Address:** croth@mhcmarlins.com. **Website:** www.mhcmarlins.com. **President:** Buddy Bengel. **General Manager:** Catherine Roth. **Head Coach:** Jason Wood.

PENINSULA PILOTS

Mailing Address: PO Box 7376, Hampton, VA 23666. **Telephone:** (757) 245-2222. **Fax:** (757) 245-8030. **E-Mail Address:** jeffscott@peninsulapilots.com. **Website:** www.peninsulapilots.com. **Owner:** Henry Morgan. **General Manager:** Jeffrey Scott. **Head Coach/Vice President:** Hank Morgan.

PETERSBURG GENERALS

Mailing Address: 1981 Midway Ave, Petersburg, VA 23803. **Telephone:** (804) 722-0141. **Fax:** (804) 733-7370. **E-Mail Address:** rmassenburg@petersburg-va.org. **Website:** www.petersburggenerals.com. **Owner:** City of Petersburg. **General Manager:** Ryan Massenburg. **Head Coach:** Matt Laney (Lander).

WILMINGTON SHARKS

Mailing Address: PO Box 15233, Wilmington, NC 28412. **Telephone:** (910) 343-5621. **Fax:** (910) 343-8932. **E-Mail Address:** info@wilmingtonsharks.com. **Website:** www.wilmingtonsharks.com. **Owners:** Smith Family Baseball Wilmington, LLC. **General Manager:** Pat Hutchins. **Head Coach:** Parker Bangs.

WILSON TOBS

Mailing Address: PO Box 633, Wilson, NC 27894. **Telephone:** (252) 291-8627. **Fax:** (252) 291-1224. **E-Mail Address:** wilsontobs@gmail.com. **Website:** www.wilsontobs.com. **Owner:** Richard Holland. **President:** Greg Suire. **General Manager:** Thomas Webb. **Head Coach:** Bryant Gaines (North Carolina).

FLORIDA COLLEGIATE SUMMER LEAGUE

Mailing Address: 2410 N Rio Grande Ave, Orlando, FL 32804. **Telephone:** (321) 206-9174. **Fax:** (407) 574-7926. **E-Mail Address:** info@floridaleague.com. **Website:** www.floridaleague.com.

Year Founded: 2004. **President:** Rob Sitz. **Vice President:** Stefano Foggi. **League Operations Director:** Phil Chinnery. **Regular Season:** 45 games. **2016 Opening Date:** June 2. **Closing Date:** August 7. **All-Star Game:** July 9. **Playoff Format:** Five teams qualify; No. 4 and No. 5 seeds meet in one-game playoff. Remaining four teams play best of three series. Winners play one game for league championship. **Roster Limit:** 28 (college-eligible players only).

ALTAMONTE SPRINGS BOOM

Operated by the league office. Email Address: altamonte@floridaleague.com. **Head Coach:** Ken Kelly. **General Manager:** TBA.

DELAND SUNS

Operated by the league office. E-Mail Address: delandsuns@floridaleague.com. **Head Coach:** Rick Hall. **General Manager:** Theresa Brooks.

LEESBURG LIGHTNING

Mailing Address: 318 South 2nd St, Leesburg, FL 34748. **Telephone:** (352) 728-9885. **E-Mail Address:** leesburglightning@floridaleague.com. **Head Coach:** Rich Billings. **General Manager:** Unavailable.

SANFORD RIVER RATS

Operated by the league office. E-Mail Address: sanfordriverrats@floridaleague.com. **Head Coach:** Kevin Davidson. **General Manager:** Phil Chinnery.

WINTER GARDEN SQUEEZE

Operated by the league office. Email Address: squeeze@floridaleague.com. **Head Coach:** Jay Welsh. **General Manager:** Adam Bates.

WINTER PARK DIAMOND DAWGS

Operated by the league office. E-Mail Address: winterparkdiamonddawgs@floridaleague.com. **Head Coach:** Scotty Makarewicz. **General Manager:** Unavailable.

FUTURES COLLEGIATE LEAGUE OF NEW ENGLAND

Mailing Address: 46 Chestnut Hill Rd, Chelmsford, MA 01824. **Telephone:** (617) 593-2112. **E-Mail Address:** futuresleague@yahoo.com **Website:** www.thefuturesleague.com. **Year Founded:** 2010. **Commissioner:** Chris Hall. **Teams (Contact):** Bristol Blues (Rick Muntean: rmuntean717@gmail.com), Brockton Rox (Todd Marlin: mcanina@brocktonrox.com), Martha's Vineyard Sharks (Shana Metzger: shana.metzger@mvsharks.com), Nashua Silver Knights (Ronnie Wallace: ronnie@nashuasilverknights.com), North Shore Navigators (Bill Terlecky: navigatorsgm@gmail.com), Pittsfield Suns (Kristen Huss: kevin@pittsfieldsuns.com), Seacoast Mavericks (Dave Hoyt: dave@usamavs.com), Torrington Titans (Chris Myslow: tortitans@gmail.com),Wachusett Dirt Dawgs (John Morrison: lefty@dirtdawgsball.com), Worcester Bravehearts (Dave Peterson: dave@worcesterbravehearts.com)

Regular Season: 56 games; 28 home, 28 away. **Playoff Format:** Six teams qualify. First round consists of two single elimination play-in games (3 seed vs. 6 seed and 4 seed vs 5 seed), two remaining teams play a best of three semi-final round followed by a best of three championship round to determine league champion. **Roster Limit:** 30. 10 must be from New England or play collegiately at a New England college.

GREAT LAKES SUMMER COLLEGIATE LEAGUE

Mailing Address: 133 W Winter St, Delaware, OH 43015. **Telephone:** (740) 368-3527. **Fax:** (740) 368-3999. **Website:** www.greatlakesleague.org.
Year Founded: 1986.
President/Commissioner: Deron Brown.
Regular Season: 40 games. **Playoff Format:** Top six teams meet in playoffs.
Roster Limit: 30 (college-eligible players only).
Teams: Cincinnati Steam, Grand Lake Mariners, Hamilton Joes, Lake Erie Monarchs, Xenia Scouts, Licking County Setllers, Lima Locos, Southern Ohio Copperheads, Lexington Hustlers, Galion Graders, Lorain County Ironmen, North Ohio Baseball Club.

JAYHAWK LEAGUE

Mailing Address: 865 Fabrique, Wichita, KS 67218. **Telephone:** (316) 942-6333. **Fax:** (316) 942-2009. **Website:** www.jayhawkbaseballleague.org. **Year Founded:** 1976.
Commissioner: Phil Stephenson. **President:** J.D. Schneider. **Vice President:** Frank Leo. **Public Relations/Statistician:** Gary Karr. **Secretary:** Cheryl Kastner.
Regular Season: 42 games. **Playoff Format:** Top three teams qualify for National Baseball Congress World Series. **Roster Limit:** Unlimited.
Teams: Bethany Bulls, Derby Twins, Dodge City A's, El Dorado Broncos, Hays Larks, Haysville Aviators, Liberal Bee Jays, Wellington Heat.

MIDWEST COLLEGIATE LEAGUE

Mailing Address: PO Box 172, Flossmoor, IL 60422. **E-Mail Address:** commissioner@midwestcollegiate league.com. **Website:** www.midwestcollegiateleague .com.
Year Founded: 2010.
President/Commissioner: Don Popravak.
Regular Season: 42 games. **2015 Opening Date:** May 27. **Closing Date:** Aug. 9. **All-Star Game:** July 8. **Playoff Format:** Top four teams meet in best of three series. Winners meet in best of three championship series.
Roster Limit: 28.

CHICAGO SOUTHLAND VIKINGS

Mailing Address: PO Box 172, Flossmoor, IL 60422. **Telephone:** (312) 420-1268. **E-Mail Address:** don@ southlandvidings.com. **Website:** www.southlandvikings .com. **General Manager:** Don Popravak. **Head Coach:** Chris Cunningham.

DUPAGE COUNTY HOUNDS

Mailing Address: 1450 S New Wilke Rd, Suite 205, Arlington Heights, IL 60005.. **Telephone:** (815) 704-3839. **E-Mail Address:** tickets@dupagehounds.com. **Website:** www.DuPageHounds.com. **General Managers:** Joe Stefani, Josh VanSwol. **Head Coach:** Sean Osborne.

LEXINGTON SNIPES

Mailing Address: 216 Prairie Ridge Drive, Lexington, IL 61753. **Telephone:** (309) 287-1668. **E-Mail Address:** billyd_73@yahoo.com. **Website:** www.lexingtonsnipes. com. **General Manager/Head Coach:** Billy Dubois.

MICHIGAN CITY LAKERS

Mailing Address: 215 Douglas Ave Michigan City, IN 46360. **Telephone:** 219-898-0191. **E-Mail Address:** tim@ voodooride.com. **Website:** www.citylakersbaseball.org General Manager/Head Coach: Tim "TJ" Jahnz.

NORTHWEST INDIANA OILMEN

Mailing Address: 1500 119th Street, Whiting, IN 46394. **Telephone:** (219) 659-1000. **E-Mail Address:** info@nwioilmen.com. **Website:** www.nwioilmen.com. **General Manager:** Chris Doherty. **Head Coach:** Adam Enright.

JOLIET ADMIRALS

Mailing Address: 1450 S New Wilke Rd, Suite 205, Arlington Heights, IL 60005. **Telephone:** 815-704-3839. **Email Address:** joe@dupagehounds.com. **Website:** Unavailable. **General Manager:** Joe Stefani. **Head Coach:** Tom Barry.

M.I.N.K. LEAGUE

(Missouri, Iowa, Nebraska, Kansas)
Mailing Address: PO Box 601, Nevada, MO 64772. **Telephone:** (417) 667-6159. **Fax:** (417) 667-4210. **E-mail Address:** jpost@morrisonpost.com. **Website:** www.mink leaguebaseball.com.
Year Founded: 1995.
Commissioner: Bob Steinkamp. **President:** Jeff Post. **Vice President:** Jud Kindle. **Secretary:** Edwina Rains.
Regular Season: 44 games. **Playoff Format:** Division winners play best of three series for league championship. Top team in each division also qualifies for National Baseball Congress World Series. **All-Star Game:** July 7 at Phil Welch Stadium.
Roster Limit: 30.

CHILLICOTHE MUDCATS

Mailing Address: 426 E Jackson, Chillicothe, MO 64601. **Telephone:** (660) 247-1504. **Fax:** (660) 646-6933. **E-Mail Address:** doughty@greenhills.net. **Website:** www.chillicothemudcats.com. **General Manager:** Doug Doughty. **Head Coach:** Eric Peterson.

CLARINDA A'S

Mailing Address: 225 East Lincoln, Clarinda, IA 51632. **Telephone:** (712) 542-4272. **E-Mail Address:** m.everly@ mchsi.com. **Website:** www.clarindaiowa-as-baseball.org. **General Manager:** Merle Eberly. **Head Coach:** Ryan Eberly.

JOPLIN OUTLAWS

Mailing Address: 5860 North Pearl, Joplin, MO 64801. **Telephone:** (417) 825-4218. **E-Mail Address:** merains@mchsi.com. **Website:** www.joplinoutlaws.com. **President/General Manager:** Mark Rains. **Head Coach:** Rob Vessell.

NEVADA GRIFFONS

Mailing Address: PO Box 601, Nevada, MO 64772. **Telephone:** (417) 667-6159. **E-Mail Address:** jpost@ morrisonpost.com. **Website:** www.nevadagriffons.org. **President:** Bob Hawks. **General Manager:** Jeff Post. **Head Coach:** Ryan Mansfield.

OMAHA DIAMOND SPIRIT

Mailing Address: 4618 N 135th Ave, Omaha, NE 68164. **Telephone:** (402) 679-0206. **E-Mail Address:** arden@omahadiamondspirit.com. **Website:** www.omaha diamondspirit.com. **General Manager:** Arden Rakosky. **Head Coach:** Adam Steyer.

OZARK GENERALS

Mailing Address: 1336 W Farm Road 182, Springfield, MO 65810. **Telephone:** (417) 832-8830. **Fax:** (417) 877-4625. **E-Mail Address:**rda160@yahoo.com. **Website:** www.generalsbaseballclub.com. **General Manager/ Head Coach:** Rusty Aton.

ST. JOSEPH MUSTANGS

Mailing Address: 2600 SW Parkway, St. Joseph, MO 64503. **Telephone:** (816) 279-7856. **Fax:** (816) 749-4082. **E-Mail Address:**rmuntean717@gmail.com. **Website:** www.stjoemustangs.com. **President:** Dan Gerson. **General Manager:** Rick Muntean. **Manager/Director, Player Personnel:** Matt Johnson.

SEDALIA BOMBERS

Mailing Address: 2205 S Grand, Sedalia, MO 65301. **Telephone:** (660) 287-4722. **E-Mail Address:** jkindle@ knobnoster.k12.mo.us. **Website:** www.sedaliabombers .com. **President/General Manager/Head Coach:** Jud Kindle. **Vice President:** Ross Dey.

NEW ENGLAND COLLEGIATE LEAGUE

Mailing Address: 122 Mass Moca Way, North Adams, MA 01247. **Telephone:** (413) 652-1031. **Fax:** (413) 473-0012. **E-Mail Address:** smcgrath@necbl.com. **Website:** www.necbl.com.
Year founded: 1993.
President: John DeRosa. **Commissioner:** Sean McGrath. **Deputy Commissioner:** Gregg Hunt. **Secretary:** Max Pinto. **Treasurer:** Brigid Schaffer.
Regular Season: 42 games. **2015 Opening Date:** June 4. **Closing Date:** Aug. 11. **All-Star Game:** July 19 in Sanford, ME.
Roster Limit: 30 (college-eligible players only).

DANBURY WESTERNERS

Mailing Address: 9 Pleasant View, New Milford, CT 06776. **Telephone:** (203) 502-9167. **E-Mail Address:** jspitser@msn.com. **Website:** www.danburywesterners .com. **President:** Paul Schaffer. **General Manager:** Jon Pitser. **Field Manager:** Ryan Smythe.

VALLEY BLUE SOX

Mailing Address: 100 Congress St, Springfield, MA 01104. **Telephone:** 860-305-1684. **E-Mail Address:** hunter@valleybluesox.com. **Website:** www.valleybluesox .com. **President:** Clark Eckhoff. **General Manager:**

Hunter Golden. **Field Manager:** Unavailable.

KEENE SWAMP BATS

Mailing Address: PO Box 160, Keene, NH 13431. **Telephone:** (603) 357-5464. **Fax:** (603) 357-5090. **E-Mail Address:** kwatterson@ne.rr.com. **Website:** www.swamp bats.com. **President:** Kevin Watterson. **VP/General Manager:** Dan Moylan.

LACONIA MUSKRATS

Mailing Address: 134 Stevens Rd, Lebanon, NH 03766. **Telephone:** (864) 380-2873. **E-Mail Address:** noah@laconiamuskrats.com. **Website:** www.laconia muskrats.com. **President:** Jonathan Crane. **General Manager:** Noah Crane. **Field Manager:** Nick Cenatiempo.

MYSTIC SCHOONERS

Mailing Address: PO Box 432, Mystic, CT 06355. **Telephone:** (860) 608-3287. **E-Mail Address:** dlong@ mysticbaseball.org. **Website:** www.mysticbaseball.org. **Executive Director:** Don Benoit. **General Manager:** Dennis Long. **Field Manager:** Phil Orbe.

NEW BEDFORD BAY SOX

Mailing Address: 427 John St, New Bedford, MA 02740. **Telephone:** 802-578-9935. **E-Mail Address:** poconnor@nbbaysox.com. **Website:** www.nbbaysox.com. **President:** Pat O'Connor. **General Manager:** Rick Avila. **Field Manager:** TBD

NEWPORT GULLS

Mailing Address: PO Box 777, Newport, RI 02840. **Telephone:** (401) 845-6832. **E-Mail Address:** gm@ newportgulls.com. **Website:** www.newportgulls.com. **President/General Manager:** Chuck Paiva. **Field Manager:** Mike Coombs.

NORTH ADAMS STEEPLECATS

Mailing Address: PO Box 540, North Adams, MA 01247. **Telephone:** 615-925-9577. **E-Mail Address:** na steeplecatsgm@gmail.com. **Website:** www.steeplecats. com. **President:** Dan Bosley. **General Manager:** Jonah Bayliss. **Field Manager:** TBD.

OCEAN STATE WAVES

Mailing Address: 1174 Kingstown Rd, Wakefield, RI 02879. **Telephone:** (401) 360-2977. **E-Mail Address:** matt@oceanstatewaves.com. **Website:** www. oceanstatewaves.com. **President:** Jeff Sweenor. **General Manager:** Matt Finlayson. **Field Manager:** Eric Cirella.

PLYMOUTH PILGRIMS

Mailing Address: 134 Court Street, Plymouth, MA 02360. **Telephone:** (508) 566-4192. **Fax:** (508) 566-4192. **E-Mail Address:** chris@pilgrimsbaseball.com.
Website: www.pilgrimsbaseball.com. **President:** Dave Dittmann. **General Manager:** Bob Kruse. **Field Manager:** Greg Zackrison.

SANFORD MAINERS

Mailing Address: PO Box 26, 4 Washington St, Sanford, ME 04073. **Telephone:** (207) 324-0010. **Fax:** (207) 324-2227. **E-Mail Address:** jwebb@nicholswebb .com. **Website:** www.sanfordmainers.com. **CEO:** Steve Cabana. **General Manager:** John Webb. **Field Manager:** Aaron Izaryk.

VERMONT MOUNTAINEERS

Mailing Address: PO Box 57, East Montpelier, VT 05651. **Telephone:** (802) 223-5224. **E-Mail Address:** gmvtm@comcast.net. **Website:** www.thevermont mountaineers.com. **General Manager:** Brian Gallagher. **Field Manager:** Joe Brown.

NEW YORK COLLEGIATE BASEBALL LEAGUE

Mailing Address: 398 East Dyke St. Wellsville, NY 14895. **Telephone:** (585) 455-2345 **E-Mail Address:** jdennste@gmail.com. **Website:** www.nycbl.com.

Year founded: 1978.

President: Steve Pindar. **Commissioner:** Jake Dennstedt. **Vice President:** Cal Kern. **Treasurer:** Dan Russo. **Secretary:** Paul Welker. **Franchise Development:** Cal Kern.

Franchises: Cortland Crush, Genesee Rapids, Geneva Red Wings, Geneva Twins, Hornell Dodgers, Niagara Power, Olean Oilers, Oneonta Outlaws, Rochester Ridgemen, Sherrill Silversmiths, Syracuse Junior Chiefs, Syracuse Salt Cats, Wellsville Nitros.

2015 Opening Date: May 30th. **Season Ends:** July 25. **All-Star Game/Scout Day:** July 16 at Damaschke Field, Oneonta, NY. **Playoff Format:** Eight teams qualify and play three rounds of best of three series.

Roster Limit: Unlimited (college-eligible players only).

CORTLAND CRUSH

Mailing Address: 2745 Summer Ridge Rd, LaFayette, NY 13084. **Telephone:** 315-391-8167. **Email Address:** wmmac4@aol.com. **Website:** www.cortlandcrush. com. **President:** Bill McConnell. **Field Manager:** Bill McConnell.

GENESEE RAPIDS

Mailing Address: 9726 Rt. 19 Houghton, NY 14474. **Telephone:** 716-969-0688. **Email Address:** rkerr@ frontiernet.net. **President:** Ralph Kerr. **Field Manager:** Unavailable.

GENEVA RED WINGS

Mailing Address: PO BOX 17624, Rochester, NY 14617. **Telephone:** 585-342-5750. **Fax:** 585-342-5155. **E-Mail Address:** gwings@rochester.rr.com. **Website:** genevaredwings.com. **President:** David Herbst. **Executive GM:** John Oughterson.

GENEVA TWINS

Mailing Address: PO BOX 17624, Rochester, NY 14617. **Telephone:** 585-342-5750. **Fax:** 585-342-5155. **E-Mail Address:** gwings@rochester.rr.com. **Website:** genevaredwings.com. **President:** David Herbst. **Executive GM:** John Oughterson.

HORNELL DODGERS

Mailing Address: PO Box 235, Hornell, NY 14843. **Telephone:** (607) 661-4173. **Fax:** (607) 661-4173. **E-Mail Address:** gm@hornelldodgers.com. **Website:** www. hornelldodgers.com. **General Manager:** Paul Welker. **Field Manager:** Unavailable.

NIAGARA POWER

Mailing Address: 2905 Staley Road, Grand Island, NY 14072. **Telephone:** (716) 773-1748. **Fax:** (716) 773-1748. **E-Mail Address:** ckern@fca.org **Website:** www. niagarapower.org. **General Manager:** Cal Kern. **Field Manager:** Josh Rebandt.

OLEAN OILERS

Mailing Address: 126 N 10th, Olean, NY 14760. **Telephone:** 716-378-0641. **E-Mail Addresses:** baseball@ oleanoilers.com, Bellr41@yahoo.com. **General Manager:** Bobby Bell. **Field Manager:** Bobby Bell.

ONEONTA OUTLAWS

Mailing Address: PO Box 608, Oneonta, NY 13820. **Telephone:** (607) 432-6326. **Fax:** (607) 432-1965. **E-Mail Address:** stevepindar@oneontaoutlaws.com. **Website:** www.oneontaoutlaws.com. **General Manager:** Steve Pindar. **Field Manager:** Joe Hughes.

ROCHESTER RIDGEMEN

Mailing Address: 651 Taylor Dr, Xenia, OH 45385. **Telephone:** (937) 352-1225. **E-Mail Addresses:** baseball @athletesinaction.org, chris.rainwater@athletesinaction .org. **Website:** www.aiabaseball.org. **General Manager:** Chris Rainwater. **Field Manager:** Unavailable.

SHERRILL SILVERSMITHS

Mailing Address: PO Box 111, Sherrill, NY 13440. **Telephone:** (315) 264-4334. **E-Mail Address:** sherrillsilver smiths@hotmail.com. **Website:** www.leaguelineup.com/ silversmiths. **General Manager:** Matthew Rafte. **Field Manager:** Unavailable.

SYRACUSE JR CHIEFS

Mailing Address: 227 Walters Dr, Liverpool, NY 13088. **Telephone:** (315) 263-3777. **E-Mail Address:** perfect. practice@yahoo.com. **General Manager:** Mike DiPaulo. **Field Manager:** Unavailable.

SYRACUSE SALT CATS

Mailing Address: 208 Lakeland Ave, Syracuse, NY 13209. **Telephone:** (315) 727-9220. **Fax:** (315) 488-1750. **E-Mail Address:** mmarti6044@yahoo.com. **Website:** www.leaguelineup.com/saltcats. **General Manager:** Manny Martinez. **Field Manager:** Mike Martinez.

WELLSVILLE NITROS

Mailing Address: 2848 O'Donnell Rd, Wellsville, NY 14895. **Telephone:** 585-596-9523. **Fax:** 585-593-5260. **E-Mail Address:** ackley8122@roadrunner.com. **Website:** www.nitros baseball.com. **General Manager:** Steven J. Ackley. **Assistant Manager:** Shelley Butler.

NORTHWOODS LEAGUE

Office Address: 2900 4th St SW, Rochester, MN 55902. **Telephone:** (507) 536-4579. **Fax:** (507) 536-4597. **E-Mail Address:** info@northwoodsleague.com.
Website: www.northwoodsleague.com.
Year Founded: 1994.
President: Gary Hoover. **Vice President, Business Development:** Matt Bomberg. **Vice President, Operations:** Glen Showalter. **Vice President, Licensing/Technology:** Tina Coil. **Vice President, Technology Development:** Greg Goodwin.
Division Structure: North-Duluth, Eau Claire, La Crosse Mankato, Rochester, St. Cloud, Thunder Bay, Waterloo, Willmar. South-Battle Creek, Green Bay, Kalamazoo, Kenosha, Lakeshore, Madison, Rockford, Wisconsin, Wisconsin Rapids.
Regular Season: 72 games (split schedule).
2016 Opening Date: May 31. **Closing Date:** August 14. **All-Star Game:** July 19 at Kenosha, Wisconsin. **Playoff Format:** 8 teams, 4 from each division, meet in single elimination games. Winners meet in best of three series for league championship.
Roster Limit: 30 (college-eligible players only).

BATTLE CREEK BOMBERS

Mailing Address: 189 Bridge Street, Battle Creek, MI 49017. **Telephone:** (269) 962-0735. **Fax:** (269) 962-0741. **Email Address:** info@battlecreekbombers.com.
Website: www.battlecreekbombers.com. **General Manager:** Tony Iovieno. **Field Manager:** Robbie Robinson Field: C.O. Brown Stadium.

DULUTH HUSKIES

Mailing Address: PO Box 16231, Duluth, MN 55816. **Telephone:** (218) 786-9909.
Fax: (218) 786-9001. **E-Mail Address:** huskies@duluthhuskies.com. **Website:** www.duluthhuskies.com. **Owner:** Michael Rosenzweig. **General Manager:** Greg Culver. **Field Manager:** Daniel Hersey. **Field:** Wade Stadium.

EAU CLAIRE EXPRESS

Mailing Address: 108 E Grand Ave, Eau Claire, WI 54701. **Telephone:** (715) 839-7788. **Fax:** (715) 839-7676. **E-Mail Address:** info@eauclaireexpress.com.
Website: www.eauclaireexpress.com. **Owner:** Bill Rowlett. **Assistant Managing Director:** Andy Neborak. **General Manager:** Spencer Larson. **Director of Operations/Field Manager:** Dale Varsho. **Field:** Carson Park.

GREEN BAY BULLFROGS

Mailing Address: 1306 Main Street, Green Bay, WI 54302. **Telephone:** (920) 497-7225. **Fax:** (920) 437-3551. **Email Address:** info@greenbaybullfrogs.com.
Website: www.greenbaybullfrogs.com. **General Manager:** Derek McCarty. **Field Manager:** Darrell Handelsman. **Field:** Joannes Stadium.

KALAMAZOOO GROWLERS

Mailing Address: 251 Mills St, Kalamazoo, MI 49048. **Telephone:** 555-555-1212.
Website: www.growlersbaseball.com. **General Manager:** Brian Colopy. **Field Manager:** Matt Lawson. **Field:** Homer Stryker Field.

KENOSHA KINGFISH

Mailing Address: 7817 Sheridan Rd, Kenosha, WI 53143. **Telephone:** 262-653-0900. **Website:** www.kingfishbaseball.com. **General Manager:** Jake McGhee. **Field Manager:** Duffy Dyer. **Field:** Simmons Field.

LA CROSSE LOGGERS

Mailing Address: 1223 Caledonia St, La Crosse, WI 54603. **Telephone:** (608) 796-9553. **Fax:** (608) 796-9032. **E-Mail Address:** info@lacrosseloggers.com.
Website: www.lacrosseloggers.com. **Owner:** Dan Kapanke. **General Manager:** Chris Goodell. **Assistant General Manager:** Ben Kapanke. **Field Manager:** Bill Sandillo. **Field:** Copeland Park.

LAKESHORE CHINOOKS

Mailing Address: 995 Badger Circle, Grafton, WI 53024. **Telephone:** (262) 618-4659. **Fax:** (262) 618-4362. **E-Mail Address:** info@lakeshorechinooks.com.
Website: www.lakeshorechinooks.com. **Owner:** Jim Kacmarcik. **General Manager:** Dean Rennicke. **Field Manager:** Eddy Morgan. **Field:** Kapco Park.

MADISON MALLARDS

Mailing Address: 2920 N Sherman Ave, Madison, WI 53704. **Telephone:** (608) 246-4277. **Fax:** (608) 246-4163. **E-Mail Address:** conor@mallardsbaseball.com.
Website: www.mallardsbaseball.com. **Owner:** Steve Schmitt. **President:** Vern Stenman. **General Manager:** Tyler Isham. **Field Manager:** Donnie Scott. **Field:** Warner Park.

MANKATO MOONDOGS

Mailing Address: 1221 Caledonia Street, Mankato, MN 56001. **Telephone:** (507) 625-7047. **Fax:** (507) 625-7059. **E-Mail Address:** office@mankatomoondogs.com.
Website: www.mankatomoondogs.com. **Owner:** Mark Ogren. **Vice President:** Kyle Mrozek. **General Manager:** Greg Weis. **Field Manager:** Ryan Kragh. **Field:** Franklin Rogers Park.

ROCHESTER HONKERS

Mailing Address: 307 E Center St, Rochester, MN 55904. **Telephone:** (507) 289-1170. **Fax:** (507) 289-1866. **E-Mail Address:** honkers@rochesterhonkers.com.
Website: www.rochesterhonkers.com. **Owner General Manager:** Dan Litzinger.
Field Manager: Trevor Hairgrove. **Field:** Mayo Field.

ROCKFORD (TO BE NAMED)

Mailing Address: 4503 Interstate Blvd., Loves Park, IL 61111. **Telephone:** 815-240-4159

ST. CLOUD ROX

Mailing Address: 5001 8th St N, St. Cloud, MN 56303. **Telephone:** (320) 240-9798. **Fax:** (320) 255-5228. **E-Mail Address:** info@stcloudrox.com. **Website:** www.stcloudrox.com. **President:** Gary Posch. **Vice President:** Scott Schreiner. **Field Manager:** Augie Rodriguez. **Field:** Joe Faber Field.

THUNDER BAY BORDER CATS

Mailing Address: PO Box 29105 Thunder Bay, Ontario P7B 6P9. **Telephone:** (807) 766-2287. **President:** Brad Jorgenson. **Field Manager:** Danny Benedetti. **Field:** Port Arthur Stadium.

WATERLOO BUCKS

Mailing Address: PO Box 4124, Waterloo, IA 50704. **Telephone:** (319) 232-0500.
Fax: (319) 232-0700. **E-Mail Address:** waterloobucks@ waterloobucks.com. **Website:** www.waterloobucks.com. **General Manager:** Dan Corbin. **Field Manager:** Scott Douglas. **Field:** Riverfront Stadium.

WILLMAR STINGERS

Mailing Address: PO Box 201, Willmar, MN, 56201. **Telephone:** (320) 222-2010.
E-Mail Address: ryan@willmarstingers.com. **Website:** www.willmarstingers.com. **Owners:** Marc Jerzak, Ryan Voz. **General Manager:** Nick McCallum. **Field Manager:** Drew Saberhagen. **Field:** Bill Tauton Stadium.

WISCONSIN RAPIDS RAFTERS

Mailing Address: 521 Lincoln St, Wisconsin Rapids, WI 54494. **Telephone:**
(715) 424-5400. E-Mail Address: info@raftersbaseball .com. **Website:** www.raftersbaseball.com. **Owner/ President:** Vern Stenman. **General Manager:** John Fanta. **Field Manager:** Craig Noto. **Field:** Witter Field.

WISCONSIN WOODCHUCKS

Mailing Address: PO Box 6157, Wausau, WI 54402. **Telephone:** (715) 845-5055.
Fax: (715) 845-5015. **E-Mail Address:** info@wood chucks.com. **Website:** www.woodchucks.com. **Owner:** Mark Macdonald. **General Manager:** Ryan Treu. **Field Manager:** Michael Gedman
Field: Athletic Park.

PACIFIC INTERNATIONAL LEAGUE

Mailing Address: 4400 26th Ave W, Seattle, WA 98199. **Telephone:** (206) 623-8844. **Fax:** (206) 623-8361. **E-Mail Address:** spotter@potterprinting.com. **Website:** www. pacificinternationalleague.com.
Year Founded: 1992.
President: Barry Aden. **Vice President:** Martin Lawrence. **Commissioner:** Brian Gooch. **Secretary:** Steve Potter. **Treasurer:** Mark Dow. **Member Clubs:** Northwest Honkers, Everett Merchants, Kamloops Sundevils (BC, Canada), Seattle Studs, Trail Orioles (BC, Canada), Burnaby Collegiate Bulldogs (BC, Canada), Highline Bears, Snoqualmie Valley Hurricane, Langley Blaze (BC Canada), West Coast Guns.
Regular Season: 20 league games. **2016 Opening Date:** Unavailable. **PlayoffFormat:** Top team is invited to National Baseball Congress World Series.
Roster Limit: 30; 25 eligible for games (players must be at least 18 years old).

PERFECT GAME COLLEGIATE BASEBALL LEAGUE

Mailing Address: 8 Michaels Lane, Old Brookville, NY 11545. **Telephone:** (516) 521-0206. **Fax:** (516) 801-0818. **E-Mail Address:** valkun@aol.com. **Website:** www.pgcbl .org. **Year Founded:** 2010.
President: Jeffrey Kunion. **Assistant to the President:**

Justin Mattingly. **Executive Committee:** Tom Hickey (Cooperstown Hawkeyes), Bob Ohmann (Newark Pilots), Paul Samulski (Albany Dutchmen).
Teams: East—Albany Dutchmen, Amsterdam Mohawks, Glens Falls Dragons, Mohawk Valley DiamondDawgs, Saugerties Stallions. **West**—Adirondack Trail Blazers, Elmira Pioneers, Newark Pilots, Utica Brewers, Victor.
Regular Season: 50. **2015 Opening Date:** June 2. **Closing Date:** July 30. **All-Star Game:** July 20. **Playoff Format:** Top three teams in each division qualify; second- and third-place finishers have one-game playoff; next two series are best of three. **Roster Limit:** 30 (maximum of two graduated high school players per team).

PROSPECT LEAGUE

Mailing Address: 59 N. Paint St., Chillicothe, OH 45601. **Telephone:** (815) 980-9045. **Fax:** n/a. **E-Mail Address:** commissioner@prospectleague.com. **Website:** www.prospectleague.com.
Year Founded: 1963 as Central Illinois Collegiate League; known as Prospect League since 2009.
Commissioner: Bryan Wickline.
Regular Season: 60 games. **2016 Opening Date:** May 26. **Closing Date:** Aug. 6. **Championship Series:** Aug 11-14. **Roster Limit:** 28.

BUTLER BLUESOX

Mailing Address: 6 West Diamond Street, Butler, PA 16001. **Telephone:** (724) 282-2222 or (724) 256-9994. **Fax:** (724) 282-6565. **E-Mail Address:** frontoffice@butler bluesox.net.
Website: www.butlerbluesox.com. **League President:** Wink Robinson. **General Manager:** TBA. **Field Manager:** Jason Radwan.

CHAMPION CITY KINGS

Mailing Address:1301 Mitchell Blvd., Springfield, OH 45503. **Telephone:**
(937) 342-0320. Fax:(937) 342-0320. E-Mail **Address:**rwhite@championcitykings.com. **Website:** www.championcitykings.com. **General Manager/ League Director:** Rick White. **Field Manager:** Rick White.

CHILLICOTHE PAINTS

Mailing Address: 59 North Paint Street, Chillicothe, OH 45601.
Telephone: (740) 773-8326. **Fax:** (740) 773-8338. **E-Mail Address:** paints@bright.net. **Website:** www. chillicothepaints.com. **League Director:** Shirley Bandy. **Field Manager:** Greg Cypret.

DANVILLE DANS

Mailing Address: 4 Maywood, Danville, IL 61832. **Telephone:** (217) 918-3401. **Fax:** (217) 446-9995. **E-Mail Address:** danvilledans@comcast.net. **Website:** www. danvilledans.com. **League Director:** Jeanie Cooke. **Co-General Managers:** Jeanie Cooke, Rick Kurth. **Field Manager:** Eric Coleman.

DUPAGE DRONES

Mailing Address: TBA. **Telephone:** TBA. **Fax:** TBA. **E-Mail Address:** info@lislebaseball.com.
Website: www.lislebaseball.com. **League Director/ General Manager:** Joshua Schaub. **Field Manager:** Joe Lincoln.

HANNIBAL CAVEMEN

Mailing Address: 403 Warren Barrett Drive, Hannibal, MO 63401.
Telephone: (573) 221-1010. **Fax:** (573) 221-5269. **E-Mail Address:** greg@hannibalbaseball.com. **Website:** www.hannibalcavemen.com. **President/General Manager:** Robert Hemond. **Field Manager:** TBA.

KOKOMO JACKRABBITS

Mailing Address: 319 S Union St, Kokomo, IN 46901. **Telephone:** (800) 525-0133. **Fax:** (414) 224-9290. **E-Mail Address:** no-reply@mkesports. **Website:** www. kokomojackrabbits.com. **League Director:** Mike Zimmerman. **Field Manager:** Greg Van Horn.

LAFAYETTE AVIATORS

Mailing Address: Loeb Stadium, 1915 Scott St., **Lafayette, IN 47904 Telephone:** (414) 224-9283. **Fax:** (414) 224-9290. **E-Mail Address:** no-reply@mkesports .com. **Website:** www.lafayettebaseball.com. **League Director:** Dan Kuenzi. **Field Manager:** Brent McNeil.

QUINCY GEMS

Mailing Address: 1400 N. 30th St., Suite 1, Quincy, IL 62301. **Telephone:** (217) 214-7436. **Fax:** (217) 214-7436. **E-Mail Address:** quincygems@yahoo.com. **Website:** www.quincygems.com. **League Director/General Manager:** Jimmie Louthan.. **Field Manager:** Zach Getsee.

SPRINGFIELD SLIDERS

Mailing Address: 1415 North Grand Avenue East, Suite B, Springfield, IL 62702. **Telephone:** (217) 679-3511. **Fax:** (217) 679-3512. **E-Mail Address:**slidersfun@spring fieldsliders.com. **Website:** www.springfieldsliders.com. **League Director:** Shane Martin.
General Manager: TBA. **Field Manager:** Zac Carbonneau.

TERRE HAUTE REX

Mailing Address:111 North 3rd St, Terre Haute, IN **47807.Telephone:** (812) 478-3817. **Fax:** (812) 232-5353. **E-mail Address:** frontoffice@rexbaseball.com. **Website:** www.rexbaseball.com.**League Director/General Manager:** BruceRosselli. **Field Manager:**Bobby Segal.

WEST VIRGINIA MINERS

Mailing Address: 476 Ragland Road, Suite 2, Beckley, WV 25801. **Telephone:** (304) 252-7233. **Fax:** (304) 253-1998. **E-mail Address:** wvminers@wvminersbaseball .com. **Website:** www.wvminersbaseball.com. **President:** Doug Epling. **League Director/General Manager:** Tim Epling. **Field Manager:** Tim Epling.

SOUTHERN COLLEGIATE BASEBALL LEAGUE

Mailing Address: 9723 Northcross Center Court, Huntersville, NC 28078. **Telephone:** (704) 635-7126. **Cell:** (704) 906-7776. **E-Mail Address:** hhampton@scbl.org. **Website:** www.scbl.org.
Year Founded: 1999.
Commissioner: Harold Hampton. **President:** Jeff Carter. **Treasurer:** Brenda Templin. **League Historian:** Larry Tremitiere. **Umpire in Chief:** Gary Swanson.

Regular Season: 42 games. **Playoff Format:** Six-team single-elimination tournament with best of three championship series between final two teams.
Roster Limit: 30 (College-eligible players only).

TEAM CHARLOTTE

Mailing Address: 7209 East WT Harris Blvd, Suite J #245, Charlotte, NC 28227. **Telephone:** (704) 668-9167. **Email Address:** baseballnbeyond@aol.com. **General Manager:** Leland Mattox. **Head Coach:** David "Doc" Booth.

CONCORD WEAVERS

Mailing Address: 366 George Lyles Parkway, Suite 125, Concord, NC 28027. **Telephone:** (704) 604-3113. **Email Address:** daviddarwin@mycoreathletics.com. **General Manager:** David Darwin. **Head Coach:** TBA.

LAKE NORMAN COPPERHEADS

Mailing Address: 8875 Bowman Barrier Rd, Mr Pleasant, NC 28124. **Telephone:** (704) 305-3649. **Email Address:** eastcoastbats@gmail.com. **General Manager:** Derek Shoe. **Head Coach:** TBA

PIEDMONT PRIDE

Mailing Address: 452 Lakeshore Parkway, Ste 205, Rock Hill, SC 29730. **Telephone:** (803) 412-7982. **E-Mail Address:** jhudak@fca.org. **General Manager:** Joe Hudak. **Head Coach:** Joe Hudak.

SBA BONES

Mailing Address: 12857 East Independence Blvd, Ste. J, Matthews, NC 28173. **Telephone:** (704) 641-1035. **E-Mail Address:** jowens@showcasebaseball.org. **General Manager:** John Owens. **Head Coach:** TBA.

UNION COUNTY VIPERS

Mailing Address: 10800 Sikes Place, Ste 205, Charlotte, NC 28227. **Telephone:** (704) 578-3468. **E-Mail Address:** mpolito@tprsolutions.com. **General Manager:** Mike Polito. **Assistant GM:** Keith Bray. **Head Coach:** Aaron Bray.

SUNBELT BASEBALL LEAGUE
Mailing Address: 3022 Liberty Way, Atlanta, GA 30318. **Telephone:** (770) 490-7912. **E-mail Address:** info@sunbeltleague.com. **Website:** www.sunbeltleague .com. **Year Founded:** 2006.
Commissioner: Bobby Bennett. **Email:** bobbybennett 27@me.com. **League Director:** Andy Collins. **President:** Todd Pratt. **Regular Season:** 28 games. **Playoff Format:** division championship series and league championship series, best of 3. **Roster Limit:** 30 (college-eligible players 22 and under).
Teams: Alpharetta Braves, Atlanta Crackers, Brookhaven Bucks, Douglasville Bulls, Gwinnett Tides, Marietta Patriots, Norcross Astros, Phenix City Crawdads

TEXAS COLLEGIATE LEAGUE
Mailing Address: 735 Plaza Blvd, Suite 200, Coppell, TX 75019. **Telephone:** (979) 985-5198. **Fax:** (979) 779-2398. **E-Mail Address:** info@tclbaseball.com. **Website:** www.texascollegeleague.com.
Year Founded: 2004.
President: Uri Geva.

Regular Season: 60 games (split schedule). **Playoff Format:** First- and second-half champions qualify, with two wild card teams. Winners of one-game divisional round meet in best of three championship series.
Roster Limit: 30 (College-eligible players only)

ACADIANA CANE CUTTERS

Mailing Address: 221 La Neuville, Youngsville, LA 70592. **Telephone:** (337) 451-6582. **E-Mail Address:** info@canecuttersbaseball.com. **Website:** www.cane cuttersbaseball.com. **Owners:** Richard Chalmers, Sandi Chalmers. **General Manager:** Richard Haifley. **Head Coach:** Lonny Landry.

BRAZOS VALLEY BOMBERS

Mailing Address: 405 Mitchell St, Bryan, TX 77801. **Telephone:** (979) 799-7529. **Fax:** (440) 425-8592. **E-Mail Address:** info@bvbombers.com. **Website:** www.bv bombers.com. **Owners:** Uri Geva. **Managing Partner:** Chris Clark. **Head Coach:** Curt Dixon.

EAST TEXAS PUMP JACKS

Mailing Address: 1100 Stone Road Suite #120, Kilgore, TX 75662. **Telephone:** (903) 218-4638. **Fax:** (866) 511-5449. **E-mail Address:** info@pumpjacksbaseball.com. **Website:** www.pumpjacksbaseball.com.

TEXAS MARSHALS

Mailing Address: 7920 Beltline Rd, Suite 1005 Dallas, TX 75254. **Telephone:** (214) 578-4388. **E-Mail Address:** info@texasmarshals.com. **Website:** www.texasmarshals.com. **Owner:** Marc Landry.

WOODLANDS STRYKERS

Mailing Address: 25009 OakHurst Dr, Spring, TX 77386. **Telephone:** (720) 205-5709. **Fax:** (281) 465-0748.

VICTORIA GENERALS

Mailing Address: 1307 E Airline Road, Suite H, Victoria, TX 77901. **Telephone:** (361) 485-9522. **Fax:** (361) 485-0936. **E-Mail Address:** info@baseballinvictoria.com, tkyoung@victoriagenerals.com. **Website:** www.victoria generals.com. **President:** Tracy Young. **VP/General Manager:** Mike Yokum. **Head Coach:** Michael Oros.

VALLEY BASEBALL LEAGUE

Mailing Address: Valley Baseball League, 3006 Preston Lake Boulevard, Harrisonburg, VA 22801. **Telephone:** (540) 810-9194. **Fax:** (540) 434-5083. **E-Mail Addresses:** don@lemish.com & baseball@shentel.net. **Website:** www.valleyleaguebaseball.com.
Year Founded: 1897.
President: Donald L. Lemish. **Assistant to the President:** Don Harper. **Executive Vice President:** Bruce Alger. **Media Relations Director:** Lauren Jefferson. **Secretary:** Stacy Locke. **Treasurer:** Ed Yoder.
Regular Season: 42 games. **2015 Opening Date:** June 5. **Closing Date:** August 9. **All-Star Game:** North vs South, July 12 at Harrisonburg. **Playoff Format:** Eight teams qualify; play three rounds of best of three series.
Roster Limit: 28 (college eligible players only)

COVINGTON LUMBERJACKS

Mailing Address: PO Box 30, Covington, VA 24426. **Telephone:** (540) 969-9923, (540) 962-1155. **Fax:** (540) 962-7153. **E-Mail Address:** covingtonlumberjacks@valley leaguebaseball.com. **Website:** www.lumberjacksbaseball.com. **President:** Dizzy Garten. **Head Coach:** Dan Scott.

ALDIE SENATORS

Mailing Address: 42020 Village Center Plaza, Suite 120-50, Stoneridge, VA 20105. **Telephone:** (703) 542-2110, (703) 989-5009. **Fax:** (703)327-7435. **E-Mail Address:** haymarketsenators@valleyleaguebaseball.com. **Website:** www.haymarketbaseball.com. **President:** Scott Newell. **General Manager:** BernieSchaffler. **Head Coach:** Justin Aspegren.

CHARLES TOWN (WV) CANNONS

Mailing Address: 2862 Northwestern Pike, Capon Bridge, WV 26711. **Telephone:** (540) 743-3338, (540) 843-4472. **Fax:** (304) 856-1619. **E-Mail Address:** bigdaddy432@verizon.net. **Website:** www.charlestowncannons.com. **President:** Brett Fuller. **Recruiting Coordinator:** Brett Fuller. **General Manager:** Steve Sabins.

CHARLOTTESVILLE TOM SOX

Mailing Address: P. O. Box 166, Ivy, Virginia 22945-0166. **Telephone:** (703)282-4425. **E-Mail:** contact@tom sox.com. **Website:** www.TomSox.com. **President:** Greg Allen. **General Manager:** Joe Koshansky.

FRONT ROYAL CARDINALS

Mailing Address: 382 Morgans Ridge Road, Front Royal, VA 22630. **Telephone:** (703) 244-6662, (540) 905-0152. **E-Mail Address:** DonnaSettle@centurylink.net. frontroyalcardinals@valleyleaguebaseball.com. **Website:** www.valleyleaguebaseball.com. **President:** Donna Settle. **Head Coach:** Jake Weghorst.

HARRISONBURG TURKS

Mailing Address: 1489 S Main St, Harrisonburg, VA 22801. **Telephone:** (540) 434-5919. **Fax:** (540) 434-5919. **E-Mail Address:** turksbaseball@hotmail.com. **Website:** www.harrisonburgturks.com. **Operations Manager:** Teresa Wease. **General Manager/Head Coach:** Bob Wease.

NEW MARKET REBELS

Mailing Address: PO Box 902, New Market, VA 22844. **Telephone:** (304) 856-1623. **Fax:** (540) 740-9486. **E-Mail Address:** nmrebels@shentel.net. **Website:** www.rebels baseball.biz. **President/General Manager:** Bruce Alger. **Head Coach:** C.J. Rhodes.

STAUNTON BRAVES

Mailing Address: 14 Shannon Place, Staunton, VA 24401.**Telephone:** (540) 886-0987, (540) 885-1645. **Fax:** (540) 886-0905. **E-Mail Address:** sbraves@hotmail.com. **Website:** www.stauntonbravesbaseball.com. **General Manager:** Steve Cox. **Head Coach:** George Laase.

STRASBURG EXPRESS

Mailing Address: PO Box 417, Strasburg, VA 22657. **Telephone:** (540) 325-5677, (540) 459-4041. **Fax:** (540) 459-3398. **E-Mail Address:** neallaw@shentel.net. **Website:** www.strasburgexpress.com. **General manager:** Jay Neal. **Head coach:** Butch Barnes.

WAYNESBORO GENERALS

Mailing Address: 435 Essex Ave., Suite 105, Waynesboro VA 22980. **Telephone:** (540) 932-2300. **Fax:** (540) 932-2322. **E-Mail Address:** waynesborogenerals@valleyleaguebaseball.com. **Website:** www.waynesborogenerals.com. **Chairman:** David T Gauldin II. **Head Coach:** Mike Bocock.

WINCHESTER ROYALS

Mailing Address: PO Box 2485, Winchester, VA 22604. **Telephone:** (540) 539-8888, (540) 664-3978. **Fax:** (540) 662-1434. **E-Mail Addresses:** winchesterroyals@valleyleaguebaseball.com, jimphill@**shentel.net.Website:** www.winchesterroyals.com. **President:** Todd Thompson. **Operations Director:** Jimmie Shipp. **Coach:** Kyle Phelps

WOODSTOCK RIVER BANDITS

Mailing Address: P.O. Box 227, Woodstock, VA 22664. **Telephone:** (540) 481-0525. **Fax:** (540) 459-8227. **E-Mail Address:** woodstockriverbandits@valleyleaguebaseball.com. **Website:** www.woodstockriverbandits.org. **General Manager:** R.W. Bowman Jr. **Head Coach:** Phil Betterly.

WEST COAST LEAGUE

Mailing Address: PO Box 20790, Keizer, OR 97307. **Telephone:** (503) 390-2543. **E-Mail Address:** dkoho@westcoastleague.com. **Website:** www.westcoastleague.com.

Year Founded: 2005.
President: Dennis Koho. **Vice President:** Eddie Poplawski. **Secretary:** Jerry Walker. **Treasurer:** Tony Bonacci. **Supervisor, Umpires:** Tom Hiler.
Division Structure: South— Bend Elks, Corvallis Knights, Klamath Falls Gems, Medford Rogues. **West**—Bellingham Bells, Cowlitz Blackbears, Kitsap Bluejackets,Victoria Harbourcats. **East**—Kelowna Falcons, Walla Walla Sweets, Wenatchee Applesox, Yakima Valley Pippins.
Regular Season: 54 games. **2015 Opening Date:** June 5. **Closing Date:** August 9. **Playoff Format:** Four-team tournament.
Roster Limit: 25 (college-eligible players only).

BELLINGHAM BELLS

Mailing Address: 1221 Potter Street, Bellingham, WA 98229. **Telephone:** (360) 746-0406. **E-Mail Address:** info@bellinghambells.com. **Website:** www.bellinghambells.com. **Owner:** Eddie Poplawski. **General Manager:** Nick Caples. **Head Coach:** Jeff James.

BEND ELKS

Mailing Address: 70 SW Century Dr Suite 100-373 Bend, Oregon 97702. **Telephone:** (541) 312-9259. **E-Mail Address:** kelsie@bendelks.com. **Website:** www.bendelks.com. **Owners:** John and Tami Marick. **General Manager:** Casey Powell.

CORVALLIS KNIGHTS

Mailing Address: PO Box 1356, Corvallis, OR 97339. **Telephone:** (541) 752-5656. **E-Mail Address:** dan.segel@corvallisknights.com. **Website:** www.corvallisknights.com. **President:** Dan Segel. **General Manager:** Bre Miller. **Head Coach:** Brooke Knight.

COWLITZ BLACK BEARS

Mailing Address: PO Box 1255, Longview, WA 98632. **Telephone:** (360) 703-3195. **E-Mail Address:** gwilsonagm@gmail.com. **Website:** www.cowlitzblackbears.com. **Owner/ General Manager:** Tony Bonacci. **Head Coach:** Grady Tweit.

KELOWNA FALCONS

Mailing Address: 201-1014 Glenmore Dr, Kelowna, BC, V1Y 4P2. **Telephone:** (250) 763-4100. **E-Mail Address:** mark@kelownafalcons.com. **Website:** www.kelownafalcons.com. **Owner:** Dan Nonis. **General Manager:** Mark Nonis. **Head Coach:** Geoff White.

KITSAP BLUEJACKETS

Mailing Address: PO Box 68, Silverdale, WA 98383. **Telephone:** (360) 692-5566.
E-Mail Address: rsmith@kitsapbluejackets.com. **Website:** www.kitsapbluejackets.com. **Managing Partner/General Manager:** Rick Smith. **Head Coach:** Ryan Parker.

KLAMATH FALLS GEMS

Mailing Address: 2001 Crest Street, Klamath Falls, Oregon 97603. **Telephone:** (541) 883-4367. **E-Mail Address:** grant@klamathfallsgems.com. **Website:** www.klamathfallsgems.com. **Owners:** Jerry and Lisa Walker. **General Manager:**
Grant Wilson. Head Coach: Mitch Karraker.

MEDFORD ROGUES

Mailing Address: PO Box 699, Medford, Oregon 97501. **Telephone:** (541) 973-2883. **E-Mail Address:** ian@medfordrogues.com. **Website:** www.medfordrogues.com. **Owner:** CSH International. **General Manager:** Ian Church. **Head Coach:** Josh Hogan.

VICTORIA HARBOURCATS

Mailing Address: 1014 Caledonia Avenue, Victoria, BC, V8T 1G1. **Telephone:** (250) 216-0006. **E-Mail Address:** jim@harbourcats.com. **Website:** www.harbourcats.com. **Owner:** John McLean. **General Manager:** Jim Swanson. **Head Coach:** Graig Merritt.

WALLA WALLA SWEETS

Mailing Address: 109 E Main Street, Walla Walla, WA 99362. **Telephone:** (509) 522-2255. **E-Mail Address:** info@wallawallasweets.com. **Website:** www.wallawallabaseball.com. **Owner:** Pacific Baseball Ventures, LLC. **General Manager:** Katie Biagi. **Head Coach:** Frank Mutz.

WENATCHEE APPLESOX

Mailing Address: PO Box 5100, Wenatchee, WA 98807. **Telephone:** (509) 665-6900. **E-Mail Address:** sales@applesox.com. **Website:** www.applesox.com. **Owner/General Manager:** Jim Corcoran. **Head Coach:** A.J. Proszek.

YAKIMA VALLEY PIPPINS

Mailing Address: 1301, S. Fair Avenue, Shattuck Bldg., Yakima, WA 98908. **Telephone:** (509) 575-4487. **E-Mail Address:** info@pippinsbaseball.com. **Website:** www.pippinsbaseball.com. **Ownership Group:** Theresa Gillespie, Greg Shaw, Jeff Cirillo, John Stanton, Mikal Thomasen, Peter van Oppen, Zachary Fraser. **Head Coach:** Marcus McKimmy.

HIGH SCHOOL BASEBALL

NATIONAL FEDERATION OF STATE HIGH SCHOOL ASSOCIATIONS

Mailing Address: PO Box 690, Indianapolis, IN 46206. **Telephone:** (317) 972-6900. **Fax:** (317) 822-5700. **E-Mail Address:** baseball@nfhs.org. **Website:** www.nfhs.org.

Executive Director: Bob Gardner. **Chief Operating Officer:** Davis Whitfield. **Director of Sports, Sanctioning and Student Services:** Elliot Hopkins. **Director, Publications/Communications:** Bruce Howard.

NATIONAL HIGH SCHOOL BASEBALL COACHES ASSOCIATION

Mailing Address: PO Box 12843, Tempe, AZ 85284. **Telephone:** (602) 615-0571. **Fax:** (480) 838-7133. **E-Mail Address:** rdavini@cox.net. **Website:** www.baseball coaches.org. **Executive Director:** Ron Davini.

Executive Secretary: Robert Colburn (St. Andrews's School, New Castle, Del.). **President:** Tim Saunders (Dublin Coffman HS, Dublin, Ohio). **First Vice President:** Steve Vickery (El Capitan HS, Lakeside, Calif.). **Second Vice President:** Mel Gardner (Delaware BCA, New Castle, Del.).

2016 National Convention: Dec. 1-4 in Columbus, Ohio.

NATIONAL TOURNAMENTS

IN-SEASON

HORIZON NATIONAL INVITATIONAL
Mailing Address: Horizon High School, 5653 Sandra Terrace, Scottsdale, AZ 85254. **Telephone:** 602-291-1952. **E-mail:** huskycoach1@yahoo.com. **Website:** www.horizon baseball.com.

Tournament Director: Eric Kibler.
2016 Tournament: March 14-17.

INTERNATIONAL PAPER CLASSIC
Mailing Address: 4775 Johnson Rd., Georgetown, SC 29440. **Telephone:** (843) 527-9606. **Fax:** (843) 546-8521. **Website:** www.ipclassic.com.
Tournament Director: Alicia Johnson.
2016 Tournament: Unavailable

LIONS INVITATIONAL
Mailing Address: 8281 Walker Street, La Palma, CA 90623. **Telephone:** (714) 220-4101x502. **Fax:** (714) 995-1833. **Email:** Pascal_C@AUHSD.US. **Website:** www. anaheimlionstourney.com.
Tournament Director: Chris Pascal.
2016 Tournament: March 26-30 (80 teams).

NATIONAL CLASSIC BASEBALL TOURNAMENT
Mailing Address: PO Box 338, Placentia, CA 92870. **Telephone:** (714) 993-2838. **Fax:** (714) 993-5350. **E-Mail Address:** placentiamustang@aol.com. **Website:** www. national-classic.com.
Tournament Director: Marcus Jones.
2016 Tournament: March 28-31 (16 teams).

USA BASEBALL NATIONAL HIGH SCHOOL INVITATIONAL
Mailing Address: 403 Blackwell St., Durham, NC 27701. **Telephone:** (919) 474-8721. **Fax:** (919) 474-8822. **Email:** markdvoroznak@usabaseball.com. **Website:** www. usabaseball.com.
Tournament Director: Mark Dvoroznak.
2016 Tournament: March 23-26 at USA Baseball National Training Complex, Cary, NC (16 teams).

POSTSEASON

SUNBELT BASEBALL CLASSIC SERIES
Mailing Address: PO Boc 20097 Oklahoma City, OK 73156.
Email: JnPickard@cox.net. **Website:** www.sunbelt classicbaseball.com.
Chairman: Jason Pickard.
2016 Junior Sunbelt Classic: June 10-15 in McAlester, OK.
2016 Sophomore Sunbelt Classic: June 24-26 at Dolese Park in Oklahoma City, OK.

ALL-STAR GAMES/AWARDS

PERFECT GAME ALL-AMERICAN CLASSIC
Mailing Address: 850 Twixt Town Rd. NE Cedar Rapids, IA 52402. **Telephone:** (319) 298-2923. Fax (319) 298-2924. **Event Organizer:** Blue Ridge Sports & Entertainment. **Vice President, Events:** Lou Lacy.
2016 Game: Aug. 14 at Petco Park, San Diego.

UNDER ARMOUR ALL-AMERICA GAME, POWERED BY BASEBALL FACTORY
Mailing Address: 9212 Berger Rd., Suite 200, Columbia, MD 21046. **Telephone:** (410) 715-5080. **Email Address:** jason@factoryathletics.com. **Website:** baseball factory.com/AllAmerica. **Event Organizers:** Baseball Factory, Team One Baseball.
2016 Game: July 23 at Wrigley Field, Chicago.

GATORADE CIRCLE OF CHAMPIONS
(National HS Player of the Year Award)
Mailing Address: The Gatorade Company, 321 N. Clark St., Suite 24-3, Chicago, IL, 60610. **Telephone:** 312-821-1000. **Website:** www.gatorade.com.

SHOWCASE EVENTS

AREA CODE BASEBALL GAMES PRESENTED BY NEW BALANCE

Mailing Address: 23954 Madison Street, Torrance, CA 90505. **Telephone:** 310-791-1142 x 4426. **Website:** StudentSports.com/baseball
Event Organizer: Kirsten Leetch.
2016 Area Code Games: Aug. 6-10 at Blair Field in Long Beach, Calif.

ARIZONA FALL CLASSIC

Mailing Address: 9962 W. Villa Hermosa, Peoria, AZ 85383. **Telephone:** 602-228-1592. **E-mail Address:** azbaseballtracy@msn.com. **Website:** www.azfallclassic. com.
President: Tracy Heid. **Directors:** Ted Heid, Matt Spring.

2016 Events

Four Corner Classic.................Peoria, AZ, June 2-5
California Classic
Qualifiers .... TBA, CA, June 3-5 & June 10-12
Arizona Summer Classic (18U) ..... Peoria, AZ, July 14-17
Arizona Summer Classic (16U) ..... Peoria, AZ, July 21-24
AZ Senior Classic Qualifier.....Peoria, AZ, Sept. 29-Oct. 2
AZ Sophomore Fall Classic...........Peoria, AZ, Oct. 6-9
AZ Senior Fall Classic (HS seniors).. Peoria, AZ, Oct. 13-16
Senior All Academic Tryout & Game.............. Oct. 13
AZ Junior Fall Classic (HS juniors) .. Peoria, AZ ,Oct. 20-23
Junior All Academic Tryout & Game.............. Oct. 20
Mizuno Universal Classic .... Peoria, AZ, Oct. 27-30

BASEBALL FACTORY

Office Address: 9212 Berger Rd., Suite 200, Columbia, MD 21046. **Telephone:** (800) 641-4487, (410) 715-5080. **Fax:** (410) 715-1975. **E-mail Address:** info@baseballfactory.com. **Website:** www.baseballfactory.com.

Chief Executive Officer/Founder: Steve Sclafani. **President:** Rob Naddelman. **CFO:** Gene Mattingly. **Executive VP, Baseball Operations/Chairman, Under Armour All-America Game Selection Committee:** Steve Bernhardt. **Senior VP, Marketing/Brand:** Jason Budden. **Senior VP, Baseball Operations:** Jim Gemler. **Senior VP, Player Development:** Dan Forester. **VP, Business Development:** Jeff Brazier. **Senior Director, Scouting/Event Operations:** Andy Ferguson. **Senior Director, College Recruiting:** Dan Mooney. **Senior Director, Event Marketing/Partnerships:** Dave Lax. **Senior Multimedia Producer:** Brian Johnson. **Senior Director, Player Development Events:** Joe Lake. **Senior Director, Web Development:** Wei Xue.

Executive Player Development Coordinator: Steve Nagler. **Senior Player Development Coordinators:** Adam Darvick, Dave Packer, John Perko. **Regional Player Development Coordinators:** Ed Bach, Drew Baldwin, Chris Brown, Nick Criscuolo, Corson Fidler, Josh Hippensteel, Rob Onolfi, Julia Rice, Matt Richter, Ryan Schweikert, Shauna Scott, Patrick Wuebben. **Director of Factory Development Institute Operations:** Mark Lemon. **Director, Social Media/Web Content:** Matt Lund. **Director, Baseball Operations/Scouting Information:** Ryan Liddle. **Director, Retail Sales:** Adam Beaver. **Director, Strategy/Development, Factory Athletics Foundation:** Anita Broccolino.

Under Armour All-America Pre-Season Tournament: Jan. 16-18, Mesa, Ariz. (Cubs Park). **Under Armour All-America Game:** July 23 Chicago (Wrigley Field)

2016 Under Armour Baseball Factory National Tryouts/College Recruiting Program: Year round at various locations across the country. Open to high school players, ages 14–18, with a separate division for pre-high school players, ages 12–14. **Full schedule:** www.baseballfactory.com/tryouts.

EAST COAST PROFESSIONAL SHOWCASE

Website: www.eastcoastpro.org. **Mailing Address:** 1 Steinbrenner Drive, Tampa, FL 33614. **E-mail Address:** info@eastcoastpro.org

Tournament Directors: John Castleberry, Howard McCullough, Sean Gibbs, Lori Bridges.

2016 Showcase: Aug. 1-4, Tampa.

IMPACT BASEBALL

Mailing Address: P.O. Box 47, Sedalia, NC 27342.

E-mail Address: andypartin@aol.com. **Website:** impact baseball.com. **Founder/CEO:** Andy Partin.

2016 Events: Various dates, May-Aug. 2016.

NORTHWEST CHAMPIONSHIPS

Mailing Address: 9849 Fox Street, Aumsville, OR 97325. **Telephone:** (503) 302-7117. **E-mail Address:** warner@baseballnorthwest.com. **Website:** www.baseballnorthwest.com. **Tournament Organizer:** Josh Warner.

2016 Events

Senior Northwest Championship Tournament
(2017-2019 grads) in Centralia, WA............Aug. 11-14
Junior Northwest Championship Tournament
(2020-2021 grads) in Centralia, WA...........Aug. 18-21

PERFECT GAME USA

Mailing Address: 850 Twixt Town Rd. NE Cedar Rapids, IA 52402. **Telephone:** (319) 298-2923. **Fax:** (319) 298-2924. **E-mail Address:** jerry@perfectgame.org. **Website:** www.perfectgameusa.com.

President/Director: Jerry Ford. **Vice Presidents:** Andy Ford, Jason Gerst, Tyson Kimm, Steve Griffin. **VP, Business Development:** Brad Clement. **VP, Tournaments:** Taylor McCollough. **International Scouting Director:** Kentaro Yasutake. **National Showcase Director:** Jim Arp. **National Scouting Director:** Greg Sabers. **National Tournament Director:** Matthew Bliven. **National BCS Director:** Justin Amidon. **Spring Swing Director:** Kevin Herlihy. **National Youth Director:** Scott Weiss. **Super25 Director:** Drake Browne. **Director, PG Crosschecker:** Allan Simpson. **College Baseball Content:** Frankie Piliere, Jheremy Brown. **Iowa League Director:** Steve James. **Scouting Coordinators:** Kirk Gardner, Jason Piddington, Brian Sakowski, Matt Huck. **Tournament Directors:** Ken Gardner, Michael Palazzone, Justin Hlubek, Mark Mathison, Breanne Schoby, Austin Bynum. **National Spokesman:** Daron Sutton. **All American Spokesman:** Trevor Hoffman.

2015 Showcase/Tournament Events: Sites across the United States, Jan. 3-Aug. 30.

PROFESSIONAL BASEBALL INSTRUCTION—BATTERY INVITATIONAL

(for top high school pitchers and catchers)
Mailing Address: 107 Pleasant Avenue, Upper Saddle River, N.J. 07458. **Telephone:** (800) 282-4638. **Fax:** (201) 760-8820. **E-mail Address:** info@baseballclinics.com. **Website:** www.baseballclinics.com/battery-invitational/.
President: Doug Cinnella.
Senior Staff Administrator: Greg Cinnella. **General Manager/PR/Marketing:** Jim Monaghan.
Event Date: November 5, 2016.

SELECTFEST BASEBALL

Mailing Address: P.O. Box 852, Morris Plains, NJ 07950. **E-mail Address:** selectfest@optonline.net. **Web site:** www.selectfestbaseball.org. **Camp Directors:** Bruce Shatel, Robert Maida.
2016 Showcase: June 24-26.

TOP 96 COLLEGE COACHES CLINICS

Mailing Address: 6 Foley Dr. Southboro, MA 01772. **Telephone:** 508-481-5935.
E-mail Address: doug.henson@top96.com. **Website:** www.top96.com. **Directors:** Doug Henson, Dave Callum.

YOUTH BASEBALL

ALL AMERICAN AMATEUR BASEBALL ASSOCIATION

Mailing Address: 331 Parkway Dr., Zanesville, OH 43701. **Telephone:** (740) 607-8531. **E-mail Address:** clw@aol.com. **Website:** www.aaaba.us.
Year Founded: 1944.
President: George Arcurio, III. **Executive Director:** Bob Wolfe.
2016 Events: AAABA Regional Tournaments—July 22-24; National Tournament—Aug. 1-7.

AMATEUR ATHLETIC UNION OF THE UNITED STATES, INC.

Mailing Address: P.O. Box 22409, Lake Buena Vista, FL 32830. **Telephone:** (407) 828-3459. **Fax:** (407) 934-7242. **E-mail Address:** debra@aausports.org. **Website:** www.aaubaseball.org.
Year Founded: 1982. **Senior Sport Manager, Baseball:** Debra Horn.

AMERICAN AMATEUR BASEBALL CONGRESS

National Headquarters: 100 West Broadway, Farmington, NM 87401. **Telephone:** (505) 327-3120. **Fax:** (505) 327-3132. **E-mail Address:** aabc@aabc.us. **Website:** www.aabc.us.
Year Founded: 1935.
President: Richard Neely.

AMERICAN AMATEUR YOUTH BASEBALL ALLIANCE

Mailing Address: 3851 Iris Lane, Bonne Terre, MO 63628. **Telephone:** (314) 650-0028. **E-mail Address:** clwjr28@aol.com. **Website:** www.aayba.com.
President, Baseball Operations: Carroll Wood. **President, Business Operations:** Greg Moore.

AMERICAN LEGION BASEBALL

National Headquarters: American Legion Baseball, 700 N Pennsylvania St., Indianapolis, IN 46204. **Telephone:** (317) 630-1213. **Fax:** (317) 630-1369. **E-mail Address:** baseball@legion.org. **Website:** www.legion.org/baseball.
Year Founded: 1925.
Program Coordinator: Mike Buss.
2016 World Series (19 and under): Aug. 11-16 at Keeter Stadium, Shelby, N.C. **2016 Regional Tournaments (Aug. 3-7):** Northeast—Bristol, Conn.; Mid-Atlantic—Leesburg, Va.; Southeast—Asheboro, N.C.; Mid-South—North Conway, Ark.; Great Lakes—Alton, Ill.; Central Plains—Bismarck, N.D.; Northwest—Cheyenne, Wyo.; West—Boulder, Col.

BABE RUTH BASEBALL

International Headquarters: 1670 Whitehorse-Mercerville Rd.,
Hamilton, NJ 08619. Telephone: (609) 695-1434. **Fax:** (609) 695-2505. **E-mail Address:** info@baberuthleague.org. **Website:** www.baberuthleague.org.
Year Founded: 1951.
President/Chief Executive Officer: Steven Tellefsen.

BASEBALL USA

Mailing Address: 2626 West Sam Houston Pkwy. N., Houston, TX 77043. **Telephone:** (713) 690-5564. **E-mail Address:** info@baseballusa.com. **Website:** www.baseballusa.com.
President: Jason Krug.

CALIFORNIA COMPETITIVE YOUTH BASEBALL

Mailing Address: P.O. Box 338, Placentia, CA 92870. **Telephone:** (714) 993-2838. **E-mail Address:** ccybnet@gmail.com. **Website:** www.ccyb.net.
Tournament Director: Todd Rogers.

COCOA EXPO SPORTS CENTER

Mailing Address: 500 Friday Road, Cocoa, FL 32926. **Telephone:** (321) 639-3976. **Fax:** (407) 390-9435. **E-mail Address:** brad@cocoaexpo.com. **Website:** www.cocoaexpo.com.
Activities: Spring training program, spring & fall leagues, instructional camps, team training camps, youth tournaments.

CONTINENTAL AMATEUR BASEBALL ASSOCIATION

Mailing Address: P.O. Box 1684 Mt. Pleasant, SC 29465. **Telephone:** (843) 860-1568. **Fax:** (843) 856-7791. **E-mail Address:** Diamonddevils@aol.com. **Website:** www.cababaseball.com.
Year Founded: 1984.
Chief Executive Officer: Larry Redwine. **President/COO:** John Rhodes. **Executive Vice President:** Fran Pell.

COOPERSTOWN BASEBALL WORLD

Mailing Address: P.O. Box 646, Allenwood, NJ 08720. **Telephone:** (888) CBW-8750. **Fax:** (888) CBW-8720. **E-mail:** cbw@cooperstownbaseballworld.com. **Website:** www.cooperstownbaseballworld.com.
Complex Address: Cooperstown Baseball World, SUNY-Oneonta, Ravine Parkway, Oneonta, NY 13820.
President: Debra Sirianni.
2016 Tournaments (15 Teams Per Week): Open to 12U, 13U, 14U, 15U, 16U

COOPERSTOWN DREAMS PARK

Mailing Address: 330 S. Main St., Salisbury, NC 28144. **Telephone:** (704) 630-0050. **Fax:** (704) 630-0737. **E-mail Address:** info@cooperstowndreamspark.com. **Website:** www.cooperstowndreamspark.com.
Complex Address: 4550 State Highway 28, Milford, NY 13807.
Chief Executive Officer: Louis Presutti. **Director, Baseball Operations:** Geoff Davis.
2016 Tournaments: June 4-Sept. 2.

COOPERSTOWN ALL STAR VILLAGE

Mailing Address: P.O. Box 670, Cooperstown, NY 13326. **Telephone:** (800) 327-6790. **Fax:** (607) 432-1076. **E-mail Address:** info@cooperstownallstarvillage.com. **Website:** www.cooperstownallstarvillage.com.
Team Registrations: Jim Rudloff. **Hotel Room Reservations:** Gina Montgomery. **Presidents:** Martin and Brenda Patton.

DIXIE YOUTH BASEBALL
Mailing Address: P.O. Box 877, Marshall, TX 75671.
Telephone: (903) 927-2255. **Fax:** (903) 927-1846. **E-mail Address:** dyb@dixie.org. **Website:** youth.dixie.org.
Year Founded: 1955.
Commissioner: Wes Skelton.

DIXIE BOYS BASEBALL
Mailing Address: P.O. Box 8263, Dothan, Alabama 36304. **Telephone:** (334) 793-3331. **E-mail Address:** jjones29@sw.rr.com. **Website:** http://baseball.dixie.org.
Commissioner/Chief Executive Officer: Sandy Jones.

DIZZY DEAN BASEBALL
Mailing Address: P.O. Box 856, Hernando, MS 38632. **Telephone:** (662) 429-4365. **E-mail Address:** dannyphillips637@gmail.com, jwahl1025@gmail.com, Bdunn39270@comcast.net, hsuggsdizzydean@aol.com. **Website:** www.dizzydeanbbinc.org.
Year Founded: 1962.
Commissioner: Danny Phillips. **President:** Jim Wahl. **VP:** Bobby Dunn. **Secretary:** Jim Dunn. **Treasurer:** Houston Suggs.
ESPN Wide World of Sports
Mailing Address: P.O. Box 470847, Celebration, FL 34747. **Telephone:** (407) 938-3802. **Fax:** (407) 938-3442. **E-mail address:** wdw.sports.baseball@disneysports.com. **Website:** www.disneybaseball.com.
Senior Manager, Sports Events: Aaron Hudson.
Senior Sports Manager: Al Schlazer.

HAP DUMONT YOUTH BASEBALL
(A Division of the National Baseball Congress)
E-mail Address: bruce@prattrecreation.com, gbclev@hapdumontbaseball.com. **Website:** www.hapdumont baseball.com.
Year Founded: 1974.
President: Bruce Pinkall

KC SPORTS TOURNAMENTS
Mailing Address: KC Sports, 6324 N. Chatham Ave., No. 136, Kansas City, MO 64151.
Telephone: (816) 587-4545. **Fax:** (816) 587-4549.
E-mail Address: info@kcsports.org.
Website: www.kcsports.org.
Activities: USSSA Youth tournaments (ages 6-18).

LITTLE LEAGUE BASEBALL
International Headquarters: 539 US Route 15 Hwy, P.O. Box 3485, Williamsport, PA 17701-0485. **Telephone:** (570) 326-1921. **Fax:** (570) 326-1074. **Website:** www.littleleague.org.
Year Founded: 1939.
Chairman: Dr. Davie Jane Gilmour.
President/Chief Executive Officer: Stephen D. Keener. **Chief Financial Officer:** David Houseknecht. **Vice President, Operations:** Patrick Wilson. **Treasurer:** Melissa Singer. **Vice President, Marketing and Communications:** Liz Brown.

NATIONS BASEBALL-ARIZONA
Mailing Address: 5160 W Glenview Pl, Chandler, AZ 85226. **Telephone:** (602) 793-8940. **Website:** Nationsbaseballaz.com. **E-Mail:** Nationsbaseballarizona@gmail.com.

NATIONAL AMATEUR BASEBALL FEDERATION
Mailing Address: P.O. Box 705, Bowie, MD 20718. **Telephone:** (410) 721-4727. **Fax:** (410) 721-4940.
E-mail Address: nabf1914@aol.com.
Website: www.nabf.com.
Year Founded: 1914.
Executive Director: Charles Blackburn.

NATIONAL ASSOCIATION OF POLICE ATHLETIC LEAGUES
Mailing Address: 1662 N. US Highway 1 Suite C, Jupiter, FL 33469. **Telephone:** (561) 745-5535. **Fax:** (561) 745-3147. **E-mail Address:** copnkid@nationalpal.org. **Website:** www.nationalpal.org.
Year Founded: 1914.
President: Christopher Hill.

PONY BASEBALL AND SOFTBALL
International Headquarters: P.O. Box 225, Washington, PA 15301. **Telephone:** (724) 225-1060. **Fax:** (724) 225-9852. **E-mail Address:** info@pony.org.
Website: www.pony.org.
Year Founded: 1951.
President: Abraham Key.

REVIVING BASEBALL IN INNER CITIES
Mailing Address: 245 Park Ave., New York, NY 10167. **Telephone:** (212) 931-7800. **Fax:** (212) 949-5695. **Year Founded:** 1989. **Senior Vice President, Youth Programs:** Tony Reagins (Tony.Reagins@mlb.com). **Senior Director, Youth Programs:** David James (David.James@mlb.com). **Vice President, Community Affairs:** Thomas C. Brasuell. **E-mail:** rbi@mlb.com. **Website:** www.mlb.com/rbi.

SUPER SERIES BASEBALL OF AMERICA
National Headquarters: 3449 East Kael St., Mesa, AZ 85213-1773. **Telephone:** (480) 664-2998. **Fax:** (480) 664-2997. **E-mail Address:** info@superseriesbaseball.com. **Website:** www.superseriesbaseball.com.
President: Mark Mathew.

TRIPLE CROWN SPORTS
Mailing Address: 3930 Automation Way, Fort Collins, CO 80525. **Telephone:** (970) 223-6644. **Fax:** (970) 223-3636. **Websites:** www.triplecrownsports.com. **E-mail:** joe@triplecrownsports.com.
Director, Baseball Operations: Joe Santilli.

U.S. AMATEUR BASEBALL FEDERATION
Mailing Address: 301 Winters Ct., San Marcos, CA 92069. **Telephone:** (760) 580-9934. **Fax:** (760) 798-9376. **E-mail Address:** usabf@cox.net. **Website:** www.usabf.com.
Year Founded: 1997.
Commissioner: Jay Gracio.

UNITED STATES SPECIALTY SPORTS ASSOCIATION

Executive Vice President, Baseball: Don DeDonatis III, 33600 Mound Rd., Sterling Heights, MI 48310. **Telephone:** (810) 397-6410. **E-mail Address:** michusssa@aol.com.

Executive VP, Baseball Operations: Rick Fortuna, 6324 N. Chatham Ave., #136, Kansas City, MO 64151. **Telephone:** (816) 587-4545. **E-mail Address:** rick@kcsports.org. **Website:** www.usssabaseball.org. **Year Founded:** 1965/Baseball 1996.

WORLD WOOD BAT ASSOCIATION

(A Division of Perfect Game USA)

Mailing Address: 850 Twixt Town Rd. NE, Cedar Rapids, IA 52402. **Telephone:** (319) 298-2923. **Fax:** (319) 298-2924. **E-mail Address:** taylor@perfectgame.org. **Website:** www.perfectgame.org.

Year Founded: 1997.

President: Jerry Ford. **National Director:** Taylor McCollough. **Scouting Director:** Greg Sabers.

INSTRUCTIONAL SCHOOLS/ PRIVATE CAMPS

ALL-STAR BASEBALL ACADEMY

Mailing Address: 52 Penn Oaks Drive, West Chester, PA 19382. **Telephone:** (610) 399-8050. **Fax:** (610)-399-8553 . **E-mail Address:** basba@allstarbaseballacademy.com. **Website:** www.allstarbaseballacademy.com. **President/CEO :** Jim Freeman. **Executive Director:** Mike Manning.

AMERICAN BASEBALL FOUNDATION

Mailing Address: 2660 10th Ave. South, Suite 620, Birmingham, AL 35205. **Telephone:** (205) 558-4235. **Fax:** (205) 918-0800. **E-mail Address:** abf@asmi.org. **Website:** www.americanbaseballfoundation.com. **Executive Director:** David Osinski.

AMERICA'S BASEBALL CAMPS

Mailing Address: 3020 ISSQ Pine Lake Road #12, Sammamish, WA 98075. **Telephone:** (800) 222-8152. **Fax:** (888) 751-8989. **E-mail Address:** info@baseballcamps.com. **Website:** www.baseballcamps.com.

CHAMPIONS BASEBALL ACADEMY

Mailing Address: 5994 Linneman Street Cincinnati, OH 45230. **Telephone:** (513) 831-8873. **Fax:** (513) 247-0040. **E-mail Address:** information@ChampionsBaseball.net. **Website:** www.championsbaseball.net. **Director:** Mike Bricker.

DOYLE BASEBALL ACADEMY

Mailing Address: P.O. Box 9156, Winter Haven, FL 33883. **Telephone:** (863) 439-1000. **Fax:** (863) 294-8607. **E-mail Address:** info@doylebaseball.com. **Website:** www.doylebaseball.com. **President:** Denny Doyle. **CEO:** Blake Doyle.

ELEV8 SPORTS INSTITUTE

Mailing Address: 490 Dotterel Road, Delray Beach, FL 33444. **Telephone:** (800) 970-5896. **Fax:** (561) 865-7358. **E-mail Address:** info@elev8si.com. **Website:** http://elev8sportsinstitute.com/

FROZEN ROPES TRAINING CENTERS

Mailing Address: 24 Old Black Meadow Rd., Chester, NY 10918. **Telephone:** (845) 469-7331. **Fax:** (845) 469-6742. **E-mail Address:** info@frozenropes.com. **Website:** www.frozenropes.com.

IMG ACADEMY

Mailing Address: IMG Academy, 5500 34th St. W., Bradenton, FL 34210. **Telephone:** 941-739-7480. **Fax:** 941-739-7484. **E-mail Address:** acad_baseball@img.com. **Website:** www.imgacademy.com.

MARK CRESSE BASEBALL SCHOOL

Mailing Address: P.O. Box 1596 Newport Beach, CA 92659. **Telephone:** (714) 892-6145. **Fax:** (714) 890-7017. **E-mail Address:** info@markcresse.com. **Website:** www.markcresse.com.

Owner/Founder: Mark Cresse.

US SPORTS CAMPS/NIKE BASEBALL CAMPS

Mailing Address: 1010 B Street Suite 450, San Rafael, CA 94901. **Telephone:** (415) 479-6060. **Fax:** (415) 479-6061. **E-mail Address:** baseball@ussportscamps.com. **Website:** www.ussportscamps.com/baseball/.

MOUNTAIN WEST BASEBALL ACADEMY

Mailing Address: 389 West 10000 South, South Jordan, UT 84095. **Telephone:** (801) 561-1700. **Fax:** (801) 561-1762. **E-mail Address:** kent@utahbaseballacademy.com. **Website:** www.mountainwestbaseball.com. **Director:** Bob Keyes

NORTH CAROLINA BASEBALL ACADEMY

Mailing Address: 1137 Pleasant Ridge Road, Greensboro, NC 27409. **Telephone:** (336) 931-1118. **E-mail Address:** info@ncbaseball.com. **Website:** www.ncbaseball.com.

Owner/Director: Scott Bankhead.

PENNSYLVANIA DIAMOND BUCKS

Mailing Address: 2320 Whitetail Court, Hellertown, PA 18055. **Telephone:** (610) 838-1219, (610) 442-6998. **E-mail Address:** janciganick@yahoo.com. **Camp Director:** Jan Ciganick. **Head of Instruction:** Chuck Ciganick.

PROFESSIONAL BASEBALL INSTRUCTION

Mailing Address: 107 Pleasant Ave., Upper Saddle River, NJ 07458. **Telephone:** (800) 282-4638 (NY/NJ), (877) 448-2220 (rest of U.S.). **Fax:** (201) 760-8820. **E-mail Address:** info@baseballclinics.com. **Website:** www.baseballclinics.com. **President:** Doug Cinnella.

RIPKEN BASEBALL CAMPS

Mailing Address: 1427 Clarkview Rd., Suite 100, Baltimore, MD 21209. **Telephone:** (410) 297-9292. **Fax:** (410) 823-0850. **E-mail Address:** information@ripken baseball.com. **Website:** www.ripkenbaseball.com.

SHO-ME BASEBALL CAMP

Mailing Address: P.O. Box 2270, Branson West, MO 65737. **Telephone:** (417) 338-5838. **Fax:** (417) 338-2610. **E-mail Address:** info@shomebaseball.com. **Website:** www.shomebaseball.com.

COLLEGE CAMPS

Almost all of the elite college baseball programs have summer/holiday instructional camps. Please consult the college section for listings.

SENIOR BASEBALL

MEN'S SENIOR BASEBALL LEAGUE

(25 and Over, 35 and Over, 45 and Over, 55 and Over)
Mailing Address: One Huntington Quadrangle, Suite 3N07, Melville, NY 11747. **Telephone:** (631) 753-6725. **Fax:** (631) 753-4031.
President: Steve Sigler. **Vice President:** Gary D'Ambrisi.
E-Mail Address: info@msblnational.com.
Website: www.msblnational.com.

MEN'S ADULT BASEBALL LEAGUE

(18 and Over)
Mailing Address: One Huntington Quadrangle, Suite 3N07, Melville, NY 11747. **Telephone:** (631) 753-6725. **Fax:** (631) 753-4031.
E-Mail Address: info@msblnational.com. **Website:** www.msblnational.com.
President: Steve Sigler. **Vice President:** Gary D'Ambrisi.

NATIONAL ADULT BASEBALL ASSOCIATION

Mailing Address: 5944 S. Kipling St., Suite 200, Littleton, CO 80127. **Telephone:** (800) 621-6479. **Fax:** (303) 639-6605. **E-Mail:** nabanational@aol.com. **Website:** www.dugout.org.
President: Shane Fugita.

NATIONAL AMATEUR BASEBALL FEDERATION

Mailing Address: P.O. Box 705, Bowie, MD 20718. **Telephone:** (410) 721-4727. **Fax:** (410) 721-4940.
Email Address: nabf1914@aol.com.
Website: www.nabf.com.
Year Founded: 1914.
Executive Director: Charles Blackburn.

ROY HOBBS BASEBALL

Open (18 and Over), Veterans (30 or 35 and Over), Masters (45 and Over), Legends (53 and Over); Classics (60 and Over), Vintage (65 and Over), Timeless (70 and Over), Forever Young (75 and Over), Women's Open, Family Ties (Father-Son) competition in February.
Mailing Address: 4301-A Edison Ave., Fort Myers, FL 33916. **Telephone:** (330) 923-3400. **Fax:** (330) 923-1967. **E-Mail Address:** rhbb@royhobbs.com. **Website:** www.royhobbs.com.
CEO: Tom Giffen. **President:** Rob Giffen.

DIRECTORIES

- ■ AGENT
- ■ SERVICE

AGENT DIRECTORY

ACES, INC.
188 Montague Street
Brooklyn, NY 11201
Phone: (718) 237-2900
Fax: (718) 522-3906
Web: www.acesincbaseball.com
E-mail: ACES@acesinc1.com
Seth Levinson, Esq.; Sam Levinson; Keith Miller; Peter Pedalino, Esq.; Brandon O'Hearn; Mike Zimmerman; Jamie Appel; Josh Yates; Josh Borkin, Esq.; Eric McQueen; Anthony Lovende, Esq.; Matt Adams; Matt Wright; Matt Harris; Allan Donato; Jason St. Clair

JACKSON MANAGEMENT GROUP, LLC
132 North Old Woodward Ave
Birmingham, MI 48009
Phone: (248) 594-1070
Fax: (248) 281-5150
Web: www.jackson-management.com
E-mail: baseball@jackson-management.com
Storm T. Kirschenbaum, Esq.; Hector Faneytt; Michael Bonanno; **Director of Taiwanese Operations**—Tony Chang; **Director of Japanese Operations**—Max Ohno; **Latin Operations**—Rafael Antun

KPT SPORTS
721 First Avenue North
St. Petersburg, FL 33701
Phone: (727) 898-5786
Fax: (727) 821-1211
Web: www.KPTsports.com
E-mail: info@KPTsports.com
Ed Kravitz, Esq., Aaron Ledesma

THE L. WARNER COMPANIES, INC
9690 Deereco Rd
Ste 650
Timonium, MD 21093
Phone: (410) 252-0808
Fax: (443) 281-5554
Web: www.lwarner.com/baseball
E-mail: roliver@lwarner.com
Chairman and CEO—Lee Warner; **President**—Rick Oliver

TLA WORLDWIDE
NEW YORK
1500 Broadway, Suite 2501
New York, NY 10036
Phone: (212) 334-6880
Fax: (212) 334-6895
Web: www.tlaworldwide.com
E-mail: info@tlaworldwide.com
Peter E. Greenberg, Esq; Edward L. Greenberg; Chris Leible; Eric Izen

CALIFORNIA
500 Newport Center Dr, Ste 800
Newport Beach, CA 92660
Phone: (949) 720-8700
Fax: (949) 720-1331
Web: www.tlaworldwide.com
E-mail: info@tlaworldwide.com
Greg Genske; Brian Peters; Brodie Scoffield; RJ Hernandez; Kenny Felder; Joe Brennan; Joe Mizzo; Scott Parker; Mike Maulini

ONYX SPORTS MANAGEMENT
60 E. Rio Salado Pkwy
Suite 900
Tempe, AZ 85281
Phone: (480) 643-9112
Fax: (480) 696-5474
Web: www.onyxsm.com
E-mail: jcook@onyxsm.com
E-mail: zprice@onyxsm.com
Jesse D. Cook; Zachary I. Price

PRO STAR MANAGEMENT, INC.
1600 Scripps Center, 312 Walnut Street
Cincinnati, OH 45202
Phone: (513) 762-7676
Fax: (513) 721-4628
Web: www.prostarmanagement.com
E-mail: prostar@fuse.net
Twitter: @prostarmgmt
President—Joe Bick; **Executive Vice President**—Brett Bick; **Recruiting Coordinator**—Jeff Gatch

SOSNICK COBBE & KARON
712 Bancroft Rd, #510
Walnut Creek, CA 94598
Phone: (925) 890-5283
Fax: (925) 476-0130
Web: www.SosnickCobbeKaron.com
E-mail: info@SosnickCobbeKaron.com
Matt Sosnick; Paul Cobbe; Adam Karon; Matt Hofer; Jonathan Pridie; Tripper Johnson; John Furmaniak

VERRILL DANA SPORTS LAW GROUP
One Portland Square
Portland, ME 4101
Phone: (207) 774-4000
Alt. Phone: (207) 774-7499
Web: www.verrilldana.com
E-mail: dabramson@verrilldana.com
David S. Abramson, Esq

SERVICE DIRECTORY

ACCESSORIES

WILSON SPORTING GOODS
8750 West Bryn Mawr Ave
13th Floor
Chicago, IL 60631
Phone: (800) 333-8326
Fax: (773) 714-4565
Web: www.wilson.com
E-mail: askwilson@wilson.com

APPAREL

DEMARINI
6435 NW Croeni Rd
Hillsboro, OR 97124
Phone: (800) 937-BATS (2287)
Fax: (503) 531-5506
Web: www.demarini.com

BAGS

DIAMOND SPORTS
1880 E. St. Andrew Place
Santa Ana, CA 92705
Phone: (714) 415-7600
Fax: (714) 415-7601
Web: www.diamond-sports.com
E-mail: info@diamond-sports.com

DEMARINI
6435 NW Croeni Rd
Hillsboro, OR 97124
Phone: (800) 937-BATS (2287)
Fax: (503) 531-5506
Web: www.demarini.com

LOUISVILLE SLUGGER
8750 West Bryn Mawr Ave
13th Floor
Chicago, IL 60631
Phone: (800) 333-8326
Fax: (773) 714-4565
Web: www.slugger.com
E-mail: customer.service@slugger.com

WILSON SPORTING GOODS
8750 West Bryn Mawr Ave
13th Floor
Chicago, IL 60631
Phone: (800) 333-8326
Fax: (773) 714-4565
Web: www.wilson.com
E-mail: askwilson@wilson.com

BASEBALLS

DIAMOND SPORTS
1880 E. St. Andrew Place
Santa Ana, CA 92705
Phone: (714) 415-7600
Fax: (714) 415-7601
Web: www.diamond-sports.com
E-mail: info@diamond-sports.com

WILSON SPORTING GOODS
8750 West Bryn Mawr Ave
13th Floor
Chicago, IL 60631
Phone: (800) 333-8326
Fax: (773) 714-4565
Web: www.wilson.com
E-mail: askwilson@wilson.com

BASES

BEAM CLAY
One Kelsey Park
Great Meadows, NJ 7838
Phone: (800) 247-BEAM (2326)
Fax: (908) 637-8421
Web: www.beamclay.com
E-mail: sales@beamclay.com

See our ad on page 312!

BATS

B45- THE ORIGINAL YELLOW BIRCH BAT COMPANY
281 Rue Edward-Assh
Ste-Catherine-de-la-Jacques-Cartier
QC G3N 1A3
Phone: (888) 669-0145
Web: www.b45online.com
E-mail: info@b45online.com

BWP BATS
80 Womeldorf Lane
Brookville, PA 15825
Phone: (814) 849-0089
Fax: (814) 849-8584
Web: www.shopbwp.com
E-mail: josh@bwpbats.com

DEMARINI
6435 NW Croeni Rd
Hillsboro, OR 97124
Phone: (800) 937-BATS (2287)
Fax: (503) 531-5506
Web: www.demarini.com

DIAMOND SPORTS
1880 E. St. Andrew Place
Santa Ana, CA 92705
Phone: (714) 415-7600
Fax: (714) 415-7601
Web: www.diamond-sports.com
E-mail: info@diamond-sports.com

DINGER BATS
109 S. Kimbro St.
Ridgway, IL 62979
Phone: (618) 272-7250
Fax: (618) 272-5705
Web: www.dingerbats.com
E-mail: info@dingerbats.com

LOUISVILLE SLUGGER
8750 West Bryn Mawr Ave
13th Floor
Chicago, IL 60631
Phone: (800) 333-8326
Fax: (773) 714-4565
Web: www.slugger.com
E-mail: customer.service@slugger.com

OLD HICKORY BAT COMPANY
P.O. Box 588
White House, TN 37188
Phone: (866) PRO-BATS
Fax: (615) 285-0512
Web: www.oldhickorybats.com
E-mail: mail@oldhickorybats.com

TRINITY BAT COMPANY
2493 E. Orangethorpe Ave
Fullerton, CA 92831
Phone: (714) 449-1275
Fax: (714) 449-1285
Web: www.trinitybatco.com
E-mail: steve@trinitybats.com

VIPER BATS
4807 Ivan Lane
Sedro Woolley, WA 98284
Phone: (360) 630-5168
Fax: (360) 630-5123
Web: www.viperbats.com
E-mail: sales@viperbats.com

BATTING CAGES

BALL FABRICS, INC.
510 W. Arizona Ave
Deland, FL 32720
Phone: (386) 740-7212
Fax: (386) 740-7206
Web: www.ballfabrics.com
E-mail: info@ballfabrics.com

BEAM CLAY
One Kelsey Park
Great Meadows, NJ 7838
Phone: (800) 247-BEAM (2326)
Fax: (908) 637-8421
Web: www.beamclay.com
E-mail: sales@beamclay.com

See our ad on page 312!

C&H BASEBALL, INC
10615 Technology Terrace, #100
Bradenton, FL 34211
Phone: (941) 727-1533
Fax: (941) 462-3076
Web: www.chbaseball.com
E-mail: sales@chbaseball.com

DIAMOND SPORTS
1880 E. St. Andrew Place
Santa Ana, CA 92705
Phone: (714) 415-7600
Fax: (714) 415-7601
Web: www.diamond-sports.com
E-mail: info@diamond-sports.com

GOLF RANGE NETTING INC.
40351 US Hwy 19N #303
Tarpon Springs, FL 34689
Phone: (727) 938-4448
Fax: (727) 938-4135
Web: www.golfrangenetting.com
E-mail: info@golfrangenetting.com

MASTER PITCHING MACHINE, INC.
4200 NE Birmingham Rd.
Kansas City, MO 64117
Phone: (800) 878-8228
Fax: (816) 452-7581
Web: www.masterpitch.com
E-mail: patrick@masterpitch.com

PROMATS ATHLETICS
PO Box 2489
Salisbury, NC 28145
Phone: (800) 617-7125
Fax: (704) 603-4138
Web: www.promatsathletics.com
E-mail: mcross@promatsathletics.com

WEST COAST NETTING
5075 Flightline Dr
Kingman, AZ 86401
Phone: (928) 692-1144
Fax: (928) 692-1501
Web: www.westcoastnetting.com
E-mail: info@westcoastnetting.com

BATTING GLOVES

DEMARINI
6435 NW Croeni Rd
Hillsboro, OR 97124
Phone: (800) 937-BATS (2287)
Fax: (503) 531-5506
Web: www.demarini.com

CAMPS/SCHOOLS

PROFESSIONAL BASEBALL INSTRUCTION
107 Pleasant Avenue
Upper Saddle River, NJ 07458
Phone: (201) 760-8720
Fax: (201) 760-8820
Web: www.baseballclinics.com
E-mail: info@baseballclinics.com

CAPS/HEADWEAR

OC SPORTS
1201 Melissa Drive
Bentonville, AR 72712
Phone: (800) 826-6047
Fax: (866) 766-1010
Web: www.ocsports.com
E-mail: teamdealer@OCsports.com

CONCESSION OPERATIONS

STADIUM1 SOFTWARE, LLC
13479 Polo Trace Drive
Delray Beach, FL 33446
Phone: (561) 498-8356
Fax: (561) 498-8358
Web: www.stadium1.com
E-mail: tim.mcdulin@stadium1.com

EMBROIDERED PATCHES

THE EMBLEM SOURCE
4575 Westgrove #500
Addison, TX 75001
Phone: (972) 248-1909
Fax: (972) 248-1615
Web: www.theemblemsource.com
E-mail: larry@theemblemsource.com

ENTERTAINMENT

SCOLLON PRODUCTIONS
PO Box 486
White Rock, SC 29177
Phone: (803) 345-3922 x43
Fax: (803) 345-9313
Web: www.scollon.com
E-mail: rickjr@scollon.com.
Contact: Rick Scollon Jr.

THE SKILLVILLE GROUP— ZOOPERSTARS!
P.O. Box 36061
Louisville, KY 40233
Phone: (502) 458-4020
Fax: (502) 458-0867
Web: www.theskillvillegroup.com
E-mail: info@theskillvillegroup.com
ZOOperstars!; BirdZerk!; Breakin' BBoy McCoy; Russian Bar Trio; and Bucket Ruckus

FIELD COVERS/TARPS

BALL FABRICS, INC.
510 W. Arizona Ave
Deland, FL 32720
Phone: (386) 740-7212
Fax: (386) 740-7206
Web: www.ballfabrics.com
E-mail: info@ballfabrics.com

BEAM CLAY
One Kelsey Park
Great Meadows, NJ 7838
Phone: (800) 247-BEAM (2326)
Fax: (908) 637-8421
Web: www.beamclay.com
E-mail: sales@beamclay.com

See our ad on page 312!

COVERMASTER, INC
100 Westmore Dr
11-D
Rexdale, ON M9V 5C3
Phone: (416) 745-1811
Fax: (416) 742-6837
Web: www.covermaster.com
E-mail: info@covermaster.com

C&H BASEBALL, INC
10615 Technology Terrace, #100
Bradenton, FL 34211
Phone: (941) 727-1533
Fax: (941) 462-3076
Web: www.chbaseball.com
E-mail: sales@chbaseball.com

FIELD EQUIPMENT

DIAMOND SPORTS
1880 E. St. Andrew Place
Santa Ana, CA 92705
Phone: (714) 415-7600
Fax: (714) 415-7601
Web: www.diamond-sports.com
E-mail: info@diamond-sports.com

FIELD WALL PADDING

BALL FABRICS, INC.
510 W. Arizona Ave
Deland, FL 32720
Phone: (386) 740-7212
Fax: (386) 740-7206
Web: www.ballfabrics.com
E-mail: info@ballfabrics.com

BEAM CLAY
One Kelsey Park
Great Meadows, NJ 7838
Phone: (800) 247-BEAM (2326)
Fax: (908) 637-8421
Web: www.beamclay.com
E-mail: sales@beamclay.com

See our ad on page 312!

COVERMASTER, INC
100 Westmore Dr
11-D
Rexdale, ON M9V 5C3
Phone: (416) 745-1811
Fax: (416) 742-6837
Web: www.covermaster.com
E-mail: info@covermaster.com

C&H BASEBALL, INC
10615 Technology Terrace, #100
Bradenton, FL 34211
Phone: (941) 727-1533
Fax: (941) 462-3076
Web: www.chbaseball.com
E-mail: sales@chbaseball.com

PROMATS ATHLETICS
PO Box 2489
Salisbury, NC 28145
Phone: (800) 617-7125
Fax: (704) 603-4138
Web: www.promatsathletics.com
E-mail: mcross@promatsathletics.com

WEST COAST NETTING
5075 Flightline Dr
Kingman, AZ 86401
Phone: (928) 692-1144
Fax: (928) 692-1501
Web: www.westcoastnetting.com
E-mail: info@westcoastnetting.com

FIREWORDS

PYROTECNICO
P.O. Box 149
New Castle, PA 16103
Phone: (800-) 854-4705
Fax: (724) 652-9555
Web: www.pyrotecnico.com
E-mail: info@pyrotecnico.com

FOOD SERVICE

STADIUM1 SOFTWARE, LLC
13479 Polo Trace Drive
Delray Beach, FL 33446
Phone: (561) 498-8356
Fax: (561) 498-8358
Web: www.stadium1.com
E-mail: tim.mcdulin@stadium1.com

GLOVES

FRANK'S SPORT SHOP
430 E. Tremont Ave.
Bronx, NY 10457
Phone: (718) 299-5223/(212) 945-0020
Fax: (718) 583-1653
Web: www.frankssportshop.com

See our ad on the divider!

LOUISVILLE SLUGGER
8750 West Bryn Mawr Ave
13th Floor
Chicago, IL 60631
Phone: (800) 333-8326
Fax: (773) 714-4565
Web: www.slugger.com
E-mail: customer.service@slugger.com.

OLD HICKORY BAT COMPANY
P.O. Box 588
White House, TN 37188
Phone: (866) PRO-BATS
Fax: (615) 285-0512
Web: www.oldhickorybats.com
E-mail: mail@oldhickorybats.com

WILSON SPORTING GOODS
8750 West Bryn Mawr Ave
13th Floor
Chicago, IL 60631
Phone: (800) 333-8326
Fax: (773) 714-4565
Web: www.wilson.com
E-mail: askwilson@wilson.com

GRAPHIC DESIGN

PROMATS ATHLETICS
PO Box 2489
Salisbury, NC 28145
Phone: (800) 617-7125
Fax: (704) 603-4138
Web: www.promatsathletics.com
E-mail: mcross@promatsathletics.com

HS SHOWCASE EVENTS

PROFESSIONAL BASEBALL INSTRUCTION
107 Pleasant Avenue
Upper Saddle River, NJ 07458
Phone: (201) 760-8720
Fax: (201) 760-8820
Web: www.baseballclinics.com
E-mail: info@baseballclinics.com

INSTILLATIONS

C&H BASEBALL, INC
10615 Technology Terrace, #100
Bradenton, FL 34211
Phone: (941) 727-1533
Fax: (941) 462-3076
Web: www.chbaseball.com
E-mail: sales@chbaseball.com

INSURANCE

K&K INSURANCE
1712 Magnavox Way
Fort Wayne, IN 46804
Phone: (800) 441-3994
Fax: (260) 459-5120
Web: www.kandkinsurance.com
E-mail: kk-sports@kandkinsurance.com
see ad on page

LIGHTING

GOLF RANGE NETTING INC.
40351 US Hwy 19N #303
Tarpon Springs, FL 34689
Phone: (727) 938-4448
Fax: (727) 938-4135
Web: www.golfrangenetting.com
E-mail: info@golfrangenetting.com

MASCOTS

SCOLLON PRODUCTIONS
PO Box 486
White Rock, SC 29177
Phone: (803) 345-3922 x43
Fax: (803) 345-9313
Web: www.scollon.com
E-mail: rickjr@scollon.com.
Contact: Rick Scollon Jr.

MUSIC/SOUND EFFECTS

SOUND DIRECTOR, INC
2918 SW Royal Way
Gresham, OR 97080
Phone: (888) 276-0078
Fax: (503) 914-1812
Web: www.sounddirector.com
E-mail: jj@sounddirector.com

NETTING/POSTS

BALL FABRICS, INC.
510 W. Arizona Ave
Deland, FL 32720
Phone: (386) 740-7212
Fax: (386) 740-7206
Web: www.ballfabrics.com
E-mail: info@ballfabrics.com

BEAM CLAY
One Kelsey Park
Great Meadows, NJ 7838
Phone: (800) 247-BEAM (2326)
Fax: (908) 637-8421
Web: www.beamclay.com
E-mail: sales@beamclay.com

See our ad on page 312!

C&H BASEBALL, INC
10615 Technology Terrace, #100
Bradenton, FL 34211
Phone: (941) 727-1533
Fax: (941) 462-3076
Web: www.chbaseball.com
E-mail: sales@chbaseball.com

GOLF RANGE NETTING INC.
40351 US Hwy 19N #303
Tarpon Springs, FL 34689
Phone: (727) 938-4448
Fax: (727) 938-4135
Web: www.golfrangenetting.com
E-mail: info@golfrangenetting.com

MASTER PITCHING MACHINE, INC.
4200 NE Birmingham Rd.
Kansas City, MO 64117
Phone: (800) 878-8228
Fax: (816) 452-7581
Web: www.masterpitch.com
E-mail: patrick@masterpitch.com

PROMATS ATHLETICS
PO Box 2489
Salisbury, NC 28145
Phone: (800) 617-7125
Fax: (704) 603-4138
Web: www.promatsathletics.com
E-mail: mcross@promatsathletics.com

WEST COAST NETTING
5075 Flightline Dr
Kingman, AZ 86401
Phone: (928) 692-1144
Fax: (928) 692-1501
Web: www.westcoastnetting.com
E-mail: info@westcoastnetting.com

PITCHING MACHINES

ATHLETIC TRAINING EQUIPMENT COMPANY - ATEC
655 Spice Island Dr
Sparks, NV 89431
Phone: (800) 998-ATEC (2832)
Fax: (800) 959-ATEC (2832)
Web: www.atecsports.com
E-mail: askATEC@wilson.com

MASTER PITCHING MACHINE, INC.
4200 NE Birmingham Rd.
Kansas City, MO 64117
Phone: (800) 878-8228
Fax: (816) 452-7581
Web: www.masterpitch.com
E-mail: patrick@masterpitch.com

SPORTS TUTOR, INC
3300 Winona Ave
Burbank, CA 91504
Phone: (818) 972-2772
Fax: (818) 972-9651
Web: www.sportstutorinc.com
E-mail: customerservice@sportstutorinc.com

PLAYING FIELD PRODUCTS

APPLIED CONCEPTS
2609 Technology Dr
Plano, TX 75074
Phone: (888) STALKER
Fax: (972) 398-3781
Web: www.stalkerradar.com
E-mail: sales@stalkerradar.com

BEAM CLAY
One Kelsey Park
Great Meadows, NJ 7838
Phone: (800) 247-BEAM (2326)
Fax: (908) 637-8421
Web: www.beamclay.com
E-mail: sales@beamclay.com

See our ad on page 312!

L.A. STEELCRAFT PRODUCTS, INC
1975 Lincoln Ave.
Pasadena, CA 91103
Phone: (800) 371-2438
Fax: (626) 798-1482
Web: www.lasteelcraft.com
E-mail: info@lasteelcraft.com

PRINTING

BALL FABRICS, INC.
510 W. Arizona Ave
Deland, FL 32720
Phone: (386) 740-7212
Fax: (386) 740-7206
Web: www.ballfabrics.com
E-mail: info@ballfabrics.com

WORLDWIDE TICKETCRAFT
3606 Quantum Blvd
Boynton Beach, FL 33426
Phone: (877) 426-5754
Web: www.worldwideticketcraft.com
E-mail: kevin@wwticket.com

PROFESSIONAL SERVICES

STADIUM1 SOFTWARE, LLC
13479 Polo Trace Drive
Delray Beach, FL 33446
Phone: (561) 498-8356
Fax: (561) 498-8358
Web: www.stadium1.com
E-mail: tim.mcdulin@stadium1.com

POINT OF SALE ITEMS

STADIUM1 SOFTWARE, LLC
13479 Polo Trace Drive
Delray Beach, FL 33446
Phone: (561) 498-8356
Fax: (561) 498-8358
Web: www.stadium1.com
E-mail: tim.mcdulin@stadium1.com

PROTECTIVE EQUIPMENT

BEAM CLAY
One Kelsey Park
Great Meadows, NJ 7838
Phone: (800) 247-BEAM (2326)
Fax: (908) 637-8421
Web: www.beamclay.com
E-mail: sales@beamclay.com

See our ad on page 312!

C&H BASEBALL, INC
10615 Technology Terrace, #100
Bradenton, FL 34211
Phone: (941) 727-1533
Fax: (941) 462-3076
Web: www.chbaseball.com
E-mail: sales@chbaseball.com

DIAMOND SPORTS
1880 E. St. Andrew Place
Santa Ana, CA 92705
Phone: (714) 415-7600
Fax: (714) 415-7601
Web: www.diamond-sports.com
E-mail: info@diamond-sports.com

PROMATS ATHLETICS
PO Box 2489
Salisbury, NC 28145
Phone: (800) 617-7125
Fax: (704) 603-4138
Web: www.promatsathletics.com
E-mail: mcross@promatsathletics.com

WEST COAST NETTING
5075 Flightline Dr
Kingman, AZ 86401
Phone: (928) 692-1144
Fax: (928) 692-1501
Web: www.westcoastnetting.com
E-mail: info@westcoastnetting.com

WILSON SPORTING GOODS
8750 West Bryn Mawr Ave
13th Floor
Chicago, IL 60631
Phone: (800) 333-8326
Fax: (773) 714-4565
Web: www.wilson.com
E-mail: askwilson@wilson.com

RADAR EQUIPTMENT

APPLIED CONCEPTS
2609 Technology Dr
Plano, TX 75074
Phone: (888) STALKER
Fax: (972) 398-3781
Web: www.stalkerradar.com
E-mail: sales@stalkerradar.com
see ad on page

SHOES

FRANK'S SPORT SHOP
430 E. Tremont Ave.
Bronx, NY 10457
Phone: (718) 299-5223/(212) 945-0020
Fax: (718) 583-1653
Web: www.frankssportshop.com

See our ad on the divider!

SPECIAL EFFECTS & LASERS

PYROTECNICO
P.O. Box 149
New Castle, PA 16103
Phone: (800-) 854-4705
Fax: (724) 652-9555
Web: www.pyrotecnico.com
E-mail: info@pyrotecnico.com

SPORTS MEDICINE

BASEBALL HEALTH NETWORK
107 Pleasant Avenue
Upper Saddle River, NJ 07458
Phone: (201) 760-8720 ext 106
Fax: (201) 760-8820
Web: www.baseballhealthnetwork.com
E-mail: info@baseballhealthnetwork.com

TICKETS

WORLDWIDE TICKETCRAFT
3606 Quantum Blvd
Boynton Beach, FL 33426
Phone: (877) 426-5754
Web: www.worldwideticketcraft.com
E-mail: kevin@wwticket.com

TRAINING EQUIPMENT

ATHLETIC TRAINING EQUIPMENT COMPANY - ATEC
655 Spice Island Dr
Sparks, NV 89431
Phone: (800) 998-ATEC (2832)
Fax: (800) 959-ATEC (2832)
Web: www.atecsports.com
E-mail: askATEC@wilson.com

LOUISVILLE SLUGGER
8750 West Bryn Mawr Ave
13th Floor
Chicago, IL 60631
Phone: (800) 333-8326
Fax: (773) 714-4565
Web: www.slugger.com
E-mail: customer.service@slugger.com

TRAVEL

SPORTS TRAVEL AND TOURS
P.O. Box 50
60 Main Street
Hatfield, MA 01038
Phone: (800) 662-4424
Fax: (413) 247-5700
Web: www.sportstravelandtours.com

UNIFORMS

WILSON SPORTING GOODS
8750 West Bryn Mawr Ave
13th Floor
Chicago, IL 60631
Phone: (800) 333-8326
Fax: (773) 714-4565
Web: www.wilson.com
E-mail: askwilson@wilson.com

WINDSCREENS

BALL FABRICS, INC.
510 W. Arizona Ave
Deland, FL 32720
Phone: (386) 740-7212
Fax: (386) 740-7206
Web: www.ballfabrics.com
E-mail: info@ballfabrics.com

BEAM CLAY
One Kelsey Park
Great Meadows, NJ 7838
Phone: (800) 247-BEAM (2326)
Fax: (908) 637-8421
Web: www.beamclay.com
E-mail: sales@beamclay.com

See our ad on page 312!

COVERMASTER, INC
100 Westmore Dr
11-D
Rexdale, ON M9V 5C3
Phone: (416) 745-1811
Fax: (416) 742-6837
Web: www.covermaster.com
E-mail: info@covermaster.com

C&H BASEBALL, INC
10615 Technology Terrace, #100
Bradenton, FL 34211
Phone: (941) 727-1533
Fax: (941) 462-3076
Web: www.chbaseball.com
E-mail: sales@chbaseball.com

GOLF RANGE NETTING INC.
40351 US Hwy 19N #303
Tarpon Springs, FL 34689
Phone: (727) 938-4448
Fax: (727) 938-4135
Web: www.golfrangenetting.com
E-mail: info@golfrangenetting.com

PROMATS ATHLETICS
PO Box 2489
Salisbury, NC 28145
Phone: (800) 617-7125
Fax: (704) 603-4138
Web: www.promatsathletics.com
E-mail: mcross@promatsathletics.com

WEST COAST NETTING
5075 Flightline Dr
Kingman, AZ 86401
Phone: (928) 692-1144
Fax: (928) 692-1501
Web: www.westcoastnetting.com
E-mail: info@westcoastnetting.com

Yankee Stadium

COURTESY THE NEW YORK YANKEES

MAJOR LEAGUE TEAMS

ONEOK Field, Tulsa, Oklahoma

MIKE JANES

MINOR LEAGUE TEAMS

Kauffman Stadium, Kansas City, Missouri

INDEPENDENT TEAMS

OTHER ORGANIZATIONS

DIAMOND IMAGES

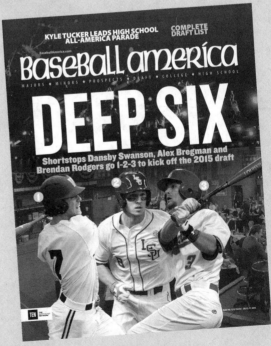